THE OXFORD HAN

WORLD PHILOSOPHY

THE OXFORD HANDBOOK OF

WORLD PHILOSOPHY

Edited by

JAY L. GARFIELD AND

WILLIAM EDELGLASS

OXFORD
UNIVERSITY PRESS

OXFORD
UNIVERSITY PRESS

Oxford University Press is a department of the University of Oxford.
It furthers the University's objective of excellence in research, scholarship,
and education by publishing worldwide.

Oxford New York
Auckland Cape Town Dar es Salaam Hong Kong Karachi
Kuala Lumpur Madrid Melbourne Mexico City Nairobi
New Delhi Shanghai Taipei Toronto

With offices in
Argentina Austria Brazil Chile Czech Republic France Greece
Guatemala Hungary Italy Japan Poland Portugal Singapore
South Korea Switzerland Thailand Turkey Ukraine Vietnam

Published in the United States of America by
Oxford University Press
198 Madison Avenue, New York, NY 10016

First issued as an Oxford University Press paperback, 2013.

Library of Congress Cataloging-in-Publication Data
The Oxford handbook of world philosophy / edited by
Jay L. Garfield and William Edelglass.
p. cm. — (Oxford handbooks in philosophy)
Includes bibliographical references.
ISBN 978-0-19-532899-8 (hardcover); 978-0-19-935195-4 (paperback)
1. Philosophy—Introductions. 2. Philosophy, Asian.
3. Philosophy, African. 4. Ethnophilosophy.
I. Garfield, Jay L., 1955– II. Edelglass, William.
BD21.O78 2010
109—dc22 2010009164

For Jiten Mohanty and in memory of Daya Krishna, two stalwarts of Cross-Cultural Philosophy

Acknowledgments

We are grateful to the subeditors for their excellent work and good spirits throughout this project: Chenyang Li (Chinese Philosophy), Nalini Bhushan (Non-Buddhist Indian Philosophy), Koji Tanaka (Japanese and Korean Philosophy), Tamara Albertini (Islamic Philosophy), Albert Mosley and Stephen C. Ferguson II (Philosophy in Africa and the African Diaspora), and Cynthia Townley (Recent Trends in Global Philosophy).

Contents

Contributors

Tamara Albertini is an Associate Professor at the University of Hawaiʻi at Manoa specializing in Islamic and Renaissance philosophy. She has a Dr.Phil. from Ludwig-Maximilians-Universität in Munich. She has published widely in Islamic philosophy. She is currently working on a book entitled *The Seductiveness of Certainty: Fundamentalists' Destruction of Islam's Intellectual Legacy.*

Dan Arnold is Assistant Professor of Philosophy of Religions at the University of Chicago Divinity School, Chicago, Illinois. He is the author of *Buddhists, Brahmins, and Belief: Epistemology in South Asian Philosophy of Religion* (Columbia University Press, 2005).

Adam Arola is a Visiting Assistant Professor at Pacific University Oregon specializing in Post-Kantian continental philosophy, ancient Greek philosophy, Christian and Islamic theology, and indigenous philosophy. He currently serves as editor of the American Philosophical Association's *Newsletter for American Indians in Philosophy* and is a descendent member of the Keweenaw Bay Indian Community of the Ojibwe Anishinaabe.

John Berthrong, educated at the University of Chicago, has taught at the Boston University School of Theology since 1989. His teaching and research interests are in interreligious dialogue, Chinese religions and philosophy, and comparative philosophy and theology. He most recently published *Expanding Process: Exploring Philosophical and Theological Transformations in China and the West* (SUNY Press, 2008).

Nalini Bhushan is Professor of Philosophy at Smith College. She recently coedited an anthology on *Transbuddhism: Translation, Transmission and Transformation* (University of Massachusetts Press, 2009) and is currently collaborating on a book project on Anglophone philosophy in colonial India.

Gillian Brock is Associate Professor in Philosophy at the University of Auckland, New Zealand. Her most recent work has been on global justice and related fields. Along with many articles that have appeared in journals such as *Ethics, Philosophy, The Canadian Journal of Philosophy, Analysis, The Monist, Philosophical Forum*, and *Utilitas*, she is the author of *Global Justice: A Cosmopolitan Account* (Oxford University Press, 2009). She has also coedited or edited three anthologies: *Current*

Debates in Global Justice (with Darrel Moellendorf, Springer, 2005), *The Political Philosophy of Cosmopolitanism* (with Harry Brighouse, Cambridge, 2005), and *Necessary Goods: Our Responsibilities to Meet Others' Needs* (Rowman and Littlefield, 1998).

ROBERT E. CARTER is Professor Emeritus of Philosophy at Trent University. He is the author/editor of several books including *Dimensions of Moral Education* (1984); *God, the Self and Nothingness: Reflections Eastern and Western* (1990); *Watsuji Tetsuro's Rinrigaku: Ethics in Japan* with Yamamoto Seisaku (1996); *Nothingness Beyond God: An Introduction to the Philosophy of Nishida Kitaro* (1998); *Encounter With Enlightenment: A Study of Japanese Ethics* (2001); and *The Japanese Arts and Self-Cultivation* (2008). He is also the author of ninety scholarly papers and reviews, and has been the recipient of the Symons Award for excellence in teaching.

AMITA CHATTERJEE is Professor of Philosophy and Coordinator of the Centre for Cognitive Science, Jadavpur University, Kolkata, India. She is the author of *Understanding Vagueness* (1994) and *Mental Reasoning: Experiments and Theories* (2009, coauthored with Smita Sirker). Her areas of specializations are logic and Navya-Nyāya, analytic philosophy, philosophy of mind, and cognitive science.

CHUNG-YING CHENG received his Ph.D. in Philosophy from Harvard University. He is Professor of Philosophy at the University of Hawai'i at Manoa, where he teaches both Western philosophy and Chinese philosophy. His special interests include philosophy of language, metaphysics, ethics, and onto-hermeneutics. He has given invited lectures at numerous universities around the world and has published over twenty-three books and more than three hundred articles in various fields of philosophy. He founded both the *Journal of Chinese Philosophy* and the *International Society for Chinese Philosophy* (ISCP).

BARBRA CLAYTON is an Associate Professor in the Religious Studies department at Mount Allison University, where she teaches Buddhism and Hinduism. She is the author of *Moral Theory in Śāntideva's Śikṣāsamuccaya: Cultivating the Fruits of Virtue*, and is coeditor of the *Journal of Buddhist Ethics*. Her research interests include Indian Mahayana ethics, Buddhist moral theory, and Buddhist environmentalism. Her current research focuses on environmental thought and practice in the Shambhala Buddhist community of Atlantic Canada.

J. ANGELO CORLETT is Professor of Philosophy & Ethics at San Diego State University. He is the author of over one hundred books and articles, including *Heirs of Oppression* (a forthcoming book on reparations); *The Errors of Atheism* (2010); *Race, Rights and Justice* (2009); *Responsibility and Punishment* (2006); *Interpreting Plato's Dialogues* (2005); *Race, Racism, and Reparations* (2003); *Terrorism: A Philosophical Analysis* (2003); and *Analyzing Social Knowledge* (1996). He is editor-in-chief of *The*

Journal of Ethics: An International Philosophical Review. His work has appeared in such journals as the *American Philosophical Quarterly; Analysis; Journal of Social Philosophy; Mind;* and *Philosophy*.

BRET W. DAVIS is Associate Professor of Philosophy at Loyola University Maryland. In addition to earning a Ph.D. in Western Philosophy, he spent over a decade in Japan working on Buddhist and Japanese philosophy. He is author of *Heidegger and the Will: On the Way to Gelassenheit* (2007); translator of Martin Heidegger, *Country Path Conversations* (2010); editor of *Martin Heidegger: Key Concepts* (2009); and coeditor of *Japanese Philosophy in the World* (in Japanese, 2005) and *Japanese and Continental Philosophy: Conversations with the Kyoto School* (2010). He has also published numerous articles in English and Japanese, including an article on the Kyoto school for the online *Stanford Encyclopedia of Philosophy*.

JOHN DUNNE (Ph.D. 1999, Harvard University) is an Associate Professor in the Department of Religion at Emory University, where he cofounded the Collaborative for Contemplative Studies. His work focuses on Buddhist philosophy and contemplative practice, especially in dialogue with cognitive science. His publications include a monograph on Dharmakīrti and scientific studies of Buddhist contemplative practice with colleagues from the Center for Investigating Healthy Minds and the Mind and Life Institute.

WILLIAM EDELGLASS is Professor of Philosophy and Environmental Studies at Marlboro College. Previously, he taught at the Institute of Buddhist Dialectics, Dharamsala, India. He is coeditor of the journal *Environmental Philosophy*, and has published widely on Buddhist philosophy, environmental philosophy, and twentieth-century French and German philosophy.

STEPHEN C. FERGUSON II is an Assistant Professor in Liberal Studies at North Carolina A & T State University. His areas of expertise include Africana philosophy, Marxist philosophy, social-political philosophy, and the history of African American philosophers. He is currently working on a book-length philosophical critique of Afrocentrism, the dominant trend in African American studies.

CHRIS FRASER is Associate Professor of Philosophy at the University of Hong Kong. He specializes in classical Chinese philosophy, with research interests in the philosophy of mind and action, epistemology, the philosophy of language, and ethics. He is the author of *The Philosophy of the Mozi*, published by Columbia University Press.

ROBERT GLEAVE is Professor of Arabic Studies at the Institute of Arab and Islamic Studies, University of Exeter, UK. He gained his Ph.D. in Islamic Studies from the University of Manchester in 1996. His research focuses on Islamic legal theory (*uṣūl al-fiqh*), and in particular Shiʿite jurisprudence. He is author of *Inevitable Doubt:*

Two Theories of Shīʿī Jurisprudence (Leiden, 2000) and *Scripturalist Islam: The History and Doctrines of the Akhbārī School of Imāmī Shīʿīsm* (Leiden, 2007).

Jay L. Garfield is Kwan Im Thong Hood Cho Temple Professor of Humanities at Yale NUS College. He teaches and pursues research in the philosophy of mind, foundations of cognitive science, logic, philosophy of language, Buddhist philosophy, cross-cultural hermeneutics, theoretical and applied ethics, and epistemology.

Barry Hallen was Reader in Philosophy at the Obafemi Awolowo University in Nigeria. He is presently Professor of Philosophy in the Department of Philosophy and Religion at Morehouse College, and an Associate in the W. E. B. Du Bois Institute for African and African American Research at Harvard University. He is the author of *A Short History of African Philosophy.*

Clevis Headley is Associate Professor and Chair of the Department of Philosophy at Atlantic University. Professor Headley also serves as the coeditor of *The CLR James Journal: A Review of Caribbean Ideas.* He has published in the areas of critical race theory, Afro-Caribbean philosophy, and analytic philosophy. His current research interests focus on Africana philosophy, deconstruction, and ontology.

Manyul Im is Associate Professor of Philosophy at Fairfield University. He has a B.A. in Philosophy from the University of California at Berkeley and a Ph.D. in Philosophy from the University of Michigan in Ann Arbor. His philosophical specialization is early Chinese philosophy.

Matthew T. Kapstein is Director of Tibetan Studies at the Ecole Pratique des Hautes Etudes (Paris) and Numata Visiting Professor of Buddhist Studies at the University of Chicago. His recent books include *The Tibetans* (Oxford, 2006), an edited volume entitled *Buddhism Between Tibet and China* (Boston, 2009), and a translation of a Sanskrit philosophical allegory, *The Rise of Wisdom Moon* (New York, 2009).

Workineh Kelbessa is an Associate Professor of Philosophy at Addis Ababa University, Ethiopia. He is the author of *Traditional Oromo Attitudes towards the Environment: An Argument for Environmentally Sound Development* (2001) and *Indigenous and Modern Environmental Ethics: A Study of the Indigenous Oromo Environmental Ethic and Modern Issues of Environment and Development* (2010). He is also the author of numerous journal articles and book chapters.

Anne Carolyn Klein/Rigzin Drolma, Ph.D., is Professor and former Chair of Religious Studies at Rice University and a founding director of Dawn Mountain in

Houston (www.dawnmountain.org). Her most recent book is *Heart Essence of the Vast Expanse, a Story of Transmission*. Other books, all examining categories of mind, include *Knowledge and Liberation; Path to the Middle; Meeting the Great Bliss Queen;* and *Unbounded Wholeness: Dzogchen and the Nonconceptual* (with Geshe Tenzin Wangyal Rinpoche).

CHRISTINE KOGGEL is Professor of Philosophy at Bryn Mawr College in Pennsylvania. She is the author of *Perspectives on Equality: Constructing a Relational Theory* (Rowman and Littlefield, 1998) and editor of the expanded three-volume edition of *Moral Issues in Global Perspective* (Broadview, 2006). Her current research is in the areas of development ethics and feminist moral and political theory.

CHENYANG LI is an Associate Professor of Philosophy at Nanyang Technological University, Singapore. Before joining NTU, he served as Professor and Chair of the Department of Philosophy at Central Washington University (1999–2010). His research interest is mainly in Chinese philosophy and comparative philosophy. His publications include *The Tao Encounters the West: Explorations in Comparative Philosophy; The Sage and the Second Sex: Confucianism, Ethics, and Gender* (ed.); and numerous articles in English and Chinese journals. He was a founding member and the first president of the Association of Chinese Philosophers in North America. He is currently completing a book on the Confucian ideal of harmony.

SHU-HSIEN LIU was Professor of Philosophy at Southern Illinois University at Carbondale. He is now Research Fellow at Academia Sinica; Chair Professor at Chengchi University, Taipei; and Emeritus Professor of Philosophy, Chinese University of Hong Kong. His publications include more than twenty books in Chinese and two books in English: *Understanding Confucian Philosophy: Classical and Sung-Ming* (1998) and *Essentials of Contemporary Neo-Confucian Philosophy* (2003).

JEFFERY D. LONG is Associate Professor and Chair of Religious Studies and Co-Director of the Asian Studies program at Elizabethtown College in Elizabethtown, Pennsylvania. He received his doctoral degree from the University of Chicago, and is the author of *A Vision for Hinduism: Beyond Hindu Nationalism* and *Jainism: An Introduction*.

JOHN C. MARALDO is Professor of Philosophy at the University of North Florida. He is the author or editor of seven books, including *Der hermeneutische Zirkel: Untersuchungen zu Schleiermacher, Dilthey und Heidegger* (1974 and 1984); *The Piety of Thinking: Essays by Martin Heidegger with Commentary* (with James G. Hart, 1976); and *Rude Awakenings: Zen, the Kyoto School and the Question of Nationalism* (with James Heisig, 1995). He has published numerous articles in Japanese and English on Japanese thought. His current concern is to foster dialogue between

Japanese and Anglo-European philosophy and provide alternatives in contemporary philosophical issues.

John H. McClendon III is Professor in the Department of Philosophy at Michigan State University. McClendon's areas of expertise include African philosophy, philosophy of African American studies, Marxist philosophy, and the history of African American philosophers. He is the author of *C.L.R. James's Notes on Dialectics: Left Hegelianism or Marxism-Leninism* (Lexington Books, 2005). He is currently the editor of the *American Philosophical Association Newsletter on Philosophy and the Black Experience.*

Mara Miller, a philosopher (Ph.D., Yale University) and Japanese art historian (M.A., University of Michigan; B.A., Cornell University), is the author of *The Garden as an Art* (SUNY Press, 1993). Three dozen of her scholarly articles have been published in the fields of aesthetics and philosophy of art, comparative selfhood, Japanese art history, women's studies, garden studies, and environmental aesthetics. Her work has been supported by an NEH Summer Seminar Fellowship in Japanese philosophy, a Mellon Post-Doctoral Fellowship at Emory University, and various other awards. She is also an abstract painter/mixed-media artist.

Albert G. Mosley is Professor of Philosophy at Smith College in Northampton, Massachusetts. He was born in Dyersburg, Tennessee; received a B.S. in Mathematics and a Ph.D. in Philosophy from The University of Wisconsin-Madison; and studied the history and philosophy of science at Oxford University. He has published on topics in logic, the philosophy of science and technology, African philosophy, African American philosophy, philosophy of sports, and philosophy of music.

Peimin Ni is Professor of Philosophy at Grand Valley State University in Michigan, and has served as visiting professor at the University of Hawai'i at Manoa and the University of Hong Kong. His publications include *On Confucius, On Reid,* and numerous articles. Ni is a former president of the Association of Chinese Philosophers in America, editor-in-chief of the ACPA book series on Chinese and comparative philosophy, and president of the Society of Asian and Comparative Philosophy.

Erik S. Ohlander is Assistant Professor of Religious Studies at Indiana University—Purdue University, Fort Wayne. A specialist in the history of Islamic mysticism, he received his Ph.D. in Near Eastern Studies from the University of Michigan, Ann Arbor (2004). He is author of *Sufism in an Age of Transition: 'Umar al-Suhrawardi and the Rise of the Islamic Mystical Brotherhoods* (Brill, 2008), and has written widely in the areas of Sufism, Qur'anic studies, and classical and medieval Islamic religious and intellectual history.

Eric Ormsby is currently Professor and Senior Research Associate at The Institute of Ismaili Studies in London. He was for many years professor and then director of The Institute of Islamic Studies at McGill University. He specializes in Islamic intellectual history with particular emphasis on theology and mysticism. His books include *Theodicy in Islamic Thought* (1984) and *Ghazali: The Revival of Islam* (2007).

Jin Y. Park is Associate Professor of Philosophy and Religion at American University. Park's research focuses on Zen and Huayan Buddhism, Buddhist-postmodern comparative philosophy, Buddhist encounters with modernity in Korea, and Buddhist ethics. Her publications include *Buddhisms and Deconstructions* (2006), *Buddhism and Postmodernity: Zen, Huayan, and the Possibility of Buddhist-Postmodern Ethics* (2008), and *Makers of Modern Korean Buddhism* (2010).

John Powers is Professor of Asian Studies and Head of the Centre for Asian Societies and Histories in the College of the Asia Pacific, Australian National University. He is the author of fourteen books and more than sixty articles, most recently *A Bull of a Man: Images of Masculinity, Sex, and the Body in Indian Buddhism* (Harvard University Press, 2009).

Rodney C. Roberts is a descendant of the African peoples who were enslaved at the Somerset Place plantation in Creswell, North Carolina. Currently Associate Professor of Philosophy at East Carolina University, his primary research interest is in the conceptual analysis of injustice and -related ideas, and the development and application of normative injustice theory—especially as it pertains to indigenous peoples and people of the African Diaspora. He is the editor of *Injustice and Rectification* (Peter Lang, 2002).

T. S. Rukmani is Professor and Chair of Hindu Studies, Department of Religion, Concordia University, Canada. Her special interests are Advaita Vedanta, Sāṃkhya, and Yoga philosophies. She is on the advisory board of the *Oxford Journal for Hindu Studies*. Her publications include an edited volume entitled *The Mahabharata: What is Not Here is Nowhere Else* (Munshiram Manoharlal, Delhi, 2005) and *Yogasūtrabhāṣyavivarana*, Volumes I and II (Munshiram Manoharlal, Delhi, 2001).

Tsenay Serequeberhan, Ph.D., is Associate Professor of Philosophy, Morgan State University. Eritrean by origin, he studied at Boston College and his work is focused on Continental and African/Africana philosophy. He has published four books: *Contested Memory* (2007), *Our Heritage* (2000), *The Hermeneutics of African Philosophy* (1994), and *African Philosophy* (1991). Presently he is working on a book-length manuscript to be titled *Existence and Heritage*.

ANDREY SMIRNOV is Head of the Islamic Philosophy Department in the Institute of Philosophy, Moscow, where he received his second Ph.D. in Philosophy (1988). His research encompasses Islamic philosophy from Mu'tazila to Ṣūfī thought. He has published Russian translations of *Fuṣūṣ al-Ḥikam* by Ibn 'Arabī, *Rāḥat al-'Aql* by al-Kirmānī, and excerpts of *Al-Muqaddima* by Ibn Khaldūn. He is the author of *Logic of Sense* (2001), *Logic and Meaning Foundations of Islamic Culture* (2005), and other books in Russian and Italian.

JOHN TABER is Professor of Philosophy at the University of New Mexico. His research interests are in the history of Indian philosophy, especially the Brahmanical and Buddhist traditions. His publications include *A Hindu Critique of Buddhist Epistemology: Kumarila on Perception* (Routledge, 2005) and several papers on Indian logic and epistemology.

KOJI TANAKA is Senior Lecturer in the Department of Philosophy at the University of Auckland, New Zealand. His research focuses on logic, history and philosophy of logic, Buddhist philosophy, classical Chinese philosophy, and Japanese philosophy.

TOM J. F. TILLEMANS holds the Chair of Buddhist Studies at the University of Lausanne in Switzerland. His initial training was in analytic philosophy, with a second training in Sanskrit, Tibetan, and Chinese. Published work has been in Buddhist Madhyamaka and epistemology, with an increasing emphasis on issues of comparative philosophy.

CYNTHIA TOWNLEY is Lecturer in Philosophy at Macquarie University, Sydney, Australia. She works in ethics, epistemology, and feminist philosophy, and has published on topics such as trust, ignorance, cyber-ethics, tolerance, and patriotism. Her current research is in trust, betrayal, and animal ethics.

JAN WESTERHOFF read Philosophy and Oriental Studies at the Universities of Cambridge and London. He is the author of *Twelve Examples of Illusion* (Oxford, 2010), *The Dispeller of Disputes: Nagarjuna's Vigrahavyavārtanī* (Oxford, 2010), *Nagarjuna's Madhyamaka: A Philosophical Introduction* (Oxford, 2009), and *Ontological Categories: Their Nature and Significance* (Oxford, 2005). He is presently Lecturer in Philosophy at the University of Durham, United Kingdom.

LIU XIAOGAN is Professor and Director of the Research Centre for Chinese Philosophy and Culture, the Chinese University of Hong Kong. He has authored, edited, or contributed to numerous books and journals in Chinese and English, including *Classifying the Zhuangzi Chapters* (2003), *Daoism and Ecology* (2001), *Companion to Daoist Philosophy* (2010), and "From Bamboo Slips to Received Versions: Common Features in the Transformation of the *Laozi*" (*Harvard Journal of Asiatic Studies*, 2003).

Hossein Ziai (Ph.D., Harvard) is Inaugural Chairholder of The Jahangir and Eleanor Amuzegar Chair in Iranian Studies, and Professor of Islamic and Iranian Studies at UCLA's Department of Near Eastern Languages and Cultures, where he has taught since 1988. He is currently the Director of the Program in Iranian Studies. His research encompasses Iranian intellectual and literary traditions with a focus on Illuminationist philosophy. Ziai has published several books and many articles on Iranian intellectual and literary traditions with a focus on Illuminationist philosophy.

Brook Ziporyn is an Associate Professor in the Departments of Philosophy and Religious Studies at Northwestern University. His published books include *Evil and/or/as the Good: Intersubjectivity and Value Paradox in Tiantai Buddhist Thought* (Harvard University Press, 2000); *The Penumbra Unbound: The Neo-Taoist Philosophy of Guo Xiang* (State University of New York Press, 2003); *Being and Ambiguity: Philosophical Experiments with Tiantai Buddhism* (Open Court Press, 2004); *Zhuangzi: The Essential Writings, with Selections from Traditional Commentaries* (Hackett, 2009); and the novels *Omnipotence for the Millions* and *The Masochistic Playpen* (iUniverse, 2001).

THE OXFORD HANDBOOK OF

WORLD PHILOSOPHY

INTRODUCTION

WILLIAM EDELGLASS
JAY L. GARFIELD

PHILOSOPHY—the aim, as Wilfrid Sellars puts it, "to understand how things, in the broadest sense of the term, hang together, in the broadest sense of that term"—has been a significant activity in many cultures for several millennia at least, even when we restrict that mode of understanding to something like *rational, analytic* understanding. It seems to be a natural development in all literate societies, and in many nonliterate societies as well, to ask difficult questions about the fundamental nature of reality, about what it is to be human, about what constitutes a good life, about the nature of beauty, and about how we can know any of these things. Any reasonably impartial view that surveys the world's cultures finds this kind of reasoned inquiry into who we are, our experience, and the nature of reality widely distributed. And not surprisingly, one finds both broad commonalities in the answers provided to these questions and important intercultural differences, commonalities and differences that are manifest in the following pages.

Curiously, the tendency to believe that one's own culture is the only one in which philosophical thought has or even could emerge is also widespread. Those readers who have come of philosophical age in Euro-American or Australasian contexts will be aware that this conceit is still alive and well in their own cultures, though now far less universally endorsed than it was only a few years ago. Western philosophers are not the only ones to have held such parochial views; there have been times when non-Chinese ideas were regarded as barbarian in China, and philosophy in India was taken to be exhausted by the six great systems. Many now still doubt the possibility of philosophical thought in cultures deemed to be too "primitive" simply because they did not employ writing.

This widespread prejudice regarding the unique ability of one's own culture to develop philosophical thought or insight was generally presupposed, or else justified in ways that seem naïve and misguided, at best, today. These views belie the long history of intercultural philosophical influence. Communication between Greek, Persian, and Indian philosophical communities was commonplace. Early European philosophy owes much to Islamic philosophy, as it does to Roman and Greek philosophy, traditions in turn influenced by Persia and India. East Asian philosophy is informed by Buddhism, Confucianism, and other views that spread along the Silk Road; and goods brought from china to the Middle East and Europe were surely accompanied by diverse ideas and cultural practices. So even the notion of hermetically sealed traditions in parallel development is largely a historical fiction. To understand the history of world philosophy is at least in part to understand the history of philosophical dialogue between, and not only within, the world's cultural traditions.

However tempting—and misleading—the view of philosophy as culturally sealed or as unique to any one particular culture may have been in the past, today there are both compelling moral and intellectual reasons for serious students of philosophy and professional philosophers to expand their gaze beyond a single culture—whether their own or that of some other. We live today in the aftermath of a long period of colonialism. One effect of colonialism has been to reinforce prejudices regarding the intellectual or cultural superiority of certain nations over others; another has been to impoverish and to disempower those who have been both colonized and disparaged. This is a serious, pervasive moral wrong.

One aspect of this disempowerment and disparagement is the neglect of the philosophical traditions of subaltern cultures. There have been attempts to justify this neglect. For example, some have insisted that non-Western intellectual traditions lack rational argument, a claim readily dismissed by anyone with knowledge of the traditions represented in the pages that follow. (Curiously, this view was never advanced by those Western philosophers actually *familiar* with non-Western traditions, but frequently by those *ignorant* of them, a fact that raises its own questions about rational argument.) Or, it was argued, that even if non-Western traditions did possess rational inquiry, this did not constitute philosophy because the inquiry took place within a religious, soteriological framework. Properly speaking, it was claimed, this was a form of religious practice and not philosophy, which is the pursuit of knowledge for its own sake. Such a narrow view, based perhaps on certain forms of recent Western philosophical practice, is blind to the varied philosophical styles and approaches that constitute the Western philosophical tradition, and would exclude from "philosophy" much of what is generally considered philosophy from the Greeks to the Early Moderns and even some contemporary philosophers.

Instead of grounding their arguments in descriptive accounts of non-Western philosophy, some Western thinkers have simply argued that "philosophy" is by definition a Greek-European project and is only mistakenly applied as a universal category to the intellectual traditions of other cultures. On this view, there may indeed be wisdom in the classic texts of other traditions, but again, these texts are not, strictly speaking, philosophical; rather, they are best approached through the methodologies of other disciplines, such as religious studies, intellectual history, anthropology, or cultural studies. Such views marginalize non-Western intellectual traditions, making them objects of cultural study, limited by their cultural particularity, and excluded from the realm of philosophy (that is, *Western* philosophy, not taken for granted as the unmarked case), which is thought to transcend cultural location in its pursuit of universal truth. We are left, on the one hand, with an often explicit claim of universal reason, and on the other, with the implicit claim that access to this universality is restricted to particular geographic locations.

Another aspect, and a curious reflection of the first, is that philosophers in subaltern cultures are encouraged, in order to work internationally, to attend primarily to the philosophical ideas, texts, and figures of dominant cultures, thus simultaneously alienating themselves from their own cultural context and reinforcing the view that there is not much there worthy of attention in the first place. However, the current global dominance of Western discourse in philosophical debates is due in no small part to the Western dominance of non-Western peoples over the last four centuries; political, military, economic, and technological power have as much to do with the framework of contemporary philosophical discourse as any alleged universal truths of Western philosophy that are unique in their transcendence of cultural and historical location. In today's multicultural world, the neglect and occlusion of non-Western thought hence constitute a kind of neocolonialism. Complicity in this occlusion of a wide range of philosophical traditions—which itself could be regarded as constituting and legitimizing violence by suppressing the perspectives of others—even if it is passive complicity, is morally unacceptable.

But even if one is not compelled by moral arguments, there are good *intellectual* reasons for studying a broad range of the world's philosophical traditions. One reason is completeness. As philosophers we should care to seek problems, solutions to problems, ideas, refutations, and arguments wherever they are to be found. People are smart and creative the world over, and there is no more reason to believe that good ideas only come from the European world, or from Australia, or from China than to believe that good ideas are only published on Thursdays, or in a Palatino font. In short, to restrict one's gaze culturally is epistemically as well as morally irresponsible.

Moreover, even if all one cares about is to understand the ideas of a single tradition (perhaps one is a specialist in the history of ideas, just as one might specialize in English literature, as opposed to being a comparativist), there is still good reason to attend to philosophy from other traditions. Hermeneutical distance is often a precondition of understanding. We can come to understand the prejudices that animate our own philosophical projects and arguments better by seeing them from the standpoint of those who do not share them. What may be mere horizon given as an unacknowledged framework can come to be seen as an object of study, and can then be subject to more reflective scrutiny.

The Western philosopher may problematize her own commitment to essence or to an antinomy between freedom and determinism by encountering a tradition in which these are absent; an Indian philosopher may suddenly see the assumption that knowledge entails certainty as called into question by Western commitments to probabilistic reasoning. Other traditions may have ontological categories, by which they divide up the things in the world, or moral intuitions that differ considerably from one's own; the study of other traditions can therefore raise important questions regarding what one takes for granted. By engaging in serious intercultural dialogue, we can provide each other with mirrors and lenses through which we may see ourselves reflected and refracted in new and philosophically fertile ways.

The occlusion of non-Western philosophy, then, is both morally and intellectual problematic. How, one might ask, ought one approach texts from other traditions? To read texts, whether in one's own tradition or in that of another, is always a historical affair. Even when the subject matter of a philosophical text is neither explicitly historical nor referential to specific past texts, the language, the problematic, and the assumptions that constitute its textual horizon derive from the tradition in the context of which it is composed. For this reason, to read cross-culturally requires one to read historically—not to read texts in isolation, but to work to understand their contexts and intertextual relations, contexts and relations that are often obscured when one reads in one's own tradition as air disappears to us, and water to a fish. For this reason, many of the articles in this volume are historical in character.

This need to attend to textual history, however, conceals its own hermeneutical danger: one might in virtue of this necessary historical orientation unwittingly succumb to a curatorial vision of the tradition with which one hopes to engage, thereby, in the very act of good-faith engagement, rendering genuine openness and communication impossible. That is, one takes the tradition that one examines to be dead, a mere historical curiosity, one that can be mined for ideas, perhaps even mourned, but not a possible dialogical partner. For this reason, we have tried in this volume not only to emphasize the history of the world's philosophical traditions, but also to indicate the current state of play, and the fact that today's philosophical world is polyglot.

This volume does not—indeed no volume could—completely cover "world philosophy." Most obviously, perhaps, there is no Western philosophy here. It is not that we forgot that there is European (in the broad sense of that term) philosophy. How could one? But we have taken it as obvious that most contemporary academic philosophers in the world are well acquainted with the European tradition, and so take "world philosophy" to be like "world music"—everything but European. There will, we hope, come a time when the European case is so unmarked that this would be an inexcusable omission. But that time has yet to come. Other lacunae are more subtle; there are important philosophical traditions that are not represented (e.g., Polynesian and Australian aboriginal traditions) and others that are underrepresented (e.g., the many Native American traditions). The bibliographies and suggested readings that follow each chapter, however, provide guidance for readers seeking further resources in any of the areas addressed here.

We present this volume in the hope that it will make salient the diversity of the world's philosophical traditions as well as the real possibility of increased interaction. We urge the reader to take seriously the possibility of fruitful philosophical engagement across cultural boundaries. Only good can come of it.

PART I

CHINESE PHILOSOPHY

EDITED BY CHENYANG LI

CHINESE PHILOSOPHY

CHENYANG LI

CHINESE philosophical thinking first emerged during the Western Zhou period (ca. 1046–771 BCE), when Chinese people began to develop theoretical concepts in a quasi-systematic fashion to formulate their understanding of the world. These concepts include *tian* 天 (Heaven), *de* 德 (virtue), *dao* 道 (the Way), *ming* 命 (mandate, the unavoidable), *qi* 氣 (energy, vital force), *yin* 陰 and *yang* 陽, *zhong* 中 (centrality, equilibrium), and *he* 和 (harmony). With these concepts, ancient Chinese philosophers not only developed their views of human society, nature, and the beyond, but also articulated their visions of the good life.

Some of these concepts evolved from primal religious thought of the Shang period (ca. 1600–1046 BCE). We have little record of the prior Xia dynasty (ca. 2200–1600 BCE), but the oracle bone inscriptions from the Shang dynasty provide rich material for helping us understand the world of the Shang people. The Shang people believed in a supreme being called "*Shang Di* 上帝," or "Lord on High," as distinct from the lord on earth. The *Shang Di* appears to possess anthropomorphic capacities, capable of rewarding good people and punishing the bad. During the Zhou period, this notion was gradually replaced by a more encompassing notion, *tian*. The original meaning of *tian* is the highest point, usually pointing to the sky. In the discourse of Chinese philosophy, *tian* acquired a broad spectrum of meaning, from the highest power in the world, to the fundamental moral order, to the sky, to nature. The notion has maintained a high level of ambiguity, and its meaning varies with different philosophers. At times it is appealed to as the supreme deity; sometimes it is just the intangible grounding of morality; and at other times it is taken simply as the natural way of the world. In mainstream Chinese philosophy, *tian* is generally understood to be in close connection to humanity as demonstrated in the broadly embraced notion of the unity of Heaven and humanity (*tian ren he yi*).

An equally important notion is *dao*, the appropriate way in the world. In most contexts, *dao* can be understood as the natural as well as moral order of the universe. In comparison with *tian, dao* is a more elusive and fluid notion, even though *tian* can also be seen as an evolving process. The *dao* of *tian* and the *dao* of humanity are often seen as inseparable. Depending on the school of Chinese philosophy, *dao* is regarded as either self-generating or generated through human activities, or both. Although *tian* is full of *de* (virtue), the latter term is mostly reserved for human beings. *De* is understood as a power or attainment that enables its possessor to function appropriately and effectively in pursuing and promoting the *dao*. Both the Shang and the early Zhou justified their legitimacy by stressing a special relationship between the rulers and *Shang Di*. An important new theme emerged during the Zhou period: that *tian* blessed the people of Zhou because they were virtuous (*de*). The *Tianxia* chapter of the *Zhuangzi* calls the study and application of these fundamental concepts the "art of the *dao* (*dao shu* 道術)," stating that the sages followed a philosophy that takes *tian* as the root and *de* as the foundation. "*Dao shu*" is probably the ancient Chinese term closest to the Western understanding of "philosophy (love of wisdom)." If we may say that in the West philosophy is mainly understood to be a search for truth, "wisdom" in China is primarily understood as the art of *dao* and philosophy is mainly taken as an activity to look for the "way." In comparison with Western philosophy, which emphasizes logical, algorithmic reasoning, Chinese philosophy is often carried out through analogical reasoning and parabolic discourse. Although logical argumentation is employed, Chinese masters tend to use heuristic methods in their teaching and help students arrive at conclusions through elicitation.

The concepts of *qi, yin*, and *yang* have played a vital role in the initial shaping and developing of Chinese thought. *Qi*, usually rendered as "energy" or "vital force," is the primary stuff-force of the universe. *Qi* is an active force in itself and can take either tangible or intangible forms. The myriad things of the world are various forms of *qi;* these forms can be changed in numerous ways. *Qi* is eternal rather than a product of divine "*creatio ex nihilo*." The *yin* and *yang* are two types of *qi:* the *yin* stands for the dark, soft, and feminine; the *yang* stands for the bright, firm, and masculine. They are present in everything and everywhere. The balance and healthy interaction of the *yin* and *yang* manifest the virtue of centrality or equilibrium (*zhong*), which leads to harmony in particular things and in the world as a whole. Harmony became a commonly shared ideal soon after it was first developed in the early Zhou period. The model of the unity between *tian* and humanity contains a prevailing theme of harmony. It is not unreasonable to argue that harmony is the highest ideal in Chinese philosophy. Virtually all early philosophers advocated harmony (*he*) as the ultimate goal of human action, even though their views of harmony sometimes differed greatly from one another.

In comparison with the philosophical traditions that developed from Greece and India, Chinese philosophy is characterized by a this-worldly, humanistic emphasis. While Chinese philosophy does not renounce the beyond, its primary concern is unmistakably this human world and this human life. This feature is evidenced not only in such early influential schools of thought as Confucianism, Daoism, Mohism, and Legalism, but also in Chinese Buddhism, in contrast with Buddhism in India. A second important characteristic of Chinese philosophy is dynamism. Such concepts as *dao*, *qi*, and other related ideas have left a defining feature in Chinese philosophy that the world is fundamentally changing and self-renewing. Constituted with the dynamic *qi*, the world is never seen as a static entity. This understanding of the world as dynamic is directly connected to a third characteristic of Chinese philosophy: contextualism. The inseparable pair of the concepts *yin* and *yang* penetrates the entire universe and defines everything as correlated and connected. Because of their interdependence, things have to be understood contextually. This, of course, does not mean that Chinese philosophers cannot see things in separation; it is that their overall tendency is to see things as connected rather than distinct, and their epistemological pattern is largely holistic. Dynamism and contextualism serve as cornerstones for the broadly shared notion of harmony as a highly valued ideal. If the world evolves without a preset form and things are fundamentally correlated, it is only logical to see the world as self-conforming and to see harmony as the optimal state of affairs.

The history of Chinese philosophy can be divided into four periods. The first period is the pre-Qin period, including early developments in the Western Zhou dynasty up to the founding of the Qin dynasty (221–206 BCE). The Zhou people's use of the Mandate of Heaven as a supernatural justification and the *de* as a moral justification of their overthrowing the Shang dynasty already demonstrated a sophisticated level of philosophical reasoning, which probably further stimulated and encouraged philosophical thinking. The fall of the Western Zhou dynasty led to the era known as "Spring and Autumn" (770–476 BCE) and then that of the "Warring States" (475–221 BCE). These were times when the previously established political and moral order collapsed and various streams of thought arose in response. Numerous schools of thought competed, engaging in sometimes heated debates. This period was the most creative and productive time for Chinese philosophy, laying much of the foundation for the later development of Chinese intellectual traditions. Both Confucianism and Daoism took shape during this period. Two other rival schools of thought, Mohism and Legalism, flourished during this time. The first five chapters of this section address this first period of Chinese philosophy.

The second period covers the Han (202 BCE–220 CE) through the Tang dynasty (618–907 CE). During this period, Confucianism was expanded and systemized. Daoism adopted an organized religious form (*dao jiao* 道教) while maintaining its philosophical attraction to free-spirited intellectuals. Buddhism was introduced from India and was transformed as the Chinese made it their own. The Han royal court made Confucianism its official philosophy, relying on its teachings to maintain order in society. Gradually, however, Buddhism replaced Confucianism as the predominant philosophy in China and from China further exerted a large influence in Korea, Japan, and Vietnam. During this period, Confucianism, Daoism, and Buddhism formed a competitive and complementary relationship, and became the three pillars of Chinese religious and intellectual culture. Chapter 6 mainly covers this period.

The third period stretches from the Song dynasty (960–1279 CE) to the Qing dynasty (1644–1911 CE). Through the great effort of Neo-Confucian scholars, Confucianism was revived and synthesized with Buddhism and, to a lesser degree, with Daoism. This is a period when Confucianism went through a major transformation and to a large degree reclaimed its influence in China. Chapter 7, on Neo-Confucianism, focuses on this period.

The final period begins in 1912 with the demise of the Qing dynasty. In this period, Chinese philosophical traditions faced tremendous challenges. Western invasions and oppression led many Chinese thinkers to question the value and viability of their own cultural traditions. With the founding of the People's Republic of China and the relocation of the Republic of China to Taiwan in 1949, Maoist-Marxism became the official ideology in mainland China. Traditional philosophies, Confucianism in particular, were criticized. For several decades, studies of Chinese philosophy could only be found outside mainland China. This situation began to change in the 1980s. In recent decades, Chinese philosophy has been undergoing a process of self-evaluation and transformation as Chinese philosophers defend, reform, and renew their heritage. The last chapter of this section, on Contemporary Confucianism, represents this still-unfolding period.

I would like to thank Raeburne Heimbeck, Yong Huang, and the editors-in-chief of this volume for their generous assistance in the preparation of this section.

BIBLIOGRAPHY AND SUGGESTED READINGS

Chan, Wing-tsit. (1963) *A Source Book in Chinese Philosophy*. Princeton, NJ: Princeton University Press.

Cua, Antonio S. (ed.). (2003) *Encyclopedia of Chinese Philosophy*. New York/London: Routledge.

Fung, Yulan. (1948) *A Short History of Chinese Philosophy*. New York: The Free Press.

Graham, A. C. (1989) *Disputers of the Tao: Philosophical Argument in Ancient China*. La Salle, IL: Open Court.

Ivanhoe, P. J., and Bryan Van Norden (eds.). (2006) *Readings in Classical Chinese Philosophy* (2nd ed.). Indianapolis, IN: Hackett Publishing Company.

Schwartz, Benjamin. (1985) *The World of Thought in Ancient China*. Cambridge, MA: The Belknap Press of Harvard University Press.

Zhang, Dainian. (2002) *Key Concepts in Chinese Philosophy*. Translated and edited by Edmund Ryden. New Haven, CT, and Beijing: Yale University Press and Foreign Languages Press.

CHAPTER 1

THE *YIJING*: THE CREATIVE ORIGIN OF CHINESE PHILOSOPHY

CHUNG-YING CHENG

Historical Background and Theoretical Presupposition

The *Yijing* 易經 (the *Book of Changes*) dates back to the beginning of the Zhou dynasty (ca. 1200 BCE). Although we do not know exactly how it was produced, it appears that the text arose as a result of sustained observations of changes in nature. The purpose of these observations was to provide the foundation for the proper judgment and conduct of appropriate human action, in light of an understanding of future events that would affect the well-being of an individual or a state. The *Xici* 繫辭[1] tells us that Fu Xi made comprehensive observations of the heavens and earth and examined things near and far, and "began to invent the eight *gua* 卦 (trigrams), so that we may reach and understand the powers of the divinity (*shenming* 神明), and classify-record the facts of the ten thousand things."[2] Thus, the system of *gua* was not invented

1. *Xici* was one of the Ten Wings or Ten Commentaries on the *Yijing* that were attributed to the authorship of Confucius. Confucius did not actually write these commentaries but inspired their composition by disciples such as Zisi or Zixia.

2. The unit of such a description is *gua*, which is composed of three *yao* lines, each of which indicates a state of change either in *yin* or in *yang*. Human beings live between heaven and earth. There are three lines, then, representing the state of heaven (the larger environment), the state of the human person, and the state of earth (the smaller environment) and in this order. Since each line could be in the state of *yin* or in the state of *yang*, we come to a system of eight *guas*.

arbitrarily but was instead purposefully established in light of comprehensive observations so that we may understand cosmic nature and relate and respond to the myriad things as part of our efforts to develop ourselves as human persons.[3]

Sima Qian (司馬遷) in his *Historical Records* informs us that King Wen (文) emended the eight-*gua* system into the sixty-four *zhonggua* (hexagrams). The so-called hexagrams are each composed of two trigrams of three *yao* lines or lines of movement in terms of *yin-yang* alternation. The doubling of two trigrams in a hexagram is an indication of how two natural states representing complexes of *yin-yang* could produce a hyperstate of reality embodied in human situations. It is interesting to note that once the double trigrams form a hexagram, the hexagram can be further explained as an ordering of the state of heaven, the human state, and the earth state, with each state represented by two lines of change or movement. We come to have sixty-four hexagrams as a result of two to the sixth power. This expansion is necessary for representing systematically all basic human situations by way of interpretation and therefore integrates situations of change with their different judgments appended, drawing from concrete cases of divination in the two previous dynasties of the Shang and Xia of more than 800 years, and probably before. The so-called judgment is a statement and foreboding on the nature of a situation as represented by a hexagram: it is an interpretation of the situation represented by a generated hexagram. No doubt, divination is an essential part of the *Yijing* tradition as a practical art to guide human action. But such divination was thought to be based on judgments derived from observed trends in nature; it was not based on the conjectured wills of deities. Even though there was shamanism in ancient China, the *wu* 巫 (shaman) and *shi* 史 (history recorder) came into being at about the same time, and eventually the *shi* became dominant. History, then—in addition to a profound understanding of the cosmos—became the basis for predicting the future: a diviner must be one who can interpret the present and its relation to the future in light of the past.

Thus, the *Yijing* embodies and presupposes a cosmic view that is consonant with human engagement with the natural environment and social practices encompassed by cultural and history. A person resolves practical life problems with reference to a comprehensive system of observation of a holistic nature that consists of heaven, earth, and humanity. In this sense, the *Yijing* is not just a text of divinatory judgments but also one that contains and presupposes theoretical and practical understanding of heaven, earth, and human being. The theoretical content generates the practical judgments in sixty-four *gua*. The foundational understanding of nature (heaven and earth) in relation to humanity in the *Yijing* marks the beginning of Chinese philosophy. And the *Yijing*, with its tradition of "comprehensive observation of changes" (*tongbian* 通變), can be regarded as a primary source of inspiration for the later development of Chinese philosophical traditions.

One may question whether the reflective understanding of nature in relation to humanity in the *Yijing* is philosophy in the proper sense of the word. If "philosophy"

3. Needless to say, Fu Xi need not be a single person. Instead, the name could refer to a tribe or group that developed a special concern with nature and the ways it is related to human living.

is inquiry into the truth of whatever matter that is important and meaningful and that may have a practical bearing on our life and actions, then what is presupposed and preunderstood in the *Yijing* is precisely what philosophy is all about. Without such philosophical activity, there is no way a deep descriptive account of change as cognized and experienced by an observer could be given. What the *Yijing* author(s) focuses on in nature reflects the philosophical interest to find out how changes take place and how we may deal with them, in such a way that the practical is built on the theoretical and the theoretical is guided by the practical.

In the original judgments (*guaci* 卦辭), many concepts are implicit; they call for definition and clarification. This is what occasioned Confucius's conscientious effort to seek their meanings and their implication for action. Therefore, the writing and development of the *Yizhuan* 易傳 as the comprehensive commentary on the *Yi* texts (forms and judgments) are a deliberate response to queries about their underlying philosophy in the fifth to fourth century BCE by Confucius and his disciples. *Shiyi* 十翼 (Ten Commentaries), especially *Tuanzhuan* 彖傳 (Commentary on Judgment), *Wenyan* 文言 (Commentary on Text and Words), *Xiangzhuan* 象傳 (Commentary on Images), and *Xici* 繫辭(Comprehensive Commentary), are explicit elucidations of the foundational philosophy of the *Yi*. In all these commentaries, concepts are explicitly defined according to reflective understanding. This understanding is based on the deep experience of and insights into cosmic reality.

The central philosophical concern of almost all of these commentaries can be described as onto-cosmological (i.e., addressing the origin of the cosmos) and cosmological (i.e., addressing the process of how the cosmos is formed), ethical (i.e., human situations and relations) and environmental-ethical (i.e., how humans relate to their environments), and philosophical-anthropological (i.e., relating to the individual) and political-philosophical (i.e., relating to the society). Even though their language is succinct and concise, they espouse a philosophy of reality and a philosophy of humanity. As such, the *Yizhuan* becomes the explicit source and beginning of Chinese philosophy, containing the implicit onto-cosmological insights uncovered by broad reflections on the part of Confucius and his disciples, just as the *Yi* text itself was formed from the reflections of King Wen and other ancient sage kings on divinatory practice. In the practice of divination, we may already discern some primary philosophical activities: making onto-cosmic discovery, doing onto-hermeneutical interpretation, exercising moral judgment on action, engaging in philosophical reflection, and providing justification.

Five Stages/Levels of Onto-Hermeneutical Formation of the *Yi* Text

The above analysis shows that the *Yijing* embodies five levels or layers of understanding and interpretation of reality (nature), conceived as five stages of development: observation (*guan* 觀), symbolization (*xiang* 象), systematization (*tong* 通), divination (*bu* 卜), and interpretation (*jie* 解). They can be described and explained in terms of key concepts or terms in the *Yijing* or the *Yizhuan*.

First, comprehensive observation (*guan*) as presented in the twentieth hexagram is the key concept to understand the formation of the *Yi* symbols in light of observation and experience of nature and reality as described in the *Xici* of the *Yizhuan*. Second, symbolization is the process of forming an image (*xiang*) of an event or a situation. All trigrams and hexagrams are images or symbols that either iconically or indexically represent real situations in nature and life. Although the *Yijing* text does not employ the word *xiang*, the *gua* symbols are iconic and indexical representations.

Third, the systematization of the *Yi* symbols, which are composed of their names and appended *gua* divinatory judgments and line (*yao* 爻) divinatory explanations, makes the *Yijing* a text (*wen* 文) or book (*shu* 書) and a system of ordered sequence of *gua*. We can understand how King Wen could come to organize the *guas* and their judgments and explanations into the present ordered sequence. He must have acquired a vision of the onto-cosmological nature with its creative development, consisting of the interactive *yin-yang* forces that lead to both differentiation and integration of things. The term "*tongbian*" (penetrating or understanding changes) indicates this understanding that inspires systematization of forms and images.

Fourth, divination is the practice of determining the nature of a present situation with milfoil stalks (*shi*) in order to produce an image of the future, the significance of which can be interpreted in light of signs as revealed in the cracks of burned oracle bones. The articulation of the meaning of the divination is called oral divination (*zhan* 占). The ancient word "*zhen*" (貞) also suggests divination using sea shells or tortoise shells.

Finally, interpretation stands for two basic concepts in the *Yi* texts: the concept of clarification or illumination (*ming* 明) and the concept of resolution (*jie* 解). In the *Tuan*, *Xiang*, and *Xici* commentaries "*ming*" is used to clarify a belief, an argument, a punishment, an administrative policy, the meaning of a time, and the moral implication of fortunate and misfortunate (*ji* and *xiong*). "*Ming*" is to interpret and explain so that a point, a truth, a fact, and a value can be clarified. But a *gua* situation also calls for resolution. The interpretation of a *gua* situation requires an informed decision on actions in light of the understanding of the situation, actions that will bring resolution to the present predicament. Here lies the relevance of the concept of "*jie*," which refers to resolution of difficulty.

With these five stages of development, in which divination plays a central role in the systematization, form judgments (*guaci* 卦辭—what diviners say about the meaning of the *gua* as a whole) and line explanations (*yaoci* 爻辭—what the diviners say about the meaning of a line in the *gua*) are generated to illuminate the *gua* symbols that accommodate observations of *yin-yang* forces and their alignments. Consequently, a primal form of onto-hermeneutic understanding[4] arises that is based on re-reading a given description in light of experience and engaging with reality.

4. If one reads meaning from the *gua* just in terms of apparent reference, one has a hermeneutic understanding. But if one understands the *gua* symbol in light of some discovered or recovered philosophy of reality (namely, ontology), one's hermeneutic understanding becomes onto-hermeneutic.

This onto-hermeneutic understanding is a matter of an onto-hermeneutic circle: an integration of the parts and whole of experiences of a situated state of reality or event. It is a circle because a circulation of attribution and regulation of meaning in light of experience and understanding of a given situation is presupposed.

We may ask how the *Yi* text comes to be formed as a result of onto-hermeneutic understanding, thereby embodying an onto-hermeneutic understanding with an epistemologically oriented methodology and an onto-cosmology, or *benti* (本體)[5]-ontology, which functions as the foundation of Chinese philosophy. To answer this is to look into the formation of the earliest *Yi* symbols and names that refer to human experiences *in* nature (heaven and earth). The trigrams are developed as an organized set of symbols to stand for the observed salient structures, events, and processes of nature. The eight trigrams (*bagua*) suggest the eight dominant natural phenomena and processes—namely, heaven and earth, fire and water, lake and hill, and wind and thunder, each indicating the presence of a potential force of formation and transformation—that are central to our understanding of nature in that they are the basis for the formation and constitution of all other events and processes of nature.

The eight phenomena-processes are also observed to be derived from even more basic forces or processes. Hence, we can speak of our experiences of *yin* (shady) and *yang* (bright), *gang* 剛 (firmness) and *rou* 柔 (softness), *dong* 動 (motion) and *jing* 靜 (rest), and related qualities such as empty and substantial, potential and actual, progress and regress, and ups and downs as basic dimensions of events such as fire and water or natural states such as hill and lake. Even heaven and earth have features we normally experience in concrete feelings and actual situations, such as nobility and fatherliness for heaven and tolerance and motherliness for earth. Based on these experienced qualities of events and things, we may reach a more generalized notion of *yin* and *yang* as the preserving force and advancing force, respectively, such that all experiences have their polar contrast and dynamic interdependence. This is what Daoism has done by introducing the concepts of *de* 德 (virtue) and *dao* 道 (the way). They can also be described as manifestations of order and vitality—*li* 理 and *qi* 氣—in Song-Ming Neo-Confucian philosophy. Insofar as we experience *de* and *dao* or *li* and *qi* in reality, we also can experience *yin-yang* qualities such as dark and bright, soft and firm, moving and still, and so forth. Such contrast and interdependence of *yin* and *yang* eventually lead to the positing of a single primary source of creativity, which is the *taiji* 太極 (the great ultimate). Hence, it is said in the *Yizhuan* that "Change has *taiji*, from which two norms (*yin* and *yang*) arise" (*Xici shang* 11). All things arise from the *taiji* by way of *yin-yang* operations, which are in turn sustained by the *taiji* as the inexhaustible source of creativity.

5. I use the term "*benti*" to refer to a unified body developed or arising from an origin that gives unity and structure to the body.

Given the primary symbols of experiences of reality, the eight trigrams can be said to be composed of these primary symbols in terms of the internal *de-dao* and *li-qi* relationships. These trigrams further combine into the larger configurations of the sixty-four hexagrams by way of binomial expansion, which logically capture the structures and vitalities of natural events and processes. The sixty-four hexagrams come to represent a usable set of basic human conditions, which we understand, manage, and act on with reason and will. Here we see how a principle of epistemic and regulative simplicity is implicitly at work: the system of sixty-four hexagrams is simply considered a representation of reality at a level consistent with our need for and capacity of understanding.

The sixty-four hexagrams, underpinned by the *yin-yang* workings, form a web of interrelated meanings that reflect the interrelatedness of things and transformation of events. It is up to the human mind, the interpreter of symbols, to make out tendencies in those changes and transformations and embark on regulative and pragmatic action. The hexagrams are simultaneously an intended objective description of natural and human processes. Thus, they are a system of images-forms-symbols, resulting from observation, reflection, and interpretation of individual and communal experiences encompassed by culture and tradition.

In short, five basic epistemological principles underlie the *Yijing* system of the dynamic and creative *yin-yang* symbols and forces: (1) the Principle of Comprehensive Observation, which ensures openness and continuity of observation from both narrowly focused and holistic points of view; (2) the Principle of Systematic (or organic) Consistency and Simplicity, which requires the whole system of observation to be organized in coherent, interdependent experiences and concepts; (3) the Principle of Polar Opposition and Complementation, which shows how production and individuation of things take place; (4) the Principle of Creative Enfolding and Development, which allows and invites new experiences of nature and reality in a growing and expanding process of life realization; and (5) the Principle of Understanding in Human Consciousness and Its Creative Self-Regulation, which points to the emergence of human consciousness and its inherent power of creative decision and action based on understanding of nature. These five epistemic-logical principles define and provide a methodological understanding of *Yi* thinking.

Benti-Ontology as Onto-Cosmology of the *Yi*

Apart from epistemology and methodology, the *Yijing* initiated an onto-cosmology, providing an onto-cosmological model of reality with lasting influence on Chinese philosophy. This model of reality may be understood by looking into the mutually defining relationship between the source-origin of creativity and the substantial development of reality. We can think of reality as representing a *benti*, a source-reality of creativity, or onto-cosmos. How do we understand this concept of source-reality of creativity, or onto-cosmos, and its referents? In the first place, all the changes observed must have an adequate source or ultimate origin so that change can happen and continue at all. This source or origin is called "*taiji*" in the *Xici*, but in the *Yi* text is referred to as the *yuan* 元 (the ultimate source). It manifests itself in *yin* and *yang* and thus has two dimensions, which are respectively referred to as *qianyuan* 乾元 (the source power of *qian*) and *kunyuan* 坤元 (the source power of *kun*); the former is the moving and creating power, while the latter is the preserving and sustaining power. But the two also belong to each other and form a unity, with an undifferentiated and yet interrelated identity. This is the great ultimate (*taiji*), the ultimate beginning of existence and hence the inceptive creativity. Hence, the root source of being and existence is a matter of unity, duality, and diversity. It is a whole body, with parts, which we can call the *ti* 體 (the body, the organic wholeness). In other words, all events and the resulting states of being form one body (*yiti* 一體); even though there is an indefinite number of individual things and events in the universe, they are organically related in one way or another.

Although the *Yi* text does not explicitly mention this concept of *ti*, it is implied in the formation of the eight trigrams or sixty-four hexagrams, which have all the qualities of one body that nonetheless exhibits interrelated differences and identities on different levels. Typically, there are levels of living beings, from the great ultimate as the starting point to the two norms, then to the four forms, and then to the eight *gua* and eventually the sixty-four *gua*, as shown in Zhang Zai's (張載) "Diagram of Ordering of sixty-four Hexagrams." Each hexagram has its internal constituent lines, which also form a body of interdependency of two trigrams, the upper and the lower, the inner and outer. But they can also be read as six interactive lines. With this conception of *ti*, we can speak of *benti* as the source-reality, original-body, or onto-cosmos, so that we may identify a body with its originating source. From the *Yijing*'s point of view, the universe or cosmos forms a *benti* by itself. In this cosmic *benti*, there is no external limitation and yet there is an inexhaustible inner force as its source. We may indeed interpret ontology in this context as the study of being as the ultimate source, and the study of the ultimate source (*benyuan* 本元 or *yuan* 元) as the study of being. But as the ultimate source is a creative power for the development of the universe, the study of being is the study of becoming, and vice versa. The universe is the onto-cosmos, or a *ti* of being, which is simultaneously becoming. This cosmic *benti* has no boundary between the inner and the outer: "Change has no body and creativity (divinity) has no direction" (*Xici Shang* 4). On the other hand, for the human being, *benti* is the emerging and self-realizing self that is rooted in the cosmos and grows and develops in its interaction with the external world, as indicated in *Zhongyong* 中庸. The human being's creativity is rooted in cosmic creativity, which should be cultivated conscientiously so that individuation can be fully realized, and simultaneously, the creative differentiation of cosmic reality (cosmic *benti*) could become richly realized in a unity of difference.

In this sense of *ti*, the *Yizhuan* speaks of a human person maintaining correct position and dwelling in her own body (*zhengwei juti* 正位居體) ("*Kun wenyan*" 坤文言). It is when a person has developed and cultivated herself into an integrative unity of mind and body and maintained her own creative force that we can speak of her *benti* as such. *Benti* thus gives rise to an onto-cosmological understanding of the universe and human being, thereby also giving rise to onto-epistemology, onto-ethics, and onto-aesthetics in which the opposition of inner and outer can be resolved in their unity. We must note that in the *Yijing*, *ben* is not a cause but a source, and *ti* is not substance in the Aristotelian sense, but organic unity. It is not transcendent as there is no real separation between the *ben* and *ti*, but it is not pure immanence either as there is always creative action to transcend one's self and state of being. The *ben* is an ultimate source of creativity without exhaustion, and *ti* is both the basis and result of actualization and achievement, which display the creativity of the *taiji*, the powerful source of creativity.

The most important feature of the *benti* concept is that the human being is creatively rooted in a creative reality and hence can continue to develop capacities for understanding and action. Thus, we can speak of developing oneself into a moral person in accordance with a paradigm of onto-cosmological creativity.

Ti-Yong and the Three Meanings of the *Yi*

We should also examine the idea of *ti-yong* 體用, which is based on *benti*. The notion of *yong* 用 is essential to the understanding of divinatory judgment, which is characterized by utility (*yong*) in the sense of making pragmatic decisions. But *yong* as a verb is the actual functioning and agency that come from understanding and engagement. Ontologically speaking, *yong* is the activity of the *ti* that gives rise to new events while fulfilling a virtual capacity for creativity. In the judgment "Do not use（用）the hidden dragon" (*Qianlong Wuyong* 潛龍勿用),[6] the energy of the hidden dragon should not be tapped because it would not be effective. *Yong* or function is the power inherent in a body that could be creatively constructive in appropriate conditions. In the divinatory judgments, there are many statements of "to use" and "not to use," based on considerations of how a body or *ti* accords with circumstances and time. In this perspective, the whole universe is a matter of the *yong* of the cosmic body, and the creative results of *yong* are the actual contents of

6. Whether the Chinese dragon—*long* 龙—in the present expression is an actual living animal the ancient Chinese saw as an open question. It is partly to do with whether there were such animals that can hide in the depth of water, can walk on the field, and can fly in the sky. There might well be. But in later use of the term *long* is often described as having a buffalo/goat head and a snake body with many small legs and being capable of flying and playing in the sky. It is obviously a product of human imagination. The purpose of such an imagined being is to focus on its being a symbol for exuberant energy, power of transformation, and the outburst of creativity.

the universe that contribute to the development and transformation of *benti*. Thus, the notion of *ti* is rooted in *ben* and realized in *yong*, thereby forming a process of creative realization of the actuality of heaven, earth, and humanity.

The self-cultivational (*xiuji* 脩己) process in Confucianism is an embodiment of such a cosmic process of creation and regeneration. A human person has his own *benti* and hence the *yong* of his *benti*. Both the *Xici* and *Zhongyong* have remarked that for ordinary people, their life functions with their inner power and yet they are not aware of it (*baixing riyong er buzhi* 百姓日用而不知). We need to become aware of our *benti* because we need to know and preserve our inner powers and cultivate them and then make proper use of them to realize our human capacities. Hence, the *benti*-cosmology has important ethical and moral implications for human development. It involves a process in which the human *benti* or the human existence with its consciousness could be cultivated to extend its sense of identity and relationships to include other people, other living things, and eventually the whole sphere of heaven and earth with their inherent and incessant creativities.

Moreover, the *yong* of the *Yi* in action is first induced by divination in a framework of understanding. One can also point to the *xiang* 象 or image system in the *Yi*. With each *xiang* one could design something useful either for oneself or others. According to the *Xici*, many of the useful inventions from the past are inspired by identifying the relevant *gua*. It suggests that to understand the images of *guas* is to relate human purposes and needs to them as they stimulate the mind toward cultural inventions.

Based on this deep understanding of the cosmic *benti*—which presents this world as a variety in unity and a change in constancy—a theory of the three meanings of *yi* was developed. First, there is the meaning of nonchange (*buyi* 不易) of change, in the sense that change is a constant activity. It is said in the *Xici* that "the life-creativity of life is called the change (*yi*)" (*Xici Shang* 5). As this is the nature of the *taiji*, which stands for the source of life-creativity, one can see how the constancy in change is in fact the creativity of the *taiji*. In this sense we may speak of a hierarchy of constancies in terms of which concrete events and individual things take place and endure for a time, only to be replaced by other events and individuals. This cosmology of constancy is rooted in the constancy of the ontology of the *taiji* and *dao*.

The second meaning of *yi* refers to the change and transformation (*bianyi* 變易 or *bianhua* 變化) of things. The *Yijing*, as a book on change, deals primarily with the forms of change in this sense and examines their relationships, so that we see how changes follow a dialectical pattern of change and nonchange. One has to learn from these forms and transformations to appreciate how the forms of change in the *Yijing* are derived, how they are related, and how, given proper conditions, predictions and decisions can be made to more fully realize one's life.

The third meaning is simplicity of change (*jianyi* 簡易). The word *jian* suggests the easy and simple way in which recording can be done on the bamboo pieces. But simplicity is also a direct experience of life, and we can sometimes see among different possibilities of life situations those that embody ease and easiness of action and movement.

With these three meanings of change, one learns that the human way of life can achieve a comprehensive content and fulfill its potentiality by following and embodying the ways of heaven and earth, which are creative development according to a deep and simple understanding of being and becoming. It is a cosmic education with profound ontological and moral significance.[7]

Diversification of the *Yi* into *Xiang-shu* and *Yi-li*

Images (*xiang* 象) and numbers (*shu* 數) are significant elements of the *Yi*. Images are forms in which we envisage events and situations so that we can have a comprehensive sense of their meanings. As they are found to be representable in terms of the *yin-yang* lines of change, odd and even numbers naturally become significant. Moreover, a holistic understanding of the process of change within the sixty-four hexagrams requires consideration of numbers. This no doubt has to do with our reflection on the observed relations among images with regard to their formation and transformation. The representation of heaven and earth in diagrams indicating positions and directions such as *River Chart* (*Hetu* 河圖) and *Luo Script* (*Luoshu* 洛書) also involves numbers. Hence, numbers become symbolic of image meanings and vice versa. To use numbers to make divination and hence to form a *gua* may have started very early in the history of the *Yijing*'s development. Although we can appropriate and explore numbers for telling the future, one cannot ignore judgments of divination made for actual life purposes and in terms of real experiences and knowledge of nature and humanity. How meanings (*yi* 義) in such judgments and the relevant principles (*li* 理) that are entailed by them are analyzed and related is not simply a matter of images and numbers.

Yet it is clear that one cannot ignore images and numbers for intuitive understanding as well as ways of transformation among hexagrams and thus real human situations. In the early study of the *Yi* system in the Han period, the school of images and numbers predominates because it wants to identify symbolic meanings for judgments through numbers of lines and *gua*. It was due to the Daoist focus on contemplative wisdom of the true meanings of words that images and numbers were dismissed. However, hexagrams can be said to be generated by numbers, and their representation in numbers is important for understanding inner and outer relations of the *gua*. It was not until Zhu Xi wrote his *Original Meanings of the Zhouyi*

7. The fact that human activity is creatively meaningful may be illustrated by two additional principles of the onto-cosmology of the *yi*: the Principle of Exchange (*jiaoyi* 交易) and the Principle of Harmonization (*heyi* 和易).

周易本义 that both judgmental meaning and implication, on the one hand, and images and numbers, on the other, became mutually supporting and complementary. The philosophy of *Yi* thus maintains a balanced and integrative position between *xiang-shu* and *yi-li*.

Rise of Daoism and Confucianism

The *Yijing* led to the rise of Daoism and Confucianism. In Daoism, the *dao* describes the way of change and transformation of things in nature. The creative function of *dao* even carries a broader meaning as a creative source than *taiji*, for it may also refer to nonbeing apart from being. In the *Daodejing*, one also sees a similar *Yi* dialectic of development. But there are differences. Daoism is relatively detached from images and forms as it concentrates on how things arise by the *wuwei* 無為 action of the *dao*. In this sense, Daoism is more retrospective than prospective, more inward looking than outward looking. Although things can be said to have risen from the *dao* according to Laozi 老子, because the *dao* cannot be positively identified—for it is beyond language and knowledge—the void of the *dao* suggests a more indeterminist approach to change, which is the process from the void to being. This may eventually lead to the notion of *wuji*, which is needed for indicating the invisible and inexhaustible origin and source of creative arising, resulting in a more complete redescription of the onto-cosmology of *wuji-taiji*, which is the essence of Zhou Dunyi's 周敦頤 onto-cosmology of *benti*.

Confucius, who studied the *Yijing* from an early age, has achieved deep understanding of the inner meanings of the system of *yi* divinations, as we have seen in the texts of the 1973 Silk Manuscripts. He regarded the natural generation and transformation of things as a creative process from the ever-present of the heaven. He also saw the development of virtues (such as *ren* 仁, *yi* 義, *li* 禮, *zhi* 智, and *xin* 信) as a timely pursuit that requires self-control for both the rectification and harmony of relations. All his remarks and observations indicate a heritage of the philosophy of the *Yijing* at work. As pointed out above, the final formation of the *Yizhuan* was inspired by Confucius's teaching and thinking about the *Yi* tradition. The Confucian quest for positive understanding, self-transcendence, and self-discipline represents the *benti* philosophy of the *Zhouyi* at its best. Confucian onto-cosmology and moral philosophy therefore can be regarded as a redevelopment and exploration of the *Yi* principles 义理. There is much from the *Yi* tradition that can be traced from Confucius, through Zisi 子思, to Mencius, and then to Xunzi 荀子.

The philosophy of the *Yijing* is further explored and expanded in Neo-Confucian philosophy, with its *yi*-inspired *benti*-ontology and onto-cosmology. Apart from breeding a distinctive philosophy of *li* and *qi*, the philosophy of *Yijing* as a way of thinking (as onto-hermeneutics) enabled Confucianism to be brought into closer contact with both Daoism and Chinese Buddhism.[8]

Conclusion

It is often claimed that the *Yijing* way of thinking characterizes the basic mode of Chinese philosophical thinking. The *Yijing* arises from a process of comprehensive observation and empathetic feeling that generates penetrating understanding. The feeling of a person toward a given situation is the reciprocation and interaction between *yin* and *yang*, which leads to one's direct experience of the dynamics of unity in duality. There are, as shown above, five steps in realizing the understanding of reality. Apart from comprehensive observation and direct, simple, and penetrating feeling, there are understanding and thinking of reality by way of images. "Images" are actually form-objects or process-events, which we may refer to as overt and ostensible (observable and felt) things in the world. Hence, they are not arbitrary mental fabrications but things in the midst of the thickness of world-reality.

As our experiences of things as images can be said to be based on our feelings (*gan* 感) as responses (*ying* 應) to things that affect our perceptions, sensations, and feelings in concrete contexts, they are related to our cognitive language, on the one hand, and idea-intentions of the mind, on the other. In contrast to the transcendent views of Neo-Daoists such as Wang Bi (226–249 CE)—who believed that language, and then images, were to be abandoned as one realized ideas in the mind—according to the *Yijing*, there is an inclusive continuum. One can see events or things in the world on one side, image-language or symbols for naming and describing them in the middle, and mental activities in our ideas or feelings on the other side, thus forming an ontological-hermeneutical circle and a creative unity of understanding. It is in this sense that we can speak of a genuine ontological understanding or interpretation of reality, which is always rooted in, and supported individually and collectively by, a history of comprehensive observations, individualized feelings, and holistic penetrating syntheses, eventually yielding an organically interrelated image of things.

We can see how the *Yijing* thinking is largely a dynamic, dialectical (as a dialogical and negotiating process), interactive and integrative process of thinking and understanding, neither fixating on objects as essences nor insisting on reducing things or presentations to pure ideation. The philosophical orientation of the *Yi* is not essentialist, nor does it follow a reductive phenomenological methodology.

8. In this connection we may also mention that Chinese Buddhism is distinct from Indian Buddhism because of the fundamental notions of *benti*-ontology, which gives rise to the notion of original-nature and Buddha-nature that underpins many Chinese schools of Buddhism.

Instead, it consists of letting reality speak to us, and of our learning from concrete reality, being both context transcendent and context inclusive. It is focal, contextual, concrete, correlative, and dynamic.

We can point to the history of Chinese philosophy and show that the main developments are guided, inspired, sustained, and enriched by the primary model of onto-cosmological and onto-hermeneutical thinking, knowing, understanding, and interpreting found in the *Yijing:* the Han Confucianism of Dong Zhongshu 董仲舒; the Weijin 魏晋 Neo-Daoism of Wang Bi 王弼 and Guo Xiang 郭象; the Sui-Tang Buddhism of Tiantai 天台, Huayan 華嚴, and Chan 禪; the Song-Ming Neo-Confucianism of Zhou Dunyi, Zhang Zai, Shao Yong, Cheng Brothers, Zhu Xi 朱熹, Lu Xiangshan 陸象山, and Wang Yangming 王陽明; and, finally, the Qing Textual Confucianism of Duan Yucai 段玉裁 and Dai Zhen 戴震. A familiarity with the *Yi* paradigms of *bento*-ontology and onto-cosmological thinking is necessary for understanding much twentieth-century Chinese philosophy. Thus, understanding the *Yijing* is an ongoing task.

BIBLIOGRAPHY AND SUGGESTED READINGS

CHENG CHUNG-YING. (2003) "*Dao (Tao)*: The Way." In *Encyclopedia of Chinese Philosophy*, edited by Antonio Cua. London and New York: Routledge, 202–205.

CHENG CHUNG-YING. (2003) "Inquiry into the Primary Way: Yijing and the Onto-Hermeneutical Understanding." *Journal of Chinese Philosophy* 30 (3&4), 289–312.

LEGGE, JAMES (trans.). (1963) *The I Ching: The Book of Changes*. Mineola, NY: Dover Publications.

MARSHALL, S. J. (2001) *The Mandate of Heaven: Hidden History in the I Ching*. New York: Columbia University Press.

RUTT, RICHARD. (1996) *Zhouyi: The Book of Changes*. Richmond, UK: Curzon Press.

SMITH, RICHARD J. (2008) *Fathoming the Cosmos and Ordering the World: The Yijing (I Ching or Classic of Changes) and Its Evolution in China*. Charlottesville, VA: University of Virginia Press.

WILHELM, RICHARD. (1967) *I Ching, or Book of Changes*, trans. in English by Cary F. Baynes (3rd ed.). Princeton, NJ: Princeton University Press.

WILHELM, HELLMUT, and RICHARD WILHELM. (1995) *Understanding the I Ching*. Princeton, NJ: Princeton University Press.

CHAPTER 2

CLASSICAL CONFUCIANISM I: CONFUCIUS

PEIMIN NI

Confucius (551–479 BCE) was born during the Spring and Autumn period in Qufu, a town in the state of Lu in central China, when the glory of the early Zhou dynasty was declining but still in fresh memory in the minds of the people. The founders of the Zhou, King Wen and his brother Duke Zhou, laid the foundation of a humanitarian government in emulation of the ancient sage kings and refined the feudal ritual system. By the Spring and Autumn period, however, the social order of the Zhou was crumbling. It was with this historical background that China had its most fertile and glorious period in philosophy.

The word "Confucianism" is unknown to most Chinese, because in China it is generally referred to as "*ru jia* 儒家"—the school of *ru*, where "*ru*" refers not to Confucius, but to the practices and the way of life most distinctively represented by Confucius. Confucius's family name is Kong 孔, and his given name Qiu 丘. "Confucius," a Latinized term for "Kong Fu-zi 孔夫子," literally means "Master Kong" in Chinese. He lost his father when he was only three. His mother, from whom he received his primary education, raised him in a relatively humble situation. Confucius set his heart upon learning at the age of fifteen, and he became a determined learner. He started his teaching career in his early thirties, and is said to have had over three thousand students during his life. Among them, seventy-two became conversant with the "Six Arts" that he taught—ritual, music, archery, charioteering, writing, and arithmetic.

Confucius considered himself a "transmitter" rather than a creator. The wisdom that he taught, according to himself, was already entailed in the ancient traditional rituals, the history, music, poetry, and limited written works, which were, though corrupted in the ages of turmoil, still available at the time. He is believed to have edited some of the most basic Chinese classic books, including the *Book of Rites*, the *Book of History*, the *Book of Odes*, the *Book of Music*, and the *Book of Changes*. His own major teachings were recorded by his students and collected into the book known as *Lunyu*, the *Analects*. Confucius spent a considerable amount of his life traveling, trying to implement his humanistic ideas in political affairs. Deeply disappointed with contemporary rulers and having survived several life-threatening situations, he returned to his home state Lu at the age of sixty-eight, and died five years later with no anticipation of his subsequent fame as China's first and foremost teacher, a supreme sage, and a "king without a crown." His teachings were taken in China as the principles of morality, law, government, education, and life in general, which everyone was supposed to follow, from the emperor down to the ordinary people. Yet at the beginning of the twentieth century, he was also taken to be responsible for all that was backward and benighted in China, because most of the repressive practices of feudal China were conducted under the name of Confucianism, though in most cases they were contrary to the real spirit of the Master's own teachings.

The *Analects*, the "Bible" of Confucianism, consists of excerpts put together with no apparent logical order, and yet the passages in it are related like different sides of a crystal that reflect the lights of each other. To "unpack" and reorganize the philosophy entailed in it in our familiar style of discourse risks simplifying the interconnectedness of the passages. Readers are therefore cautioned to take this chapter as a guide and not as a substitute for reading the original work.[1]

The Unity between Heaven and Human Being

There is a spiritual and religious dimension in Confucianism, which contains a strong sense of mission, a journey that is not supposed to end before one's death (8.7), and an aim even more important than life itself (15.9). But there is neither deity worship nor priesthood in Confucianism. Confucian temples are more like monuments than monasteries.

Confucius's own attitude toward issues regarding deities and life after death is skeptical and pragmatic. "The Master did not talk about strange phenomena, . . . or spiritual beings" (7.21). His advice is to "Keep a distance from spiritual beings while showing them due reverence" (6.22). "If you are not yet able to serve people, how can you serve spiritual beings?" "If you do not yet understand life, how can you understand death?" (11.12). Zi Gong once asked Confucius whether those who were

1. The translations in this article are based on the books listed in the bibliography at the end, with some occasional modifications. Citations from the *Analects* are given in parentheses with the chapter and section numbers. For example, "(2.1)" means chapter 2, section 1 from the book of the *Analects*.

dead had consciousness. The Master said, "When you die, you will eventually know. It will not be too late to know by then."[2] These responses show a strong this-worldly attitude, with an openness to the possibility of the other world. They also show that for the Master, living a decent human life in this world will not cause regret regardless of whether or not there is an afterlife.

The spirituality of Confucianism is mostly associated with *tian* 天, usually translated as "Heaven." Confucius's Western Zhou predecessors had already replaced and gradually depersonalized the Shang dynasty notion of Shang Di 上帝, "Lord on High," with the notion of Heaven, without losing its sense of being a reality that governs worldly affairs, and they had brought the being from on high down to the human realm. Human beings began to be seen as a part of Heaven. The will of Heaven was no longer the will of an anthropomorphic deity that issued orders and gave blessings and sanctions from above; it immanently exhibited itself in popular consensus and in regular patterns of discernible social and natural events, and it could be affected by the moral undertakings of people. Under such a notion, rulers were considered sacred only so long as they were able to continue to be entrusted with the Mandate of Heaven (*tian ming* 天命).

Because Heaven is immanent, it is possible for humans to know its Mandate. Confucius says: "At the age of fifty, I knew the Mandate of Heaven (*tian ming* 天命)" (2.4). He did not explain specifically how he came to know it, but "Does Heaven speak? And yet the four seasons turn and the myriad things are born and grow within it" (17.19), says the Master. The will of Heaven is displayed through patterns of social and natural events, but unlike laws of nature, it seems inexplicable through words and needs to be experienced directly and embodied before one is able to know it. The Master shows a strong confidence that Heaven has bestowed virtue in him (7.23). Since the word for virtue, *de* 德, also means power, his confidence is derived from his faith in the power of the virtue given to him by Heaven. Even though otherwise Heaven often appeared to be at odds with him, the Master believed that "It is the human who is able to make the Way great, not the Way that can make the human great" (15.29). This statement also sheds light on "the Way" (*dao* 道), because it suggests that the Way is more a trajectory, a mode of acting, which is itself road building, than a metaphysical entity that is purely objective and external to human conduct.

Confucius sometimes talked about *ming* 命, a term usually translated as "destiny." Since the word for mandate is also the same character, and it is sometimes used interchangeably with *tian* (Heaven), it is easy to confuse it with *tian ming*. *Ming* is different from the Mandate of Heaven in that the latter is more of a moral imperative, and the former is more of a determination of certain phenomena, usually in a particular order or sequence. For instance, when a natural event happens beyond a person's control, it would be considered *ming* (see, for example, 6.10 and 12.5). Similarly, whether the Way eventually prevails or not, given the human efforts

2. Sun Xing Yan and Guo Yi, Kong Zi Ji Yu Jiao Bu [孔子集语校补 Collected Sayings of Confucius, Proofread and with New Additions] (Shangdong: Qi Lu Shu She, 1998), p. 21.

involved, is determined by *ming* (14.36). Since Heaven is more like nature that is beyond personal control, so what is by "*ming*" is also by "*tian*," Heaven.

Ren—Human-heartedness

Variously translated as "benevolence," "human-heartedness," "authoritative person/conduct," "altruism," "humanity," "goodness," and so forth, *ren* 仁 is a concept most prominent in Confucius's philosophy. Yet the Master never offered a precise definition of it, nor have translators been able to come up with a uniform English translation.

Some observations, however, can help us understand it. First, the word "*ren*" is occasionally used in Confucian texts as somewhat synonymous to "human" or "person"—*ren* 人—which is, in Chinese, homophonic to it (see *Mencius*, 1B.15 and *Zhongyong* 20). This fact shows that "the distinction between the two terms [人 and 仁] must be qualitative: two distinguishable degrees of what it means to be a person" (Hall & Ames, 114). Thus, the word "*ren* 仁" can be interpreted as a quality that makes a person an authentic human being, which every biological human needs to strive toward. Second, the word consists of two elements, "person 人" and the number "two 二." This etymological analysis, says Ames and Rosemont, "underscores the Confucian assumption that one cannot become a person by oneself—we are, from our inchoate beginnings, irreducibly social" (Ames & Rosemont, 48). Indeed, many descriptions of *ren* in the *Analects* are about interpersonal relations. "*Ren*" is to "love people" (12.22), says the Master, and the method to be *ren* is "*shu* 恕"—comparing one's own heart with other hearts with compassion (6.30). Third, we observe that when asked about *ren*, Confucius gave different answers to different disciples according to their particular needs for personal development. This fact suggests that *ren* is more like an art that needs to be mastered, embodied, and displayed in one's gestures and manners, rather than a formula to be understood or accepted by the intellect. *Ren*, then, is a quality pertaining to one's caring dispositions toward others that has to be developed and fully embodied before a biological person can become an authentic human being.

Twice when asked about *ren*, Confucius answers in the form of the negative version of the "Golden Rule"—"Do not impose upon others what you yourself do not want" (12.2, 15.24)—and he endorses a positive version of it also, for he says: "If you want to establish yourself, establish others. If you want to promote yourself, promote others" (6.30). However, while taking the "Golden Rule" as a rule has the problem of basing rights and wrongs on unqualified personal likes and dislikes, Confucius never took it as a rule, much less as "Golden." He states clearly that a morally exemplary person, *jun zi* 君子, "is never for or against anything invariably. He is always on the side of the appropriate" (4.10). Confucius "rejects ... inflexibility and rigidity" (9.4, see also 15.37). Confucius himself was characterized as a sage who acted according to circumstances rather than rules (*Mencius*, 5B.1). The art of flexibility is deemed by the Master so high that he says to find a partner good enough in the exercise of *quan* 權 (discretion) is more difficult than finding a partner good enough in taking a stand or in the pursuit of the Way (9.30). The word "*quan*" originally means "scale," and thus the action of "weighing" as well. According to *Gong Yang Zhuan* 公羊傳, a Chinese classic from as early as the Zhou dynasty, "*quan* means moral goodness resulting from transgressing well-established classics" ("The 11th Year of the Duke of Huan").

Confucius is not uncritical of desires and wants. In fact, one of Confucius's major descriptions of *ren* is "To restrain the self" (12.1). When a disciple asked, "Is there one expression that can be acted upon throughout one's entire life?" the Master replied, "There is *shu* 恕. Do not impose on others what you yourself do not want" (15.24). In another passage, right after the statement of his positive version of the "Golden Rule," the Master says: "Taking an analogy near at hand is the method of becoming *ren*" (6.30). The word "*shu*" consists of two parts: the upper part, "*ru* 如," means "like," "as if," or "resemble," and the lower part, "*xin* 心," means "heart-mind." This etymological analysis helps us to understand that for Confucius, the application of the "Golden Rule" is to take one's own heart as an analogy near at hand and to extend one's considerations to the wants and needs of others empathically.

According to such a reading, the "Golden Rule" is no different from "*shu*," a *method* to be *ren*. Even though there is no guarantee for the method to lead to right actions all the time, it helps a person to become sensitive to the interests of others. In contrast to a rule, which allows no exceptions and is imposed upon the agent as an obligation, proscribing certain acts, a method is mastered by the agent, enables the agent to perform the right action, and is not to be used when its application is unwarranted.

Confucius also characterizes *ren* as to "love the people" (12.22). Extending beyond personal interest and into interpersonal caring, love is characteristic of human-heartedness. Love must be from the heart and not merely from the rational faculty of the mind. Whether in daily life or in governmental affairs, a *ren* person is always considerate and has others' interests in mind. In running a government, the *ren* ruler "is frugal in his expenditures and loves his subordinates, and puts the common people to work only at the proper season of year" (1.5). In daily life, he "loves the multitude broadly" (1.6).[3]

One of the Confucian qualifications for proper love is to love with distinction. Confucius differentiates according to relationships and social roles. "When his stables caught fire, the Master hurried back from court and asked, 'Was anyone hurt?' He did not inquire after the horses" (10.17). It does not mean that he cared nothing about animals. "The Master fished with a line, but did not use a net; he used an arrow and line, but did not shoot at roosting birds" (7.27). Among humans, he also believes

3. Indeed, the statement that all men "should act towards one another in a spirit of brotherhood" in the United Nations' Declaration of Human Rights is derived from the Confucian saying that "all within the four seas are brothers" (12.5).

that one should start with loving one's own parents and gradually extend the love to others according to degrees of closeness in relations. Filial piety (*xiao* 孝) is considered the very root of a proper social order. "The morally exemplary person concentrates his efforts on the root; for the root having taken hold, the Way will grow therefrom. Aren't filial piety and fraternal deference the roots of becoming human-hearted indeed?" (1.2). Here we find the love to be both a characteristic of the *ren* person and a method of becoming *ren*. By practicing *ren*, *ren* grows. If we do not start our love from the immediate context of our life and with those whom we immediately encounter, it will not start at all. As a method, it is not to be confused with a moral imperative or principle. Confucius's reference to his fellow villagers' way of dealing with one's own family member's misconduct by mutual concealment (13.18) becomes a defense of injustice if we take it to be an ethical principle, but it becomes sacrificing a branch for the sake of saving the root when we treat it as a method.

Confucius also differentiates love according to circumstances. He would rather help the needy than make the rich richer (6.4). Unlike "eye for an eye and tooth for a tooth" or Jesus Christ's exhortation to turn the other cheek, Confucius repays ill will with uprightness or straightforwardness (*zhi* 直). If you repay ill will with kindness, says the Master, "then how would you repay kindness?" (14.34). In classic Chinese grammar many words can serve as verb, noun, or adjective; thus, *zhi* may also mean "to straighten" or "to correct."

Ren is also what makes a person worthy of respect. According to Kant, rational beings are ends in themselves because they can make free choices and are therefore the source of value. For Confucius, however, one earns reverence from others by being respectful oneself. "If one is respectful, one will not suffer insult" (17.6, 1.13). Confucius says, "The exemplary person does not speak more than what he can accomplish, and does not behave across the line of proper conduct, people revere him without being forced to" (*Book of Rites*, ch. 27). The respect one deserves is therefore in proportion to the level of one's cultivation. But this teaching aims at reminding everyone to cultivate oneself rather than serving as a reason for disrespecting others. Repeatedly Confucius reminds his students to set strict standards for themselves and to be lenient to others (see 15.15, 4.14, 14.30, 15.19, and 15.21).

Yi and *Li*—Appropriateness and Ritual Propriety

While *ren* is the internal quality or disposition that makes a person an authentic person, *yi* 義 is the appropriateness of actions that typically originates from *ren*. For being appropriate in one's action, however, one also needs the guidance of *li* 禮, ritual propriety; otherwise, a person of *ren* can still go astray. Confucius says, "not being mediated by the observance of the ritual propriety, in being respectful a person will wear himself out, in being cautious he will be timid, in being bold he will be unruly, and in being forthright he will be rude" (8.2).

The word *li* originally meant holy ritual or sacrificial ceremony. It was used more broadly by Confucius to mean behavior patterns established and accepted as appropriate through history by a community, including what we call manners, etiquette, ceremonies, customs, rules of propriety, and so forth. The metaphor of holy ritual serves as a reminder that the most ordinary activities in our life can also be ritualistic or ceremonial. When a disciple asked about filial conduct, the Master replied: "Those who are called filial today are considered so because they are able to provide for their parents. But even dogs and horses are given that much care. If you do not respect your parents, what is the difference?" (2.7). By serving and dining with respect and appreciation in a proper setting, the mere physical nourishment becomes a ceremony, and thereby becomes human. Learning rituals is therefore no different from learning to be human. Through ritual propriety, social activities and human relations are coordinated in a civilized way. The relevance of a ritual setting to humanity is further illustrated by the Master's interesting comparison of a disciple to a sacrificial vase of jade (5.4), for the vessel's sacredness does not reside in the preciousness of its material or in its beauty. It is sacred "because it is a constitutive element in the ceremony.... By analogy, Confucius may be taken to imply that the individual human being, too, has ultimate dignity, sacred dignity by virtue of his role in rite, in ceremony, in *li*" (Fingarette, 75).

Confucius values ritual proprieties so highly that he says, "If for a single day one were able to return to the observance of ritual propriety, the whole empire would defer to *ren*" (12.1). One reason for this is that humans are like raw materials—they need to be carved, chiseled, grounded, and polished to become authentic persons (1.15). Learning ritual propriety is such a process. By practicing ritual propriety, a person can be transformed and established (8.8). Most people learn their basic moral lessons in their youth, not by studying Kantian formulations of the categorical imperative or utilitarian calculations, but by repeated use of rituals such as saying "thank you," which increases one's sense of appreciation, and "I am sorry," which increases one's sensitivity to others' pain.

This learning is basic but not at all primitive. The skill of dealing with subtle and sophisticated human relationships has to be learned from actual life. It is more a knowing "how" than knowing "what." Only from this perspective can we understand and appreciate the passages in the *Analects* that give detailed accounts of how the Master greeted his guests, dressed himself, ate, sat, and so forth. The subtlety and complexity of the coordinated ritual acts are certainly beyond what can be encapsulated in any abstract principle.

Though Confucius advocated the traditional ritual proprieties, nowhere did he say that they must be unchangeable (see, for example, 9.3). When asked about the root of observing ritual propriety, the Master replied, "What an important question! In observing ritual propriety, it is better to be modest than extravagant; in mourning, it is better to express real grief than to worry over formal details" (3.4). The principle behind this is the humanitarian spirit, *ren*, not the mere traditional formality (see also 11.1).

Zheng—Social and Political Philosophy

Just as the role of a vessel in a ceremony is specific, ritual proprieties also serve as fabrics of a social order. In the ideal Confucian society, everyone knows his or her own social position and conducts his or her life according to the rituals appropriate to it, though this does not entail the rigidity of one's social position. The Master is himself a role model: "At court, when speaking with lower officials, he was congenial, and when speaking with higher officials, straightforward yet respectful. In the presence of his lord, he was reverent though composed" (10.2). In these rituals the social roles and relationships are confirmed and communicated, the responsibilities that come with them are taken, and the human-heartedness is displayed.

Confucius explicitly regarded administrative rules and law enforcement as inferior to the way of ritual propriety and moral excellence for achieving social order. "Lead the people with administrative injunctions and keep them orderly with penal law, and they will avoid punishments but will be without a sense of shame. Lead them with excellence (*de* 德) and keep them orderly through observing ritual propriety, and they will develop a sense of shame, and moreover, will order themselves" (see 2.3). The Master said, "In hearing litigation, I am no different from anyone else. But if you insist on a difference, it is that I try to get people to have no need to resort to litigation in the first place" (12.13). In public affairs, if those who are in superior positions are fond of ritual propriety, the common people will be easy to command (14.41), so easy that they will even follow without any command (13.6, 15.5). Confucius believed that the way to conduct *zheng* 政 (to govern) requires one to be *zheng* 正, a homophone that means "being proper," "straight," "orderly," "to correct," or "to make straight." The two words are not merely homophonous; they have an intrinsic affinity. "Being proper (*zheng* 正) in their own position, what difficulty would the rulers have in governing? But if not able to set themselves proper, how can they set others proper?" (13.13; see also 12.19 and 12.17). This is the Confucian notion of *wu wei* 無為—action by nonaction, a notion more well known for its Daoist affiliation. While the Daoist *wu wei* is to do things naturally and spontaneously, the Confucian *wu wei* is to accomplish intended results by ritual proprieties enlivened by moral virtue.

The kind of order secured by ritual propriety and moral excellence is also totally different from what law and administrative enforcement can achieve. It is not only more penetrating and less coercive, but more importantly, it harmonizes. "Achieving harmony is the most valuable function of observing ritual propriety" (1.12). Harmony (*he* 和) is different from conformity (*tong* 同). "The exemplary person pursues harmony rather than conformity; the petty minded is the opposite" (13.23). While the parts forced into conformity are in agreement with each other at the cost of their individuality, the parts of a harmonious whole mutually enhance each other without sacrificing their uniqueness. People in harmonious relations *participate in* social activities and construction, not merely being *constituents of* them. In this order there is hierarchy, but it is supposed to be one of deference to excellence and reciprocity rather than an order of aristocracy.

Exemplary persons do search for agreement on principal matters such as humanheartedness and *dao*, the way, as "People who have chosen different ways (*dao*) cannot make plans together," says the Master (15.40). But the way is not formulated as a set of abstract universal principles. The agreement is based on *zhengming* 正名, ordering or rectifying names, so that each person will know what is expected of him or her in a given web of particular relationships. When asked about what would be the priority in bringing order to a state, Confucius replied, "Without question it would be to order names properly" (13.3). Using names, for Confucians, is like implementing strategies or devices that stipulate expectations. "The ruler must rule, the minister minister, the father father, and the son son" (12.11). Each "name" carries with it a norm that whoever bears the name is expected to follow. When Confucius was editing the *Spring and Autumn Annals*, he paid special attention to the use of words, since words carry the force that can affect reality 名可制實. That is why Confucius advises people to "speak cautiously" (2.18). In the Confucian rectification of names, reality is supposed to match words, and the aim of rectification is to ensure that, as pegs of role expectations, the names are acceptable. In contrast, in the referential use of language familiar to philosophies preoccupied with obtaining truth and knowledge, words are supposed to match reality, and the aim of rectification is to ensure that they represent reality.

It would be inadequate to take Confucius's teachings as merely advocating a social and political moral theory, because they also aim at achieving personal freedom and aesthetic creativity. In his famous short autobiography, Confucius says, "At the age of seventy, I was able to follow my heart-mind's (*xin* 心) will (*yu* 欲) without overstepping the line" (2.4). Unlike the freedom of indifference in which one does not know which choice is better, this freedom of cultivated spontaneity frees one even from making choices! Just like any decent human being would not deliberate on whether or not to kick an innocent child for fun, a well-cultivated person will have no need for deliberation in most cases. Of course, for Confucius freedom is not a personal matter, for a person is so inseparable from others that her domain of choice is itself defined and transformed by her interaction with others.

Xue—Learning to Be Human

As a system of teachings that oriented toward personal cultivation and manifestation of *ren* and *li*, the topics of learning, thinking, and attaining knowledge are important to Confucianism.

One distinctive feature of the Confucian way of dealing with learning, thinking, and knowledge is that they all contain the *heart* part of the *xin* 心, heart-mind. The heart is engaged in the process of reaching a deeper understanding, of critical evaluation, and of appropriating what is learned so that one is able to apply it creatively and artistically. Responding to a disciple's question about mourning his parents,

Confucius asked, "Would you feel at ease?" (17.21). This question forces the disciple to bring whatever feelings and ideas that he encounters in front of his moral subjectivity and examine whether or not he can accept them at ease. When another disciple asked Confucius about the exemplary person, the Master said, "The exemplary person is free from worry and apprehension. . . . If there is nothing to be ashamed of upon self-reflection, what can the person be worried about and afraid of?" (12.4). It is no coincidence that the Chinese language contains lexicons that can be illustrative of the bodily characteristic of the Confucian way of thinking and knowing, such as "*ti yan* 體驗," bodily experience; "*ti hui* 體會," bodily understanding; "*ti cha* 體察," bodily examination; "*ti zhi* 體知," bodily knowing; and "*ti ren* 體認," bodily recognition. The subject does not passively receive impressions, nor does she merely reason intellectually. She experiences with the body engaged, understands with her heart in empathy, examines with the sensitivity of the body, and knows with the body dispositioned to act upon what is known.

The entire process of learning and reflection involves the body, and thus requires practice. The outcome is not an accumulated body of propositional knowledge but a set of abilities, which Song and Ming dynasty Confucians call "*gongfu* 功夫" (*kungfu*), usually obtained through receiving training from masters and through one's own diligent practice. The *Analects* shows that when asked about *ren* by the disciples, Confucius never tried to describe *ren* per se. He talked about what a *ren* person would be like and how she would act, and he gave instructions according to each disciple's particular condition, letting them know on which level and which aspect they should start or continue their practice. The teaching method is indeed more typical of *gongfu* masters than of philosophy teachers in the common sense of the term.

The Confucian *gongfu* culminates with *zhongyong* (see 6.29). "*Zhong* 中" means "centrality," or "not to be one-sided." "*Yong* 庸" means "ordinary" or "commonality," "practicality," and "constancy." When "*zhong*" and "*yong*" are used together as one term, it can be translated as "centering the commonality." There is considerable overlap between the Confucian doctrine of *zhongyong* and the Aristotelian Golden Mean. Both mean the virtue (not necessarily moral virtue), or excellence, of avoiding two extreme vices—deficiency and excess (see 11.16, 11.22, and 20.1), and not a state of being mediocre. By associating "*zhong*" with "*yong*," Confucius advises people to constantly practice *zhong* in the ordinary or common life that makes our heart-mind always at ease when we do the appropriate things. Since everyday life situations are dynamic and there is no rigid rule to follow, the person has to embody the *gongfu* to respond to differing situations in a consistent way, and be creative, as a cocreator of the universe. After all, the unity between Heaven and humanity is not a combination of two entities, or a human's ascendance to another world. It is rather one's becoming truly human in serving parents, taking care of children, respecting teachers, helping friends, and finding enjoyment in these activities (see 7.19).

Unlike the common conception of art that associates artworks with studios and galleries, the Confucian art is a way of life itself. If a master of conventional arts is one who dissolves the opposition between the mind and the "hands" and between the hands and the objects, the Confucian aesthetic life is one in which the person achieves unity with Heaven and is able to participate with Heaven in creation. The person embodies *zhi*, knowledge or wisdom, and is therefore not perplexed; she embodies *ren*, human-heartedness, and is therefore not worrisome; she is courageous, and is therefore not timid (9.29). The person enjoys water, for wisdom is like water, dynamic and creative. The person enjoys mountains, for human-heartedness is like the mountains, enduring and full of dignity (6.23). The Confucian artistic creation is displayed in one's entire life, including ordinary daily activities.

BIBLIOGRAPHY

AMES, ROGER T., and HENRY ROSEMONT, JR. (1998) *The Analects of Confucius: A Philosophical Translation.* New York: Ballantine Books.

Book of Rites (LI CHI). (1967) Translated by James Legge. New Hyde Park, NY: University Books.

CHEN, WING-TSIT. (1963) *A Source Book in Chinese Philosophy.* Princeton, NJ: Princeton University Press.

FINGARETTE, HERBERT. (1972) *Confucius—The Secular as Sacred.* New York: Harper and Row.

GRAHAM, A. C. (1989) *Disputers of the Tao.* La Salle, IL: Open Court.

HALL, DAVID L., and ROGER T. AMES. (1987). *Thinking Through Confucius.* Albany, NY: State University of New York Press.

NI, PEIMIN. (2002) *On Confucius.* Belmont, CA: Wadsworth.

CHAPTER 3

CLASSICAL CONFUCIANISM II: MENCIUS AND ZUNZI

MANYUL IM

MENCIUS 孟子 (ca. 370–289 BCE) and Xunzi 荀子 (ca. 310–220 BCE) are the only two early scholars in the Confucian lineage (known as the *ru* 儒, or "Ritualists," in the period) whose teachings were handed down in relatively complete, eponymous form. Additionally, the high quality of their teachings has led the tradition to regard them as the two most prominent Confucians after Confucius. Mencius was generally considered to be superior to Xunzi by practicing Confucian scholar-gentlemen. This was due in part to strong Han dynasty (202 BCE–220 CE) biases against Xunzi based on the notoriety of his most famous student, Han Feizi (280–233 BCE), the Legalist. During the great Song dynasty (960–1279 CE) revival of Confucianism, Zhu Xi (1130–1200 CE) institutionalized Mencius's favored position by establishing the *Mencius* as one of "the Four Classics" along with the *Analects* of Confucius, the *Great Learning*, and the *Doctrine of the Mean*. More recently, Xunzi has become the object of much scholarly interest and commentary.

In both cases, their teachings are directed toward improving the justification of Confucian social and political norms during a time when philosophical challenges to traditional mores and institutions were proliferating. However, they proceed through very different strategies of justification. Mencius, in effect, argues that Confucian norms are best suited to express innate, central facets of human psychological dispositions. Xunzi appeals to the transformative effect of Confucian ritual training and education in producing the most desirable state of affairs—a state in which both intrapersonal and interpersonal desire-satisfaction is efficient, harmonious, and orderly. Interestingly, given the emphasis on rituals in the *Analects* of Confucius and in the *Xunzi*, and the relative lack of direct discussion of ritual in the *Mencius*, the continuity of teachings attributed to Confucius with those of Xunzi is arguably stronger than with those of Mencius.

Philosophical Contexts

Confucius and his detractors set the stage for both Mencius's and Xunzi's philosophical agendas, and it is important to see how they acknowledge this. The vision implemented by Confucius called for the agents of governance, from the lowest knight-scholars in training up to the highest ministers, dukes, and the emperor, to return and adhere to traditional forms of cultural and ethical education. Such forms were established, Confucius believed, in the early days of the Zhou dynasty (ca. 1040–256 BCE). Enculturation and education of this kind involved instilling in the student—or in oneself in the case of self-cultivation—traditional norms concerning proper conduct and feeling, both in mundane activity and in formal ceremony. The texts associated with such education consisted of poetry, historical documents, and ceremonial ritual manuals, all of which required careful study and correct interpretation for achieving proper moral, social, and political guidance, that is, for achieving the proper *dao*. Hence, textual and ritual mastery were the marks of the gentleman, or *junzi*, the model for properly cultivated personhood.

The tradition-centered justification of social and political norms implicit in Confucius's teachings was opposed in immediately subsequent generations by those who did not share his optimism about the efficacy of the Zhou cultural template. Particularly influential in Mencius's era were the teachings of Mozi (400s BCE) and his followers, who argued that social and political action should be guided by considerations of increasing benefit (*li*利) for all people in all places. The key to accomplishing this, they argued, was for everyone to adopt universally inclusive affection (*jian ai* 兼愛) for fellow humans. Based on direct reports in the *Mencius* and other extant philosophical literature of the era, it is clear that during Mencius's time there were at least two other influential movements, though their details are very sketchy. One involved an apparent form of individualism or egoism coupled with a tendency toward eremitism. The other involved some kind of agro-primitivism that promoted a return to simpler modes of thinking, feeling, and living together, while rejecting ideals of enculturation and civilization.

Mencius was acutely concerned by the Mohist threat to Confucian teachings. This is evident in some of Mencius's own reasoning directed toward production of beneficial consequences, which bears some resemblance to the Mohists, though it is clear that he thought *direct* concern with benefit should be avoided (*Mencius* 1A.1). His more emphatic criticisms of Mohism are directed toward the latter's doctrine that adoption of universally inclusive affection is both necessary and possible for social harmony (3A.5). So, Mencius's agenda is shaped by his concern with correcting what he took to be an erroneous mode of practical reasoning and an implausible theory of psychology. His emphasis on innate elements of human psychology and the guidance they provide in the direction of a traditional form of life takes aim, in large part, at the Mohists.

A generation later, Xunzi felt the threat of at least six types of errant teachings, roughly hedonism, asceticism, Mohism, legalism, logical paradox mongering, and less-than-competent forms of Confucianism. In addition to these teachings, he perceived an unfortunately strong tendency toward superstition among the people, particularly with regard to appeasing Heaven—which Xunzi regarded as an impersonal and constant force or process—and with physiognomic divination. Against these teachings, Xunzi asserts a carefully crafted set of arguments and analyses aimed at showing how education and self-cultivation based on traditional forms of literature, music, and ritual transform what might be a life that is beastly at worst and coarse at best into a life of refinement and nobility. Along the way, he provides observations and arguments that he believes dismiss the multifarious theoretical errors of his day regarding both the natural world and important aspects of human artifice, including the nature of language.

Mencius: The Power and Availability of Virtuous Rulership

One of the ways in which Mencius is portrayed by the author(s) of the eponymous text is as a kind of gadfly to the ambitious rulers of Liang, Qi, and other kingdoms of the Warring States period (479–221 BCE). It was a period of political and social unrest that emerged during the final, waning years of the Zhou dynasty. Each of these rulers sought to expand his power and unify the perceived civilized world under a new dynastic order. Mencius is shown making the most of the audiences he is given—he is often critical, didactic, and encouraging in the same passages. In these exchanges Mencius discourses on moral and political responsibility, as well as providing important outlines of his moral psychology. His focus is always on the responsibilities that someone in the ruler's position has toward his people and toward implementation of the ritual, ceremonial, and interpersonal norms that are contained in benevolence (*ren* 仁), rectitude (*yi* 義), ritual propriety (*li* 禮), and wisdom (*zhi* 智), the four central Mencian virtues (2A.6). Other character traits a ruler or subject might have are subsumed under these virtues. For example, courage (*yong* 勇) is dependent on rectitude (2A.2) for ethical utility; compassion (*en* 恩) must be guided by benevolence and sometimes checked by ritual propriety (1A.7).

Two main points Mencius emphasizes with these rulers are (1) that they can only unify the kingdoms under their power by implementing the virtues in themselves and (2) that they are themselves responsible for such implementation. It is important to disambiguate the first point. Mencius does not regard the virtues as mere means to the end of unifying the kingdoms. Rather, they are constitutive of the type of governance that Mencius thinks will naturally draw other people and rulers to the virtuous ruler because others will recognize the ideal state that results from it. This seems to be Mencius's construal of the very important concept of *de* 德, which is frequently translated as "virtue," but is better glossed as "power to influence." It also encompasses issues that have to do with the Warring States concept of the Mandate of Heaven (*tian ming* 天命). The Mandate of Heaven to rule over the empire seems to receive a naturalistic interpretation in Mencius's idea that a ruler is only fit for such a position *and* sufficiently capable of attaining it through possession and implementation of the virtues.

The second point, often understated in secondary literature, is one to which Mencius seems to return quite often: each of these rulers has only himself to blame for lack of success in unifying the kingdoms. For each of them, the necessary virtues are readily available should they desire them. It is the ruler's desire for the virtues and the implementation of the actions and policies that the virtues dictate that is lacking. Most often it seems to be due to insufficient benevolence—a virtue quite accessible to these particular rulers, Mencius thinks—that their ambitions are not realized. Could it really be that Mencius thinks the virtues are readily available to these rulers, should they only desire them? That would perhaps be in keeping with the statement in the *Analects* that as soon as one desires benevolence, it is available (7.30). However, some prominent commentators have interpreted this sort of criticism of the rulers by Mencius less than literally. The idea that these kings actually have the virtues so readily available to them seems at odds with the assumption that the stringent work of self-cultivation is necessary for such attainment. One way in which Mencius might be understood nonliterally would be to interpret his ruler-directed injunctions to "just do it" (*wei zhi er yi yi* 為之而已) (1A.7) to apply not so much to virtuous action, but to the necessary prior work of self-cultivation. Another possibility would be that Mencius is not entirely sincere in his remarks to the rulers and instead is overstating their abilities for virtue in order to encourage them toward some approximation of true virtue. Whatever the reading, the struggle to influence these rulers, in which Mencius ultimately fails, speaks to his high—perhaps naive—optimism about human nature. To this subject we now turn.

Mencius: Natural Human Capacities and the Confucian Life

The other main portrayal of Mencius is as a teacher to particular disciples and as a participant in disputes with other thinkers, some Mohist, others harder to identify. In these exchanges, it is clear that Mencius employs techniques of disputation that are evident in other Warring States texts as well. For example, he is familiar with the rhetoric of pointing out similarities between cases and pressing for consistency in his opponents' attitudes toward them (5B.4, 6A.7, 6A.12, and 7B.31)—what some commentators have called "analogical reasoning." In other instances of intense debate, most famously in the disputes with an opposing philosopher named Gaozi (6A.1–6), Mencius's reasoning is less clear. It is, however, in these more ambiguous disputes that we find the most historically prominent aspects of Mencian thought. In the Gaozi exchanges, Mencius lays out an important connection between the activities of the heart and human nature (*ren xing* 人性). He then defends the contention that human nature is good (*shan* 善) against Gaozi's claim that it is neither good nor bad (*e* 惡). (Xunzi held a third view, discussed below—that human nature is bad.)

Mencius's position on human nature seems grounded in his belief that the human heart is the source of the judgments, feelings, and motivation that are associated with the central virtues (benevolence, rectitude, ritual propriety, and wisdom). There are other sources of judgment and motivation, broadly speaking, of an aesthetic kind. However, these other sources, which include the eyes, ears, nose, mouth, and limbs, lack the capacity for reflection (*si* 思) and require the heart to provide a kind of internal governance (6A.7, 14, 15). Mencius believes that the heart both reflectively and spontaneously makes superior judgments and, if allowed, provides the right feelings and motivations for being virtuous. Hence, though there are a variety of potential sources within the human organism for normative judgment, he defends a naturally normative hierarchy among these sources. The heart has a special ability that makes it naturally more fit to "lead" the organism. Mencius regards the capacities of the human heart to be possessed by all humans by nature. The heart and its capacities are endowments (*cai* 才) of Nature, or Heaven (6A.6, 15). Further, these capacities, Mencius thinks, are naturally disposed to engage in certain situations or toward certain kinds of objects. In short, all humans have natural dispositions to judge some things as admirable, objectionable, honorable, or shameful and to feel compassion, familial affection, respect, and so forth for the right sorts of people (2A.6, 6A.6).

As already noted, this interest in the human heart serves the Mencian defense of Confucian norms that are derived from the models of action, feeling, ceremony, and governance of Zhou dynastic culture against those, such as the Mohists, who propose more radical systematic principles of action and feeling. Mencius pursued the systematic grounding of Confucian norms in the nature of the human organism. The natural needs, reactions, judgments, and tastes with which a typical person is born determine, he thought, the type of life that is good for people. Such a life should accommodate those natural aspects, in particular as reflected in the naturally superior reactions and reflective normative judgments of the heart. Mencius connects such accommodation of human life to the practices of traditional culture, for example, through the defense of traditional mourning periods and burial rituals against Mohist criticism (3A.2, 5). Those defenses rely on the argument that such practices serve to satisfy the desires that are naturally generated by the heart's judgments about what is proper to feel toward one's deceased parents. In Mencius's analysis such feelings and judgments that sometimes spring spontaneously from the human heart and sometimes emerge from careful reflection reveal that the type of life that is best for humans is one supported by Confucian norms.

How does a life guided by Confucian norms accommodate human nature, according to Mencius? First, it is a life that nurtures those feelings and judgments so that they are not damaged or suppressed. Second, it is a life that expresses the variations in strength and quality such feelings and judgments have as they apply to different people and circumstances within an individual's life. The first aspect of such a life includes the principle that generates Mencius's aforementioned discourses on the proper way to rule and legitimize political governance: nurture and guard the feelings and judgments that are natural to people. This is why Mencius focuses his conversations with rulers on providing benevolently for the economic, social, and educational well-being of the people. This principle also underlies the aforementioned theoretical disputes about human nature. The second aspect of the best human life includes the justification for a specifically structured society, one that is primarily derived from the structure and norms of traditional Zhou society. Because there are specifically graded feelings and judgments based on gradations and qualities of relationship among people, the best society for humans must recognize such nuances of relationship and express the sometimes hierarchic and asymmetric structure of the associated feelings. For Mencius, Confucian rituals and norms for proper conduct and feeling provide guidance for this kind of society.

Xunzi: The Transformative Power of Confucian Education

Whereas Mencius is portrayed from a third-person perspective in the *Mencius*—in the doxographic style of the era—Xunzi seems more likely to be the "first-person" author of the text that bears his name. Perhaps because of this the *Xunzi* exhibits extraordinary systematicity and flair in its organization and rhetorical style. The most impressive sections and books are both lengthy and sharply focused. They also reveal a sharp analytical and speculative style that serves Xunzi's goals of correcting existing philosophical errors and explicating the true nature of the universe and human life. These are lofty, but they are also the goals of a Confucian who, in a fiercely combative intellectual context, is faced with the task of rationally defending contemporary adherence to traditional social and political ideas that Confucius traced back to an ever-receding, distant past. Xunzi's defense may be said to consist of three broad philosophical projects: providing an analysis of the process and benefits of a Confucian-style education; providing an account of the historical and practical grounds for Confucian sociopolitical ideals; and settling the more abstract disputes concerning nature, knowledge, and psychology. Xunzi relies on several modes of analysis throughout these projects. The most frequent seem to be drawing on analogies from the natural world and from skill-crafts, construction of hypothetical thought experiments, and pointing out facts or phenomena that are clearly observable to all.

What ties together much of Xunzi's work is his emphasis on the transformative effects of education and self-cultivation, largely through the poetry, music, and rituals of Confucian life, incorporating traditional texts, forms, and activities. This is the backbone of Xunzi's thought. In education and self-cultivation, it is the refined and noble quality of a person's demeanor, inner psychological state, and activity that justifies the program of education and regimen of self-cultivation. The knowledge contained in the Zhou-derived rituals, music, odes, and historical documents and records, according to Xunzi, enters the heart, disperses throughout the body, and is manifested both in activity and in rest (*Xunzi* 1.9). In books 19 and 20, Xunzi argues that both at the individual level and at the social level, the transformative effects of music and ritual are not only desirable but also absolutely necessary for social life. They are needed in order to turn potential, individual psychological turmoil as well as public, social chaos into something orderly, effective, and refined. *What it is* that makes the refinement and nobility of the educated and self-cultivated gentleman desirable reveals the axiological underpinning of Xunzi's views.

There is a deeply aesthetic sensibility underlying Xunzi's theory of value, not unlike the one that often surfaces in Aristotle's—and the ancient Greeks' more generally—view of what is good: the fine or beautiful (*kalon*). This is most evident in Xunzi's discussions of human nature in book 23. The nature (*xing*) of humans is bad (*e*), according to Xunzi. A more accurate rendering of *e* translates to the view that human nature is "ugly" or "repulsive." This rendering is borne out by Xunzi's analysis. The reason that human nature is bad is because natural human tendencies are driven by desires that, if indulged, would cause complete chaos. They would do so because they are, in their untutored state, blind to important social distinctions that divide objects of desire into categories of acceptable and unacceptable, and into ranked orderings of distribution based on seniority of honor and age. Much as in Hobbesian moral theory, the "state of nature" for Xunzi is one that is fearful and, more important, disorderly. According to Xunzi, from the ancients to his own day what everyone has called good is what is upright, patterned, peaceful, and regimented (23.3). Hence, the results of letting human nature determine the actions and feelings of individuals would be far from good.

Xunzi: Confucian Life as a Corrective to Human Nature

According to Xunzi, his own analysis of human nature stands in stark contrast to-and corrects—Mencius's view that human nature is good. As we have seen, Mencius does consider the capacities of the heart to be the saving grace bestowed on humans by Heaven. Without the judgments, desires, and feelings of the heart that are inborn, there would be no guidance for humans. Xunzi is perhaps most famous, or notorious, among those with a passing familiarity for this unilateral debate with Mencius regarding human nature. Scholars of Confucianism through the ages have argued variously that Xunzi either misunderstood Mencius's view or that he was simply wrong about the constituents of human nature.

But it is useful to note how the differences in their views may be analyzed by more even-handed scholarship (for example, by D. C. Lau in Kline and Ivanhoe, 2000). On the one hand, Mencius's focus is on what he takes to be a natural ability of discernment, expressed either in judgments or in feeling, regarding what is proper or called for. On the other hand, Xunzi's focus is on what he takes to be the lack of natural ability to produce results of a particular kind, namely, a peaceful, principled, harmonious, and regimented life. What this reveals about these two thinkers is that they had what might be called differing *success-conditions* for natural human endowments to be considered good. For Mencius, it was enough to have native discernment. For Xunzi, it required ability to produce a certain type of result. Here is where the interesting difference seems to lie between them.

Xunzi's point about "what everyone has called good" is germane to this point. Xunzi's analysis depends on an ordinary-use analysis of language for identifying the nature of what is good and hence desirable. But it is not simply that what we happen to desire is desirable; rather, it is what, upon historical reflection, we see everyone agreeing upon as good that is desirable. This reflects something we might call a constructivist or conventionalist view about the human good, in contrast to Mencius's moral sensibility view. Furthering this broadly humanistic point, Xunzi argues that "Heaven" (*tian*), from which humans receive their natural endowments, is not even an indirect source of judgments about what is good. In book 17, Xunzi argues that the work of Heaven is fixed and constant, with no regard for human life. True "divination" of Heaven's ways lies in aligning human activity to the expectable activities of Heaven based on its regularity, especially agricultural activity in relation to meteorological regularity. In book 9, Xunzi goes so far as to formulate a doctrine of the "triad" formed by Heaven, Earth, and the gentleman, in which the gentleman is central—without the gentleman, Heaven and Earth have no principles of order, no ritual or rectifying principles.

Despite their unruly natural endowments, Xunzi believes that humans can save themselves from ruin through education and self-cultivation. Since neither the endowments nor willful aid of Heaven is available for this task, it is only accomplishable through consciously self-guided activity (*wei* 為). The nature and scope of such activity is of the sort, however, that is not naturally apparent to humans. Fortunately, Xunzi believes, two things are available for just this task. On the one hand, there is a distinctively human ability to categorize things (5.4). This provides the wherewithal to make social distinctions among people, based on their relationships to each other. Second, the ingenuity of certain people, historically, has already generated the principles and practices of effective and orderly social distinction that one may adhere to in one's own activity to attain the circumstances befitting a good human life. It would be folly to ignore the wisdom handed down by such men. Not that such men as the ancient sages—who were "pitch pipes of the *dao*" (8.7)—differ in natural constitution or capacity from anyone else. They did not receive any special favor or endowment from Heaven (23.4), but they distinguished themselves through extraordinary ability (23.5) that was the result of accumulated effort (8.11, 23.4–5).

So, for Xunzi, the defense of traditional culture is derived from its role in transforming untutored human life into something that makes it worth living. In that sense, traditional culture in the form of rituals, music, poetry, and the other subjects of traditional education may seem to possess instrumental value for making human life refined and beautiful. Some hardworking people, who in retrospect are regarded as sages, discovered the value of these cultural forms, Xunzi thinks. However, there may be more to the value of traditional culture than this instrumental role. The ultimate goods in Xunzi's view seem to be order and refinement in human life, as opposed to chaos and coarseness. But order and refinement are found within the practice of just such rituals, music, and texts that were produced by the sages and passed down. The aesthetic/ethical value of these things is not constituted by a separate state that results from them; such value supervenes on their actual form and content. So, the actual value of traditional culture is not solely instrumental; it is constitutive of the ultimate goods—order and refinement—that stand in opposition to psychological chaos and a chaotic, coarse life.

Conclusion

Broadly speaking, then, the differences between Mencius and Xunzi may be characterized by the ways in which each attempted to defend visions of the good life for humans in some systematic way. What they have in common is their championing of the connection between the good life and the conception of tradition-based society handed down from Confucius. Their views changed the character of justification within Confucianism. No longer was simple recitation of sage-king myths or recounting the actions of historical Zhou-culture heroes sufficient for making the Confucian vision of social order necessary or appealing. There were new and opposing viewpoints with powerful justifications or popular appeal that challenged Confucian teachings. Mencius's and Xunzi's participation in the resulting philosophical disputes revealed views with complexity and sophistication that have held the interest of scholars through the ages.

BIBLIOGRAPHY AND SUGGESTED READINGS

Cua, Antonio S. (1985) *Ethical Argumentation: A Study in Hsun Tzu's Moral Epistemology.* Manoa, HI: University of Hawaii Press.

Eno, Robert. (1990) *The Confucian Creation of Heaven.* Albany, NY: State University of New York Press.

Fingarette, Herbert. (1972) *Confucius: The Secular as Sacred.* San Francisco, CA: Harper San Francisco.

Graham, A. C. (1990) *Studies in Chinese Philosophy & Philosophical Literature.* Albany, NY: State University of New York Press.

Hansen, Chad. (1992) *A Daoist Theory of Chinese Thought: A Philosophical Interpretation.* Oxford: Oxford University Press.

Kline, T. C., and Philip J. Ivanhoe (eds.). (2000) *Virtue, Nature and Moral Agency in the Xunzi.* Indianapolis, IN: Hackett Publishing Company.

Knoblock, John. (1988) *Xunzi: A Translation and Study of the Complete Works,* Volume I. Stanford, CA: Stanford University Press.

———. (1990) *Xunzi: A Translation and Study of the Complete Works,* Volume II. Stanford, CA: Stanford University Press.

———. (1994) *Xunzi: A Translation and Study of the Complete Works,* Volume III. Stanford, CA: Stanford University Press.

Lau, D. C. (trans.). (2003) *Mencius* (revised edition). New York: Penguin Group.

Liu, Xiusheng, and Philip J. Ivanhoe (eds.). (2002) *Essays on the Moral Philosophy of Mengzi.* Indianapolis, IN: Hackett Publishing Company.

Nivison, David S. (1996) *The Ways of Confucianism: Investigations in Chinese Philosophy,* edited with an introduction by Bryan W. Van Norden. Chicago, IL: Open Court.

Schwartz, Benjamin I. (1985) *The World of Thought in Ancient China.* Cambridge, MA: Belknap Press of Harvard University Press.

Shun, Kwong-loi. (1997) *Mencius and Early Chinese Thought.* Stanford, CA: Stanford University Press.

CHAPTER 4

DAOISM: LAOZI AND ZHUANGZI

LIU XIAOGAN

IT has long been common knowledge that the two earliest representative thinkers of Daoism are Laozi 老子 and Zhuangzi 莊子, and the two texts that carry their names are likewise recognized as Daoist philosophical classics. The Chinese term for Daoism, *Dao jia* 道家, is a retrospective label for this strain of Chinese thought; it first appeared in the work *Shi-Ji* 史記 (*Historical Records*) by the Han court historian Si-Ma Qian 司馬遷 (ca. 140–86 BCE), written hundreds of years after the two philosophers lived. Strictly speaking, however, the word "Daoism" is not a translation of any Chinese term, but a word coined in the nineteenth century by Westerners to denote both Daoist philosophy and the indigenous religious movements (*dao-jiao* 道教) that took shape at the end of Eastern Han (25–220 CE). Being aware that early Daoist groups were not institutionalized helps us avoid the largely misguided assumption that struggles occurred between Confucianists and Daoists, a dramatic and appealing theory that has been broadly used as a framework for understanding Daoist thought and textual history. In addition to the thought of Laozi and Zhuangzi, Daoism in its modern usage also includes the Huang-Lao 黄老 (legendary emperors Huang and Laozi) and Xuan Xue 玄學 (mysterious learning) schools that prevailed in the Western Han (206 BCE–8 CE) and Wei-Jin (220–420 CE) periods, respectively.

Laozi

Laozi, according to the *Historical Records* by Sima Qian, is believed to have been an elder contemporary of Confucius and the author of the *Laozi* or *Daodejing* 道德經, a work of roughly five thousand characters. The traditional account of the person, as well as the dating and authorship of the work, has been seriously challenged. Nevertheless, the three incomplete Guodian bamboo versions of the *Laozi* excavated in 1993 prove that the text was extant and in circulation in the fourth century BCE, and may have been composed still earlier.

Dao

Laozi may have been the first person in Chinese intellectual history to develop a theory about the source and ground of the universe and all things; this theory is represented in the concept "Dao" (Tao). The key term in the *Laozi*, Dao is commonly described as invisible, inaudible, subtle, formless, infinite, vague, mysterious, oneness, and so on. There is no single word or term in modern Chinese, let alone English, to adequately gloss Dao. *Dao* literally means "way" and is often extended to imply various political or moral principles. What is noteworthy is that Laozi attributed a new meaning to it: "Dao generated the one, the one generated the two, the two generated the three, and the three generated the ten thousands things" (*Daodejing*, ch. 42). Here the one, two, and three do not seem to indicate anything specific, but instead present a general cosmological formula: from nothing to being, one to multitude, and simplicity to complexity.

Dao is the primordial root of all beings and creatures; all beings and creatures in turn depend on it, and it never turns away from them. As the ultimate source and ground of the universe, Dao seems equivalent to a metaphysical concept in Western philosophy. But in Daoism there is no dichotomy between the metaphysical and the physical, the ontological and the axiological, the descriptive and the prescriptive. Dao runs through the whole universe and human life and is simultaneously both transcendent and immanent. As the model for human behavior and the object of ultimate human concern, Dao seems similar to God, but has nothing to do with will, feelings, and purpose. Dao runs through and is manifest in all things, including human beings, as *de* (*te* 德), the power or virtue embodied variously in individuals. We may say, then, that Dao is a quasi-metaphysical concept, and *de* is its manifestation in all beings.

One persistent issue of interest to scholars is whether or not Dao is *wu* 無 (nothing or nonbeing). Laozi never answers this question explicitly, but chapter 40 presents a relationship between *you* 有 and *wu*. "All things in the world come from *being* (*you*), and being comes from *non-being* (*wu*)" (Chan 1963, 173). The myriad things come from *you*, and *you* in turn comes from *wu*; thus, *you* and *wu* represent two phases in a sequence, not a pair at the same level of meaning in cosmological context. *Wu* is thus the ultimate origin. Since, according to chapter 42, Dao produces ten thousand things, it is easy for one to infer from chapters 40 and 42 that Dao is equal to *wu* as the ultimate source of the universe, though the *Laozi* does not make this claim. This position was later clearly articulated by Wang Bi (226–249). Wang Bi takes Dao to be *wu* and makes *wu* the ground of all beings, instead of their ultimate source. Therefore, *wu* in Wang Bi's philosophy can be rendered as an ontological concept of nonbeing, while in Laozi's text, it can be better understood as simply "nothing" or "what is not there" in a cosmological sense, though we should not take the difference strictly and dogmatically.

In Laozi's discussion, Dao embodies features of both *you* and *wu*. Chapter 1 of the silk manuscript version (excavated in Changsha, China, in 1973) can be rendered, "Nameless (*wu-ming* 無名), it (Dao) is the beginning of ten-thousand things (*wan-wu*); Named (*you-ming* 有名), it is mother of ten-thousand things (*wan-wu* 萬物)." Unlike received versions, this couplet repeats "ten thousand things" in association with both *wu-ming* and *you-ming* characteristics, which suggests that *wu-ming* and *you-ming* are equally features of Dao. *Wu-ming* reflects Dao as *wu*, or nothing, while *you-ming* represents it as *you*, or something. In this context, *you* and *wu* are equals in a pair, as distinct from their relationship in the cosmological process.

You and *wu* as features of Dao should not be confused with *you* and *wu* in the physical world and human life. Chapter 2 says: "What there is (*you*) and what there is not (*wu*) generate each other"; this by no means applies to Dao or to the general relationship of *you* and *wu*. *Wu* seems to function as a critical concept here, but this theory cannot be verified by textual analyses. We find 130 references to *wu* in most versions of the *Laozi*, but many of these are in the form of negative adjectives and adverbs; the term itself is generally not used in a technical way to discuss philosophical issues. Only in three cases is *wu* used as a philosophical term: one occurs in chapter 40, in discussion of the ultimate source; one appears in chapter 2, regarding the mutual independence of *wu* and *you* in empirical life; and the third such mention is in the chapter 11 discussion of advantages and utility *wu* presents in real-world situations. The *Laozi* never explicitly claims that Dao is *wu*, or nonbeing.

Naturalness

Another key concept in Laozi's philosophy is *zi-ran* 自然, or naturalness. Laozi advocates: "Man models himself on the earth, the earth models itself on heaven, heaven models itself on the Dao, and the Dao models itself on *zi-ran*" (ch. 25). The compound *zi-ran* consists of "self" (*zi* 自) and "so" or "such" (*ran* 然). Its essential meaning is "so of (it)self." This term is often confused with some notion of the natural world because it is used in modern Chinese to denote the Western idea of Nature. In classical Chinese, however, the natural world is encompassed in the terms *tian* 天 (Heaven), *di* 地 (Earth), and *wan-wu* (ten thousand things).

In another misconception, *zi-ran* rendered as "nature" is confused with Hobbes's "state of nature," the hypothetical that supposes, prior to the advent of the state, that everyone engaged in constant warfare against everyone else. In striking contrast, Laozi's *zi-ran* refers to an ideal condition of human societies; it is the highest principle and core value of his philosophy, and is embodied and promoted by Dao. The true meaning and message of the formula above about the structure of the moral universe is that humans should put the principle of naturalness into practice and engage in natural harmony in their lives and with their surroundings. Natural harmony and natural order are valuable and desirable compared with either forced order or chaos. Human nature prefers natural order to societal order achieved only under high pressure. *Zi-ran* also pertains to the individual condition. Thus, Laozi (in the bamboo version) contends, "The sage is able to assist the naturalness of ten thousand things and unable to take action." This leads us to the next fundamental Daoist concept—*wu-wei* 無為 (nonaction).

Nonaction

Wu-wei also consists of two parts: "no" (*wu*) and "action" (*wei*). Superficially, then, *wu-wei* means "no action." But in fact, *wu-wei* negates only certain kinds of action, not all action. Obviously, it does not negate such actions as the above-mentioned "assist(ing) the naturalness of ten thousand things." The agent of *wu-wei* in Laozi's theory is essentially the sage, or leader of society, who takes "assisting" as the key principle of action instead of directly ordering, pushing, interfering, and interrupting. Therefore, *wu-wei* has two aspects: its negative expression suggests restraining and preventing the usual operations of power, such as oppression, confrontation, and strife; its positive meaning advocates an alternative and nuanced manner and style of behavior, such as assisting, waiting, and watching, that lead toward natural development and harmony in society. In his famous formula "doing nothing and leaving nothing undone," Laozi clearly points to the positive objective of *wu-wei:* "doing nothing" is the means to realize the end of leaving nothing undone; that is, things develop or are accomplished according to their own processes. *Wu-wei* actually asserts superior approaches and the consummate result of human activities. It derives from comprehensive and humanistic perspectives and considerations, and is not pushed by fashions and trends to realize immediate benefits.

Dialectics

Another distinctive feature of Laozi's philosophy is his dialectical or paradoxical thinking, in which the unity and transformation of pairs of contradictions are a basic operating principle. Take, for instance, the interdependence between opposite things and concepts: "Calamity is that upon which happiness depends; happiness is that in which calamity is latent" (Chan 1963, 167). Another example is the reversibility of opposites, such as "correctness can become the perverse, and good may become evil" (ibid.). According to Laozi, all things are in flux: changing and moving toward their reversal. Thus, humility produces greatness and ambitions bring about failure. The obverse and the reverse often exchange positions. Things both in human societies and in the natural world change to become the opposite of our expectation and will. Human beings make two kinds of mistakes. One is that they do not make enough of an effort, and the other is that they overdo. The former mistake is easy to remedy because it does not waste too many resources or shake morale. The second is much more difficult to correct. This is another argument for the reasonableness and significance of *wu-wei.*

We may conclude that Laozi's thought possesses a perceptible structure: *wu-wei* is the methodological principle by which *zi-ran*, its core value, can be realized. Dao as the ultimate source and ground of the universe provides both quasi-metaphysical and axiological foundations for *wu-wei* and *zi-ran*, while the theory of dialectics supports these key concepts from the perspective of human experience.

ZHUANGZI

The earliest official biography of Zhuangzi was also provided by Si-ma Qian in his *Historical Records.* As with other figures of antiquity, Zhuangzi's life and writings have generated numerous debates. In Si-ma's account, his given name was Zhou, and he is identified by the honorific "Zi," as was Laozi. He was born sometime after 369 BCE and died before 286 BCE—roughly the middle of the Warring States period. He once served as officer-in-charge at a royal lacquer garden, which may have been his highest position. It was said that King Wei 威 of Chu 楚, having heard of his reputation, once sent messengers with gifts to invite him to his state, promising to make him chief minister. Zhuangzi, however, merely laughed and said to them: "Go away, do not defile me.... I prefer the enjoyment of my free will." It was said that Zhuangzi wrote a book of more than one hundred thousand characters, in fifty-two chapters. Today, the only available version of the *Zhuangzi* consists of approximately seventy thousand characters in thirty-three chapters, divided into three parts: the Inner, Outer, and Miscellaneous chapters. Based on the textual tradition and textual analyses, most scholars believe that the Inner chapters were probably written by Zhuangzi himself and the others by his followers or disciples. This introduction will focus on the Inner chapters.

Most scholars believe that the central theme of the *Zhuangzi* is freedom of the mind, presented as the metaphor of soaring above the world and enjoying all manner of wonders without becoming attached to any of them. In the words of Burton Watson, Zhuangzi addresses the spiritual rather than the political or the intellectual elite (Watson 1968, 5). Yet spiritual freedom is based on the recognition of bondage and liberation from frustrations into a realm without limits. This breakthrough is achieved by realizing the true equality of all things. For Zhuangzi, right and wrong, good and bad hold the same values, while life and death, fortune and adversity are equally as acceptable as the alternating day and night. Thus, Zhuangzi's thought involves an ideal notion of human existence. Unlike most other thinkers, Zhuangzi develops and conveys his philosophical ideas and theories mainly through fables, tales, anecdotes, and dialogues. The *Zhuangzi* is a literary, as well as a philosophic, classic.

Logically, Zhuangzi's thought starts with the idea of fate and ends with the notion of carefree wandering. The knowledge of truth and a vision of the equality of things are conjoined bridges connecting one end to the other. Accordingly, we can understand Zhuangzi better by examining four unique aspects of his thought: the idea of being at ease with or indifferent to one's destiny, the carefree wandering of the mind, the theory of true knowledge, and the equality of the myriad things. Upon careful exploration of these concepts and their implications, we may reasonably argue that the notions of being at ease with one's destiny and wandering carefree capture the Zhuanzian attitude to life as it is, while insights on the ideal state of mind and the vision of equality across the cosmos lead him to propose the characteristics of an ideal life.

Being at Ease with Destiny

The first theme Zhuangzi deals with is the problem of undesirable social realities. The situation that constrains one's life and will was called *ming* 命, which is often roughly translated as fate or destiny, though its various meanings are complex and defy straightforward definitions.

The general notion of *ming* took shape in the early stages of Chinese civilization during the Shang dynasty (sixteenth to eleventh centuries BCE). However, from the Western Zhou dynasty (1027–770 BCE) onward, the fatalism usually associated with this term was challenged by social turbulence as well as by daring minds. Both the Duke of Zhou (eleventh century BCE) and Confucius expressed doubt about the political extension of *ming*, Heaven's Mandate (*tian ming* 天命). The sporadic sayings regarding *ming* occurring in Confucius's *Analects* amount to a claim that destiny is not an important Confucian theme. Another philosopher, Mozi, launched a vehement attack on the notion of *ming*.

But the *Zhuangzi* makes frequent reference to one's *ming*, or destiny. *Ming* in Chinese generally implies an inevitable and usually adverse outcome that originates with the Mandate of Heaven and is therefore inescapable. Zhuangzi's theory of *ming* carries on the general meaning that human beings are bound by external inevitabilities and are not free in social life, and simultaneously combines this idea of an inevitable *ming* with Laozi's exceptional concept of *wu-wei*. Hence, Zhuangzi's theory of *ming* features the doctrine that one should have a peaceful and even accepting mind and do nothing about or against one's *ming*. The *ming* is just as natural as the cycle of day and night and of the four seasons. It is determined by Heaven or Dao and the function of Heaven or Dao is completely spontaneous, with no meaning or retribution to assign to human beings; thus, people should accept *ming* peacefully without pain or complaint, as one faces the annual cycle of seasons. We might consider this kind of *ming* as a "naturally given situation" to distinguish it from general accounts of *ming* as retribution decided by gods or Heaven with will and purposes. In this theory Laozi's *wu-wei* is transformed into a new idea that insists that people should do nothing against or for *ming*, so they can keep their mind in harmony and at ease. This distinguishes Zhuangzi's doctrine of *ming* from the views of most thinkers, including Confucius and Laozi.

Most Confucians talked about the Mandate of Heaven but simultaneously advocated a determined effort to exert oneself. Confucius expressed his "awe towards Heaven" and advised his disciples to be content with what they encounter in life; yet he also encouraged them to "try" even though they may "know their goal is impossible." This is the very opposite of Daoist *wu-wei*, though Confucius himself once mentioned *wu-wei* in a positive manner. The general theory of *wu-wei*, which advocates spontaneity and the elimination of ambitious striving, does not necessarily propose being content with fate. For instance, in Laozi's thought, *wu-wei* encompasses overcoming the strong by being soft and weak, so fatalism or determinism is marginal to it. Few early Daoist texts assert that *wu-wei* pertains to fatalism at all, with perhaps the sole exception being the *Zhuangzi*: admitting and accepting one's destiny is the premise from which one must begin in order to reach the state of mind in which one can enjoy true freedom.

The *Zhuangzi*'s notion of *ming* is also distinct from theological fatalism, in that destiny is ascribed not to God or Heaven but to the inevitabilities of social and natural reality. This "naturally given situation" springs from a spontaneity that has its origins in Dao and Heaven. What the *Zhuangzi* makes clear is that human desires are not to be fulfilled in earthly life. Thus, *ming*, or the "naturally given situation," is simply the unavoidable context one encounters in every aspect of life, things that have nothing to do with punishment, retribution, judgment, or reward. The point is neither to explain the source or content of destiny nor to emphasize its irresistible power; instead, the *Zhuangzi* argues that one should accept the inevitable and be at ease with it—only then can spiritual freedom arise. Accordingly, practicing *wu-wei* and being content with one's *ming* are the keys to leading a successful life. To sum up, for Zhuangzi, *ming* or destiny is not something to be upset about; if one accepts it as a kind of natural phenomenon, one can learn to be carefree.

Carefree Wandering

Zhuangzi is unique in his associating the acceptance of destiny with spiritual freedom. That spiritual freedom is powerfully conveyed in his vision of carefree wandering, the topic of the very opening chapter and a running theme throughout the book. As scholars have agreed, carefree wandering is grounded in the freedom of the mind, and this is the *Zhuangzi's* central theme and the goal of its philosophy of life.

The meaning of carefree wandering can be understood by examining the constituent words *xiao-yao* 逍遥 and *you* 游. *Xiao-yao* appears in other Chinese classics such as the *Shi-jing* 詩經, *Chu-ci* 楚辭, and *Liji* 禮記, where it refers to a carefree or unfettered condition of the body. In the *Zhuangzi*, this condition is more closely related to the mind: "Why don't you plant it (the huge tree) in Never-never Land with its wide open spaces? There you can roam in non-action by its side and sleep carefree beneath it" (Mair 1994, 9). This suggests an imaginary and purely spiritual freedom, a connotation that only the *Zhuangzi* ascribes to *xiao-yao.*

In comparison with *xiao-yao, you* is found more frequently in the Chinese classics, where its common meaning is an easy or comfortable "trip" or "tour." Again the *Zhuangzi* attributes to the word other implications, namely, that the place in which one roams freely is mysterious as well as remote. The wilderness or the "Never-never Land" (*wu-he-you-zhi-xiang* 無何有之鄉) refers to such a place, far beyond the world. Moreover, the compound *you-xin* 游心 (mind's wandering) appears repeatedly, indicating quite directly that it is the mind, rather than the body, that roams. Thus, by combining *xiao-yao* and *you,* the *Zhuangzi* depicts a free soul roaming in the boundless world of imagination where the mysterious union with Dao can be attained. *Xiao-yao* and *you* mean gaining access to the infinite panorama of a spiritual world.

The *Zhuangzi* illustrates the spiritual experience of freedom and independence through the metaphor of traveling in the company of exotic and imaginary figures and fabulous animals. For example, "[Someone] could ride upon the truth of heaven...could chariot upon the transformations of the six vital breaths and thereby go wandering in infinity" (Mair 1994, 5). A godlike person could "ride on the clouds, drive a flying dragon, and wander beyond the fours seas [in east, west, north, and south]" (7). People who so wander "roam beyond the dust and dirt of the mundane world, carefree in the career of non-action (*wu-wei*)" (61). As spiritual freedom, then, carefree wandering represents the ideal in human life, and follows from an emptiness and stillness of the mind. It can be realized in the Daoist states of no-thinking (*wu xin* 無心) and no-feeling (*wu qing* 無情), both representing basic attitudes toward society and mundane life that manifest one's ease with destiny and facilitate carefree wandering. To reach the states of no-thinking and no-feeling, one must pursue serious self-cultivation in the Daoist arts of mind-fasting (*xin-zhai* 心齋) and sitting-and-forgetting (*zuo-wang* 坐忘).

The Theory of True Knowing

The term "true knowing" (*zhen-zhi* 真知) first appears in chapter 6: "Only when there is a true man is there true knowing." True knowledge means the experience of Dao, that is, an intuitive realization of Dao that in effect annuls mundane knowledge obtained via the senses. True knowledge is not knowledge in the common sense; it is ignorance or "not knowing" in everyday life.

The *Zhuangzi*'s theory of knowledge is laid out in skeptical arguments that deny the reliability of knowledge obtained through the senses and reason. This is taken to its logical extreme in stories that show ignorance to be the way to true knowledge. The text also claims that one can directly see or know Dao, the root of the world, through certain meditative practices. Knowledge can thus be ascribed a kind of intuitiveness, and its realization a mysterious union with Dao. Skepticism and intuitiveness are two terms often used to describe this theory of knowledge.

Zhuangzi likes to raise issues and provoke discussion or reflection, leaving all questions open ended. This reflects the fact that, in his opinion, there are no fixed solutions to any problem in earthly life. Thus, doubt is not regarded as problematic; rather, it is seen as the solution to human misery. Ignorance is esteemed as real knowledge and achieving it is counted as the very first step toward living a spiritually satisfactory life. Zhuangzi insists that we cannot possibly know anything with real certainty, whether or not the normal "knowledge" guiding our lives is reliable or true. But he does not simply arrive at the reductive answer "we know nothing"; instead, what he provides is the subtler formulation, "we do not know if we do know or if we do not know."

Like a skeptic, Zhuangzi first of all realizes the limitations of human faculties for knowing. He points out that knowing relies on specific conditions and perspectives, which can hardly lead to absolute knowledge in the strict sense. The human ability to capture the world effectively, and in particular the reliability of rational thought, is dubious at best. Zhuangzi was the first Chinese thinker to problematize the limitations of human knowledge. In his analysis of binary opposites such as right/wrong, good/bad, true/false, and so forth, he points out that universally reliable standards are unattainable. All such dichotomies are subject to individual preferences and produce no absolute knowledge or truth. Furthermore, things are forever in the process of natural change, with life and death, dreaming and wakefulness ever shifting and unpredictable. This is a further check on our assumed claims to possessing reliable knowledge.

While suspicious of the human ability to know, Zhuangzi is firmly convinced of the value and validity of intuitive experience. In spite of his skepticism concerning standards of right and wrong or good and bad, he has absolute faith in the ultimate Dao. This intuitivism proceeds from a direct perception of Dao, the *Zhuangzi*'s idea of true knowledge. So both ignorance and experiencing Dao are equally true knowing.

The Equality of Things

Related to Zhuangzi's theory of true knowledge, his insight about the equality of things also points to the ideal in human life. The theme of the second chapter counters those thinkers who try to distinguish between alternatives and argue about right and wrong, good and bad. According to the *Zhuangzi*, true knowledge goes beyond all dichotomies.

Certainly, Zhuangzi realizes the power of contradictions. He notices that dichotomies prevail in the natural world and in social life as well as in human knowledge and values. He elaborates on a number of binary pairs such as "this" (*ci* 此) and "that" (*bi* 彼), "that's it" (*shi* 是, right) and "that's not" (*fei* 非, wrong), death and life, being and nonbeing, self and other, affirmation and denial, and so forth. What concerns him is the role of each of the opposites. He shows that opposites generate each other and that recognition of one depends on the function of the other. Thus, he demonstrates their relativity:

> Everything is "that," everything is "this." . . . So I say, "that" comes out of "this" and "this" depends on "that"—which is to say that "this" and "that" give birth to each other. But where there is birth there must be death; where there is death there must be birth. . . . Where there is recognition of right there must be recognition of wrong; where there is recognition of wrong there must be recognition of right. Therefore the sage does not proceed in such a way, but illuminates all in the light of Heaven. He too recognizes a "this" but a "this" which is also a "that," a "that" which is also a "this." (Graham 1981, 35)

Zhuangzi believes there is a way to get beyond opposites. By highlighting the interrelations of opposite concepts, he indicates clearly that each term derives its meaning from the other and eventually they should be seen as indistinguishable from each other; that is, oppositions are no longer significant and should be ignored. From a transcendent point of view, the myriad things are essentially without differences. By illuminating the ultimate equality of all things, he concludes that one need not deliberate on differences, but should enter directly into union with Dao. Thus, if we possess a comprehensive understanding of his thought, we cannot fairly call Zhuangzi a relativist.

Like all great thinkers, Zhuangzi was firmly grounded in his own time and place. Witnessing social chaos and feeling despair at human weakness led Zhuangzi to decide that it was more important to free oneself from the grip of the world. It is fair to say that the *Zhuangzi* suffers from a degree of absurdity produced by its contradictory values and judgments, yet at the same time, the author of its Inner Chapters clearly yearned for a world without conflict and discord. Thus, it is easy to understand that the *Zhuangzi*'s exposition on opposites embraces both dialectical and transcendental elements. Zhuangzi may have begun his theoretical reflection with dialectical problems, but he reached the conclusion that indifference is the highest state of mind, a state reached by self-cultivation.

In conclusion, theories about knowing the world and expectations about human life are usually linked in Chinese philosophy. This is true even in the unique early Daoist works such as the *Zhuangzi*. For Zhuangzi, the highest level of knowing conforms to the highest state of human existence in the sense that by grasping both true knowing and the equality of things, one can achieve the highest state of spiritual life, namely, rambling along on a delightful and purposeless journey with no attachments to burden one's spiritual universe.

This project was supported by the Hong Kong Government RGC General Research Fund 2009-10 (447909).

BIBLIOGRAPHY AND SUGGESTED READINGS

Chan, Wing-tsit. (1963) "The Natural Way of Lao Tze." In *A Source Book in Chinese Philosophy.* Princeton, NJ: Princeton University Press, 136–176. (This includes a translation of the received version of the *Laozi*.)

Graham, A. C. (trans.). (1981) *Chuang-tzu, The Seven Inner Chapters and Other Writings from the Book Chuang-tzu.* London: George Allen & Unwin.

———. (1989) *Disputers of the Tao: Philosophical Argument in Ancient China.* La Salle, IL: Open Court.

Hansen, Chad. (1992) *A Daoist Theory of Chinese Thought: A Philosophical Interpretation.* New York: Oxford University Press.

Henricks, Robert G. (2000) *Lao Tzu's Tao Te Ching: A Translation of the Startling New Documents Found at Guodian.* New York: Columbia University Press. (This is the translation of bamboo versions excavated in 1993.)

LaFargue, Michael. (1994) *Tao and Method: A Reasoned Approach to the Tao Te Ching.* New York: State University of New York.

Lau, D. C. (trans.). (2001). *Tao Te Ching: A Bilingual Edition.* Hong Kong: The Chinese University Press. (This is the translation of silk versions excavated in 1973.)

Liu, Xiaogan. (1994) *Classifying the Zhuangzi Chapters.* Ann Arbor, MI: Center for Chinese Studies, the University of Michigan.

———. (1998) "Naturalness (tzu-jan), the Core Value in Taoism: Its Ancient Meaning and Significance Today." In *Lao-tzu and Tao-te-ching*, edited by Livia Kohn and Michael LaFargue. Albany, NY: State University of New York Press, 211–228.

———. (2001) "Non-Action and the Environment Today: A Conceptual and Applied Study of Laozi's Philosophy." In *Taoism and Ecology: Ways within a Cosmic Landscape*, edited by Norman Girardot, James Miller, and Liu Xiaogan. Cambridge, MA: Harvard University Center for the Study of World Religions, 315–340.

———. (2009) "Daoism (I): Lao Zi and the Dao-De-Jing." In *History of Chinese Philosophy*, edited by Bo Mou. London and New York: Routledge, 209–236.

Mair, Victor H. (trans.). (1994) *Wandering on the Way: Early Taoist Tales and Parables of Chuang Tzu.* Honolulu, HI: University of Hawaii Press.

Slingerland, Edward. (2003) *Effortless Action: Wu-wei as Conceptual Metaphor and Spiritual Ideal in Early China.* New York: Oxford University Press.

Watson, Burton (trans.). (1968) *The Complete Works of Chuang Tzu.* New York: Columbia University Press.

CHAPTER 5

MAJOR RIVAL SCHOOLS: MOHISM AND LEGALISM

CHRIS FRASER

Viewed through the lens of much later developments, Confucianism and Daoism might seem to have dominated the intellectual discourse of China's Warring States era (481–221 BCE). In fact, however, at the time, the Confucians, or *Ru*, were just one of several widely recognized social or ethical movements, and the figures and texts we now call "Daoist" did not represent an organized school or movement at all, but only a loose network of mentors and pupils with a roughly overlapping doctrinal orientation. Neither can be considered to have approached the status of philosophical orthodoxy or dominance, and numerous other thinkers and ideological communities flourished alongside them in what later became known as the age of the "hundred schools," perhaps the most intellectually fertile period in Chinese history. This chapter introduces two of these rival strands of early Chinese thought, Mohism (*Mo Jia*) and Legalism (*Fa Jia*).

But for their shared opposition to Confucianism, the Mohists and the Legalists had little in common. The Mohists were a well-organized, grassroots social movement deeply committed to moral, political, and religious ideals and particularly concerned for the welfare of the common people. Mo Di, the charismatic teacher from whom the movement took its name, was arguably the first real philosopher in the Chinese tradition. He and his followers developed a systematic set of moral, political, and epistemological doctrines, supported by detailed arguments, that include history's earliest version of a consequentialist ethics. Mo Di—or Mozi ("Master Mo"), as he became known—flourished in the middle decades of the fifth century BCE, near the beginning of the Warring States era, and the movement he founded continued for two to three centuries after his death. The Mohists deeply influenced the development of early Chinese ethics, political theory, epistemology, philosophy of language, and logic. They also contributed to early Chinese science and mathematics. Some groups of Mohists even became experts in military engineering and defense tactics and were renowned for their defense of besieged cities.

By contrast, Legalism was not an actual school or movement at all, but a taxonomical category invented by Han dynasty historians, who classified the thinkers of the classical age into six major *jia*, or schools of thought. Under the rubric of the *Fa Jia*, or "School of *Fa*"—commonly translated as "Legalism"—they grouped together a disparate set of statesmen and political thinkers who lived at different times, in different states, and advocated no unified doctrine or way of life. What linked these men is that all were theorists or practitioners of a realistic, amoral brand of statecraft aimed at consolidating and strengthening the power and wealth of the state and its autocratic ruler. Their thought was realistic in being premised on what they took to be brute facts about how people actually behave, rather than optimistic beliefs about how people morally ought to or could be led to behave, and on the central fact of their political era, that the world consisted of numerous competing, potentially hostile autocratic states. It was amoral in that they were utterly unconcerned with whether the institutions and methods they advocated were morally justified. These characteristics bring to mind Machiavelli, to whom the Legalists are indeed similar in some respects. But where Machiavelli focused on the arts of the individual ruler, the Legalists were more like social engineers attempting to create foolproof, mechanically reliable institutions for controlling the officials who administer the state and the populace who are the source of its wealth and military power.

Unfortunately, neither the Chinese nor the English label for these political thinkers is particularly apt. The English "Legalism" derives from interpreting the Chinese word *fa* as "law." In ancient times, however, *fa* connoted not laws specifically but models or standards, of which laws were one kind. The stock examples of *fa* were tools that provide objective standards of shape, weight, and length, such as the carpenter's compass, setsquare, and level or the merchant's weights and measures. As these thinkers use it, *fa* is conceptually closer to a performance standard, backed by incentives for success and disincentives for failure, than to our notion of law. So "the School of Standards" would be a more accurate translation of *Fa Jia* than "Legalism" is. In any case, *Fa Jia* is itself something of a misnomer, since these men were interested in a range of methods of government and not all emphasized *fa* as a focal concept. The "realists" or "authoritarians" might be more accurate labels for them. For the purposes of this chapter, however, we will stick with the conventional designation, the "Legalists."

Despite their radical difference in orientation, the Mohists and Legalists have at least three conspicuous similarities. One is that *fa*, or explicit, easily applied standards of conduct, have a prominent role for both, Mozi's conception of *fa* being in effect the ancestor of the Legalists.' Whereas the Mohists aimed to articulate standards of morality, however, the Legalists see standards as determined arbitrarily by the ruler as his purposes require. The Mohists and Legalists also both advocated a centralized bureaucracy staffed by officials appointed on the basis of merit, the

Legalists effectively adopting and developing the Mohist doctrine of "promoting the worthy." In the Legalist version of the idea, however, merit is judged purely in terms of how effectively officials perform their tasks, while for the Mohists it includes moral worth. A third similarity is that both traditions died out during the Western Han dynasty (206 BCE–8 CE). The Mohist movement was rendered obsolete by political unification, changing customs, economic development, absorption of their major ethical doctrines into Confucianism, and the unappealing harshness of their frugal, self-sacrificing way of life. The Legalists were discredited by the excesses of the totalitarian Qin dynasty, though many of their administrative methods were adopted by the Han and subsequent empires. Aspects of Legalist thought may have lived on for some time in a syncretic combination of Legalist and Daoist ideas known as "Huang-Lao," named after the mythical Yellow Emperor (Huang Di) and the legendary Daoist sage Laozi.

Mohism

Among the various early Chinese schools of thought, the Mohists were the main rivals to the Confucians in promoting a way of life centered on moral teachings. But where the Confucians were elite ritual specialists, the Mohists came mainly from subelite groups, including artisans, small landholders, merchants, and soldiers. (Mo Di himself is likely to have been an artisan, perhaps a carpenter.) They rejected the traditional rituals and music central to the Confucian way of life, seeing them as wasteful and pointless, and instead emphasized thrift and practical utility. Rather than ground their ethics in morally fallible customs or traditions, as the Confucians did, they sought to identify objectively justified moral standards. The central standard they proposed was that morally right practices are those that promote the welfare of all.

The major source text for Mohist thought is an anthology called the *Mozi*, which contains a diverse collection of essays, anecdotes, dialogues, and notes written and compiled by different hands over the course of two centuries or more after Mo Di's lifetime. Though the names of a handful of Mohist leaders besides Mo Di have come down to us, none are known to have promulgated original philosophical views of their own. All of the doctrines in the *Mozi* are either attributed to the master or presented anonymously. However, most writing in early China was anonymous, and it was common to attribute one's own ideas to a venerated teacher or wise man, partly out of respect and partly to give the writer more authority. The various writings in the *Mozi* appear to represent different stages in the development of Mohist doctrines and perhaps the views of several distinct Mohist factions. So it is likely that many of the views in the anthology are not Mo Di's own, but developments, revisions, or new ideas introduced by his followers.

The Mohist movement seems to have originated in Mozi and his early followers' dismay at the war, feuding, crime, exploitation of the poor and weak, and other wrongdoing they saw as endemic to their world. They urgently sought to find a way to restore order (*zhi*) to human society. The Mohists saw people as naturally social, and thus concerned about their family and community, and generally committed to doing what they take to be morally right. But if people have different ideas about what is right, or if they fail to distinguish right from wrong properly—as is likely without proper education and political leadership—conflicts will arise, leading to disorder. The Mohists thus offered two main diagnoses of the causes of disorder. The first was moral disagreement. People followed a plurality of different moral standards, in most cases presumably in ignorance of the right standard. If people are strongly committed to morality yet apply different, incompatible moral standards, they are likely to end up quarreling, and such quarrels will eventually descend into widespread, possibly violent disorder. The Mohists' second diagnosis—partly a consequence of the first—was that, ignorant of the proper moral standards, many people acted in disregard for the welfare of others. So they did not hesitate to injure others in order to benefit themselves.

As moral activists, the Mohists aimed to rectify this moral disagreement and ignorance and thus achieve social order. They proposed to do this by training everyone to follow a unified moral code. Ideally, this project would be carried out through a government administered by wise, virtuous leaders, who at each level of the state hierarchy—from the village up to the entire world—would teach everyone to draw moral distinctions in the same way. The major method of education would be model emulation: the leaders would set practical examples of distinguishing right from wrong, which everyone would learn from. This training would be reinforced by an incentive scheme in which good conduct was praised and rewarded and bad conduct criticized and punished.

This political and educational system would provide a means for training everyone to apply a unified moral code. But proper order could be achieved only if the content of the shared code was correct. The Mohists thus mounted a search for objective moral standards, or as they saw it, reliably correct, easily applicable models or standards (*fa*) by which to guide judgment and action. These would guide everyone to distinguish right from wrong correctly, just as a straight-edged tool clearly and reliably guides a carpenter in sawing a straight line. The models would provide the content of the unified morality.

In choosing such a model, however, we must be cautious. Human role models, such as parents, teachers, and rulers, and traditional customs, such as the Confucian rituals, are all potentially unreliable. If we model ourselves on them, we might inadvertently follow the wrong kind of example. Instead, the Mohists proposed, we should take as our model the noblest and wisest moral agent in the cosmos, Heaven (*tian*, also nature or the sky), whom they worshipped as a personal god. The Mohist proposal is not a divine command theory, but an epistemic appeal to a conception of an ideal moral agent, by reference to which we can identify impartial, objectively correct moral standards. Since Heaven is an infallible moral agent, which is benevolent, impartial, and consistent, it will unfailingly set a correct example of what is morally right.

Heaven has not handed down any scriptures we can consult. But what we can do is observe its intentions, as manifested in its actions, and take those as our guide. When we do, what we find, according to the Mohists, is that Heaven all-inclusively cares about and benefits all humanity. It gives us all life and the resources needed for survival. According to traditional lore, it rewarded the ancient sage kings who advanced the welfare of all and punished the vicious tyrants who mistreated their subjects. Examples such as these show that Heaven desires that people "inclusively care about each other and in interaction benefit each other" and that moral right and wrong can be distinguished by the standard of "promoting the benefit of all under heaven and eliminating harm to all under heaven." Morally right practices, policies, and acts are just those that tend to advance the benefit of or eliminate harm to all.

The Mohists' notion of the "benefit of all" is a general conception of the public good consisting of material wealth, an abundant population, and sociopolitical order (*zhi*). Core features of order are the absence of war, strife, crime, and hostility and the universal virtuous performance of the paradigmatic social roles of ruler, subject, father, son, and brother. More broadly, order may include things such as people being willing to share knowledge, surplus labor, and surplus resources and the government administering the penal system properly. As this list of goods indicates, Mohist ethics is communitarian, not individualistic. The goods that serve as criteria of morality are collective or public, in contrast, for instance, to individual happiness or well-being, the basic goods in most familiar Western forms of utilitarianism or consequentialism.

Drawing on this framework of political, epistemological, ethical, and religious doctrines, the Mohists offered systematic arguments for why wars of conquest, extravagant funerals, excessive state spending, and other practices were morally wrong. In their view, each of the rejected practices was detrimental to the general welfare. Their consequentialism led them to develop a platform of ten ethical and political doctrines—some rather idiosyncratic—that they aimed to persuade rulers of their day to adopt. A summary of the ten doctrines provides a quick synopsis of the Mohist moral and political reform program.

According to the doctrine of "identifying upward" (*shang tong*, also interpretable as "promoting unity"), the aim of government is to achieve a stable social, economic, and political order by promulgating a unified conception of morality. This project of moral education is carried out by encouraging everyone to "identify upward" with the good example set by social and political superiors. Those who do are rewarded; those who do not are punished. Government is to be structured as a centralized, bureaucratic state led by a virtuous monarch and managed by a hierarchy of appointed officials. According to the doctrine of "promoting the worthy" (*shang xian*), appointments to the bureaucracy should be made on the basis of competence and moral merit, without regard for candidates' social status or origin.

"Inclusive care" (*jian ai*) was the Mohists' signature doctrine. To achieve social order and exemplify the virtue of *ren* (moral goodness), people must inclusively care about each other, having as much concern for others' lives, families, and communities as for their own, and in their interactions with others seek mutual benefit. The Mohists' second most prominent doctrine was "condemning aggression" (*fei gong*). Military aggression is morally wrong, for the same reasons that theft, robbery, and murder are: it harms others in pursuit of selfish interest, while failing to benefit Heaven, the spirits, or human society.

According to "moderation in use" (*jie yong*), wasteful luxury and useless expenditures should be eliminated, so as to benefit society and ensure the welfare of the populace. The doctrine of "moderation in burial" (*jie zang*) contends that to promote social order and the economic welfare of the common people, the morally good person avoids wasting resources on extravagant funerals and protracted mourning (early Chinese customs staunchly defended by the Confucians).

The doctrine of "Heaven's intention" (*tian zhi*) holds that Heaven is the noblest, wisest moral agent in the cosmos, so its intentions are a reliable, objective standard of what is morally right and thus should be respected. Heaven rewards those who obey its intentions and punishes those who defy it, so people should strive to be morally good and to do what is morally right. "Elucidating ghosts" (*ming gui*) contends that social and moral order can be advanced by encouraging belief in ghosts and spirits who reward the good and punish the wicked.

According to "condemning music" (*fei yue*), the morally good person opposes the extravagant musical entertainment and other luxuries enjoyed by rulers and high officials, since they waste resources that would be better used to feed and clothe the general populace. "Condemning fatalism" (*fei ming*) argues that, by teaching that our lot in life is predestined and human effort is useless, fatalism interferes with pursuit of the basic goods that constitute the welfare of all. It is thus wrong and must be rejected.

As these ten core doctrines illustrate, the Mohists saw themselves mainly as a moral, political, and religious advocacy group devoted to pursuing their vision of a morally right society and way of life, one that promotes the welfare of all. Because of this practical orientation, their ten-doctrine platform alludes only indirectly to the underlying ethical and epistemological theories that support their proposals. To philosophical readers today, however, the latter are the Mohists' main legacy.

LEGALISM

According to the *Han History*, the "School of *Fa*" included Li Kui (fl. ca. 500 BCE), chief minister of Wei; Shang Yang (d. 338 BCE), chief minister of Qin; Shen Buhai (d. 337 BCE), chief minister of Han; Shen Dao (fl. 310 BCE), a thinker associated with the Ji Xia academy in Qi; and Han Fei (d. 233 BCE), a member of the ruling house of Han, who briefly served as an envoy to Zhao Zheng, the king of Qin who later became China's first emperor. To this list is often added Guan Zhong (d. 645

BCE), chief minister of Qi. Anthologies of writings are associated with all of these men. In Warring States practice, however, attribution of such a compilation to a historical figure did not imply authorship, but only that the person was an appropriate figurehead for the writings in it. The *Guanzi*, for instance, is not a work by Guan Zhong, but a compendium of fourth- through second-century BCE texts from his home state containing Confucian, Mohist, and Daoist works as well as writings on statecraft. The *Book of Lord Shang* is mainly devoted to statecraft, but probably dates to roughly 240 BCE, about a hundred years after the death of Shang Yang. Significant portions of the *Hanfeizi*, the most important of these anthologies, are unlikely to be by Han Fei himself, though scholars generally agree that the main essays on statecraft are. The text named after Li Kui is lost, and only fragments remain of those of Shen Buhai and Shen Dao (the titles of both books are romanized as *Shenzi*, though they are written and pronounced differently in Chinese).

With the possible exception of Shen Dao—about whose thought early texts give widely varying accounts—none of the Legalists were really part of Warring States philosophical discourse in the way the Mohists or Confucians were. Shang Yang and Shen Buhai were highly influential in shaping government institutions, but they were statesmen, not theorists. Han Fei, the grand synthesizer of Legalist thought, influenced the first and second emperors and their chancellor, Li Si, but lived near the end of the classical period and thus had little or no role in preimperial discourse. Indeed, while Han Fei is undoubtedly a major political theorist, one could argue that he is not really a political *philosopher* at all. Political philosophy is primarily a normative field, and Han Fei is not the least interested in normative issues such as the justification of political authority, the legitimate scope of state power, or social justice. In contrast to the Mohists and Confucians, who see government as responsible for the welfare of all and the ruler's mandate as resting partly on how well he cares for the populace, Han Fei simply assumes that the aim of government is to promote the interests of the ruler and the state. He takes for granted the legitimacy of a totalitarian autocracy and seeks to articulate institutions and methods by which to maintain stability, consolidate the ruler's power, and increase the state's economic wealth and military might. He does hold that the populace fares better under his system, a version of rule by law, than under the traditionalist, Confucian system, a version of rule of man. But this point is not offered as a justification, only as a claim about the relative potential for misgovernment under the two systems.

One starting point for Legalist thought is the conviction that, contrary to Confucian traditionalism, the ruler must be free to modify or introduce standards and customs, because socioeconomic conditions change over time. Specifically, as the population grows and resources become scarce, different systems of government become appropriate. Daoist laissez-faire policies and Confucian rule by the morally worthy are thus not mistaken so much as obsolete. Long ago, when the populace was small and resources plentiful, people could have lived in an orderly way without government. As the population grew, conflicts became common but could be resolved by appeal to the moral teachings of worthy leaders. Now, however, the population is enormous and resources limited. Social order can be maintained only through a system of controls enforced by a hierarchy of officials working under the unifying leadership of a ruler. The Legalists can thus grant that Daoist or Confucian political ideals might have worked at earlier stages of history. But once political society grows to a certain scale, these ideals are superseded.

The Daoists and Confucians both held a regressive view of history, seeing their age as the outcome of a long decline from the ideal society of the ancient sage kings. By contrast, the Legalist view of history is purely descriptive. Society is not better or worse than it used to be, but simply different, so different means of government are called for. Nor does society's tendency to fall into disorder show that people are by nature wanton or unruly—the view of the Confucian Xunzi, under whom both Han Fei and Li Si are said to have studied. The problem is only that mouths are many, resources few. As Han Fei sees it, people in the past were generous not because they were kind, but because resources were abundant; people in his day fight and steal not because they are dishonest, but because resources are scarce. His own approach to government rests on no stronger claim about human nature than that people by nature have likes and dislikes, and so rewards and punishments can be used to make them obey.

How, then, should the state maintain order? The Legalists proposed a number of keys to successful government, which Han Fei draws together into a coherent system. He credits his predecessors with articulating three crucial concepts in particular: *fa* (standards, laws), which he attributes to Shang Yang; *shu* (arts, techniques), which he attributes to Shen Buhai; and *shi* (position, power), which he attributes to Shen Dao. He criticizes shortcomings in the approaches of all three men while showing how their core ideas can be combined into a cogent, unified theory.

The first element in this theory is *fa*. *Fa* are explicitly codified, publicly promulgated standards, including laws, standards for satisfactory job performance, and criteria for promotion in the military or the bureaucracy. The aim of *fa* is to clearly specify the standards of conduct people are expected to meet, so that all will understand exactly what they must do and their performance can be evaluated with measurement-like precision. According to Han Fei, *fa* are to replace the moral teachings passed down in books, and the officials who promulgate the *fa* are to replace the virtuous example of the sage kings. To ensure people conform, the *fa* are backed by reliable, generous rewards for compliance and inescapable, heavy penalties for noncompliance. (Such penalties would have included the traditional "five punishments": tattooing the face, cutting off the nose, chopping off one or both feet, castration, and death.) If the *fa* are clear and appropriate and the rewards and punishments robust and inevitable, the system will work mechanically to achieve the goals of the state whether or not the ruler and administrators are particularly talented or worthy. Han Fei concedes that such a system may seem harsh in the short term but insists that it works to the long-term benefit of all. He offers this contention not as a justification for why people should submit to the system, but simply as a claim about its effectiveness.

The ruler, too, must conform to the *fa* without exception, never allowing personal preferences or choices to influence his decisions. He may revise the *fa*, if needed, but for the system to work, whatever explicit, objective standards he sets up must be applied rigorously and consistently. The standards will thus prevent him from being deceived or manipulated by cunning officials. The system of *fa* is to be so transparent and reliable that it eliminates any opportunity for official corruption or abuse. Since the standards are exact, explicit, and known to all, supposedly no one can get away with bending or violating them. The *fa* are thus a way both of controlling the populace and of limiting officials' power. The system contrasts dramatically with the older, traditional system of rule of man, under which officials punished crimes without appeal to explicit, publicly promulgated laws. In the older system, such laws were rejected as opening up opportunities for litigation and narrowing the scope of officials' discretionary power. The Legalists saw such power as harmful to the ruler's interests, since officials could use it to build their own clout and wealth at his expense. For related reasons, they eliminated traditional differences in treatment between the general population and the officials or aristocracy. Traditionally, those of high rank had been exempt from common punishments or were offered alternatives, such as suicide instead of execution. The Legalists applied a unified system of rewards and punishments to all, recognizing no differences in rank.

Fa, then, are explicit, public standards for regulating the behavior of the general populace. But besides controlling the populace, the ruler must also manage the officials in his administration, ensuring that they do their jobs properly and serve his interests, rather than their own. For this, he needs *shu*, managerial arts or techniques. In contrast to *fa*, which are codified and known by all, *shu* are undisclosed, uncodified methods. They are not to be revealed even to the ruler's closest associates, lest those around him use their knowledge of his actual thoughts and desires to manipulate him or curry favor. Techniques to be used by the ruler include appointing officials on the basis of merit, holding them strictly accountable for the tasks corresponding to their job title, and employing the "two handles" of life and death—or reward and punishment—to ensure they perform their duties. The first of these points is an extension of the Mohist doctrine of promoting the worthy: officials are to be appointed on the basis of demonstrated competence. The second is an extension and modification of the doctrine of the rectification of names (*zheng ming*) endorsed in Confucian and other early texts. Han Fei's version of the doctrine is called *xing ming* (forms and names), which he tells us refers to "speech and duties" (or "words and deeds"). Officials are assigned duties on the basis of "speech," here referring to either their job title or their administrative proposals. Their achievements are then measured against their assigned duties and their duties against their words. If all three are in accord, they are amply rewarded; if not, they are severely punished.

The proper functioning of both *fa* (standards) and *shu* (techniques) rests on a third factor: *shi*, a word meaning basically "position," but usually connoting a powerful or advantageous position. *Shi* is the institutional power of the ruler's position, which he wields to implement standards of conduct and exercise his administrative techniques. Just as the Legalist system of *fa* contrasts with the Confucian ideal of rule by the morally worthy, the Legalist view that successful rule derives from the ruler's institutional power contrasts with the Confucian view that it rests on the ruler's moral worth. Han Fei sees the Confucian view as foolishly unrealistic, on two counts. First, since truly talented and worthy leaders are few and far between, a system of rule by the moral authority of the worthy would condemn us to almost constant misgovernment, interrupted at best only occasionally by the emergence of a sagely ruler. The political system should be designed not around rare, exceptional great men but around the average ruler, who is neither as worthy as the sage kings of old nor as vicious as the tyrants. Second, without institutional power, even a great sage cannot rule more than a handful of people. Moral authority and charisma are simply not enough to control a large populace; only power and position can ensure that all will submit to government. Moral worth is thus redundant. To govern successfully, one need only employ *fa* from a position of power (*shi*) while using judicious techniques (*shu*) to manage one's administration. From his position of power, the ruler establishes standards and wields the "two handles" of life and death to ensure that his prohibitions are observed and decrees carried out, and "the way of order is complete."

BIBLIOGRAPHY AND SUGGESTED READINGS

Creel, Herrlee G. (1974) *Shen Pu-hai.* Chicago, IL: University of Chicago Press.

Duyvendak, J. J. L. (trans.). (1928) *Book of the Lord Shang.* London: Probsthain.

Fraser, Chris. (2002) "Mohism." In *The Stanford Encyclopedia of Philosophy* (Winter 2002 edition), edited by Edward Zalta. http://plato.stanford.edu/archives/win2002/entries/mohism. Stanford, CA: The Metaphysics Research Lab.

Graham, A. C. (1989) *Disputers of the Tao.* LaSalle, IL: Open Court.

Hansen, Chad. (1992) *A Daoist Theory of Chinese Thought.* Oxford: Oxford University Press.

Ivanhoe, Philip J. (1998) "Mohist Philosophy." In *The Routledge Encyclopedia of Philosophy*, edited by Edward Craig, Volume 6. London: Routledge, 451–455.

Ivanhoe, Philip J., and Bryan W. Van Norden (eds.). (2000) *Readings in Classical Chinese Philosophy.* New York: Seven Bridges Press.

Liao, W. K. (trans.). (1939) *The Complete Works of Han Fei Tzu.* 2 vols. London: Probsthain.

Lowe, Scott. (1992) *Mo Tzu's Religious Blueprint for a Chinese Utopia.* Lewiston: Edwin Mellen.

Lundahl, Bertil. (1992) *Hanfeizi: The Man and the Work.* Stockholm: Institute of Oriental Languages, Stockholm University.

Mei, Yi-pao (trans.). (1929) *The Ethical and Political Works of Motse.* London: Probsthain.

Rickett, W. Allyn (trans.). (1985) *Guanzi: Political, Economic, and Philosophical Essays from Early China*, Volume I. Princeton, NJ: Princeton University Press.

——— (trans.). (1998) *Guanzi: Political, Economic, and Philosophical Essays from Early China*, Volume II. Princeton, NJ: Princeton University Press.

Schwartz, Benjamin I. (1985) *The World of Thought in Ancient China.* Cambridge, MA: Belknap Press.

Thompson, Paul M. (1979) *The Shen Tzu Fragments.* Oxford: Oxford University Press.

Watson, Burton (trans.). (1963) *Mo Tzu: Basic Writings.* New York: Columbia University Press.

——— (trans.). (1964) *Han Fei Tzu: Basic Writings.* New York: Columbia University Press.

CHAPTER 6

CHINESE BUDDHIST PHILOSOPHY

BROOK ZIPORYN

CHINESE Buddhism represents one of the first extended encounters between two radically different cultural worlds, an early attempt to find a common ground and develop a synthesis that simultaneously satisfies their very dissimilar demands. The Indic religions stressed transcendence of and redemption from earthly life, while early Chinese thought focused on human ethical interactions and the art of rulership, taking it as axiomatic that life was in its essence finite and physical, and that the creation of value on earth, personally and socially, was the highest good. Chinese Buddhist philosophy can be viewed in terms of its development of conceptions of transcendent value accessible within the confines of this-worldly existence, its ways of utilizing the tools of radical world-denial to yield a form of extreme world-affirmation.

This chapter introduces the three traditions within Chinese Buddhism that alter the face of Indian Buddhism most distinctly. The earliest attempt at a thoroughgoing Sinitic reworking of the Buddhist tradition is found in the Tiantai 天台 school, founded in the fifth century CE. Close on its heels, the Huayan 華嚴 school and the Chan 禪 (Japanese: Zen) school emerged. All three schools succeeded in creating elaborate syntheses of indigenous and Indian Buddhist thinking, with varying emphases. While the Chan school sheds much of the scholastic theoretical baggage of Indian Buddhism, or at least streamlines and marginalizes it in favor of modes of practice and affect that owe much to indigenous traditions, the Huayan and Tiantai schools remained committed to elaborate theoretical expositions of metaphysical ideas derived from the framework of Indian religious categories. But all of these schools may be seen as emphasizing and extending the valorization of the phenomenal world, found also in some Mahayana scriptures, and a down-playing of the need for literal transcendence of the cycle of rebirth in the world. In so doing each in its own way develops a doctrine of what might be called "omnisolipsism": the notion that each and every entity is actually all entities, that each particular thing in the world *is* the totality of the world. This idea allows for a strong affirmation of immanence of Buddhahood in the world, and the interfusion and identity between sentient beings and Buddhas, between samsara and Nirvana. The three schools arrive at this conclusion by means of different sets of premises and deductions, with significantly varying implications. Of particular philosophical interest are their differing assumptions about what counts as a real entity and what as a merely illusory entity, and the practical consequences of this difference.

Tiantai: Delusion as Local Coherence as Global Incoherence as Ultimate Reality

Tiantai Buddhist theory, as developed by its de facto founder Zhiyi 智顗 (538–597), rests on the doctrine of the Three Truths (三諦 *sandi*).[1] This is an expansion of the Indian Madhyamaka distinction between Conventional Truth and Ultimate Truth. Indian Buddhism makes use of the notion of "Emptiness" (*sunyata*), the denial of any intrinsic or independent "own-nature" for any putative entity, as a method by which to refute all views about the ultimate nature of things. This is considered liberating, because the Buddhist tradition regards attachment as the primary cause of suffering, and the predication of absolute facts about things is considered a form of attachment, correlative with a notion of a substantial self and a blindness to conditionality that engenders desire and suffering. Since every putative entity and each of its apparent attributes arise only through dependence on multiple causes and conditions, no predicates can legitimately be attributed to any entity considered independently, not even "existence" or "nonexistence," and this abandonment of all predications is what is meant by "Emptiness." Things are neither existent nor nonexistent: they are empty.

But the *concept* of "Emptiness" itself is here considered an instance of what is called Conventional, not Ultimate, Truth. Conventional Truth is composed of (1) commonly accepted ordinary speech (e.g., "self," "other," "cause," "effect") *in addition*

1. These doctrines are given their classical expression in the records of Zhiyi's lectures recorded by his disciple Guanding in the *Miaofalianhuajingxuanyi* (also known as the *Fahuaxuanyi*) ("Profound Meaning of the Lotus Sutra") and in the *Mohezhiguan* ("Great Calming and Concentration"), both collected in the *Taishô Shinshû Daizôkyô* (henceforth "T") (*The Buddhist Canon, New Edition of the Taishô Period*), volumes 33 (T33) and 46 (T46), respectively.

to (2) Buddhist terminologies (e.g., "nonself," "impermanence," "karma," "emptiness"), all of which are seen as aids to the realization of Ultimate Truth, which is not a set of cognitive claims at all but rather precisely freedom from all predicative views, which is thus by definition inconceivable. Absolutist claims of non-Buddhist religions and philosophies are thus not included in the category of Conventional Truth, nor are individual fantasies and unshared cognitive errors, for none of these is viewed as an aid to the realization of Ultimate Truth. An assertion qualifies as a Conventional Truth, then, if and only if it is capable of leading beyond itself, of self-overcoming: only those views that are conducive to the ultimate overcoming of views (= Ultimate Truth) are Conventional Truths. Emptiness is not to be taken as a view about things in its own right, but rather as a heuristic whose sole purpose is to overturn all possible views. When this work is done, it, too, is to be discarded, negated by the "Emptiness of Emptiness." The operative *concept* of Emptiness is to be contrasted to the absolute unspeakability of the experience of Ultimate Truth.[2]

Tiantai alters this picture decisively by speaking of not two but three types of truth, which are further said to be "interfused." These are Ultimate Truth, Conventional Truth, and the Center (真諦，俗諦，中諦 *zhendi, sudi, zhongdi*), also identified as Emptiness, Provisional Positing, and the Center (空假中 *kong, jia, zhong*). Tiantai regards as self-contradictory the idea that Ultimate Truth is beyond all views rather than being a view in its own right. It thus also rejects the gap between attributive predication and the experience of liberation beyond all predicates. If either conceptual Emptiness (a Conventional Truth) or experienced Emptiness (Ultimate Truth) does anything, even if only to refute the ultimacy of all views or bring cognitive error and suffering to an end in however attenuated, qualified, or self-canceling a way, then it is *ipso facto* a something, and entails a kind of predicative view or position of its own. Instead, Tiantai takes the deployment of Emptiness as *merely* Ultimate Truth—not yet the Center—but then asserts that the Three Truths "interfuse," meaning that Emptiness, both as a concept and as an experience, is itself a Provisional Posit. Hence, Emptiness, the negation of all characteristics, is no different from any other view or putative entity: it is a position taken on things that is provisionally assertable and conceivable, for the temporary pragmatic purpose of leading beyond itself, although it is itself ultimately insupportable, empty. But the same applies to all Provisional Posits, for this is the only kind of predication there is. In short, rather than separating all possible experience into two categories, the conceivable (susceptible to predication) and the inconceivable, Tiantai asserts that each putative entity is constitutively both conceivable *and* inconceivable. The conceivable is always also inconceivable, and vice versa. Indeed, "conceivability" is itself inconceivable, and "inconceivability" is, to exactly the same extent as any other putative cognitive object, conceivable. More radically, it is just its conceivability that is its inconceivability. This last point is the third Tiantai truth, the Truth of the Center.

2. For more on Indian Buddhist accounts of emptiness, see the chapters in this volume by John Dunne, John Powers, and Matthew Kapstein.

We may better understand the Tiantai position by retranslating the terms "provisional positing" and "emptiness" as "local coherence" and "global incoherence," respectively. Provisional Truth is the apprehension of some qualium X as having a certain discernible, graspable, coherent identity. Emptiness is the revelation that this coherent identity is only provisionally coherent, that it fails to be coherent in all contexts and from all points of view, and thus is globally incoherent. X appears exclusively as X only when our field of attention is arbitrarily narrowed to exclude some of the relevant ways it can be considered; attention to its constitutive elements, antecedents, and contexts reveals that this very same item, X, is also readable as non-X. But these particular contexts derive their own determinate identities to their further contextualizations; the call for identity-granting contextualization, once begun, can have no nonarbitrary stopping point. Since identity is context dependent, each identity requires the context of all possible existents. But all possible existents can grant no particular determinacy. Whatever is true of "all" of reality is by definition indeterminate, for a determinacy requires a contrast between itself and some other existent that it is "not." "Determinacy" is synonymous with "non-allness." So since each determinacy also involves a claim about the identity of all things (namely, "the universe must be such that X is thus and so"), each determinacy is self-undermining. To be coherent is thus also to be incoherent. And this fact, that conventional and ultimate truths—coherence and incoherence—are synonymous, but only by means of their necessary contrast, giving ultimacy to neither, is what is meant by the Center, the Third Truth.

From this idea of Centrality, Zhiyi deduces the omnisolipsist claim that each thing is the entirety of reality, that all things are everywhere at once. Centrality means "intersubsumption." For if to be definitively X and not to be definitively X are merely alternate ways of stating the same fact about X, the contrast between the absence and presence of X is annulled, and X is no more present "here and now" than it is present "there and then." It pervades all possible times and places to exactly the extent that it is present here at all. It can be read into any experience, and is here and now only because it has been so read into the here and now. X, in other words, is eternal and omnipresent, but only as "canceled," divested of the putative opacity of its simple location. Any entity is the whole of reality, is the sole reality. All determinations are locally coherent, globally incoherent, and the absolute reality manifesting as all other realities. The "incoherence" of X does not undermine the "coherence" of X, or vice versa. Rather, X interfuses with non-X precisely by means of its separation and difference from non-X, from the provisional contrast that is constitutive of the being of both the coherence and the incoherence of X. X is present *as* both X and non-X, and only by means of the ineradicable contrast between the two. X, as a particular determination, is *more* real than it appears: it is inextricable from any possible reality, discoverable in all times and places.

This reconfiguration has two direct consequences: first, the hierarchy between conventional and ultimate truth is canceled; they are no longer describable as a one-way means and ends structure, where the means can be discarded when the end is reached. Second, the category of "plain falsehood," which was often understood to be implied by the Madhyamaka idea of Two Truths, is here eliminated entirely: all claims of whatever kind, including heretical metaphysical views and idiosyncratic personal delusions, are equally conventional truths, and thus of equal value to and ultimately identical with ultimate truth, or the conception of Emptiness. This is because the truth of a statement consists simply in its coherence to some given perspective, which is always the effect of arbitrarily limiting the horizons of relevance. Hence, any view of any putative matter that might be adduced for consideration (1) is now seen to be a conventional truth that can lead beyond itself, and (2) is what is beyond that view, and all views, and (3) is the ultimate interfusion and interidentity of that view, and all views, and what-is-beyond-all-views. This applies also to these three statements themselves.

Every instant of experience is thus the whole of existential reality, manifesting in this particular form, *as* this particular entity or experience. But this "whole" is irreducibly multiple and irreducibly unified at once, in the following way: all possible conflicting, contrasted, and axiologically varied aspects, the "three thousand natures and characteristics," are irrevocably present—in the sense of "findable"—in each of these totality-effects. Good and evil, delusion and enlightenment, Buddhahood and deviltry, are all "inherently entailed" (性具 *xingju*) in each and every event. More important, however, these multiple entities are not "simply located" even virtually or conceptually: the "whole," which is the agent performing every experience, is not a collection of these various "inherently entailed" entities or qualities arrayed side by side, like coins in a pocket. Rather, they are intersubsumptive. Each part is the whole, each quality subsumes all other qualities, and yet none are ever eradicable. A Buddha in the world makes the world all Buddha, saturated in every locus with the quality "Buddhahood"; a devil in the world makes the world all devil, permeated with "deviltry." Both Buddha and devil are always in the world. So the world is always both *entirely* Buddhahood and *entirely* deviltry. Every moment of experience is always completely delusion, evil and pain, through and through, and also completely enlightenment, goodness and joy, through and through.

We have seen that in Tiantai there are no errors, only local coherences of varying ranges of applicability: all experiences and assertions of any kind are conventional truths, and all conventional truths may lead beyond themselves to reveal themselves to also be ultimate truth and the intersubsumption of the two types of truth and, further, of all local coherences. But what is most remarkable is that we can with equal validity also put this point the other way around: instead of saying there are no errors, we can say there are *nothing but errors*. Even enlightenment can never be separated from cognitive error, false views, unsustainable positions, or delusion. For in Tiantai, enlightenment is always and only enlightenment *about delusion*. Truth is a deeper knowledge *about errors*—that is, in this context, one-sided, self-contradictory, and ultimately unsustainable views. There is simply nothing else for there to be truth about; there is nothing else to know about. And this knowledge about errors is not an elimination or refutation of the errors only; it is rather a way of allowing them to exist *more clearly and fully as what they are*. An error is a particular local coherence, the global incoherence of this local coherence, and the fact that these are merely alternate ways of saying the same thing. So in allowing the error to become more manifest as itself, the error (local coherence) is both more fully established as this particular coherence and undermined, and these are seen to be identical. Enlightenment is not the elimination of delusion, then, but the full realization of delusion: delusion is the content and object of enlightenment. This is the basis for the unique Tiantai doctrine that "the Buddha-nature inherently entails evil," that even for a Buddha, the intrinsic nature of evil, and all the characteristics of hell and hell-beings, can never be destroyed, only recontextualized. It is this ineradicable pluralism as integration that is most distinctive to Tiantai thought. To see is always to also see otherwise; to be sentient is always to have double vision, to be experiencing things from more than one point of view. Delusion is always Enlightenment/Delusion. Enlightenment is always Delusion/Enlightenment. Enlightenment is a structural rearrangement that supplements and recontextualizes Delusion, rather than replacing or destroying it.

Huayan: Interdependence as Interidentity

Huayan Buddhist doctrine, as found in the works attributed to its putative founder Dushun 杜順 (557–640) and its great systemizer Xianshou Fazang 法藏 (643–712), gives a more detailed and single-minded account of omnisolipsism, a streamlined working through of the Tiantai views but resting on rather different premises and bringing somewhat divergent results. The divergences can be seen most clearly in the works of Chengguan 澄觀 (738–839) and especially Guifeng Zongmi 圭峰宗密 (780–841), where the emphasis on the "One True Mind" as the omnipresent principle instantiated in all reality assumes greater importance, providing a convenient theoretical complement to Chan theory and practice.

The thought of Dushun and Fazang begins from considerations that can be stated as follows. To ask "What is X?" means, "What are the characteristics that really belong to X," where "really" means "intrinsically, inalienably, through its own power alone, under all conditions, from all perspectives, at all times." We have here a definitional assumption that derives squarely from Buddhism's Indo-European sources. X is "really" what X is in isolation from all relations, what X is intrinsically, what X is "absolutely."

But the Mahayana Buddhist premise that all components of experience (*dharmas*) arise in dependence on multiple causes brings with it a distinctive twist to this definition: the insight that nothing could possibly meet it. In other words, for any and all existent things of whatever kind, there is in fact only one characteristic that meets this definition: the characteristic of having no characteristics that meet this definition, except this one. All things have the nature of "having no nature," the intrinsic character of "having no intrinsic characteristics."[3] But even "the definitive excluding of characteristics, or indeed of any single possible characteristic," would be a characteristic, and even this cannot be intrinsic. So to be any apparent X is really to be "neither intrinsically possessing nor capable of excluding any possible characteristics." This means that the ability to take on characteristics, or to appear to have characteristics, or to temporarily (i.e., nonintrinsically) assume characteristics, is itself the *only* intrinsic characteristic of all things. This one intrinsic characteristic is in Huayan thought identified with "Emptiness," and renamed as "Principle" (*li* 理).[4]

The relation between this intrinsic Principle of taking on characteristics and all the extrinsic characteristics that it appears to take on is determined as one of neither sameness-nor-difference, or more exactly, both sameness-and-difference, where they are the same *because* they are different and different *because* they are the same. From this it is concluded that every particular event is both identical to Principle (this is all that is truly intrinsic to it) and different from it (the nature of Principle is precisely to exclude the intrinsic being of whatever this particular event determinately purports to be). These are not two different facts, but alternate ways of stating the same fact. As the *Huayan fajieguan*, attributed to Dushun, puts it, "The not-sameness is the not-difference."[5] Dushun gives three alternate explanations of the proposition that "form is the same as emptiness *because* form is different from emptiness, and this is the real meaning of the sameness between form (events) and emptiness (principle)":

1. Form is different from the deludedly conceived annihilationist sense of emptiness (the definitive exclusion of all characteristics) and emptiness is different from form conceived as self-standing and intrinsically existing. This difference is precisely what makes the *real* (dependently coarisen) form the same as the *real* (nonannihilationist) emptiness.
2. The particularity of the characteristics of any event is different from the universal principle of noninclusion-as-nonexclusion of all characteristics that is its only truly intrinsic characteristic; they are conceptually

3. This is applicable at all levels. That is, if X is a thing with apparent characteristics A, B, and C, and by the above premises it is concluded that A, B, and C are not the true nature of X (i.e., do not intrinsically belong to X), the same question can then be asked of A, B, and C themselves (i.e., "What is A, what is B, what is C?") with the same result: the only characteristic intrinsic to any of them is affectability, the ability to take on characteristics. The true nature of each of these elements or characteristics is also none other than "having no nature."

4. This character of emptiness or principle constitutes the *whole real* being of each and every particular. It is not a part of its real being, but *all* that is really intrinsic to it, in the above sense. Moreover, this character of emptiness or principle is indivisible. It cannot be partially possessed; to have this character is to have it in its entirety. The character of "being susceptible to otherness, to other characteristics" is thus possessed *in its entirety* by every being and state. The assumption is that this character does not admit of degrees, because it is the character of having no fixed character, and divisibility presupposes parts or characteristics that can be distinguished.

5. The text appears at T45.687b-c, with Zongmi's commentary.

distinguishable aspects. But it is precisely this difference that makes each particular characteristic an instantiation of this universal characteristic of "allowing any characteristic." Each particular being an instantiation of this universal principle is the sameness between them.

So far this amounts to an alternate and much streamlined derivation of what Tiantai thought called "the Center." But Huayan adds to this a specification that is alien to Tiantai thought:

3. Their sameness is their difference because there is a relation of one-way *dependence* between "principle" and "event." Events are dependent (依 *yi*) on principle, and principle is what events depend on. This is their difference. Their sameness depends on the distinctive Huayan assertion that all dependence relations are really relations of sameness as well, already implied in the Tiantai conception of intersubsumption, but further explored in Fazang's doctrine of the "Six Characteristics."

This doctrine is presented at the end of the *Huayan yisheng fenqi zhang*, where Fazang asserts that a true and comprehensive view of any entity or event must simultaneously apprehend that it is (1) itself the whole of reality, identical to the whole; (2) one differentiated part, a particular event within reality; (3) the same as all other entities or events; (4) different from all other entities or events; (5) bringing to completion the whole of reality and each other entity within it; and (6) undermining the whole of reality and each entity within it. Fazang illustrates this with his analogy of the pillar and the house.[6] The pillar is precisely the house. The reason for this is that if the pillar is lacking, the house cannot come into existence, and whenever the pillar exists, the house exists. This last point depends on a distinction between a "real pillar" and a mere plank of wood, and also on the distinction between a "good house" (好舍 *hao she*) and a "broken house" (破舍 *po she*)—the latter meaning not a real house, not a genuine, successful example of a house. Fazang's point is that, in the absence of the existing completed house, the pillar is simply not a pillar: it is merely a plank of wood. It cannot be accurately named a "pillar" unless the whole house is there. In this sense, Fazang can say that the one pillar alone makes the house. The same argument is used to assert that the pillar is also identical to all the other parts of the house, each being identical to the whole house in the same way. For if the pillar is gone, the house cannot exist, and without the house, the walls, roof, and so on are not "really" walls, roof, and so on, but merely chunks of wood. The other five points above depend on the same type of reasoning.

This is an understanding of omnisolipsism and interpenetrating identities that is mediated by each part's identity with the whole. What interpenetrates in each case is not what we normally call a pillar, if we are deluded about interpenetration and think of it as a separable single part of the house. *That* pillar simply does not exist,

6. T45.507c-508a.

and cannot interpenetrate with other particulars, or do anything else for that matter. The only pillar that qualifies as a pillar is the one that is seen to be interpenetrating. Here we see the persistence of the Indo-European dichotomy between appearance and reality, which does not apply in Tiantai thought. Now we can always move the analysis to other levels, and say that while the pillar-without-a-house is not really a pillar, it is really a plank of wood, and exists interpenetratingly in other totalities that way. Each entity is the whole universe, because to really be "this entity" means for the universe to be as it is; this entity is only really "this entity," only has the characteristics attributed to it, because of its contextualization by every other entity being what and how it is. Outside of these relationships, it does not have any of the characteristics or identities that putatively pertain to it. This is simply a way of thinking through the relation of dependence thoroughly, so that interdependence, with no remainder, is seen to be none other than interidentity. But this recourse to "really qualifying to be called X" already introduces a level of final adjudication that limits the possibility of multiperspectivism and surreptitiously posits a meta-perspective, with at best a one-way hierarchy of levels of reality and interpervasion.

One helpful formula developed to illustrate Huayan thought is the doctrine of the "Four Dharmadhatus" (四法界*si fajie*), which describe four alternate ways in which all of reality is to be viewed:

1. All dharmas seen as particular separate events
2. All events seen as Principle
3. Principle seen as interfusing, interidentical, with all events, and all events seen as interfusing with Principle
4. Each event seen as interfusing, interidentical, with every other event[7]

These are four alternate ways of viewing the totality of all that exists, representing ascending levels of spiritual attainment. All things can be seen as events, as Principle, as events-that-are-Principle, and as events-that-are-all-other-events. We can observe here an attempt to move beyond the transcendental dimension of Principle, bringing its significance back into the phenomenal world, into the "horizontal" relation between events. However, as Peter Gregory and others have pointed out, there is a tendency in later Huayan thought, particularly in the work of Zongmi, to move the emphasis to the Third Dharmadhatu, the immanent relationship between Principle and each event. Principle in this context also tends to become associated with the "One True Mind," the undifferentiated awareness that is always operating even in deluded thought. The logic of this identification of Principle or Emptiness with the True Mind can easily be deduced, for the characteristic of neither-inclusion-nor-exclusion translates neatly into "reflectivity per se," that is, perceptivity per se, awareness: something whose only self is its unending and ineradicable relation to some other, with

7. This schema, though implicit in early Huayan works, is not given this definitive form until Chengguan's *Huayan fajie xuanjing*, which can be found at T45, #1883.

which it is, at the moment of awareness, indistinguishable. We will find here a convenient point of contact between Huayan and Chan.

Huayan thought differs from Tiantai thought in its handling of the reality/appearance problem. In Huayan, there is a real, right view of all that is; it is the view of interdependence itself, in which alone all things are ontologically grounded, and which accounts for their being the way they are. But this is conceived on a Two Truths model, so that the notion of separable things—that is, the content of the vast majority of sentient experience—is now viewed as simply a mistake. What does not exist cannot interpenetrate, nor cause enlightenment; it cannot have any function whatsoever. The Three Truths model of Tiantai, in contrast, means that all the putative entities mistakenly conceived by deluded sentient beings also interpenetrate, and delusion itself, together with all its concomitants, is itself identical to enlightenment. In Huayan, enlightenment is a realization of the truth about all actual things: they are actually inseparable, interpenetrating, and interidentical. In Tiantai, enlightenment is a realization about all possible views and experiences of things: they are locally coherent, globally incoherent, and intersubsumptive, and these three are synonymous. Later Tiantai writers such as Siming Zhili 四明知禮 (960–1028) thus criticize the Huayan interpretation of the Mahayana scriptural assertion of interpenetration of value opposites—for example, "Defilement is itself enlightenment," "samsara is identical to nirvana," and "form is identical to emptiness." Zhili asserts that the Huayan reading of these statements, in particular in the works of Guifeng Zongmi, fails to grasp any actual identity of opposites, and thus establishes no true interpenetration. For the reality/appearance dichotomy in Huayan thought necessitates that there is "really" no such thing as defilement, samsara, or form—these are just deluded attributions of separability based on a failure to understand interdependence. Hence, what was called defilement was all along "really" nothing but enlightenment, and so on.[8] Therefore, according to Tiantai, Huayan thought falls short because it does not really teach a real interpenetration of genuinely distinct entities. Huayan writers, on the other hand, tend to see the Tiantai doctrine of ineradicable inherent evil as morally questionable, and at odds with the basic soteriological aims of Buddhism.

Chan: The Self-overcoming of Absolute Subjectivity

Chan (Jap. Zen) is a movement within Chinese Buddhism with a very complex history, and a rather tangled relationship to what is normally called "philosophy." If we sift through all the obfuscations and legends, as well as the rhetorical attacks on the

8. Cf. T46.707b.

kind of scholastic philosophizing we find in Tiantai and Huayan, we can perhaps discern an evolving series of positions that can survive translation into philosophical terms. Chan begins as an affirmation of original enlightenment and the identification of the mind of sentient beings with Nirvana and Buddhahood, as asserted in some of the Indian Tathagatha-garbha literature. The real meaning of Emptiness is on this view not what is reached at the end of dialectical reasoning, but what is prior to all such reasoning: the mind itself. It is this mind, functioning right now, that is really beyond all predicates and all conditionality, as Nirvana and Emptiness were asserted to be. The primary mistake is to think of these as objects, as experiences to be grasped or reached, as concepts posited out before us. They are rather, as it were, "we ourselves." This means, first, that all the complex terminologies developed in Buddhist philosophy and scripture are really just ways of talking about the mind of the sentient being. Hence, in the earliest strata of Chan literature, we see an emphasis on a kind of demythologizing, where all concrete, "objective" aspects of Buddhist practice and attainment turn out to be metaphors for states of mind of the Buddhist practitioner. A further step is taken, perhaps represented by the famous mythology of the Northern-Southern schism, when the full inherence of all these aspects of Buddhahood, rather than their attainment as special states of mind, is stressed. In the *Platform Sutra* (eighth century), we have the figure of Huineng 慧能 (638–713), an illiterate layman from the barbarian south, representing the universality of Buddha-nature prior to any special attainments or practices. Instead, somewhat in line with indigenous Daoist and Confucian ideas, Buddhahood is what all creatures originally possess, which is not attained by producing some special deliberate state of mind, but rather exactly what the mind is when undisturbed by all such efforts to make it one way or another. Hence, Buddhist morality, meditative concentration, and wisdom are no longer concrete facts in the world, nor metaphors for particular states to be attained by the mind, but rather three intrinsic characteristics of the original mind of all beings: the mind is intrinsically pure (morality), is concentrated (meditation), and discloses particular forms without distortion (wisdom). Huineng is made to compare the "self-nature" of all beings to empty space, which here both contains and produces all the particular objects within it. The self-nature is also said to "flow unobstructedly," to be in essence "nondwelling." Like space, it is the pure unobstructedness that allows any and every object to manifest, without getting "stuck" in or as any of them.

A further following through of the logic of nonobjectification is taken here: for even to say "the mind is the Buddha," while de-objectifying the Buddha, now objectifies the mind. Anything that can be named or indicated at all, anything determinate, is *ipso facto* an object, not pure subjectivity. Hence, "mind" is not the real mind. As the *Surangama Sutra*, a Chinese apocryphal scripture that spells out many crucial Chan themes, puts it, "When seeing is seen, it is no longer seeing." Chan asserts that "the eye cannot see itself": whatever is seen is not the eye. Whatever is known is not the mind, not the real Buddha. Hence, we find Huineng pushing the metaphor of mind as mirror—with no particular color or shape of its own, but capable of revealing any and every color and shape—a step further. If the metaphor is taken uncritically, the materiality of the mirror is not yet metaphoricized away. Hence, we have the representative of the "Northern School" in the *Platform Sutra* asserting intrinsic enlightenment with the exhortation to simply keep this mirror clean, wipe the dust away constantly. Nothing need be added, but obstructions must be removed. Huineng is made to respond that there is originally no thing there, no mirror—"mirror" was just a temporary metaphor for this absence of any "thing"—so there is nowhere for the dust to settle: nothing need be wiped away, the appearance and disappearance of particular thoughts and perceptions are to be released into free-fall, into unobstructed, nondwelling flow. Since the original mind can never be seen as an object in itself, it is seen only in the continual unobstructed upsurge of particular objects and events. Hence, Chan, in the formulation of the Hongzhou school that was to become dominant from the late Tang dynasty (618–907) forward, comes to assert that the Buddha-nature is just "pure Function" itself. Not any particular object, not the elimination of all objects, but the preobjectified moment of coming-to-appear of any and every object or action is the Buddha-nature, our real, unconditional selves. This also means that the primal error is precisely "seeking" Buddhahood in any particular form, for it is the Function that is doing the seeking that is really the Buddha. One is "riding a horse in search of a horse," or, in the parable of the *Surangama Sutra*, one is seeking one's own head after seeing one's own reflection: that person over there in the mirror has such a clear, distinct, objective thing there up on top of his neck, a "head," whereas I, over here, have just a blank from my neck on up. It is of course this blank, this emptiness, this space, that is the real head—the eye that cannot see itself. But it mistakenly attributes "reality" only to what is determinate, what has a visible or conceivable form, and projects value into it. The real head is the seeing of the fake head, and the real value is the projecting of value into some false object. Seeking any "reality," then, is precisely what at once separates us from reality—the pure presubjective function—but also, in another way, is always revealing it.

From this time forward we find Chan masters demonstrating but not explaining the Buddha-nature—any explanation would have to be in the form of already objectified and hence distorted terms. It can be demonstrated by any function whatsoever—lifting the eyebrows, rolling on the ground—but only as the in-process occurrence, not the already complete, describable, determinate something. Here also we find the use of blows and shouts as an expedient by which to fly "under the radar" of conceptual thought, of already complete determinations: the element of quickness, of surprise, discloses the occurrence of function "as it's happening," before it has solidified into a particular something. This also means that, in that instant when it is still dawning, Function is neither subjective nor objective, neither my own nor another's: it is the self-manifestation of Buddha-nature. We find these techniques especially pronounced in the Linji 臨濟 (Jap. Rinzai) school.[9] The full

9. Other methods of focusing on the unknowable, the preobjective/presubjective, are developed in the Caodong school, drawing on Daoist motifs of the interfusion of light and darkness; unfortunately, there is no space to go into these here.

spontaneity of preobjectified function is here first a kind of extreme and virulent rejection of all objectivity, and in that sense radical subjective megalomania. We find the eponymous founder of the school Linji Yixuan 臨濟義玄 (d. 866) famously saying, for example, "If you meet the Buddha, kill the Buddha; if you meet the patriarchs, kill the patriarchs," and so on. All particular objects and values must be negated and destroyed—nothing should be clung to—for all of these obtain their objecthood, their substantiality, their characteristics, and their value solely from the ongoing function of the mind itself, the Buddha-nature, at any given moment. This Function going on right now is what gives them their being and value, is the real "master" of all, and it can also freely remove them. But this goes also for the "self" as ordinarily conceived. The willfulness of Linji is meant to be self-destroying. In the moment of the upsurge of Function, we have something even "closer to ourselves" than what we normally call a subjective willful action: it is not a deed committed in order to attain a particular preconceived end, it has no particular purpose, and it is not part of any system, whether of my own aims or of objective truth. We might see in this a kind of self-overcoming of subjectivity. Pushed to its extreme, the rejection of all determinate objects is also the rejection of any determinate self, or indeed any fixable determinate deed.

What is left is the pure Function that can never be captured in any determinate descriptions, which can only be indicated by contradictory statements and deeds. In later Chan the "public case" (Ch. *gong-an* 公案; Jap. *koan*) technique is developed as a systematic means of training students in sensitivity to this radical presubjectivity. A famous example is Zhaozhou's "No": a monk asked, "Does a dog have Buddha-nature?" Zhaozhou 趙州 answered, "No!" This example is drawn out of the collected sayings of the Tang monk; in other dialogues, Zhaozhou answers the same question, "Yes!" It is accepted Mahayana doctrine, of course, that all beings have the Buddha-nature, so on the first level this example is singled out to undermine the attachment to objectified doctrine. What is real about the Buddha-nature is the contradiction of all already solidified objectified terms, so this contradiction actually reveals the Buddha-nature. On another level, it is Zhaozhou's speaking of the word "No!"—this pure Function unentangled in the net of self-created objectifications—that is the manifestation of Zhaozhou's own Budhha-nature and also the Buddha-nature that is the dog. On yet another level, we may say that the dog really does not "have" the Buddha-nature, for that would imply a separation between the dog and the Buddha-nature. Rather, the dog *is* the Buddha-nature, like all other sentient beings. But what one *is*, the presubjective function going on at this instant, one does not *have:* what one *has* is only the world of already objectified objects, concepts, selves. The eye does not see itself: the dog does not have Buddha-nature—and this "not" is precisely its Buddha-nature, or is itself *as* the Buddha-nature.

In Chan, then, all attempts to state the what lies outside all statements, or to reach the Absolute, the unconditioned, Nirvana through a chain of conditional premises or procedures, are doomed in advance; anything that is a conclusion is *ipso facto* wrong. But the very stating and failing are themselves a manifestation of the Function that is absolute. Every Function is the absolute. We end up here with a kind of omnisolipsism not of entities, but of moments in time, of functions, assimilating nicely to what the Huayan school calls "events." As a description, as philosophy, this is rejected, but we can trace a similar point of view in the indirections of the Chan texts. There exists nothing beyond this present Function, this present moment, this present event. All other events are manifestations, projections, objectifications actualized by this function occurring right here and now.

In all these forms of Chinese Buddhism, then, we find an omnisolipsism that brings Buddhahood into the present world of human life, radicalized in various ways so that Buddahood is not only revealing itself in "the world" as such, which is still an objectification and a deluded thought, but into each and every sentient occurrence. Buddhahood manifests itself in Tiantai in delusion as delusion, even precisely as misconceived purposes and volitions; it is precisely *because* they are deluded that Buddhahood manifests in them. Interpenetration is revealed precisely as isolation and separation, as the negation of interpenetration. In Tiantai, then, Buddhahood is *this* specific deluded purpose and volition. In Huayan, Buddhahood is manifested in each event when seen truly as *really* the interpenetration of all real events, of *all* purposes and volitions. In Chan, Buddhahood manifests itself as each and every function when seen as *freed from any* specific and determinate conception, volition, or purpose.[10]

BIBLIOGRAPHY AND SUGGESTED READINGS

Chang, Chung-yuan. (1995) *Original Teachings of Ch'an Buddhism.* New York: Pantheon Press.

Chang, Garma. (1974) *The Buddhist Teaching of Totality: The Philosophy of Hwa Yen Buddhism.* State College, PA: Pennsylvania State University Press.

Cleary, Thomas. (1983) *Entry into the Inconceivable: An Introduction to Hua-yen Buddhism.* Honolulu, HI: University of Hawaii Press.

Cook, Francis. (1977) *Hua-Yen Buddhism: The Jewel Net of Indra.* State College, PA: Pennsylvania State University Press.

Donner, Neal, and Daniel B. Stevenson. (1993) *The Great Calming and Contemplation: A Study and Annotated Translation of the First Chapter of Chih-I's Mo-Ho Chih-Kuan.* Honolulu, HI: University of Hawaii Press.

Swanson, Paul L. (1995) *Foundations of T'ien-t'ai Philosophy: The Flowering of the Two Truths Theory of Chinese Buddhism.* Fremont, CA: Asian Humanities Press.

Watson, Burton. (trans.). (1999) *The Zen Teachings of Master Lin-Chi.* New York: Columbia University Press.

Ziporyn, Brook. (2000) *Evil and/or/as the Good: Omnicentrism, Intersubjectivity and Value Paradox in Tiantai Buddhist Thought.* Cambridge, MA: Harvard University Press.

———. (2004) *Being and Ambiguity: Philosophical Experiments with Tiantai Buddhism.* Chicago, IL: Open Court Press.

10. For more on how Chinese Buddhism was developed in Japan and Korea, see the chapters in the section on Japanese and Korean Philosophy in this volume.

CHAPTER 7

NEO-CONFUCIANISM

JOHN BERTHRONG

NEO-CONFUCIANISM designates a galaxy of thinkers of various Confucian lineages beginning in the late Tang dynasty (post-840s) through the Qing dynasty (1644–1911) in China. As an international movement, it incorporated profound contributions by scholars in Korea, Japan, and Vietnam. It constitutes the Second Epoch of Confucian philosophy, at the midpoint between the Classical Confucianism of antiquity and New Confucian Movement of the contemporary world. In Neo-Confucian terms, to tell the story of philosophy, we must also attend to the history of the intellectual culture that has sustained Neo-Confucianism as the dominant philosophy in East Asia since the eleventh century. Social and intellectual history, along with an understanding of philosophical lineages, is crucial for Confucian self-understanding. No philosophical culture saw itself as more historically conditioned and concerned than the Neo-Confucians. Confucians never saw themselves as individualistic creative thinkers. Rather, Confucians all strive to sustain, even elaborate, what Confucius called "this culture of ours" (*siwen* 斯文) down the long river of East Asian philosophical history. Creative advance there is in abundance, but it is always viewed as part of the revered historical development of the Confucian Way.

The Neo-Confucians revived classical Confucian thought through an extended dialogue with Daoists and Buddhists. Neo-Confucians formulated a series of highly complicated cosmological, axiological, hermeneutic, and political theories about how to understand and promote human flourishing. The various lineages of Neo-Confucianism cluster around the understanding of four major intersecting concepts: *li* 理, coherent principle; *qi* 氣, vital energy; *xing* 性, nature; and *xin* 心, the mind-heart. The expansion of Neo-Confucian discourse revolved around alternative definitions of the meanings of these terms and the cosmological and axiological visions that evolved in the debate about how these terms were related to each other in one form or another. For instance, one paradigmatic Neo-Confucian debate swirled around the relationship or priority of coherent principle and vital energy. Which was the primary cosmological category of explanation and reality? The Neo-Confucians greatly expanded Confucian philosophy by elaborating on older theories of social ethics and personal transformation and adding great new cosmological, epistemological, hermeneutical, historical, practical, and axiological systems over eight centuries. Moreover, the movement was not only immensely productive in China but also equally creative in Korea and Japan. In Confucian social theory, the Neo-Confucians were exploring the connections of the *waiwang* 外王 ("the king without") and the *neisheng* 內聖 ("the sage within"). In the modern world the "king" could definitely be the citizens of a democratic society. In short, they explored the cosmos and the moral mind-heart within each person and tried to discern the patterns of order to be found in a relational, realistic, and processive manifestation of the supernal connection of heaven, earth, and humanity.

As we shall see, Zhu Xi's 朱 熹 (1130–1200) philosophy of the relationship of coherent principle (*li*) and vital energy (*qi*) and Wang Yangming's 王 陽明 (1472–1529) philosophy of intuitive exploration and cultivation of the mind-heart (*xin*) represent the two most critical philosophical achievements of Neo-Confucianism's search for the unity of the king without and the sage within and made permanent contributions to East Asian and world philosophy. No one can understand the development of modern East Asian thought without understanding the development and contributions of Neo-Confucian philosophy. In a sense, the debate about coherent principle and vital energy framed the debates about the cosmological patterns and dynamics of the world just as arguments about human nature and the mind-heart grounded the disputes over ethics and the cultivation of human character.

Late Tang Origins

To discern the origins of Neo-Confucian thought, we must return to the end of Tang (618–907). In the ninth century the trio of Han Yu 韓愈 (768–824), Li Ao 李翱 (ca. 772–836), and Liu Zongyuan 柳宗元 (773–819) began the late Tang Confucian revival by seeking to revive knowledge of the true Dao. Ultimately, Song masters consolidated an intellectual revolution in favor of Confucian thought in the eleventh century. It is crucial to remember that without the flowering stimulus of Chinese Buddhist philosophy in the late Tang and early Song, there would never have been a revival of the Confucian Way. As Han Yu taught about the origin of the *dao* 道, he was also inventing a Neo-Confucian discourse on the connections of cosmology and morality more profound and complex than had been the case in earlier Confucian thought. By using the Confucian classics, Han, Li, and Liu showed how classical Confucian doctrines such as the Dao, human nature as coherent principle, vital energy, the mind-heart, and the virtue of humaneness (*ren* 仁) provide the underpinnings of a comprehensive cosmological and cultural vision founded on a revival of the thought of Master Kong and Master Meng. Rather than merely expanding the word-by-word exegetical traditions of the classics favored by Han and Tang dynasty scholars, Han, Li, and Liu boldly argued that they could find a deeper philosophical meaning in the classical Confucian texts. They began an attempt to explain the role of human beings set within the ongoing creative flourishing of the Dao.

Development in the Northern Song Dynasty

By the 1020s, Song China was undergoing a major cultural and philosophical transition. Social and philosophical reform was in the air and one influential advisor and social philosopher was Fan Zongyan 范仲淹 (989–1052). Although his reforms were never adopted, they did inspire a maturing group of younger intellectuals to develop a whole new philosophical approach to human culture and the understanding of the cosmos. Along with seeking ways to improve Song governmental institutions, the Confucian reformers denounced what they took to be the pernicious influences of Daoism and Buddhism on Chinese society and suggested a wide range of Confucian alternatives.

In the midst of the great reform of Song social and philosophical culture stands the imposing figure of Wang Anshi 王安石 (1021–1086), probably the greatest political reformer of the Song or any other Chinese dynasty. Wang proposed an ambitious reformation of every aspect of Song political life ranging from founding government schools in every village in the land, a new tax code, and improved and expanded medical care to restructuring the imperial examination system. Along with his political projects, Wang also wrote commentaries on books such as the *Rituals of the Zhou* to provide an exegetical and philosophical defense of his exhaustive reform program.

Not every Neo-Confucian agreed with Wang's reform program. Ouyang Xiu 歐陽脩 (1007–1072), historian, public intellectual, and philosopher, became a persistent critic of Wang Anshi's vision of China's Confucian future. Along with playing a major role in the politics of the day, Ouyang was famous for his belief that there was a coherent principle (*li* 理) to be found in all the canonical texts; Ouyang asserted that we must study both history and philosophy and recognize that history and reason do not always go hand in hand. We often fail to impose correctly the abstract order of *li* on the messy complexity of the dynamic (*qi*) flux of history. Moreover, Ouyang had the rare courage and scholarly discernment as a historian and philosopher to question the historical authenticity of many of the classical texts so highly regarded by Wang Anshi. His work raised Confucian philosophical hermeneutics to new critical heights.

The great historian Sima Guang 司馬光 (1019–1086) offered a fascinating metaphor for any successful reform project. Reforming government was like the complicated renovation of a vast mansion. If you wanted to save the house, you must carry out your restorations one item at a time with prudence and care that the changes never harm the basic structure or foundation of the house itself. In order to bolster his case, Sima composed one of the great works of Chinese history, *The Comprehensive Mirror for the Aid in Government*. In this text he argued that while there are indeed coherent principles such as the five cardinal virtues, human beings are also subject to the vagaries of historical circumstance and need to take a prudent approach to governmental and social reform.

Another vibrant voice in the Northern Song symphony of creative intellectual ideas was the philosopher-poet Su Shi 蘇軾 (1037–1101). Su, along with being a first-rate poet, also broke ranks with his fellow Neo-Confucians in maintaining that they could learn a great deal from Buddhist philosophy and self-cultivation. He was of course correct that the Neo-Confucians created their own form of meditation modeled on Chan Buddhist meditation. Moreover, Su pointed out that cultural activities and achievements such as poetry and the fine arts were just as important for a flourishing civilization as the active manifestations of coherent principle in systematic historical and philosophical reflection on cosmology and self-cultivation, much less on good government.

The work of these great historians, civil servants, and poets provided the vibrant matrix in which the famous Northern Song philosophical masters produced a new vision of the Dao—the fusion of what *is* as a comprehensive cosmology along with what *ought to be* as an axiological ethics of social and personal conduct and self-cultivation. One of the strongest consistent Confucian claims is that the *isness* of anything and the *oughtness of the thing* are everywhere and always conjoined. This persistent Neo-Confucian and New Confucian claim about the unity of is/ought has made for a lively debate with the heirs of Hume and Kant.

The Northern Song Philosophers

Borrowing the felicitous phrase of Tillman (1992), the Northern Song revival is a broad *fellowship* of Confucian scholars that includes the traditional five great Northern Song cofounders of Neo-Confucian speculative philosophy. The five philosophical masters in chronological order are Shao Yong 邵雍 (1011–1077), Zhou Dunyi 周敦頤 (1017–1073), Zhang Zai 張載 (1020–1077), Cheng Hao 程顥 (1032–1085), and Cheng Yi 程頤 (1033–1107). (Zhang Zai was the uncle of the brothers Cheng Hao and Cheng Yi.)

As a private scholar, Shao desired to understand the cosmos and define the place of human beings in the world as he understood it by speculating on the role of number in cosmic evolution. Shao was impressed with the ceaseless transformations and changes that seemed to define every aspect of our creative and processive cosmos. And while other Song Confucians might quarrel with how Shao went about the description of the generative, creative Dao, they would all agree with the underlying insight into the ceaseless creativity of the cosmos governed by numerical order that could be comprehended by a sophisticated objective epistemology. Moreover, Shao was convinced that he could depict the essential features of the coherent principle that defines the nature of the changing cosmos by means of the epistemological principle of objective observation of things without interjecting subjective human prejudices.

Shao was convinced that the coherent principle could be comprehended by paying careful attention to the images, symbols, and numerology of the *Yijing*. Shao persevered in his search for the coherent principle of the cosmos within the *Yijing* and ultimately called it *taiji* 太 極 (the Supreme Ultimate or Supreme Polarity). Shao made a great contribution to Neo-Confucian epistemology with his explanation of how the mind-heart interprets the coherent principle of the things and events of the cosmos by the method of *fanquan* 反 觀 (recursive reflection). Shao believed that this method enabled one to objectively observe the cosmos by finding phenomenological methods to see the world the way it truly is without allowing cultural or personal preconceptions to obscure philosophical investigation.

Zhou Dunyi shared Shao Yong's conviction that the world is characterized by ceaseless creation and change. He enshrined this vision of a processive cosmos in the famous opening line of "An Explanation of the Diagram of the Supreme Polarity [Ultimate]" (*wuji er taiji* 無 極 而 太極). The line can be translated in a number of ways: "The Ultimateless and the Supreme Polarity," or "The Ultimateless and yet the Supreme Polarity." The problem with the epigram is that *wuji* was considered more a Daoist than a Confucian concept, though *taiji* had an impeccable Confucian pedigree in the *Yijing*, the most universal of all of the early Classics. Zhou rejects a false reification of *taiji* as something concrete and qualifies it with the notion of *wuji*. The Supreme Polarity or Ultimate as *taiji* is the ceaseless, transforming, processive coherent principle of the emerging cosmos; his philosophical intent is to defend a pluralistic, coherent, and realistic cosmology based on an omni-centric pattern and order. There is a supreme order, the *taiji*, and hence each and every object or event in the cosmos manifests the Supreme Polarity as becomes what it ought to be in relationship with all the other myriad things.

In *Penetrating the Yijing*, Zhou describes *cheng* 誠 (authentic sincerity and self-realization) as the key to Confucian self-cultivation, expanding the traditional meaning as sincerity or authenticity to explain the process of the moral self-actualization of the human person. The self-cultivation process of *cheng* is what ultimately gives full actualization and manifestation of all the Confucian virtues, and is literally the root of becoming a sage as outlined in the Diagram of the Supreme Polarity. Zhou takes a classical Confucian ethical notion and expands its meaning in order to demonstrate its cosmological and axiological function as part of the Confucian Way. As a microcosm of the dynamic vital energy of the Dao, a person can manifest the true nature of coherent principle.

Among the Northern Song masters, Zhang Zai became the great proponent of the theory of *qi* 氣. *Qi* has been translated in various ways, including "vital force," "energy," "vital energy," or "material force." *Qi* represents the vast field of ever-circulating force or dynamic energy that is the matrix of the *yin-yang* forces as the constant and ceaseless root of all the things and events of the cosmos. According to Zhang and all the other Song masters, there is nothing in the cosmos that is not *qi*. Spiritual beings are *qi* and the most mundane material clay cup or paper and bamboo fan also manifests various aspects of *qi*. Many later Neo-Confucians argued that the most fundamental expression of the Dao is *qi*. It was precisely in *qi* that Zhang and those who followed him found the source of the endless processive and creative traits of the cosmos.

For Zhang, *qi* is as spiritual as it is material. However, he also affirmed the role of the coherent principle in the cosmos. He was insistent that there were all kinds of important patterns of order to be found within *qi*. His favorite term for these coherent patterns or principles was *tianli* 天理 (supernal coherent principle). Zhang argued that if we do not pay attention to the coherent principle, we will become lost through error and ignorance of the moral pattern of the cosmos.

No other Northern Confucian Master better defines the spiritual sensibility of Song thought as a deeply profound axiological vision of an interconnected and ethically conjoined cosmos. In the famous "Western Inscription," Zhang writes

> Heaven is my father and Earth is my mother and even such a small creature as
> I finds an intimate place in their mists. Therefore that which fills the universe
> I regard as my body and that which directs the universe I consider as my nature.
> All people are my brothers and sisters, and all things are my companions.
> (Chan 1963, 497)

Song Confucians believed that we must display a profound and coherent care not only for our immediate family but also for all of humanity, and that this care is not complete until we extend it fully toward the whole of creation. And of course, for Zhang, this could only happen through the wondrous and all-pervasive matrix of *qi*. The New Confucian scholar Xu Fuquan 徐 復 觀 (1903–1982), closely followed by his colleague Mou Zongsan 牟 宗三 (1909–1995), called this insight into the moral axiology of the cosmos "concern consciousness" (*youhuan yishi* 憂患意識). All the Neo-Confucians believed that cosmology has an ethical component: we cannot understand the world unless and until we discover the ethical imperatives that are part and parcel of the coherent principles of *tianli*, the coherent principles of heaven, earth, humanity, and the Dao.

The last of the great Northern Song philosophers were the Cheng brothers, Cheng Hao and Cheng Yi. The Cheng brothers are the great theorists of coherent principle *li*. They wrote, "All things have [coherent] principles, for instance *that by which* fire is hot and that by which water is cold." Further, "If we exhaust the [coherent] principles in the things of the world, it will be found that a thing must have a reason why it is and rule to which it should conform, which is what is meant by [coherent] 'principle'" (Graham modified 1992, 8). "What is called heaven (*tian* 天) is self-dependent (*ziran* 自然) coherent principle" (Graham modified 1992, 23).

There is a coherent principle for the cosmos and each thing or event has its own coherent principle that forms part of the order of the entire field for the dynamic forces of the Dao, demonstrating, as Cheng Yi would say, *liyi fenshu* 理一分殊 (the coherent principle is one but its manifestations are many). In terms of ethical self-cultivation, Cheng Hao asserted, "[One's duty] is to understand this [coherent] principle (*li*) and preserve *ren* (仁 humaneness) with sincerity and seriousness (*jing* 敬), that is all" (Chan 1963, 523). In another famous saying, Cheng Hao likened the lack of humaneness (*ren*) to being paralyzed, to lacking concern or consciousness for the things and events of the cosmos. With the clear articulation of the nature of coherent principle by the Cheng brothers, all the various elements for a grant synthesis were in place.

The Southern Song Synthesis

Zhu Xi 朱熹 (1130–1200) was a scholar of immense range, publishing far more essays, letters, poems, histories, ritual studies, and philosophical commentaries and dialogues than any of his colleagues. A true polymath, he was best known for his ability to give a complex, exhaustive, and coherent structure to the Northern Song speculative vision of the cosmos, a project he called "The Transmission of the Way" (*dao-tong* 道統). He sought to elaborate, explain, and defend the complex axiological cosmological vision of the Northern Song masters. For instance, he constructed a philosophical architectonic that had a logical place for coherent principle, vital energy, human nature, and the mind-heart—all key terms for the emerging schools of Neo-Confucianism.

Having in his late thirties and early forties experienced a series of intense debates with good friends about key terms such as human nature, the mind-heard, the examination of things and events, and self-cultivation, Zhu began to doubt the coherence of the hermeneutical methods of self-cultivation he learned from his teachers. In the midst of struggling to understand the various teachings of his Northern Song masters, he remembered a key definition of the *xin* 心 (the mind-heart) given by Zhang Zai: *xin tong xing qing* 心通性情 (the mind-heart unifies [human] nature and emotion). On a more abstract level Zhu then explained how the coherent principle (*li*) unified and ordered the person by providing a pattern for the ever-creative and dynamic *qi* (vital force) endowed by heaven. Human beings illustrate the process of how we become what we ought to be by embodying the coherent principle, informed by the cultivation of moral action *li* 禮 (ritual civility), within the matrix of the dynamic *qi*. The mind-heart is the subtlest expression of *qi* and allows the person to identify with or embody the coherent principle of heaven's "oughtness" that is the pattern for our psychophysical person and provides a proper moral compass. The goal of becoming a morally and intellectually exemplary person can only be achieved by the reverential self-cultivation of the mind-heart and the examination (*gewu* 格物) of the things and events of the external world.

The complex and subtle interplay of the coherent principle and *qi*, and the mind-heart and its exemplification in personal and communal flourishing became the mark of Zhu's cosmological vision. Zhu argued that this philosophical architectonic explains the notion that the coherent principle is one but its manifestations are many. The "one" is the essential goodness and ceaseless creativity of the Dao and the "many" are the myriad persons, things, and events that flow from this boundless creativity of the cosmos. The marker for this unity of the one and many, both for a person and for the cosmos, was the *taiji* (Supreme Polarity) as the Dao.

In terms of epistemology, in order to achieve the proper ethical outcome, each person was obliged to practice *gewu* 格物 (the examination of things). Zhu's notion of the examination of things included the mind-heart, the things of the mundane world, and the words of the sages as recorded in the classics and historical records that were the patrimony of any true scholar. The person's mind-heart needed to be examined in order to manifest its latent seeds of virtue, but this was not enough. Because Zhu believed that other persons, things, and events were just as real as one's own mind-heart, a person must examine the things and events of the cosmos in order to discover and understand the coherent principle of myriad things and events of the cosmos. And being a humanistic scholar, Zhu was particularly partial to the study of the classical and contemporary texts of the Chinese world.

Many later scholars disagreed with Zhu's cosmological architectonic and also with his disciplined method of study and ethical self-cultivation. Two of the most important immediate critical responses to Zhu's synthesis were provided by Lu Xiangshan 陸象山 (1139–1193) and Chen Liang 陳亮 (1143–1194). Lu was concerned that Zhu forced the student into a form of study that was a needlessly complicated empirical examination of the outside world. Lu provided an alternative self-cultivation that aimed at the rectification of the mind-heart as the true font of wisdom. The aim to become a worthy was the same for both Lu and Zhu, yet the methods of study and self-cultivation were dramatically different.

> The Teacher [Lu] said: Investigate the principle of things. Bormin said: The ten thousand things under Heaven are extremely multitudinous; how, then, can we investigate all of them exhaustively? The teacher replied: The ten thousand things are already complete in us. It is only necessary to apprehend their [coherent] principle. (Huang 1977, 31)

Chen Liang, conversely, was the great pragmatist and defender of the importance of good public policy for humane flourishing. He articulated a Confucian philosophy in a much more pragmatic light: true scholarship was not to be found in a search for perfected personal character—though there was nothing wrong in this per se. Rather, real scholarship ought to be in service to common good and governance of the empire. Chen believed Zhu's system both was too subjective and found too much cosmological coherence in human affairs. He urged a greater appreciation of the empirical complexity of the cosmos and the untidy, conflicted nature of human history. Careful empirical study was important for anyone seeking to improve the common good rather than endless moral, rigorous self-cultivation. In this regard

Chen prefigures the great Qing dynasty critics of Zhu's *daoxue* 道學 study of the way. These more practically oriented scholars argued that the philosophies of Zhu and Liu both fell into the personal solipsism of Buddhism and Daoism.

Internalization of Neo-Confucianism Self-Cultivation

With the fall of the Southern Song to the conquering Mongol Yuan dynasty, Confucian teachers kept the Song legacy alive in difficult times. Scholars define the philosophical sensibility of this period as a turn inward—that is, a predilection for and preoccupation with the cultivation of the mind-heart instead of an intense examination of the external world as Zhu Xi would have urged. For instance, Zhen Dexiu 真德秀 (1178–1235) wrote the *Classic of the Mind-Heart* with a special focus on the use of reverence (*jing* 敬) as the key to the cultivation of the mind-heart and is a paradigmatic example of the turn inward upon introspection and less of an engagement with the mundane world. Along with the "turn inward," other Yuan scholars such as Wu Cheng 吳澄 (1249–1333) speculated that Zhu's theory of the relationship of the coherent principle and vital energy did not mesh nearly as neatly as Zhu's followers would like to believe, causing doubt as to whether Zhu's grand synthesis was as comprehensive and persuasive as Zhu's followers maintained. Wu often wondered if Zhu's theory with its two vectors verged on a theory of a dual origin of the cosmos with pride of place going to the abstract coherent principle at the expense of the dynamic reality of vital energy. Wu's research on Zhu's *daoxue* caused him to keep asking one of the great Neo-Confucian questions: what is the balance of empirical study and intuition in the formation of a vision of the cosmos? What is the true relationship of coherent principle and vital energy?

However, the greatest challenge to Zhu's grand synthesis came from Wang Yangming 王陽明 (1472–1529). Wang was a poet, famous general, and charismatic teacher. During a forced period of exile in south China, it suddenly dawned on Wang that Zhu was wrong about the theory of the investigation of things and events both in the mind-heart and in the external world. In a moment of sudden enlightenment, Wang realized that the coherent principle was to be found via intuition in his moral mind-heart and not through the endless empirical study of things external to the mind-heart. Wang countered Zhu's theory of *gewu* by arguing that the moral rectification of things and events resides within the mind-heart because we only actually experience things and events in the mind-heart and not as external objects. The things might seem external, but they are to be examined phenomenologically in the mind-heart in the first instance. It is only when we realize the fundamental lucidity of the mind-heart and its coherent principles that we can use "the investigation of things" as the proper moral ordering of our perceptions. Wang's philosophy was therefore called *xin-xue* 心學, the teaching of the mind-heart, in order to distinguish it from Zhu's *li-xue* 理學, the teaching of the coherent principle.

Wang also provided another signal teaching in his theory of the unity of knowledge and action. Zhu had argued that we must first "know" the things and objects of the world by empirical examination before we can act rationally and morally. But Wang countered by arguing that if the rectification of things and events cannot be subtracted from the moral mind-heart, then knowledge was the direction of action and action was the effort needed to complete knowledge. If we can achieve this state of moral intuition of the truly good mind-heart, then we become capable of the extension of the highest discernment (*liang-zhi* 良知) of the mind-heart as the full extension of the Way. Wang's challenge to Zhu provided a reformation of the development of Neo-Confucian philosophy.

Late Ming Developments

One of the impacts of Wang's teachings was the creation of a space for voices not previously heard among the Neo-Confucian fellowship by opening philosophical debate to those without a great deal of formal education but who practiced his form of the perfection of knowledge and action through the intuition of the moral nature of the mind-heart. For instance, we find the radical egalitarian social theories of thinkers such as Li Zhi 李贄 (1527–1602), He Xinyin 何心隱 (1517–1579), and Jiao Hong 焦竑 (1540–1620) defending the notion that common people of innate good character had just as much access to the Dao as great scholars. Some of these radical philosophers even included women in the list of potential profound students of the Way. Jiao went even further and explored the possibilities of uniting Confucianism, Daoism, and Buddhism. He Xinyin was famous for his expansive defense of the role of friendship as critical for humane flourishing, and Li promoted a radical defense of the role of emotion (*qing* 情) as a vital trait of Confucian self-cultivation as well as the education of women. Many of these scholars questioned the neglect by *lixue* scholars of the positive impact of emotion for a fully formed human life. They reminded their readers that the emotions represented the dynamic character of vital energy in the lives of every person. We can no more live without emotion than we can without rational study, reflection, and wise discernment of the Way.

This question about the role of emotion had the unanticipated effect of inviting educated Chinese Confucian women to join the debate. These highly educated women, although excluded from the public political and intellectual arena, argued that we must know something about the emotions in order to be fully human. Pressing even deeper, many women maintained that the entangled world of romantic love exemplified in the arts needed analysis from a Confucian perspective. Even romantic love could and should become a noble and worthy partner of a truly Confucian life when put into proper ethical perspective. Not to establish a positive interpretation of the integration of the full range of human emotions, they argued, was a failure of Confucian nerve and meant that Confucians capitulated to the negative view of emotions attributed to Daoist and Buddhist philosophies of life.

Internationalization in Korea and Japan

It was during the Ming period that Neo-Confucianism became not just a Chinese philosophical movement but spread to Korea and Japan. A strong case can be made that some of the most profound Neo-Confucian philosophy in the sixteenth, seventeenth, and eighteenth centuries took place in Korea and Japan. For instance, the two most famous philosophers in Korean history, Yi T'oegye (1501–1570) and Yi Yulgok (1536–1583), carried on a celebrated and extended philosophically sophisticated debate on the first principles of Zhu's *lixue* and the role of emotion within Confucian philosophy. T'oegye provided a brilliant defense of Zhu's basic position that the coherent principle did indeed embody a living quality that helped to inform the emotions in a positive sense. Yulgok, on the other hand, emphasized the primordial role of vital energy, with coherent principle as an informing pattern with it, as the matrix out of which human emotion emerged and was morally manifested. While respecting the role of coherent principle, Yulgok constructed a viable philosophy of ordered vital energy.

Another fascinating example of the elaboration of Neo-Confucian thought is found in the Japanese scholar Kaibara Ekken's (1630–1714) *Precepts for Daily Life*. In this work Ekken provides an interpretation of the Confucian personal and social ethical program that could be applied to the conduct of daily life in Tokugawa Japan. Like Master Zhu, he also was fascinated by the examination of things and wrote extensively about the flora and fauna of Japan, even including wonderful illustrations of the wildlife he found. Furthermore, at the end of his life he wrote a small treatise, entitled *The Record of Great Doubts*, in which Ekken affirmed that *qi* was truly the most important Neo-Confucian philosophical concept; one suspects that Zhang Zai would have treasured this Japanese philosopher, civil servant, and naturalist. Along with many scholars in China during the same period, Ekken reaffirmed the primordial role of vital energy in any proper Confucian philosophical argument.

Qing Critics

Returning to China, Wang Fuzhi 王夫之 (1619–1692) provided a new philosophical vision that helped set the tone for Qing thought. He inquired into the question of what was necessary for understanding the cosmos, humanity's place within it, and how the myriad things and events come to be, flourish, change, and ultimately dissipate. Wang's sensibility challenged the emphasis on speculative Song philosophical ideas, such as the highly abstract notion of the coherent principle. His philosophy came to be known as the school of evidential research. Wang was deeply committed to a careful historical and hermeneutical examination of Confucian thought.

Wang developed a sophisticated theory of the change and transformation of vital energy to understand the cosmos. He returned to Zhang's vision of the ceaseless creativity of vital energy, which became the first principle of his philosophy. Wang stressed vital force as *shen* 神 (spirit) in order to emphasize the fact that one simply cannot rationally predict the outcome of the creative patterns of vital energy. Coherent principle exists but only as the pattern or order of the things found within the dynamics of vital energy.

Gu Yenwu 顧炎武 (1613–1682) was likewise revered as one of the founders of the school of evidential research. Scholars such as Gu and Wang believed their research to be an authentic return to the foundational Han and pre-Han sources (*hanxue* 漢學, Han Study) of the Confucian tradition without the accretions of Song and Ming speculative philosophy. In order to achieve this scholarly restoration, Gu became a master of phonetics, ancient history, archaeology, and classical studies in order to find the facts in the things themselves. One of the philosophical epigrams of the movement was to find the truth of things in the things themselves. By moving Qing scholarship away from speculative philosophy toward historical and philological studies, Gu and Wang dreamed that the literati would become effective civil servants who might actually benefit the lives of the people. In Confucian philosophy there is always the tendency to create a practical guide to daily life based on a careful historical examination of the records of the sages. In a sense, this is something like the Confucian quest "for the historical Kongzi" based on the strong belief that if the scholar could only discover the historical reality of the early sages, this knowledge could become applied to contemporary social problems and efficacious governmental policy.

The most renowned of Evidential Research scholars, Dai Zhen 戴震 (1724–1777) realized that no research project is ever innocent of a speculative philosophical vision. Dai held that we must know as much history as possible of the ritual institutions of the primordial sages in order to elucidate the philosophical principles derived from the ordered pattern of ritual action. He was convinced that the Song-Ming philosophers who began with speculative philosophical ideas about the coherent principle neglected the tedious yet necessary work of historical, phonetic, and philological studies.

Dai Zhen never abandoned the explanation of the role of the coherent principle in the vital energy of *qi*. The coherent principle is the special pattern of vital energy that manifests and patterns distinctive things. It is always and everywhere the order to be found in the things and events of the cosmos and not some abstract transcendental formalism. Dai's conclusion is that however brilliant Zhu and his colleagues were, they were seduced away from proper, concrete, social Confucian research programs by accepting, even if unwittingly, Daoist and Buddhist philosophy about transcendental theories. In a way Dai, as a careful historian and speculative philosopher, sums up two of the major paths followed by the Neo-Confucian quest: cosmology and social ethics.

Dai would have been astounded to see what would happen to all forms of Neo-Confucian philosophy in the century after his death. Following the Opium War of 1839, the traditional Confucian world was violently swept away by the intrusive and relentless Western imperial powers. In 1905, the civil service examination, the bulwark of Confucian dominance of Chinese civil society, was replaced with attempts at founding a Western-styled educational system. To the next few generations of Chinese revolutionaries who struggled to free China from its semicolonial status and counter Japanese aggression, Neo-Confucianism was regarded as irrelevant, a relic of Chinese intellectual history. The inferiority of Neo-Confucianism had been demonstrated, they believed, by its incapacity to respond to the challenges of modernity.

However, Neo-Confucianism lives on as one of the basic building blocks of what is now called New Confucianism. New Confucianism is a movement three generations old that contends that while much in need of reform, there is also a great deal of merit in both classical and Neo-Confucian thought. In the world of modern China, Neo-Confucianism persists as people continue to ask about the role of coherent principle, vital energy, human nature, and the mind-heart.

BIBLIOGRAPHY AND SUGGESTED READINGS

Berthrong, John H. (1998) *Transformations of the Confucian Way*. Boulder, CO: Westview Press.

Bol, Peter K. (1992) *"This Culture of Ours": Intellectual Transition in T'ang and Sung China*. Stanford, CA: Stanford University Press.

Chan, Wing-tsit. (1963) *A Source Book in Chinese Philosophy*. Princeton, NJ: Princeton University Press.

Ekken, Kaibara. (2007) *The Philosophy of Qi: The Record of Great Doubts*, translated by Mary Evelyn Tucker. New York: Columbia University Press.

Graham, A. C. (1992) *Two Chinese Philosophers: The Metaphysics of the Brothers Ch'eng*. La Salle, IL: Open Court.

Huang, Siu-chi. (1977) *Lu Hsiang-shan: A Twelfth Century Chinese Idealist Philosophy*. Westport, CT: Hyperion Press.

Mote, Frederick W. (1999) *Imperial China 900–1800*. Cambridge, MA: Harvard University Press.

Tillman, Hoyt Cleveland. (1992) *Confucian Discourse and Chu Hsi's Ascendancy*. Honolulu, HI: University of Hawaii Press.

Yao, Xinzhong (ed.). (2003) *Encyclopedia of Confucianism*. 2 vols. London and New York: Routledge Curzon.

Zhang Dainian. (2002) *Key Concepts in Chinese Philosophy*, translated and edited by Edmund Ryden. New Haven, CT, and Beijing: Yale University Press and Foreign Languages Press.

CHAPTER 8

CONTEMPORARY CONFUCIANISM

SHU-HSIEN LIU

INSTITUTIONAL Confucianism came to an end when the last dynasty (Qing 清) was overthrown in 1912 and replaced by the Republic of China. As all governmental and educational systems changed, Confucianism was displaced from the center of Chinese cultural and political life. No longer regarded as the pride of Chinese civilization, the Confucian tradition was blamed for its inability to withstand the onslaught of a superior, modern Western civilization. Slogans such as "Down with the Confucian shop!" were popular in the cultural movement symbolized by May Fourth, 1919 (see Chow 1960).

The undisputed leader for the trend to westernize or modernize was Hu Shi 胡適 (1891–1962), who upheld the ideals of freedom, democracy, and science. He studied under John Dewey at Columbia University and promoted pragmatism in China. However, his proposal for gradual reform could not meet the demands of the time. China faced both serious internal problems and domination by foreign powers, culminating in the Japanese invasion that led to World War II. China adopted more and more radical means for her survival. Eventually, this led to the establishment of the People's Republic of China (1949–) under the leadership of Chairman Mao Zedong 毛澤東 (1893–1976), and drove the Nationalist government to the island of Taiwan. The official ideology of the Communist regime on Mainland China is Marxism-Leninism-Maoism, another foreign import adapted to the Chinese environment. Under the direction of Mao and the Gang of Four, the Anti-Confucius Campaign reached its climax during the disastrous Cultural Revolution (1966–1976). It was only after the death of Mao that China returned to a more moderate policy that opened the door to the outside world, and the fortunes of Confucianism have gradually improved since then. Now it is thriving in the new millennium, like a phoenix reborn from ashes.

Confucianism means different things to different people. My effort here will concentrate on an inquiry into spiritual Confucianism only. This refers to the tradition of Confucius, Mencius, Cheng 程 and Zhu 朱, and Lu 陸 and Wang 王 that has been revived by Contemporary Neo-Confucians (Liu 1998, 13–14). In 1986, Mainland China designated Contemporary New Confucianism (*xiandai xin ruxue* 現代新儒學) as a national research program for a period of ten years. At first its scope was not clearly defined; after extensive discussion and debate, a list of fifteen scholars was adopted. The list is generally accepted by scholars in the field. I have assigned these fifteen thinkers to four groups in three generations (Liu 2003, 24–25):

The First Generation

Group I: LIANG Shuming 梁漱溟 (1893–1988), XIONG Shili 熊十力 (1885–1968), MA Yifu 馬一浮 (1883–1967), and ZHANG Junmai 張君勱 (Carsun Chang, 1887–1969)

Group II: FENG Youlan 馮友蘭 (Fung Yu-lan, 1895–1990), HE Lin 賀麟 (1902–1992), QIAN Mu 錢穆 (1895–1990), and FANG Dongmei 方東美 (Thomé H. Fang, 1899–1977)

The Second Generation

Group III: TANG Junyi 唐君毅 (1909–1978), MOU Zongsan 牟宗三 (1909–1995), and XU Fuguan 徐復觀 (1903–1982)

The Third Generation

Group IV: YU Yingshi 余英時 (Yu Ying-shih, 1930–), LIU Shuxian 劉述先 (Liu Shu-hsien, 1934–), CHENG Zhongying 成中英 (Cheng Chung-ying, 1935–), and DU Weiming 杜維明 (Tu Wei-ming, 1940)

There have been four waves in Contemporary New Confucianism, each lasting about twenty years. In the 1920s, Liang initiated the movement. In the 1940s, during the war, Feng and Xiong formulated their philosophies. The 1960s saw Tang and Mou do their most important work, after they fled to Hong Kong and Taiwan, respectively, and after they issued their famous "Manifesto on Chinese culture and the World" on New Year's Day in 1958; this manifesto was later seen as an important landmark for Contemporary Neo-Confucianism in the narrower sense (Chang 1962, 455–483). In the 1980s with the Third Generation, Contemporary Neo-Confucianism added an international dimension (see Bresciani 2001, ch. 14). As my interest here is primarily philosophical, my attention will be on Liang and Xiong in Group I, Feng in Group II, and Tang and Mou in Group III.

The First Generation

Liang, Xiong, and Ma are recognized as the three elders of the First Generation. Xiong was the spiritual leader of Contemporary Neo-Confucianism in the narrower sense, as he was the teacher of Tang, Mou, and Xu in the Second Generation. But his influence was only deeply felt in the circles after the 1940s, so I will discuss him in the context of the Second Generation. Liang is generally regarded as the one who initiated Contemporary Neo-Confucianism. In 1917, he was invited to teach Indian philosophy and Consciousness-Only Buddhism at Peking University, where he became a colleague of Hu Shi, and declared his intention to defend Confucius and the Buddha. When the May Fourth Movement broke out in 1919 and turned into the iconoclastic New Culture Movement, Liang was engaged in developing his ideas of comparative culture. In 1922, his book *Eastern and Western Cultures and Their Philosophies* was published by Commercial Press. It immediately became a best seller, and has been influential ever since. He took a comparative approach, and found that Western, Chinese, and Indian cultures have opted for three different directions in life. The guiding spirit of Western culture is a belief that the Will always strives forward, with its characteristics of the conquest of nature, scientific method, and democracy. The guiding spirit of Chinese culture, on the other hand, is that the Will aims at achieving harmony and equilibrium, with its characteristics of contentment, adjustment to the environment, and acceptance of authority; such a culture, he argued, would not invent steamships and trains, or democracy. Finally, the guiding spirit of Indian culture is that the Will looks backward; the only thing it cares about is religious aspiration and liberation from worldly cares. Thus, Western culture values material gratification, Chinese culture social life, and Indian culture transcendence.

After examining these three directions of life, Liang felt he was ready to address the question of which attitudes we should adopt today. He found that Indian and Chinese cultures were premature and failed to fully develop their potentialities. His conclusion was threefold. First, as the Indian attitude looks backward, it must be totally excluded. Second, Western achievements must be adopted in China without reservation, but the Western attitude of exclusively striving forward would cause serious social and political problems and eventually must be changed so that its undesirable consequences could be avoided. And finally, the middle way of the Chinese culture, which looks both forward and backward, should be revived from a critical point of view. According to Liang, Confucius's strength was derived from resources in life itself, and both traditional shortcomings and modern challenges could be overcome by a Contemporary Confucian approach. Liang never showed how such a synthesis could actually be achieved, but he was the first to suggest the revival of the Confucian Way as a response to the contemporary situation.

How did the emergence of Contemporary Neo-Confucianism come right after the iconoclastic May Fourth Movement of 1919? Liang distinguished between what we call spiritual Confucianism and institutional Confucianism. The rigid system of rites and rituals had died with the fall of the last dynasty; the remnant of the system was denounced by the New Culture Movement. The spirit of Confucianism, however, symbolized by Confucius himself and transmitted by Neo-Confucians, especially Wang Yang-ming 王陽明 (1472–1529), Liang maintained, teaches a perennial philosophy that has significance not only for the Chinese but also for the whole world. This is indeed the fundamental message transmitted by Contemporary Neo-Confucianism, even though expressions of the insight vary widely from one individual to another. It is for this reason that Liang is honored as the first to initiate the movement.

After the Japanese invasion of China in World War II, Western liberalism, with its ideas of gradual reform as represented by Hu Shi, lost its appeal. More and more, Dialectical Materialism with its tendency to radicalism captured the minds of the young. Nevertheless, in the 1940s, under difficult circumstances, some Neo-Confucian scholars continued to develop their systems of thought. One key figure was Feng Youlan (see Liu 2003, ch. 3). Feng was a college student when Hu Shi and Liang Shuming taught at Peking University and was influenced by both. In 1919, Feng went abroad. He followed the footsteps of Hu Shi to Columbia University, where he also studied under John Dewey. But he was more influenced by New Realism—an early twentieth-century philosophical movement—than Pragmatism. At Columbia, Feng argued that China opted for the Confucian way, which emphasizes seeking lasting peace in the mind, and thus, there had been no drive to develop science. The West is extroverted, while the East is introverted. In the future, Feng claimed, when humanity becomes wiser and seeks lasting peace and happiness in the mind, then Chinese wisdom will also be appreciated. This argument is similar to Liang's account of the relationship between Eastern and Western cultures. After studying world philosophies at Columbia, however, Feng moved away from Liang's emphasis on Bergsonian creative evolution toward "intuition," and put more emphasis on philosophical analysis. Feng regarded "intuition" as vague and not very useful in constructing a philosophical system.

In 1923, Feng returned to China, where he worked intensively on his *History of Chinese Philosophy*. The publication of his book in two volumes (1931 and 1934) was a major milestone in Chinese philosophy.[1] Feng paid tribute to Hu Shi, who started the new approach to Chinese philosophy with his volume on ancient Chinese thought published in 1919. But with the publication of his history, Feng quickly eclipsed Hu's influence. Feng elevated Confucius's position by claiming that before Confucius, there was no private authorship. Even more striking was his interpretation of Zhu Xi 朱熹 (1130–1200) in terms of certain concepts he adopted from New

1. Feng's student Derk Bodde translated this work into English; the two volumes were published in 1952 and 1953 by Princeton University Press. It has been used as a standard text ever since, and exerted profound influence on study of Chinese philosophy worldwide.

Realism. Hu, in turn, felt that Feng was making a mistake and writing from the perspective of Confucian orthodoxy.

Feng, however, was not satisfied to be only a historian of Chinese philosophy. During the dark time, when the Japanese invasion forced the universities to move from Beijing to the interior, Feng conceived and constructed his philosophical system. He published his so-called *Six Books from Zhen to Yuan* 《貞元六書》 from 1939 to 1946. Feng's ideas were taken from the *Book of Changes. Zhen* 貞 (firmness) is the last and *yuan* 元 (origin) the first of the four heavenly virtues. After descending to the lowest point, there will be hope for ascendancy.[2] The situation is not unlike seasonal changes: after a severe winter, spring will come. That was why Feng saw glimpses of hope for national rebirth. Feng's originality lay in that he borrowed concepts from New Realism to reinterpret Zhu Xi's philosophy of *li* 理 (principle) and *qi* 氣 (material force) in response to challenges against metaphysics from logical positivism. He made the attempts to transform some Neo-Confucian concepts into what he understood as logical concepts devoid of content; as a result, he transformed the fundamental character of Neo-Confucian philosophy, shifting the emphasis from *xin-xing* 心性 (mind-heart and nature) discipline to logical, philosophical analysis. His thoughts were novel and ingenious, but problematic as well.

There are four main metaphysical concepts in Feng's philosophy: principle (*li* 理), material force (*qi* 氣), the substance of Dao (*daoti* 道體), and the Great Whole (*daquan* 大全). The first concept is derived from the proposition that "as there are things, their specific principles must be implicit therein." The second concept is derived from the proposition that "if there is principle, there must be material force for its embodiment." The third concept is derived from the Neo-Confucian proposition of "the Ultimate of Nonbeing and also the Great Ultimate." This means that the universe is a "great functioning" through the processes of "daily renewal" and incessant change. This concept shows the relation between principle and material force. The fourth concept is the equivalent of Dao, or Heaven. This is a formal concept, because it is the general name for all and not an assertion about the actual world. It is comparable to the Absolute in Western philosophy, just as the first three concepts may be compared to the concepts of being, nonbeing, and becoming, respectively. Such abstract philosophical analysis may be applied to practical affairs. According to Feng, universals are transferable; they transcend the difference between Ancient and Modern, East and West. Particulars, however, are confined to specific times and places, and there is no need to demand conformity on this level.

In 1947, Feng was visiting in America; he decided to go back to China against the advice of his friends. After the establishment of the People's Republic of China in 1949, intellectuals faced the harsh reality of living under the strict control of thought

2. According to the Commentaries of the *Book of Changes* (*Yijing*), a Confucian classic, there are four heavenly virtues: origination, flourish, advantages, and firmness; one succeeds the other, and they go by cycles. They match with four seasons: spring, summer, autumn, and winter (cf. Chan 1963, 594).

by the Communist regime. Feng was forced to write one confession after another after 1950 and to fully denounce his own philosophy. During the Anti-Confucius Campaign in 1973, Feng turned around to side with the "people." He served as an adviser to a team writing under the guidance of the notorious Gang of Four.

In the 1980s, Feng acknowledged that he had not been true to himself during the Cultural Revolution, the darkest time in his life. Now his thought reverted to the philosophy he developed during the war. For a decade Feng devoted himself to rewriting his new *History of Chinese Philosophy*, published in seven volumes from 1982 to 1992. This history was written principally from a Marxist viewpoint. He did pay tribute to Mao Zedong, but criticized Mao in his later years, turning to radical leftist ideologies without paying attention to the actual state of affairs. In the concluding chapter of the seventh volume, he pointed out that while Mao's guiding principle is strife, for Neo-Confucian philosophy, it is harmony. This volume was not allowed to be published on the Mainland for some years.

While Feng believed that the future of Chinese philosophy lies in a reconstruction of *li-xue* 理學 (learning of principle), his colleague He Lin believed it lies in a reconstruction of *xin-xue* 心學 (learning of mind-heart). But He Lin did not complete the project. This line of thought found its expression in a surprising source. In 1944, Commercial Press published the vernacular version of Xiong Shili's *Xin Weishi Lun* 新唯識論 (New Doctrine of Consciousness-Only), which was recognized as an original work at the time. A number of bright students, including Tang Junyi and Mou Zhongsan, were attracted to his teaching and inadvertently he became the spiritual leader of the Neo-Confucian Movement (see Liu 2003, ch. 4). Xiong was ten years older than Feng, but achieved fame much later. When he was young, he was engaged in revolutionary activities against the Manchu dynasty. In middle age he experienced a spiritual crisis. Following the advice of Liang Shuming, he entered the Institute of Buddhism to study under Ou-yang Jingwu 歐陽竟无 (1871–1943). When Liang resigned from Peking University, he recommended Xiong to teach Buddhism in his place. But Xiong soon became dissatisfied with the Consciousness-Only doctrine, as he felt that in its cosmology the realm of origination and destruction was cut off from the realm that transcends origination and destruction. Hence, he returned to the insights of a philosophy of creativity implied in the *Yijing* 易經 (*Book of Changes*) and developed a "New Consciousness-Only" doctrine that opened a new direction for Contemporary Neo-Confucian philosophy.

From Xiong's perspective, even though the world does not stand still even for an instant, as taught by Buddhism, it is not something from which we need to escape. It is an ever-creative universe, the message of which can be realized by attending to our own being. Xiong believed that Heaven is the ultimate, creative metaphysical principle that works incessantly in the universe, and that we are endowed with the kind of nature we have through the decree of Heaven as taught by the *Doctrine of the Mean*. If we can realize the creativity within ourselves, then we can also realize the creativity of Heaven. There is a correlation between microcosm and macrocosm. As Xiong loved to say: when you taste a drop of water in the ocean, you taste the whole ocean.

Although Xiong did not write a treatise on epistemology and methodology, they are inseparable from his metaphysics. He followed the lead of Indian logic and studied *liang* 量 (*pramānā*, means of knowledge). According to some Indian logicians, there are four means of knowledge: perception, inference, analogy, and testimony.[3] Empirical knowledge can be built on sense perception and logical inference. By treating sense perception and logical inference, Xiong was able to absorb Western logic and science into his system. But he felt deeply that beyond the objects of sense perception and logic, there is a world to which one can gain access only via meditative contemplation beyond logical thought and through self-realization beyond words. To achieve this, analogy and testimony from an enlightened person are most helpful. They are most relevant to the Oriental, especially the Confucian, tradition. Thus, he made a crucial distinction between what he called *liangzhi* 量智 (measuring wisdom) and *xingzhi* 性智 (original wisdom). From the former is derived knowledge by measurement and from the latter knowledge by nature. *Liangzhi* depends on sense perception to function, but one must resist the tendency to assume that external objects are metaphysically real. In contrast, *xingzhi* refers to a kind of self-illumination through self-realization. But self-realization requires life experience in the world. Thus, there is a dialectical relationship between *xingzhi* and *liangzhi*, as *liangzhi* has no source other than *xingzhi*, and *xingzhi* has to manifest itself through *liangzhi*.

Another pair of related concepts are *benxin* 本心 (the original mind) and *xixin* 習心 (the habitual mind). The latter always directs its attention outward to things. The original mind is empty, because it is not identified with any concrete forms, and yet it is illuminating, as it realizes the creative power of the Way as inexhaustible so that substance (transcendence) and function (immanence) are nondual; it should not be seen as the opposite of matter. It is the habitual mind that is the opposite of matter and the correlate with matter. This explains why Xiong rejected both materialism and idealism, since both matter and mind are manifestations or functions of the metaphysical principle of creativity. It is only through the realization of the original mind that we can establish any metaphysical knowledge at all.

Xiong was firmly in the Confucian tradition; he cared not only for *neisheng* 內聖 (inward sageliness), which emphasized personal cultivation, but also for *waiwang* 外王 (outward kingliness). For Xiong, socialist ideals were proposed by Confucius some two thousand years ago. But Confucius's ideal of Great Unity (*dadong* 大同) was lost after his death as later scholars, including Mencius, became slave-scholars who supported monarchy, the ideal of Small Peace (*xiaokang* 小康). But Xiong's scholarship has been questioned by other scholars, and many regard his ideas as impractical; not even his closest students could support his views. Under communist rule Xiong was allowed to publish his works in small quantities, and he appeared to be the only Contemporary Neo-Confucian who did not write a single

3. For more on Indian theories of valid cognition, see the chapters by Dan Arnold and Tom Tillemans in this volume.

confession to criticize himself. Nevertheless, he was abused by the Red Guards during the Cultural Revolution and died under miserable conditions.

While Feng Youlan and Xiong Shili remained in Mainland China, Fang Dongmei, Mou Zongsan, and Xu Fuguan chose to flee to Taiwan, and Qian Mu and Tang Junyi started New Asia College in Hong Kong. These thinkers exerted a profound influence over the next generations of scholars in these areas and overseas.

Fang Donmei started out with Western philosophy, especially Pragmatism, but he turned to Chinese philosophy, writing in English, during World War II.[4] He had taught Tang Junyi in the Second Generation, and Liu Shuxian and Cheng Zhongying in the Third Generation (see Liu 2003, ch. 5).

Tang and his friend Mou became the leading proponents of Contemporary Neo-Confucianism in the narrower sense. Most of Tang's important works were published after he arrived in Hong Kong. He shared with Fang an interest in comparative philosophy and culture, but confessed that he only reached a proper understanding of the fundamental insights in Chinese philosophy through Xiong, and he found his closest ally in Mou (see Liu 2003, ch. 6). Tang drafted the famous "Manifesto for a Reappraisal of Sinology and Reconstruction of Chinese Culture," signed by Zhang Junmai, Xu Fuguan, and Mou Zongsan. They urged Sinologists to study Chinese culture not just through the eyes of missionaries, archaeologists, or political strategists. The wisdom of Chinese philosophy, he insisted, is crystallized in its philosophy of mind and human nature, an unmistakable reference to Neo-Confucianism. Although recognizing the need for Chinese culture to learn from the West by absorbing its achievements in science and democracy, they also suggest that the West may learn from Eastern thought in the following five areas:

1. The spirit asserting what is here and now and letting everything go (in order for nature to take its own course)
2. The pervasive and all-embracing understanding or wisdom
3. A feeling of warmth and compassion
4. The wisdom of how to perpetuate the culture
5. The attitude that the whole world is like a family

In his later years, Tang devoted himself to tracing the origins of insights in traditional Chinese philosophy, publishing six monumental volumes on the subject. His last work is a comprehensive system of philosophy he conceived over the course of his life. This book deals with the whole existence of man and tries to understand the various activities of the mind. Owing to these activities, there are different views of things. These views may be horizontal, straightforward, or vertical. Correlating to these views, there are objects of the mind. They may be represented as either substance, form, or function. Then they may be regarded as either the objective

4. Fang Donmei's *magnum opus, Chinese Philosophy: Its Spirit and Its Development* (1981), was published posthumously. He also formulated a grand system of comparative philosophy, which was left unfinished at his death.

existents grasped by the mind, or the subjective activities of the mind, or the aspired ideals of the mind that transcend both the subject and the object. When these are combined together, there are nine worlds (spiritual spheres) of the activities of the mind, as follows:

1. The world of discrete things
2. The world of species and genus in terms of empirical generalization
3. The world of functional operation
4. The world of perceptions interpenetrating with one another
5. The world of contemplation of what is transcendent and vacuous
6. The world of moral practice
7. The world of aspiration to God
8. The world of *shunya* (emptiness) of both the self and the *Dharma* (the Law)
9. The world of the embodiment of heavenly virtue

The first three worlds are the worlds of the object, the next three worlds are the worlds of the subject, and the last three worlds are the worlds that transcend both the subject and the object. Tang's formulation of his philosophical system was influenced by Hegel, but Tang avoided using a deductive model that would force empirical data into his system in a rigid fashion. Tang tried hard to find a proper place for the insights discovered in the Indian and Western traditions. But the world he admired most was still the world of heavenly virtue manifested in the Confucian philosophy of humanity and creativity through *The Book of Changes.*

Tang's colleague Mou Zongsan was a graduate of Peking University, but he felt alienated from dominant figures there, such as Hu Shi. The teacher who influenced him most was Xiong Shili.[5] Mou's early interest was in logic and epistemology. He later turned to Chinese philosophy and published his important works in Taiwan and Hong Kong. Mou's study of Song-Ming Neo-Confucianism far surpassed his teacher; he brought great conceptual rigor to the field. Mou also opened up new vistas to Contemporary Neo-Confucian philosophy, and he was one of the most original and influential thinkers of his generation (see Liu 2003, ch. 7). Although Mou inquired deeply into his own tradition, his thought never lacked a comparative perspective, which was brought into focus in the last stage of his writing. In *Intellectual Intuition and Chinese Philosophy*, he pointed out that the major difference between Chinese and Western philosophies lies in the fact that the three major Chinese traditions, Daoism, Buddhism, and Confucianism, all believe in the

5. Mou later told a story of when he was a junior student, and Feng Youlan paid a visit to Xiong. They had a discussion on Wang Yang-ming's *liangzhi* 良知 (innate knowledge of what is morally good). Feng was of the opinion that *liangzhi* is a postulate; Xiong disagreed and said that it is a presence for it requires self-consciousness here and now, affirmation here and now. This shocked Mou; he felt his consciousness at the moment was raised to the level of that realized by Song-Ming Neo-Confucian philosophers. This story illustrates that the fountainhead of Contemporary Neo-Confucianism in the narrower sense was Xiong, not Feng.

possibility of intellectual intuition, whereas major Western traditions deny that there is such a possibility. Mou especially appreciated Kant, whom he used as his point of departure. Kant made a sharp distinction between phenomenon and noumenon; he believed that all human knowledge depends on sensible intuition and only God has intellectual intuition. Hence, Kant could only develop a metaphysics of morals, not a moral metaphysics; owing to his Christian background, he could only hope to formulate a moral theology. Consequently, freedom of the will for Kant can only be a postulate of practical reason; the same is true for immortality of the soul and the existence of God.

For the major Chinese traditions, however, even though it is clearly recognized that humans are finite beings, they have been endowed with the ability to have a firm grasp of the Way as both transcendent and immanent, regardless of whether the Way is understood to be Daoist, Buddhist, or Confucian. Since the Chinese believe that they have the ability to penetrate reality, the wide gap between phenomenon and noumenon is transcended. Mou insisted that intellectual intuition is possible and therefore humans are capable of participating in the Way through personal realization. But Mou readily admitted that the Chinese were short in purely theoretical pursuits; in this regard, they have a great deal to learn from the Western tradition. In the meantime, going beyond Kant's position would help the West to overcome the dualism between the supernatural and the natural. Confucianism in particular offers a truly humanistic philosophy that transmits the message of the earth. Mou criticized Martin Heidegger's attempt to reconstruct metaphysics as being inadequate and misguided, because it loses the true meaning of transcendence. Only the Confucian philosophy has been able to take care of the perspectives of both the transcendent (Heaven) and the immanent (humans). In *Phenomenon and the Thing-in-itself*, Mou made a distinction between what he called "ontology with attachment" and "ontology without attachment." The former has been highly developed in the Western traditions, and the latter has been elaborately formulated in the Asian traditions. When the infinite mind puts restrictions on itself, the knowing subject is formed; this is a dialectical process. The attachment of the knowing mind and the realization of the infinite mind actually share the same origin. It is here that a foundation can be found for the unity of the two perspectives.

From the above, we can see that Tang and Mou formulated their philosophies through sophisticated Western philosophical concepts. The central philosophical insight, however, goes back to their teacher Xiong Shili. The next generation, including Du Weiming at Harvard and myself, faces a very different situation. They went abroad to study and made their careers overseas. They are concerned much less with China as a nation than with the so-called cultural China, and Confucianism is seen as one of the spiritual traditions in a pluralistic setting. They no longer care to defend Confucianism as orthodoxy as the previous generation did. The far more urgent problem for them is that, as the world has turned into a global village, how is it possible for different peoples and cultures to live harmoniously together on the same earth? I do believe that the Confucian idea of *zhonghe* 中和 (equilibrium and harmony) could have a role to play. And the Neo-Confucian dictum of *liyifenshu* 理一分殊 (one principle, many manifestations), which steers a middle course between universalism and particularism, likewise could have contemporary significance. In order to develop a global ethic, the inductive method, which used to emphasize commonality at the expense of difference, is inadequate. A creative interpretation of *liyifenshu* would look for the transcendent ideal of commonality (*liyi*) and encourage different expressions (*fenshu*) of the Way. Only if both the transcendent and immanent perspectives are addressed can we hope to move toward the right direction for the future (see Liu 2003, ch. 8).

BIBLIOGRAPHY AND SUGGESTED READINGS

Bresciani, Umberto. (2001) *Reinventing Confucianism: The New Confucian Movement.* Taipei: Taipei Ricci Institute for Chinese Studies.

Chan, Wing-tsit (ed. and comp.). (1963) *A Source Book in Chinese Philosophy.* Princeton, NJ: Princeton University Press.

Chang, Carsun (Zhang Junmai) and others. (1962) "A Manifesto for a Reappraisal of Sinology and Reconstruction of Chinese Culture." In his *The Development of Neo-Confucian Thought*, Volume 2. New York: Bookman Associates.

Chow, Tse-tsung. (1960) *The May Fourth Movement: Intellectual Revolution in Modern China.* Cambridge, MA: Harvard University Press.

Liu, Shu-hsien (Shuxian). (1998) *Understanding Confucian Philosophy: Classical and Sung-Ming.* Westport, CT, and London: Greenwood Press and Praeger Publishers.

———. (2003) *Essentials of Contemporary Neo-Confucian Philosophy.* Westport, CT, and London: Praeger Publishers.

Mou, Bo (ed.). (2009) *History of Chinese Philosophy.* London and New York: Routledge.

Tu, Weiming, and Mary Evelyn Tucker (eds.) (2004) *Confucian Spirituality.* New York: The Crossroad Publishing Co.

PART II

NON-BUDDHIST INDIAN PHILOSOPHY

EDITED BY NALINI BHUSHAN

NON-BUDDHIST INDIAN PHILOSOPHY

NALINI BHUSHAN

India has a long and rich philosophical tradition that stretches back for a thousand years. It has its origins in the ancient Vedic poetic hymns, and especially in their more reflective aspects, compiled in treatises called the Upanisads. The established view is that there are four Vedas and 108 Upaniṣads. On some accounts, the *Bhagavad Gīta* should be regarded as an additional original source. Others argue that Bharata's *Natya Shāstra* should be regarded as a fifth Veda. Regardless, together these constitute the fundamental original "texts" whose explication, interpretation, and critique have resulted in distinctive philosophical schools of thought in India, each with its own rich commentarial tradition.

This section on India is divided into six chapters representing the principal orthodox schools of Indian philosophy, Jain philosophy, and more recent Anglophone Indian philosophy. Jain philosophy is included in this section along with the orthodox schools because it is a distinctively Indian philosophical tradition. Buddhism, the other major heterodox Indian philosophical school, is omitted, treated instead in the next section due to its greater philosophical extent and cultural reach. Also included is a section addressing the very fertile period of Indian philosophy from the late nineteenth century (the period of the "Indian Renaissance") to the present, in which many of the Indian traditions engage creatively with Western philosophical traditions.

Freedom (*mokṣa*) is an ultimate value that is recognized by all Indian philosophical schools and is the underlying goal of all philosophical reflection. Differences between the schools lie in their respective characterization of freedom's experiential and metaphysical nature (bliss, oneness, nonduality, access to divinity); the epistemic modes of access to freedom (religious devotion, yogic training and training under a teacher, study of the "texts," intuition); and the relation between freedom of various kinds (positive [freedom *to*] and negative freedom [freedom *from*]) and being-in-the-world (detachment from the material world of objects, service to humanity, mastery over oneself).

Freedom in the Indian tradition is intrinsically tied to self-knowledge. Opinions differ as to what is required for self-knowledge as well as to what constitutes it. Is knowledge of the self to be regarded as relational or nonrelational? For instance, is there a form of knowing the self that does not reduce the self to the status of an object (i.e., where knowledge consists in the apprehension of the properties of the self as an "object" to be in this way known)? Or is this self-knowledge in some sense nonconceptual? The notion of *ātman*—the real self as opposed to the empirical self—is central in all discussions.

The distinction between valid and invalid knowledge is critical to all Indian philosophical schools and so the *pramāṇas*—different means of obtaining knowledge—are the subject of careful scrutiny. The *pramāṇas* fall into three broad categories: *pratyakṣa,* or perception; *anumāna,* or inference; and *śabda,* or verbal testimony. While the first two *pramāṇas* are relatively uncontroversial cross-culturally, the third arguably is unique to the Indian tradition. What constitutes valid verbal testimony? Is it primarily the testimony of the revealed texts (*śruti*)? What is the relation between text and interpretation? (See Arnold's essay for a detailed discussion of *śabda pramāṇa* by the Mīmāṃsā School.) The Nyāya (and Navya-Nyāya) School develops a unique system of logical inference as it puts the *anumāna pramāṇa* at the center of its investigations (see Chatterjee's essay). The result of such avenues of knowledge is *darśana* (sight), that is, truth that is revealed to one who embarks on such a mission. For this reason, the different schools, emphasizing as they do different avenues to such truth, are also called the *darśanas.* While these orthodox schools defend some notion of absolute truth, the one heterodox school represented in this section, Jainism, articulates and defends a nonabsolutist or perspectivalist approach to truth (*syādvāda*) (see essay by Long).

One who is free (i.e., is in possession of the highest form of knowledge, which inextricably involves self-knowledge) is thereby in touch with Ultimate Reality or the Absolute (*Brahman*). The different schools have subtle and nuanced views about the best way to characterize *Brahman* or the Absolutely Real and its relationship to empirical reality. One might characterize this as the debate about the One and the Many. Indian philosophical schools range from the Realist to the Idealist. Thus, for the Nyāya-Vaiśeṣikas, the empirical world is real; not so for Vedānta. How does the Absolute appear in the way that it empirically does for us? Who or what is responsible for this appearance? For some schools the concept of *māyā* is central in accounting for this apparent dichotomy between the Apparent and the Real (see Taber's essay on Vedānta for a useful discussion of *māyā,* as well as Bhushan's essay for more contemporary interpretations). Also, is Ultimate Reality without characteristics (*nirguna*) or with characteristics (*saguna*)? To the extent that I can say (or think) the characteristics of Ultimate Reality (e.g., as all-loving, radiant, all-powerful, all-encompassing—as *saguna*), is this in effect a conceptualized, and thereby diminished, grasp of Ultimate Reality?

All the schools have an interest in the kinds of action (*dharma*) that will best serve human beings in the empirical world in their quest for metaphysical and experiential freedom. These actions—which are differentially emphasized in the different schools—include the intellectual (study of the texts), the devotional, the communal (service to others), and the ethical (restraints on the individual). For instance, a detailed ethical regimen involving physical and mental training and a prescription of moral duties is a primary concern of the Yoga School (see Rukmani's essay). Also, since the Jain school does not have transcendental concerns, being as it is a reaction to the orthodox Indian schools, its central focus is on the delineation of moral precepts for the best ethical life, with *ahiṁsā* (noninjury) at its center.

Materialism and a robust form of skepticism is considered in India by the Cārvākas (or Lokāyatas), as is a thoroughgoing fatalism by the Ājīvikas. On both of these accounts, freedom is displaced as the central Indian philosophical concern, and the conventional nature of morality is stressed. However, since most of these texts have been destroyed or lost, there is no sustained discussion of their arguments to which we have access. More moderate forms of skepticism, on the other hand, as in Jainism and Buddhism, gain a foothold in the Indian consciousness as the different schools of thought (represented in four essays in this section) develop in India in part as a response to those skeptical voices.

Indian philosophy becomes fraught and creative as a consequence of the British presence, on topics ranging from political identity to metaphysical freedom (see Bhushan's essay). The old philosophical chestnuts are articulated using modern vocabulary; Western texts are juxtaposed with Indian texts; and Indian voices—now in English—incorporate their Western educational training to simultaneously present and challenge the assumptions of their discipline, as arguments are reworked, reframed, defended, and further developed for a global audience.

CHAPTER 9

NYĀYA-VAIŚEṢIKA PHILOSOPHY

AMITA CHATTERJEE

The Nyāya and the Vaiśesika systems are two orthodox (*āstika*) systems of Indian philosophy—meaning they admit the Vedas as eternal and infallible[1]—that preexist the Common Era. According to tradition, the Vaiśeṣika system is older than the Nyāya system; some scholars even trace it back to the thirteenth century BCE. In their early histories, the Nyāya and Vaiśeṣika were two independent systems with their own respective metaphysics, epistemology, logic, ethics, and soteriology. Over time, the Vaiśeṣika system became so entwined with the Nyāya that until recently (Thakur 2003), there was no independent history of the Vaiśeṣika as a basic system. One reason for addressing these two systems together is that they share many important tenets (*samānatantra*): both systems are committed to common-sense realism and pluralism in their ontology; believe in the creation of the world from material atoms that conjoin to generate this world by the will of God and in accordance with the accumulated merits and demerits (*adṛṣṭa*) of individual agents; accept a theory of causation according to which a new effect is produced by its cause (*asatkāryavāda*) and is not a mere manifestation of the cause; and admit that liberation means absolute cessation of suffering, a state where the liberated self is without any consciousness. However, there are important differences, too. The Vaiśeṣika world is composed of seven categories, six positive and one negative, while in the Nyāya world there are sixteen categories. The Vaiśeṣikas admitted two valid means of cognition (*pramāṇa*-s), while the Naiyāyikas admitted four. The two systems were amalgamated into the syncretic system of the Nyāya-Vaiśeṣika when the Navya-Naiyāyikas expanded their scheme by including the seven Vaiśeṣika categories.

1. Śaṃkarācārya, however, regarded the Vaiśeṣika system as *ardhavaināśika*, meaning antagonistic to Vedic culture.

Keeping in mind these developments, we shall first discuss the main tenets of the Vaiśeṣika and the Nyāya systems separately, highlighting their points of divergence, and then focus on important developments in Navya-Nyāya.

Ontology

Kaṇāda (second century CE) is said to be the author of the first Vaiśeṣika treatise, the *Vaiśeṣikadarśana*,a collection of aphorisms. After Kaṇāda's treatise, the oldest extant Vaiśeṣika text is Praśastapāda's (fifth century CE) *Padārthadharmasaṃgraha*, popularly known as *Praśastapādabhāṣya* (i.e., a commentary by Praśastapāda). Praśastapāda's text follows Kaṇāda, but he freely adds his own views in order to systematize the Vaiśeṣika tenets. Later extant commentators and contributors to the Vaiśeṣika tradition include Śankaramiśra (*Upaskāratīkā*, fifteenth century), Vyomaśiva (*Vyomavatī*, tenth century), Udayana (*Kiraṇāvalī* and *Lakṣaṇāvalī*, tenth century), Śrīdhara (*Nyāyakandalī*, tenth century), Śivādityamiśra (*Saptapadārthī*, eleventh century), Candrānanda (*Vṛtti*, sixth century circa), Bhaṭṭa Vādīndra (*Kaṇāda-sūtranibandha* and commentaries on Udayana's texts, thirteenth century), Śrīvallabha (*Nyāyalīlāvatī*, twelfth century), Raghunātha (*Padārthatattvanirūpaṇam*, sixteenth century), and Jayantabhaṭṭa (ninth century) and Bhāsaravajña (tenth century), two Kashmiri Naiyāyikas.

The Vaiśeṣikas begin their enquiry with the question of what entities they would admit in their ontology. Kaṇāda lists six positive categories (*bhāva-padārtha*-s), namely, substance (*dravya*), quality (*guṇa*), action (*karma*), universal (*sāmānya*), ultimate differentiator (*viśeṣa*), and the relation of inherence (*samavāya*). Later stalwarts up to Vyomaśiva tacitly admit and Śivādityamiśra adds the negative category of absence (*abhāva*) to the list. Absence, he points out, is not merely a logical or linguistic operator; it is as objectively real as a positive entity. The system derives its name from *viśeṣa* (ultimate differentiator), the fifth category, which is a unique feature of this tradition; no other Indian philosophical system except Navya-Nyāya admits *viśeṣa* as a basic category (*padārtha*).

"*Padārtha*" literally means the reference of a word. Though a *padārtha* is defined as knowable (*jñeya*) and nameable (*abhidheya*), it is said to exist independently of the cognizing subject (*jñatā*)—a view that makes the Vaiśeṣikas robust realists. As J. N. Mohanty notes, "The categories are the highest non-formal genera under which all entities fall" (Mohanty 2006, 30). (Early scholars considered the list of seven categories to be fixed; nothing could be added to or deleted from this list. Some later scholars questioned this assumption.)

The Vaiśeṣika scheme includes detailed subcategorization. They divide substances into nine kinds, qualities into twenty-four kinds, actions (mainly movements) into five kinds, and universals into three kinds; ultimate differentiators being unique particulars do not have any internal differentiation; inherence is a relation *par excellence* without any internal type-distinction; and absences are of four types.

The nine substances are earth, water, fire, air, *ākāśa*,[2] space, time, self, and mind. Of these nine, the first four are of two varieties, eternal and noneternal. Substances of atomic magnitude are eternal, whereas compound substances are noneternal. *Ākāśa*, space, and time are eternal and all-pervasive. The number of each of them is one, though for our convenience we introduce conceptual divisions such as past, present, and future. Both self and mind are eternal and many. A self is all-pervasive, while mind, the internal sense organ, is of atomic magnitude. Self is different from other kinds of substances because it alone is potentially conscious. Consciousness, however, is an adventitious quality of self because a self gets endowed with consciousness only when it is embodied. Interestingly, in the Vaiśeṣika scheme, conscious self can freely interact with material body without falling prey to the problems of Cartesian dualism because they subscribe to a different theory of causation.

The Vaiśeṣikas do not give any explicit account of their deduction of categories. It appears, however, that they derive their list of natural classes not *a priori*, but through empirical methods. Some scholars believe that the Vaiśeṣikas were mainly guided by prevalent linguistic usage. By introducing a scheme of subclassification and justification thereof, they have also blurred the distinction between the pure doctrine of categories and an empirical theory of their exemplification—a stance that enables them to derive a natural science from the doctrine of categories.

The order in which the categories have been enumerated has a special significance. Substance, for instance, is the entity in which all things belonging to other positive categories reside by the relation of inherence. All substances possess qualities, but not all of them possess action; hence, the quality category precedes the action category. Next comes universal, as it inheres in substance, in quality, or in action. An ultimate differentiator, on the other hand, resides only in an eternal substance. Noneternal substances, qualities, actions, universals, and ultimate differentiators reside in their respective substratum in the relation of inherence; hence, inherence appears as the sixth category. Since an absence cannot be understood without referring to the thing of which it is an absence and since every absence has an ultimate reference to a positive entity, this negative category is mentioned last.

Let us elucidate the nature of these categories with the help of some examples. Consider, for instance, a red earthen pot. The pot is the substance and it possesses red color, which is a quality. Each quality in the Vaiśeṣika scheme is a particular instantiation of the corresponding universal. A quality resides in a substance by the relation of inherence and a universal also resides in its instances by the same relation. So the red color of the earthen pot inheres in it and the universal redness also inheres in the particular instance of the color red. When the earthen pot we are talking about is broken, we get smaller parts made of earth, which in turn can be broken down to smaller and smaller parts until we reach its atomic constituents. We have already seen that atoms, according to the Vaiśeṣika philosophers, are qualitatively different. To

2. *Ākāśa* cannot be accurately translated in English. It is accepted as the substratum of sound in the Vaiśeṣika system.

differentiate between two atoms of the same type, or two liberated selves that cannot be distinguished otherwise, they introduced a category, namely, the ultimate differentiator (*viśeṣa*). Inherence (*samavāya*) is the only relation admitted in the Nyāya-Vaiśeṣika ontology. This relation obtains, generally across categories, between five pairs of entities: (1) a whole and its parts[3] (e.g., a pot and the potsherds), (2) a substance and its qualities (e.g., a pot and its red color), (3) a substance and its action (e.g., fire and its upward movement), (4) a universal and its instances (e.g., cowness and individual cows), and (5) an ultimate differentiator and an eternal substance (e.g., a unique particular and an atom). There are four types of negation or absence admitted in the system: (1) mutual absence (*anyonyābhāva*) (e.g., a jar is not a pen and vice versa), (2) absence of the not-yet type (*prāgabhāva*) (e.g., absence of a bread in flour before it is baked), (3) absence of the no-more type (*dhvaṃsābhāva*) (e.g., absence of a vase in its broken pieces), and (4) absolute absence (*atyantābhāva*) (e.g., absence of color in air).

I consider next the Old Nyāya philosophy. Akṣapāda Gautama (second century) is recognized as the compiler of the first Nyāya treatise, the *Nyāyasūtra*. Vātsyāyana (fourth century) wrote an elaborate commentary (*bhāṣya*) on *Nyāya-sūtra*, which was severely criticized by Buddhist scholars such as Diṅnāga (fifth century). Uddyotakara (seventh century) took up the cudgel against Diṅnāga and defended the Nyāya position in his *Nyāyavārttika*. Vācaspati Miśra (ninth century) wrote an explanatory treatise entitled *Nyāyavārttika-tātparya-ṭīkā* on Uddyotakara's work, which was itself clarified by Udayanācārya in *Tātparyaṭīkā-pariśuddhi* (tenth century). According to the tradition, Udayana's works formed the watershed between the Old and the Navya-Nyāya, which in the process of defending and explicating the Nyāya tenets also anticipated many theses and approaches of the later Naiyāyikas.

The Nyāya also had a list of categories (*padārtha*-s). These sixteen categories are valid means of knowing (*pramāṇa*), objects of knowing (*prameya*), doubt (*saṃśaya*), aim (*prayojana*), example (*dṛṣṭānta*), established conclusion (*siddhānta*), members or constituents of an argument (*avayava*), hypothetical reasoning or supportive argument (*tarka*), settlement or decision (*nirṇaya*), an honest debate (*vāda*), a tricky debate (*jalpa*), a destructive debate (*vitaṇḍā*), fallacy (*hetvābhāsa*), underhand tricks (*chala*), false rejoinder (*jāti*), and defeat situations (*nigraha-sthāna*). According to Akṣapāda Gautama, correct knowledge of these categories leads to liberation, and misconception about them is at the root of our bondage.

True to its name, "Nyāya," meaning argumentation, is dedicated to formulating principles of valid reasoning. Its attitude is rational and intellectual, while its method is analytic. However, the early Naiyāyikas were not radical enough to accept whatever conclusions their logic arrived at. They opposed upholding conclusions that contradicted scriptural tenets and eschewed them as *nyāyābhāsa*-s, or pseudoarguments. It is evident from the list of the Nyāya categories that unlike the Vaiśeṣika scheme, the Nyāya scheme of categorization was guided mainly by epistemological considerations.

3. A whole, according to them, is not a mere collection of parts but is over and above its parts.

Ontological entities admitted in the system[4] are all included in the second category (i.e., objects of knowledge). This should not lead us to think that the Naiyāyikas are compromising on realism. No doubt, they are talking about objects as known and not about objects as such. But that is because they were interested in attaining truth by accredited means of knowing and then defending these truths from irrational attacks. All fourteen categories starting with doubt relate to the process of effective argumentation and rules of debate; the first seven constitute the "prior stage" and the last seven, beginning with debate, constitute the "posterior stage" of the Nyāya method. That is, an argument, according to Nyāya, starts with an initial doubt and ends with the establishment of a hypothesis by evidence, having demolished all objections raised by the opponents. The Navya-Naiyāyikas shifted their concern from the techniques of debating to the valid means of knowing and developed an elaborate theory of inference, thus dissociating logic from the art of debate.

Here is a brief introduction to entities admitted in the Nyāya system. *Átmā*, or soul, according to Nyāya, is to be inferred from its qualities, namely, desire, aversion, volition, pleasure, pain, and cognition, which reside in the soul-substance. Body is the substratum of effort, senses, and pleasure and pain (i.e., body is the site of all sorts of experiences). The Naiyāyikas as well as the Vaiśeṣikas admit five external sense organs—visual, auditory, gustatory, olfactory, and tactual, which are produced from fire, *ākāśa*, water, earth, and air, respectively. Color, sound, taste, smell, and touch are the objects of the respective sense organs. Intellect is the same as apprehension or cognition. *Manas* is the internal sense organ with the help of which we introspect our inner states. *Pravṛtti* is that which leads to physical and mental acts. Affection, aversion, and stupidity are listed as faults. Transmigration means the series of births and deaths through which an individual soul travels until attaining liberation. Birth means connection of a soul with body, senses, and so forth; death means their dissociation. Consequences of activities are of two types: pleasure and pain. Pain produces distress and liberation is the absolute cessation of pain. This is the Nyāya account of all possible experiences of soul. The means of release from the cycle of life and death, then, is the correct knowledge of the categories, which enables one to distinguish self from not-self.

Epistemology: Valid Means of Cognition (*Pramāṇas*)

In epistemology, the Vaiśeṣikas admit two independent means of knowing—perception (*pratyakṣa*) and inference (*anumāna*). The Naiyāyikas add two more to the list—comparison (*upamāna*) and testimony, or authority (*śabda*). Both schools

4. These are soul (*ātmā*), body (*śarīra*), senses (*indriya*), objects of sense (*artha*), intellect (*buddhi*), mind (*manas*), activity (*pravṛtti*), fault (*doṣa*), transmigration (*pretyabhāva*), consequences of acts (*phala*), pain (*duhkha*), and liberation (*apavarga*).

acknowledge the important role played by sense organs in perception[5] and offer a causal definition. In order that a perceptual cognition may arise, a series of contacts must take place. The self should come in contact with the mind and the mind with the sense organ and the sense organ with its object. Of these three contacts, the first one is necessary for any noneternal cognition. The second contact is not required in internal perceptions, though it is indispensable for any type of external perception. The third contact is the uncommon cause of all perceptions. Since perception cannot arise if there is no sense-object contact, it turns out to be an intentional state *par excellence.* It is different from inference because it is characterized by immediacy, which an inferential cognition lacks. Another interesting feature of this theory of perception is that perception always results in action. The perceiver is guided by the desire to seek, shun, or ignore the object of perception.

That all knowledge cannot be grasped by any one sense organ is a platitude. Our eyes cannot see sound, nor can our ears hear smells. So each sense organ has its special range of objects. Besides, different types of contacts (*sannikarṣa*) are needed to perceive different types of objects. The Naiyāyikas divide contacts into two types—ordinary (*laukika*) and extraordinary (*alaukika*). Uddyotakara first listed six types of ordinary contacts. In perceiving a substance by visual or tactual sense, the specific contact involved is conjunction (*saṃyoga*). When a quality or an action or a universal inhering in a substance is to be perceived, the contact required is inherence in the conjoined (*saṃyukta-samavāya*). The contact needed for perceiving a universal in a quality is inherence in the inherent in the conjoined (*sammyukta-samaveta-samavāya*). In the auditory perception of a sound the contact involved is inherence (*samavāya*), and to perceive soundness in a sound, the required complex relation is inherence in the inherent (*samaveta-samavāya*). In perceiving an absence, the contact involved is known as "characterizer-characterized" (*viśeṣya-viśeṣaṇa-bhāva-sambandha*).

Three types of extraordinary contacts have been elaborated by the Navya-Naiyāyikas—*sāmānyalakṣaṇa, jñānalakṣaṇa,*and *yogaja.* Here also the principle of division is the difference in contact. *Sāmānyalakṣaṇa* is that type of perception which gives us knowledge of all the instances of a class, when a single instance of the class is presented to a sense organ. The class-character or *sāmānya*, which is present in the single perceived instance, functions as an operative relation between the sense organ and all the instances of the class. Thus, when we perceive one instance of smoke, we come to recognize all instances of smoke via our prior knowledge of its class-character smokeness. Admission of such perception is necessary for establishing universal generalization, the knowledge of which is a prerequisite of inference. In the *jñānalakṣaṇa* variety of perception the contact involved is memory. Thus,

5. Perception is the cognition, different from inference, that arises when the self is in contact with a sense organ and the sense organ with an object (*Vaiśeṣika-sūtra*,3.1.17). Perception is the cognition arising out of the sense-object contact and which is certain, nondeviating, and nonverbal (*Nyāya-sūtra*, 1.1.4).

when one sees sandalwood as fragrant, the visual perception of sandalwood stimulates the memory of fragrance as experienced in the past. This memory somehow puts the eye in contact with fragrance in an extraordinary way when we see sandalwood at a distance. The Naiyāyikas make use of this type of perception in their account of perceptual error, of after-perception (*anuvyavasāya*), of recognition, of our awareness of the negatum of an absence, and of *upamiti*, where the knowledge of similarity is acquired through some extraordinary means. In the third type of extraordinary perception, the contact involved is a kind of supernatural power developed by the practice of yoga. It enables a yogin to perceive objects that are very subtle or remote in space and time.

The second *pramāṇa*, inference or *anumána*, according to Gautama, is directly based on perception of sign (*hetu*) in the locus of inference (*pakṣa*), which is invariably concomitant with the thing to be inferred (*sādhya*). To explain, a man sees smoke spiraling up from a hilltop. This man has seen smoke before coming from a kitchen fire and has acquired the knowledge that whatever has smoke has fire. Now when he sees the column of smoke on the hilltop, he remembers the universal correlation between smoke and fire. This knowledge makes him see smoke as that which is invariably co-present with fire on the hill. If there is no strong impediment, this knowledge will lead him to conclude that the hill has fire. Here smoke is the *hetu*, fire is the *sādhya*, hill is the *pakṣa*, and the relation of invariable concomitance between smoke and fire is the *vyāpti*. The man could not infer fire on the hill upon seeing smoke there if he had not known that smoke is invariably concomitant with fire. Hence, knowledge of *vyāpti* between *hetu* and *sādhya* is the logical ground of any inference.

Both the Vaiśeṣikas and the Naiyāyikas divide inference broadly into two types. Inference-for-oneself (*svārthānumāna*) deals with the psychological conditions (i.e., causally connected cognitive states leading to one's own inferential cognition). Inference-for-others (*parārthānumāna*) essentially deals with the proper linguistic expression of this inference with a view to communicating it to others. Inference-for-others has five constituents arranged in the order of assertion (*pratijñā*), reason (*hetu*), example (*udāharaṇa*), application (*upanaya*), and conclusion (*nigamana*). The typical example of an inference-for-others is the following:

Pratijñā: The hill possesses fire (stating what is to be proved).
Hetu: The reason is smoke (stating the ground of inference).
Udāharaṇa with *vyāpti:* Wherever there is smoke, there is fire, as in a kitchen.
Upanaya: The hill is similar (in possessing smoke).
Nigamana: The hill possesses fire.

Though the conclusion appears the same as the first step, these two perform two different tasks. The first step just asserts the thesis, while the conclusion declares that what is to be proved has been proved. According to the tradition, the first step is said to be generated by verbal cognition; the second is established by inference; in the third step, example is acquired through perception; and the fourth step is based on cognition of similarity. Since these four steps are established by four sources of true cognition admitted in the Nyāya school, the Naiyāyikas consider this five-membered argument as the demonstration *par excellence* (*parama-nyāya*). The Nyāya-Vaiśeṣika philosophers then proceed to classify inference, adopting different criteria of classification, and specify the marks of a legitimate sign, violation of which leads to different types of fallacies.

The next two means of cognition—comparison and testimony—are admitted by the Naiyāyikas, but the Vaiśeṣikas attempt to reduce them to inference. Comparison (*upamāna*) is defined as the instrument of that cognition which depends on the perception of similarity between two objects. It leads to the cognition of relation between a name and the thing it names. Suppose a man hears that a new animal called "*gavaya*" has been found in the forest lying at the outskirts of his village. Enquiring from an expert who lives in the forest, he comes to know that a *gavaya* is like a cow. Now when he goes to the forest and sees an animal that looks like a cow, he remembers what the forester has said and he has the knowledge "this animal is a *gavaya*." Thus, he learns the reference of the name "*gavaya*." The Naiyāyikas give elaborate arguments to establish comparison as an independent means of true cognition. Comparison cannot be reduced to perception because perception of similarity between a cow and a *gavaya* is not sufficient for knowing the reference of the word "*gavaya*." Nor can it be reduced to testimony (*śabda*) because the words of the forester only lead to the knowledge of similarity. It also cannot be reduced to inference because this type of cognition does not depend on the knowledge of relevant *vyāpti*.

Verbal testimony (*śabda*) is defined as the instructive utterance of a reliable person. A reliable person may be a wise man (*ṛṣi*), an ordinary knowledgeable person, or even a nonbeliever in the Vedas, but he must be an expert in a certain matter and willing to communicate his knowledge of it. Verbal testimony is of two kinds, namely, that which relates to matters seen and that which relates to matters that cannot be empirically determined. The first kind of cognition is amenable to empirical verification, but the second kind cannot thus be ascertained, for example, assertion in the Scriptures that one attains Heaven (not liberation) by performing the *agnihotra* sacrifice. The Vaiśeṣikas are against autonomy of verbal testimony mainly for two reasons. First, they maintain that just as in an inference, where fire is inferred from smoke on the basis of the knowledge of invariable concomitance between smoke and fire, similarly, on hearing a word, we arrive at the cognition of its referent on the basis of the invariable concomitance between a particular word and its referent. This referential relation is learned in one's childhood from observing the verbal behavior of elders and the acts that follow. Second, the validity of information received from others needs to be established through inference from the reliability or trustworthiness of the speaker and hence cannot be an independent means of cognition. The Naiyāyikas, however, point out that like cognition based on similarity, information received through verbal testimony too cannot be dependent on the knowledge of invariable concomitance. For, how can one have the knowledge of invariable concomitance between words that are about imperceptible objects and their references? We can understand words such as "*svarga*" (heaven), and so forth, based on the words of trustworthy persons. Besides, in our after-perception (*anuvyavasāya*), verbal cognition is never grasped as a case of inference, so one should grant autonomy to verbal testimony.[6]

Navya-Nyāya

By combining the Nyāya epistemology with the Vaiśeṣika ontology, Gaṅgeśa initiated a new trend of philosophizing in Mithila—northeastern India—in the thirteenth century. It is Gaṅgeśa who integrated and popularized the technique of subtle argumentation in his magnum opus *Tattvacintāmaṇi* (*TCM*) and is regarded as the founder of the Navya-Nyāya tradition. The tradition was carried forward by Vardhamāna (fourteenth century), Yajñapati Upādhyāya (fifteenth century), and Pakṣadhara Miśra (fifteenth century), among others. The novelty and originality of the Navya Nyāya school is found not in introducing new topics of philosophical discussion but in the method employed, in devising a precise technical language suitable for expressing all forms of cognition. They formulated their approach against their principal opponents—the Mīmāṃsákas.

From Mithila, Navya-Nyāya traveled to Navadwīpa, in Bengal. The unorthodox logician, Raghunātha Siromaṇi (sixteenth century) of Navadwipa, wrote a commentary on *TCM* entitled *Dīdhiti*, in which he went far beyond Gaṅgeśa by introducing changes in Navya-Nyaya metaphysics and epistemology. Subsequent prominent proponents of Navya-Nyāya in Bengal—including Bhavānanda Siddhantavāgīśa, Mathurāntha Tarkavāgīśa, Jagadīśa Tarkālaṇkāra, and Gadādhara Bhattacharyya—wrote commentaries on *Dīdhiti*, which contributed to the fullest development of Gaṅgeśa's technique of reasoning. The fame of Navadwīpa Naiyāyikas spread all over India and scholars from other schools adopted the Navya-Nyāya language. This highly technical language became the medium for all serious philosophical discussion by the sixteenth century, irrespective of the ontological, epistemological, and moral commitments of the discussants.

The use of Navya-Nyāya language outside Nyāya philosophy is evidence of its strength. But unfortunately, this has led to the misconception that Navya-Nyāya is a mere tool of theoretical discussion. We must remember that though the Navya-Nyāya language can be successfully dissociated from its context, Navya-Nyāya was developed as a complete system of philosophy. Gaṅgeśa's *TCM*, for example, begins with an invocation to the three-faced (*trimūrti*) Lord and ends with sections on liberation (*mukti*), with epistemological, logical, and ontological discussions in the middle.

6. Jagadīśa, the famous Navya-Naiyāyika, offers a more sophisticated form of this argument in his *Śabdaśakti-prakāśikā*.

The Navya-Nyāya language, despite its aspiration for complete precision, is still composed in Sanskrit. Sanskrit grammar is rigorous, yet Sanskrit being a natural language it is not entirely free from ambiguities and uncertainties. Besides, Sanskrit as the First Order Language, which expresses objects and events of the world, fails to make the structure of the cognitive content perspicuous. Suppose we have a perceptual cognition of the form "The pot is black." In Sanskrit, one does not usually differentiate between "The pot is black" and "The black pot" (i.e., between a sentence and a complex term). In fact, in ordinary Sanskrit, "is" is considered superfluous, though the grammarians maintain that a sentence must contain a finite verb and in the absence of a finite verb, one must posit it. The Naiyāyikas, however, follow the common linguistic practice and that is why in this tradition we do not find any distinction between a fact and a complex object. Nor do they admit propositions as abstract entities. Hence, according to them, a cognitive content is nothing but a complex object, expressible in a complex term.

According to Navya-Nyāya, the basic combination that expresses a cognitive content is a locus-locatee combination of the form "a has f-ness"/"f-ness in a" ("the pot has blackness"/"blackness in pot" in this case). In a perspicuous account of a cognitive content, the Navya-Naiyāyika would like to make explicit the connection between the pot and its color in consonance with their own categorical framework. Sanskrit as an object language is either neutral to metaphysical questions or bears the burden of the grammarian ontology.[7]

Now the color black may be located in a pot in different relations. In object language, the relation between blackness and pot is never specified. There is a rule in Navya-Nyāya that whatever can be expressed in the object language ceases to be a relation but becomes a term of a relation. For example, if one says, "The hill has fire," she means that fire is related by the unmentioned relation *saṃyoga* (contact) with the hill. But, if on the other hand, someone says, "The hill has contact (*saṃyoga*) with fire," "contact" here does not act as the relational component but as the third term of the cognition in question. The second piece of cognition, thus, points to another unmentioned relation, namely, inherence (*samavāya*) of the contact with the hill,[8] on the one hand, and fire on the other. It is, therefore, obvious that relations involved in cognition must be specified if one wants to make the structure of a cognitive content transparent—hence the need for a Second Order Language, which talks about the First Order Language. The Navya-Nyāya language is a Second Order Language because it is where the structure of a cognitive content expressed in the First Order Language is made explicit.

The second important reason behind developing a higher-order technical language relates to the identification of a true sentence. In the absence of a proposition,

7. In the object language, a Sanskrit grammarian would be content to show the relation of identity between "pot" and "black color," which he would express by applying the same suffix to the noun phrase and the adjective phrase. Identity, however, is not the relation that we grasp in our reflective cognition (*anuvyavasāya*).

8. Contact in the Nyāya-Vaiśeṣika ontology is a quality and a quality inheres in a substance.

the cognitive content has been taken to be the truth bearer in the Indian analytical tradition. To state the Navya-Nyāya definition of truth in a simplistic way: to know of what something is that it is and of what something is not that it is not, is true. In the course of explaining their definition of truth, the Navya-Naiyāyikas always give a *de re* reading of a cognitive content. The content of any cognition has at least three elements—*viśeṣya* (qualificandum), *prakāra* or *viśemaṇa* (qualifier), and *saṃsarga* or the qualification relation between them. If, for example, my cognitive content is a-R-b (i.e., b is located in a by the relation R), then, says the Naiyāyika, we are directly aware of a, b, and R where a and b are things in the real world and not mere representations of things and the relation R actually obtains between a and b. So a cognitive content a-R-b is true if and only if b is located in a by the relation R. So, when I have a cognition of a black pot, my cognitive content will be true if and only if blackness characterizes the pot by the relation of inherence.

Sanskrit as an object language does not make quantifiers explicit. Though sometimes "all" (*sarva*) or "some" (*kiñcit*) prefix a subject term, we do not come across any expression indicating the quantity of the predicate. Usually when someone says, "The hill is fiery," it is not indicated whether a particular hill is fiery or all hills are fiery. The problem becomes all the more acute when the content is negative. When someone says "absence of pot," it may mean "absence of all pots," "absence of a particular black pot," or "absence of some pots." Hence, the Naiyāyikas had no option but to introduce some technical terms in their higher-order language, such as limitor (*avacchedaka*), "limitor-hood" (*avacchadakatā*), and so forth, to compensate for this lacuna.

The Navya-Naiyāyikas are of the opinion that only qualificative cognition of the form a-R-b leads to action/behavior. An unstructured nonqualificative cognition can never be the cause of behavior. The presence of a qualificand and the qualifier, however, does not make a cognition qualificative. As we have already seen, the qualifier must also qualify the qualificand in a specific manner (i.e., the qualificand and the qualifier must be related by some specific relation). So in Navya-Nyāya logic and language, relations play a crucial role. Over and above *saṃyoga* and *samavāya*, two relations admitted by the Vaiśeṣikas, they defined a number of new relations because they realized that these two relations are not sufficient to explain how different individuals belonging to different ontological categories are related to one another and also how these related complexes appear in our cognition. All relations admitted in Navya-Nyāya are dyadic relations, however complex they may appear. There is some difference of opinion among the Naiyāyikas regarding the ontological status of these new relations. Some take them as epistemic categories; some are ready to accept them as ontologically real. In spite of this debate, all admit that these are efficient tools of precisification.

A minimalist definition of relation, which has been admitted by the stalwarts of Navya-Nyāya, is:

> x is a relation iff x governs a qualificative cognition.

Jagadiśa amends this definition to:

> A relation is the object of a qualificative cognition, which is other than the qualificand and the qualifier.

Gadādhara finally defines relation in terms of subjuncts/superstratum (*anuyogī*) and adjuncts/substratum (*pratiyogī*).

> When xRy is a cognitive content, R is a relation of x to y iff x is the adjunct of R (one which is related) and y is the subjunct (to which x is related) of R.

The Nyāya way of expressing a relation is always as xRy, where the entity to the left of R is the adjunct and the entity to the right of R is the subjunct. The Navya-Naiyāyikas admit two types of relation, occurrence-exacting (*vṛtti-niyāmaka*) and non–occurrence-exacting (*vṛtti-aniyāmaka*). An occurrence-exacting relation always gives the impression that one entity is located in another entity, while a non–occurrence-exacting relation does not do so. The latter only makes us aware that the two terms are related. It is easier to identify the adjunct and subjunct of a relation of the former type; the adjunct is that which is located and the subjunct is that where the adjunct is located but in the second type adjunct and subjunct are identified depending on the fiat of the cognizer. The Navya-Naiyāyikas mainly use four types of relation: (1) contact (*saṃyoga*), (2) inherence (*samavāya*), (3) *svarūpa*,[9] and (4) identity (*tādātmya*). Of these, the first two are occurrence-exacting, *svarūpa* is sometimes so, and identity is not.

A minimal analysis of the component of Navya-Nyāya language is given below:

> The primitive terms of the language are the nouns or nominal stems like *ghata* (pot), *dhūma* (smoke), *kapi* (monkey), etc.

By adding the simple suffix "*tva*" or "*tā*," many new terms are generated. For example, by adding "*tva*" to *dhūma*, abstract terms like *dhūmatva* (smokeness or smokehood), which is a universal (*jāti*), can be generated. The suffix "*tā*" is used to generate relational abstract expressions such as causehood (*kāraṇatā*), locushood (*ādhāratā*), and their corresponding inverse relational expressions such as effecthood (*kāryatā*), located-hood, or superstratumhood (*ādheyatā/vṛttitā*).

In the Navya-Nyāya language, we also find some determining or conditioning operator that when combined with a relational expression forms a more precise term. The causehood is a relational abstract that can be employed in the context of any cause. But to signify some specific cause (e.g., cause of smokeness), the Navya-Naiyāyikas take recourse to this conditioning operator that enables them to generate an expression, causehood determined by smokehood (*dhūmatva-nirūpita-kāraṇatā*).

Another very important operator is *avaccehadakatā*, or limitorhood. This operator performs multiple functions. But without entering into the details of this

9. *Svarūpa* will be left untranslated because any English term is bound to distort its meaning; it is identical with either one or both of the relata.

complex notion, let us understand this operator with a simple example. Smoke may have different causes. Suppose we want to identify a specific cause of smoke, say, fire, then we shall have to say following a Navya-Naiyāyika that causehood determined or conditioned by smokehood is limited by firehood (*vahnitvāvacchinna-dhūmatva-nirūpita kāraṇatā*). Thus, the Naiyāyikas have developed a mechanism to generate relations wherever necessary for expressing an event precisely.

To make these technical concepts more intelligible, let us take another example. Let us once again look at the adjunct and the subjunct of a relation. The *Rámáyaṇa* says that Kauśalyā is the mother of Rāma. So the relation from the side of Kauśalyā is "being the mother of" and the corresponding abstract property is motherhood (*mātṛtva*). The relation from the side of Rāma is "being the son of" and the corresponding relational abstract is sonhood (*putratva*). The adjunct (*pratiyogī*) of the relational abstract "motherhood" is Rāma and the subjunct (*anuyogī*) is Kauśalyā. The Naiyāyikas describe this relational abstract as "the motherhood of Rāma in Kauśalyā." In case of absence, however, adjunct and subjunct are understood in a different way.

An absence is always of something, and that something is called the counterpositive or the negatum (*pratiyogī*) of that absence. Consider the absence of smoke in a lake. Smoke is the counterpositive (*pratiyogī*) of the absence of smoke and *pratiyogitā*, or the relation of counterpositiveness, is the relation between an absence and its counterpositive. Here, the lake is the locus (*anuyogī*) of the absence. Hence, *anuyogitā* connects the absence in question with its locus. Here absence is that of smoke in general (*dhūma-sāmānya*) and not this or that particular smoke; hence, it is called *dhūma-sāmānyābhāva*. Next, let us explain the notion of a limitor and the limiting relation. When x is in y, x is related to y in a particular relation and that relation is the limiting relation. Similarly, when there is an absence of x in y, a counterpositiveness must be in x and there must be a relation to limit that counterpositiveness. Suppose there is smoke on a mountain. Here the limiting relation is contact (*saṃyoga*). There is at the same time absence of smoke on the same mountain by the relation of inherence because smoke never resides in a mountain by the relation of inherence. Again, smoke is absent on the mountain by the relation of identity or *tādātmya*, since smoke and mountain cannot be identical. So counterpositiveness in the first case is limited by the relation of inherence, whereas in the second case the limiting relation is identity. At the same time, counterpositiveness so related determines (*nirūpaka*) the absence. Thus, the first absence is determined by the counterpositiveness residing in smoke limited by the relation of inherence (*samavā yasambandhāvacchinnapratiyogitā-nirūpita-dhūma-sāmānyābhāva*) and the second absence is determined by the counterpositiveness residing in smoke limited by the relation of identity (*tādātmyasambandhāvacchinna-pratiyogitā-nirūpita-dhūma-sāmānyābhāva*).

We shall now see the application of these technical expressions in connection with the definition of pervasion (*vyāpti*), the most important and foundational concept of the Nyáya theory of inference. *Vyāpti* is the relation of universal concomitance between the thing to be inferred and the ground of inference. It is a lawlike connection that enables one to infer a property in a new situation from a second property depending on the knowledge of lawlike connection between the first property and the second property. Gaṅgeśa in the *Vyāptivāda* of *TCM* rejects definitions of *vyāpti* given by his opponents, only the first of which will be analyzed here. Simply stated, the definition runs thus: pervasion, or *vyāpti*, is the absence of occurrence of the *hetu* in every locus of absence of the *sādhya*.[10] This definition, however, has been amended quite a number of times to free it from the charges of overcoverage (*ativyāpti*) and undercoverage (*avyāpti*).[11] A ramified version of the definition, though it is not the final version, is:

> The *hetu* is pervaded by the *sādhya* if the *hetu* is in no way occurrent by the relation of *hetutāvacchedaka* in any locus of the absence of the *sādhya* which is characterized by the *sādhyatāvacchedaka dharma* and also by the *sādhyatāvacchedaka sambandha*.

We have said before that pervasion is the relation of invariable concomitance of the ground of an inference (*hetu*) and the thing to be inferred (*sādhya*). Without the knowledge of this relation, it is not possible to infer. In a valid inference, "The hill has fire because it has smoke," the *sādhya* is fire, the *hetu* is smoke, and *pakṣa*, or the locus, is the hill. *Sādhyatāvacchedaka-sambandha* is the relation in which the *sādhya* resides in the *pakṣa*. As fire resides in the hill by the relation of contact (*saṃyoga*), the limiting relation is contact. The property that is the limitor of the *sādhya* in this case is fireness (*vahnitva*) and not the property of producing burns (*dāhajanakatva*). Similarly, by *hetutāvacchadkasambandha* is meant the relation in which the *hetu* resides in the *pakṣa*. In the given instance, that relation is also contact, as smoke too resides in the hill by contact. This absence of occurrence of smoke is again absence of occurrence of smoke in general and not of any particular smoke. So there is the relation of pervasion between the *hetu*, smoke, and *sādhya*,fire, as there is general absence of occurrence of the *hetu*, smoke, by the limiting relation of contact, determined by every locus of absence of the *sādhya*, fire, counterpositiveness of which is limited by the relation of contact and the limitor firehood. Fire pervades smoke because no smoke ever resides by way of contact in a lake or anywhere else that is the locus of absence fire qua fire.

Such concern for precision might appear obsessive, but if one qualification is left out, the definition of pervasion will be either incomplete or defective, leading to fallacious reasoning and unsound conclusions. The Navya-Nyāya logicians achieved analytical precision by the use of their technical language, which can serve as a model of regimentation of natural languages.

10. *Sādhyābhāvavadvṛttitvam*.

11. Overcoverage means that the definition is too wide, for example, when a cow is defined in terms of attribute, having horns, which is not a distinguishing mark of a cow. Undercoverage means the definition is too narrow, for example, when a cow is defined as possessing brown color, which is not present in all cows.

BIBLIOGRAPHY AND SUGGESTED READINGS

Bhattacharya, Gopinath. (1976) Translated and elucidated. *Tarkasaṃgrahadīpikā on Annaṃbhaṭṭa's Tarkasaṃgraha*. Calcutta: Progressive Publisher.

Ganeri, Jonardon. (2008) "Towards a Formal Regimentation of Navy-Nyāya Technical Language I & II." In *Logic, Navya-Nyāya & Applications: Homage to Bimal Krishna Matilal*. Volume 15: *Studies in Logic*, edited by Mihir K. Chakraborti, et al. London: College Publications, 105–138.

Gangopadhyay, Mrinalkanti (trans.). (1982) *Nyāyasūtra with Vātsyāyana's Commentary*. Calcutta: Indian Studies.

Guha, Dinesh Chandra. (1979) *The Navya-Nyāya System of Logic*. Delhi: Motilal Banarasidass Publishers Private Limited.

Jha, Ganganatha. (1982) *Padārthadharmasaṃgraha of Praśastapāda*. Varanasi: Chowkhamba.

——— (trans.). (1984) *The Nyāyasūtra of Gautama (with the commentaries of Vātsyāyana and Uddyotakara)*. 4 vols. Delhi: Motilal Banarassidass Publishers Private Limited.

Matilal, B. K. (1977) *Nyāya-Vaiśeṣika*. Wiesbaden: Otto Harrassowitz.

———. (1998) *The Character of Logic in India*, edited by J. Ganeri and H. Tiwari. Albany, NY: SUNY.

Mohanty, J. N. (1989) *Gangeśa's Theory of Truth*. Delhi: Motilal Banarasidass Publishers Private Limited.

———. (2006) "Categories in Indian Philosophy." *Philosophical Concepts Relevant to Sciences in Indian Tradition*,Volume I, edited by Pranab Kumar Sen. New Delhi: Centre for Studies in Civilizations, 30.

Phillips, Stephen H. (1995) *Classical Indian Metaphysics*. Chicago and La Salle: Open Court.

Phillips, Stephen H., and Ramanuja N. S. Tatacharya (2008) *Epistemology of Perception*. Delhi: Motilal Banarasidass Publishers Private Limited.

Potter, K. H. (ed.). (1977) *Encyclopedia of Indian Philosophy*, Volume 2: Nyāya-Vaiśeṣika. Delhi: Motilal Banarasidass Publishers Private Limited.

Potter, K. H., and Sibajiban Bhattacharya. (1993) *Encyclopedia of Indian Philosophy*, Volume 6: Navya-Nyāya. Delhi: Motilal Banarasidass Publishers Private Limited.

Thakur, Anantalal. (2003) *Origin and Development of the Vaiśeṣika System*. New Delhi: Centre for Studies in Civilizations.

CHAPTER 10

SĀṂKHYA-YOGA

T. S. RUKMANI

Darśana (vision/insight) is the standard term that denotes a philosophical school in Indian thought. Many *darśanas* are recognized in Indian thought. Some are called orthodox (*āstika*) as they accepted the authority of the Vedas, while others are called unorthodox (*nāstika*) as they do not accept the Vedas as authoritative. In extant literature we find the philosophical schools mentioned without taking into account the orthodox/unorthodox distinction. Thus, Haribhadra Suri (ninth century) in his *Ṣaḍdarśanasamuccaya* mentions six schools of philosophy—Buddhism, Nyāya, Sāṃkhya, Jainism, Vaiśeṣika, and Mīmāṃsā—thus finding a place for Buddhism and Jainism, which do not accept the Vedas as authoritative. Sāṃkhya is enumerated as a philosophical system, but there is no mention of Yoga as a school. We then have Jayanta Bhaṭṭa (tenth century), who writes of the *ṣaṭ tarkī*, or six logical schools, in his *Nyāyamanjarī*, in which he includes Mīmāṃsā, Nyāya, Sāṃkhya, Jainism, Buddhism, and Cārvaka. In this list we find the three unorthodox schools (i.e., Cārvaka [materialist], Jainism, and Buddhism) given a place as systems of philosophical thought. Mādhava (fourteenth century) refers to sixteen philosophical systems in his *Sarvadarśanasaṇgraha*, in which Sāṃkhya and Yoga are mentioned as separate schools but which also mentions Buddhism and Jainism. Thus, the convention of enumerating only the six orthodox schools as philosophical systems was not the norm in the Indian context well into the fourteenth century.

While it is not certain precisely when the convention came into existence, it has become widely established. Satchidananda Murthy believes that the first Sanskrit book to mention these six orthodox schools together is the *Viśvasāratantra*, in the twelfth century (1957, vi). It is reasonable to think that after the advent of Buddhism and other schools, when a number of changes both political and cultural had taken place in the period between 500 BCE and 400 CE, the desire to preserve Vedic culture might have had something to do with bringing the orthodox schools under one umbrella. Thus, while systems that accepted the Vedas and those that did not were included together under the category of philosophy (*darśana*) in general, the common element of acceptance of the Vedas gradually helped in bringing together these six as the standard Indian philosophical schools by the twelfth century in the *Viśvasāratantra*. Sāṃkhya and Yoga are included in the six schools of Indian philosophy that accept the authority of the Vedas, along with Vaiśeṣika, Nyāya, Pūrvamīmāṃsā, and Uttaramīmāṃsā or Vedānta.

While the textual history of Sāṃkhya, as known to us, begins with the *Sāṃkhyakārikā* (SK) (ca. 350–450 CE), the terms Sāṃkhya and Yoga themselves are integral to a much older religious and philosophical tradition. They constitute part of the cultural and religious/spiritual landscape, occurring as they do in many different cultural contexts. Thus, we find these terms in the *Upaniṣads*, the *Mahābhārata*, and the *Bhagavadgītā* as well as in a number of the Purāṇas. However, whether they each refer to independent systems of Sāṃkhya and Yoga philosophy is not easy to determine. The *Mahābhārata* uniformly depicts Sāṃkhya as a nontheistic school that does not believe in an Īśvara, as opposed to Yoga, which is spoken of as a theistic school (cf. Chakravarti 1975, 54). The *Mahābhārata* also gives evidence of Sāṃkhya not having a consistent view regarding both *puruṣa* and *prakṛti* (ibid.). All this suggests that many ideas were being discussed as Sāṃkhya ideas before they were systemized later into the Sāṃkhya school with which we are currently familiar. The *Bhagavadgītā* again treats Sāṃkhya in many sections and sometimes not uniformly. The general meaning of Sāṃkhya and Yoga that one derives from the *Gītā* is knowledge (*jñāna*) and disinterested action (*karmayoga*), respectively. Chakravarti is of the view that Sāṃkhya as we know it today was already "systemized before the composition of the *Gītā*" (ibid., 56), a view supported by the *Gītā*'s application of the three-*guṇa* category of the Sāṃkhya philosophy to analyze many of its own categories. Larson and Bhattacharya call the presence of all these different views—as well as the presence of both Sāṃkhya and Yoga ideas in the spheres of religion, philosophy, medicine, art, and so forth—proto-Sāṃkhya and pre-Kārikā-Sāṃkhya (1987).

Among the six orthodox schools as well we have scholars who hold the view that Sāṃkhya is the oldest philosophical thought and that it has influenced all the other schools in their development (Mainkar 1964). Others like Larson believe that even though Yoga ideas must have been present in the milieu as a "characteristic dimension of Indian spirituality" (Larson and Bhattacharya 2008, 24), Sāṃkhya was one of the earliest schools to develop systematically and Yoga philosophy developed by piggy-backing on the metaphysics of Sāṃkhya. There is also the argument that Sāṃkhya is the earlier school that was later modified or revised as Yoga, when it came into confrontation with Buddhist Abhidharma traditions somewhere in the third and fourth centuries CE (Larson and Bhattacharya 2008). Scholars such as Hauer, on the other hand, believe that Yoga philosophy was an independent school even while acknowledging its connection with Sāṃkhya. On the other hand, Hiriyanna is of the opinion that the differences between the two may be derived from "differentiations in an originally single doctrine" (1951). It is difficult to resolve this question one way or the other. This essay shall treat Sāṃkhya and Yoga as independent schools of philosophy in spite of some metaphysical and other similarities between them.

The Classical Age of the *Sūtras*

It is instructive to divide the early period of Indian history into the Vedic age (ca. 2000–500 BCE) and the post-Vedic age, also called the classical age (500 BCE–500 CE). By the late classical age (ca. 200 BCE–500 CE), foundational texts advocating the various schools of Indian thought written in a *sūtra* style had come into existence. These different *sūtra* texts do not represent the beginnings of any of these schools but are summary statements of the various approaches to philosophical questions that were in the milieu. Because of the terse style of the *sūtra* texts, a tradition of commentaries developed for each of these schools, and it is due to the efforts of the commentators that one is able to piece together, in a cogent manner, the philosophy of the respective schools. Just as Patañjali is connected to the *Yogasūtras* (YS) as its author, tradition associates Kapila as the propounder of the Sāṃkhya school. Nevertheless, the *Sāṃkhyasūtras* of Kapila that we have today is uniformly considered to be a late fourteenth-century work and so is not the earliest Sāṃkhya *sūtra* text. Sāṃkhya alone, then, stands out among the six schools in lacking an original *sūtra* text from the late classical age. The oldest systematic text in the Sāṃkhya tradition is the *Sāṃkhyakārikā* (SK) by Īśvarakṛṣṇa (ca. fourth to fifth century CE) (Larson and Bhattacharya 1987). It is in this composition that we find the principles of Sāṃkhya clearly spelled out. However, like the *sūtra* texts, the SK is also not easily understood without the help of commentaries, of which there are many. The earliest extant commentary is the *Suvarṇasaptati*, and there are at least eight more (ibid., 20). Vindyavasin's *Yuktidīpikā* and Gauḍapāda's commentary on the SK are also important commentaries. However, the one that really became popular and the standard for understanding Sāṃkhya philosophy, as represented in the SK, is Vācaspati Miśra's *Tattvakaumudī* (ninth to tenth century CE).

The basic project that concerned all the classical philosophical systems, including Sāṃkhya and Yoga, was to understand the nature of ultimate reality and to explore the role of the human person in it. In this context the use of the term *darśana* (vision) for Indian philosophy is significant in that the search for reality was not just an attempt to explain the physical world but to probe deeper and see the correlations between the inner make-up of the individual and outer reality. This is a search that is already in evidence in the ṚgVeda (RV), where both reason and intuitive insight were recruited to unravel the mystery of ultimate reality. There were two distinct philosophical trends noticeable in the RV. One is to view the ultimate reality as a Unity (RV I.164), and the other is an intuitive belief in the close relationship between the microcosmic and the macrocosmic dimensions of the universe (RV X.90; X.16–18). This twofold trend could be the result of an intuitive feeling that the ultimate "Single Truth" is not just a transcendental Unity principle standing over and above the universe but one that also finds expression in the universe through the various phenomena. It is this belief that eventually led to the development of the various schools of Vedānta, such as nondualism, which believed in the reality of only the Ultimate Single Truth, Brahman, while others opted for various forms of a difference/nondifference relationship between the Ultimate, the universe, and the individual selves.[1]

In the classical *Upaniṣads* (900–400 BCE), inquiries into these basic matters go in a number of directions. The *Upaniṣads* are testimony to the fact that vigorous philosophical activity was present in the milieu from pre-Buddhistic times and diverse views were prevalent. One has to imagine that these orthodox schools were all engaged simultaneously in their separate ways to understand the deeper philosophical questions, borrowing from each other when their ideas agreed and asserting their views in their separate ways. Thus, a horizontal playing field, rich in philosophical speculation both orthodox and nonorthodox, was the norm in this period. The inquiry finally culminated in an equation of identity between the ultimate reality, called Brahman, and the inner reality of the human, called *ātman*, in the *Upaniṣads*. There is no evidence to suggest that there was a systematic attempt to construct systems of thought in the *Upaniṣads*. But with the appearance of the Buddhists and Jains, who rationally questioned the validity of the Vedas, the orthodox schools were forced to defend themselves using rational means as well. It was probably this compulsion that resulted in the compiling of the foundational *sūtra* texts for each of the six schools, wherein their ideas were laid out in a systematic manner.

Sāṃkhya and Yoga were also engaged in their own separate ways to find answers to some of these questions, and we find them represented in the *Sāṃkhyakārikā* of Īśvarakṛṣṇa and Patañjali's *Yogasūtras*, respectively.

Sāṃkhya

The word Sāṃkhya, derived from *saṃkhyā* (number), has many meanings. It is understood as both right knowledge or correct knowledge (*samyak-khyāti*) as well as enumeration. It is the right knowledge or discernment of the difference between *prakṛti* (a material principle) and *puruṣa* (a spiritual reality) that is the aim of this philosophy, and so the word Sāṃkhya can be understood as "right knowledge." The second meaning of enumeration comes from Sāṃkhya's counting the basic principles of reality as twenty-four in its scheme of evolution of the categories described below.

1. See Taber in this volume.

Sāṃkhya advocates two eternal realities called *prakṛti* and *puruṣa* (conceived pluralistically though singular in nature). *Prakṛti* (material reality) contains all the worldly effects within itself that can manifest later given the right conditions. Sāṃkhya arrives at its twofold reality not because it is so stated in the sacred books but by a process of reasoning. The following fivefold reasoning is given by Īśvarakṛṣṇa in SK 10 to prove the existence of *prakṛti:* (1) If the effect does not preexist in the cause, it cannot be produced by any means of production. (2) Cause and effect have an invariable connection with each other and are each manifestations of their material make-up. (3) Everything cannot be produced from everything. (4) A cause produces only that effect for which it has the capacity. (5) The effect is in essence not different from the material cause itself.

In connection with the origin of things and therefore finally of the universe, the different schools of philosophy propounded two theories. One was known as the *satkāryavāda*, which believed in a primal cause potentially holding all that would come into existence later, given the right conditions for its production. The other was the *asatkāryavāda*, which argued for new effects that come into existence from the first cause. Sāṃkhya took the stand that all effects or all that exists in the material world, including space and time, have evolved from *prakṛti*, which is inferred to be the first cause and thus supported the *satkāryavāda*.

While the reasoning for the existence of *prakṛti* seems to follow the familiar role of the relationship between a cause and its effect, another fivefold reasoning is given for the inference of *puruṣa* in SK 17 and is based on a subject/object divide drawn from everyday experience and a teleological principle to which Sāṃkhya subscribes. The reasoning is as follows: (1) *Prakṛti* and its evolutes all serve the purpose of the self (consciousness); thus, evolution is teleological. (2) This other whose purpose is served by *prakṛti* and the evolutes must be different from everything composed of the three *guṇas* (*sattva, rajas*, and *tamas*, to be elaborated upon below). (3) Experiences suggest a "transcendental synthetic unity of pure consciousness to coordinate all experiences"; all knowledge necessarily presupposes the existence of the self" (Sharma 1987, 156). (4) The physical universe needs a sentient *puruṣa* to experience it (i.e. there is need of a subject to experience the objects). The *guṇas* generate pleasure, pain, and delusion. But these qualities have meaning only when there is an intelligent principle to experience it. Therefore, there is *puruṣa*. (5) Finally, one sees that there is a longing to escape from *saṃsāra* in some people. This desire can be meaningful only if there is something other than *prakṛti* that tries to escape from *prakṛti*. This is *puruṣa*.

Instead of positing a designer or architect or Īśvara (God) who brings the world into existence, Sāṃkhya also argues that since *prakṛti* evolves for the sake of a subject (i.e., *puruṣa*), there is no necessity for an Īśvara. Therefore, Īśvara does not figure in the Sāṃkhya of the SK.

Scholars have commented on the predilection of Sāṃkhya to reach conclusions based on reasoning as opposed to depending heavily on Vedic authority. T. G. Mainkar refers to this when he writes, "The main difference between the traditional approach and that of the Sāṃkhyas appears to be that the Sāṃkhyas insisted upon the use of Logic in philosophical matters and regarded it as having a far greater scope than the one given to it by those who admitted absolute authority of the Āgamas" (1964, 1). This dependence on reason has also been critiqued by commentators belonging to other *āstika* schools, in particular by Pūrvamīmāṃsā and Vedānta, which heavily relied on Vedic authority. The *Brahmasūtra* (BS) and Śaṅkara's commentary (BSBh) on some of the relevant *sūtras* of the BS characterize Sāṃkhya reasoning as *śuṣkatarka*, or dry logic without substance. The second chapter of the BS deals with Sāṃkhya as a school to be dismissed as it is not based on *śruti* (*Upaniṣads*) but on *smṛti* (logic).[2] It is clear from the BS and the BSBh of Śaṅkara that Sāṃkhya was still considered a rival even in the eighth century, for Śaṅkara makes it clear that he is opposing Sāṃkhya in such great detail because he considers it to be the chief rival (*pradhāna-malla*) and by defeating the main enemy the others can be silenced (see BS and BSBh I.1.5–12; I.1.18; I.4.1–28; II.1.1–11; II. 2.1–10 etc). Śaṅkara concludes forcefully by stating that reasoning may be useful in some instances but not in the case of ascertaining the reality of the cause of the universe, which then leads to the goal of liberation for which only the Vedas can help. The knowledge arising from the *Upaniṣads* is alone true knowledge and is opposed to reasoning that has no Vedic foundation and that springs from the imagination of people like Kapila, Kaṇāda, and others who lack authority (BS and BSBh II.1.1–12). One can perhaps wonder whether Sāṃkhya was indeed initially based on the *Upaniṣads*, yielding its premier position eventually to Vedānta as the dominant view. One also can see in Bādarāyaṇa's and Śaṅkara's vehement Vedantic opposition to Sāṃkhya that they wanted to distance themselves from Sāṃkhya, whose theory of knowledge resembles that of Advaita Vedānta closely.

Through reasoning, Sāṃkhya also arrives at the three-*guṇa* nature of *prakṛti*. It goes somewhat like this in *Sāṃkhyakārikā* 12: all worldly things possess some characteristics that "are capable of producing pleasure, pain, and indifference" (Sharma 1987, 153). These are *guṇas* or qualities of the mind in the wake of certain experiences; since logically all effects must share the characteristics of the cause (*prakṛti*) in some significant way, Sāṃkhya infers that *prakṛti* also is composed of the three *guṇas: sattva, rajas*, and *tamas*. (Sharma 1987, 153). One must understand these *guṇas* as being both physical and psychical from the way their products are described. They are also behind the evolution of psychic entities such as *mahat* (intelligence), ego, and mind. Though they are called *guṇas* (qualities), they are not qualities in the ordinary sense of the term. They are so called because "they by intertwining make a rope (*guṇa*) or forge a chain for binding the self [*puruṣa*]." Another explanation as to why they are called *guṇas* is because they "form a category" that is inferior (*gauṇa*) to *puruṣa* (Hiriyanna 1951, 271). These meanings, however, are derived from the etymological meaning of the word *guṇa* itself and need not necessarily indicate the actual character of their operations. In the end, the *guṇas* are viewed as intrinsically part of *prakṛti* and cannot be considered as separate entities.

2. *Śruti* and *smṛti* are also used frequently in the sense of direct perception and inference in the BS and BSBh (BS I.3.28; III.2.24; IV.4.20).

Among the *guṇas, sattva* represents whatever is luminous and light, *tamas* whatever is dark and heavy, and *rajas* activity. Thus, *prakṛti*, the primary cause, is viewed as constituted by the three *guṇas*, and all subsequent effects are also considered to contain the three *guṇas*. The difference in the effects is due to the preponderance of one or the other *guṇa*. The school believes that *prakṛti* is in constant motion and reproduces itself when the *guṇas* are in equilibrium, but when there is disequilibrium in the *guṇas*, evolution is set in motion. According to the *satkāryavāda*, then, there is nothing new created but what is potential comes into existence. The three *guṇa*s can be viewed as competing as well as cooperating with each other constantly. They are compared to the oil, the wick, and the flame of a lamp, which cooperate in order to produce light (SK 13). *Prakṛti* is both the material and efficient cause in Sāṃkhya as seen from the SK. Even though there is presence of the other eternal entity *puruṣa/puruṣas*, it has no active role in the emergence of the world.

From *prakṛti* evolve the twenty-three principles that constitute both the physical and psychological world. The first is *mahat* (intellect). Even though *mahat* is material, having arisen from *prakṛti*, the material reality, since it is composed of the finest *sattva guṇa* it is capable of reflecting the *puruṣa*, which alone is pure consciousness in the system. Knowledge/experience is explained through a psychic medium consisting of *mahat, ahaṃkāra* (ego), and *manas* (usually translated as "mind"). When this complex is affected by an object, external or internal, *mahat* itself assumes the image of the object in question and there is a modification of the intellect assisted by both the ego and the mind, called a *vṛtti*. This *vṛtti* is capable of receiving the reflection of *puruṣa* like a well-polished mirror, for instance, which can reflect one's face clearly. The intellect then becomes conscious and intelligent because of this reflection of *puruṣa*, which is known as knowledge/experience.

Mahat in turn gives rise to *ahaṃkāra*, the sense of individuality. Ahaṃkāra has a threefold evolution from its three aspects of *sattva, rajas*, and *tamas*. From the *sāttvika* aspect comes into being *manas*, the five sense-organs of knowledge (sound, touch, vision, taste, and smell), and the five sense-organs of action (speech, movement in the hands, movement in the feet, excretion, and reproduction). From the *tāmasika* aspect arise the subtle elements of sound, touch, taste, vision, and smell, which give rise to the gross elements. The *rājasika* aspect provides the energy for these combinations to come into being. All these *guṇas* also have their psychological/emotional side as good, indifferent, and passionate. Thus, a preponderance of *sattva* leads to good thoughts and deeds, *tamas guṇa* is indicative of dull and indifferent attitudes and deeds, and *rajas* generates the energy for bad deeds (see Sharma 1987). The evolution of *prakṛti* is to serve the purpose of each individual *puruṣa* and is thus teleological. *Prakṛti* can only stop evolving when all the *puruṣas* have attained liberation and thus, in a sense, is always evolving. *Puruṣa*, in its embodied existence, can be satisfied by *bhoga*, or ordinary everyday experiences, when it accumulates the results of its *karma* and keeps going around the circle of births and deaths. On the other hand, the real aim of *prakṛti* can also be to help each *puruṣa* attain its final liberation.

There is no satisfactory answer to what causes the initial disequilibrium in the three *guṇas* in order to set in motion the manifestation of the universe. Sāṃkhya tries some explanations, but they are not philosophically satisfying. The mere presence or proximity of *puruṣa* is supposed to trigger this change, but since *puruṣa* is also an eternally present reality and is omnipresent, there must always be disequilibrium in *prakṛti*. But if so, evolution must be a constant process without being able to accommodate the cyclical periods of evolution and dissolution that Sāṃkhya believes in. Since Sāṃkhya also admits many *puruṣas*, it is not clear which *puruṣa* will trigger this change. In order to circumvent these difficulties, some scholars have posited that the collective *karma* of all embodied *puruṣas* starts the process. But that is also not satisfactory. This is because the whole evolution of *prakṛti* has to be viewed as teleological and not mechanical, since it has the purpose of *puruṣas* realizing their true nature as distinct from *prakṛti*.

The fundamental postulate of Sāṃkhya is that life in the lived world is essentially painful. Even the so-called pleasures are eventually tinged with pain and therefore a wise person seeks eternal freedom from this misery. Since the *puruṣa* in its intrinsic nature is pure consciousness and suffers only because of its association with *prakṛti*, the attempt must be to attain insight into the difference between *puruṣa* and *prakṛti* through *viveka*, or discriminate discernment. The conception of *prakṛti* as without sentience and of *puruṣa* as without activity is compared to the analogy of a lame man sitting on the shoulder of a blind man; the blind one is *prakṛti* who has no sentience, while *puruṣa* is the lame one without activity but who has the ability to see/know. It is in *puruṣa*'s hands to use the evolutes of *prakṛti* either for pure enjoyment/worldly experience (*bhoga*) or for attaining final liberation (*apavarga*). What transmigrates is a subtle body composed of the intellect, sense of individuality, *manas* (mind), five knowledge senses, and five motor senses along with the five subtle elements and not the gross body. All past traces (*vāsanās*) of *karma* are stored in this subtle body until such time that it is cleansed of the wrong identity of *puruṣa* with *prakṛti*. Through perception, inference, and the testimony of Vedic utterances, one needs to cultivate the insight of the difference between *puruṣa* and *prakṛti*, which is a liberating insight; it can happen even in an embodied state. Sāṃkhya, however, does not lay down the methodology for acquiring this release except to state that it is by meditation on the truth of the difference between *puruṣa* and *prakṛti* (SK 64).

Philosophers in general find that this evolution of *prakṛti* for the sake of the individual *puruṣas* does not address the question of the transcendental self. As it stands, Sāṃkhya in the SK has reduced the ontological absolute to the phenomenal ego. Without the ontological dimension being taken into consideration, Sāṃkhya has only partially addressed the philosophical problem of the ultimate reality without finding an answer to it even partially. Hiriyanna argues that one can assume a cosmic *puruṣa* and "regard the whole process of evolution as presented to him [that cosmic *puruṣa*]" (1951, 286–287). Then *mahat* can be cosmic liberation and enlightenment in which the cosmic *puruṣa* is illumined and the next stage occurs; that is, "*ahaṃkāra* will stand for the sense of self-hood which arises in him ... [thus there can be] on the one hand the objective series and on the other the subjective series [i.e.] the apparatus of thought adapted to cognize it" (ibid.). This way of understanding Sāṃkhya can bring it closer to its own claim of being based on the *Upaniṣads*. According to Sharma, some of the proof for the existence of *puruṣa* in SK can only apply to a purely phenomenal self. As *puruṣa* is called the enjoyer and *prakṛti* the enjoyed, there is a fundamental flaw in positing enjoyment/experience in the transcendental *puruṣa*, who is never the enjoyer. *Puruṣa* is also never bound if it is ever free (1987, 167–168). Thus, Sāṃkhya of the SK, which is the earliest source we have for a systematic presentation of the Sāṃkhya school, fails to take this transcendental dimension into consideration.

Yoga

The basic *sūtra* text for Yoga is Patañjali's *Yogasūtras* (YS) and the commentary on it by Vyāsa. There are other important commentaries on both the *sūtra* text and Vyāsa's commentary, such as the *Tattvavaiśāradī* by Vācaspati Miśra (the same individual who wrote the Sāṃkhya commentary *Tattvakaumudī*), Bhoja's *Rājamārtāṇḍa* called the *Bhojavṛtti*, the *Yogavārttika* of Vijñānabhikṣu, and the *Yogasūtrabhāṣyavivaraṇa* of Śaṅkara (not Śaṅkara of Advaita fame).[3]

Yoga, like Sāṃkhya, starts with two ontological realities, *puruṣa/puruṣas* and *prakṛti*, and takes for granted the evolutes without enumerating them. However, it does not list the intellect, sense of individuality (*asmitā*, not *ahaṃkāra* here), and *manas* separately but subsumes them under the category of *citta* (mind-stuff), which is all-pervasive. It is this *citta* that helps in the acquisition of knowledge and also serves the function of the Sāṃkhyan subtle body for transmigration purposes. Yoga also believes in an Īśvara, not in the usual theistic sense, but as a special *puruṣa* (*puruṣa-viśeṣaḥ*) who is beyond the afflictions that affect ordinary *puruṣas*. This *puruṣa* in the YS has no role to play in the manifestation of the world, though later commentators such as Vijñānabhikṣu regard Īśvara as an efficient cause, going against the grain of Yoga as presented in the YS. While Sāṃkhya depends on a reflective process for gaining insight into the difference between *prakṛti* and *puruṣa*, Yoga relies on a transformation of the material body, mind, and intellect in order to receive that insight. "Yoga's principal concern is with purposeful strategies, both physical and psychological, to be employed in order to achieve the requisite reflective discernment" (Larson 2008, 51) (YS I.1). The state of liberation is also identified with what is known as seedless meditation or contentless meditation (*asaṃprajnāta/nirbīja-samādhi*) in Yoga, which is the last of the eight means described in the YS for liberation.

3. For probable dates consult Larson 1987.

The eightfold path of Patañjali's Yoga requires at its outset ethical practices called *yama*, which are nonviolence, truth, nonstealing, self-control, and nongreed, as well as external observances called *niyama*, which are described as cleanliness, contentment, reading sacred literature, austerities such as fasting, and meditation on Īśvara. These are followed by any posture that can help one to hold the body steadily and practice regulation of one's inhalation and exhalation of breath (*āsana* and *prāṇāyāma*). This is followed by withdrawing the mind from external objects (*pratyāhāra*), which leads to developing concentration on any mental object (*dhāraṇā*), which can then gradually lead to meditation on that same object (*dhyāna*), and finally to a state of oneness with the object (*saṃprajñāta-samādhi*), culminating in an objectless state of *samādhi* (*asaṃprajnāta-samādhi*). At this stage, there is a separation of *puruṣa* from the intellect, which is equivalent to *kaivalya* (liberation). "If we compare our common mental state to the ruffled surface of water in a lake which reflects an object like a tree on the bank as a distorted image, the *saṃprajnāta* [*samādhi* with content] may be likened to the calm surface containing a steady and faithful image of it and the *asaṃprajnāta* [contentless, *samādhi*] to the condition where the tree is by itself and there is no image at all for the lake has dried up" (Hiriyanna 1951, 296).

The eightfold process is dealt with in great detail in four chapters containing 195 *sūtras* in the YS. Describing the *citta* as having the five basic afflictions (*kleśa*)—ignorance (*avidyā*), I-sense (*asmitā*), attachment and hatred toward sense objects (*rāga* and *dveṣa*), and clinging to life (*abhiniveśa*)—everyday life is consumed with experiences through the modifications of the *citta* by knowing, misapprehension (*viparyaya*), constructed reality (*vikalpa*), sleep, and memory. The attempt is therefore to transform the basic three *guṇa-citta* into a predominantly *sattva* one with both *rajas* and *tamas* completely inhibited by a process of attenuating the five afflictions in which altered state it can realize its difference from the material reality with which it was confused earlier.

Ethics

Both Sāṃkhya and Yoga accept direct perception, inference, and Vedic testimony as guidance for correct action. Starting with the assumption that life in the world is full of pain (*duḥkha*), Sāṃkhya classifies pain in the world as of three kinds. The first is that caused by mental and bodily suffering; the second is due to natural causes such as men, beasts, and so forth; and the third is brought about by supernatural causes. However, in their scheme of prevention of these miseries they do not hesitate to condemn the practice of animal sacrifice prescribed in the Vedas. Their reasoning is that it is not conducive to *dharma*. Gauḍapāda, while commenting on SK 2, unequivocally states that even if the Vedas declare that *dharma* is acquired through animal sacrifice, it is still impure. Thus, the revealed means (Vedas and other sacred texts) and evident means for the removal of pain are both impure. It is only through an inquiry into the nature of the manifest (worldly phenomena), the unmanifest (*prakṛti*), and the knower (*puruṣa*) that the threefold misery can be finally eradicated. This is also corroborated in Vyāsa's rather elaborate commentaries on YS II.30 and II.33–34. Violence done by one, caused to be done by another, or approved when done by another are all unequivocally condemned by Vyāsa (see YS II.34). Other commentators on both the SK and the YS and YSBh are in agreement with the overall principle of *ahiṃsā* (nonviolence) being the highest ethical virtue mentioned in the first means to Yoga as *yama* (the set of ethical practices referred to earlier that must be followed by one who aspires to the eightfold path to enlightenment).

In a climate of philosophical apologetics where the prevalent norm of animal sacrifice was justified in a ritual context as nonviolence itself, even while condemning it unequivocally in a nonritual context, it was a courageous stand for Sāṃkhya/Yoga to take up and to condemn violence under all circumstances.

BIBLIOGRAPHY AND SUGGESTED READINGS

Bhattacharyya, Ramshankar. (1977) *Sānkyasūtram with Vijñānabhikṣu's commentary along with Jyotiṣmatī ṭīkā* (Hindi). Delhi: Bharatiya Vidya Prakashan.

Chakravarti, Pulinbihari. (1975) *Origin and Development of the Sāṃkhya System of Thought*. New Delhi: Oriental Books Reprint Corporation.

Halbfass, Wilhelm. (1991) *Tradition and Reflection*. New York: State University of New York Press.

Hiriyanna, M. (1951) *Outlines of Indian Philosophy*, second impression. London: George Allen and Unwin Ltd.

Larson, James Gerald, and Ram Shankar Bhattacharya (eds.). (1987). *Samkhya: A Dualist Tradition in Indian Philosophy*. Princeton, NJ: Princeton University Press.

———. (eds.). (2008) *Yoga: India's Philosophy of Meditation*. Delhi: Motilal Banarsidass.

Mainkar, T. G. (trans. with notes). (1964) *The Sāṃkhyākarikā of Īśvarakṛṣṇa with the commentary of Gauḍapāda*. Poona: Oriental Book Agency.

Miśra, Adyaprasād (trans.). (1966) *Sāṃkhyatattvakaumudī-Prabhā* (Hindi). Allahabad: Satya Prakashan.

Murty, K. Satchidananda (trans. with notes). (1986) *Ṣad-Darśana-Samuccaya by Haribhadra*, (revised ed.). Delhi: Suman Printers.

Rukmani, T. S. (trans. with notes). (1981–1989) *Yogavārttika of Vijñānabhikṣu*, Volumes I–IV. Delhi: Munshiram Manoharlal Pvt. Ltd.

———. (trans. with notes). (2001) *Yogasūtrabhāṣyavivaraṇa of Śankara*, Volumes I–II. Delhi: Munshiram Manoharlal Pvt. Ltd.

———. (1999) "Sāṃkhya and Yoga: Where They Do Not Speak in One Voice." In *Asiatische Studien Etudes Asiatiques*, LIII-3. Berlin: Peter Lang.

Sharma, Chandradhar. (1987, reprint 2003) *A Critical Survey of Indian Philosophy*, Delhi: Motiala Banarsidass.

CHAPTER 11

MĪMĀṂSĀ

DAN ARNOLD

Mīmāṃsā (more precisely, Pūrva Mīmāṃsā) names one of the six major Brahmanical schools of Indian philosophy. Its principal concern is with the interpretation and appropriate use of those Vedic texts that involve the performance of sacrificial rituals. The school is most familiar to philosophers for its influential contribution to epistemological discourse in India: the doctrine of the *svataḥ prāmāṇya* ("intrinsic reliability") of doxastic practices. In ways comparable to the approach of some contemporary proponents of "reformed epistemology," this view has it that the truth-conduciveness of doxastic practices cannot be demonstrated without epistemic circularity; hence, defeasible justification is all that our ways of knowing can yield. Along with the view that the Vedic texts are eternal and authorless, this epistemology is taken by proponents of Mīmāṃsā ("Mīmāṃsakas") to support their claims about the uniquely authoritative status of the Vedas. Reflecting this epistemic deference to a body of texts, Mīmāṃsakas typically upheld a robust form of linguistic realism (particularly opposed to nominalist Buddhist views). The more significant influence of the school was thus in the areas of hermeneutics and philosophy of language. The characteristic atheism of Mīmāṃsā was among the points that put its proponents at odds with some other Brahmanical philosophers.

The word "Mīmāṃsā" is a desiderative form of the verb √*man*, "to think," and thus means something like "close reflection." It typically names one of the main Brahmanical (or as many anthologies would have it, "orthodox") schools of thought in Indian philosophy. Properly speaking, the tradition of thought usually meant is *Pūrva* ("prior") Mīmāṃsā. This is in contrast to "*Uttara*," or "subsequent," Mīmāṃsā. Both strands of Mīmāṃsā have as their guiding concern the interpretation and right use of Vedic texts, which these schools agree in thinking to be uniquely authoritative for matters of ultimate concern. These schools differ chiefly over which portion of this vast corpus of texts should be thought definitive, for "Veda"—a scriptural category that is arguably definitive of "Hinduism"—represents a status traditionally claimed for a huge range of texts, composed over a large period of time (from c. 1200 BCE to early in the first millennium and even later), exemplifying a wide spectrum of literary genres and characteristic doctrines. Advocacy of the "Pūrva" Mīmāṃsā position involves commitment to the authority particularly of that portion of the Vedic corpus, culminating with the so-called *Brāhmaṇas*, that chiefly concerns the performance of ritual sacrifice (of the sort exemplified in Frits Staal's controversial but interesting film *Altar of Fire*). Hence, this school of thought was also well known as *Karma Mīmāṃsā* ("Mīmāṃsā regarding ritual action") and *Adhvara Mīmāṃsā* ("Mīmāṃsā regarding sacrifice"). Since *Uttara Mīmāṃsā* instead takes its bearings from that portion of the Vedic corpus (consisting of the *Upaniṣads*) that was traditionally styled "Vedānta" ("culmination of the Veda"), Uttara Mīmāṃsā is more popularly referred to by that name.

Just as texts in the many strata of the Vedic corpus mostly represent themselves somehow as commentaries on their predecessors, so, too, the philosophical tradition of Pūrva Mīmāṃsā (henceforth simply "Mīmāṃsā"), typically of the generally scholastic style of Indian philosophy, developed in the form of commentaries on the foundational texts of the tradition (and commentaries on the commentaries, etc.). Mīmāṃsakas thus take their bearings from the *Mīmāṃsā Sūtras* attributed to one Jaimini, who is thought to have flourished near the beginning of the first millennium CE. Typifying the "sūtra" genre of mnemonic concision, the first of Jaimini's aphorisms names "the desire to know *dharma*" (*dharmajijñāsā*) as the constitutive concern of Mīmāṃsā. Also typical of the genre, Jaimini's text is generally found intelligible only with reference to commentaries. The earliest of the completely available commentaries on Jaimini's sūtras is that of Śabara (fl. c. 400 CE), whose commentary (which quotes from some earlier commentaries that are no longer extant) defines the basic parameters of the tradition's unfolding. Mīmāṃsā then divides chiefly along two lines of further commentary on Śabara: those who take their bearings from Kumārila (c. 620–680 CE) are typically styled "Bhāṭṭas" (followers of Bhaṭṭa, as Kumārila is sometimes called), while those who defer to Prabhākara (fl. c. 700 CE) are similarly called "Prābhākaras." Like many general discussions of Mīmāṃsā, the present introduction is based chiefly on the works of Kumārila, the Mīmāṃsaka whom later Indian Buddhist philosophers, too, most often had in their sights.

As constitutively concerned with the understanding and proper use of Vedic texts, the Mīmāṃsā project raises issues especially in hermeneutics, philosophy of language, and epistemology. In regard to these, many of the hermeneutical tools that figure most centrally in later philosophy and poetics were first developed in Mīmāṃsā discourse. When faced, for example, with a Vedic text that seemed to enjoin two mutually exclusive ritual actions, Mīmāṃsakas had to establish criteria for resolving the tension. With such interpretive situations in view, Mīmāṃsakas argued—in ways that bring to mind Grice's ideas regarding conversational implicature—that one can know that a word or phrase is being used in a secondary sense if its primary sense makes the sentence incoherent or otherwise absurd. Again, Mīmāṃsakas gave careful consideration to the possibilities for difference in the scope of negation. Their recognition that there is a significant difference between, for example, "this is not a Brahmin" and "there is no Brahmin" would later be enlisted by some proponents of the Buddhist Madhyamaka school of thought.

At the same time, proponents of Mīmāṃsā also recognized that their project required arguing for the epistemic authority of the Vedic texts—for their status, as the Indian philosophical tradition characteristically puts it, as a *pramāṇa*, a valid "criterion" of knowledge (or, we might also say, a reliable doxastic practice). Mīmāṃsaka arguments in this regard advanced a case for epistemologically "realist" views very much like those characteristically elaborated by Thomas Reid (as also by contemporary "reformed epistemologists"). As direct realists in their epistemology, Mīmāṃsakas will have no truck with sense data and the like; what you see is what you get. "What you see," however, finally confers only defeasible justification, which is all we can coherently be taken to get from any of our epistemic practices.

On the view thus advocated by Mīmāṃsakas, we are justified in entertaining those beliefs that have not been falsified, but we can never finally *demonstrate* the veridicality of any awareness as such without epistemic circularity. This is because any such demonstration must itself depend on some awareness already taken to be veridical. Mīmāṃsakas framed their account in terms of the expression generally taken to name their epistemological position: *svataḥ prāmāṇya*. Just what is claimed by this expression depends largely on what we take "*prāmāṇya*" to mean. The word is a secondary derivative from the word *pramāṇa*, and therefore literally denotes secondary properties like "of or relating to *pramāṇa*" or "being a *pramāṇa*." Insofar, then, as the doctrine clearly concerns *epistemic* attributes, it may not be helpful to follow some modern interpretations in taking this to mean *truth*. Whatever the epistemic attributes in virtue of which *pramāṇas* are what they are (reliability, say, or credibility, or truth-conduciveness), though, Mīmāṃsakas claim they are somehow *intrinsic* (*svataḥ*) to any cognition's being a *pramāṇa*.

A cognition's being a *pramāṇa* cannot be thought to depend, then, on some other cognition, since that would in turn have to be taken as itself a *pramāṇa*. Thus, if one wants to know not whether some particular perception of a tree is veridical, but whether perception, as such, is a reliable way of knowing this, the answer cannot be that this is known based on something else. This is because the only thing such knowledge could be based on would be other *pramāṇas*, and whether these are reliable is just what we want to know in this case. More precisely, any attempt to *show* the reliability of perception will turn out already to presuppose its reliability. An appeal to the testimony of others, for example, would depend on the reliability of *their* perceptions, and any inference regarding this will eventually involve perceptually warranted premises. The status of a doxastic practice *as* the reliable practice it is cannot, then, be shown without epistemic circularity.

That being the case, however, it is not reasonable to think one is entitled to a belief only when one can *show* (by an appeal, presumably, to perception) that one is. With respect, then, to a stock example of a Vedic injunction (*svargakāmo yajeta*, "one desirous of heaven should perform the sacrifice"), Mīmāṃsakas would respond to demands for the justification of the claims implicit therein (*show* me someone going to heaven!) with the claim that one is entitled to the beliefs so long as they have not been falsified or otherwise overridden; that is all the more justification one can have even based on perception. Since, then, someone's *not* going to heaven is also not seen, the commitments implicit in the Vedic injunction are not shown by an appeal to perception to be unjustified. (If defeasible justification seems like settling for less, proponents of this epistemology can ask whether it could make sense to want anything more than that; what could it look like, epistemically, not only to be *justified* in holding a belief, but also to know it is *true?* This is already just what one is entitled to think in virtue of being justified.)

One might respond that the case of knowing something based on a Vedic text is not analogous to that of knowing something perceptually; indeed, one might argue that what the argument from epistemic circularity shows is that it is just *perception* that is presupposed by any account of the reliability of our doxastic practices, and that perception should therefore be reckoned, uniquely, as epistemically basic. Against this, the Mīmāṃsakas enlist arguments that reveal a very strong commitment to the reality and power of language. Specifically, proponents of this school think we have good reason to take authoritative testimony to make at least as strong a claim on us as sense perception does. On this view, there is a significant sense in which it is right to say that Vedic injunctions really do *engender* justified beliefs—and this insofar as language is finally one of the most "real" things there are.

The strong linguistic realism of Mīmāṃsā relates closely to another of the commitments that figure centrally in the deployment of the doctrine of *svataḥ prāmāṇya* to warrant the authoritative status of the Vedas. The characteristically Mīmāṃsaka epistemology is held, then, together with a commitment to the view that the Vedas are authorless and eternal—*apauruṣeya* ("not of persons"), as Mīmāṃsakas typically say. This view, along with certain ideas about how linguistic knowing generally works, is taken by Mīmāṃsakas to mean that the Vedic texts, uniquely among valid criteria of knowledge (*pramāṇas*), are not subject to falsification (indeed, that they never *can* be falsified); for insofar as there is no agent whose intention could be thought to be expressed by the Vedas, there is no basis for the kinds of faults with a speaker (e.g., mendacity, epistemic deficiency) that could falsify the beliefs these texts engender.

If Vedic injunctions (and all that they entail) thus cannot be falsified by faults with the author whose intention they express, they cannot be falsified by any other *pramāṇas*, either. This is because the other *pramāṇas* are all ultimately parasitic on sensory perception, and Vedic texts essentially bear on something constitutively inaccessible to perception. Specifically, as Jaimini's first sūtra has told us, they have to do with *dharma*, which is defined at one point in Śabara's commentary simply as "what connects a person with the highest good." To the extent that Vedic injunctions are paradigmatically exemplified by *svargakāmo yajeta* ("one desirous of heaven should perform the sacrifice"), *dharma*'s inaccessibility to perception could be taken as a function of its having to do with the alleged postmortem (or otherwise supersensible) results of ritual action. This would not be altogether misleading, since it is indeed characteristic of Mīmāṃsā not to share the generally Indian preoccupation with an axiological framework centrally involving "release" (*mokṣa*) from *saṃsāra*, but rather, to hold that what we should want (and what proper Vedic practice will yield) is more of the same *kinds* of good things we typically want—material prosperity, progeny, continued existence.

There is, however, a more nuanced and metaphysically general view of *dharma*, considered as what proper Vedic practice is concerned to cultivate or realize, that finds expression in some characteristically Mīmāṃsaka hermeneutical principles. On this view, the salient point about *dharma* is that it is never already "existent" (*bhūtam*), but always "yet to be realized" (*bhaviṣyat*, "going to be"). Insofar as they centrally concern *dharma*, then, Vedic injunctions (*codanā*)—which for Mīmāṃsakas represent the primary unit of Vedic text—essentially enjoin the ongoing *bringing into being* of a ritual world that must continually be renewed. Indeed, the Vedic picture here involves the idea that the world itself is sustained by Vedic sacrifice. Seen this way, the *dharma* that Mīmāṃsā constitutively concerns is not chiefly a matter of individual gain; rather, the person of the sacrificer himself becomes merely instrumental to the larger ritual act that is itself the real locus of significance. *Dharma* is not perceptible, then, insofar as never yet fully realized, never (as Heidegger might say) "ready-to-hand." On the hermeneutical principle related to this point, reference in a sentence to something *bhūtam*, "already existent," should always be understood as subordinate to whatever state of affairs the sentence says or implies is *bhavya*, "to be realized."

While perception constitutively bears only on presently sensible existents, then, Mīmāṃsakas urged that language is unique in its capacity to give us knowledge concerning states of affairs that are not available to sense perception—and *dharma*, as always *yet to be realized* (*bhaviṣyat*, *bhavya*), paradigmatically involves such states of affairs. The Vedic text, in particular, is authoritative with regard to matters that thus transcend individual epistemic perspectives just insofar as it is held by Mīmāṃsakas to be authorless and eternal. Among the Mīmāṃsakas' intuitions here is that only *language itself*, as abstract and universal in character, can inform us of things essentially unavailable to a single epistemic agent. (That Mīmāṃsakas argued strenuously against Buddhist and Jaina claims about the possible cultivation of omniscience reflects the stake they thus had in denying that there could be an epistemic perspective that somehow takes in everything; language, in contrast to such individual knowers as the Buddha and the Jina, is not itself a limiting perspective.)

Given the Mīmāṃsaka view that the linguistic artifact that is the Vedic text is eternal, it must also be true that language as such is eternal. Proponents of Mīmāṃsā were thus committed to an unusually thoroughgoing realism about linguistic universals. Arguing that the very *relation* between language and nonlinguistic fact is primordial, Mīmāṃsakas challenged (chiefly Buddhist and Nyāya) proponents of contract- or convention-theories of linguistic origins to explain how any *particular* linguistic act could coherently be imagined to be the *first* such act. The problem is that any particular linguistic act is intelligible *as* a linguistic act only given the prior understanding that the meaning-creating utterance itself *means* something. One person could, that is, propose to another that this thing here be called a "cow" only by *telling* her so—but the possibility of his doing so is just what we want to understand. Language, Mīmāṃsakas argue, must therefore be eternally available as a condition of the possibility of there being any particular speech acts. (The same argument—familiar to readers of Herder's *Essay on the Origin of Language*—was also defended by Indian philosophers in the tradition of the so-called grammarians. A strikingly similar argument is deployed by the cognitive-scientific philosopher Jerry Fodor, who urges that this kind of regress can only be stopped by positing the sort of neuropsychological capacities that he figuratively refers to as a "language of thought." Fodor agrees, to that extent, that our coming to know a language is intelligible only given our already having one.)

It should not be surprising, given this strong view about the reality of language, that Mīmāṃsakas were characteristically realists about such linguistic universals as *concepts*. This comes through in the context of Mīmāṃsā epistemology, which commonly holds that *perceptions*, properly speaking, yield justified beliefs regarding things *as* the kinds of things they are. Buddhist philosophers were the principal adversaries of the Mīmāṃsakas in this regard, as an influential Buddhist line of argument has it that perception is constitutively *non* conceptual. Against such arguments, Mīmāṃsakas urged that one perceives, for example, not only this particular bovine critter, but the fact of its instantiating *go-tva*, the property of "being a cow"; this is what it means to perceive it *as a cow*. Universals are thus among the things perceived since they are, for Mīmāṃsakas, real. Among the arguments for this is one based on the *svataḥ prāmāṇya* doctrine sketched above; it's not right to say that the property of "being a cow" is not real since there is nothing that finally falsifies our valid cognitions of things as exemplifying this property. Hence, the belief that such general properties as "being a cow" are real is justified.

Mīmāṃsaka arguments for the reality of linguistic universals were particularly developed against Buddhist interlocutors, whose *apoha* ("exclusion") account of semantics is not unreasonably characterized as strongly nominalist. Buddhist proponents of *apoha* characteristically argued that the content of a concept could be explained simply in terms of its exclusion-range ("cow" refers to "whatever is not a *non*-cow"), and that one therefore need not posit a real universal (either intensional or extensional) as its content. Proponents of Mīmāṃsā argued that this account was circular, and ultimately presupposes precisely the kinds of universals it claims to explain; for we can only know *what to exclude* in any case given some idea of sameness—can only know what is a *non*-cow if we already know what a *cow* is. As an alternative, Mīmāṃsakas held a complex view of universals as related to individuals or particulars. Mīmāṃsakas like Kumārila refused the characteristically Nyāya claim that universals exemplify the relation of "inherence" (*samavāya*) in their tokens, on the grounds that thus positing an intermediary category to do the work of *relating* the two different kinds of things just opens up an infinite regress. (We can always ask how this property of "inherence" is itself related to these relata.) Mīmāṃsakas instead held that "universal" and "particular" simply represent different aspects of the same things.

These issues are in play when it is asked how some particular utterance of a word can be said to be the utterance *of a universal*, when the "word" *exists* only for as long as the utterance lasts. Mīmāṃsakas characteristically explain that any particular utterance "manifests" an enduring linguistic relation that must be in play if we are even to say that any two utterances might count as utterances *of the same word*. The question of what is being argued here is complicated by the fact that the Sanskrit word here translated as "word" (*śabda*) is ambiguous—it refers both to *language*, as such (described, that is, in the synchronic kinds of terms that characterize what the structural linguist Saussure distinguished as *langue*), and to "sound" or "noise" (hence, one might suppose, to the particular acoustic events that are speech acts—what Saussure called *parole*). If, with the former idea in mind, one considers the Mīmāṃsakas' arguments as meant to show the ineliminable reality of linguistic abstractions, then one of the stock Buddhist counterarguments (that *śabda* is impermanent just insofar as it is produced on particular occasions) seems rather to miss the point; if, in contrast, the Mīmāṃsakas' arguments are read as meant to show the permanence of *uttered phonemes*, then the Buddhist objection may have more purchase. To further complicate the issue, some Mīmāṃsakas held that *śabda* in *both* senses is eternal—that what must be part of a final ontology is not only, say, the kinds of conceptual items that must figure in any intentional characterization of experience, but also the relation of those to particular sounds. (This view relates to some characteristically Vedic ideas, centering on that of *mantra*, about the inherent power not only of language in general, but of correctly pronounced Sanskrit in particular.)

The Mīmāṃsā commitment to the eternality of language in general (and that of the Vedic texts in particular) was thought by most Mīmāṃsakas to commit them to arguing against the existence of God (insofar as God, or *īśvara*, is conceived as the eternal agent who created the universe; reference to the characteristically Vedic pantheon is of course allowed to figure in Mīmāṃsā practice). Mīmāṃsakas thus realized that language could not be as metaphysically basic as their system requires if it can itself be explained as created by a God who would therefore be metaphysically prior. (Some proponents of the Brahmanical Nyāya school of philosophy enlisted something very much like the Mīmāṃsaka argument for the eternality of language in service of the conclusion that *God* must have created it; this argument thus credits the Mīmāṃsaka claim that an infinite regress will ensue if we posit some particular speech act as first, and differs only in taking God as reasonably terminating the regress.) Precisely in the course, then, of arguing for the eternality of linguistic relations, Mīmāṃsakas such as Kumārila advanced several arguments against the coherence of theism. Interestingly, many of these arguments—such as that the very idea of God's having a *desire* to create could only reflect a deficiency on God's part—were essentially similar to atheistic arguments made by Buddhist philosophers.

For the theistic Nyāya philosopher Jayanta Bhaṭṭa (who likely flourished in the late ninth century), the atheism entailed by characteristically Mīmāṃsaka commitments shows that many Mīmāṃsaka arguments need to be reversed, and that there are specific limits of properly Mīmāṃsaka concern. Jayanta, a Naiyāyika devotee of Śiva, held that the authoritative status of the Vedas must finally involve its having been authored by God. Thus, it is chief among the tasks of Jayanta's monumental *Nyāyamañjari* to argue that Nyāya, not Mīmāṃsā, represents the definitive defense of Vedic authority. Mīmāṃsā, in contrast, should be thought paramount only in matters of hermeneutics—which is, after all, what Mīmāṃsakas themselves were all along chiefly concerned to address.

Other important Indian philosophers who influentially engaged Mīmāṃsā include the Buddhists Śāntarakṣita (died 788 CE) and his pupil Kamalaśīla (died 795 CE). The former's massive *Tattvasaṃgraha*, together with the commentary of the latter, contains lengthy sections purportedly refuting such Mīmāṃsaka doctrines as (especially) *svataḥ prāmāṇya*. (Śāntarakṣita's engagement with this doctrine preserves many quotations from a no-longer-extant work of Kumārila's, and thus represents an important source for the study of Mīmāṃsā.) In thinking through the Mīmāṃsā positions, these Buddhists had available to them the texts of Śabara and Kumārila, the latter with the commentary of one Bhaṭṭa Uṃveka (fl. c. 710 CE). Like the later commentaries of Sucaritamiśra (fl. c. 1120 CE) and Pārthasārathimiśra (fl. c. 1075 CE), this often frames Kumārila's thought against that of the Buddhist Dharmakīrti (c. 600–660 CE); Kumārila himself had often targeted Dharmakīrti's predecessor Dignāga (c. 480–540 CE). The close relationship between "Pūrva" and "Uttara" Mīmāṃsā is reflected in the career of Maṇḍaṇamiśra (fl. c. 690 CE), who wrote significant works from both points of view. The polemical character of the long-debated relationship between these broad streams of "Mīmāṃsā" is evident in the work of Appayya Dīkṣita (fl. late sixteenth century), who challenged the idea that "Pūrva" and "Uttara" Mīmāṃsā (i.e., Vedānta) should be thought to exemplify a single school of thought.

While Mīmāṃsā epistemology and metaphysics thus contributed to rich Indian philosophical debates concerning such questions as the nature and status of *pramāṇas*, the conceptual character of perception, and the reality of linguistic universals, the most pervasive influence of the school is probably on such constitutively hermeneutical discourses as law and (perhaps especially) poetics. This is perhaps not surprising, given that Mīmāṃsā is not only a school of thought fundamentally concerned to elaborate principles of hermeneutics, but also one more generally committed to the view that thought and language are about things in a real world—that *what there is* (namely, relatively enduring tokens of such recognizable types as cows and pots and selves) is pretty much what language leads us to expect.

BIBLIOGRAPHY AND SUGGESTED READINGS

Arnold, Dan. (2005) *Buddhists, Brahmins, and Belief: Epistemology in South Asian Philosophy of Religion*. New York: Columbia University Press.

Bhatt, G. P. (1962) *Epistemology of the Bhāṭṭa School of Pūrva Mīmāṃsā*. Varanasi: Chowkhamba Sanskrit Series Office.

Clooney, Francis X. (1990) *Thinking Ritually: Rediscovering the Pūrva Mīmāṃsā of Jaimini*. Vienna: Institut für Indologie der Universität Wien.

Jha, Ganganath. (1964) *Pūrva-Mīmāṃsā in Its Sources*. Varanasi: Banaras Hindu University Press.
———. (1978) *The Prābhākara School of Pūrva Mīmāṃsā*. Delhi: Motilal Banarsidass.
Matilal, B. K. (1990) *The Word and the World: India's Contribution to the Study of Language*. New Delhi: Oxford University Press.
———. (2005) *Epistemology, Logic, and Grammar in Indian Philosophical Analysis*. New Delhi: Oxford University Press.
McCrea, Lawrence. (2000) "The Hierarchical Organization of Language in Mīmāṃsā Interpretive Theory." *Journal of Indian Philosophy* 28, 429–459.
Pollock, Sheldon. (1989) "Mīmāṃsā and the Problem of History in Traditional India." *Journal of the American Oriental Society* 109/4, 603–610.
———. (2004) "The Meaning of *Dharma* and the Relationship of the Two Mīmāṃsās: Appayya Dīkṣita's 'Discourse on the Refutation of a Unified Knowledge System of Pūrvamīmāṃsā and Uttaramīmāṃsā." *Journal of Indian Philosophy* 32, 769–811.
Taber, John. (1992) "What Did Kumārila Bhaṭṭa Mean by *Svataḥ Prāmāṇya?*" *Journal of the American Oriental Society* 112(3–4), 204–221.
———. (2005) *A Hindu Critique of Buddhist Epistemology: Kumārila on Perception*. New York: Routledge Curzon.

CHAPTER 12

VEDĀNTA

JOHN TABER

Vedānta refers to the collection of schools of Indian Brahmanical (Hindu) thought devoted to expounding the metaphysical and spiritual teachings of the Upaniṣads. The Upaniṣads, the oldest of which were composed approximately 800 to 500 BCE, are said to comprise the end (*anta*) of the Veda, coming last in the usual arrangement of Vedic texts, hence the term "Vedānta" (*veda-anta*). In addition to the Upaniṣads, the *Bhagavad Gītā* and the *Brahmasūtra* (or *Vedāntasūtra*)—a collection of about 550 short statements (*sūtras*) summarizing the doctrines of the Upaniṣads—are considered the three "foundations" (*prasthānas*) of Vedānta. Much of the literature of each school consists of commentaries and subcommentaries on these texts. The *Brahmasūtra* (BS), however, which was composed 200 to 400 CE and is ascribed to Bādarāyaṇa, is regarded as the authoritative exposition of the system. Yet the ambiguous nature of the *sūtras* allows for widely divergent interpretations. Over time quite different Vedānta philosophies evolved, typically distinguished in terms of their positions regarding the relation of the Absolute—Brahman—to the world.

Advaita Vedānta, the school of Absolute Nondualism, holds that reality consists of just one entity, Brahman, which is completely devoid of "difference" (*bheda*)—parts, divisions, or attributes—and change. Hence, it is strictly ineffable and indescribable; one may characterize it only by saying that it is in its essence Being, Consciousness, and Bliss (*sac-cid-ānanda*). All the diverse phenomena of the experienced world, including individual selves and bodies, are merely an illusion (*māyā*) appearing in (or projected on) Brahman. Taking the Upaniṣadic declaration "That thou art" literally, Advaita holds that, despite appearances, everything is in fact numerically identical with Brahman. The so-called Bhedābheda—Identity-in-Difference—school of Vedānta, on the other hand, while agreeing that Brahman is the only thing that exists, stops short of saying that it is devoid of difference and change. Rather, Brahman transforms itself into the diverse phenomena of the experienced world, which constitute its parts. Brahman is both one and many, like a tree with many leaves, roots, and branches; it is both the same as and different from the world, like the ocean and its waves.

Viśiṣṭa Advaita Vedānta or the Qualified Nondualism school conceives of Brahman as God, who in the religious circles in which this school developed is identified as Viṣṇu, the deity who appears as Kṛṣṇa in the *Bhagavad Gītā*. Although still one, Brahman is not featureless and impersonal. Rather, it or He is endowed with many powers and auspicious qualities: omniscience, omnipotence, benevolence, and so forth. Individual souls and the natural world are different from God but cannot exist separately from Him. God is related to them as a substance is to its attributes, or the soul to the body. (God is "the soul of the soul.") Finally, in Dvaita or Dualistic Vedānta, Brahman, again conceived as Viṣṇu, is quite separate from His creation, which nevertheless owes its existence to His Will or Grace.

It may seem strange that so many conflicting views could be based on a single body of texts. The Upaniṣads themselves, however, are by no means consistent at first glance; in fact, they contain the philosophical and ritualistic speculations of diverse Vedic communities. While their main thrust is clearly monistic (in many different passages it is asserted that Brahman is the only reality and is one) and idealistic (Brahman is also conceived as spirit), there are also many statements that ascribe personal characteristics to Brahman: it is "the Lord" (Īśa or Īśvara), "the inner controller" (*antaryāmin*) of everything, and so forth. Depending on which statements one takes literally, and which figuratively, one may arrive at vastly different views of reality. Each school developed its ideas, over many generations, with great dialectical and hermeneutical sophistication. The arguments for each system are so well crafted and polished that it is difficult to adjudicate them. Not the least interesting aspect of Vedānta is its discussion of the principles of scriptural exegesis, which it took over from Pūrva-Mīmāṃsā, the Vedic science concerned with the interpretation of sacrificial texts. Indeed, Vedānta is often referred to as "the later Mīmāṃsā" (Uttara Mīmāṃsā; *mīmāṃsā* is an analytic investigation), that is, the study of the Upaniṣads, which is supposed to follow upon "the prior Mīmāṃsā" (Pūrva Mīmāṃsā), that is, the study of the Brāhmaṇas (the Vedic texts concerned with mythical and symbolic interpretations of the Vedic sacrifice).[1] Vedānta philosophy, especially Advaita, had a profound influence on other Indian philosophical traditions, including the "Word Monism" (Śabda Advaita) of the Grammarian school, Śaiva Siddhānta, and Kāśmīrī Śaivism (whose most outstanding figure was the great eleventh-century thinker Abhinavagupta).

1. See Arnold in this volume.

Vedānta Literature

The *Brahmasūtra* Commentary (*Brahmasūtrabhāṣya,* BSBh) of Śaṅkara (commonly known as Śaṅkarācārya, also Śaṅkarabhavatpāda, early eighth century) is the oldest extant commentary on the BS and forms, together with Śaṅkara's commentaries on individual Upaniṣads and the *Bhagavad Gītā,* the starting point of systematic Vedānta philosophy. (Śaṅkara also authored an independent treatise, the *Upadeśasāhasrī,* and probably also a commentary on the *Yogasūtrabhāṣya.* These, together with his commentaries on the three *prasthānas,* comprise his known works. Many others of undetermined authenticity are attributed to him.) Two other Vedānta treatises prior to Śaṅkara's works have come down to us: the *Vākyapadīya* of Bhartṛhari (fifth century) and the *Āgamaśāstra* of Gaudapāḍa (seventh century). The former, an investigation into problems of philosophy of language, which is part of Vyākaraṇa, the ancient Indian science of grammar, identifies Brahman as the primordial "Word" (*śabda*), which gives rise to the world through its myriad "potencies" (*śakti*) of sound and meaning. The latter, which is ascribed to Śaṅkara's *paramaguru,* the teacher of his teacher, is noted for making extensive use of Buddhist arguments and vocabulary to demonstrate the unreality of causation and change and the reality of unchanging, nondual consciousness. The views of other ancient precursors of Śaṅkara whose dates cannot be determined and whose writings are now lost or preserved only in fragments are mentioned, and sometimes criticized, by Śaṅkara and his successors: Bhartṛtprapañca (a leading proponent of the Bhedābheda view), Upavarṣa, Baudhāyana, and Taṅka or Brahmanandin. Other ancient authorities of Vedānta and (Pūrva) Mīmāṃsā are mentioned in the *Brahmasūtra* itself: Bādarāyaṇa, Auḍulomi, Kāśakṛtsna, Bādari, Āśmarathya, and Jaimini. (Although Bādarāyaṇa and Jaimini are identified by classical Vedāntins as the authors of the *Brahmasūtra* and the *Mīmāṃsāsūtra* [the foundational text of the Pūrva Mīmāṃsā], respectively, both are cited in both treatises. It seems likely that the BS and the *Mīmāṃsāsūtra* are compilations of the teachings of numerous ancient experts, among whom Bādarāyaṇa and Jaimini loomed large.) Thus, Vedānta thought has a rich, though primarily reconstructed, history prior to Śaṅkara.

Another major Vedānta author roughly contemporaneous with Śaṅkara, Maṇḍanamiśra, expounded Advaita relying less on scriptural exegesis and more on independent reasoning, offering formulations of its doctrines attuned to contemporary epistemological theories. In the second part of his *Brahmasiddhi* he attempts to show that none of the recognized means of knowledge (*pramāṇas*), in particular, perception and inference, is able to establish that the world consists of discrete objects differing from each other in nature or even location in time and space, thereby defending the scriptural (Upaniṣadic) view of reality as nondual.

Much of Advaita literature after Śaṅkara consists of commentaries and subcommentaries on his works, especially his *Brahmasūtrabhāṣya.* Sureśvara, his immediate successor and, by tradition, his direct disciple, wrote commentaries on Śaṅkara's commentaries on the *Taittirīya* and *Bṛhadāraṇyaka* Upaniṣads. His

Bṛhadāraṇyakabhāṣyavārttika runs to over 11,000 verses! He also composed the *Naiṣkarymayasiddhi,* an independent treatise that, among other things, criticizes the views of Maṇḍanamiśra. Another reputed disciple of Śaṅkara, Padmapāda, composed the *Pañcapādikā,* intended as a commentary on Śaṅkara's commentary on the first five *sūtras* of the BS but preserved only through the fourth *sūtra.* An important commentary on this work in turn, the *Pañcapādikāvivaraṇa* by Prakāśātman (tenth century), defined one of the two main tendencies of interpretation of Śaṅkara's system, the so-called Vivaraṇa school. The other main tendency, the Bhāmatī school, began with Vācaspatimiśra's (ninth century) *Bhāmatī* subcommentary on Śaṅkara's *Brahmasūtrabhāṣya.* Other important early Advaita authors and their principal works were *Sarvajñātman* (ninth century, *Saṅkṣepaśārīraka*), Vimuktātman (tenth century, *Īṣṭasiddhi*), Śrīharṣa (twelfth century, *Khaṇḍanakhaṇḍakhādya;* this work uses *reductio*-type arguments to refute definitions of the *pramāṇas* and other categories of realist metaphysics), and Citsukha (thirteenth century, *Tattvapradīpikā*). Prominent authors of the later period were Vidyāraṇya (fourteenth century, *Jīvanmuktiviveka, Pañcadaśī*), Madhusūdhana Sarasvatī (sixteenth century, *Advaitasiddhi*), and Appaya Dīkṣita (sixteenth century, *Siddhāntaleśasaġraha*). The *Vedāntaparibhāṣā* of Dharmarāja (also sixteenth century) together with its many commentaries serves today in India as a standard introduction to Advaita Vedānta for beginning students.

The oldest preserved works of Viśiṣṭa Advaita literature are those of Yāmunācārya (eleventh century), though the school identifies three preceptors prior to Yāmuna, beginning with Nāthamuni. In his *Āgamaprāmāṇya,* Yāmuna defends the authority of the Pañcarātra Āgama, an extensive collection of Vaiṣṇava tantric texts. Viśiṣṭa Advaita in effect systematizes the theology of the Śrī Vaiṣṇava religious sect of South India, which combined popular devotion to Viṣṇu with Vedic teachings and practices. Yāmuna's *Siddhitraya,* "Three Demonstrations," includes an *Ātmasiddhi,* demonstration of the existence of an individual self; an *Īśvarasiddhi,* demonstration of the existence of God; and a *Saṃvitsiddhi,* demonstration of the reality of the sensible world. It was Rāmānuja (twelfth century), however, who gave definitive shape to the system in his commentary on the BS, known as the *Śrībhāṣya.* This work rivals Śaṅkara's *Brahmasūtra* commentary in scope and profundity. Other important works of Rāmānuja are a *Bhagavad Gītā* commentary, the *Vedārthasaṅgraha,* and the *Vedāntasāra.* The most important of the numerous subcommentaries on the *Śrībhāṣya* is the *Śrutaprakāśikā* of Sudarśana Sūri (fourteenth century). Perhaps the most famous post-Rāmānuja Viśiṣṭa Advaita figure was the prolific Veṇkaṭanātha or Vedānta Deśika (fourteenth century), who also composed a *Śrībhāṣya* subcommentary among many other works.

Dvaita Vedānta literature begins with the writings of Madhva or Madhvācārya (twelfth century). Many titles are ascribed to him, including commentaries on the *Bhagavad Gītā,* various Upaniṣads, the *Bhāgavata Purāṇa, Mahābhārata,* and even the *Ṛg Veda,* as well as numerous independent treatises. As in other Vedānta schools, the interpretation of the BS was of particular importance. Madhva wrote four works on the BS: a longer *Brahmasūtrabhāṣya;* an *Anubhāṣya* ("Supplementary

Commentary") in thirty-four verses; the *Nyāyavivaraṇa,* a summary of the topics and arguments of the BS in prose; and the *Anuvyākhyāna,* another more extensive, critical exposition, which is considered Madhva's *magnum opus.* In these works he vigorously attacks the interpretations of Śaṅkara. A subcommentary on the *Anuvyākhyāna* by Jayatīrtha (thirteenth century), the *Nyāyasudhā,* is another foundational work of the school, which polemically engages later Advaita thinkers. Other prominent Dvaita dialecticians were Viṣṇudāsa (fifteenth century, *Vādaratnāvalī*) and Vyāsatīrtha (sixteenth century, *Nyāyāmṛta, Tarkatāṇḍava*).

The Identity-in-Difference (Bhedābheda) school of Vedānta was overshadowed by the others, but an early commentary on the BS by Bhāskara, perhaps Śaṅkara's younger contemporary, was written from this perspective. Much later the Bhedābheda doctrine was revived by Nimbārka (probably fourteenth century), who also identified Brahman as Kṛṣṇa-Viṣṇu. Another influential theistic version of Vedānta that has affinities with the *bhedābheda-vāda* is the so-called Śuddhādvaita system of Vallabhācārya (sixteenth century), who was founder of a sect of Kṛṣṇa worship known as the Puṣṭimārga.

Advaita Vedānta

The main thesis of the system of Advaita Vedānta is that what the Upaniṣads identify as reality—Brahman—is one in every sense. It is the only reality, and it is perfectly one in nature, that is, without "difference"—divisions, parts, or attributes. Passages such as *Muṇḍaka Upaniṣad* 2.2.11: "It is Brahman alone that extends over this whole universe"; *Chāndogya Upaniṣad* (ChU) 6.2.1: "In the beginning... this world was simply the existent—one only, without a second"; *Bṛhadāraṇyaka Upaniṣad* (BĀU) 2.4.6: "All these—the priestly power, the royal power, worlds, gods, beings, the whole—all that is nothing but this self"; and BĀU 4.4.19: "From death to death goes he who sees any diversity here,"[2] are taken as proof texts for this view. Brahman also does not undergo change in any way. Yet it is the cause of this diverse world—this is taken to be asserted by BS 1.1.3: "It is that from which the origin [subsistence and dissolution] of this [world] proceed"—and, according to the *satkārya-vāda,* the doctrine of "the [pre-] existence of the effect in its cause," which Śaṅkara adopted from Sāmkhya philosophy and understood to entail the *continued identity* of cause and effect after the latter's emergence, the world is identical with Brahman. The incongruity of the complete identity of two things contradictory in nature, one devoid of difference and change (Brahman), the other endowed with them (the world), is possible insofar as one of them is *not real.* Indeed, allegedly according to another text, ChU 6.1.4, "It is like this... By means of just one lump of

2. Passages from the Upaniṣads are cited according to Olivelle 1996.

clay one would perceive everything made of clay—the transformation [into a pot, etc.] is a verbal expression, a name, while the reality is just this: 'It is clay!,'" the world that arises, as it were, out of Brahman is an illusion. The world, thus, is the *same thing* as Brahman and does not exist apart from it, in the same way an imaginary snake is nothing other than the rope one mistakes it for. This illusion is due simply to ignorance (*avidyā*) of Brahman as the reality of the universe, including one's own self, just as the illusion of the snake is due simply to failing to see that it is really a rope. The world can thus be said to be an *illusory* transformation (*vivarta*) of Brahman. The notion that the world is a *real* transformation (*pariṇāma*) of it is associated with the Bhedābheda doctrine and is considered incompatible with the orthodox Advaita teaching of Śaṅkara.

The Upaniṣads also declare the nature of Brahman to be consciousness, as well as being and, less explicitly, bliss. Śaṅkara and later Advaitins put the emphasis on consciousness. (Maṇḍanamiśra, interestingly, emphasizes bliss.) Thus, *Taittirīya Upaniṣad* 2.1: "He who knows Brahman as truth, knowledge, and infinite... he obtains all desires." That is to say, Brahman is pure consciousness, "a mass of consciousness" as stated at BĀU 2.4.12. Its consciousness is not its property as a knowing subject but what it *is*. Since its consciousness does not involve any distinction of subject and object—"For when there is duality of some kind, then the one can smell the other, the one can see the other, the one can hear the other.... When, however, the Whole has become one's very self, then who is there for one to smell and by what means....?" (BĀU 2.4.14)—the term "consciousness" is applied to it only figuratively, not literally. In truth, Brahman is "unqualified" (*nirviśeṣa*), devoid of all attributes; it is indescribable and unthinkable. The most precise characterization of it, according to Śaṅkara, was made by the Upaniṣadic sage Yājñavalkya: "About this self, one can only say 'Not, not'" (BĀU 3.9.26). And yet there are indeed also passages that depict Brahman as the Supreme Being, the efficient cause of the universe, endowed with omniscience, grace, and so forth. Such texts, however, according to Advaita, present Brahman only under the aspect of ignorance (*avidyā*). As Śaṅkara explains in a key passage of his *Brahmasūtra* commentary, "The Lord's being a Lord, his omniscience, his omnipotence, etc., all depend on the limitation [of his/its nature] due to adjuncts [such as a divine intellect and body] of the nature of *avidyā*, while in reality none of these qualities belong to the self, whose true nature is cleansed, by means of knowledge, of all adjuncts whatsoever" (BSBh 2.1.14).[3]

Although Brahman, then, is only in a manner of speaking "cause" (or Creator) of the universe, since the latter is really illusory—moreover, as seen, Brahman's status as Creator is illusory—nevertheless Advaita Vedānta, in identifying *consciousness* as the "cause," as it were, sharply distinguishes itself from other realist-oriented Brahmanical philosophies such as Sāṃkhya and Vaiśeṣika, which trace the origin of the world back to some material first principle, such as atoms (Vaiśeṣika) or prime

3. Thibaut 1962, I, 329, emended.

matter (*prakṛti*) (Sāṃkhya). Śaṅkara went to some lengths to refute the physical theories of these other systems.

Being the reality of everything, Brahman is *a fortiori* the reality of individual selves; indeed, in some of the Upaniṣadic passages quoted above the word "self" is substituted for "Brahman." Due to a mutual "superimposition" (*adhyāsa*), which again is grounded in *avidyā,* of Brahman and the properties of the individual psychophysical organism, an individual living self (*jīva*) appears. The mind, senses, and body, which are in fact material in nature, seem endowed with consciousness, on the one hand, and Brahman, the true Self, which is infinite and without activity, seems limited and active, on the other. The goal of spiritual practice, which consists primarily in reflecting on key Upaniṣad passages such as "That thou art" (*tat tvam asi,* ChU 6.8.7; such passages are referred to as *mahāvākyas,* "great statements")[4] until one realizes their full significance, is to dispel this superimposition and experience the true nature of the self as Brahman. As a consequence, the journey of the living self through the (inherently painful) cycle of rebirth (*saṃsāra*) is brought to an end—one is "liberated" (*mukta*). As *Muṇḍaka Upaniṣad* 3.2.9 puts it, "When a man comes to know that highest Brahman, he himself becomes Brahman"; that is to say, he loses his status as an individual, transmigrating being. And yet, Brahman, consisting of pure knowledge or consciousness, is always, eternally enlightened and liberated. Even the contrast of states of bondage and liberation is an illusion! Śaṅkara, finally, is adamant that liberation results just from comprehending the meaning of scripture (i.e., the *mahāvākyas*). The practice of yoga and various meditations described in the Upaniṣads and the performance of obligatory rituals such as the Agnihotra, the daily fire sacrifice, serve only a preparatory purpose. If indeed the individual self and the natural world with all its distinctions are but insubstantial figments of ignorance, like a snake seen instead of a rope, then nothing more nor less than right knowledge is required to make them vanish. (If they do not altogether disappear, then they are seen for what they really are, illusions.)

Advaita authors after Śaṅkara grappled with metaphysical and epistemological ramifications of the system that Śaṅkara himself appears not to have been interested in. For one, what is the ontological status of *avidyā?* If it is real (*sat*), then it must be of the nature of Brahman, in which case it would never cease and could never be dispelled. If it were unreal (*asat*), then, like a sky-flower or a hare's horn (standard Indian examples of impossible objects), it would not appear at all. In response to this problem, the Advaitins developed the theory that *avidyā,* hence the empirical world that is its product, is "inexpressible" (*anirvacanīya*); that is to say, it is neither real nor unreal. They came to this solution through a critical examination of the theories of error of other schools (the *akhyāti* theory of Prābhākara Mīmāṃsā, the *anyathākhyāti* theory of Bhāṭṭa Mīmāṃsā, and so on). An error, like the silver

4. This famous phrase is translated by Olivelle as "And that's how you are," following the seminal study by Joel Brereton, "*Tat Tvam Asi* in Context," *Zeitschrift der deutschen morgenländischen Gesellschaft* 136 (1986): 98–109.

that one apprehends instead of a piece of mother-of-pearl, they maintained, is a "false appearance" (*mithyāvabhāsa*), which is something positive in nature (*bhāvarūpa*). It is produced under certain circumstances—the presence of an object similar to another object, the lack of ideal viewing conditions, and so forth—by an *avidyā-śakti,* a cosmic ignorance-force or potency. The same factor, also known as *māyā,* which has the two basic functions of "concealing" and "projecting"—it obscures the real and causes something else to appear in its place—is originally responsible for the appearance of the world of plurality within Brahman. In this way some Advaitins considered *māyā* the "material cause" of the universe, parallel to the *prakṛti,* primal or unmanifest "nature," of Sāṃkhya philosophy, and sometimes even referred to it by that term. Other Advaitins, however, were uncomfortable with this view, seeing in it a tendency to reify *avidyā* into a second thing alongside Brahman.

Another question that occupied Advaitins and also gave rise to tensions within the school was, What is the bearer (or substratum: *āśraya*) of *avidyā?* As for knowledge, which normally involves a knowing subject and an object, ignorance must also have someone or something to whom it belongs and some object that it misapprehends. Obviously, it is problematic to suggest that Brahman, which is self-luminous consciousness, could be ignorant in any way. The living self (*jīva*), on the other hand, being part of the world of appearance, has *avidyā* as its condition. If it were also the bearer of *avidyā,* there would be the fault of mutual dependence. Advaitins, however, were forced to opt for one or the other unsatisfactory alternative. Those who chose the individual self as the bearer of *avidyā* emphasized that both the self and *avidyā* are, according to Śaṅkara, beginningless. Thus, while *avidyā* may be the condition for the existence of the *jīva,* the *jīva* could have been its substratum prior to that, *avidyā* the condition for the *jīva* prior to that, and so on forever into the past. Those who chose Brahman or the Self as the bearer of *avidyā* point out that the *jīva* is, in the end, really just Brahman; the distinction between the two is illusory. (In later Advaita the *jīva* is often described as a "reflection" [*pratibimba*] of Brahman, like that of the moon in a body of water. Exactly in what way and to what extent the distinction between a thing and its reflection can be said to be false was also a matter of some discussion.) Or else, Brahman is all there is, so *avidyā has* to belong to it. Although Brahman is of the nature of knowledge itself, it could not in any way be diminished by ignorance, since ignorance is not real. It does not amount to a real limitation or defilement of Brahman. To the objection that Brahman would seem to be more appropriate as the *object* of *avidyā* than its bearer (i.e., as that which is falsely taken to be something else), it is pointed out that object and bearer needn't always be different. Just as darkness is *in* the house that it conceals, so *avidyā* may be both *in* Brahman and conceal it.

Ultimately, Advaitins recognized that neither solution to the problem of the bearer of *avidyā* is entirely coherent. But that is as it should be, since, as explained above, *avidyā* is neither real nor unreal. If it made sense, it wouldn't be *avidyā.* This is probably why Śaṅkara avoided discussing issues pertaining to *avidyā.* In one passage of his BSBh where the question of the bearer of *avidyā* comes up, he deftly turns it aside: "Whose is this lack of knowledge?" an opponent is allowed to ask. "It belongs to you who are asking." "But am I not said by scripture to be the [omniscient] Lord?" "If you have become awakened in this way, then lack of knowledge belongs to no one" (BSBh 4.1.3).

A final example of a problem considered in post-Śaṅkara Advaita is, How can one really *know* Brahman? Advaita insists that scripture is the sole means of knowing it. Yet scripture consists of sentences, that is, language. How can language precipitate an experience of that which is supposedly beyond all words, beyond all thought? To answer such questions, Advaitins offered detailed analyses of *mahāvākyas* such as "That thou art" and "I am Brahman." Since the words "that" and "thou," for instance, cannot be taken fully literally when occurring as subject and predicate in an identity judgment—for "that" refers to the omniscient cause of the world, bliss, and so forth, while "thou" refers to a finite conscious subject who undergoes suffering—the hearer, as the result of a careful process of reflection, is compelled to abandon the incompatible aspects of their meanings and focus on that which they have in common, namely, the idea of consciousness itself. The sayings of the Upaniṣads thus have a unique capacity to propel the awareness of the listener beyond language, or at least beyond its literal meaning. The Advaitins drew on theories of Indian poetics (Alaṃkāra Śāstra) in arriving at this solution.

Viśiṣṭa and Dvaita Vedānta Critiques of Advaita Vedānta

The most formidable objections to the Advaita position, of course, came from outside the tradition, and less from realist Brahmanical philosophers (Naiyāyikas, Vaiśeṣikas, and Mīmāṃsakas), who tended to ignore it, than by theistic Vedānta thinkers, who accepted the basic premise of the supreme authority of the Upaniṣads.

In the introduction to his *Śrībhāṣya* commentary on the BS, the Viśiṣṭa Advaita philosopher Rāmānuja, who is considered by his followers to be equal in stature to Śaṅkara, presents trenchant criticisms of the main Advaita tenets. It would appear, however, that the object of his criticisms is not so much Śaṅkara himself as his rival Maṇḍanamiśra.

There is no proof of reality—Brahman—as being devoid of all difference, whether by means of scripture, perception, or reasoning, Rāmānuja argues. Scriptural passages such as "From death to death goes he who sees any diversity here" only deny plurality in the sense of separateness and independence from Brahman. The meaning of the unity of the world with Brahman is not that Brahman is *absolutely* identical with it, but rather that Brahman is its (real) cause and inner controlling principle (the *antaryāmin*). Texts such as ChU 6.2.3, "May I become many, may I grow forth," even suggest that Brahman transforms itself into the world, hence that plurality is part of its nature. It would be ridiculous if scripture were to teach this and then turn around and deny that Brahman is without any diversity. Nor are there any passages that unambiguously teach that Brahman, in its *true* nature, is without attributes, "unqualified" (*nirviśeṣa*). Texts such as "He who knows Brahman as truth, knowledge, and infinite..." actually imply that Brahman *is* possessed of different features that justify applying different predicates to it. The denial of the existence of anything besides Brahman, a "second," moreover, can only mean that Brahman is possessed of manifold powers capable of giving rise to this vast universe.

Nor can perception or inference establish the existence of an entity devoid of difference. In general, all means of knowledge (*pramāṇas*) present us with objects that are determinate in nature. "All states of consciousness," Rāmānuja writes, "have for their object something that is marked by some difference, as appears in the case of judgments like 'I saw this [determinate thing].'" Nor are the differences revealed by perception and inference unreal because they negate each other, as some Advaitins maintained: I see a pot one moment, a cloth the next; the perception of the pot is "negated" by the perception of the cloth! For, obviously, different things perceived at different times and places cannot be said to contradict each other. Nor am I presented, in the first moment of perception, with a direct experience of pure, undifferentiated Being, which in the next moment is covered over by differences imagined by the mind making comparisons and distinctions, as was again held by certain Advaitins (Maṇḍana in particular). If we really apprehended perceptually that there is no difference among objects, says Rāmānuja, then a man seeking for a horse would be satisfied with finding a buffalo!

In short, the *pramāṇas* reveal difference over and over. Even scripture, which consists of language, combines individual words that mean different things to express complex states of affairs. One may hold that reality is really one undifferentiated substance—Being or Consciousness—only at the cost of being contradicted by experience at every turn.

Another central claim of Advaita is that the living self is not an individual knowing subject but in reality pure consciousness. This, again, flies in the face of experience, reflected in judgments such as "I know X" and "I am conscious of Y," which imply that consciousness is always a state of an agent of knowledge directed toward an object. Consciousness itself is not the agent. Consciousness, moreover, is not permanent; we experience it arising and ceasing (for instance, in waking and sleeping). The self, on the other hand, is permanent, as revealed by memory: it is the same self who remembers now what it experienced before, and so has continuously existed from the past to the present. Thus, consciousness and the self cannot be identical. The Advaita notion that the self is a figment of ignorance that is dispelled upon becoming enlightened, moreover, is tantamount to saying that liberation is self-annihilation. If someone seeking to be relieved of pain were told he could escape it by bringing it about that "he" no longer exists, he would hardly be encouraged. Nor would he be consoled if he were told that in the state of liberation pure consciousness *will* continue to exist. "No sensible person exerts himself under the influence of the idea that after he himself has perished there will remain some entity termed 'pure light'!" quips Rāmānuja. As for the apparent statements of the identity of Brahman and the self in the Upaniṣads, they do not assert the absolute, numerical identity of Brahman and the self. Rather, they affirm that Brahman, as the omniscient cause of the universe, has become embodied in His creation, including individual selves. Thus, such passages teach plurality, not complete unity: Brahman exists in different forms, as the Supreme Being and also as the world.

When it comes to attacking the Advaita doctrine of ignorance (*avidyā*), Rāmānuja exploits all the weaknesses of the theory that the Advaitins themselves grappled with. There is no conceivable substrate for it. The individual soul is the consequence of it, and Brahman, on the Advaita view, is pure knowledge. Nor is it true that the Upaniṣads teach that liberation results simply from knowledge of the true nature of Brahman as completely one and identical with the world. Rather, they teach that liberation results from knowledge of Brahman as qualified by His manifold, auspicious qualities (i.e., as God [Viṣṇu]) and of the self as a part of the living body of God.

In summary, the Viśiṣṭa Advaitins insist that the Upaniṣads could not possibly be telling us that reality is a single, attributeless, impersonal substance; rather, they are telling us that it is God. Salvation comes about as a result of surrender (*prapatti*) to God and the practice of constant devotion (*bhakti*) to Him—as illustrated particularly in scriptures such as the *Bhagavad Gītā* and the *Bhāgavata Purāṇa*—in the form of loving meditation on his nature and one's relation to Him. A full, immediate experience of Brahman or God is realized only through God's grace, and takes place in heaven after the soul has been released from the physical body.

Many of the Viśiṣṭa Advaita criticisms of Advaita were adopted by the Dvaita school, which developed later. But they also came up with some of their own, as well as arguments against Viśiṣṭa Advaita positions. (Although both Dvaita and Viśiṣṭa Advaita are theistic in orientation, Dvaita particularly objected to the Viśiṣṭa Advaita theory that God transforms Himself into the world.) One of Madhva's cleverest moves was to read the *mahāvākya* of ChU 6.8.7, *tat tvam asi*, as *a-tat tvam asi*, "Thou art *not* that"! He argues that such a reading is more justified by the context, which gives several examples of beings returning to their point of origin—a bird settling on its post, rivers flowing into the sea, and so forth—which actually implies difference rather than complete oneness. Madhva, of course, does not deny that there are many statements in scripture that suggest the unity of Brahman with the world, but there are many ways of interpreting them. (Viṣṇudāsa will offer twenty different explanations of *tat tvam asi!*) The interpretation that Madhva favors is utter dependency on a transcendent, higher power. Again, the apparently monistic assertions of the Upaniṣads ("One only, without a second...," etc.) do not mean that God is all there is, but that God is all that matters. To claim that one actually *is* God is not only absurd, in light of a vivid awareness of one's imperfections and limitations, but also blasphemous. Later Dvaita figures such as Jayatīrtha, Viṣṇudāsa, and Vyāsatīrtha were especially occupied with refuting Advaita *reductio* arguments against the reality of difference and attacking the Advaita concept of "falsehood" (*mithyātva*), the ontological category to which the world supposedly belongs, as incapable of a coherent, precise definition.

Extending from the first half of the first millennium BCE to the present day—significant Vedānta works were still being produced in the twentieth century—Vedānta has to be the oldest continuously practiced tradition of philosophical reflection in the world. It is rich and diverse, containing a veritable ocean of ideas and arguments, and presenting a gargantuan clash of fundamentally opposed yet compellingly articulated perspectives on reality.

BIBLIOGRAPHY AND SUGGESTED READING

ALSTON, A. J. (1989) *A Śaṃkara Source-Book.* 6 vols. London: Shanti Sadan.

BALASUBRAMANIAN, R. (1976) *Advaita Vedānta.* Madras: University of Madras.

CARMAN, JOHN BRAISTED. (1974) *The Theology of Rāmānuja: An Essay in Interreligious Understanding.* New Haven, CT: Yale University Press.

COMANS, MICHAEL. (2000) *The Method of Early Advaita Vedānta.* Delhi: Motilal Banarsidass.

DASGUPTA, SURENDRANATHA. (1962–1968) *A History of Indian Philosophy.* 5 vols. Cambridge: Cambridge University Press.

HACKER, PAUL. (1995) *Philology and Confrontation: Paul Hacker on Traditional and Modern Vedānta,* edited by Wilhelm Halbfass. Albany, NY: State University of New York Press.

NAKAMURA, HAJIME. (1983, 2004) *A History of Early Vedānta Philosophy.* 2 parts. Translated by Trevor Leggett et al. Delhi: Motilal Banarsidass.

OLIVELLE, PATRICK. (1996) *Upaniṣads.* Oxford: Oxford University Press.

SATCHIDANANDENDRA SARASVATI, SWAMI. (1989) *The Method of the Vedanta,* translated by A. J. Alston. London: Kegan Paul International.

SHARMA, B. N. K. (1981) *History of the Dvaita School of Vedānta and Its Literature.* Delhi: Motilal Banarsidass.

Thibaut, George (trans.). (1962) *The Vedānta Sūtras of Bādarāyaṇa, with the Commentary by Śaṅkara.* New York: Dover.

WOOD, THOMAS E. (1990) *The Māṇḍūkya Upaniṣad and the Āgama Śāstra. Monographs of the Society for Asian and Comparative Philosophy,* no. 8. Honolulu, HI: University of Hawaii Press.

CHAPTER 13

JAIN PHILOSOPHY

JEFFERY D. LONG

THOUGH less known in the West than Vedānta and Buddhism, the contributions of Jainism to Indian philosophy are both extensive and profound. Perhaps its most striking departure from these traditions rests with its defense of a thoroughgoing metaphysical realism, in contrast with the idealism predominant in, for example, Advaita Vedānta and Yogācāra Buddhism. Sharing the soteriological concerns of these two traditions, many of Jainism's criticisms of them are based on the perception that idealism is detrimental to spiritual practice. As in most systems of Indian philosophy, Jain philosophical activity is carried out in the service of the pursuit of *mokṣa*—spiritual release and liberation from *saṃsāra*, the cycle of birth, death, and rebirth.

In terms of the traditional taxonomy used to categorize the various Indian schools of philosophy, Jainism is classified, along with Buddhism and the Lokāyata or Cārvāka system of materialism, as a *nāstika* or "heterodox" system, due to its explicit denial of the authority of the Veda. Among the standard list of six "orthodox" or Vedic systems of philosophy, Jainism most closely resembles the Sāṃkhya and Yoga systems, particularly with regard to the strong dualism of spirit and matter that these systems affirm. It differs from these two systems with its distinctive affirmation of the material nature of karma.

Possibly the most distinctive Jain contribution to Indian philosophical discourse is the pluralistic ontology that is affirmed in its "many-sided doctrine" or "doctrine of nonabsolutism" (*anekāntavāda*) and the corresponding relativistic epistemology affirmed in its "doctrine of perspectives" (*nayavāda*) and its doctrine of conditional predication or "maybe doctrine" (*syādvāda*). This complex of doctrines is seen by contemporary Jains as an extension into the intellectual realm of the principle of nonviolence (*ahiṃsā*). This, however, is a relatively recent interpretation of what were originally polemical doctrines.

Jainism shares the soteriological orientation of the Vedic systems and Buddhism, thereby blurring, as these systems do, the line drawn in the West between "philosophy" and "religion." This article will focus on those dimensions of Jainism of most interest to philosophers in the West—ontology, epistemology, logic, linguistics, and ethics—setting aside such dimensions as ascetic practice, meditation, and ritual activity, though with the understanding that these "religious" dimensions of the tradition are of vital importance to the Jains themselves, and important constituents of the total environment in which Jain philosophical reflection has occurred.

Intellectual History

The earliest extant Jain texts, which form the basis of the subsequent intellectual development of the tradition, are the canonical *Āgama* literature of the Śvetāmbara sect of Jainism. The oldest texts of this collection contain materials dating back to the third or second centuries BCE, and possibly earlier, though the bulk of them seem to have been composed in the early centuries of the Common Era. These texts present themselves as containing the teachings of Mahāvīra, who lived, according to Jain tradition, from 599 to 527 BCE. Because he is presented in both Jain and Buddhist sources as a contemporary of the Buddha, however, recent scholarship, which suggests a somewhat later date for the Buddha than the dates given by Buddhist traditions—perhaps as late as the fourth century BCE—requires a similar readjustment of the period of Mahāvīra's life.

Mahāvīra, an epithet meaning "Great Hero," can be regarded as the founder of the Jain tradition in only a limited sense. Though he is the founder of the community and the tradition as it exists today, he is regarded by Jains as only the most recent in a series of twenty-four *Tīrthaṅkaras*, or "Ford-makers"—enlightened beings who appear periodically in the world to create a crossing or "ford" (*tīrtha*) over the waters of rebirth. At least one Ford-maker prior to Mahāvīra—his immediate predecessor, Pārśva, the twenty-third Ford-maker—is accepted by modern scholarship as an actual historical figure. The first Ford-maker, Ṛiṣabha, is held by some Jain scholars to be the Ṛiṣabha mentioned in the *Ṛg Veda*.

Mahāvīra emerged from the same northern Indian ascetic culture of the mid-first millennium BCE that produced the Buddha and the *Upaniṣads*. Jain literature presents a picture of the life of Mahāvīra with a number of similarities to that of the Buddha. Both are depicted as members of the ruling Kṣatriya *varṇa*, or Warrior class, who give up lives of privilege and power in search of wisdom and spiritual liberation. Both renounce the world to take up the lifestyle of a wandering ascetic. Although the paths they take and will ultimately recommend to their followers are distinct, both are presented as achieving the goal of liberation and as attaining a state of perfect enlightenment. And finally, both establish communities of male and female ascetics with broader communities of male and female lay supporters.

By the fifth century CE, and for reasons that remain somewhat obscure, Mahāvīra's community had split into two sectarian divisions—the Śvetāmbara, or "white-clad" Jains, whose male and female ascetics wear simple white garments, and the Digambara, or "sky-clad" Jains, whose male ascetics wear nothing at all. Although the Digambaras reject the authority of the Śvetāmbara canon because it depicts Mahāvīra as engaging in activities that they believe inappropriate for an enlightened being, there are remarkably few philosophical differences between these two Jain traditions. Both groups accept the authority of the *Tattvārthasūtra*, or "Text on the True Nature of Reality." This central text for Jain philosophy was composed by Umāsvāti, a figure of the second or third century CE who seems to have predated the division of the Jain community into its Śvetāmbara and Digambara sections. The *Tattvārthasūtra* has been commented upon by both Śvetāmbara and Digambara scholars over the centuries, and is the closest thing available to a universally accepted foundational Jain text. Essentially, it is a summary of the philosophical teachings scattered throughout the Śvetāmbara canon. Despite considerable internal diversity regarding ritual, ascetic practice, and monastic organization, the Jain tradition has been remarkably uniform with regard to issues that are of interest to philosophers, perhaps because of widespread acceptance of Umāsvāti's text.

A distinctively Digambara bent toward mysticism, however, emerges within the writings of Kundakunda, who may have lived as early as the fifth or as late as the eighth century CE. As shall be seen below, Kundakunda, a highly regarded *ācārya*, or teacher, of the Digambara tradition develops a distinctively Jain version of the "two truths" doctrine articulated in the Buddhist tradition by Nāgārjuna and in Vedānta by Śaṅkara. Departing somewhat from the metaphysical realism insisted upon by the rest of the Jain tradition, Kundakunda develops what could broadly be called a gnostic stance toward the Jain spiritual path, emphasizing the realization of the true nature of the soul or *jīva* over ascetic practice as the true means to liberation. This emphasis places him closer to Buddhist and Vedāntic understandings of liberation, one could argue, than Jain thought normally goes. It should be added, though, that in practice, Kundakunda's followers are no less committed to asceticism than are other Jains. Kundakunda's writings, particularly his *Pravacanasāra*, or "Essence of the Doctrine," and his *Samayasāra*, or "Essence of the Soul," continue to exert a strong influence among Digambara intellectuals, especially in the modern period, in which his thought has experienced something of a resurgence.

Another important Digambara figure of the early Common Era is Samantabhadra, whose *Āptamīmāṃsā*, or "Analysis of the Nature of the Authoritative Teacher," is central to understanding the doctrine of conditional predication, applying it to a variety of topics that were current in Samantabhadra's time (roughly the fourth or fifth century CE). Finally, Akalaṅka (c. eighth century CE) is renowned for his critique of the work of the Buddhist logician, Dharmakīrti (c. seventh century CE).

The Jain doctrines of relativity are further developed by the Śvetāmbara thinkers, Siddhasena Divākara (c. fifth century CE) and Haribhadrasūri (c. eighth century CE). In particular, Haribhadrasūri is associated with the accommodating attitude toward non-Jain systems of thought that contemporary Jains see these doctrines as expressing. Additional renowned intellectuals of the Śvetāmbara tradition include Hemacandra (1089–1172 CE) and the relatively recent Yaśovijaya, who flourished in the seventeenth century.

Jain Ontology: The Nature of the Soul and *Anekāntavāda*

According to Jain ontology, the fundamental categories of being are soul (*jīva*), matter (*pudgala*), space (*ākāśa*), time (*kāla*), the principle of motion (*dharma*), and the principle of rest (*adharma*). Soul is sentient and nonmaterial. Matter is nonsentient and, of course, material. Space, time, and the principles of motion and rest are neither sentient nor material.

Besides being sentient, soul is characterized by infinite knowledge (*jñāna*), bliss (*sukha*), and energy (*vīrya*). Souls are also many, their number corresponding to that of the number of living beings in the universe. The number of souls, though it is not, strictly speaking, infinite, is virtually infinite. Because knowledge is one of its essential traits and because it is not one, but many, the soul, as conceived in Jainism, is close to the *puruṣa* concept of the Sāṃkhya and Yoga systems.

In Sāṃkhya and Yoga, however, the soul, or *puruṣa*, finds itself bound to the cycle of rebirth because it has mistaken the qualities (*gunas*) of matter or nature (*prakṛitī*) for its own. It has misidentified itself with the world of matter.

In Jainism, however, the soul, or *jīva*, is bound to the cycle of rebirth because tiny, subtle particles of matter (*pudgala*) have actually embedded themselves within it. This subvariety of matter, called *karma*, is the cause of the *jīva*'s bondage to *saṃsāra*, and it is this karmic bondage that Jainism, as a spiritual path, seeks to overcome.

The *jīva* itself, according to Jainism, is not a material substance. But it does have a few qualities in common with matter, such as extension in both time and space and the ability to bond with karmic matter, that make the Jain conception of the soul distinctive among the schools of Indian philosophy.

In terms of temporal extension, the *jīva* is infinite, having no beginning or end. In terms of spatial extension, the soul takes on the shape of the body it currently occupies. This is sometimes compared with the light from a lamp that takes the shape of the room in which it is located. The *jīva* expands or contracts to fill its physical container.

The ability of the *jīva* to bond with karmic matter is compared to a cloth that becomes sticky when wet. It thus attracts dust, which is comparable to karmic matter. The water that wets the cloth, giving it its stickiness, is compared to the passions. The passions are deformations of the essential nature of the *jīva*, which, again, is intrinsically conscious, blissful, and energetic. The passions are evoked by experiences, which arise due to the karmic particles that have previously bonded with one's soul. Passions attract karmic particles of various kinds into the soul—the kind of particle depending on the kind and the intensity of the passion in question. Karmic particles are compared to seeds, which ripen and bear fruit at a given time, depending on what kind of seed they are and the condition of the spiritual "soil" in which they are planted. The "fruit" that the seed bears takes the form of a particular kind of experience. Experiences are pleasant, painful, or neutral, and evoke corresponding passions of attraction, aversion, or indifference. The passions, in turn, attract more karmic particles, or seeds, and the entire process repeats itself.

The goal of Jainism, as a spiritual path, is to purify the soul of karmic matter, to clean away the karmic "dust" that obscures the true nature of the soul, thus allowing the soul to shine forth in its intrinsically omniscient, blissful, and energetic nature. Ascetic practice is essential to this process, in order both to calm the passions, thus preventing further karmic influx, and to "burn off" the existing karmas already abiding in the soul.

Karmic matter is of various kinds, and an extensive Jain technical literature has emerged that divides this matter into various categories, based on its effects, and that goes into considerable detail regarding what these effects are, what kinds of actions cause them to be bound to the soul, and what one must do to rid oneself of them. In terms of the rebirth process, the most important karmic effects are those that determine the type of body the soul will inhabit in a given lifetime, what status it will have in the cosmic and social scheme of things, and how long its lifespan will be. The most destructive karmas are those that obscure knowledge, for these prevent one from understanding the true nature of reality and acting upon it, thus enabling one to fall even deeper into bondage.

Jain "karmic realism" has had a profound effect on the subsequent development of the Jain philosophical tradition, given it the sharply realist bent mentioned earlier. Due to karma being not simply the inevitable result of earlier actions, as in most of the Vedic systems of thought, or a kind of psychic energy that needs to be worked out, as is often found in Buddhist thought, but an actual, physical substance that has bonded with the soul, the emphasis of Jainism has overwhelmingly been ascetic practice—what one must do, and avoid doing, in order to reverse the process of karmic bondage. Philosophical claims are thus evaluated in terms of their ability to support spiritual practice. Idealistic tendencies that downplay the reality of the material world—views collectively called in the Jain tradition by the pejorative term *māyāvāda*, or "doctrine of illusion"—are rejected as undermining practice. A realist doctrine is affirmed instead, which seeks to account for all the dimensions of experience without relegating any to the realm of illusion.

At its most systematic, this realism is expressed in the "many-sided" doctrine, or *anekāntavāda:* the doctrine of the irreducible complexity of reality. According to the Jain critique of Vedānta and Buddhism, each of these systems clings, respectively, to a one-sided conception of reality as characterized by either permanence or impermanence. The Jain view, however, is presented as one that includes the fundamental insights of both traditions. According to the Jain view, reality is characterized by both permanence and impermanence, for both of these aspects of reality are disclosed in our experience of existence. To reject the ephemeral as illusory, as Advaita Vedānta does, for example, in favor of that which is permanent, or to reject continuity as illusory, as Buddhist schools of thought do, in favor of a view of reality as fundamentally impermanent, is, according to Jain thought, to take a biased and partial perspective. Our experience is characterized by continuity and change, by permanence and impermanence. Our conception of reality should therefore be able to accommodate both. According to the Umāsvāti, "Origination, cessation, and persistence constitute existence."[1] Karmically determined states come and go, but the essential nature of the *jīva* remains.

Jain Epistemology: *Nayavāda*

The epistemology that develops from this understanding of reality as irreducibly complex is one that has enabled Jain philosophers to take stances toward other schools of thought that are both strikingly charitable and yet deeply critical. To continue with the theme of permanence and impermanence, Vedānta and Buddhism are both valid and true conceptions of reality, from their respective points of view (*nayas*). Haribhadrasūri, in his "Collection of Views on Yoga" (*Yogadṛṣṭisamuccaya*), is thus able to make charitable assertions about these and other rival systems reminiscent of the claims of modern or "neo" Vedāntins, such as Sri Ramakrishna and Mahatma Gandhi, that the world's religions are all true, or that they are so many paths to a common goal or destination:

> The highest essence of going beyond *saṃsāra* is called "*nirvāṇa*." The wisdom gained from discipline is singular in essence, though heard of in different ways.
>
> "Eternal Śiva, Highest Brahman, Accomplished Soul, Suchness": With these words one refers to it, though the meaning is one in all the various forms.[2]

Haribhadra depicts non-Jain systems, such as Vedānta and Buddhism, as well-intentioned attempts to achieve the common goal of *nirvāṇa*. Wisdom is to be respected, whatever its source, and in whatever terminology it is expressed.

At the same time, their approach allows the Jains to affirm that their system alone is the most comprehensive, and so the most true, incorporating, as it does, the essential truths of all the others. Hemacandra, employing the same approach in his revealingly titled "Ripper Apart of Other Systems of Thought" (*Anyayogavyavacchedika*), writes:

> Being contrary to one another, the other systems are partial and mutually exclusive.
>
> But your system [Mahāvīra's] is impartial, desiring all perspectives in their totality.[3]

1. Umāsvāti, *Tattvārthasūtra* 5:30. Translation by Tatia.
2. Haribhadrasūri, *Yogadṛṣṭisamuccaya* 129–130. Translation by Chapple.
3. Hemacandra, *Anyayogavyavacchedika* 30. Translation mine.

Other systems, such as Vedānta and Buddhism, are depicted by Hemacandra as partial, favoring their particular insights into reality as characterized by either permanence or impermanence, unlike the impartial and more complete Jain system.

The epistemology of multiple perspectives (*nayavāda*) is intimately connected to the claim, made in the earliest extant Jain texts, of Mahāvīra's omniscience. Recall that according to Jain ontology, the *jīva* has infinite knowledge as one of its inherent qualities. This knowledge is obscured by the presence of knowledge-obscuring karma. But once a spiritual aspirant begins practicing ethical restraint and ascetic disciplines, these karmas begin to drop away, and the pure knowledge that is the soul's intrinsic nature begins to shine through in stages. One begins with the mundane forms of knowledge, which the *Tattvārthasūtra* characterizes as "empirical" (*mati*) and "linguistic" (*śrutā*). These refer, respectively, to the knowledge gained through the senses and through linguistically based concepts—the latter including both the knowledge received through the verbal testimony of another and the knowledge arrived at through logical reflection. As the knowledge-obscuring karmic matter is expelled from the *jīva*, one also develops clairvoyance (*vadhi*) and, at a more advanced stage, telepathy (*manaḥparyāya*). When all the karmic material is gone, and the intrinsic nature of the *jīva* is fully revealed, one experiences *kevalajñāna*—"unique" or "absolute" knowledge—which is defined as perfect omniscience.[4]

The Jain claim of absolute omniscience for enlightened beings, or *jinas*, such as Mahāvīra, has been a controversial one in the history of Indian philosophy, for the other systems of thought have not made such claims for their founding figures. The Buddhists do designate the Buddha as *sarvajña*, or "all-knowing." But they qualify this claim with the explanation that the Buddha knows all that needs to be known in order to bring beings to *nirvāṇa*. He knows everything that he needs to know to save suffering beings. But he does not know, literally, everything. But this is precisely the claim that the Jains make for *jinas* such as Mahāvīra.

This claim of omniscience for Mahāvīra is foundational for Jain perspectivalism because it is this claim that enables the Jain view not to lapse into a debilitating form of relativism. The views of various systems are all partly true, but a standard for evaluating *how* true they are, and in what senses, exists in the form of Mahāvīra's teaching.

In order to illustrate this point, Jain philosophers often invoke the story, the oldest extant version of which is actually found in a Buddhist scripture, of the Blind Men and the Elephant.

According to this famous story, a group of blind men come upon an elephant and begin to debate its nature. Being blind, each man grasps a particular part of the elephant and bases his assessment on that particular part, combined with his own past experiences. One man, grasping the trunk, claims that the elephant is like a

4. Umāsvāti, *Tattvārthasūtra* 1:9–30.

snake. Another, feeling its side, says that the elephant is like a wall. Yet another, feeling a leg, says that the elephant is like a tree trunk. The one who grasps the elephant's tail claims that it is like a broom hanging from a ceiling, while the one who grasps a tusk finds it to be like a spear. And the one who grasps an ear says that the elephant is like a large winnowing fan.

Hearing such divergent descriptions and finding them to be unlike what his own experience reveals to him, each blind man begins to argue with the others until they are about to come to blows. Finally, a person who can see comes upon them and gently tells them that they are all partially correct and partially incorrect, for the elephant does have all of the characteristics that the blind men are ascribing to it, but it is reducible to none of them. Only a sighted person is capable of perceiving the entire elephant in its true, complex nature and explaining to the blind men how they are each partly right and partly wrong.

On a Jain interpretation, the blind men represent the adherents of the various rival systems of Indian philosophy, disputing with one another about the ultimate nature of reality. Is it permanence? Is it impermanence? The elephant is reality itself. And the person who can see is Mahāvīra, the enlightened *jina*, whose omniscience enables him to perceive the true nature of reality and assign each of the partial perspectives expressed by the other systems of thought to its proper place in the total scheme of existence. It is the absolutist affirmation of the omniscience of the *jina* that makes logically possible the nonabsolutist interpretation of non-Jain systems of thought.

Jain Logic and Linguistics: *Syādvāda*

An important implication of the Jain epistemology of multiple perspectives, each of which corresponds to a different aspect of reality (as affirmed in the Jain doctrine of the irreducible complexity of existence), is that all philosophical claims, in order to fully capture the truth, must be qualified. The Jain conception of language is not, as one finds in some forms of Vedānta and Buddhism, one that it is wholly inadequate for capturing the nature of reality. Nor, on the other hand, do the Jains hold the view of the Mīmāṃsakas that the Sanskrit language corresponds perfectly to the realities it describes. The predominant Jain view is that language can describe reality in a provisional way, and that this ability can be enhanced through the proper qualification of one's claims. One cannot capture reality perfectly with language. But one can approach this goal by conditional predication.

What this means, essentially, is that proper philosophical discourse involves the specification of the perspective (*naya*) from which one's claims are made: the part of the elephant that one is grasping at a particular moment in time, to continue with the elephant metaphor. From one point of view, it is true that reality is characterized by permanence. From another point of view, it is true that reality is characterized by impermanence. The simple, unqualified or absolute claims that "reality is characterized by permanence" and that "reality is characterized by impermanence" are partially true and partially false: true to the degree that each captures a facet of the total complexity of reality, as it is disclosed in our experience, and false to the degree that it denies the truth of its contrary. But the qualified statements, "reality is, in one sense, or from one point of view, characterized by permanence" and "reality is, in yet another sense, or from yet another point of view, characterized by impermanence" are literally and absolutely true, so long as one specifies the senses in which they are true in terms that are logically compatible with the overall worldview of Jainism. The intrinsic nature of the soul, for example, is permanent, while the karmic states that it undergoes are impermanent.

The Jain expression of this principle is the doctrine of conditional predication, or *syādvāda*. The third-person singular, optative tense form of the Sanskrit verb "to be" is *syāt*, which, in ordinary discourse, would mean, "it may be," "it could be," or "it should be." In Jain technical usage, however, this verb becomes a *nipāta*, or particle, meaning, "in some sense," or "from a certain point of view it is the case that...." In order for a philosophical claim to be properly true, it needs to be made *syāt*—in a certain sense, or from a certain point of view—rather than absolutely.

According to the Jain logicians, there are seven possible truth-values that a claim can possess, once one allows for the various points of view from which it can be made:

1. In a certain sense, or from a certain point of view (*syāt*), the claim is true.
2. In a certain sense, or from a certain point of view (*syāt*), the claim is false.
3. In a certain sense, or from a certain point of view (*syāt*), the claim is both true and false.
4. In a certain sense, or from a certain point of view (*syāt*), the truth of the claim is inexpressible (i.e., it is neither true nor false).
5. In a certain sense, or from a certain point of view (*syāt*), the claim is true and its truth is inexpressible.
6. In a certain sense, or from a certain point of view (*syāt*), the claim is false and its truth is inexpressible.
7. In a certain sense, or from a certain point of view (*syāt*), the claim is both true and false and its truth is inexpressible.

The first four truth-values are more or less intuitive, and analogous to a similar fourfold model of truth developed in the Buddhist tradition. The latter three constitute all of the possible logically nonredundant combinations of the first four.

With *syādvāda*, Jain philosophers are able to take the substantive claims made by various systems of thought and analyze them into their constituent truth values, showing them to be merely relative assertions of the truth as understood by the Jain tradition.

Syādvāda as Intellectual *Ahiṃsā*?

The central ethical principle of Jainism is *ahiṃsā*. This term, often translated as "nonviolence," actually has a far more holistic meaning beyond the simple avoidance of physical harm that the English word "nonviolence" suggests. *Ahiṃsā* means the absence of even the desire to do harm in thought, word, or deed. Though critics of Jainism have at times suggested that *ahiṃsā* is a negative virtue, implying an attitude of indifference toward other beings—simply not harming as opposed to actively helping—this is not the predominant view within the Jain community, where *ahiṃsā* is often described in terms of compassion for all living things. The observance of *ahiṃsā* is the basis of most of the strict ascetic practices for which Jain monks and nuns are known, and for the moral rules governing lay activity as well. It is the cardinal virtue of Jainism and a central emphasis of even the earliest Jain scriptures, attributed to Mahāvīra himself.

The emphasis on *ahiṃsā* in one's speech does lead to rules governing the speech of ascetics, such as when the canonical *Daśavaikālikasūtra* enjoins ascetics not only to tell the truth, but also to avoid speaking harshly, even if one's words are true.[5]

Though it might be quite natural to see *syādvāda* as having evolved from such injunctions, the extensive polemical use to which it is put by traditional Jain logicians—even by the relatively charitable Haribhadrasūri—suggests that, historically, it has been more of a polemical tool evolving out of the distinctive, pluralistic conception of reality entailed by the worldview of early Jainism as expressed in the *Tattvarthasūtra* and the Śvetāmbara canon.

Contemporary Jains, however, do see in *anekāntavāda, nayavāda*, and *syādvāda* a powerful logical tool for expressing an open and pluralistic attitude in philosophical and religious discourse—for showing that the views of others have truth and value, while at the same time not compromising the truth and value of one's own perspective. And non-Jain authors have also begun to look seriously at these doctrines for their possibilities as tools for developing a logically rigorous philosophy of religious pluralism.[6]

BIBLIOGRAPHY AND SUGGESTED READINGS

Chapple, Christopher Key. (1993) *Nonviolence to Animals, Earth, and Self in Asian Traditions*. Albany, NY: State University of New York Press.

———. (2003) *Reconciling Yogas: Haribhadra's Collection of Views on Yoga*. Albany, NY: State University of New York Press.

Daśavaikālika Sūtra. (1973) Translated by Kastur Chand Lalwani. Delhi: Motilal Banarsidass.

5. *Daśavaikālikasūtra* 7:2–3, 11, 13.
6. See, for example, Sharma 2001 and Long 2007.

Dundas, Paul. (2002) *The Jains* (2nd ed.). London and New York: Routledge.

Gopalan, S. (1991) *Jainism as Meta-Philosophy*. Delhi: Sri Satguru Publications.

Haribhadrasūri. (2003) *Reconciling Yogas: Haribhadra's Collection of Views on Yoga*, translated by Christopher Key Chapple. Albany, NY: State University of New York Press.

Jaini, Padmanabh S. (1979) *The Jaina Path of Purification*. Delhi: Motilal Banarsidass.

Johnson, W. J. (1995) *Harmless Souls: Karmic Bondage and Religious Change in Early Jainism with Special Reference to Umāsvāti and Kundakunda*. Delhi: Motilal Banarsidass.

Kumar, Rai Ashwini, T. M. Dak, and Anil Dutta Mishra (eds.). (1996) *Facets of Jain Philosophy, Religion and Culture: Anekāntavāda and Syādvāda*. Ladnun, Rajasthan: Jain Vishva Bharati Institute.

Long, Jeffery D. (2007) *A Vision for Hinduism: Beyond Hindu Nationalism*. London: I.B. Tauris.

———. (2009) *Jainism: An Introduction*. London: I.B. Tauris.

Sharma, Arvind. (2001) *A Jaina Perspective on the Philosophy of Religion*. Delhi: Motilal Banarsidass.

Tatia, Nathmal. (1951) *Studies in Jaina Philosophy*. Banaras: Jain Cultural Research Society.

Umāsvāti. (1994) *Tattvārtha Sūtra: That Which Is*, translated by Nathmal Tatia. New York: Harper Collins Publishers.

CHAPTER 14

ANGLOPHONE PHILOSOPHY IN COLONIAL INDIA

NALINI BHUSHAN

ANGLOPHONE philosophy in India (from 1850 to 1947 and thereafter) is shaped by at least three distinct historical phenomena: Thomas Macaulay's "Minute on Education" in 1835 that makes English the medium of instruction in Indian education and Protestant missionary professors at the center of philosophical learning in Indian colleges and universities; the social and religious reform movements of the Arya and Brahmo Samaj that sweep the country, resulting in a revaluation of the orthodox Hindu philosophical systems[1] and a move to a return to the original, "purer" Vedas and Upaniṣads; and the presence of the British as an occupying force, which generates a politico-cosmopolitan awareness and a distinctive approach to imagining the modern Indian nation in academic and nonacademic philosophical circles. This essay addresses some of the distinctly philosophical contributions in the fields of metaphysics and epistemology, comparative philosophy, aesthetics, ethics, and social and political philosophy that were generated as a consequence of the interface of these three axes in colonial India and thereafter.

METAPHYSICS AND EPISTEMOLOGY

What is the relation between a self and the external world? Is the external world real? Is the self a real entity? Is there a reality beyond the one that we can experience

1. For a detailed discussion of each of these systems, see earlier essays in this section on Indian philosophy.

via our senses? If so, what is the relation between the empirical world and that Ultimate Reality? Can either be known? If so, in what ways? These metaphysical and epistemological questions are developed in a very particular way in colonial India. In this period, methods, vocabularies, and reference points from outside of India are creatively appropriated and fashioned by philosophers in service of anchoring, articulating, and, crucially, rendering accessible to a global audience Indian philosophical issues in a modern context.

A.C. Mukerji (1888–1968) grapples with issues of subjectivity in his two volumes, *The Concept of Self* (1933) and *Self, Thought and Reality* (1938), and a number of essays in the journal *Allahabad University Studies.* His focus is on epistemological questions that stem from the egocentric predicament, one that he traces past Descartes and all the way back to the Bṛhadhāraṇyaka Upaniṣad and the voice of Yajñavālkya. The problem is this: how does the knower know itself? If knowledge is always of an object, then to know a subject must involve knowledge of a subject as an object and not of subjectivity as such. If so, the subject qua subject must remain unknowable. The goal of the two volumes is to provide an argument to the effect that such a subject can be known, but not in the way that knowing is traditionally understood; instead, it is a knowing that is direct and nonrelational.

This alternative way of knowing—one that is not reducible to either the intellectual or the perceptual—sometimes called the "intuitive" or "direct" or "nonconceptual" way, is the subject of clarification and further analysis in the work of many Indian thinkers, including, most famously, S. Radhakrishnan (1888–1975), M. Hiriyanna (1871–1950), S. Dasgupta (1887–1952), and R. D. Ranade (1886–1957).

The concepts of "subject" and the "object," and of the difficult relation between them, are analyzed by perhaps the best-known Indian philosopher of this period, Krishna Chandra Bhattacharyya (1875–1949). His essays "The Concept of Philosophy" (1936) and "The Subject as Freedom" (1930) in particular stand as modern-day Indian classics. Bhattacharyya is particularly interested in the relationship between levels of subjectivity and the corresponding levels of freedoms, both phenomenological and metaphysical, that they make possible. Many of his ideas and concerns are taken up by his sons Kalidas Bhattacharyya and Gopinath Bhattacharyya, who, like their professorial father, trained many intellectuals in the Indian academy.

The dichotomy between Idealism and Realism—two views ordinarily taken to be at opposite ends of the metaphysical spectrum—is rejected by many of these thinkers[2] as a false and pernicious one. This is an important philosophical issue during this period, since of the six orthodox schools of Indian philosophy, it is the

2. See, for instance, Mukerji 1927, "The Realists' Conception of Idealism," *Allahabad University Studies*, vol. 3, pp.207-243. Also, H. Haldar, "Realistic Idealism," in Radhakrishnan and Muirhead 1936, pp. 215–232.

Vedānta school,[3] and Advaita Vedānta in particular, often characterized as "Advaitic Idealism," that flourishes in colonial India and in particular in the work of these thinkers. In exposing the falsity of the dichotomy, they argue for a conception of our proper relation to the universe that cannot be reduced to received views of Idealism, mystical or otherwise. Take Mukerji, for instance, who in 1927 writes: "if we are to retain the terms Idealism and Realism, we must give up the old method of contrasting them, and define Realism as *the habit of accepting the facts as out there, unconditioned and absolute.* Idealism, on the contrary, *insists on the conditioned nature of the ordinary facts of experience* and holds that apart from their conditions, the so-called facts are reduced to non-entities" (Mukerji 1927, 210, emphasis added). In his focus on the distinction between the unconditioned and the conditioned as the real source of the debate between the Realists and the Idealists, he anticipates the arrival on the global metaphysical stage of more nuanced forms of Realism that view the conditioned nature of the world as one of its fundamental aspects.[4]

Another significant philosophical task was to clarify the meaning of a number of concepts within Vedānta philosophy. Thus, for instance, the central concept of *mayā* in Vedāntic philosophy, which is essential to an understanding of the observed world, is subject to careful articulation and clarification in the works of Swami Vivekananda and V. Subrahmanya Iyer. Vivekananda (1862–1902) in his *Jnana Yoga* makes the case for an understanding of the concept *māyā* that is not reducible to illusion or delusion, to magic, or to a nonperceptible veil that distorts what we see around us. Rather, for Vivekananda, *māyā* captures the essential nature of anything that is empirical—namely, that which is subject to change, to error, to misperception. Rather than having it be a metaphysical notion that is layered upon an empirical reality, he proposes it as a way of capturing the very heart of empirical reality. V. S. Iyer (1869–1949), arguing more broadly for a Vedānta that is secured more firmly on philosophical than religious grounds, also addresses and corrects common misperceptions of *māyā* among scholars (1955).

In addition to the importance of clarifying the concept of *māyā*, another issue that is at the forefront of discussion among Vedāntins is whether or not it is right to focus on *māyā* in the first place as the central concept of Advaita Vedānta. Aurobindo (1872–1950) in *The Life Divine* (1949) argues for the centrality of *līlā* (play), rather than *māyā* (illusion), in the metaphysical relation between the empirical world and reality. Aurobindo argues that the operation of *māyā* is due to the self and lies in the epistemological domain; it is not due to *Brahman* (Ultimate Reality), whose

3. See Taber in this volume.

4. Donald Davidson's essays in the seventies and eighties on the scheme-content distinction (collected in *Inquiries into Truth and Interpretation*, Oxford University Press, 1984) offer arguments in support of what Mukerji would call a 'conditioned' realism as the only form of Realism worth serious consideration. For Mukerji, of course, this very view would be an Idealism worth having! If one were forced to choose, the decision of whether to term the position 'Realism' or 'Idealism' may arguably be based on the reigning metaphysical fashion of one's day.

operation is *līlā*. Aurobindo's work was critical in generating a deep and sustained discussion on this subject among philosophers, finding its most famous scholarly expression in a symposium held by the Indian Philosophical Congress, entitled "Has Sri Aurobindo refuted Maya Vada?" (1950). One consequence of going with a *līlāvāda* rather than a *māyāvāda* emphasis in understanding Advaita philosophy is that it produces an understanding of our presence as selves in the empirical world that is less at odds with what is ultimately required for self-realization. On the *līlāvāda* perspective, the relationship between the realized self and the world is one of immanence rather than of separation, distance, or transcendence.

Finally, and importantly, modernist interpretations of Islamic philosophy include Syed Ameer Ali's (1849–1928) *The Spirit of Islam*, Muhammad Iqbal's (1873–1938) *The Reconstruction of Religious Thought in Islam*, and Abul Kalam Azad's (1888–1958) commentary on the Quran.

In sum, this period of Anglophone Indian philosophy saw a revisiting of ancient metaphysical and epistemological problems, but with a particular focus, within the context of a university-style philosophical training that required an awareness of habits and styles of philosophizing the world over. There was a will to render accessible to a global audience the problems and arguments and the habits and styles of the Indian philosophical traditions with which they were intimately familiar (in part from informal training in the home as well as from formal teachings by Sanskrit pandits outside of the university setting). An instance of this cross-fertilization in metaphysics and epistemology is the spread of neo-Hegelianism in India, inspired by the German philosopher G. W. F. Hegel. While the neo-Vedāntins H. Haldar, S. K. Maitra, and B. N. Seal all cite Hegel as a formative influence, their acquaintance with Hegelian ideas was via the British Idealists such as F. H. Bradley, E. Caird, J. H. Stirling, and T. H. Green. One of their projects as Vedāntins was to creatively appropriate the Hegelian concept of the Absolute, both to illuminate and to render accessible to a global philosophical public the Vedāntic concept of *Brahman*.

Comparative Philosophy

B. N. Seal (1864–1938) is regarded as the founder of the field of comparative philosophy. More accurately, he proposed the comparative method in philosophy. In 1899, at the International Conference of Orientalists, in a paper that undertook a comparative study of Vaishnavism and Christianity, Seal proposed an approach to philosophizing that was bold and innovative for its time. "Comparison," Seal argued, "*presupposes* that that which is compared is of coordinate rank" (McEvilley 2002, ix). This implies that regardless of its *fruits*, the very *act* of comparison in India *presumed* the equality of Indian and Western philosophy and of the philosophers who chose to engage in philosophical comparisons. It is part of Seal's legacy that the strategy of comparison and the move to a "synthesis" of Eastern and Western ideas came to play a central role in Indian philosophical thought. The work of Seal's students S. K. Maitra and Rasvihari Das is an important part of his legacy.

Comparative philosophy in this period was pursued, for instance, in the philosophy of religion, with a focus on Hinduism and Christianity. Ram Mohan Roy (1772–1833) and Keshub Chunder Sen (1838–1884) of the Brahmo Samaj famously engaged the missionaries in philosophical debates on the comparative merits of the two religions and, in particular, whether it could be argued that the two religions were radically different. While Roy and Sen in Bengal, as well as S. Subrahmanya Sastri in Madras, chose to emphasize the similarities, even as they made the case for the ability of Hinduism to shed light on otherwise problematic theological questions, some missionaries, most famously A. C. Hogg (1875–1954), who was also a professor of philosophy, argued for an essential and ineliminable difference between the two religions.[5] The Theosophical Society, headed by Annie Besant, was also active in the philosophical conversation about the relative merits of the different religious traditions.

In the Indian academy, the field of metaphysics and epistemology in particular saw the explosive publication of many comparative essays on Śaṅkara and Kant, and on Hegel and Vedānta, by H. Haldar, A. C. Mukerji, and P. T. Raju, and more broadly on Eastern versus Western styles of philosophizing by S. Radhakrishnan, T. M. P. Mahadevan, Aurobindo Ghose, and R. Tagore, among others. The comparative method itself came under scrutiny and severe criticism post-1947. However, as early as 1928, A. C. Mukerji, himself engaged in part in philosophical comparisons, worried about comparative work being undertaken by some of his colleagues (notably that of S. Radhakrishnan) that was overly historical or descriptive, where the goal was either to showcase what was prestigious about each tradition or to find the tradition of the other in one's own cultural heritage. In both cases what was lost was an opportunity to subject each set of ideas to critical scrutiny with the goal of "mutual supplementation of arguments and consequent clarification of issues" (Mukerji 1933, vi). He wrote: "If... we want to profit by thinking modern problems of European philosophy in Indian terms, without misrepresentation of either and yet with a considerable clarification of both methods of thought, *we must give up the practice of finding Kant and Hegel... in the Upanishads;* these are misrepresentations which do not clarify but confound problems" (Mukerji 1928, 379, emphasis added).

The field of comparative philosophy today thus owes both it fecundity and its vastly changed contours to the work done by these philosophers in the hey-day of philosophical comparisons as well as to their thoughtful critiques. Cross-cultural philosophy today is less comparative in nature, but its driving force is the same as

5. The debate between Sastri and Hogg on the subject of Hinduism and Christianity, notably on the subject of karma and redemption, appears in *The Madras Christian College Magazine*, 1908–09. Hogg's views subsequently appear in book form in 1909, entitled *Karma and Redemption* (Madras: Diocesan Press). One of Hogg's students at Madras Christian College was S. Radhakrishnan. W. S. Urquhart's work from this period is also relevant.

the one that led Seal into this field in 1899—the instinct to consider all philosophical traditions the world over, *prima facie*, as of equal worth.

Aesthetics

The central aesthetic concept of *rasa* (a distinctive taste or essence that is evoked in an appreciator by a good artwork) is traceable back to Bharata's *Natya Shāstra*, a text on dance-drama, regarded by some as a fifth Veda, and famously reinterpreted by Abhināvagupta in the eleventh century CE. Indian aesthetic theory and art criticism, and *rasa* in particular, takes on a particular modern cast in the nineteenth and twentieth centuries. The ways in which aesthetic issues are conceptualized, framed, discussed, and criticized by scholars vary in intriguing ways in the colonial context.

M. Hiriyanna, in a number of essays dating back to 1919, was perhaps the first philosopher in the Indian academy to argue for the indispensable place of aesthetics in Indian philosophical thought. While acknowledging the centrality of traditional metaphysical and epistemological concerns—of a quest for truth, knowledge, and Ultimate Reality—he uses the notion of the *jivanmukta* (a person who is free on this earth, rather than in the hereafter) to argue for (both) aesthetic (and ethical) practice as making possible a freedom for an individual that comes not from an extinction or suppression of instincts and interests, but rather from their expansion. Consequently, the cultivation of the emotions is one of the aims of art and must be on par with a cultivation of the intellect. In addition, while art does not have anything directly to do with morality so that "a moral *aim*" is not required as a precondition for aesthetic practice (as it is often required as a precondition for intellectual practice), Hiriyanna argues that art must have "a moral *view*, if it should fulfil its true purpose" (Hiriyanna 1954, 59). This purpose is to free the human being from all strife and secure a form of unique joyful experience. In this way, the metaphysical idea of *mokṣa* (ultimate freedom) gets yoked to the aesthetic, and thereby to the world of the here and now. While Hiriyanna is among the first to underscore the role of the aesthetic in questions concerning freedom, there are many who continue to develop this theme, albeit with different emphases.

Mulk Raj Anand wrote *The Hindu View of Art* (1933) with a view to rendering accessible to a global audience Indian aesthetic concepts and their connection to more fundamental philosophical and soteriological concerns. Anand shows the essential connection between the Hindu view of art and the Hindu view of life by arguing that the concept of *rasa* in the aesthetic domain is not different from the concept of *ānanda* (bliss) in the metaphysical domain nor the concept of *Īṣvara* (God) in the religious domain.

Ananda K. Coomaraswamy (1877–1947), in a string of essays on Indian aesthetics, provides the concept of *rasa* with a nationalistic slant. He argues for the presence of a distinctive Indian-ness to the best Indian art and identifies that distinctive Indian essence with *rasa. Rasa* comes to be evocable only in a subject immersed in Indian culture and aesthetic theory and by art objects that are traditionally Indian. Art works with national themes are regarded as the ones most likely to evoke *rasa.* Thus, Abanindranath Tagore's artistic rendition of *Bhārat Mata* becomes, for the philosophical, art historical, and artistic community of that period, simultaneously quintessentially authentically Indian and the work that evokes *rasa* in the clearest way to the most discerning of appreciators (*rasikas*).

The debate between the "Revivalists" and the "Modernists" in this period turns on the question of whether Indian aesthetic theory is uniquely applicable to Indian subject matter, techniques, and artists immersed in the Indian cultural and religious tradition, or whether *rasa* can be evoked universally from a range of subject matters, techniques, and cultures. If Coomaraswamy is the paradigmatic nationalist Revivalist, then B. K. Sarkar is India's universalist Modernist. In a section entitled "View-Points in Aesthetics," Sarkar argues against a conception of *rasa-vidya* that requires that it be rooted in any specific religious, cultural, or philosophical tradition. While he acknowledges that the significance of a work of art for a religious devotee or an art historian or a nationalist depends on the religion, art historical training, or nation from which the individual springs, he argues that for a *rasika,* one who is to appreciate a work on purely aesthetic grounds, the work is universal: "Paintings and sculptures are... universal in their appeal because their spiritual basis is geometry, the most abstract and cosmopolitan of all *vidyas*" (Sarkar 1922, 138).

Sarkar makes the case for the sculpture of the Tamil *Natarāja* (the god of dance) as one of the permanent glories of the human creative genius in the following way: "Nataraja is a most original creation in the ripple of bends and joints. The balancing of diverse masses in motion, the swaying of the volumes away from one another, the construction of imaginary circles within circles, the grouping of unseen parallels in movements and poses, and the gravitation of all the varied shapes to a common center of dynamic rhythm—all these constitute an epoch-making attainment of unity in diversity, of the correlation of matter and motion, which possesses a meaning in the idiom of *rupam* as much to the Western as to the Eastern artist" (Sarkar 1922, 140). In this way, Sarkar illustrates the kind of universal language and the universal structural forms that, no matter from where and by whose hand they originate, when wielded by the artist in his or her appropriate genre, can evoke *rasa* in the *rasika* who comprehends and appreciates that language.

K. C. Bhattacharyya, in what many regard as the seminal academic essay on *rasa* from this period ("The Concept of Rasa" [1930], in Bhattacharyya 1958), provides an analysis of this concept that is striking in its distance from religious or even explicitly Indian philosophical vocabulary. Bhattacharyya's approach to *rasa-vidya* is subjective rather than objective, focusing more on the levels of feeling that are evoked in a subject in the presence of an object rather than on the compositional and structural properties of the work itself, as does Sarkar. And yet, the kind of subjectivity that occupies his attention is as distanced from the kinds of religious and national focus that are central to Coomaraswamy, Hiriyanna, and Anand in their respective interpretations of Indian aesthetic theory.

Bhattacharyya distinguishes between three levels of feeling with respect to an object. The first is direct feeling, as in the case of a child who enjoys a toy. There is no felt distance between the subject and object. The next level involves the feeling of a feeling, rather than of an object per se. Sympathy is an example of this level of feeling, as is the case when I enjoy the enjoyment of my child with her toy. At this level of feeling there is a felt distance from the object (the toy), in that I would not be personally upset if the toy were no longer present, as indeed the child would. So there is a freedom of sorts, but a connection (or un-freedom) remains in my connection to the child (and my investment in her feeling, which manifests itself as sympathy). There is a third level of feeling that is more detached or free—which Bhattacharyya characterizes as "sympathy with sympathy," or "duplicated sympathy." Consider a stranger who accesses my feeling as a mother in the presence of the child's feeling. At this level, the investment in the feeling of a feeling ceases to be grounded in the particular (this mother's enjoyment of this child's enjoyment of her toy): "Since it is altogether detached from the particularity of fact, it is a kind of eternal reality, a real eternal value" (Bhattacharyya 1958, 352).

Aesthetic enjoyment belongs to this third level of feeling, a contemplative rather than a sympathetic joy. There is a disinvestment in the particularity of the feeling that the mother has as she sympathizes with her child's feeling and an expansion instead to something more universal, to the essence of the emotion that begins with the child's enjoyment of the toy and continues through the mother's enjoyment to that of the stranger who knows neither particular and so is able (paradoxically) to feel the most freely. Bhattacharyya calls this feeling the "heart universal" (*sahṛdaya*). Despite the fact that the feeling is contemplative rather than sympathic or primary, *rasa* nonetheless has neither an intellectual nor a spiritual component, and is to be explicated purely in terms of feeling. Aesthetic questions that stem in part from Bhattacharyya's work but that have much broader implications are taken up in a sustained way by his son Kalidas Bhattacharyya (1911–1984) and further developed by subsequent generations of his students at Shantiniketan and elsewhere.

It is fitting to end the section on the aesthetics of this period with the poet-philosopher Rabindranath Tagore, who delivered the Presidential Address at the very first session of the Indian Philosophical Congress (hereafter IPC) in 1925 on the subject of the relation between philosophy and poetry, or, more broadly, between art and life. Tagore's own written and artistic work contains aspects that are Revivalist and Modernist. His early work as a writer and poet—including Bengali Baul songs in translation and, most famously, his work *Gitānjali,* for which he won the Nobel Prize for Literature in 1912—is arguably Revivalist, in part an attempt at making the connection between the classical, the vernacular, and the religious in a national context. However, Tagore's later writings and especially his work as a painter reveal modernist susceptibilities, as he breaks in his later years in both painterly style and philosophy from his famous artist-nephew A. Tagore. This latter susceptibility, in his artistic work, to a modernism that is more international than national in character is most clearly seen in his more political writings on the issue of nationalism (see below).

Ethics and Social and Political Philosophy: Imagining and Working Toward a Nation

The spiritual goal of the major Indian philosophical traditions—that of self-realization—is understood in a quite distinctive way in the colonial period of Indian philosophy. In a shift in emphasis to the role of the individual in society and away from the more traditional detachment and distance of the individual from society, the metaphysical goal of individual liberation (*mokṣa*) from this world of suffering is yoked to the ethical goal of selfless activity in this world as a response to suffering. The *Bhagavad Gita* in particular becomes for many philosophers a text from which to fashion an ethics and a politics.

Hiriyanna is as celebrated for his ethics[6] as he is for his aesthetics. In his IPC address in 1939 (Dubey 1998, v. 1, 285–297) entitled "Subjective Self-less-ness: The Message of Indian Philosophy," Hiriyanna argues that it is "unselfishness" that Indian philosophical systems in general have emphasized as the ideal of life. While this might suggest that renunciation of various worldly goods and activities is the route to such an ideal, Hiriyanna argues that it is in fact "self-renunciation and not world-renunciation" (288) that is recommended, and refers to the core message of the *Gita* with its insistence on a life of incessant activity. Self-renunciation, then, is consistent with a self that acts in the world; indeed, service is not merely consistent with renunciation, but is rather "the very means of cultivating it. Consequently, the aim is not renunciation *and* service, but renunciation *through* service" (Dubey 1998, 289). This form of argument, one that kept intact the fundamental ideal of renunciation as it made service integral to its very conception, was fashioned in different contexts during this period. Aurobindo's *Essays on the Gita* (1950) is a sustained argument for the indispensable role of action in the liberation of the individual. Vivekananda, critical of the kind of Vedāntic approach that was more inward looking, argued for an interpretation of Advaita that could lead to the active transformation of society.

Anglophone Indian philosophy coincides with and contributes to the Indian Renaissance (or Resurgence, as Vivekananda chose to characterize it). Traditional philosophical concerns were linked to the social and political movements that swept India during this period. For instance, individual subjectivity gets linked to an essential Indian identity; Indian aesthetics gets linked to *swadeshi* ("one's own land"; more descriptively, the name Gandhi gave to the practice of a way of life that would ensure economic self-sufficiency on one's own land and with local, rather than foreign, resources); and philosophical debates about the concept of the nation itself and the relation between nationalism and internationalism come to the fore within the philosophical community in a new way.

6. Hiriyanna's seminal *Indian Conception of Values* (1950) is a more wide-ranging work that makes the case for a distinctive approach to ethics, aesthetics, and metaphysics in different Indian philosophical traditions.

Aurobindo's *The Renaissance in India* (1918) is a classic from this period. He sees the Indian renaissance as a "reawakening" rather than the "overturn" or "reversal" that was true of the renaissance in Europe, preferring instead to see in India "a resemblance to the recent Celtic movement in Ireland, the attempt of a reawakened national spirit to find a new impulse of self-expression... after a long period of eclipsing English influences" (Aurobindo 1918, 2). In a shift from individual subjectivity to the Indian nation as subject, Aurobindo concludes in the following way:

> India can best develop herself and serve humanity by being herself.... This does not mean, as some blindly and narrowly suppose, the rejection of everything new that comes to us... [that] happens to have been first developed or powerfully expressed by the West. Such an attitude would be intellectually absurd, physically impossible, and above all unspiritual; true spirituality rejects no new light, no added means or materials of our human self-development. It means simply to keep our center... and assimilate to it all we receive, and evolve out of it all we do and create. (Aurobindo 1918, 25)

A. K. Coomaraswamy worries about the ability of the Indian to maintain the center or core of which Aurobindo speaks, if the new ideas to which India is exposed are tainted by a legacy of Imperialism.

> Our struggle is part of a wider one, the conflict between the ideals of Imperialism and the ideals of Nationalism.... [W]e believe in India for the Indians... not merely because we want our own India for ourselves, but because we believe that every nation has its own part to play in the long history of human progress, and that nations, which are not free to develop their own individuality and own character, are also unable to make the contribution to the sum of human culture which the world has a right to expect of them. (Coomaraswamy 1909, 2)

Coomaraswamy, in his defense of Indian nationalism, argues for a link between nationalism and internationalism with the idea that each nation gets the freedom to develop its ideas in its own way, free from external interference. This optimism as to the consequences of adopting a robust nationalist approach is not shared by Rabindranath Tagore, as we shall see below, in his debates with M. K. Gandhi on the subject of the nation.

Two cultural icons, nonacademic philosophers with pan-Indian and international reputations, were Rabindranath Tagore (1861–1941) and M. K. Gandhi (1869–1948). The disagreements between Tagore and Gandhi on the concept of nation and on the appropriate route to political independence were real, even as they also had much more in common than was evident on the surface. Tagore, in his essays on nationalism (1916, 1917), worries about the divisive effects of the idea of Nation on its peoples. He says: "A nation... is that aspect which a whole population assumes when organized for a mechanical purpose. Society as such has no ulterior purpose" (Das 1996, 421). He argues that there is an oppressive and stultifying aspect to the very concept of the nation. About the British he says: "I have a deep love and a great respect for the British race as human beings.... We have felt the greatness of this people as we feel the sun; but as for the Nation, it is for us a thick mist of a stifling nature covering the sun itself" (Das 1996, 424). Tagore runs an analogous argument for a separation between a concern for Indian peoples and the concern for an Indian nation. The symbolism of Bharat Mata (Mother India) worries him, as does that of the Charka (the spinning wheel),[7] as symbols that are more inclined to impose a unity from without rather than encourage a creative and organic unity from within. This concern, however, is not shared by Gandhi.

Gandhi creatively combines the metaphysics of the *Gita,* the perspectival epistemology of Jain philosophy, with its corresponding prescription of *ahiṃsā,*[8] and Thoreau's notions of a return to nature and the justifiability of civil disobedience to craft a distinctive philosophical politics for the Indian nation in its struggle for independence. He argues that political freedom (*Swaraj* as self-government) is genuinely possible only when individuals are free (*swaraj* as mastery over oneself). The cultivation of self-mastery is far from being a purely individual pursuit. In expanding the scope and conception of *dharma* (variously translated as duty, ethics, and service, to mention just a few examples), Gandhi includes the social ideal of selfless service we encountered earlier with Hiriyanna, but goes further in proposing a political ideal of a citizenry united under one nation.

B. K. Sarkar shares with Tagore his criticism of the political and cultural arguments in support of nationalism more generally and of conceiving of India as a nation in particular. Sarkar criticizes those, such as A. K. Coomaraswamy, who would put forward the "hypothesis as to the 'Indianness' of Indian inspiration, that is, the distinctiveness of Hindu [or 'Indian'] genius" (Sarkar 1922, 117), arguing that this would be as bizarre as an Indian physics or chemistry. Sarkar goes on to develop a sustained argument for a pluralistic India. "There is no one India" he writes, "there are Indias" (Sarkar 1922, 298). He emphasizes the heterogeneity rather than the homogeneity of Indian historical, cultural, and religious experience and articulates a vision of India that is united in virtue of, rather than despite, its plurality.

In this way Sarkar and Tagore's notions of modern India and of what it means to be authentically Indian contrast markedly from those of Coomaraswamy and Gandhi. We may locate Aurobindo somewhere between these two positions, for while he argues that India *has* a center, he sees no need to ensure its protection as a nation or culture, seeing in such efforts a fossilization rather than the much-needed rejuvenation.

A different trajectory of argument on the subject of nationalism occurs in the context of the Young India movement. At the forefront is Lajpat Rai of the Arya Samaj, who published *Young India* (1917) in London (by the Home Rule for India League), a book that was banned almost immediately as seditious in nature. The book documents the different approaches to nationalism that sprouted in India during this period and analyzes their similarities and differences. M. N. Roy

7. See Tagore 1925, "The Cult of the Charka." See also the film by Satyajit Ray based on Tagore's novel *The Home and the World* (translated from the Bengali) for an excellent depiction of the different philosophies of nation and patriotism of Tagore and Gandhi.

8. See Long, this volume.

(1889–1954) is a noteworthy philosopher as well, representing a minor but insistent Marxist philosophical voice among the more dominant voices already mentioned.

Philosophy in English in India and the Diaspora after 1947: A Sketch

Indian philosophy in English has exploded globally. The focus on Vedānta philosophy and idealism, so central in the colonial period, has shifted to other Indian philosophical schools, expanding more broadly into areas of logic, language, and phenomenology.

In India, four philosophy projects are of particular interest. One is D. P. Chattopadhyaya's ongoing project of producing a comprehensive survey of Indian Civilization in a Series, containing several volumes, entitled *History of Science, Philosophy and Culture in Indian Civilization*. It is an interdisciplinary project that includes philosophy, political theory, economics, history, and science.[9] The second is the *Samvada* Project begun by M. P. Rege in 1983 and championed most recently by Daya Krishna (1924–2007). The purpose is to facilitate a dialogue between two sets of scholars of the Indian philosophical tradition, those trained primarily in Sanskrit and those trained primarily in English. The third is the philosophy in vernacular languages project. It is a recovery project of philosophers writing in the vernacular languages during the period of British Rule, and while it is not in English, the project warrants mention in this essay as philosophy in the vernacular was and continues to be underappreciated, as was the work of those writing in English (and documented in this essay). A. Chakrabarti[10] has taken a particular interest in furthering the documentation of the vernacular philosophical work from this period. The fourth is a project undertaken under the auspices of the Indian Council of Philosophical Research (ICPR) and the editorship of S. P. Dubey: the publication of all of the Presidential Addresses of the Indian Philosophical Congress from 1925–1995. A study of these addresses offers a perspective on the development of philosophy in India during this 70-year period.

More globally, the East-West philosophy conferences at Hawaii and the work of the journal by the same name have been critical in furthering the work of cross-cultural philosophy. The work of Karl Potter and Elliot Deutsch has been influential,

9. Of particular interest is Volume X, Part 1 in the series, entitled *Developments in Indian Philosophy from Eighteenth Century Onwards: Classical and Western*, 2002, edited by Daya Krishna.

10. Currently holding positions at the University of Hawaii and at the Indian Institute for the Advancement of Science, Bangalore, India.

as has the work of B. K. Matilal in the United Kingdom and that of J. L. Mehta and J. N. Mohanty in the United States. Most recently, in the social and political domain, philosophers such as Amartya Sen and Martha Nussbaum have crafted cosmopolitan models of citizenship, patriotism, and economic development, with a particular interest in the complex and multidimensional example of India.

BIBLIOGRAPHY AND SUGGESTED READINGS

ANAND, MULK RAJ. (1933) *The Hindu View of Art.* London: George Allen and Unwin.

Aurobindo. (1918) *The Renaissance in India.* http://inyoga.online.fr/rii.html.

———. (1949) *The Life Divine.* New York: The Greystone Press.

———. (1957) *The Synthesis of Yoga.* Pondicherry: Sri Aurobindo Ashram.

BHATTACHARYYA, GOPINATH (ed.). (1958) *K.C. Bhattacharyya: Studies in Philosophy,* Volumes 1 and 2. Calcutta: Progressive Publishers. (Recent edition in 2008 at New Delhi: Motilal Banarsidass.)

CHATTERJEE, MARGARET (ed.). (1997) *Contemporary Indian Philosophy Series II.* New Delhi: Motilal Banarsidass. (Original edition edited by H. D. Lewis in 1974 in London in the Muirhead Library of Philosophy.)

CHATTOPADHYAYA, D. P. (general ed.). (2001) *History of Science, Philosophy and Culture in Indian Civilization,* Volume X. New Delhi: Center for Study in Civilizations.

COOMARASWAMY, A. K. (1909) *Essays in Indian Idealism* Colombo: Colombo Appothecaries Co. Ltd. (First Indian edition published by Munshiram Manoharlal Publishers, New Delhi, 1981.)

———. (1910) *Art and Swadeshi* Madras: Ganesh Press. (Second edition published by Munshi Manoharlal Publishers, New Delhi, 1994.)

DAS, SISIR KUMAR (ed.). (1996) *The English Writings of Rabindranath Tagore,* Volume II. Kolkata: Sahitya Akademi.

DASGUPTA, S. (1922) *A History of Indian Philosophy,* Volumes 1–5. Cambridge: Cambridge University Press. (Indian edition first published in 1975 in Delhi: Motilal Banarsidass.)

DATTA, D. M. (1934) *The Six Ways of Knowing.* London: George Allen and Unwin. (Reprinted in 1960 in a 2nd ed. Calcutta: University of Calcutta.)

———. (1950) *The Chief Currents of Contemporary Philosophy.* Calcutta: University of Calcutta.

DAYA KRISHNA. (1991) *Indian Philosophy—A Counter Perspective.* Delhi: Oxford University Press. (Revised and enlarged edition by Sri Satguru Publications, Delhi, 2006.)

———. (2001) *New Perspectives in Indian Philosophy.* Jaipur and New Delhi: Rawat Publications.

DUBEY, S. P. (ed.). (1998) *Facets of Recent Indian Philosophy,* Volumes 1–4. (Presidential Addresses of the Indian Philosophical Congress from 1925–1995.) New Delhi: Indian Council of Philosophical Research.

GANDHI, M. K. (1909) *Hind Swaraj and Other Writings,* edited by A. J. Parel in 1997. Cambridge: Cambridge University Press.

HIRIYANNA, M. (1950) *Indian Conception of Values* Mysore: Kavyalaya Publishers.

———. (1954) *Art Experience.* (Republished in 1997 by the Indira Gandhi National Center for the Arts, New Delhi.)

HOGG, A. C. (1909) *Karma and Redemption*. Tambaram: Madras Christian College Magazine Publications. (Reprinted in 1970 at Madras: The Diocesan Press.)

IYER, V. S. (1955) *The Philosophy of Truth or Tattvagnana*. Salem: Sri Ramakrishna Mission.

LARSON, G., and E. DEUTSCH (eds.). (1989) *Interpreting across Boundaries: New Essays in Comparative Philosophy*. Delhi: Motilal Banarsidass.

MAHADEVAN, T. M. P. (1985) *Superimposition in Advaita Vedanta*. New Delhi: Stirling Publishers.

MAHADEVAN, T. M. P., and G. V. SAROJA (eds.). (1981) *Contemporary Indian Philosophy*. New Delhi: Sterling Publishers.

MATILAL, BIMAL K. (1986) *Perception: An Essay on Classical Indian Theories of Knowledge*. Oxford: Oxford University Press. (Indian edition published in New Delhi, 2002.)

———. (1990) *The Word and the World: India's Contribution to the Philosophy of Language*. New Delhi: Oxford University Press.

———. (2002) *The Collected Essays of Bimal Krishna Matilal*. Vol. 1: *Mind, Language and World*, edited by J. Ganeri. New Delhi: Oxford University Press.

———. (2002) *Philosophy, Culture and Religion*, edited by J. Ganeri. New Delhi: Oxford University Press.

MCEVILLEY, T. (2002) *The Shape of Ancient Thought*. New York: Allworth Press.

MOHANTY, J. N. (2000) *Classical Indian Philosophy*. New Delhi: Oxford University Press.

———. (2000) *The Self and Its Other: Philosophical Essays*. New Delhi: Oxford University Press.

———. (2001) *Explorations in Philosophy*, edited by Bina Gupta. New Delhi: Oxford University Press.

MOORE, CHARLES (ed.). (1967) *The Indian Mind: Essentials of Indian Philosophy and Culture*. Honolulu, HI: University of Hawaii (East-West Center) Press.

MUKERJI, AC. (1927) "The Realist's Conception of Idealism," *Allahabad University Studies* III, pp. 207-243.

———. (1928) "Some Aspects of the Absolutism of Shankara (A Comparison between Shankara and Hegel)," *Allahabad University Studies* IV, pp. 375-429.

———. (1933) *The Nature of Self*. Allahabad: The Indian Press.

MURTY, SACHIDANANDA K. (1967) *Readings in Indian History, Politics and Philosophy*. London: Allen and Unwin.

MURTY, SATCHIDANANDA K., and RAMAKRISHNA K. RAO (eds.). (1972) *Current Trends in Indian Philosophy*. London: Asia Publishing House.

NIKHILANANDA, SWAMI (ed.). (1953) *Vivekananda: The Yogas and Other Works*. New York: Ramakrishna-Vivekananda Center.

POTTER, KARL. (1963) *Presuppositions of India's Philosophies*. Westport: Greenwood Press.

RADHAKRISHNAN, S. (1923) *Indian Philosophy*. 2 vols. London: George Allen and Unwin. (Oxford India paperbacks 10th impression in 2003.)

———. (1932) *An Idealistic View of Life*. London: George Allen and Unwin.

———. (1939) *Eastern Religion and Western Thought*. Oxford: Clarendon Press, Humphrey Milford.

RADHAKRISHNAN, S., and J. H. MUIRHEAD. (eds.) (1936) *Contemporary Indian Philosophy*. London: George Allen and Unwin.

RAGHURAMARAJU, A. (2006) *Debates in Indian Philosophy: Classical, Colonial and Contemporary*. Delhi: Oxford University Press.

RAJU, P. T. (1937) *Thought and Reality: Hegelianism and Advaita*. London: George Allen and Unwin.

Ranade, R. D. (1926) *An Encyclopedic History of Indian Philosophy*, Volume 2. Poona: Oriental Book Agency.
Sarkar, B. K. (1922) *The Futurism of Young Asia*. Berlin: Julius Springer.
Seal, B. N. (1899) *Comparative Studies in Vaishnavism and Christianity*. Calcutta: Hare Press.
Sen, A. (2005) *The Argumentative Indian*. New York: Farrar, Straus and Giroux.
———. (2006) *Identity and Violence*. New York: W.W. Norton and Co.
Sen, K. C. (1909) *Lectures in India*. London: Cassell and Company, Ltd.
Urquhart, W. S. (1928) *The Vedanta and Modern Thought*. London: Oxford University Press.
Vivekananda, Swami. (1915) *Jnana Yoga*. Kolkata: Advaita Ashrama.

PART III

INDO-TIBETAN BUDDHIST PHILOSOPHY

EDITED BY WILLIAM EDELGLASS AND JAY L. GARFIELD

INDO-TIBETAN BUDDHIST PHILOSOPHY

WILLIAM EDELGLASS AND JAY GARFIELD

From the standpoint of every Buddhist tradition, the central event in the history of Buddhism was the historical Buddha, Siddhartha Gautama, achieving awakening at Bodh Gaya, India. According to these traditions, his awakening under the bodhi tree consisted in his attainment of profound insight into the nature of reality, which in turn enabled the solution of the central problem toward which Buddhism is oriented—the universality and pervasiveness of suffering. The Buddha argued that this suffering is caused most immediately by attraction and aversion, and that the root cause of attraction and aversion is confusion regarding the fundamental nature of reality. As a consequence, the Buddha taught that his liberating insight into the nature of reality is the antidote to the confusion, and hence to the attraction and aversion it causes, and therefore, in the end, to suffering itself. This is the core content of the four noble truths expounded in his first discourse at Sarnath, the *Dhammacakkappavattana-sutta* (*Discourse That Sets in Motion the Wheel of Doctrine*), and is the foundation of all Buddhist philosophy.

The Buddhist world, however, is vast, and generated numerous schools of thought and philosophical systems elaborating these fundamental insights, with a substantial and internally diverse philosophical canon comparable to that of Western philosophy. Though there are important core views that characterize a philosophical approach as Buddhist, there is considerable variety in detail.

While Buddhist philosophy as a whole is aimed at soteriological concerns, involving the goal of attaining release from suffering or the insight into the nature of reality that enables it, Buddhist philosophical concerns are principally metaphysical, epistemological, and ethical. Metaphysics is foundational simply because the root of samsara—of the world of suffering—is confusion regarding the nature of reality, and liberation from suffering requires insight into that nature. Thus, it is not surprising that much Buddhist philosophy is concerned with an analysis of the fundamental nature of reality. But in order to attain liberation, one must come to *know* this nature, in a direct and immediate way, and cease to be deceived by merely apparent reality. Epistemology is hence a central concern of the tradition. The path to liberation sketched by the Buddha is a path of ethical perfection as well, as he held that morality is central to developing a real appreciation of the nature of reality and that a great deal of the suffering we encounter is caused by immorality. Buddhist ethics is hence a rich tradition.

Central to any Buddhist view of reality is the insight that all phenomena are impermanent, without essence (or selfless), and interdependent. The confusion the Buddha aimed to extirpate is the view that phenomena are enduring, are independent, and have essential cores. Impermanence is understood in a Buddhist framework in two senses, usually referred to as "gross" and "subtle" impermanence. The gross impermanence of phenomena consists simply in the fact that nothing has been here forever, and nothing lasts forever. All phenomena arise at some point, when the proper constellation of causes and conditions is present; age constantly during their existence, changing in various ways as they age; and eventually pass out of existence. At a more subtle level, on this view, all phenomena are merely momentary. Since to be identical is to share all properties, and later stages of any object fail to share all properties, nothing retains its identity from one moment to the next. Everything arises, exists, and ceases at each and every moment. On this view, the observable phenomena that we take to be enduring, including ourselves, are causal continua of momentary phenomena to which we conventionally ascribe an identity that is nowhere to be found in the things themselves.

Selflessness and interdependence are closely connected to impermanence. Most Western philosophers are accustomed to thinking of selves as personal, and as attached to human beings, and perhaps also to animals. Buddhist philosophers refer to the self so conceived as "the self of the person," connoting the self attributed by subjects of experience to themselves. But the more general idea of self at work in Buddhist philosophy is broader than this, further encompassing what is referred to in Buddhist traditions as "the self of phenomena." The idea is this: just as when we ascribe a self to ourselves as subjects we ascribe to ourselves a permanent, independent, enduring entity that is the ultimate referent of the term "I" and the possessor of our body and mind and the subject of our experience, so when we experience the objects around us as relatively permanent, independent, and substantial we thereby, at least implicitly, ascribe to them a substantial core that endures through superficial changes, that is the possessor of their parts, and that is the ultimate referent of a demonstrative "that," or of a noun phrase denoting the object in question. The idea of a self, then, is the idea of this enduring, independent core, common to the attribution of the self to persons or subjects and to external phenomena or objects.

Buddhists argue that there is no such self, either in the case of persons or external phenomena. Persons, as well as the objects of their experience, in virtue of being merely continua of causally connected episodes, lack a substantial core. Moreover, since all phenomena, including persons, exist only as causally connected continua, and since the causes and conditions of any episode in any continuum are themselves dependent on indefinitely many causes and conditions, both within and external to the conventionally identified continuum of a person or an object, all things exist only in thoroughgoing interdependence on countless other things. In short, things arise in dependence on innumerable causes and conditions, endure in dependence on innumerable causes and conditions, and cease in dependence on innumerable causes and conditions.

The analysis of phenomena, especially persons, and the emphasis on dependent origination and impermanence are already articulated in the early *suttas*, discourses attributed to the historical Buddha, often embedded in narratives with rich uses of metaphor. The collections of texts known as the "Abhidharma" (supplement to the doctrine) arose in the third and second centuries BCE, as systematic explications of the ideas articulated in the *suttas*, which present arguments that appeal both to reason and to the *suttas* to clarify philosophical claims in the discourses of the Buddha. The Abhidharma texts also seek to provide comprehensive classifications of experience, including the moral dimension of thoughts, feelings, sensations, and volitions, thereby supporting meditators in avoiding harmful experiences on the path to realization and cultivating experiences that are conducive to liberation.

In addition to cataloguing the moral and affective dimensions of experience, the Abhidharma texts also emphasize ontology, with their comprehensive presentations of the possible objects of experience. In "Abhidharma Philosophy," Jan Westerhoff situates the Abhidharma historically and then presents the Abhidharma treatments of a number of significant areas of Buddhist philosophy, including consciousness, time, ontology and metaphysics, and epistemology. Some Ābihdharmikas developed an exhaustive distinction between primary and secondary existents. Secondary existents, they argued, are phenomena that can be analyzed into their constituent parts. Eventually, however, the analysis arrives at partless atoms or partless moments of consciousness, which are said to withstand analysis, and are thus primary existents to which all secondary existents are reducible. For, the Ābihdharmikas argue, there has to be some foundational level upon which secondary existents are dependent.

Nāgārjuna (second to third centuries CE) and his Mādhyamika followers reject the Abhidharmic distinction between primary and secondary existents, arguing instead that because everything is dependently originated, there is nothing that is not susceptible of further analysis and nothing that exists independently as an ontological foundation. According to Nāgārjuna, we are mistaken in attributing essence, or substance, or any kind of irreducible existence to things, for to conceive of an essence is to conceive of something that is unchanging, and thus is not dependently arisen. Following earlier Buddhist accounts, Nāgārjuna distinguished between conventional and ultimate truths or conventional and ultimate reality. Conventionally, things exist as we take them to exist. But, Nāgārjuna argues, the conventional truth of things is, from the ultimate perspective, mentally imputed; thus, things lack essence. Ultimately, that is, things are empty of essence.

It would be a mistake, though, to take this to mean that for a Mādhyamika emptiness is the ultimate nature of things; emptiness, on this view, is itself dependently originated and therefore *also* empty of inherent existence. This is why Nāgārjuna famously defends the doctrine of the emptiness of emptiness, a doctrine that exerted enormous influence in later Buddhist thought in India, and especially Tibet, China, and East Asia. John Dunne, in "Mādhyamika in India and Tibet," discusses Nāgārjuna's relationship to the Ābihdharmikas, presents Nāgārjuna's own account, and then traces the diverse interpretations of Nāgārjuna's philosophy as it came to dominate much later Indian Buddhist thought and virtually all Tibetan Buddhist philosophy.

Mādhyamikas regarded their account as a middle way between the extremes of reification (taking things to exist as unchanging substances) and nihilism (the view that nothing endures at all). For a Buddhist, either one of these views undermined the path to liberation: reification precludes the possibility of the kind of radical change that is the overcoming of suffering; nihilism renders the soteriological path pointless and renders our everyday experience nonsensical, even as illusion. By defending conventional existence but regarding it as ultimately empty, Mādhyamikas take themselves to provide a metaphysical account that also made sense of the path to liberation.

While Yogācārins (also called Cittamātrins or Vijñānavādins) share a Mahāyāna soteriological framework with the Mādhyamikas, they took the Madhyamaka philosophical account to be a form of nihilism. The Yogācāra view, which evolved in the centuries following Nāgārjuna, also distinguishes between conventional and ultimate truth. And like the Mādhyamikas, Yogācārins regarded conventional existence as ultimately empty. But, as John Powers notes in his chapter on Yogācāra philosophy in this section, for the Yogācārins, conventional existence is empty because it consists of mental impressions; there is no access to objects external to the mind. Thus, they argue, the proper understanding of emptiness requires the rejection of any subject-object duality. Emptiness, on this view, is not emptiness of *essence*, but emptiness of *external* existence, or of subject-object duality.

While today there is some debate regarding whether Yogācārins were ontological or only epistemological idealists (or perhaps phenomenologists), Buddhist traditions in India and Tibet have generally viewed Yogācārins as rejecting the existence of external objects of phenomena and thus defending a form of ontological idealism.

Buddhist debates concerning the nature of reality and truth naturally lead to concern with questions of how knowledge is attained. Dignāga (fifth to sixth centuries) and Dharmakīrti (seventh century) inaugurated a program of systematic Buddhist epistemology, addressing the causal basis of knowledge and the structure of epistemological warrant. The central philosophical construct in this enterprise is *pramāṇa*, a term deriving from a root that means *to measure. Pramāṇa* denotes the quality of being a reliable source or instrument of knowledge, as well as the quality of being a warrant, or validator of a claim. Buddhist epistemologists generally regarded perception and inference as the only two *pramāṇas* and rejected other candidates accepted as warrants by other Indian schools such as testimony or scripture. Buddhist epistemology emerged as a prominent tradition and exerted significant influence on rival Buddhist schools and also non-Buddhist traditions, which often drew on the work of the Buddhist epistemologists to articulate and defend their own views. Tom Tillemans, in his chapter on "Buddhist Epistemology (*pramāṇavāda*)," provides a historical introduction to the movement that began with Dignāga, and then discusses Dignāga's and Dharmakīrti's views on epistemology and ontology, concepts and language, logic, argumentation, the philosophy of logic, and soteriology.

Indian Buddhist scriptures and philosophy were enthusiastically assimilated by Tibetans. Indeed, it was Tibet more than any other country that embraced the great Indian Buddhist philosophical traditions after the demise of Buddhism in the land of its birth. Matthew Kapstein, in "Buddhist Thought in Tibet: An Historical Sketch," presents an overview of the main movements, thinkers, and topics in Tibetan Buddhist thought. One of the important traditions in Tibet that has recently aroused significant interest in the West is Dzogchen, or "Great Completeness," an esoteric movement within the Nyingma school of Tibetan Buddhism. Drawing on elements of both the Madhyamaka and Yogācāra traditions, but taking them in a very different direction, Dzogchen presents a view of our ultimate nature as primordially, naturally aware and pure. As Anne Klein argues in her chapter in this section, Dzogchen thus stands in contrast with some Buddhist traditions that regard practice as the cause of eradication of mental afflictions, which discloses the fundamental emptiness of the mind; it is this emptiness, some Buddhists argue, that is Buddha-nature itself, the enlightened mind. For Dzogchen, however, the enlightened empty mind is itself luminous, with pure, positive qualities that manifest upon the removal of mental afflictions. According to Dzogchen, the ultimate nature of the mind is luminosity.

While Buddhists generally understand insight into the nature of reality to be necessary for liberation, it is not regarded as sufficient. Insight is an antidote to ignorance, but liberation also requires the overcoming of attachment and aversion, which is achieved through the cultivation of moral discipline and mindfulness. For this reason Buddhists have devoted much thought to the question of which acts, intentions, consequences, virtues, and states of mind lead to this kind of mental transformation and thereby the alleviation of suffering. In moral thought there is more agreement than in other areas of Buddhist philosophy, yet there is still a great diversity of approaches to moral questions in Buddhist traditions, as Barbra Clayton makes clear in the final contribution in this section. As Clayton notes, ethics was a central component of Buddhist theory and practice from the very first discourse of the Buddha. Clayton gives a systematic presentation of Buddhist moral thought, covering fundamental questions such as the place of ethics in Buddhist theory and soteriology; karma; intentions; merit; precepts and virtues; the distinction between "good" and "bad," or skillful or unskillful; contemporary Buddhist ethics, especially socially engaged Buddhism; and Buddhist moral theory.

CHAPTER 15

ABHIDHARMA PHILOSOPHY

JAN WESTERHOFF

The Abhidharma is one of the three collections that make up the Buddhist canonical scriptures (the other two are the *sūtras*, the Buddha's discourses, and the *vinaya*, the rules of monastic discipline). All three are usually referred to as the "three baskets" (*tripiṭaka*), indicating the way in which the original palm-leaf manuscripts were stored. The etymology of the term "Abhidharma" is controversial[1]; a plausible reading understands the prefix *abhi* as "with regard to," and *dharma* as referring to the Buddha's teachings. The Abhidharma therefore is a collection of texts intended to deal with what the Buddha taught.

While the *sūtras* and the *vinaya* are traditionally supposed to record the Buddha's teachings to various audiences and the rules he laid down for the monastic community he founded, the Abhidharma clearly plays a supplementary role: it is meant to explicate and systematize various aspects of the Buddha's teaching that are spread across his discourses. This difference is reflected in its style. While the *sūtras* speak in a colloquial manner, explaining points by metaphors and similes, the Abhidharma is written in a highly technical language, relying heavily on a framework of definitions and classifications.

The texts in the *sūtra* and *vinaya* collections adopted by the different schools of early Buddhism are very similar, yet the content of their Abhidharma collection varies. Two Abhidharma collections have been preserved in their complete forms: the Theravāda Abhidharma and the Sarvāstivāda Abhidharma. These are the ones on which our discussion will mainly focus. Both were most likely compiled in the last 250 years before the beginning of the Common Era. Both Abhidharma collections consist of seven treatises; the Theravāda Abhidharma is preserved in the original

1. Various alternative interpretations are listed in Cox 1995, 3–4.

Pāli. For the study of the Sarvāstivāda Abhidharma, we have to rely on Chinese and Tibetan translations.[2]

The discussion found in the Abhidharma texts comprises two main elements: categorizing lists (*mātṛkā, mātikā*) and explicatory discussion of points of doctrine. The lists present an exhaustive and highly intricate classification of the world of experience comprising both a soteriological and an ontological component. Classifying the various phenomena the meditator will encounter during his practices allows him to cultivate the virtuous ones leading to liberation and give up those not conducive to liberation. As these classifications are intended to be exhaustive, they also provide an ontological framework in the sense of a structured theory of the most general kinds of things that exist.[3] Explicatory discussions intend to bring out explicitly certain philosophical points that were only implicitly presented in the *sūtras*, usually by a mixture of reasoned argument and appeal to the canonical scriptures.

Considering the sheer amount of Abhidharma literature, it is not possible to come anywhere near a comprehensive survey within the limits of an essay such as this. I have therefore selected three topics that are of particular philosophical interest and relate to questions in ontology, the philosophy of time, and metaphysics.

Ontology: Two Types of Existence

The ontology of the Sarvāstivāda Abhidharma distinguishes between two fundamentally different classes of existents: primary existents (*dravyasat*) and secondary existents (*prajñaptisat*). All secondary existents ultimately depend for their existence on primary existents, though some may do so by depending on other secondary existents, which in turn depend on primary existents. Secondary existents are sometimes defined as objects that "disappear under analysis" (Cox 1995, 138–139). The idea here is that if we mentally break down an object, such as a chariot, into its constituent parts, then break these down further, and so on, until we reach its ultimate material constituents, the chariot will have disappeared and all we are left with is an agglomeration of atoms. Primary existents, such as partless atoms, or partless moments of consciousness, on the other hand, cannot be broken down in this manner and therefore "withstand analysis." Primary existents constitute the level we reach if we follow a chain of dependence relations (such as mereological dependence) to its very end. Since the Ābhidharmikas do not hold that such a chain of dependence relations could go on infinitely, a foundational level has to be reached somewhere. Objects at the fundamental level do not depend on their parts for their existence

2. For a description of the different treatises contained in these collections see Frauwallner 1995, 13–37, 39–95; and Cox 1995, 30–37.

3. For a useful survey of these categorizing lists see Hirakawa 1990, ch. 10.

and are considered to be the only things that truly exist—everything else is a conceptual superimposition upon them. Unlike secondary existents, primary ones do not depend on linguistically induced conceptualizing activity, nor do they depend on anything else (Williams 1981, 240).

We can qualify the last part of this statement by pointing out that while the Sarvāstivāda Abhidharma denies that the primary existents are in any way dependent on their parts or the conceptualizing mind, it does not claim that they are independent in terms of *every* dependence relation. In particular, they are not causally independent. Unlike the atoms postulated in other systems of Indian philosophy, the atoms of the Abhidharma are not eternal. As we will see below, they are in fact extremely short-lived. They pass in and out of existence in dependence on causes and therefore must not be understood as initial members of the chain of *causal* dependence relations. The primary existents do not constitute a first cause.

Primary existents are also the only phenomena that possess *svabhāva* (*sabhāva* in Pāli). This notion, which becomes very important in later Buddhist philosophy as the concept the Madhyamaka school wants to deny,[4] can be literally translated as "own (*sva*) being (*bhāva*)." For present purposes, it may be most helpful to render it as "substance" or "intrinsic existence," both of which indicate that an object thus characterized exists independently of other objects.[5]

It is interesting to note that the distinction between primary and secondary existents is sometimes identified with that between absolute (*paramārtha*) and conventional truth (*saṃvṛtisatya*) (Williams 1981, 237). This distinction—which initially arose from a discussion of the question concerning which of the Buddha's teachings were to be understood literally, and which had to be interpreted relative to the specific context in which they were given—proved to be very influential throughout the history of Buddhist philosophy. Its interpretation in Abhidharma philosophy provides an interesting example of how an originally hermeneutic or epistemological question ("Which description or understanding of the world is accurate without further qualification?") later acquired an additional ontological dimension ("What are the most fundamental kinds of things?").

The ontological emphasis displayed in the Sarvāstivāda discussion of the two types of existence is, however, not something that applies across the whole of the Abhidharma. In particular, the Theravāda Abhidharma appears to have placed considerably less emphasis on using the canonical sources for building a comprehensive ontological theory, a fact that also manifests in its treatment of the concept of *svabhāva* (Ronkin 2005, ch. 2 and 112–120). While the Sarvāstivādins regard it as a mark of ontological status, singling out the primary existents, the Theravādins understand it in epistemological terms: an object's *svabhāva* indicates its distinguishing or unique characteristics. It allows us to individualize and speak about

4. For more on this see Williams 1980.

5. The term *svabhāva* is also sometimes used to indicate an object's specific or essential quality, such as the heat of fire. For a more detailed discussion see Westerhoff 2007 and Williams 1981, 242–243.

objects (in particular in the context of contemplative analysis) but does not indicate their place in some ontological hierarchy (Ronkin 2005, ch. 4).

Time: The Theory of Momentariness

The theory of momentariness denies the view that objects that are causally produced are in any way temporally enduring through time. In itself it is not a theory of the nature of time,[6] but of the existence of objects in time. According to this theory, things do not lose one property and acquire a new one while staying fundamentally the same in some way (as a banana changes color from green to yellow and yet remains a banana all the time). Rather, things pass out of existence as soon as they have arisen and do not possess any "temporal thickness." Immediately after ceasing to exist, they produce a discrete new object, very much like the old one, which is also immediately going to disappear to give rise to yet another, and so on. We might call this view a cinematographic conception of reality. When watching a film, we have the impression of witnessing gradual processes and temporally thick objects, yet all there really is is a rapid succession of images projected at the wall in front of us. In a similar manner the conception of reality postulated by the theory of momentariness assumes that what appears to be a temporally thick banana is just a succession of clusters of indivisible atoms flashing up one after the other, doing so at such a high speed that we cannot tell them apart. The analogy is not perfect because the individual frames in a film are not causally connected, whereas the clusters of objects are. An image flashing up on the projection screen is not the cause of the next image immediately following it (this is caused by the fact that the frames are arranged in a certain order within the reel); however, the present banana cluster is part of the cause of the next banana cluster, which is very much like it.

It is a curious fact that the doctrinal support for a philosophical position as distinctive and important as the theory of momentariness is rather thin. Searching for a precise formulation of this theory in the Buddha's discourses, it is hard to come up with anything definite. The doctrine of universal impermanence (of which the theory of momentariness constitutes an extreme case) is indeed espoused by the Buddha; in fact, it is one of the "three seals," a characteristic that all phenomena are supposed to have—the other two are unsatisfactoriness (*duḥkha, dukkha*) and lack of substance (*anātman, anatta*). But while impermanence is implied by the theory of momentariness, it does not imply it in turn.

6. The Sarvāstivāda Abhidharma does accept an atomistic conception of time according to which the temporal instants (*kṣaṇa*) cannot be subdivided. Nevertheless, each atomic instant is supposed to contain in itself the four moments of origination, subsistence, decay, and destruction. Attempts at reconciling these two assumptions generated considerable philosophical discussion, some of which is described in von Rospatt 1995, 44–46, 97–98; and Ronkin 2005, 61–62.

Both extant systems of Abhidharma, the Theravāda and Sarvāstivāda, endorse the theory of momentariness.[7] It remains an interesting question how the move from the weaker theory of impermanence to the stronger theory of momentariness came about. The loss of the relevant texts describing the view of the earliest Buddhist schools, together with the fact that some of these texts may never have been committed to writing, makes it difficult to come to any definite conclusions regarding this matter (see von Rospatt 1995, 15–39; Ronkin 2005, 59–60).

In the same way in which the mereological reductionism of the Abhidharma entails that our perception of spatially extended objects cannot be veridical, since these, as secondary existents, do not exist at the fundamental level of reality, the theory of momentariness implies that our perception of motion, change, and causality cannot be a reflection of how things really are either. Since there is no temporally enduring banana, our perception of a green banana turning yellow cannot present us with an adequate account of what happens. Since no object lasts for more than an instant, there cannot be any causal processes that involve temporally enduring objects. The theory of momentariness therefore not only faces the challenge of having to explain why we experience the world in a fundamentally different way—that is, why we do not perceive a world of objects flashing in and out of existence, but gradual changes in persistent objects—but also the problem of how to reconcile it with other philosophical theories, such as an account of causation.

The Ābhidharmika here faces the problem that while causation is a two-place relation, only one of its relata will exist at a given time. When the effect has arisen, the cause will already have disappeared, and during the existence of the cause there is no effect yet arisen. This is closely related to the problem faced by the presentist who regards only the present but not the past or the future as real. If he wants to make the commonsensical claim that the present is the way it is because of causal influences from the past, he will have to address the worry that one of the two relata of the causal relation is completely nonexistent (Markosian 2004). But this seems to be as methodologically problematic as attempting to account for the belief in Santa Claus by postulating a "believes in" relation between a person and a nonexistent object.

This worry manifests in a variety of guises whenever causal processes are in play. Since perceptual cognition takes time, it could never be veridical in the sense that it connects with an existent object. The things we perceive have already ceased to exist when we form a cognition of them, so that all we could ever have knowledge of are nonexistent objects.

7. The matter is more complicated than I present it here. The Theravādins, for example, hold that one moment of existence of a material object lasts sixteen or seventeen times as long as one moment of existence of a mental object (Kim 1999, 130–147; Ronkin 2005, 62–63). But this would mean that a material object does not immediately disappear after arising since we can squeeze in a succession of mental moments between its production and cessation. In this case the theory of momentariness as described here would not be applicable to material objects. For further details the interested reader is referred to von Rospatt 1995, whose focus is, however, primarily on Sarvāstivāda material. The theory of momentariness in the Theravāda is dealt with in an unpublished doctoral thesis by Wan Doo Kim (Kim 1999).

The Sarvāstivāda Abhidharma tried to address this difficulty by claiming that past, present, and future objects all exist. It is from this idea that "everything exists" (*sarvam asti*) that the school takes its name. During its history, it developed various ways in which this idea could be squared with the idea of momentariness. Traditionally, it distinguishes four accounts put forward by four different authors.[8]

Dharmatrāta regarded "being past" and "being future" as modes of existence that an object could acquire without changing its underlying substance. He gives the example of a golden vessel that is melted down to make another golden thing. The idea appears to be that temporal change is regarded to be on the very same level as change of form. When we speak of the golden statue and the golden vessel that provided the raw material as both existing, we mean the gold that has endured during the transformation. In the same way, regarding the past and future as real means that as a future object becomes present, or a present object becomes past, there is an underlying real substance, the transformation of which produces these different temporal "forms" or modes of existence.

A second explanation, due to Ghoṣaka, argues that the very same object can be past, present, and future. He illustrates this initially counterintuitive claim by the example of a man attached to one woman, who is thereby not deprived of his capacity to feel attachment to other women. What is presumably meant here is that in the same way as a man can feel attached to three different women, an object can have three temporal properties and therefore exist in all three times. However, the connections to these properties may not all be of the same strengths, as the man might not feel attached to all three women equally. In fact, he might love one most, then the second, and then the third. This is probably the model of temporal change Ghoṣaka has in mind: something future becomes present if its connections with the future and past become weaker, and its connection with the present becomes stronger. It becomes past when its connections with the present and future grow weaker, and that with the past grows stronger.

The third approach, attributed to Vasumitra, regards temporal properties as relational properties in the same way as Ghoṣaka, but according to Vasumitra's model, an object cannot have all three temporal properties. He cites the example of a placeholder in a calculating device, such as a ball in an abacus. The value of the ball depends on where it is put, that is, on its relation to other balls. Whether it represents ones, tens, hundreds, and so forth is not a property of the ball but a property of our regarding it as a specific representation in relation to the other balls. We might apply this example to the temporal case by considering the relation of an object to its function. Water that can quench our thirst is present water; water that can no longer do so, past water; water that cannot quench our thirst now but can do so later, future water. The temporal predicates would then not indicate any intrinsic change in the water, but merely different relations between the water and its ability to perform a function.

8. For details of the four explanations see Stcherbatsky 1923, 78–80; Frauwallner 1995, 188–193; Cox 1995, 139–140; and Dhammajoti 2007b, 147–157.

The final account, due to Buddhadeva, shares Vasumitra's relational conception of change. However, relationality is here not spelled out in terms of relation to an object's functionality, but merely in terms of its relation to other times. Something is past in relation to present and future objects but future relative to some (even earlier) past objects, in the same way in which the same woman is a mother relative to one person and a daughter relative to another. Once again, these different predicates do not indicate a change in substance.[9]

Since all the records we have of these four theories are very brief second-hand accounts, it is relatively difficult to get a clear idea of the philosophical details of the positions involved, as well as what kinds of answers to objections the authors might have provided. Some issues, however, can be raised immediately.

Concerning Dharmatrāta's theory, it is evident that we would not want to think of the transformation of the substance as taking place in some temporal medium, so that some object *first* has the temporal form that makes it present and *later* has the temporal form that makes it past (as something first has the spatial form of a vessel and then the form of a statue). This would then make it necessary to account for the temporal medium and we would have to repeat the entire account at a more fundamental level, well on our way to an infinite regress. We therefore have to conceive of a nontemporal notion of transformation, the results of which could nevertheless be regarded as temporally distinct objects. A useful model might be the transformation of one mathematical object into another, such as the transformation of an equation into a different form. Both forms are forms of the same equation (and therefore "have the same substance"), but they do not stand in any relation of temporal priority. So it seems that we can make sense of the transformation of an object that does not require a temporal medium in turn. How to build a coherent theory of temporal relations on this is of course another matter.

Ghoṣaka's theory, claiming that objects can be related to the past, present, and future yet to different degrees, may strike us as particularly difficult to render intelligible. After all, "being present" and "being past" are mutually exclusive properties, so how could an object be connected to both the present and the past? But then "seeing blue" and "seeing green" and "seeing red" are mutually exclusive, too, yet the trichromatic theory of vision tells us that we see colors by the cones in our retina being affected simultaneously by light of the respective wavelengths. Conceived in this way, the theory has the advantage of being able to account for every point in the temporal continuum in terms of a combination of the degrees to which an object is connected to the past, present, and future.

Conceiving of temporal properties as purely extrinsic appears to be the most elegant way of reconciling the existence of past, present, and future objects with the idea that nothing lasts for more than an instant. It is this construction that the Sarvāstivādins eventually adopted, though not in the form of Buddhadeva's theory but by following Vasumitra's suggestion. The substance (*svabhāva*) of an object is

9. For a more detailed discussion of Buddhadeva's account see Williams 1977.

taken to exist in all three times, while its temporal properties are to be understood as manifestations of its relation to its efficiency (*karitrā*).[10] Depending on causes and conditions, an object, the substance of which always exists, becomes efficient. If this happens, the object is called "present." An object that is efficient at a moment, then not efficient, is past at the second moment; an object that is not efficient at a moment, then efficient, is future at the first moment.

An obvious objection to this theory is presented by objects that are present yet nevertheless unable to fulfill their function and therefore inefficient. Assuming that the function of the eye is to see, if we are locked in a dark room it will no longer be efficient. But we would not want to conclude from this that therefore the eye does not presently exist. To answer this objection, we have to take into account that the Sarvāstivādin understands efficiency in a very specific sense. It is not just any power to perform a function, but an object's ability to produce its next moment (i.e., a different object that is nevertheless very much like it and therefore conventionally regarded as the temporal continuation of that past object). To this extent, the eye in darkness is still efficient, even though it is not able to see, as long as it manages to ensure the existence of its own temporal successor.

A more important worry seems to be the fact that the existence of an underlying substance not subject to temporal qualifications contradicts the Buddha's teaching of impermanence, a notion that lies at the center of Buddhist thought and finds ample support in canonical material.[11] Is postulating such a permanent substance not an obvious violation of the assertion that all objects are marked by impermanence? The Sarvāstivādin replies that it is in fact the defender of the exclusive existence of the present moment who violates the doctrine of impermanence. This doctrine establishes that things change and do not remain fixed. But if an object passes out of existence the moment it has arisen, only to be replaced by another object, nothing changes at all; there is just a sequence of unchanging objects succeeding one another. There is no change in past or future objects, since these are nonexistent, and no change in the present, since this has no temporal thickness. To have change, rather than a sequence of distinct objects, something has to remain the same throughout the change. If we open one box and find a green banana, then open another box and find a yellow one, we do not think any change has happened unless we also assume that it is the same banana in the two boxes. This basis of change is the object's substance (*svabhāva*). This substance, however, is not permanent since it is not distinct from various changes affecting that object. It is also not identical with it, since it constitutes the basis on which the change takes place.

This reply is fine as far as it goes, yet it does not help us to understand why an object's substance should be anything more than a conceptual superimposition projected onto a series of momentary objects in order to make sense of our notion

10. For further discussion of the notion of *karitrā* see Dhammajoti 2007b, 157–165.

11. Saṃghabhadra's treatment of the question of the permanence of substance is summarized in Dhammajoti 2007b, 172–176.

of change. Even if we assume that a substance has to be postulated to make sense of the Buddha's teaching of impermanence, this does not give us a notion of substance (*svabhāva*) as a primary existent (*dravya*). All we have here is a convenient conceptual fiction, but not a solid ontological notion on which to build a comprehensive theory of what exists.

Epistemology: The Status of Perceptual Objects

The Sarvāstivāda Abhidharma defines an existent as something that produces in us a cognition of it (Williams 1981, 235). It regards perception as a process by which a representation of an externally existent object is produced in consciousness by the combination of that object and the necessary sense-faculty (including the five sense-faculties as well as the mind). Together with the theory of momentariness, however, this seems to entail that our perceptions are never veridical. During the moment when the consciousness of an object (the effect) exists, the object it is a perception of as well as the sense-faculty that allows us to perceive it (the causes) have already ceased to exist, since their respective moments have passed. But then our perception never presents anything real to us, since it only acquaints us with things that have just passed out of existence (Kim 1999, 107–108; and Dhammajoti 2007a, 42, 152–153).

The Theravāda Abhidharma appears to have solved the problem by its unique theory of the different speeds of mental and physical phenomena. Given that mental processes are claimed to run faster than material processes (there are sixteen or seventeen moments of a mental object for each moment of a material object), our perception, which necessarily requires some processing time, is allowed to catch up: we can conclude a full mental unit of a thought process during a time when the same material object still exists. In this way the perception of an object and the object itself can actually exist at the same time (Kim 1999, 107). Traditional sources illustrate this theory with the simile of two men of different height who still manage to walk side by side. Even though the tall man covers more ground with a single stride, the short man takes sixteen short steps during the time it takes the tall man to make one. In this way they can be perfectly aligned despite the different lengths of their legs (Kim 1999, 129–130).

The Sarvāstivāda Abhidharma offers two replies to this problem of nonexistent objects of perception. First, it uses the problem as an argument for the existence of past objects (Dhammajoti 2007b, 208, 345–346). Since the objects we perceive are real and must, by the doctrine of momentariness, have just passed out of existence, past objects must be real. A similar argument can be run for the existence of future objects, which are the objects of mental perception. In this way the existence of veridical perception is used to argue for the existence of objects in the three times.

Second, the Sarvāstivādin argues that cause and effect exist simultaneously, rather than successively (Cox 1988, 35; and Dhammajoti 2007a, 137). In this way, when the perception of some object arises in consciousness, its two causes, the instants of the object and of the sense-faculty, are still around. This notion of simultaneous causality is of course not without problems. It does avoid the Humean problem of everything happening at once (given that simultaneity is symmetric and effects of a cause are causes of further effects). This is because the Sarvāstivādin does not argue for the simultaneity of cause and effect in all cases, but only in certain contexts, such as that of perception (Dhammajoti 2007b, 202). Traditional examples of simultaneous causation include the relation between the flame and the wood it burns, and that between the different wooden stalks in a bundle mutually supporting each other. We may add the Kantian example of the lead ball and its impression on a cushion, as well as that of the opposite ends of a see-saw.

There are a variety of difficulties distinct from that observed by Hume. If we consider the stalks in the bundle, it is difficult to see how we can regard one as a cause and the other as an effect without appealing to the notion of temporal priority. Since stalk A is supporting B and C, B is supporting A and C, and C is supporting A and B, are they not all equally cause and effect? The distinctness of cause and effect in supposed cases of simultaneous causation also becomes problematic if we consider cases like the flame and the firewood, or the two ends of a see-saw. It is tempting to assume that we are really just dealing with one process, such as the burning fire or the moving see-saw, different aspects of which we label as "cause" and "effect." We would then say that there are not really two distinct entities here, but that the causal relata involved are merely convenient distinctions the analyzing mind has forged. This, however, is not an account the Sarvāstivādin could adopt concerning objects supposedly linked by simultaneous causation, since he would want to assume that the perception of an object arising in consciousness (the effect) and the external object and sense-faculty (the cause) are two objectively distinct phenomena standing in a simultaneous causal relation, rather than two hypostasized aspects of a single event.

The Abhidharma regards perception first and foremost as perception of something real. The Sarvāstivādins argue that what we perceive directly when we see a material object is an assemblage of atoms (i.e., an agglomeration of primary existents). That we perceive the object as a vase, a car, and so forth, rather than as a conglomeration of indivisible entities is the work of a succeeding mental consciousness that superimposes the perception of a secondary existent on the prior perception of a primary object (Dhammajoti 2007a, 142). It is important to note that at least according to some authors, the conglomeration of the atoms perceived by visual consciousness is *not* regarded as a secondary existent, while perception as a specific object, such as a vase, which is carried out by the mental consciousness, is only a secondary existent. Both the indivisible atoms and their conglomeration are regarded as similarly substantially existents (*dravya*) (Dhammajoti 2007a, 147). They obviously differ in epistemological status (we can observe the collections of atoms, but not the atoms themselves), but this is merely a reflection of the fact that our senses have threshold beyond which they cannot make distinctions, not an indication of their different ontological status.

There is a certain tension between this view and the mereological reductionism favored by the Ābhidharmikas. For if a conglomeration of atoms is a primary existent, is it not the case that there must be at least one example of a primary existent being dependent, since conglomerations depend on their parts for their existence? A reply one might make is that what is meant by saying that conglomerations are as real as the atoms they consist of is that their existence is similarly mind independent. The atoms that make up a chariot are not put into their specific spatial arrangement by the categorizing mind but are conglomerated in the way they are by their own force. (That it still takes a mind to perceive this conglomeration as a chariot is another matter). Atoms and their conglomerations are both substantially existent since neither bears the mark of the mind's handiwork. If we accept this interpretation, we might want to distinguish between two notions of primary existents: a "strong" one, which includes mereological independence and mind independence, and a "weak" one, which only includes the latter. Atoms would then come out as primary existents in a strong sense, while conglomerations of atoms are only primary in a weak sense. Chariots, vases, and so forth, however, are not primary existents in either sense.

Given that according to the Sarvāstivāda Abhidharma, perception is regarded as giving us access to what is real in the sense of primary existence, even perceptions that appear to be perceptions of nonexistent objects, such as optical illusions, objects seen in a dream, the self (which is rejected by the Buddhist doctrine of selflessness), or the mental perception of things like a hare's horn, have to be understood as endowed with real bases. In all cases the Sarvāstivādin will argue that there are real entities that are the actual objects of perception, such as the five psychophysical constituents of a person (the *skandhas*), the previous perception of objects similar to those seen in a dream, and separate perceptions of hares and horns, and that the illusory perceptions are merely superimposed on these without having any existential status in themselves (Dhammajoti 2007b, 346–348). The basis of cognition therefore does not need to exist in the manner in which it is cognized; for the Sarvāstivādin there may be a substantial difference between the characteristics of a cognition and the characteristics of the object in itself (Cox 1988, 61, 66).

This position differs crucially from that of the Sautrāntikas (a later offshoot of the Sarvāstivāda), who do accept nonexistent objects of cognition (Dhammajoti 2007a, 44–48). This is entailed by the fact that they, like the Sarvāstivādins, accept the doctrine of momentariness, yet neither presuppose that past and future objects exist as well as present ones, nor that perception constitutes an example of simultaneous causation. Therefore, by the time our mind has grasped some conglomeration of atoms as a chariot, the momentary objects so grasped have already ceased to exist. In this way our perception of the chariot is the perception of a nonexistent object (Cox 1988, 43). The Sautrāntikas also argue that present objects of perception can be nonexistent. The arguments presented for this are generally based on the fact that the same object is conceptualized differently by different people: a woman may be regarded as desirable by her lover, as hateful by her rival, as commanding respect by her son. Because these properties are not properties of the woman but rather created by the minds of the beholders, their perceptions are perceptions of something that does not exist at the fundamental level. It is easy to see how further developments of these arguments can be used in support of the Yogācāra position that all objects are nothing but a superimposition upon consciousness itself.

BIBLIOGRAPHY AND SUGGESTED READINGS

Readers who want to learn more about the issues discussed here are advised to begin with Dhammajoti 2007b and Ronkin 1995, which provide good philosophical introductions into the Sarvāstivāda and Theravāda Abhidharma. More historical background can be found in Hirakawa 1990. This book also contains a very useful "bibliographical essay" (pp. 333–334), which lists further primary and secondary Abhidharma sources available in Western languages.

Cox, Collett. (1988) "On the Possibility of a Nonexistent Object of Consciousness: Sarvāstivādin and Dārṣṭāntika Theories." *Journal of the International Association of Buddhist Studies* 11(1), 31–87.

———. (1995) *Disputed Dharmas. Early Buddhist Theories on Existence.* Tokyo: International Institute fore Buddhist Studies.

Dhammajoti, K. L. (2007a) *Abhidharma Doctrines and Controversies on Perception.* Hong Kong: Centre for Buddhist Studies.

———. (2007b) *Sarvāstivāda Abhidharma.* Hong Kong: Centre for Buddhist Studies.

Frauwallner, Erich. (1995) *Studies in Abhidharma Literature and the Origins of Buddhist Philosophical Systems.* Albany, NY: State University of New York Press.

Hirakawa, Akira. (1990) *A History of Indian Buddhism. From Śākyamuni to Early Mahāyāna.* Honolulu: University of Hawaii Press.

Kim, Wan Doo. (1999) *The Theravādin Doctrine of Momentariness: A Survey of its Origins and Development.* Unpublished D. Phil. thesis, University of Oxford.

Markosian, Ned. (2004) "A Defense of Presentism." In *Oxford Studies in Metaphysics*, Volume 1, edited by Dean Zimmerman. Oxford: Oxford University Press, 47–82.

Ronkin, Noa. (2005) *Early Buddhist Metaphysics. The Making of a Philosophical Tradition.* London and New York: Routledge.

von Rospatt, Alexander. (1995) *The Buddhist Doctrine of Momentariness. A Survey of the Origins and Early Phase of this Doctrine up to Vasubandhu.* Stuttgart: Franz Steiner.

Stcherbatsky, Theodore. (1923) *The Central Conception of Buddhism and the Meaning of the Word "Dharma."* London: Royal Asiatic Society.

Westerhoff, Jan. (2007) "The Madhyamaka Concept of *svabhāva:* Ontological and Cognitive Aspects." *Asian Philosophy* 17(1), 17–45.

Williams, Paul. (1977) "Buddhadeva and Temporality." *Journal of Indian Philosophy* 4, 279–294.

———. (1980) "Some Aspects of Language and Construction in the Madhyamaka." *Journal of Indian Philosophy* 8, 1–45.

———. (1981) "On the Abhidharma Ontology." *Journal of Indian Philosophy* 9, 227–257.

CHAPTER 16

MADHYAMAKA IN INDIA AND TIBET

JOHN DUNNE

The Mahāyāna Buddhist philosophy of India and Tibet contains several major strands, and while some strands were eventually construed to be flawed, one became dominant in Indian Mahāyāna. Its hegemony continued in Tibet, where it became the largely unquestioned pinnacle of Buddhist thought. It is the Mādhyamika or "Middle Way" philosophy, initially developed by Nāgārjuna (fl. third century).

In the context of Mahāyāna Buddhism, sweeping claims rarely survive a careful review of the historical evidence, but in saying that the Mādhyamika eventually became the pinnacle of Indo-Tibetan Mahāyāna thought, one is unlikely to run afoul of historical contradictions. The superiority of the Mādhyamika is nevertheless not a simple matter, for the term applies to a wide range of stances. In Tibet especially, the great variety of systems called "Mādhyamika" (Tib. *dbu ma*) might lead one to conclude that the term simply became an obligatory epithet for a tradition's most cherished philosophy, whatever it might be. This conclusion, however, would belie the commonalities that Mādhyamika thinkers share—commonalities that become evident when they trace themselves back to Nāgārjuna, the revered originator of Mādhyamika thought.

This essay will thus focus on Nāgārjuna's initial articulation of Mādhyamika, and it will then examine the central developments in the Indian and Tibetan traditions he inspired.

Nāgārjuna

Traditionally depicted as being at once philosopher, contemplative adept, and alchemist, Nāgārjuna composed various texts that provide the philosophical underpinning for the burgeoning Mahāyāna influences in Indian Buddhism. Chief among his texts is *Wisdom: Root Verses on the Middle Way (Mūlamadhyamakakārikā)*, which received the most commentarial attention and has had the greatest impact. Although sometimes questioned in their authorship, five other texts are also especially important sources for his philosophical views, including the *Precious Garland (Ratnāvalī)*, in which his arguments are integrated with aspects of Buddhist practice. In various ways, these philosophical works evince the forces at work in the rise of Indian Mahāyāna.

One aspect of the Mahāyāna especially important to Nāgārjuna's philosophy arises from the shifts in attitudes and practices that bear on the nature of a Buddha or "awakened" being. Prior to Nāgārjuna, visual depictions of the historical Buddha represented him not iconically as present, but aniconically as absent. Such depictions include an empty throne or a set of footprints. As these depictions suggest, all that remained were traces of the Buddha, including his relics and, most important, his teachings. Around Nāgārjuna's time, however, new depictions arise in which the Buddha is fully present in a remarkable physical form. The Buddha thus reemerges in the Buddhist world, and in part this must mean that, for him, *nirvāṇa* did not signify an utter cessation or end. Instead, this period witnesses the development of a new notion of *nirvāṇa* as "unlocated" (*apratiṣthita*). The Buddha is not situated in the suffering world of cyclic existence (*saṃsāra*), nor is he located in some quietistic cessation (*nirodha*). Instead, he is not bound by either state but remains free to continue expressing enlightened activity in the world.

Whatever may have motivated such shifts in attitudes about the Buddha, the result is a corresponding reconfiguration of *nirvāṇa* as the final goal of Buddhist practice. Earlier Buddhism emphasizes the cessative quality of *nirvāṇa;* it is the end of suffering, an escape from the "prison of *saṃsāra*." In the Mahāyāna, however, mere cessation is no longer the final goal. *Nirvāṇa* becomes a radical transformation that is indeed the cessation of *saṃsāra*, but also the full "blossoming" or "awkening" (*bodhi*) of a buddha's capacities to aid others in their search to end suffering. In a typical trope, one Mahāyāna literary text presents the figure of Śāriputra, a disciple of the Buddha, who rhetorically represents a pre-Mahāyāna view. Assembled with others to hear the Buddha's teaching, Śāriptura overhears someone speak of how beautiful the setting is, but as he surveys the environment, all he sees are the peaks and valleys of *saṃsāra*, a world filled with ordure. His thoughts become known to the Buddha, who, to make a dramatic point, momentarily alters Śāriputra's perception, such that now he beholds the environment as a magnificent and breathtakingly beautiful heaven. The point is an obvious one: achieving freedom from *saṃsāra* no longer requires an escape to *nirvāṇa*, but rather a transformation such that *saṃsāra* itself becomes *nirvāṇa*.

This literary reconfiguration of *nirvāṇa* crucially requires a philosophical complement, for it poses insurmountable problems for the form of philosophy, generally characterized as the Abhidharma, that precedes Nāgārjuna and the Mahāyāna. For Abhidharma theorists, the constituents of body and mind—and indeed, the world itself—are all products of *karma*. That *karma* is caused by "ignorance" (*avidyā*), whose distortions lead inevitably to suffering. Thus, as the products of ignorance, the constituents of mind, body, and world are *saṃsāra*, an incessant stream of suffering. Moreover, since ignorance is central to the causal process that produces those constituents, they are by their very "nature" (*svabhāva*) products of ignorance. Thus, the cessation of ignorance—the root cause of *saṃsāra*—must also lead to the cessation of those constituents. In this way, on the Abhidharma view the cessation of *saṃsāra* does not permit a continued presence in the world because with the cessation of ignorance comes not only the cessation of *saṃsāra* for the one who has ended ignorance, but also the end of that being's mind and body in a final *nirvāṇa* (*parinirvāṇa*) where no products of ignorance are possible. To accommodate the notion that the attainment of final *nirvāṇa* no longer entails a Buddha's utter absence, the Mahāyāna thus requires a philosophical view whereby the end of suffering still permits participation in the world—a view whereby the constituents of mind, body, and world are not, in their very nature, the products of ignorance. The need for such a philosophy is central to Nāgārjuna's context, and it is answered by one of his best-known aphorisms:

> *Saṃsāra* is not at all different from *Nirvāṇa*. *Nirvāṇa* is not at all different from *saṃsāra*. (*Wisdom* 25.19)

From the perspective of early Buddhism, Nāgārjuna here presents so radical a view that one might consider him to be breaking entirely with his Buddhist predecessors. His writings, however, rely heavily on the Abhidharma, and his philosophical project rests on some fundamental presuppositions that he inherits. One issue in particular is the notion, cited above, that ignorance fuels *saṃsāra*, and that the way out of *saṃsāra* requires the elimination of ignorance. This principle lies at the core of the Four Noble Truths of Buddhism, most especially the claim that suffering (the first truth) has an origin (the second truth). For the Abhidharma traditions, suffering's origin was generally conceived as the aforementioned ignorance: a cognitive defect that distorted each moment of awareness. Articulated as a belief, it is the notion that for each person there is an absolute, unchanging, nondependent Self (*ātman*) that is the one who perceives, who acts as an agent, who controls the mind and body, and so on. For Abhidharma theorists, this distorted belief in an absolute Self not only leads to ineffective actions motivated by the belief, but also drives the causal process of compulsive rebirth in *saṃsāra*. And Nāgārjuna very much agrees when he says that "when [the attitudes] 'I' and 'my' have ceased, the appropriation [of the next embodiment] ceases. Through the cessation of appropriation, birth ceases" (*Wisdom* 18.4).

Early Buddhist arguments against this notion of an absolute Self take various forms, but they often refer to the constituents of the mind and body, known as the "aggregates" (*skandha*). One well-known strategy is a mereological critique, whereby this alleged Self is analyzed in relation to its constituents, the aggregates. Just as a chariot, when analyzed in terms of its parts, cannot exist as either identical to or different from those parts, so, too, the Self cannot exist as identical to or different from the aggregates. Nāgārjuna also endorses this argument (e.g., *Wisdom* 18.1), whose intricacies deserve more attention than is possible here. Nāgārjuna's key revision is to move beyond a critique merely of a Self in persons; instead, he redirects and sharpens the analysis in an attempt to demonstrate that even the aggregates lack any essential identity.

The word "essence" here renders a key Sanskrit term, *svabhāva*, which is the main object of Nāgārjuna's critiques. In part to serve the mereological analysis mentioned above, the Abhidharma traditions formulated precise accounts of the constituents of mind, body, and world. In the Abhidharma of the Sarvāstivāda, one of Nāgārjuna's main objects of critique, these constituents are termed "elements" (*dharma*s), and they are "substantially real" (*dravyasat*) or "ultimately real" (*paramārthasat*) in that they are irreducible. In contrast, things that are reducible to these primary elements are real only in terms of designations (*prajñaptisat*); that is, they are only conventionally real (*vyavahārasat*). On this analysis, a vase, for example, would exist only conventionally because it can be reduced to the particles that compose it. In contrast, the particles themselves, being irreducible, exist ultimately. Moreover, a thing that exists ultimately—or "substantially" in Abhidharma terminology—is not only irreducible; it also exists in terms of its "own nature" (*svabhāva*). In this way, the Abhidharma formulates the notion of "two truths" or "two realities" (*satyadvaya*), the ultimate reality of substantially existent things and the conventional reality of whatever is made from them.

Although Nāgārjuna does not always clearly target a particular Abhidharma tradition, he indisputably focuses on the notion that an ultimately existent thing—be it a material element or an irreducible component of mind—exists in terms of its *svabhāva*. For Nāgārjuna, this means at least that if an entity exists "essentially" (*svabhāvataḥ*), its identity—what it truly is—must be established without any dependence on any other entity for its existence. In contrast, an entity might exist *parabhāvataḥ*, that is, in terms of another (*para*) entity's nature (*bhāva*). To return to the example of the vase, it exists not in itself (*svabhāvataḥ*), but rather by virtue of the existence of something else, namely, the particles that compose it. As such, the vase only exists conventionally; to exist ultimately, it must exist in itself, that is, *svabhāvataḥ* or in terms of its *svabhāva*. It is this sense of *svabhāva*—as marking what is intrinsic or essential to an ultimately real thing—that Nāgārjuna targets in his arguments. He will seek to demonstrate that any search for an ultimately real entity—something that exists with *svabhāva* or essential identity—always ends in failure.

In targeting *svabhāva* or "essence," Nāgārjuna expands the definition of ignorance. Later commentators note that, in addition to the "essencelessness of persons" (*pudgalanairātmya*) that the Abhidharma philosophers seek to demonstrate, Nāgārjuna argues for the "essencelessness of things" (*dharmanairātmya*). Hence, while Abhidharma thinkers maintain that the world's basic elements (*dharmas*) are ultimately real because they are irreducible, for Nāgārjuna even these basic building blocks do not ultimately exist. In short, the upshot of Nāgārjuna's arguments is that no person or thing whatsoever exists essentially (*svabhāvataḥ*), and since essential existence is what constitutes ultimate existence, no person or thing whatsoever exists ultimately. Instead, all things are "empty of essence" (*svabhāvaśūnya*), and this "emptiness" (*śūnyatā*) is the final answer to any inquiry into whether any entity exists ultimately.

Some of Nāgārjuna's detractors interpret his philosophy of emptiness as nihilism, but on examination, a nihilistic interpretation is difficult to defend. *Wisdom*'s first chapter argues against the possibility of ultimately real causation. The crux of the argument appears in this aphorism:

> A causal condition for either an already existent thing or a not yet existent thing does not make sense. A causal condition for something non-existent is a condition for what? And what would be the purpose of a causal condition for something that already exists? (*Wisdom* 1.6)

The argument here plays on the fundamental problem that Nāgārjuna sees in asserting the identities of things. To say that the essence or intrinsic nature (*svabhāva*) of a seed is to be a cause for an effect such as a sprout, one must define that essential nature in terms of the effect, for as he later says, "It does not make sense for something that is not producing anything to be a cause" (*Wisdom* 20.22). If, however, the cause can only be defined in terms of an effect, then the effect must already exist at the time of the cause because it makes no sense to define an entity's identity in relation to an entity that does not exist. Or, as Nāgārjuna puts it, "A causal condition for something non-existent is a condition for what?" On the other hand, if the effect does indeed exist such that another entity can be defined as its cause, then what purpose does that cause serve? The effect exists, so the cause is unnecessary.

This analysis of identity rests on a dyadic relationship, and although Nāgārjuna examines more complicated relations, the dyadic analysis is the most straightforward and the most frequently employed. The dyadic argument is clearest, perhaps, in his analysis of the relationship between desire (*rāga*), thought to be an irreducible mental constituent, and a desirous mind (*rakta*)—that is, one in which desire is occurring. In that analysis he begins, "If the desirous mind, in exclusion from desire, existed before desire, then desire would exist in dependence on the desirous mind such that when the desirous existed, there would be desire" (*Wisdom* 6.1). The problem, of course, is that to define that moment of mind as by its nature desirous, one must appeal to the presence of desire, but desire cannot itself be defined except as that which is occurring in a desirous moment of mind. One response would be to claim that the two occur simultaneously, but Nāgārjuna responds, "It is not possible for desire and the desirous to arise simultaneously because desire and the desirous would then not depend upon each other" (*Wisdom* 6.3). A response might be that they mutually define each other, but in order for them to be defined in relation to each other, they must be separately established—they must be distinct things, which means that they each already have an essential identity or *svabhāva*. And so Nāgārjuna asks, "If desire and the desirous, while different, arise together, then do they arise together because they are already established separately? If desire and the desirous are already established separately, then why do you imagine that they arise together?" (*Wisdom* 6.6–7). There is no need to appeal to their mutual co-arisal because they are already established separately. But of course, they cannot be established separately, for neither makes sense except in relation to the other. And so Nāgārjuna concludes, "Thus, desire is not established either with the desirous or without the desirous. And as with desire, none of the elemental things (*dharmas*) are established either together or separately" (*Wisdom* 6.10).

The point of this analysis is that any candidate for a thing's true identity—any alleged essential nature or *svabhāva*—inevitably requires an appeal to something other than that thing. And then the same problem appears: to be real, that other thing must likewise have an essential nature, which again leads to the same appeal. Thus, when Abhidharma theorists claim that an ultimately existent thing must exist with an essential nature, they create an impossible requirement: that there be at least one entity whose essential identity involves no appeal to anything else. But Nāgārjuna seeks to demonstrate that all notions of identity are necessarily interdependent; hence, if essential identity of this kind is required for an entity to ultimately exist, one must conclude that ultimate existence is impossible. Instead, all things must be empty of any such ultimate essence. As Nāgārjuna puts it, "There is no thing whatsoever which occurs independently. Therefore, there is no thing whatsoever which is not empty" (*Wisdom* 24.19).

To construe Nāgārjuna's philosophy of emptiness as nihilism, one must make a crucial mistake that he explicitly warns against. One way to express Nāgārjuna's conclusion is to say that when analyzed in terms of whether they ultimately exist—that is, whether they have an essence or intrinsic nature—things cannot be said to exist ultimately. In short, all things are ultimately empty of essence, and that emptiness is the final outcome to any examination of their true or essential existence. The tempting mistake here is then to conclude that emptiness—the utter lack of any essence—is itself an ultimately real nothingness that is the essence of things. In other words, one can construe emptiness as a new, ultimate essence itself, and one thus concludes that, being ultimately empty, all things are ultimately nothing.

This nihilistic interpretation would hold if emptiness itself were immune to the critiques that Nāgārjuna raises against any entity that is alleged to be ultimately real, but he explicitly applies the same critique to emptiness. He says, "If there were some [entity that is] the non-empty, then there would be some [entity that is] the empty. There is no non-empty; how could there then be the empty?" (*Wisdom* 13.7). Emptiness itself faces the same problem of the dyadic relation cited above, for it can only be defined in terms of the nonempty. But since the nonempty is equally contingent (on emptiness), neither can exist ultimately. Emptiness, too, is only contingently or conventionally real. In this way, no philosophical truth can withstand analysis, and all views—including the philosophy of emptiness—are contingent. Not heeding this argument, those who insist on turning emptiness into a "view" (*dṛṣti*)—that is, those who seek to proclaim its ultimate, noncontingent truth—are indeed nihilists. And as Nāgārjuna said, "The victors [i.e., the Buddhas] have said that emptiness is the death of all views, but they said that, for those whose view is emptiness, there is no cure" (*Wisdom* 13.8).

For Nāgārjuna, not only does the view of emptiness require a rejection of nihilism, but it must also be understood in tandem with interdependence. That is, in saying that no thing is ultimately real, Nāgārjuna is not denying any reality whatsoever. Instead, in saying that, in ultimate terms, all things are empty of essence, he is also saying that to the extent that things exist conventionally, they are necessarily interdependent. And in a crucial aphorism, he therefore remarks, "We say that emptiness is that which is interdependence" (*Wisdom* 24.18). And this clarifies his remark that *nirvāṇa* and *saṃsāra* are not different. They cannot be ultimately distinct because neither can be ultimately established in its own identity. Instead, *saṃsāra* and *nirvāṇa* exist only conventionally in mutual interdependence.

Indian Developments

In penning *Wisdom* and his other philosophical texts, Nāgārjuna probably had no intention to spawn a new "school" of thought. Indeed, the notion of a "school" (*siddhānta*, Tib. *grub mtha'*) is a later development in Indian thought whereby various seminal thinkers and their texts were sorted under rubrics that later became central to Tibetan exegesis. Nevertheless, not long after Nāgārjuna, Indian commentators began to identify themselves as adhering to a philosophy that they call "Mādhyamika," and numerous commentators appear all the way up to the virtual disappearance of Buddhism in India in the fourteenth century. Immediately after Nāgārjuna comes Āryadeva, who may have been his student. He writes his own independent work on Mādhyamika that further integrates Nāgārjuna's thought with Buddhist practice. After Āryadeva comes Buddhapālita, the first significant commentator on Nāgārjuna's *Wisdom*. The next major commentator is Bhāvaviveka (fl. sixth century), who critiques some features of Buddhapālita's work, and then Candrakīrti (fl. c. 625), who critiques Bhāvaviveka in turn. Candrakīrti's two major works are the *Prasannapadā* ("Clear Words"), a commentary on Nāgārjuna's *Wisdom*, and the *Madhyamakāvatāra* ("Entry into Mādhyamika"), an independent work; both texts are especially important to the development of Mādhyamika in Tibet. He and Bhāvaviveka are later seen by Tibetan exegetes as espousing significantly different approaches to Nāgārjuna's basic thought, as will be discussed below. Near Candrakīrti's time comes Śāntideva (fl. c. 675); like Āryadeva, he combines Mādhyamika with contemplative practices in a way that is seminal for the Tibetan spiritual exercise tradition (*blo sbyong*). Three subsequent philosophers are important for understanding late Indian Mādhyamika and Tibetan developments: Jñānagarbha (fl. c. 700), Śāntarakṣita (fl. c. 725–788), and Kamalaśīla (fl. c.740–795). The last two are especially central figures, for they actually traveled and taught in Tibet. Śāntarakṣita and Kamalaśīla do not comment directly on Nāgārjuna, but rather compose independent works. Several other Indian thinkers write Mādhyamika treatises, but those mentioned here are the most relevant to the overall arc of Indian Mādhyamika, especially in relation to its continuation in Tibet.

To understand the history of Mādhyamika after Nāgārjuna, one must take account of two important developments in Mahāyāna thought. First, perhaps within a century after Nāgārjuna's death, a new form of Mahāyāna philosophy arises. This new trend, the Yogācāra, also speaks of "emptiness" (*śūnyatā*), but with a new meaning. Initially articulated in a systematic way by Asaṅga and Vasubandhu (both probably active in the fourth to fifth centuries), for the Yogācāra emptiness is interpreted within the framework of the "three natures" (*trisvabhāva*). In brief, for ordinary beings the flow of experience—or mind itself—arises such that an experiencing subject appears to be established in opposition to experienced objects. Innovatively, the Yogācāra maintains that this subject-object duality is the subtlest manifestation of ignorance, and thus that this duality is actually a distortion. Described as the "constructed nature" (*parikalpitasvabhāva*), this duality within ordinary experience is a false overlay on the "relative nature" (*paratantrasvabhāva*), the causal flow of experience or mind itself. When mind is seen as it truly is—undistorted by that duality—one experiences the "perfect nature" (*pariniṣpannasvabhāva*), namely, the causal flow of mind *empty* of subject-object duality.

Bhāvaviveka, Candrakīrti, and Śāntideva will all strive to refute the Yogācāra interpretation of emptiness, for they see it as affirming the possibility of ultimate existence. Indeed, Yogācāra thinkers explicitly affirm that mind itself exists ultimately, although only in a form that makes naïve essentialism about perceiving subjects and perceived objects impossible. Certainly, all Indian Mādhyamika thinkers reject the notion that even mind could ultimately exist, but by the eighth century, some Indian Mādhyamikas are willing to employ Yogācāra techniques and arguments in the service of a Mādhyamika analysis. Thus, Śāntarakṣita and Kamalaśīla, unlike their predecessors, do not see Yogācāra as entirely flawed, and they make free use of Yogācāra methods. They endorse a sequence of analyses that lead from the Abhidharma mereological reduction of things into irreducible elements, a Yogācāra reduction of those elements to mind itself, and then finally a Mādhyamika analysis that demonstrates that not even mind ultimately exists. Integrated into a contemplative practice most clearly articulated by Kamalaśīla, this approach eventually becomes known as "Yogācāra-Mādhyamika," and it is the form of Mādhyamika that first reaches Tibet.

A second crucial development that significantly impacts Indian Mādhyamika is the formation of the Buddhist epistemological tradition. Arising within the context of Yogācāra thought, the epistemological tradition begins with Vasubandhu, but it is first systematically articulated by Dignāga (fl. c. 500). His project is then taken up by Dharmakīrti (fl. c. 625), whose rigorous reworking of Dignāga's thought becomes paradigmatic for the Buddhist epistemological tradition. The articulation of Buddhist epistemology is embedded in a context cutting across Indian philosophical traditions, and it largely concerns the question of what constitutes a "valid cognition" or *pramāṇa*. Particularly important in the Mādhyamika context is the status of perception (*pratyakṣa*) and inference (*anumāna*), which Dignāga and Dharmakīrti consider to be valid. Dharmakīrti gives a particularly thorough account of inference, in part because it is crucial to the reasoning that Buddhist thinkers use in their analyses, but also because it is the main tool that Indian philosophers use to defend their positions in debate.

While Bhāvaviveka and Candrakīrti agree in their dismissal of Yogācāra thought and method, they diverged strongly in their attitudes toward Buddhist epistemology. Bhāvaviveka, to whom only Dignāga's theories were available, readily adopted the tools of Buddhist epistemology, and he critiques his predecessor Buddhapālita for failing to do so. For Candrakīrti, however, the epistemological tradition endorses a subtle version of essentialism, and he thus strongly criticizes Bhāvaviveka for adopting its methods. In part, Candrakīrti objects to the notion that a Mādhyamika thinker can defend any thesis at all, and he harkens back to the statement, "I have no thesis," found in Nāgārjuna's *Vigrahavyāvartanī*. Although variously interpreted, Candrakīrti's main point is that the inferential reasoning of the epistemological tradition occludes the interdependence that pertains between, for example, the negation of a thesis and its affirmation. Likewise, inference requires a subject of the thesis to be established by the inference, but in a debate, how could a Mādhyamika thinker and his opponent agree on a thing, such as an effect, as the subject of the thesis? For Mādhyamikas, there is ultimately no such thing as effects, so how can they agree sufficiently with their opponents about what an effect is before going on to prove its essencelessness? In the end, the Mādhyamika who used inferential proof statements might have to accept implicitly the opponent's essentialist views in order for those proof statements to have any traction. For these and other reasons, Candrakīrti maintains that a Mādhyamika can only use "consequences" (*prasaṅga*), whereby one points out the inconsistencies in the opponent's position without resorting to an "autonomous inference" (*svatantrānumāna*), in which the Mādhyamika would seek to prove his own thesis.

Candrakīrti's rejection of the Buddhist epistemological tradition involves other issues such as the alleged essentialism in its account of perception. Yet despite Candrakīrti's efforts, his critique received little attention in India, and his texts held little sway among Indian commentators. Indeed, Śāntarakṣita and Kamalaśīla both readily embrace the epistemological tools developed by Dharmakīrti, and they see no problem in using inferences to prove their points. Their use of Yogācāra methods and Buddhist epistemology were central to the Mādhyamika that they brought to Tibet, and the epistemological orientation of their work was especially influential for Tibetan thinkers. At the same time, Candrakīrti's critiques finally found a ready audience when they crossed the

Himalayas, for the Tibetans eventually consider his version of Mādhyamika to be supreme.

Mādhyamika in Tibet

The Tibetan reception of Mādhyamika helped create a vibrant philosophical tradition that remains vital in many Tibetan institutions of Buddhist learning. The sheer magnitude of the commentarial literature—exceeding many thousands of pages—is often matched by exegetical brilliance and striking innovation. It is thus not possible to do justice here to the full range of Tibetan Mādhyamika thought. Nevertheless, although traditional Tibetan thinkers remain prolific in their philosophical writings, the overall contours of Tibetan debates on Mādhyamika were largely in place by the fifteenth century, and those contours themselves spring from crucial developments some three hundred years earlier. In many ways, these developments focus on the challenges raised by Candrakīrti.

The Tibetan reception of Buddhism is generally depicted through two "Diffusions of the Teaching" (Tib. *bstan dar*), the Early and the Later Diffusions. The former begins in the period of the Tibetan empire. During this time, a large number of Buddhist texts are translated from Sanskrit into Tibetan. The Early Diffusion ends in the ninth century with the empire's collapse and an ensuing period of turmoil in central Tibet. The Later Diffusion begins in the tenth and eleventh centuries from eastern and western Tibet, and the task of translation is renewed with vigor. A number of previously untranslated epistemological works by Dharmakīrti greatly impact Tibetan thinkers, but of perhaps even greater significance is the translation of other previously unavailable works: the main oeuvres of Candrakīrti.

In the Early Diffusion, Mādhyamika thought reached Tibet through the efforts of Śāntarakṣita and Kamalaśīla, both of whom taught in Tibet. As noted above, they articulated Mādhyamika through the tools of the epistemological tradition, and they employed Yogācāra arguments as steps toward a final Mādhyamika negation of essence. At the same time, other trends strongly influenced the transmission of Buddhism to Tibet. Indian tantric Buddhism and, to a lesser extent, Chinese Chan Buddhism impacted the interpretation of Mādhyamika within Buddhist practice. Buddhist tantras speak of emptiness, but their interpretation trends more toward the Yogācāra. Thus, to realize emptiness is to be absorbed in the direct intuition of the mind in its true nature, devoid or empty of the "adventitious defilements" (*aguntakamala*), especially subject-object duality, that make the mind into the locus of *saṃsāra*. In the tantras is also found the notion of the "Buddha-nature" (*tathāgatagarbha*), a facet of Yogācāra thought, whereby all beings are understood to have the potential—or even the actuality—of buddhahood fully present within them. In many tantric contexts, the goal of practice is to allow this innate buddhahood to emerge unobstructed, in part through ritual identification with a Buddha, but also through yogic techniques that physiologically induce states in which these adventitious obstructions are allegedly weakened or suspended. While highly varied, Chan practice shares some of these features, in that many contemplative techniques aim to clear away ordinary mind so as to allow one's original mind (i.e., one's own Buddha-nature) to manifest spontaneously.

Tantric and Chan influences probably account for the emergence of a notion of "sudden" enlightenment in the early period, and traditional sources maintain that Kamalaśīla debated with a Chinese Chan master, Moheyan, so as to defend an approach that becomes known as "gradual." One of the main distinctions between these two is the role of reason, especially the highly systematic inferential reasoning found in the Buddhist epistemological tradition. In his *Bhāvanākrama* ("Stages of Meditation"), Kamalaśīla argues against Moheyan's view, which he depicts as maintaining that "one should not think anything at all" (*na kiṃcic cintayitavyam*). For Kamalaśīla, this view leads to a disastrous abandonment of moral practice, but it also blocks the realization of emptiness because it makes rational analysis impossible. He asks, "Without analysis of what is real, how is the essencelessness of things realized? For without some analysis of it, such as, 'In their very nature things are empty,' how would there be the penetrating realization of emptiness?" For Kamalaśīla reason plays a central role, for on his view liberative insight does not spontaneously emerge from simply stopping thought; it must instead arise through the careful cultivation of a particular realization that results from rational analysis. Traditional accounts maintain that Kamalaśīla prevailed over Moheyan, but the role of reason remained a crucial issue.

In many ways, reason's role is central to the controversy evoked by the translation of Candrakīrti's major works at the outset of the Later Diffusion. Although Candrakīrti's round rejection of the Buddhist epistemological tradition found little favor among his fellow Indian scholiasts, the Later Diffusion witnessed a further influx of philosophical and tantric materials that leaned toward an interpretation of enlightenment as "sudden." It appears that Candrakīrti's skepticism about the reach of reason cohered with these materials. So, too, it coincided with a growing community of practitioners who rejected (or did not receive) training in the intricacies of Buddhist scholasticism—a scholasticism that was only growing more technical with the new translation of Dharmakīrti's works.

Whatever led to the sudden relevance of Candrakīrti, the debates that began around his works in the twelfth and thirteenth centuries continue to this day. Recently recovered materials (previously thought to be lost) have energized academic research on this crucial period in Tibetan intellectual history, and as new publications appear, previous work will undoubtedly face revision. Nevertheless, in general terms, the debates spurred by Candrakīrti's works can be roughly situated between two camps: on the one hand, defending the Mādhyamika interpretation of Kamalaśīla and Śāntarakṣita are the scholars of Sangphu (gsang phu) monastery, founded by the renowned translator and exegete Ngog Loden Sherab (rNog blo ldan shes rab, 1059–1109). Here, the sixth abbot Chapa Chokyi Senge (Phya pa chos kyi seng ge, 1109–1169) plays an especially important role. In the other camp stand those who promulgate Candrakīrti's view, necessarily supplanting the approach of Śāntarakṣita and Kamalaśīla. Here one finds Patsab Nyima Drag (Pa tshab nyi ma grags, b. 1055), who eventually took up residence in Gyel Lhakhang monastery (rGyal lha khang) after a long sojourn in Kashmir where he translated Candrakīrti's two major works. In this camp also stands the Kashmiri scholar Jayānanda (fl. twelfth century), who traveled in the Tibetan cultural region and there composed his commentary on Candrakīrti's *Entry into the Mādhyamika*. Another key figure is Mabja Changchub Tsondrü (rMa bya byang chub brtson 'drus, 1109–1169). Although initially one of Chapa's top students, Mabja switched camps and studied perhaps with both Patsab and Jayānanda. In some ways, his views bridge the two camps, though in the end he effectively abandons Chapa's interpretation by favoring Candrakīrti's approach.

As mentioned above, the crux of this debate is the role of reason, but this issue can be articulated through Candrakīrti's notion of buddhahood, especially as interpreted by Jayānanda. Clearly, to eliminate ignorance one must realize emptiness, but according to Jayānanda, Candrakīrti says: in knowing emptiness, a Buddha is not knowing anything at all. Instead, this knowing is actually a nonknowing that only metaphorically can be referred to as a cognition of emptiness. Thus, in the liberative awareness of the ultimate that is emptiness, there is no object known, nor any mind engaged in the act of knowing. Moreover, in the state of buddhahood, ignorance cannot be active. In lieu of cognitions distorted by ignorance, a Buddha has only uncontaminated gnosis of the ultimate. And since that gnosis is not a knowing of anything at all, Candrakīrti concludes that in a Buddha's awareness "mind and mental facets" (*cittacaitta*) have ceased. It is only from the perspective of ordinary beings that a Buddha appears to make decisions so as to engage in compassionate activities that lead beings out of suffering. From a Buddha's own perspective, no conscious decisions are made, no deliberate actions are taken, and no cognitions occur.

The obverse of this radical view of buddhahood is that all cognitions necessarily involve ignorance, and hence, from an ultimate perspective no cognition could be fully reliable. Here, Candrakīrti's rejection of the epistemological tradition makes good sense, for that tradition confidently asserts the full reliability of perception and well-formed inference. Thus, following the epistemologists, Mādhyamikas such as Śāntarakṣita and Kamalaśīla maintain that, if one employs inferential reasoning properly, one can carefully rehearse arguments that lead to a correct understanding of emptiness. At first, this understanding will only be conceptual, but by employing the contemplative techniques recommended by Kamalaśīla, one can eventually attain a direct intuition of emptiness that no longer relies on reasoning and concepts. On this model, inferential reasoning initially determines the proper object of one's meditation on emptiness; only then may one attempt to cultivate a direct intuition of that object. For Candrakīrti—at least as Jayānanda interprets him—this approach is wrongheaded because it begins from the false assumption that the meditation on emptiness could involve any object at all. Reason does have a role: to negate all essence, and then eventually to negate itself, for reasoning requires conceptual structures (*prapañca*) that are themselves manifestations of ignorance.

Thus interpreted, Candrakīrti's thought has far-reaching implications for Buddhist thought and practice, but it also may have especially suited the early part of the Later Diffusion. The scholasticism of Chapa's approach, heavily reliant on advanced training in the technicalities of Dharmakīrti's epistemology, may have run counter to much Tibetan Buddhist practice at that time. The Later Diffusion witnessed, for example, the rise of the Mahāmudrā tradition, which drew on Indian sources that often circumvented—or even derided—philosophical technicalia. In Mahāmudrā, the target state of meditative practice involves the complete suspension of all conceptual structuring (*prapañca*) so as to experience the nature of mind itself, which is the locus of both *saṃsāra* and *nirvāṇa*. Here, the scholastic emphasis on determining the meditative object through inferential reasoning would not only be unuseful, but would also actively create more conceptual structuring, which would further occlude the mind's nature. Perhaps Candrakīrti's rejection of Buddhist epistemology offered an opportunity to bring the burgeoning monastic academies more in line with such styles of Buddhist practice, which were only becoming more widespread.

Whatever the reasons may be, Chapa's defense of Śāntarakṣita and Kamalaśīla largely failed, and Candrakīrti's interpretation—filtered through Patsab, Jayānanda, and others—became dominant. Harkening back to Candrakīrti's warning against the use of "autonomous inferences" (*svatantrānumāna*), Tibetan exegetes began to speak of the Svātantrika (Syllogistic) Mādhyamika as a moniker for the approach defended by Chapa. In contrast, the Candrakīrtian interpretation became known as Prāsaṅgika (Consequentialist), reflecting Candrakīrti's admonition that Mādhyamikas should use "consequences" (*prasaṅga*) in debates with opponents, rather than asserting their own theses to be proven.

The shift away from the Syllogistic approach, while perhaps more suited to the practices of the time, came at a price recognized by Mabja, Chapa's wayward student. Candrakīrti's works imply that ordinary human cognition cannot be epistemically reliable, and some of his interpreters enthusiastically endorse this position. Patsab in particular maintains that, even in relation to conventional reality, no cognition is a *pramāṇa* (i.e., a fully reliable "valid cognition"). This radical position clearly calls into question not only ultimate analyses of essence, but even conventional concerns about morality, proper ritual practice, and so on. Mabja begins the task of restoring a place for valid cognition in the Mādhyamika fold, but this task is left to Je Tsong Khapa.

Je Tsong Khapa (rJe tsong kha pa blo bzang grags pa, 1357–1419) is a towering figure of Tibetan intellectual history, and his impact on the course of Tibetan Mādhyamika is prodigious. In the centuries between his birth and the translation of Candrakīrti's major works, a number of influential thinkers leave their mark on Tibetan Mādhyamika, and he inherits their efforts. By his time, Tibetan traditions have become organized into three overall sects: the Ancients (rNying ma), who identify as the tradition established by Indian masters active in the Early Diffusion, and the Sakya (Sa skya) and the Kargyü (bKa' brgyud), two diverse traditions that trace themselves back to India through lineages that arrive at the outset of the Later Diffusion. Je Tsong Khapa receives instruction in all three lineages, but his Mādhyamika learning is indebted especially to the Sakya philosopher Rendawa (Red mda' ba gzhon nu blo gros, 1349–1412). The Sakyapas have become the acknowledged masters of Buddhist epistemology, especially through the works of Sakya Paṇḍita (Sa skya paṇḍita Kun dga' rgyal mtshan, 1182–1251), but Sakya Paṇḍita himself continued to see a limited role for inferential reasoning in the context of Mādhyamika. Je Tsong Khapa will argue against this position, and in doing so, he creates an entirely new and innovative synthesis of Indian Mādhyamika thought. His efforts will lead to the formation of what eventually is known as the Gelug (dGe lugs, the "Virtuous tradition"), the sect that becomes dominant and maintains political control over the central government until the loss of Tibetan independence in 1951.

Je Tsong Khapa's interpretation of Mādhyamika is intricate, and it is not easily treated briefly. One can nevertheless point to several features at the core of his innovative approach. The first is a return to Candrakīrti's rejection of Yogācāra, even as a provisional step in Mādhyamika analysis and practice. Although the triumph of Consequentialist (Prāsaṅgika) Mādhyamika at the outset of the Later Diffusion rested on Candrakīrti's skepticism about the role of Buddhist epistemology, his concerns about Yogācāra went largely unheeded. All of the practice lineages in Tibet continued to employ techniques and interpretations drawn from the Yogācāra, and Mādhyamika texts generally still reflected the integration of Yogācāra and Mādhyamika promulgated by Śāntarakṣita and Kamalaśīla. Je Tsong Khapa eschews that integration, and he pointedly critiques Yogācāra philosophy and methodology. One possible motivation for this choice is the "other-emptiness" (*gzhan stong*) view of Kunkyen Dölpopa (Dol-po-pa Shes-rab-rgyal-mtshan, 1292–1361). Espousing what he called the "Great Mādhyamika" (*dbu ma chen po*), Dölpopa developed a unique synthesis of Mādhyamika and Yogācāra thought that rested on a strongly ontological interpretation of Buddha-nature. For Dölpopa, all of the qualities of buddhahood, even the physical marks and signs, were already fully present in the nature of the mind, and this nature is "empty" not of its own essential nature; rather, it is empty of all that occludes it, namely, all of conventional reality itself. For Je Tsong Khapa, this was an especially egregious misinterpretation of both Mādhyamika and Yogācāra, but it rested primarily on the ontologizing of the mind's nature that is fundamental to Yogācāra.

Je Tsong Khapa's efforts to refute Dölpopa fall within a larger concern about two tendencies that Je Tsong Khapa saw in Mādhyamika interpretations. These can be termed "undernegation" and "overnegation." The flaw of undernegation leads to absolutism (*yod mtha'*), while overnegation entails nihilism (*med mtha'*). Dölpopa's radical notion of other-emptiness clearly failed to negate the essential nature (*svabhāva*) of Buddha-nature itself, but even less obviously absolutist approaches can still miss the mark. Two problems can cause undernegation. First, one must properly "recognize the negandum" (*dgag bya ngos bzung*); that is, in order to refute essential nature, one must precisely identify what it is. Here, careful attention to phenomenal experience is necessary so as to identify the essentializing habits that underlie ordinary cognition, but reason also plays a crucial role. Indeed, it is only through inferential analysis that one can clearly determine precisely what is meant by the "essential nature" that is refuted by Mādhyamika analysis.

The second problem that incurs undernegation stems from a failure to employ the proper mode of negation. Drawing on earlier Indian and Tibetan precedents, Je Tsong Khapa emphasizes the distinction between an "affirming negation" (Skt. *paryudāsa;* Tib. *ma yin dgag*) and a "nonaffirming negation" (Skt. *prasjyapratiṣehda;* Tib. *med dgag*). Although originally drawn from Sanskrit grammar, for Je Tsong Khapa these modes of negation amount to the distinction between a negation that implies something in place of what has been negated, and a negation that makes no such implication. Thus, one might ask, "Is the soup hot?" A negative response shows that it is not hot, but it also implies that it is some other temperature. In contrast, one might ask, "Are square circles green?" Here, a negative response does not imply that square circles are some other color, but rather that there are no such things as square circles, such that they could have any color. For Je Tsong Khapa, it is crucial to understand that the negation of essential nature must be of the latter kind.

Already it is clear that Je Tsong Khapa's Mādhyamika returns inferential reasoning (and its operations such as negation) to a central role in Mādhyamika discourse, despite Candrakīrti's qualms. The role of reason and the Buddhist epistemological tradition become even clearer when one considers the problem of overnegation. For Je Tsong Khapa, the Mādhyamika critique of essence must not negate the viability of all conventional activities (*bya byed thams cad*), including especially the use of inferential reasoning in conventional contexts. Overnegation occurs when conventional reality is negated in this way, and it is avoided by positing two modes of analysis: the ultimate and the conventional. Ingeniously drawing on Dharmakīrti's theory of probative nonperception (*anuplabdhihetu*), Je Tsong Khapa notes that when a valid cognition fails to find (*ma rnyed*) an object that should otherwise be found in the locus under examination, that object necessarily does not exist in that locus. For example, an apple on the table should be perceived by valid visual cognition when the proper conditions are in place, and if it is not then perceived, the apple does not exist there. However, if the form of valid cognition in question does not have the capacity to detect the object in question, the nonfinding of that object does not prove its absence. Thus, an apple on the table would not be perceived by valid aural cognition, so even if I do not hear it, that nonhearing does not establish the absence of the apple there. In an analogous manner, a valid cognition analytic of the ultimate (*don dam du dpyod pa'i tshad ma*)—that is, one that seeks essences—will fail to find an essentially real apple on the table (or anywhere), and this establishes that there is no essentially real apple. But since its scope of analysis is the ultimate, that cognition's failure to find an *ultimately real* apple in no way negates the existence of a *conventionally real* apple. Indeed, if an apple is there, the appropriate valid cognition analytic of the conventional (*tha snyad du dpyod pa'i tshad ma*) will find it.

In this way, Je Tsong Khapa not only restores the place of inferential reasoning at the heart of Mādhyamika thought and practice, but also strongly endorses the validity of reasoning in conventional contexts, where decisions about monastic codes, ritual procedures, and the like can be fully and rationally adjudicated. But as with Patsab's sweeping dismissal of valid cognition, Je Tsong Khapa pays a price for his embrace of it. In the conventional contexts, the Gelug tradition often tends toward a narrow epistemological realism that has implications for institutional conservatism. In ultimate contexts, the embrace of Buddhist epistemology leaves unanswered the question of whether the mental structures required for reasoning are themselves expressions of essentialism. Je Tsong Khapa's system requires, for example, that although it is a negation, emptiness must nevertheless be an existent (*yod pa*), knowable (*shes bya*) object (*yul*) that is realized in meditation.

Here, Je Tsong Khapa's critics, such as the incisive Sakya thinker Gorampa Sönam Senge (Go rams pa Bsod nams seng ge, 1429–1489), see major flaws in Je Tsong Khapa's Mādhyamika. For Gorampa, reason does indeed play a crucial role, but in the final analysis, even the structures that would permit emptiness to be presented as an object in cognition must themselves be negated by Mādhyamika analysis so as to result in a realization that is utterly unstructured (Tib. *spros bral*). Although initially suppressed, Gorampa's works have sparked much fertile debate among Gelug thinkers and their critics. They also informed the thought of a more recent Tibetan philosopher, the revered Ju Mipham ('Ju mi pham rnam rgyal rgya mtsho, 1846–1912), whose innovative philosophy stands in some ways between Gorampa and Je Tsong Khapa. In any case, Tibetan intellectuals continue to ponder the intricacies of Mādhyamika, and their debates clearly animate their vibrant traditions.

BIBLIOGRAPHY AND SUGGESTED READING

Arnold, Dan. (2005) *Buddhists, Brahmins and Belief: Epistemology in South Asian Philosophy of Religion*. New York: Columbia University Press.

Burton, David F. (1999) *Emptiness Appraised: A Critical Study of Nāgārjuna's Philosophy*. Curzon critical studies in Buddhism. Richmond, Great Britain: Curzon Press.

Cabezón, Jose Ignacio, and Geshe Lobsang Dargyay. (2006) *Freedom from Extremes: Gorampa's "Distinguishing the Views" and the Polemics of Emptiness*. Studies in Indian and Tibetan Buddhism. Boston: Wisdom Publications.

Dreyfus, Georges B. J., and Sara L. McClintock. (2002) *The Svātantrika-Prāsaṅgika Distinction: What Difference does a Difference Make?* Studies in Indian and Tibetan Buddhism. Boston, MA: Wisdom Publications.

Eckel, Malcolm David. (2008) *Bhāvaviveka and his Buddhist Opponents*. Harvard Oriental Series 70. Cambridge, MA: Harvard University Press.

GARFIELD, JAY L. (2001) *Empty Words: Buddhist Philosophy and Cross-Cultural Interpretation*. New York: Oxford University Press.

HUNTINGTON, C. W. (1989) *The Emptiness of Emptiness: An Introduction to Early Indian Mādhyamika*. Honolulu, HI: University of Hawaii Press.

JINPA, THUPTEN. (2002) *Self, Reality and Reason in Tibetan Philosophy: Tsongkhapa's Quest for the Middle Way*. Richmond, Great Britain: Routledge-Curzon.

NĀGĀRJUNA. (1995) *The Fundamental Wisdom of the Middle Way: Nāgārjuna's Mūlamadhyamakakārikā*, translation and commentary by Jay L. Garfield. New York: Oxford University Press.

RUEGG, DAVID S. (1981) *The Literature of the Madhyamaka School of Philosophy in India*. History of Indian Literature. Wiesbaden: Otto Harrassowitz.

SIDERITS, M. (2003). *Personal Identity and Buddhist Philosophy: Empty Persons*. Burlington, VT: Ashgate Publishing Company.

THURMAN, ROBERT A. F. (1984) *Tsong Khapa's Speech of Gold in the Essence of True Eloquence: Reason and Enlightenment in the Central Philosophy of Tibet*. Princeton, NJ: Princeton University Press.

VOSE, KEVIN A. (2009) *Resurrecting Candrakīrti: Disputes in the Tibetan Creation of Prāsaṅgika*. Studies in Indian and Tibetan Buddhism. Boston, MA: Wisdom Publications.

WALSER, JOSEPH. (2005). *Nāgārjuna in Context: Mahāyāna Buddhism and Early Indian Culture*. New York: Columbia University Press.

WESTERHOFF, JAN. (2009) *Nāgārjuna's Madhyamaka: A Philosophical Approach*. New York: Oxford University Press.

CHAPTER 17

YOGĀCĀRA

JOHN POWERS

The Two Main Philosophical Traditions of Indian Buddhism

Indian Buddhist thinkers considered a wide range of philosophical problems, and each school was concerned with distinctive issues and adopted characteristic approaches. The Middle Way School (Madhyamaka) was mainly concerned with dialectical debate and applied a *reductio ad absurdum* (*prasaṅga*) approach to analysis of various philosophical systems. The Yogic Practice (Yogācāra) tradition, the other major philosophical strand of ancient and medieval Indian Buddhism, produced a number of influential treatises on epistemology and logic, and it dismissed the Madhyamaka focus on argument as a waste of time and as antithetical to the pursuit of liberation from cyclic existence, which for its proponents was founded on introspective meditation.

These differences reflect their respective orientations: Madhyamaka philosophers beginning with Nāgārjuna (c. second century) emphasize metaphysics and highlight the use of dialectical argumentation in refuting opponents' positions, while Yogācāra is more concerned with issues of epistemology, soteriology, and phenomenology. Madhyamaka claims to follow a "middle way" (*madhyama-pratipad*) between the extreme philosophical views of eternalism (*śāśvata-vāda*) and cessationism (*uccheda-vāda*). The former posits that all the phenomena of the universe are evolutes of an eternal ground of being that itself remains unchanged despite the transformations of phenomena. The latter position claims that everything we experience exists for a finite time and is then destroyed. The Mādhyamikas rejected both of these notions and claimed that phenomena are products of causes and conditions, but they are ultimately empty of inherent existence. Their Yogācāra opponents asserted that the Madhyamaka critique of rival views shaded into the realm of nihilism, and they adopted an idealist position that viewed phenomena as products of mind, but mind is also said to be ultimately empty.

Both schools place fundamental emphasis on the doctrine of emptiness (*śūnyatā*), which denies any substantial essence of phenomena, but their perspectives are subtly different. Madhyamaka links emptiness with dependent arising (*pratītya-samutpāda*), the notion that phenomena are products of causes and conditions, composed of parts and constantly changing. Because of the partite nature of phenomena and the effect of causes and conditions, they change from moment to moment and thus lack an enduring nature. Yogācāra philosophers accepted these notions in their discussions of emptiness, but also contended that all we ever know of objects are mental impressions of them. Consciousness is aware of its own products, and its perceptions of objects are derived from sense impressions filtered through sensory apparatus and then interpreted, but sentient beings have no way of directly contacting objects. Thus, for Yogācāra emptiness also relates to a denial of subject-object duality. Sense impressions arise along with objects, and so Yogācāra philosophers contend that the phenomena of perception do not exist as external objects.

Yogācāra Scriptural Sources

The major scriptural source for Yogācāra is the *Discourse Explaining the Thought* (*Saṃdhinirmocana-sūtra*), attributed to the Buddha, but probably composed around the third century CE. This is a work of great philosophical subtlety, which considers the problem of conflicting statements credited to the Buddha and provides hermeneutical guidelines for resolving them. The text has ten chapters, in each of which a tenth-level (*bhūmi*) bodhisattva poses doctrinal conundrums to the Buddha, who articulates a number of philosophical notions that came to be closely associated with Yogācāra and that were developed in the treatises of the philosophers of the school.

In the first four chapters, the Buddha discusses the relation between phenomena and ultimate truth (*paramārtha,* which is equated with emptiness). He declares that ultimate truth is the final nature of phenomena, and it cannot be ontologically separated from them. The two can, however, be differentiated by thought. Ultimate truth and phenomena are said to coexist like sound and the musical instrument that produces it, or the white color of a conch shell and the shell itself. They are two perspectives on the same thing, and cannot exist apart from each other.

Chapter 5 presents the doctrine of the "basis consciousness" (*ālaya-vijñāna*), which is the subtle substratum underlying all aspects of consciousness. It is said to be composed of the "seeds" (*bīja*) created by a person's volitional actions. Every action creates predispositions that tend to habituate consciousness to continue acting and perceiving in a particular way. The basis consciousness at any particular moment is the sum total of the seeds that comprise it. If one makes a life-altering decision—for instance, a resolve to enter the Buddhist path and begin cultivating positive mental states—one alters the constitution of this subtle mind, and as one replaces negative seeds with positive ones, the basis consciousness becomes progressively purified. When it is entirely composed of positive seeds, one undergoes a profound existential change, "reversal of the basis" (*āśraya-parāvṛtti*), and the basis consciousness is henceforth referred to as "stainless consciousness" (*amala-vijñāna*).

The basis consciousness is foundational, as its name implies, but because it is simply the sum total of its component seeds with no residual essence, it is also empty. Yogācāra epistemology developed a system of eight consciousnesses; the other seven emerge from the basis consciousness and are characterized by its constitution. The eight consciousnesses of the Yogācāra system are the five sense consciousnesses (seeing, hearing, touch, taste, and smell), mental consciousness, afflictive mentality (*kliṣṭa-manas*, which is responsible for the arising and perpetuation of afflictive mental factors), and the basis consciousness. In the idealist system of Yogācāra, the basis consciousness is fundamental, and the other seven are adventitious. Sense impressions, including perceptions of external objects and subject-object duality, are produced by seeds contained in the basis consciousness that are conditioned by past perceptions and that remain in its continuum until the time is ripe for their full maturation.

The basis consciousness has important ramifications for Buddhist meditation theory. Buddhist meditation literature discusses a number of trance states in which consciousness is suspended, and because Buddhism asserts that consciousness is momentary, there were significant questions regarding how it could resume after one emerges from these meditations, and how one could still retain memories. The basis consciousness theory provides a mechanism for the reemergence of consciousness, and it also accounts for continuity throughout a particular life and between successive lives.

The *Discourse Explaining the Thought* is also concerned with hermeneutical issues. The Buddha is credited with thousands of discourses, many of which contain contradictory ideas, and later exegetes were faced with the task of reconciling them and developing philosophical frameworks in which certain doctrines took precedence while others were relegated to the status of "interpretable" (*neyārtha*) teachings. In most chapters of the *Discourse Explaining the Thought*, questions are asked and the Buddha answers them, presenting the basics of the perspective that came to be identified with the Yogācāra tradition, but in several places he also provides guidelines for reconciling contradictions in works attributed to him. The most important of these are the three characters (*lakṣaṇa*), the three entitylessnesses (*niḥsvabhāva*), and the three wheels of doctrine (*dharma-cakra*). The third of these is discussed in the seventh chapter, in which the Buddha declares that the many doctrines attributed to him were presented to different types of people with varying capacities and perspectives. The first wheel comprised teachings found in the Pāli Nikāyas and Sanskrit Āgamas and focused on fundamental doctrines like the four noble truths (*ārya-satya*: suffering, its causes, its cessation, and the path that makes cessation possible) and dependent arising. These were intended for followers of the Inferior Vehicle (Hīnayāna) and were only delivered for a pragmatic purpose as a way of helping them transcend non-Buddhist philosophical systems and various sorts of mistaken ideas, but they were not his final thought.

In the second wheel of doctrine, he declared that all phenomena, as well as all concepts, are empty of inherent existence, which undermined the dogmatic adherence that many of his followers had developed toward the literal reading of his teachings. When they realized that even the word of the Buddha does not enjoy a privileged truth status and is devoid of inherent existence, this allowed them to break free from their previous cognitive attachments, but led some to an extreme of nihilism. Some took emptiness too far and conceived it as a denial of the existence of anything at all.

In the third wheel, the Buddha sorted out exactly what is being negated in discussions of emptiness. All phenomena can be viewed in terms of three characters: (1) the imputational (*parikalpita*), (2) the other-dependent (*paratantra*), and (3) the thoroughly real (*pariniṣpanna*). The first refers to the conceptual overlay ignorant consciousnesses superimpose on their perceptions of phenomena. It is compared to the yellow hue perceived by people with jaundice or floating objects perceived by people with damaged eyes. One aspect of the imputational is the false notion that people or things have inherent existence, that they possess an enduring essence or substance that remains constant throughout the vicissitudes of change to which all things are subject. This is completely false, and it can be weakened by a combination of empirical observation and reasoning. It is only fully eliminated by introspective meditation conjoined with reasoning.

The other-dependent character refers to the fact that things are products of causes and conditions that come into being, change from moment to moment, and eventually pass away. This is not their ultimate truth, but is true on a conventional level, and those who realize this have a more correct understanding than others who operate on the imputational level. The thoroughly real character is equated with emptiness and ultimate truth: it is the way things really exist, and is described as the absence of the false conception of the imputational that is superimposed on the other-dependent. It is understood only by advanced meditators, and only fully comprehended by buddhas. It also serves an important soteriological function: it is an "object of observation for purification" (*viśuddhālambana*), meaning that when one takes it as a meditative object, it eliminates afflictive mental states.

The three characters are discussed in conjunction with the notion of three entitylessnesses: (1) entitylessness in terms of character, (2) entitylessness in terms of production, and (3) entitylessness in terms of the ultimate. Each indicates a particular way in which phenomena lack any real or enduring nature. The first refers to qualities that are only designated by conceptuality and language, such as subject-object duality. The characteristics they impute do not exist, and so they lack entity. The second type refers to dependent arising: phenomena are produced and change due to causes and conditions outside of themselves, and so they lack entityness (that is, autonomy) in terms of production. The third nonentityness is equated with emptiness and ultimate truth: phenomena are ultimately empty of any enduring essence, and this is said to be ultimate entitylessness.

The imputational character is related to entitylessness in terms of character because it is not produced, does not cease, and so is devoid of the characteristics mistakenly attributed to imputational phenomena. They do not exist by way of their own character and so cannot be said to be produced.

Other-dependent phenomena are also not produced by way of their own character because they depend on causes and conditions for their arising, alteration, and cessation. Thus, they are empty of inherent existence and characterized by entitylessness in terms of production. Even the thoroughly real nature is characterized by entitylessness—entitylessness in terms of the ultimate—because it is empty of inherent existence and is the mere absence of false imputations superimposed on the other-dependent.

The *Discourse Explaining the Thought* is the major scriptural source for Yogācāra, but many of its ideas are undeveloped. Other scriptures that contain Yogācāra-related doctrines include the *Discourse on the Ten Levels* (*Daśabhūmika-sūtra*), which describes the bodhisattva's path to buddhahood, and the *Descent into Laṅka Discourse* (*Laṅkāvatāra-sūtra*), which is generally not categorized by Buddhist doxographers as a Yogācāra text but discusses Yogācāra concepts such as the basis consciousness and echoes Yogācāra idealism in its statement that all phenomena are mind-only (*citta-mātra*).

Asaṅga, Vasubandhu, and Their Commentators

The two most important early philosophers of Yogācāra were the brothers Asaṅga and Vasubandhu, who probably flourished during the fourth century. Asaṅga's contributions to Buddhist philosophy were primarily scholastic. He authored the *Compendium of the Great Vehicle* (*Mahāyāna-saṃgraha*), which outlines the major topics of Mahāyāna philosophy from a Yogācāra perspective; the voluminous *Levels of Yogic Practice* (*Yogācāra-bhūmi*), which comprehensively discusses both Hīnayāna and Mahāyāna philosophical systems; and the *Compendium of Higher Doctrine* (*Abhidharma-samuccaya*), which develops a scholastic system from a Mahāyāna perspective.

Vasubandhu was a philosopher and scholar of great philosophical acumen, with a critical mind that was able to size up any argument and critique it. He is credited with authorship of the monumental scholastic treatise *Storehouse of Higher Doctrine* (*Abhidharma-kośa*), which is one of the most influential philosophical works of Indian Buddhism. According to tradition, Vasubandhu composed the root verses after a period of study with the Vaibhāṣikas of Kashmir. In one account, he was an itinerant monk who supported himself by challenging opponents to public debate. After finalizing a verse of his treatise, he would carve it on a metal plate, which was tied onto the neck of an elephant. Vasubandhu would lead the elephant through the streets, daring any rival philosophers to dispute the proposition. As the treatise developed, however, he became increasingly disenchanted by the flaws of the Vaibhāṣika system. He sent a written copy of the work to his former teachers in Kashmir, and they declared it to be the finest exposition of their philosophical system. Some parts remained obscure, however, and so they sent gold to Vasubandhu with instructions to write a commentary that would elucidate the pithy verses he had composed, which contained brief summaries of the primary tenets of the Vaibhāṣikas.

As he composed his commentary, he adopted the perspective of the rival Sūtra school (Sautrāntika), and freely critiqued the doctrines of his former teachers. When they read the finished treatise, they were reportedly outraged and denounced him as an apostate, but Vasubandhu was an independent thinker who was concerned with articulating a consistent philosophical system, and not adherence to any orthodoxy.

After his conversion to Mahāyāna, he retained many of the doctrines articulated in his early works, but also moved into new philosophical territory. In keeping with the Yogācāra interest in epistemology and reasoning, he composed the highly influential treatise *Differentiation of the Middle Way and Extremes* (*Madhyānta-vibhāga*), which examined the operations of consciousness and the relation between apprehending subject and apprehended object. He rejected as extreme the Madhyamaka concept of emptiness and argued that it fails to recognize the true ontological status of subject and object and the interrelationship between the two. He summarized his understanding of emptiness in the opening chapter:

> Imagination of the unreal exists.
> But emptiness exists in it, and that [imagination] in it [emptiness].
> Thus it is said that all phenomena are neither empty nor non-empty,
> Because of [imagination's] existence, [the object's] non-existence, and
>   [emptiness'] existence.
> This is the middle way.

A number of important notions are encoded in this. Gadjin Nagao (1978) noted that this verse closely parallels one in Nāgārjuna's *Fundamental Verses on the Middle Way* (*Mūlamadhyamaka-kārikā*) and appears to be a challenge to his claim to have articulated the true "middle way" of the Buddha:

> Whatever is dependently arisen
> Is explained to be emptiness.
> That, being dependently arisen
> Is simply the middle way. (XXIV.18)

Vasubandhu indicates that imagination of the unreal (*abhūta-parikalpa*) creates mental images, and people act on them. Thus, it has effects, even though its referents are based on false conceptions. Because of its effects, it cannot be dismissed completely, like a square circle or the son of a barren woman. It is conceptually linked to emptiness, and Vasubandhu claims that Nāgārjuna's reading of this doctrine leaves no room for empirical objects, which are empty, but emptiness itself depends on an empty thing as its referent. Emptiness—equated with the ultimate truth and the thoroughly real nature—is ultimately real, but at the same time is empty, and in this sense has the same ontological status as phenomena.

Vasubandhu also composed an influential treatise on debate, the *Rules for Reasoning* (*Vāda-vidhi*). Public philosophical disputations between rival philosophers were a form of public entertainment in ancient India, and were often sponsored by rulers. The combatants generally represented specific philosophical systems, and the winners commonly won royal support, new recruits, and public prestige. The defeated party could face exile or forced conversion to a rival's school, so the stakes were very high. When these contests involved Buddhists and non-Buddhists, neither could cite their own scriptures in support of an argument because the other party did not accept their authority, and Vasubandhu detailed a set of rules within which opponents from different traditions could engage in debate on the basis of shared epistemological premises and rules of logic.

His *Twenty Verses* (*Viṃśatikā-kārikā*) and *Thirty Verses* (*Triṃśikā-kārikā*) are among his most influential works. Both are concerned with establishing the validity of cognition-only. In the *Twenty Verses*, Vasubandhu argues that people with ocular disorders perceive nonexistent objects that appear to be real, and the same is true of dream images. For someone immersed in a dream, the phenomena she experiences appear incontrovertibly real, but are seen as illusions upon awakening. In the same way, the perceptions of ordinary beings appear as real external objects, but are products of mind, but Buddhas see them as they really are. Vasubandhu further argues for idealism from an ontological point of view: he asserts that a realist must accept some form of atomism, but he contends that there is no coherent way to account for extension in this view. If phenomena are composed of tiny parts, these must have sides, top, and bottom in order to be able to contact other atoms and create composite things. But if an atom has sides, it can still be further broken down. Taking this process to its conclusion, at some point there must be a particle so small that it has no extension at all, which Vasubandhu asserts is contradictory to the very notion of atomism. If something is so subtle that it has no sides, top, or bottom, how could it create something with extension in a conglomeration with other such particles? He claims that

> A sense object is neither a single thing nor several things, from the atomist point of view, nor can it be an aggregate (of atoms).
>
> Therefore, atomism cannot be demonstrated. (*Viṃśatikā-kārikā*, v. 12)

The *Thirty Verses* argues for idealism from an epistemological point of view. Vasubandhu asserts that all mental events are merely permutations of consciousness. He details the various categories of mental states and discusses how apparently external objects appear as the result of the maturation of seeds in the basis consciousness. As long as one remains within the subject-object dichotomy, these mental perceptions will appear, but "when consciousness no longer apprehends any object of consciousness, it abides in cognition-only." At this point mind in the conventional sense ceases to operate and one understands (mental) reality as it truly is. This is associated with the state of buddhahood. The two treatises are often treated together and referred to as the *Establishment of Cognition-Only* (*Vijñapti-mātratā-siddhi*).

Yogācāra and Idealism

The notion of cognition-only is one of the most hotly debated topics among contemporary scholars of Yogācāra. From at least the fifth century, Buddhist Yogācāras have read this concept as a form of idealism entailing a denial of the existence of external objects. The first articulation of cognition-only is probably the eighth chapter of the *Discourse Explaining the Thought*, in which the Buddha informs the bodhisattva Maitreya that the object of observation of a meditating consciousness is not different from the mind that contemplates it. Alex Wayman (1979) contended that the denial of the separate existence of external objects was only postulated within the context of a state of introspective meditation, but the text goes on to extend the idea to all objects of knowledge. Maitreya asks, "are the appearances of the forms and so forth of sentient beings, which abide in the nature of images of the mind, not different from the mind?" The Buddha replies: "Maitreya, they are not different. However, because childish beings with distorted understanding do not know cognition-only just as it is in reality, they misconstrue them."

There has been considerable controversy among contemporary nontraditional scholars regarding how this idea should be understood: some read it as implying that mind alone exists and external objects are its products. For others it refers to the fact that every impression of an external object is known only in the mind. The idealist reading is a denial of the real existence of external objects, and most traditional Buddhist commentators have adopted this perspective. Dan Lusthaus (2002) has forcefully argued for an alternative interpretation, according to which cognition-only implies a bracketing of the ontological status of external objects, similar to that of Husserl's phenomenology.

Indian Buddhist philosophers who composed treatises exploring the ramifications of this notion have consistently adopted an idealist reading. The Korean scholar Wonch'uk (613–696), who wrote the most extensive commentary on the *Discourse Explaining the Thought*, states: "objects of direct perception arise from the entity of the consciousness itself. . . . [T]hose objects that are images are also not different from the mind." He adds: "when [beings] abandon [the notion of the existence of] external objects, they pacify incorrect minds; when they pacify incorrect minds, they realize the middle way" (Wonch'uk 1985). Thus, he characterizes the idealist position rejecting the existence of external objects as the true purport of the Buddha's doctrine.

The idealist tendencies of Yogācāras were criticized by rival schools, and the response of later philosophers such as Sthiramati (c. sixth century) and Dharmakīrti (c. sixth century) was to make their commitment to idealism even more explicit. In his *Commentary on Valid Cognition* (*Pramāṇa-vārttika*), Dharmakīrti declares that his final position is that "external objects do not exist."

Yogācāra as a "School"

In the present state of our knowledge of Yogācāra, it is not clear to what extent it constitutes a definable school. Certainly there is a lineage of people beginning with Asaṅga and Vasubandhu and commentators including Sthiramati, Asvabhāva (c. late sixth century), and Sumatiśīla (c. mid-eighth century) who focused on a core group of texts and who shared some similar concerns related to doctrine and practice, but there is also considerable divergence of views among these thinkers. Moreover, there is no evidence that they considered themselves to be proponents of a "Yogācāra school." This label was probably invented by later doxographers, who created often artificial divisions within Buddhist literature in an attempt to make sense of the vast array of texts and teachings they had inherited.

Despite this caveat, there is a lineage of philosophers who share similar epistemological and soteriological concerns and who view a corpus of texts, particularly the *Discourse Explaining the Thought* and the Perfection of Wisdom sūtras, as authoritative. Credit for systematizing the doctrines of this tradition and providing the most influential commentaries on the treatises of Vasubandhu should probably be mainly given to Sthiramati, who composed a number of treatises that developed the philosophical implications of core Yogācāra doctrines and forcefully argued its idealist position.

The Buddhist Epistemologists Dignāga (c. fourth century) and Dharmakīrti, who are commonly viewed by Buddhist doxographers as members of an offshoot of the Yogācāra tradition, concentrated primarily on issues relating to epistemic validity and logic, and later Mahāyāna philosophers such as Śāntarakṣita (c. eighth century) and Kamalaśīla (c. eighth century) developed syncretic systems that attempted to bridge conceptual differences between Yogācāra and Madhyamaka. In his *Entry into the Middle Way* (Madhyamakālaṃkāra), Śāntarakṣita argued that the doctrine of cognition-only can be reconciled with both systems. In his interpretation, both Madhyamaka and Yogācāra claim that all objects are empty of inherent existence. Yogācāra contends that they are empty in that they are merely products of mind, and also adds that mind itself is empty. The nature of mind is neither simple nor complex. If there were such a thing as a truly existent nature, it would have to accord with one or the other of these alternatives, and since it does not, the only valid conclusion is that mind lacks any inherent nature. He extends this logic to all the things of experience, and concludes that conditioned phenomena like dharmas (which according to the scholastic Buddhist Abhidharma system are the ultimate real constituents of complex phenomena) and unconditioned phenomena like nirvana do not have either simple or complex natures. Thus, they utterly lack self-nature (*svabhāva*). This, he contends, is the ultimate position of both Madhyamaka and Yogācāra, and so from this point of view they are in agreement.

To date, even some of the most important Yogācāra works have not been fully translated, and in several cases existing translations contain significant problems. This is hardly surprising given that a number of Indian Yogācāra works, such as the *Discourse Explaining the Thought* and Asaṅga's *Compendium of Ascertainments* (*Viniścaya-saṃgrahaṇī*), are no longer extant in Sanskrit and are found only in Tibetan or Chinese translations. To further complicate matters, many Sanskrit manuscripts are quite corrupt, and even some published Sanskrit editions of Yogācāra texts are so flawed as to be worthless. Given these difficulties, translation and study of each of the often voluminous texts of Yogācāra require years of careful work that compares existing versions in Sanskrit, Tibetan, and Chinese; Sanskrit fragments in other works; and relevant commentaries (manuscripts of which are also found in a variety of languages). Added to this is the fact that Yogācāra literature is notoriously difficult reading because of the complexity of its doctrines and the scholastic prolixity that characterizes many texts of Asaṅga, Vasubandhu, and their commentators. Given all of these factors, it appears likely that advances in the study of Yogācāra will occur incrementally, one text and one doctrinal study at a time, and it will probably be several decades before the outlines of Yogācāra literature and doctrines become fully clear.

BIBLIOGRAPHY AND SUGGESTED READINGS

Anacker, Stefan. (1984) *Seven Works of Vasubandhu, The Buddhist Psychological Doctor.* Delhi: Motilal Banarsidass.

Buescher, Hartmut. (2008) *The Inception of Yogācāra-Vijñānavāda.* Vienna: Österreichische Akademie der Wissenschaften.

Garfield, Jay L. (2002) *Empty Words: Buddhist Philosophy and Cross-Cultural Interpretations.* New York: Oxford University Press.

Hopkins, Jeffrey. (1999) *Emptiness in the Mind-Only School of Buddhism: Dynamic Responses to Dzong-ka-ba's The Essence of Eloquence: 1.* Berkeley, CA: University of California Press.

———. (2002) *Reflections on Reality: The Three Natures and Non-Natures in the Mind-Only School.* Berkeley, CA: University of California Press.

Kritzer, Robert. (2005) *Vasubandhu and the Yogācārabhūmi: Yogācāra Elements in the Abhidharmakośabhāṣya.* Tokyo: The International Institute for Buddhist Studies.

Lusthaus, Dan. (2002) *Buddhist Phenomenology: A Philosophical Investigation of Yogācāra Buddhism*. London: Routledge.

Nagao, Gadjin. (1978) "What Remains in Śūnyatā: A Yogācāra Interpretation of Emptiness." In *Mahāyāna Buddhist Meditation*, edited by Minoru Kiyota. Honolulu, HI: University of Hawaii Press, 66–82.

Powers, John. (1991) *The Yogācāra School of Buddhism: A Bibliography*. Metuchen, NJ: Scarecrow Press.

———. (1992) *Two Commentaries on the Saṃdhinirmocana-sūtra*. Lewiston and Queenstown: Edwin Mellen Press.

———. (1993) *Hermeneutics and Tradition in the Saṃdhinirmocana-sūtra*. Leiden: E. J. Brill.

———. (1995) *Wisdom of Buddha: The Saṃdhinirmocana-Sūtra*. Berkeley, CA: Dharma Publishing.

Schmithausen, Lambert. (1987) *Ālayavijñāna: On the Origin and the Early Development of a Central Concept in Yogācāra Philosophy*. 2 vols. Tokyo: The International Institute for Buddhist Studies.

Siderits, Mark. (2007) *Buddhism As Philosophy: An Introduction*. Indianapolis, IN: Hackett Publishing.

Wayman, Alex. (1979) "Yogācāra and the Buddhist Logicians." *Journal of the International Association of Buddhist Studies* 2.1, 65–78.

Wonch'uk. (1985) *Ārya-gambhīra-saṃdhinirmocana-sūtra-ṭīkā*; Tibetan: *'Phags pa dgongs pa zab mo nges par 'grel pa'i mdo'i rgya cher 'grel pa*. Delhi: Delhi Karmapae Choedhey, Gyalwae Sungrab Partun Khang, 1985, *mdo 'grel* vol. thi (119), 217.5.

CHAPTER 18

BUDDHIST EPISTEMOLOGY (*PRAMĀṆAVĀDA*)

TOM J. F. TILLEMANS

WHILE arguments on philosophical and doctrinal issues abound in early Buddhist writings, *theoretical perspectives* on argumentation and analysis developed in bits and pieces in the works of a number of thinkers of different orientations from about the second century CE on. Some of the first such theorizing is to be found in writings of the Mādhyamika, or Middle Way, philosopher Nāgārjuna, who in his *Vaidalyaprakaraṇa* and *Vigrahavyāvartanī* saw the necessity to sketch out Buddhist positions on epistemology and related metaphysical issues in order to establish his philosophy that things were all free of, or empty of, intrinsic natures. The oldest Buddhist treatise dedicated specifically to reflection upon argumentation and issues of right reasoning is the **Upāyahṛdaya*,[1] sometimes attributed to Nāgārjuna, and in any case only extant in a Chinese translation, the *Fang bian xin lun*, made in 472 CE. Debate and argumentation were also treated by such famous fourth- to fifth-century authors as Vasubandhu and Asaṅga and became the subject of a genre of literature known as the *vāda* (debate) treatises, some of the main texts being Vasubandhu's *Vādavidhi* (Rules of Debate) and *Vādavidhāna* (Methods of Debate), as well as the *Nyāyamukha* (Gateway to Reasoning) and a now lost *Vādhavidhānaṭīkā*, both by the great fifth- to sixth-century thinker Dignāga. By the end of Dignāga's philosophical output, however, justificatory issues of knowledge-claims had come to the fore, gradually giving rise to the extensive literature concerning *pramāṇa*, "sources/means of knowledge," "standards," or, less literally, "epistemology." The key text that began this epistemological turn was Dignāga's

1. An asterisk prior to a Sanskrit term here indicates a Sanskrit reconstruction from Tibetan or Chinese, which may not be found in any extant Sanskrit text.

Pramāṇasamuccaya (Compendium of Epistemology); this text then led to the *Pramāṇavārttika* and other works of Dharmakīrti (seventh century) with their considerable commentarial literature both in India and in Tibet. It is fair to say that after Dharmakīrti, the *vāda* literature diminished in importance, being superseded by epistemology, as is evidenced by the fact that the topic of debate tended to become one chapter among others in larger works on *pramāṇa* that dealt with a wide-ranging ensemble of justificatory issues, including the reliability of perception, testimony and scripture, and a host of loosely related matters, both philosophical and religious, from the problem of universals to reincarnation and omniscience.

Curiously enough, this school of Dignāga and Dharmakīrti actually had no official or widely used name in Sanskrit. Tibetan scholastics did give it a number of names, namely, the "Idealist school that follows reasoning" (*rigs pa rjes su 'brang ba'i sems tsam pa*) and "the Sautrāntika school following reasoning" (*rigs pa rjes su 'brang ba'i mdo sde pa*), reflecting the fact that Dignāga's and Dharmakīrti's stance on idealism and the existence/nonexistence of the external world was complex and nuanced, with external objects and atomic matter often provisionally accepted, only to be denied in the final analysis. Nowadays, for convenience, it is often known as the "*pramāṇa*-school," or "*pramāṇavāda,*" and hence "The Epistemological School"/"Erkenntnistheoretische Schule," because of its focus on standards for and evaluation of knowledge-claims.[2] While it might have had no name in India, it was nonetheless very influential, being itself one of the main Buddhist schools as well as a major influence upon rival Buddhist schools, which often borrowed its logical and epistemological theories when they needed sophisticated tools to establish and defend their own positions. It was undoubtedly the Buddhist school that provoked the most elaborate responses by non-Buddhist Brahmanical thinkers, such as Uddyotakara, Kumārila (seventh century), and many others, who took Buddhist *pramāṇavāda* very seriously as a threat to their own positions. In what follows, for the sake of simplicity, we'll flatten out a number of the philosophical and exegetical differences between major Buddhist Epistemologists and concentrate primarily on Dharmakīrti's views. Historically, Dharmakīrti (rather than Dignāga) was the main source for important Buddhist writers on epistemology from the seventh to ninth centuries, such as Devendrabuddhi, Śākyabuddhi, Dharmottara, Śāntarakṣita, Kamalaśīla, and Prajñākaragupta, as well as for the influential later Indian philosophers, Jñānaśrīmitra, Ratnakīrti, and Mokṣākaragupta (eleventh to twelfth centuries); Dharmakīrti's "seven works on epistemology" (*tshad ma sde bdun*) were also *the* source for the rich Tibetan traditions of *tshad ma*-studies (i.e., *pramāṇavāda*).

2. For a bibliography of the works of the school and modern research upon them, see Steinkellner and Much 1995.

Epistemology and Ontology

Dignāga and Dharmakīrti formulated an extremely parsimonious ontology in direct correlation with a twofold scheme of sources of knowledge (*pramāṇa*), namely, perception (*pratyakṣa*) and inference (*anumāna*). Just as there are two ways and only two ways to know, that is, to have reliable (*avisaṃvādin*) new understanding, there are only two kinds of entities that can be objects of knowledge, viz., universals and particulars. The baroque ontologies of the non-Buddhist are explained away in terms of the pared-down twofold typology of objects, while the sources of knowledge recognized by non-Buddhist schools (e.g., scriptural testimony, verbal usage, analogy, and others) are reduced to specific cases of the twofold *pramāṇas*. As we shall see, it is also in dependence on that binary organization of entities and corresponding ways of knowing that Buddhist accounts of concepts, language use, and logical thinking and even knowledge of religious dogma are made possible.

The interlocking series of epistemic and ontological categories leads to potential problems that Buddhists recognized and confronted with considerable dexterity. To see these problems more clearly, we need to delve a bit deeper into the system's workings. First of all, this Buddhist school (contrary to certain globally antirealist Buddhist schools like the Madhyamaka) recognizes that there are, indeed must be, some entities that are fully real. It is a school that is thoroughly *nominalist:* what is real for them is only particular (*svalakṣaṇa*), punctual in time (*anitya*), extensionless, and endowed with causal powers (*arthakriyāsāmarthya*); anything that is a universal (*sāmānyalakṣaṇa*) or extended in time and space and hence causally inefficient is fictional (i.e., fabricated by thought and language). Particulars are known directly by perception, which is purely nonpropositional, while conceptual thought (*kalpanā*) is based on language and apprehends only fictional proxies that stand in for particulars. Perception as a source of knowledge (to be differentiated from nonconceptual hallucinations and the like) is thus "fixed" (*niyata*) by its objects in that it is directly causally bound to particulars: the image or representation (*ākāra*) that appears to it is causally determined by and mirrors the characteristics of the particular. Conceptual thought, on the other hand, which does proceed by propositional attitudes, is not fixed in this way by particulars and can to a large degree "spin freely," thinking what it will about whatever object it chooses in function of human interests and needs. When conceptual thought is a source of knowledge (and not just a thoroughly wrong understanding), it operates via logical reasons (*hetu*), basing itself on properties that are indices (*liṅga*) showing other properties—in this case it is known as "inference" (*anumāna*), literally an "understanding that follows upon, or is in conformity with."

Now, since language and concepts and hence logical thinking proceed by fictional universals while the real is purely particular, real things cannot be directly described, nor directly thought about conceptually. How, then, can one ever know reality, and especially with the degree of diversity and subtlety needed for the sophisticated tasks of human life? On the one hand, while pure perception is in contact with the real, it is bereft of judgment and propositional attitudes and thus gives little usable information apart from brute sense data. On the other hand, while conceptual thinking does provide subtle information, the objects it treats are fictions. Hence, the iterated binary structures in the system lead to the central epistemological concern that the Buddhist addresses throughout his philosophy, namely, to account for a nonarbitrary connection between describable conceptual fictions and the ineffable real particulars only accessible to perception in a way such that at least some thoughts and words are nonetheless linked (*sambaddha*) to real entities, that is, can "make one reach" (*prāpaka*) reality. The Buddhist Epistemologists are, in effect, to borrow an idea of Donald Davidson, subscribers to a rigid separation between a conceptual *scheme* and a perceptual *content* free from the scheme's additions and distortions, and their problem then becomes how to bridge that very scheme-content gap.

Concepts and Language

There are, broadly speaking, two distinct approaches in Buddhist Epistemology to bridge the scheme-content gap: what we could call "top-down" approaches and "bottom-up" approaches. By "top-down" we shall mean an account that maintains that it is because of some specific (and perhaps ingenious) features of the fictional proxy, or concept, that it pertains to particular things, even though it does not have the ontological baggage of a real universal. On a top-down approach, the fictional stand-in for a universal like "blueness" would behave like a property, a sense or a meaning, that belongs to the conceptual scheme but would nonetheless qualify and serve to pick out the real blue particulars in the world. This can be accomplished, according to Buddhist Epistemologists, because the fictional proxies are, or can be analyzed to be, "exclusions of what is other" (*anyāpoha*), a type of double negation that applies to particular patches of blue in the sense that each such patch is non-non-blue. Dignāga and his followers appealed to a recurrent intuition that mere absences of properties are simply mind fabricated, whereas positive presences would have to be real parts of the furniture of the world—negative facts like X not being blue, heavy, and so forth, are constituted by our mere interests (i.e., we seek a blue thing at such and such a location and come away empty-handed), and are less real than X being blue, which is what it is objectively and independently of interests. As the "exclusion of what is other" is itself only a negative property/absence of something rather than a presence, we are spared commitment to there being real universals in addition to real particulars. This approach is primarily that of Dignāga in the fifth chapter of *Pramāṇasamuccaya,* and is how the "exclusion theory" (*apohavāda*) is generally presented in the works of non-Buddhist opponents of Dignāga, as well as in modern works treating the subject. What is far from clear, however, is how genuine nominalist mileage is to be gained in this way. The usual charge against it by its (seventh-century) non-Buddhist critics, like Kumārila and Uddyotakara, is a type of argument from compositionality: understanding any negation presupposes understanding the negandum, so that understanding what non-non-blue is would depend on understanding blueness.

On a "bottom-up" approach, on the other hand, the double exclusion plays a relatively minor role: causal chains and error are what serve to bridge the scheme-content gap, rather than the logico-metaphysical features of exclusions (*apoha*). Strikingly, such reliance on causality is entirely absent in Dignāga: it is Dharmakīrti's major contribution to the theory. The way words link to things is thus primarily explained through the existence of a causal chain from particular things to perceptions to thoughts and then to the utterances of words. What is at stake is a version of what is usually called nowadays a "causal theory of reference," that is, a type of theory that explains how Mr. X can refer to such and such an object in the world by detailing a complex and long causal chain from the object, via Mr. X's language learning and concept acquisition, to the representation of the object and then to the use of the word on a specific occasion. "Bottom-up" *apoha*-theory is not much different on that score in relying on a chain of causal links as a necessary condition for successful reference to things in the world. Here are the details: Mr. X sees particular things and has perceptual images (*ākāra*) of them; these images regularly cause—due in part to "imprinted tendencies" on the mind—the same type of judgment, "This is an instance of *U*," a judgment to which appears an *apoha* (i.e., a generic image of non-non-*U*); because the particular perceptual images all have the same effect in leading to the same judgment, they are all the same in their causal power and can be grouped together. The link to the specific word is made by a speaker's speech intention (*vivakṣā*): he or she wishes to use a specific word to express/mean such and such a generic image, so that it is the intention that causally conditions the utterance of the word.

The dominant direction of Dharmakīrti's causal account seems to be that of a *naturalistic* explanation. (In what follows, I'll be speaking of a "naturalized theory of reference" in much the same way as, since W. V. Quine, we can speak of "naturalized epistemology," a theory that places the emphasis on what human beings do in knowing, referring, etc., rather than on philosophically *certifying* the rationality and justification of what they do.) Dharmakīrti is trying to account for the cognitive events that supposedly happen when people refer to things with words, and this he does by specifying a chain of events in which each event is causally linked with the next. Notable is the fact that Dharmakīrti at crucial stages in his "exclusion theory" actually relinquishes the quest to ground or certify reference and seems to say, in effect, that we do such and such types of things and make such and such judgments, but at a certain point no more philosophically satisfying justification can or need be given. For example, various particular perceptual images are grouped together because they all do in fact cause the *same judgment* (*ekapratyavamarśa*), "This is a *U*," and not because there is anything "in them" that they have in common. A critic might then object that in order to certify that judgments are the same, the exclusion theorist would have to say that they all cause the same meta-judgment, and in that case an obvious regress would loom. Dharmakīrti, in *Pramāṇavārttika* I, was aware of that regress and refused to give a further justificatory account in terms of the same meta-judgments; instead, he just appealed to the fact that this is how the judgments appear to us (i.e., as all seeming to have the same content).[3] Certification seems to come to a clear end at this stage, replaced by a mere pointing out of some complex facts.

Logic and Philosophy of Logic

The way the *vāda* and *pramāṇa* literature, and many other types of texts, represent the mental process of reasoning is that one thinks: "*A* is *B* because of being *C*, like *D*," where one invokes a logical reason, *C*, to prove the truth of the conclusion *A* is *B*. The example *D*, which is actually sometimes omitted, is a commonly acknowledged case of *B*-ness and *C*-ness that permits an individual to understand that all *C*'s are indeed *B*'s. The latter generalization is known as "pervasion" (*vyāpti;* Tibetan *khyab pa*) of *C* by *B*—a universally generalized material implication, *for all x: if x is C then x is B,* with the interesting feature that the quantification ranges over both actual and nonactual items. (The indispensability or dispensability of the example for one to understand/establish the pervasion becomes a hotly debated topic among later theoreticians.)

There is also an important variant where the truth of "*A* is *B*" is not being established, but only the fact that it would follow from an *acceptance* (*abhyupagama*) of *A* being *C*. Thus, a debater can present an opponent with a *prasaṅga* (consequence) of the sort: "It would follow absurdly that *A* would be *B*, because of being *C*." Such a consequence will constitute the key step in a proof by *reductio ad absurdum*, a proof that will culminate in a type of contraposition, turning on *modus tollens.* When the pervasion in the consequence holds and the opponent understands that *A* is not in fact *B*, the opponent will then be lead by a "contraposition of the consequence" (*prasaṅgaviparyaya,* literally "reversing the consequence") to understand that *A* is not in fact *C* because of not being *B*. Both these structures (i.e., proofs by logical reasons and consequences) are to be found in Indian and Tibetan writing on a variety of subjects.

Since T. Stcherbatsky's two-volume study and translation of Dharmakīrti's *Nyāyabindu*, entitled *Buddhist Logic* (i.e., Stcherbatsky 1930–1932), one often sees the Buddhist theory of reasons/indices designated as "logic," a term that sometimes has the unwanted effect of leading readers to think that good reasons for Buddhists are simply those that are formally valid. In fact, the notion of formal validity (i.e., the conclusion's being guaranteed true, *provided* the premises are true) is not itself

3. For the details in Dharmakīrti, Śāntarakṣita et al., see Dunne 2004, 121–126.

explicitly discussed by Buddhist theoreticians; it is in any case not distinguished from other, more informal, considerations. Instead of formally valid reasons, Buddhist theoreticians developed the notion of a good reason (*saddhetu*, Tibetan *rtags yang dag*), that is, one that satisfies a triple criterion (*trairūpya*). These three criteria for "goodness" are given in the following fashion from Dharmakīrti on:

(a) *pakṣadharmatva* (the logical reason's being a property of the subject): the subject, A, is ascertained (*niścita*) as having the property C;
(b) *anvayavyāpti* (pervasion [that is formulated] as copresence): C is ascertained as present in only instances similar to A insofar as they possess B;
(c) *vyatirekavyāpti* (pervasion [formulated] as coabsence): C is ascertained as wholly absent from instances dissimilar to A insofar as they do not possess B.

True, in texts like the *Hetucakra* of Dignāga (also taken up by Dharmakīrti), a version of the triple criterion (*trairūpya*) for good reasons and the operators "partial presence," "complete presence," and "complete absence" were correlated to yield a series of nine *types* of reasons, types that are abstracted from content and subject matter. Not inappropriately, the great historian of logic Innocentius Bocheński, in the chapter on Indian Logic in his *History of Formal Logic*, stated that the *Hetucakra* thus suggested an awareness of formal considerations. R. S. Y. Chi, in his *Buddhist Formal Logic* (reprint Delhi: Motilal, 1984), went several steps further and attempted to show that the *Hetucakra*, taken in its formal aspects, might present a number of interesting features to a modern logician. That being said, there is much more to "good reasons" satisfying the triple criterion than simple formal validity: the term "ascertained" (*niścita*), when unpacked by Dharmakīrti and his commentators, demands that good reasons must be sound (i.e., the premises must in fact be true and the conclusion must follow from them) and that they must be convincing to the opponent who has the appropriate "desire to know" (*jijñāsā*) something he does not already know. This latter demand leads to a host of other requirements: in order to be convinced of something new, the opponent must have the requisite doubt, understand the terms, and accept the subject of debate. In short, good reasons involve formal considerations (what follows from what?); factual considerations (what is so? what is true?); epistemic considerations (what does one need to know in order to know such and such? when is doubt possible?); and what can be termed "rhetorical considerations" (what is newly convincing to whom?). The weighting of these aspects in the theory of the "triple criterion" changes over history in complex fashions.[4]

Later theoretical elaborations by Dignāga, Dharmakīrti, and others about how to *present* publicly (i.e., verbally) a good reason (*saddhetu*) to an adversary in a debate prescribe the use of complex verbal forms known as *prayoga* (formal reasonings). Thus, for example, the standard formal reasoning that Dharmakīrti and his Indo-Tibetan successors prescribed was a two-membered form known as an "inference-for-others" (*parārthānumāna*):

4. See Tillemans 2008, 6.

All *C's* are *B's*, like *D*.
A is *C*.

Commentators make an explicit correlation with the triple criterion (*trairūpya*). Thus, the first statement perspicuously expresses the pervasion (i.e., the *anvayavyāpti* and *vyatirekavyāpti*) and the second expresses the fact of the reason being a property of the subject (*pakṣadharmatva*). The conclusion, *A* is *B*, is omitted, indeed ruled out in later prescriptive accounts of how Buddhists should argue. This is supposedly because the only function of such a form is to show "provers" (*sādhana*), and a conclusion cannot prove itself: *A* is *B*, that is, "what is to be proved" (*sādhya*), can be understood indirectly but should not be stated. While the inference-for-others has often been thought to somehow formally resemble a syllogism in Aristotelian logic, it is apparent that the presence and absence of conclusions in syllogisms and inferences-for-others, respectively, as well as the idea of what constitutes a "prover" for Buddhists, means that *parārthānumāna* and Aristotelian syllogisms are accounted for in terms of considerably different philosophies of logic.[5]

Another distinctive feature of the Buddhist philosophy of logic is its intimate link with the "exclusion theory" described above: provers (*sādhana*) are things, or states of affairs, and not words, propositions, or simple inventions of thought unconnected with reality. They can of course be expressed in words, as in a "public" inference-for-others, but they are not themselves words. Although Dharmakīrti and others speak in realist terms of one state of affairs, or one entity (*artha*), proving another, in fact the picture has all the complex features of the scheme-content gap and its bridges: logical reasoning is a mental process that directly treats of fictional proxies (i.e., concepts), which are in turn connected in *apoha*-fashion to real particular entities.

One of the main innovations Dharmakīrti and his school made in the Buddhist philosophy of logic was that pervasion, and indeed all three criteria of the reason (see above), had to be *ascertained* (*niścita*) and thus not be subject to doubt and fallibility—it seems clear that this idea was due to Dharmakīrti and was not present in Dignāga's system, and especially not in the earlier commentator on Dignāga, Īśvarasena (sixth century), whose interpretation of *Pramāṇasamuccaya* spurred Dharmakīrti to write the first chapter of *Pramāṇavārttika* as in part a refutation of that commentator's view that pervasion could be claimed to hold simply on the basis of one not seeing any counterexamples. Dharmakīrti thus deemed it essential to good reasoning, if it was not to be fallible, that the concepts constituting the prover and property to be proved (*sādhyadharma*) exhibit a relation, a type of necessary connection (*sambandha; pratibandha*), between terms. Now, given the standpoint of logic as at least indirectly dealing with reality rather than just concepts alone, this relationship too must be anchored in features of reality: the particulars covered by the concepts that constitute the prover and proved must bear a "natural connection" (*svabhāvapratibandha*) to each other. Such a natural

5. See Tillemans 1999, 69–87.

connection between particulars, say *x* and *y*, can be of two sorts: either *x* and *y* are causally connected (*tadutpatti*) or are identical (i.e., $x = y$) (*tādātmya*).

Not surprisingly, the idea that natural connections of this sort can somehow ground logical thought and prevent it from being fallible has its philosophical complexities. First of all, when a pervasion is bidirectional, as in the case of being impermanent (*anityatva*) and being produced (*kṛtakatva*), it's easy to see that the impermanent particulars will be identical with produced particulars, and that identity of the two sets provides "grounding" in that it is a necessary and sufficient condition for the bidirectional pervasion. When the pervasion holds in only one direction, however, as in the case of being a *śiṃśapa*-tree and being a tree, the identity is between *śiṃśapa*-trees and some particulars in the set of trees. In that case the identity of these selected particulars is only a necessary condition for grounding the pervasion and needs to be supplemented by an account of how one set is the pervader (*vyāpaka*) and one is the pervaded (*vyāpya*). The theory of concepts is invoked by Dharmakīrti to account for one set being included in another, but as concepts are fictions the problem of how the mere fact of identity grounds pervasion would seem to remain.

Secondly, in cases of a bidirectional pervasion (Tibetan *yin khyab mnyam*), like that between impermanence and being produced, the extension of the concepts (i.e., the set of impermanent particulars and the set of produced particulars) is the same, but substitution of one for the other would seem to lead to an invalid inference where the premises are true but the conclusion is not. To bring out the problem, take the following tempting, but invalid, inference:

> Being a product is a good reason for proving that sound is impermanent
> Being a product is coextensive with being impermanent (i.e., for all x: x is a product if and only if x is impermanent)
>
> ---
>
> Therefore (by substitutivity of identicals for identicals), being impermanent is a good reason for proving that sound is impermanent.

We would seem to go from two true premises to a false conclusion, for it is clear that for a Buddhist (as for most people) arguing that something is so simply because it is so is *not* giving a good reason. And yet we would also seem to be using the acceptable principle of substitutivity of identicals for identicals *salva veritate*. What went wrong?

Dharmakīrti, in *Pramāṇavārttika* I verse 40 et sq. and *Svavṛtti*, diagnosed the problem as one of bidirectional pervasions (i.e., coextensive concepts) seeming to force us to accept *pratijñārthaikadeśahetu* "reasons that are one part of the thesis" (e.g., when one says "sound is impermanent because it is impermanent," then the reason "being impermanent" is also a part of what is being proved). He saw this undesirable consequence as one of the main challenges to logical thought, that is, "inference," being a source of knowledge (*pramāṇa*), for unless one can somehow rule out the problematic substitutions in what I have called the "tempting inference," we would be saddled with having to accept as good a huge number of singularly uninformative reasons.

The problem is recognizably the familiar one of substitutivity in referentially opaque contexts, such as propositional attitudes and modal contexts.[6] Talk of good reasons being ones where the debater has a desire to know *P* but not an equivalent *Q* is indeed an opaque context. To analyze what goes wrong in the tempting inference, Dharmakīrti, in effect, made a usual move by distinguishing between types of identities: "being impermanent" and "being produced" are extensionally identical, but somehow not intensionally so—what he terms being the same concept, that is, exclusion (*apoha; vyāvṛtti*). And in the opaque context, substitution could only be made between conceptually identical terms.

In fact, though, it could be said that the usual idea of an intensional identity (one that is understood to hold between properties *F* and *G* when the biconditional *for all x: x is F if and only if x is G* is true in all possible worlds) will not get us very far out of the woods, as being impermanent and being produced *are* arguably identical in that way, and it would thus seem that if *that* is what conceptual identity is about for a Buddhist Epistemologist, it should *be* possible to make the substitution in the opaque contexts under discussion. Dharmakīrti's idea of concepts *F* and *G* being identical thus demands a much stronger criterion than the necessary truth of the biconditional *for all x: x is F iff x is G.* In his *Svavṛtti* ad verse 40 and in considerable detail in the Tibetan "Epistemological Summaries" (*tshad ma bsdus pa*) and "Collected Topics" (*bsdus grwa*) literature, we find the makings of an idea of "conceptual identity/difference" (Tibetan *ldog pa gcig/tha dad*) such that to each meaningful subject or predicate term in a language there is a different concept—synonyms, for example, will express different concepts. Interestingly enough, although this individuation of exclusions/concepts might seem to lead to an undesirable proliferation of strange ultra-intensional entities, at least certain Epistemologists—for example, Śāntarakṣita, Kamalaśīla, and very clearly the twelfth- to thirteenth-century Tibetan Saskya Paṇḍita (in the first chapter of his *Tshad ma rigs gter*)—emphasized that concepts were just fictions, *façons de parler* for different states of mind, and even that concepts were not to be reified as a kind of object (*viṣaya; yul*). The states of mind could be individuated unproblematically, and so derivatively we could individuate the concepts too without committing ourselves to a plethora of occult objects, one for each word.

Religion

Indian and Tibetan writers have held various views on what constituted the principal goal of Buddhist Epistemology, some seeing it as a predominantly secular philosophy, one of the "five sciences" on a par with medicine and grammar, and others seeing the theory of sources of knowledge as above all to be used to establish Buddhist religious doctrines, like the Four Noble Truths, the proofs of the Buddha being an

6. See Tillemans 1986.

authoritative/reliable person (*pramāṇapuruṣa*, Tibetan *tshad ma'i skyes bu*), the law of retribution of acts (*karman*), reincarnation, omniscience, the innate Buddha-nature, absence of real personal identity, and so forth. In any case, all these topics are treated *in extenso* in the second chapter of *Pramāṇavārttika*, and some form the subject of independent treatises by later Epistemologists. It is impossible to summarize these discussions here, but suffice it to say that Indian Buddhist Epistemologists were indeed not only theoreticians of knowledge, but also very strong defenders of their religion in the face of a period of forceful challenges to Buddhist institutions and power by reinvigorated Brahmanism. This historical situation had its influence on their philosophy.[7] For example, arguably, it could be said that one of the important motivating factors in the Epistemologists' critique of universals (*sāmānya; jāti*) and their embrace of nominalism was to undercut the Brahmanical idea of castes (*jāti*) being real, naturally existing (and hence fixed) properties in individuals, with the social consequences that such fixed stratification entails.

The debate with Brahmanical schools on specific doctrinal questions moved to issues of scriptural authority, especially when confronted with the Mīmāṃsaka school's justification of the *Vedas* as being eternal, uncreated by humans (*apauruṣeya*) and hence authoritative because free from any human influence. (The Buddhist retort is essentially that speakers' intentions are determinate in words having meaning, so that if *per impossibile* scriptures were uncreated by humans, they would be incomprehensible.) On the role of scripture, Dharmakīrti actually had a nuanced position. In *Pramāṇavārttika* I.213–217 et sq. and in IV.48–108, he maintains that scripture shouldn't be used on factual or rationally decidable matters; perception and logical reasoning trump the scriptures of one's own school; one is not to be faulted for rejecting one's school's scriptures when reason dictates it; on rationally undecidable matters, however, that is, on so-called "radically inaccessible things" (*atyantaparokṣa*), like the specific details of the law of karman (exactly what actions in past lives lead to what results in the future?), scriptural accounts need to be relied on because of the absence of any other means (*agatyā*) (I.216); if it passes the requisite threefold tests (I.214–215), scripture is designated as being an inferential source of knowledge, but is always fallible and *not* to be considered a full-fledged source of knowledge, as it has no claim to certainty (*nāto niścayaḥ*), unlike bona fide inferences (*Svavṛtti* ad I.318). The eighth-century commentator Śākyabuddhi summarizes things interestingly in his commentary to I.216: scripture is simply needed by (indeed, indispensable to) those who wish to set out upon the spiritual path (*pravṛttikāma*), but it is not grounded in any objective facts (*vastutas*). Over history, however, the later Indo-Tibetan Buddhist scholastic apologists transformed this surprisingly fallibilist and pragmatic position about scripture into a much more rigid edifice, indeed often turned the idea of "scriptural inference" (*āgamāśritānumāna*) into a rationale for a type of fundamentalism.[8] Such was the use of a potentially radical philosophy of religion by very conservative religious institutions.

7. See Eltschinger 2007.
8. See Tillemans 1999, 37–51.

BIBLIOGRAPHY AND SUGGESTED READINGS

DREYFUS, GEORGES B. (1997) *Recognizing Reality. Dharmakīrti's Philosophy and its Tibetan Interpretations.* SUNY Series in Buddhist Studies. Albany, NY: State University of New York Press.

DUNNE, JOHN D. (2004) *Foundations of Dharmakīrti's Philosophy.* Studies in Indian and Tibetan Buddhism. Boston, MA: Wisdom.

ELTSCHINGER, VINCENT. (2007) *Penser l'autorité des Écritures. Autour de Pramāṇavārttika I.213–268 et Svavṛtti: traduction française et édition de la version tibétaine, précédées d'une introduction historique et doctrinale.* Vienna: Verlag der Österreichischen Akademie der Wissenschaften.

HATTORI, MASAAKI. (1968) *Dignāga on Perception, being the Pratyakṣapariccheda of Dignāga's Pramāṇasamuccaya.* Harvard Oriental Series 47. Cambridge, MA: Harvard University Press.

KAJIYAMA, YŪICHI. (1989) *An Introduction to Buddhist Philosophy,* an annotated translation of the *Tarkabhāṣā* of Mokṣākaragupta. Kyoto: Memoirs of the Faculty of Letters of Kyoto University 10, 1966. Reprinted in *Yūichi Kajiyama. Studies in Buddhist Philosophy,* edited by K. Mimaki et al. Kyoto: Rinsen.

MATILAL, BIMAL K., and R. D. EVANS (eds.). (1986) *Buddhist Logic and Epistemology. Studies in the Buddhist Analysis of Inference and Language.* Studies of Classical India 7. Dordrecht: D. Reidel.

STCHERBATSKY, THEODORE. (1930–1932) *Buddhist Logic.* 2 vols. Leningrad: Bibliotheca buddhica 26. (Reprinted by Mouton and Co., The Hague, 1958.)

STEINKELLNER, ERNST. (1971) "Wirklichkeit und Begriff bei Dharmakīrti." *Wiener Zeitschrift für die Kunde Südasiens* 15, 179–211.

———. (1982) "The Spiritual Place of the Epistemological Tradition in Buddhism." *Nanto Bukkyō* 49 (Nara, Japan).

STEINKELLNER, ERNST, and TORSTEN MUCH. (1995) *Texte der erkenntnistheoretischen Schule des Buddhismus.* Systematische Übersicht über die buddhistische Sanskrit-Literatur 2. Abhandlungen der Akademie der Wissenschaften in Göttingen. Göttingen: Vandenhoeck and Ruprecht.

TILLEMANS, TOM J. F. (1986) "Identity and Referential Opacity in Tibetan Buddhist *apoha* Theory." In *Buddhist Logic and Epistemology. Studies in the Buddhist Analysis of Inference and Language.* Studies of Classical India 7, edited by Bimal K. Matil and R. D. Evans. Dordrecht: D. Reidel.

———. (1999) *Scripture, Logic, Language. Essays on Dharmakīrti and his Tibetan Successors.* Studies in Indian and Tibetan Buddhism. Boston, MA: Wisdom Publications.

———. (2000) *Dharmakīrti's Pramāṇavārttika. An Annotated Translation of the Fourth Chapter (parārthānumāna),* Volume 1 (k. 1–148). Österreichische Akademie der Wissenschaften, Philosophisch-Historische Klasse, Sitzungsberichte, 675. Band. Vienna: Verlag der Österreichischen Akademie der Wissenschaften,

———. (2008) "Introduction: Buddhist Argumentation." *Argumentation* 22 (Springer Verlag), 1–14.

CHAPTER 19

BUDDHIST THOUGHT IN TIBET: AN HISTORICAL INTRODUCTION

MATTHEW T. KAPSTEIN

The intellectual history of Tibetan Buddhism is only imperfectly understood. Although abundant new textual sources have been discovered in recent decades, it will take some time before scholars have assimilated this growing documentation, which, considering only what is pertinent to the history of philosophical thought, amounts to many thousands of individual works composed over a millennium. Accordingly, we can do no more here than to furnish a concise introduction, touching upon selected topics that are now generally agreed to be of importance for the history of Tibetan Buddhist thought overall.

The Beginnings of Tibetan Buddhism: Its Indian, Chinese, and Indigenous Sources

Tradition considers Buddhism to have been first adopted in Tibet by the monarch Songtsen Gampo (Srong-btsan sgam-po, reigned ca. 617–650), who unified his nation and set it on the path of imperial expansion in Central Asia. His Chinese and Nepalese brides are said to have encouraged the king and his court to adhere to the Buddha's teaching. Nevertheless, there is little evidence that the new religion had much success in Tibet until the early eighth century, when another Chinese princess,

Jincheng (d. 739), married Songtsen's descendant Tri Detsuktsen (Khri Lde-gtsug-btsan, reigned 712–755) and sponsored a monastic community from Khotan, a Buddhist state then under Tibetan rule. Despite this royal support, an anti-Buddhist reaction on the part of nobles who favored native Tibetan religious traditions (later referred to in general as "Bön") led to the expulsion of the Khotanese monks following the princess's death.

It was Tri Detsuktsen's son and heir, Tri Songdetsen (Khri Srong-lde-btsan, reigned 755–ca. 797), who firmly adopted Buddhism as the religion of his dynasty and committed considerable state resources to its promotion. Several of the edicts promulgated by this remarkable ruler survive, and in them we find indications of his understanding of and interest in Buddhist doctrine. He writes, for instance, that

> All those who are born and revolve among the four sorts of birth,[1] from beginningless origins to the infinite end, become as they are owing to their own deeds (*karman*).... That which is neither good nor evil is unspecified. The result of what one does to another ripens upon oneself. One may be born as a god among the heavenly stages, or as a human on earth, or as an anti-god, a hungry ghost, an animal or a subterranean creature of the hells—all born in these six have done so owing to their own deeds.
>
> Transcending the world are those who become Buddhas, and those who make progress as bodhisattvas, self-awakened ones (*pratyekabuddha*), and pious attendants (*śrāvaka*)—all of them have done so owing to the provisions of merit and gnosis that they themselves have amassed.

Besides the adherence to Buddhist normative doctrine that is evident here, it is striking that Tri Songdetsen was particularly interested in the means whereby we may *know* the truth of religious claims. For he goes on to say:

> If one investigates what is found in the Dharma [the Buddha's teaching], some points are immediately evident in their good or evil consequences, while others that are not immediately evident may nevertheless be inferred on the basis of those which are, and so are also fit to be held with certainty.[2]

In other words, he was familiar with, and sought to introduce his subjects to, the view of the Indian Buddhist epistemologists that knowledge may have two valid sources (*pramāṇa*): direct perception (*pratyakṣa*) of what is evident to the senses and intellectual intuition, and inference (*anumāna*) of what is "hidden," that is, not directly evident.

Tri Songdetsen established Tibet's first full-fledged monastery, called Samyé (Bsam-yas), in about 779, which housed an important translation academy. Its scholars, including Tibetans and foreign Buddhist monks, rendered large numbers

1. Birth from an egg, from the womb, due to heat and moisture, or miraculous birth.

2. Following the text as established in Hugh Richardson, "The First Tibetan *Chos-'byung*," in his *High Peaks, Pure Earth: Collected Writings on Tibetan History and Culture*, ed. Michael Aris (London: Serindia), pp. 89–99. Unless otherwise stated, this and all translations in the present chapter are my own.

of Indian Buddhist scriptures and treatises from Sanskrit into Tibetan and achieved an outstanding level of accuracy, an important result of which was the formation of a well-standardized philosophical vocabulary in Tibetan. The project of creating in this way a canonical literature was continued under Tri Songdetsen's successors, until the collapse of the dynasty during the mid-ninth century, by which time many hundreds of Indian religious and philosophical texts were available in Tibetan versions. At the same time, Tibetan translators also begin to author manuals introducing the new vocabulary together with elements of Buddhist thought. Some of these works are notably philosophical, such as the treatise entitled *Distinctions of Views* (*Lta ba'i khyad par*) by the renowned ninth-century translator Yeshé-dé (Ye-shes-sde), in which, for example, he summarizes a key argument of the Madhyamaka school:

> In accordance with the system formulated by Ācārya Nāgārjuna, all outer and inner entities are explained to be interdependently originated. Relatively, because they have arisen from cause and condition, they exist just apparitionally, whereas ultimately, entities are without production, [as is demonstrated] by the fourfold proof that states that they are not born from self, other, both, or causelessly.
>
> "Not born from self" means precisely not born from itself. For if entities were born from themselves, they would have to be said to be born from a self whose own coming-into-being was completed, or else from one that has not come into being. On the one hand, were it born from what had already come into being, it could never be the case that it does not come into being, and this leads to an endless regression. But on the other hand, were it born from what had not come into being, then the rabbit's horn and the barren woman's son might also come into being![3] Therefore, it is not born from self.
>
> It is also not born from other, for that implies the fault of everything's coming into being from everything. Nor is it born from both self and other, for in that case both of the aforementioned faults are combined. Neither is it born causelessly, for in that case there are these faults: it would always arise with dependence on anything at all, everything would emerge from everything, and all purposeful undertakings would be fruitless.
>
> Thus, because the birth of the entity is not established, therefore there can be no birth. Birth-talk is no more than conventional utterance.[4]

Tibetan thinkers thus began to become familiar with the major traditions of Indian Buddhist philosophy: Vaibhāṣika, Sautrāntika, Yogācāra, and Madhyamaka. Yeshé-dé recognized two main divisions of the latter: one, following Bhāvaviveka, adhered to Sauntrāntika conventions in their treatment of relative reality, while the other, following Śāntarakṣita, adopted the idealist approach of the Yogācāra. Both would be later classified as divisions of the Svātantrika-Mādhyamika, the school

3. The "rabbit's horn" is a standard example, in Indian philosophy, of an empirical impossibility, the "barren woman's son" of a logical contradiction.

4. Ye-shes-sde, *Lta ba'i khyad par*. Archaic version, ms. Pelliot Tibetain 814, reproduced in Macdonald and Imaeda, *Choix de documents tibetains* (Paris: Bibliotheque Nationale, 1978), vol. 1, plates 210–225.

that sought to demonstrate the thesis of universal emptiness by means of direct, or "autonomous," proof. The Prāsaṅgika-Mādhyamika, which favored indirect proof and would later become the dominant trend in Tibetan Madhyamaka thought, was as yet unknown.

During the same period, Chinese Buddhism made inroads in parts of the Tibetan world. Teachers affiliated with the teaching of Chan ("meditation," or Zen in Japanese) introduced Tibetans to the idea that enlightenment, or awakening, was immediately, intuitively present, without striving for numberless lifetimes as the mainstream of Indian Buddhism affirmed. This led to a protracted dispute in Tibet between partisans of "sudden" versus "gradual" enlightenment, the former sometimes associated with a teaching of mystical intuition, and the latter with the methodical application of reasoned analysis. The controversy resurfaced repeatedly in later times owing to its implications for concepts of our prospects for spiritual progress and, indeed, our very nature: are we essentially flawed creatures, for whom self-perfection is a far distant goal, or are we, and all creatures, already in fact Buddhas? Does the latter position entail a kind of gnosticism, according to which ignorance and knowledge are all that really matter, and moral effort merely an illusion?

Traditional sources recount that the first actual debate over these issues took place at Samyé during the late eighth century, and that the disputants were the Chinese Chan master Moheyan and the Indian philosopher Kamalaśīla. The accounts that have come down to us are mostly late, and tend to caricature the Chan perspective:

> When master Kamalaśīla asked for his opponent's position, saying, "What is the Chinese religious tradition like?" the Chinese responded, "Your religious tradition, beginning with going for refuge and the cultivation of an enlightened attitude, is an ascent from below, like a monkey climbing a tree. Because one will not be awakened as a Buddha by such contrived doctrines, it is in this tradition of ours, having meditatively cultivated the nonconceptual, that one becomes awakened by realizing the nature of mind itself. So this is like the eagle's alighting from the sky upon the top of a tree; it is a 'pure panacea' because it is a doctrine that thus descends from on high."
>
> To this the master said, "Your example and its significance are both invalid. For the eagle alights upon the tree, either spontaneously generated in the sky with its wings fully grown, or born in its eyrie, where its wings have gradually matured. Only then does it alight. The first is an impossibility and the second should be a gradualist example, but is inappropriate as an example of sudden enlightenment."[5]

Though this exchange may be a pious fiction, it does reflect the important role, inherited from Indian systems of argument, of exemplification and counterexample in the accepted procedures of reasoning. At the same time, it underscores the great gulf that separated rationalist from intuitionist approaches to Buddhist insight.

5. *Sba-bzhed ces-bya-ba-las Sba Gsal-snang-gi bzhed-pa bzhugs* (Beijing: Nationalities Press, 1980), pp. 64–76.

The currents entering Tibet from India and China provoked dynamic responses, both harmonious and hostile, on the part of indigenous Tibetan traditions as well. It was this process that gave birth to the native religion of Bön (Bon), which, from about the tenth century on, established its own monastic communities and scriptural canons, in many respects resembling those of Buddhism. Nevertheless, the elaboration of Bön literary traditions also encouraged efforts to give written form to autochthonous techniques and beliefs. Though Bon thinkers often used the Buddhist philosophical apparatus, they also developed an almost anthropological interest in documenting the practical means whereby Tibetans have traditionally interacted with the natural world, seen as an abode of benign and malignant spirits. Here, a twelfth-century author summarizes the "priestly way of the realm of appearance" (*snang-gshen*):

> The four gates of incantation are the gate of worship of the divine spirits, the gate of expulsion and cleansing, the gate of liberation and ransom, and the gate of creation, fortune and power. [...] One enters [this priestly way] unerringly, in accord with the chants of thanksgiving and the methods of playing the drum.
>
> As for practical action: because all that appears and comes into being is present as gods and demons, in order to deal with obstacles and spirits [...] one amasses the stipulated requisites and ritual items. Having distinguished between beneficial deities and harmful spirits, one beseeches the deities to fulfill one's final purposes, and offers a refuge as befits the lords and patrons of the priesthood.[6]

In time, the ancient traditions reflected here, which sought not transcendence, but instead a mastery of the forces inhering in the phenomenal world, would become part and parcel of Tibetan Buddhist thought and practice as well. Inclinations toward holism and a view of the world as the play of divine and quasi-divine energies would be regularly reasserted throughout the history of Tibetan religious thought. Thus, esoteric (or "tantric") Buddhism, with its emphasis on ritual agency and its philosophical grounding in the Mahāyāna conception of the ultimate identity of worldly existence (*saṃsāra*) and transcendent peace (*nirvāṇa*), introduced not just an Indian pantheon, but embraced also the native gods and demons of Tibet.

The Formation of the Major Buddhist Traditions

The century or so following the collapse of the Tibetan empire is traditionally remembered as a dark age, when Buddhism was suppressed and learning and letters were no more. Although recent scholarship shows this to be much exaggerated, translation activity and the scholarship associated with it were severely

6. *Gal mdo* (Dolanji: Tibetan Bonpo Monastic Centre, 1972), p. 167.2ff.

reduced until the end of the tenth century, when the West Tibetan kingdom of Gugé began to patronize Buddhist art and learning on a large scale once again. Henceforth, conditions favoring doctrinal and philosophical investigations gradually reemerged.

Central to this revival was the long, influential sojourn of the Bengali scholar and saint Dīpaṃkaraśrījñāna, better known as Atiśa, first in Gugé (1042–1045) and then in central Tibet until his death in 1054. Atiśa sought to emphasize above all the ethical grounding of Mahāyāna Buddhism, and his teachings became the basis for subsequent Tibetan education with respect to the Mahāyāna path, including the substantial literature on "training the mind," or "spiritual exercise" (*blo-sbyong*). The essential framework for instruction in this area was a moral anthropology that recognized three grades of aspirant, as defined by Atiśa in his widely read *Lamp on the Path of Enlightenment* (*Bodhipathapradīpa*):

> Whoever by whatever means strives for his own sake
> Only for saṃsāra's pleasures—that one is the lesser person.
> Turning his back to worldly pleasure, and shunning sinful deeds,
> The soul who strives for his own peace is called the middling person.
> One who, owing to the pain of his own existence, wholeheartedly seeks to end
> All the pain of others—that is the superior person.[7]

Atiśa's overriding concern to encourage the practice of such "superior persons" is evident, too, in his reserve with respect to aspects of philosophical activity. While he promoted the study of Madhyamaka, and in particular the work of Candrakīrti, he wished to emphasize meditation on emptiness as a necessary component of the path of practice, and not dialectical reasoning per se. Thus, he famously wrote:

> [Investigations of] perception and inference are unnecessary.
> They have been formulated by the learned to refute the disputations of extremists.

Nevertheless, an analysis of the phenomena of everyday experience is essential, so as to arrive at the insight that:

> There is neither seeing nor seer, but peace without beginning or end,
> Abandoning substantiality and insubstantiality, free from conceptions, free from objectives,
> Neither an abode, nor that which abides, no coming or going, unexemplified,
> Ineffable, not to be viewed, unchanging, uncompounded—

7. Atiśa, *Bodhipathapradīpa*, verses 3–5.

If the adept realizes that, the affective and cognitive obscurations are abandoned.[8]

In brief, Atiśa, following Candrakīrti in what became known as the Prāsaṅgika-Mādhyamika (the Madhyamaka school that admits only indirect proof, *prasaṅga* in Sanskrit), held that relative, or ostensible reality (*saṃvṛtisatya*), is best described in accord with the conventions of everyday language. The special role of philosophical discourse is not system building, but the criticism of our assumptions about reality, dismantling them until we arrive at the profound realization of emptiness.

Atiśa's disciples established a distinctive monastic order, called Kadampa (Bka'-gdams-pa), meaning the "adherents of the canon and practical instructions" of the Mahāyāna. During the same period, a number of other new orders were founded that would similarly shape the later history of Tibetan Buddhism. Foremost among them were the Kagyüpa (Bka'-brgyud-pa) "adherents of the oral lineage," stemming from the followers of the translator and tantric adept Marpa Chöki Lodrö (Mar-pa Chos-kyi blo-gros, 1012–1096), and the Sakyapa (Sa-skya-pa) "adherents of Sakya," referring to the monastic center founded by the aristocratic Khön family in 1071. The differences among these and other contemporaneous orders reflected primarily differing lineages and traditions of esoteric ritual and yoga rather than philosophy and doctrine, though as they developed through the generations they also began to elaborate distinctive doctrinal positions, as will be seen below. At the same time, lines of teaching that traced their antecedents back to the earlier imperial period sought to retain their distinct identity over and against the newer orders, and so came to be known as Nyingmapa (Rnying-ma-pa), the "Ancients." The latter, together with the Bön, considered the highest realizations to be embodied by the Great Perfection (*rdzogs chen*), a system of abstract contemplation that was sometimes attacked as a resurgence of the Chan teaching of sudden enlightenment. The Kagyüpa, for their part, promulgated the Mahāmudrā—the "great seal" delimiting the parameters of all possible experience—an esoteric approach to meditation that, in some of its forms at least, became the object of similar criticism. Both of these systems, however, served as important stimuli for later doctrinal investigations.

Tibetan Scholasticism

From the late eleventh century onward, Tibetan monastic colleges emphasized a highly rationalized approach to Buddhist doctrine, over and against one dominated primarily by faith. At the forefront of this development was the college of Sangpu

8. Both this and the preceding quotation are from Atiśa, *Satyadvayāvatāra*. The affective obscuration (Skt. *kleśāvaraṇa*) includes all dispositions underlying the emotions that bind us to worldly patterns; the cognitive obscuration (*jñeyāvaraṇa*) the inability to penetrate to a full realization of the true nature of things.

(Gsang-phu), established in 1073 by one of Atiśa's foremost disciples, Ngok Lekpé Sherab (Rngog Legs-pa'i shes-rab), whose nephew Ngok Loden Sherab (Rngog Blo-ldan shes-rab, 1059–1109) was responsible for its preeminence in philosophical education. The younger Ngok was an excellent scholar of Sanskrit, who studied Buddhist philosophy in Kashmir and who, despite Atiśa's reservations, was much inspired by the rigor of Indian epistemological theories. The curriculum he formulated required the careful study of philosophical writings, with the epistemological and logical works of Dharmakīrti (c. 600) supplying the major methodological organ. Other required topics included the monastic code or Vinaya (*'dul-ba*), the "meta-doctrine" or Abhidharma (*chos-mngon-pa*), the Perfection of Wisdom or Prajñāpāramitā (*phar-phyin*), and the teaching of the Middle Way (*dbu-ma*), that is, the Madhyamaka dialectic of the Indian philosopher Nāgārjuna. Henceforth, this would become the core curriculum of Tibetan monastic colleges, regardless of the order to which one belonged.

Instruction at Sangpu emphasized the practice of debate. Precise definition of key terms and the understanding of their relations with regard to a number of basic logical operations formed the foundations of the Tibetan debate logic. Relations among terms were defined in terms of "invariable concomitance," or "pervasion" (Skt. *vyāpti*), a technical concept derived from Indian logic that refers to the extension of terms (i.e., what the term "covers"). When two terms are mutually pervasive—they cover the same ground, as we would say colloquially—they are treated here as synonyms. Understanding such relations—whether terms are synonyms, contradictories, or contraries—allows one to draw out their implications. What this system of reasoning in fact seeks to do is to explore the implications of the terms proposed until one arrives at the recognition that one's initial premises were inconsistent or otherwise defective, or else one reaches those fundamental assumptions that must be accepted as intuitively valid, without further possibility of dispute. The debate is thus at once an inquiry that seeks to arrive at sound and valid conclusions and at the same time a game, in which one deploys all the dialectical skill one can muster with the sole objective of defeating one's opponent. In this respect, the debate becomes also a dramatic performance, in which exaggerated movements, verbal tricks, and sometimes humorous asides are deployed to drive home the point.

Each argument is part of a larger discussion and introduces further possible lines of inquiry, in accord with the overall architecture of the Buddhist philosophical edifice. On the analogy of a game, the individual argument may be seen as a single round or innings. The dialectical method that is employed here is often described as a threefold procedure, consisting of, first, a refutation of erroneous positions (*dgag*), followed by the definition of the position one wishes to defend (*bzhag*), and, finally, the refutation of challenges to that position (*spong*). As the debaters develop their skill through practice, like chess players who thrive on constant competition, they pursue the analysis of the entire range of topics treated in the monastic curriculum, examining in full detail the concepts of fundamental reality, the path to spiritual awakening, and the nature of the Buddha's enlightenment itself as these were elaborated in the four principal schools of Indian Buddhist philosophy mentioned above. The practice aims to sharpen and deepen one's sense of the conceptual relations among Buddhist ideas, and so reinforces a ready familiarity with the conceptual scheme as a whole, fixing it as one's way of spontaneously engaging with the world.

The Sangpu curriculum was refined by a succession of brilliant teachers, including Chapa Chöki Senggé (Phya-pa Chos-kyi seng-ge, 1109–1169), who is often credited with giving definitive form to the system of debate logic overall. One of the scions of Sakya, famed as Sakya Paṇḍita (1182–1251), also received his early philosophical education at Sangpu, and then, after 1204, continued his studies with the Kashmiri master Śākyaśrībhadra, who arrived in Tibet accompanied by an entourage of Indian scholars. Sakya Paṇḍita was one of a number of Tibetan clerics who were inspired by this opportunity to learn directly from knowledgeable Indian teachers and he applied himself to mastering Sanskrit grammar and other aspects of Indic learning, a training that would lend a notably "Indological" perspective to his scholarship in later years. In his treatise, the *Scholar's Gate (Mkhas-pa 'jug-pa'i sgo),* he sets forth a general program representing his scholarly ideals, detailing a trivium based on the mastery of composition, rhetoric, and debate.

Indian traditions of logic and epistemology figured prominently among Sakya Paṇḍita's major concerns. His key contributions included the final redaction of the Tibetan translation of Dharmakīrti's masterwork, the *Pramāṇavārttika,* and his own synthesis of Indian Buddhist epistemology, the *Treasury of Epistemology* (*Tshad-ma rigs-gter*), which enjoys a singularly extensive commentarial tradition. In other writings he commented at length on current doctrinal debates, voicing trenchant criticisms of various developments in Tibet. Among his foremost targets was the notion of sudden enlightenment, which he often characterized as the "Chinese Great Perfection" (*rgya-nag rdzogs-chen*). But he found many other issues to be problematic as well, including the claims of everyday language philosophy:

> Some sophists, conforming with master Candrakīrti, establish the relative as according with ordinary worldly conventions, and they say that, though the individual may not be a worldling, he nevertheless engages [in activity] conforming to the unanalyzed, unexamined engagement of a worldly mind. But if this be examined [in terms of] the logic and epistemology of conventional signs, it is [shown to be] unsound. For, to a mind that has not investigated them, there are no engagements involving [well-formed notions of] perception, inference, proof, elimination of the exclusion,[9] and so on, and therefore the entire order of epistemic criteria and their opposites, that are explained in the seven treatises [of Dharmakīrti], are brought to decline. If you wish to follow those who thus affirm a worldly philosophy, then [you are already refuted], because among

9. The elimination of the exclusion (Skt. *anyāpoha*) was the centerpiece of the Buddhist theory of meaning, developed by Dignāga. According to this theory, which accords with aspects of modern semantics, the content of a term or concept is a function of its range of exclusion. That is, "cow," which excludes all things that are not cows, is conceptually richer than "living being."

> the objects of knowledge [you may admit] there are only entities and nonentities, and among the entities only inanimate matter and awareness, and every way of affirming inanimate matter has already been refuted, while, as for awareness, except for Mind Only nothing else is sound.[10]

In short, everyday conventions are inevitably unsustainable. To elaborate a sound approach to relative reality some system building must be countenanced, even though, like everyday discourse, this will *ultimately* give way under the assault of the Madhyamaka dialectic.

The traditions of Sangpu and Sakya were largely responsible for the content, style, and method of subsequent Tibetan Buddhist scholasticism, which came to be characterized by close study of the major Indian Buddhist philosophers—Nāgārjuna, Asaṅga, and Dignāga, and their commentators Candrakīrti, Vasubandhu, and Dharmakīrti, above all—rigorous adherence to the canons of argument, and precise and elegant use of language. Nevertheless, despite the resulting edification of exegetical systems in which the Buddha's teaching was subject to thoroughgoing rationalization, skeptical undercurrents still sometimes rose to the surface. Thus, the second Karmapa hierarch, Karma Pakshi (1206–1283), authored a catalogue of disputed opinions, in which he writes:

> It is held that saṃsāra has a beginning and end, and it is held that saṃsāra is without beginning or end. It is held that minds are of identical nature throughout all saṃsāra and nirvāṇa, and it is held that all minds are of differing natures. It is held that sentient beings are newly produced, and it is held that sentient beings are not newly produced.... But whatever such tenets—whether good, bad, or mediocre—one might harbor are the causes of good, bad, or mediocre [conditions of] saṃsāra. They are devoid of the life-force of nirvāṇa. Therefore, whatever tenets, hankerings or particular philosophical positions you hold, they cause you to be buddhaless, and make you meet with saṃsāra. You should know in this way the whole mass of tenets, [each one] in particular.[11]

Buddha-Nature and the Luminosity of Mind

The fourteenth century saw deepening interest in topics associated with the so-called "third turn of the doctrinal wheel": Buddha-nature or the "matrix of the tathāgata" (*tathāgatagarbha*), the "consciousness of the ground-of-all" (*ālayavijñāna*), and the "luminosity of mind" (*cittaprabhāsa*) foremost among them. There can be little doubt that the effort to elaborate satisfactory intellectual frameworks for the investigation of these and related topics received its impetus in part from the spread of

10. Sa-skya Paṇḍita Kun-dga'-rgyal-mtshan, *Tshad ma rigs gter* (Beijing: Nationalities Press, 1989), pp. 43–60.

11. *'Dod pa rgya mtsho mtha' yas*, in Karma Rang-byung-rdo-rje, *Rgya mtsho mtha' yas skor* (Gangtok, 1978), vol. 1, pp. 625–626.

contemplative and yogic techniques, which made use of these same concepts in the practical context of spiritual disciplines. The presence of similar terminology in some branches of the Indian scholastic literature and in certain of the sūtras led a growing number of scholars to argue that the highest teachings of the Buddha were to be found in such texts and to elaborate an exegetical program in support of that position. The debates to which this gave rise became some of most hotly contested areas of Tibetan Buddhist thought, and among the richest in terms of the range of perspectives that emerged. A strong current of idealist influence may be detected in many authors, though most, who were well aware of the critiques of idealism on the part of the Indian Madhyamaka philosophers, steered clear of any commitment to the ultimate viability of metaphysical idealism.

The efforts expended by Indian Buddhist writers in order to distinguish the teachings of *ālayavijñāna* and *tathāgatagarbha* from various "doctrines of self" (*ātmavāda*) demonstrate that they were felt to be problematic almost from the time that they were first introduced. D. S. Ruegg has argued that interpretive approaches to them exhibited two broad tendencies: on the one hand there were those who sought to show that the doctrines in question were not literally intended, but regarded as deriving from a soteriological strategy tailored for the needs of those not yet ready to apprehend the genuine purport of the Buddha's teaching; and on the other there were those who maintained that they had been so intended, adding only that their proper relationship with other discourses on the absolute, especially the concept of emptiness, had to be understood correctly.[12] It was this latter approach that was most obviously problematic, as it seemed to suggest that, once emptiness was comprehended, there was nevertheless something more to be known.

The Third Karmapa Rangjung Dorjé (Karma-pa Rang-byung-rdo-rje, 1284–1339) was one of the most influential figures in connection with the developments with which we are concerned. His views are set forth in his celebrated treatise, *Profound Inner Meaning* (*Zab mo nang don*), summarized here in the remarks of Jamgön Kongtrül ('Jam-mgon Kong-sprul, 1813–1899):

> That reality, or suchness, that is the ground of all saṃsāra and nirvāṇa, is referred to by many names, such as the "primordial, indestructible, great seminal point," "Prajñāpāramitā," "inborn gnosis," and "ordinary cognition." When it is stirred by the agitating vital energy of intellect, extraneous thoughts grow active. Owing to the appearance of dichotomized phenomena, one adopts the convention [of distinguishing between] the "gnosis of the ground-of-all" (*ālayajñāna*) and the "consciousness of the ground-of-all" (*ālayavijñāna*).
>
> Regarding the gnosis of the ground-of-all: it is buddha-nature, and in the *Prajñāpāramitā* and the *Uttaratantraśāstra* it is called the "nature of mind."... That, moreover, is the homogeneous causal basis of nirvāṇa, and the dominant or appropriating causal basis of saṃsāra. And because it abides latently in the consciousness of the ground-of-all, in the manner of water and milk mixed

12. Refer to Ruegg 1989.

> together, those who are bewildered about the definitive significance do not recognize the gnosis of the ground-of-all, and maintain that there are only the six aggregates of consciousness; and even if they maintain there to be eight aggregates, they apprehend the ground-of-all as consciousness alone.[13]

Passages such as this, taken out of context, may lead one to suppose that Karmapa Rangjung Dorjé favored a substance ontology similar to that sometimes associated with idealist traditions. Other passages from the Karmapa's work, however, suggest that the fundamental ground, as he understood it, was something far more diaphanous than some sort of "mind-stuff." Indeed, in the verses in which he comes closest to characterizing it directly, he deliberately undercuts the tendency to substantialism:

> The causal basis is mind-as-such that is beginningless.
> Though it is without interruption and imbalance,
> Through its unimpeded play—
> Empty in essence, radiant in nature, unimpeded in features—
> It arises as anything whatsoever.[14]

And elsewhere he describes the significance of the ground in the altogether normal Madhyamaka terms of "uncompounded reality, surpassing thought, neither indicated by affirmations, nor refuted by negations."[15]

The figure most often associated with controversial ontological speculations, however, was a junior contemporary of the Karmapa, Dölpopa Sherab Gyeltsen (Dol-po-pa Shes-rab-rgyal-mtshan, 1292–1361), whose radical teaching asserted that emptiness was not the intrinsic nature of the absolute, which was in fact to be realized as a plenitude. It is thus only extrinsically empty, that is, empty of all that constitutes relative reality:

> The intention is to distinguish intrinsic emptiness (*rang-stong*) from extrinsic emptiness (*gzhan-stong*). As for those who do not do so and who say that all is only intrinsic emptiness, and that emptiness is not determined in terms of extrinsic emptiness, but that only intrinsic emptiness determines emptiness, and who maintain that all [the Buddha's] statements that ultimately there is existence, permanence, self, purity and truth are of provisional meaning, while all statements of nonexistence, impermanence, non-self, impurity and rottenness are of definitive meaning, and that the [...] absolute, the ultimate body of reality, the essential body, natural luminosity, natural coemergence, natural great bliss, the

13. Kong-sprul Yon-tan rgya-mtsho, *Rnal 'byor bla na med pa'i rgyud sde rgya mtsho'i snying po bsdus pa zab mo nang gi don nyung ngu'i tshig gis rnam par 'grol ba zab don snang byed*, in *Bka' brgyud pa'i gsung rab pod nyi shu pa: thabs grol* (Xining: Mtsho sngon mi rigs dpe skrun khang, 2001), pp. 69–70.

14. Karma Rang-byung rdo-rje, *Zab mo nang gi don zhes bya ba'i gzhung*, in *Bka' brgyud pa'i gsung rab pod nyi shu pa: thabs grol*, pp. 3–4.

15. *Nges don phyag rgya chen po'i smon lam*, op. cit., p. 892.

naturally innate, natural nirvāṇa, the natural and spontaneously achieved maṇḍala, etc., as well as the natural abiding buddha-family with its many classifications, the ultimate buddha-nature endowed with many attributes, etc., are held with respect to reality but that reality is itself intrinsically empty—these and more are so many perverse views, coarse and bad views, without number.[16]

Dölpopa's thinking sparked a prolonged dispute and he was condemned in some circles as a tacit adherent of the Hindu teaching of the *ātman*. After the order to which he adhered, the Jonangpa, was suppressed by the Fifth Dalai Lama for political reasons, his writings were even banned, and many believed the suppression itself to be due to perceived heresy. Nevertheless, Dölpopa's insistence that the absolute could not be conceived as a mere nothingness had touched a sore nerve in Tibetan Buddhist thought, so that his teaching has been repeatedly revived, albeit with various modifications, down to the present time. His work had made clear the great difficulties involved in reconciling the teachings of the "third turn," as described above, with those of the "second turn," that is, the Perfection of Wisdom sūtras with their emphasis on emptiness. The noted editor of the canon, Butön Rinchendrup (Bu-ston Rin-chen-grub, 1292–1364), for instance, insisted against Dölpopa that the Buddha's definitive teachings were to be found just there, and not in the third turn. Their disagreement in matters of hermeneutics was not without significant philosophical ramifications.

The great interest aroused by discussions of luminosity and Buddha-nature may be seen, too, in the work of Longchen Rabjampa (Klong-chen Rab-'byams-pa, 1308–1364), the greatest theoretician of the Nyingmapa teaching of the Great Perfection. Nowhere is this more evident than in his treatment of the "ground" (*gzhi*), the basis for the actualization of the "fruit" (*'bras-bu*) that is buddhahood. In his conception of the emptiness of the absolute, he avoids Dölpopa's position, but is nevertheless similarly concerned not to embrace what he regards as the nihilistic tendencies of some Tibetan scholars:

The primordially luminous reality that is unconditioned and spontaneously present, from the perspective of emptiness is in no way established as entity or characteristic, and so is in no way divided into saṃsāra, nirvāṇa, etc., for which reason it is free from all elaborated extremes, like space. From the perspective of lucency, being primordially endowed with the nature of body and gnosis, there is spontaneous presence and luminosity, like the maṇḍalas of sun and moon....

Nowadays, most of the teachers and all of the hermits alike make out the ground to be a bare vacuity, nothing at all, and this does not accord with the intention of the significance of the matrix. By experientially cultivating a ground that is nothing at all, the fruit of awakening as buddha, with all enlightened attributes, will not emerge, because the trio of ground, path, and result has been confounded. This is because the awakened buddha, unconditioned and possessing the spontaneously present enlightened attributes, is a disclosure of the

16. *The 'Dzam-thang Edition of the Collected Works of Kun-mkhyen Dol-po-pa Shes-rab-rgyal-mtshan* (New Delhi: Shedrup Books and Konchhog Lhadrepa, 1992/1993), vol. 5, pp. 335–343.

> result of a separation [of adventitious taints from the primordially pure ground].... Here, on the other hand, it is the unconditioned and spontaneously present luminosity that is held to be the ground. From the inherent structure of such a ground, when not recognized as it is, there comes to be unawareness. Due to that, having errantly constructed the apprehending subject and apprehended object, one turns through the three realms.[17]

Tsongkhapa and His Critics

The fourteenth century was in many respects the golden age of Tibetan Buddhist philosophy. Besides the figures just surveyed, a host of scholars, many of whom were educated in the Kadampa and Sakyapa traditions, contributed to the elaboration of every aspect of Buddhist thought, engendering lively controversies in most areas. It became customary for aspirants to move from one center to another, studying with different masters and honing their debating skills on the way. One of those who entered this world of itinerant scholars was Jé Tsongkhapa Lozang Drakpa (Rje Tsong-kha-pa Blo-bzang-grags-pa, 1357–1419). Originally from the far northeastern Tibetan province of Amdo (modern Qinghai), he came to central Tibet as a teenager and pursued rigorous studies with all the foremost luminaries of the various orders. His dedication to the Kadampa teaching of the progressive path of the bodhisattva was such that he and his successors often came to be thought of as "new Kadampa" (*bka'-gdams gsar-ma*) and his treatise the *Great Exposition of the Stages of the Path (lam-rim chen-mo)* is renowned as a definitive expression of this approach. From his Sakyapa teacher, Remdawa Zhönu Lodrö (Red-mda'-ba Gzhon-nu-blo-gros, 1349–1412), he acquired a special concern for the interpretation of the Prāsaṅgika-Mādhyamika philosophy of the Indian master Candrakīrti, and it was in collaboration with Remdawa that he undertook his celebrated reform of the practice of the monastic code, or Vinaya. He thoroughly rejected the "extrinsic emptiness" doctrine of Dölpopa, regarding it as an extreme representative of persistent Tibetan misunderstandings of the Yogācāra philosophy of India, and, though accepting the authority of the Prāsaṅgika-Mādhyamika, he developed his own distinctive interpretation thereof, that in many respects was not anticipated in the work of Remdawa or earlier thinkers. In contradistinction to Atiśa's reservations with regard to the utility of Buddhist epistemology, for instance, Tsongkhapa sought to forge a viable synthesis between Dharmakīrti's approach to logical analysis and Candrakīrti's conception of the two truths. In Tsongkhapa's formulation of the lat-

17. Kloṅ-chen Rab-'byams-pa Dri-med-'od-zer, *Sems dang ye shes kyi dri lan*, in *Miscellaneous writings (Gsuṅ thor bu) of Kun-mkhyen Klon-chen-pa Dri- med-'od-zer* (Delhi: Sanje Dorje, 1973), vol. 1, pp. 377–392.

ter, the absolute did not override conventional reality, but in the highest insight one arrived at a seamless integration of the two. As he himself expressed it:

> The Buddha's realization is not comprehended so long as the infallible conditionality of appearance and emptiness-without-assertion[18] are both understood as separate. When [they arise] simultaneously, without alternation, so that in just perceiving the infallibility of conditioned origination all positions apprehending the ascertained object dissolve, at that time the analysis of viewpoints is concluded.[19]

In short, though drawing on earlier tradition, Tsongkhapa formulated a novel synthesis of the Indian Buddhist legacy, strongly emphasizing careful textual study and the demands of logic. After founding his own monastic center of Ganden in 1409, his followers gradually came to be established as a distinctive new order, which eventually adopted the name Gelukpa (Dge-lugs-pa) and to which the Dalai Lamas adhere.

Tsongkhapa clearly perceived that the many contested topics in the Buddhism of his day could not be resolved by appealing to scriptural authority alone and wrote:

> A scriptural passage which merely says "this [text] is of this [level of meaning]" cannot establish that to be so, for, as there is in general no such invariable concomitance [relating statements of the form given to the levels of meaning to which they refer], the mere statement, "this [scripture] is of this [level of meaning]" cannot prove a particular instance of interpretable or definitive meaning.[20]

The would-be interpreter is therefore thrown back on the operations of natural reason if he is to cut through the conundrums posed by doctrinal texts.

In connection with the Prāsaṅgika-Mādhyamika philosophy, in particular, there were principally eight such conundrums about which Tsongkhapa proposed new solutions. One of his chief disciples, Gyeltsab-jé (Rgyal-tshab-rje, 1364–1432), lists them as follows:

18. In adopting this expression, Tsong-kha-pa emphasizes his commitment to the Prāsaṅgika tradition of Candrakīrti, over and against the Svātantrika-Mādhyamika, associated with such figures as Bhāvaviveka and Śāntarakṣita, for whom emptiness is asserted in the positive conclusion of a formal demonstration.

19. Rje Tsong-kha-pa Blo-bzang-grags-pa, *Lam gyi gtso bo rnam gsum*, in *Rje tsong kha pa chen po'i bka' 'bum thor bu* (Xining: Mtsho sngon mi rigs dpe skrun khang, 1987), pp. 344–346.

20. Rje Tsong-kha-pa Blo-bzang-grags-pa, *Drang nges legs bshad snying po*, Sarnath ed., p. 3.

21. In the system of Dignāga and Dharmakīrti, the "self-marking particular" (*svalakṣaṇa*) is the discrete phenomenon that bears those qualities that establish its unique identity for a perceiver who is not subject to error. This, the elementary building block of their ontology, was accepted by many Tibetan thinkers as conventionally true, even in Madhyamaka contexts, but by Tsongkhapa to be not even conventionally acceptable for the Prāsaṅgika.

22. For Dignāga and Dharmakīrti, reflexivity or apperception (*svasaṃvittiḥ*) was the elementary unit of consciousness, paralleling, in their system, the self-marking particular as the minimal object. Tsongkhapa, true to his own principles, in rejecting one, rejected equally the other.

> In relation to the ground: (1–2) the denials of the ground-of-all and the self-marking particular,[21] and (3) the affirmation of outer objects. In relation to the path: (4–5) the denials of the autonomous syllogism [i.e. direct proof] and reflexive awareness[22] as the means for realizing just what is as it is, and (6–7) the affirmation of [a unique approach to the explanation of] how the two obscurations are established and of the realization, among pious attendants and self-centered buddhas, of the absence of the substantial nature of principles.[23] And in relation to the result: (8) [a unique approach to the explanation of] how the Buddha cognizes the extension of things.

Each of these topics is complex, and each occasioned extensive discussion. As we have seen aspects of the earlier treatment of the consciousness of the ground-of-all, some extracts of Gyeltsab-jé's comments on this may be taken as illustrative:

> Some hold that, if virtuous or unvirtuous deeds were to abide until the maturation of the result, then they would be permanent, so that [one who affirmed this] would fall into the extreme of eternalism, while if, on the other hand, the deed that was performed were to be annihilated in the second instant, then, because the annihilated cannot be an entity, it could not generate the mature result, wherefore completed deeds would vanish without trace.
>
> Some respond to this argument, saying that, even though the deed be annihilated, there is a ground for the successive emergence of the potency of the deed, which is considered to be the ground-of-all, while others affirm this to be the continuous stream of intellectual consciousness. And some respond by holding that, even though the deed be annihilated, the deed's acquisition remains in existence, while others hold there to be some other principle, called "inexhaustion," that is like the seal witnessing a debt. Our own response is that, even without affirming any of those four propositions, beginning with the ground-of-all, it is implied that the completed deed will not vanish without trace. For even if those [four theories] are not affirmed, there is no contradiction involved if we assume that it is the annihilated deed that generates a result. If [our opponent counters,] saying, "Unproven! For what is annihilated cannot be an entity," then [we respond that] that is unproven, for, though the annihilated cannot be an entity if you affirm the self-marking particular [to be the defining entity], we do not affirm the self-marking particular even as a matter of convention, wherefore both annihilated and unannihilated deeds are equivalent with respect to whether or not they are entities.[24]

Tsongkhapa's solution to the problem of *karma* and causation, that the annihilation or destruction (*zhig-pa*) of a thing could act in a causal stream just as does an entity, may appear to be a rabbit pulled from the hat just in order to preserve his system. This, indeed, is how his critics perceived it and, together with many other of

23. The more prevalent view was that *śrāvaka*-s and *pratyekabuddha*-s, who exemplified the highest goals of the "lesser vehicle" (*hīnayāna*), realized the insubstantiality ("selflessness") of persons, but not of the principles (*dharma*) upon which persons supervene.

24. This and the preceding quotation from Rgyal-tshab-rje Dar-ma rin-chen, *Dbu ma rtsa ba'i dka' gnad chen po brgyad kyi brjed byang*, in *Dbu ma'i lta khrid phyogs bsdebs* (Sarnath: Central Institute of Higher Tibetan Studies, 1985), pp. 154–187.

the distinctive aspects of his thought, it was universally rejected by those outside of the Gelukpa order he had founded. One of his sharpest opponents, the Sakyapa Gorampa Sonam Senggé (Go-rams-pa Bsod-nams seng-ge, 1429–1489), for instance, argued that it had the absurd entailment that "karma and its effects are different since at the level of conventions, they are set off from one another by an intermediary, namely 'destruction *qua* real entity,' just like two mountains that face each other are set off from one another by the river [that runs between them]."[25] Much of the later history of Buddhist thought in Tibet, in fact, may be interpreted in terms of the continuing debate between Tsongkhapa's critics and defenders. Among the former, besides Gorampa, particularly notable philosophers include the Sakyapa master Serdok Paṇchen (Gser-mdog Paṇ-chen, 1428–1507) and the Eighth Karmapa hierarch Mikyö Dorjé (Mi-bskyod rdo-rje, 1507–1554), while, among the latter, Sera Jetsün Chöki Gyeltsen (Se-ra rje-btsun Chos-kyi rgyal-mtshan, 1469–1546) is famed for his detailed defenses of Tsongkhapa's thinking against all three of the critics mentioned here.

Later Developments

Political turmoil in Central Tibet throughout much of the seventeenth and eighteenth centuries, in tandem with changing relations with Tibet's Mongol and Manchu neighbors, contributed to a remarkable shift in Tibet's cultural geography. Whereas Central Tibet had been, throughout the preceding centuries, the unrivaled heart of Tibetan religious life, new centers of intellectual and artistic activity now emerged in Tibet's far eastern regions of Amdo and Kham. In the latter, with the patronage of the rulers of Dergé (Sde-dge), Karmapa and Sakyapa masters contributed to the foundation of Tibet's greatest publishing house, the Dergé Printery, which made canonical and other works widely available. At the same time, the Gelukpa monasteries in Amdo for the first time also became important centers of learning in their own right, for instance at Kumbum (Sku-'bum), near Tsongkhapa's birthplace not far from the city of Xining (Qinghai Province), and Labrang (Bla-brang), founded by Jamyang Zhepa ('Jam-dbyangs-bzhad-pa, 1648–1721) in southern Gansu. Scholars associated with these latter centers were often not ethnic Tibetans, and they frequently enjoyed the patronage of the Manchu court, which regarded Tibetan Buddhism as supplying a cultural lingua franca for the peoples of Inner Asia.

The prominence of the east in this period is very well illustrated in the life and work of the great eighteenth-century master Changkya Rolpei Dorjé (1717–1786). Born among the Monguor of Qinghai, he was identified at the age of four as the

25. Cabezón and Dargyay 2007, 137.

incarnation of a famous lama and sent to Beijing to be educated at the court. There he became the fast friend of a Manchu prince, who later succeeded to the throne as the emperor Qianlong (reigned 1736–1799), the greatest of the Qing monarchs. Changkya rose with his boyhood friend to become the empire's preeminent Buddhist clergyman, as well as the confidante and biographer of the Seventh Dalai Lama Kelzang Gyatso (Bskal-bzang rgya-mtsho, 1708–1757). As Changkya's writings make clear, he adhered closely to Tsongkhapa's ideal of reason in seeking to resolve for himself the conflicted points of Buddhist teaching.

One of Changkya's most esteemed and puzzling works, called the "Epistemological Path" (*Tshad ma lam rim*), records a dream-vision in which the relationship between the systematic study of Dharmakīrti's epistemology and progress on the Buddhist path is set out in general terms. Changkya, by placing his sketch of Buddhist rationalism in the context of a dream-vision, effectively annuls the gulf separating religious experience from reason. In his dream, a voice instructs him:

> You must reflect on your understanding of Dharmakīrti, intermingling your intellectual insight with your present experience: these varied pleasures and pains that occur to you now in the course of things are ephemeral occurrences. These pleasures and pains are experientially proven to occur on the basis of causes and conditions.... Thus you arrive at the thought that the Buddha's teachings of impermanence, suffering, and causality are established by reason and verified experientially...."[26]

Hence, for Changkya, the reasoned investigation of the teaching is to be intermingled with one's experiences; it must flow from, and in turn inform, one's engagement in the self-cultivation that characterizes the Buddhist path.

The position of the non-Gelukpa orders was relatively stronger in Kham, where, during the nineteenth century, a dynamic movement often characterized as "eclectic" or "universalist" (*ris-med*) sought to defuse the intense sectarianism that had often plagued Tibetan Buddhism. The encyclopedic writings of Jamyang Khyen-tse ('Jam-dbyangs Mkhyen-brtse, 1820–1892) and Jamgön Kongtrül (1813–1899) became in some respects a new canon for the adherents of this movement. One of their disciples, Mipam Namgyel (Mi-pham rnam-rgyal, 1846–1912), also elaborated a new scholastic curriculum emphasizing the doctrinal standpoint of the Nyingmapa order, and engaged in wide-ranging debates with some of his Gelukpa contemporaries. Like his teachers, however, Mipam was convinced that the Tibetan Buddhist orders had more in common than sectarian polemicists were readily willing to admit. In a satirical essay, after noting some of the strengths and vulnerabilities of the four major orders, he concludes:

> The philosophical systems of the teaching in Tibet began at the time of the [...] the religious king [Tri Songdetsen]. From that ancient and excellent legacy, all [the Tibetan orders] are alike in affirming the four seals that mark the transmitted precepts of the teaching.[27] Above and beyond that, they all affirm the

26. *Tshad ma lam rim*, in *Lcang skya rol pa'i rdo rje'i rnam thar*, pp. 635–638.

27. The four seals of the teaching are that conditioned entities are impermanent; that corruptible things involve suffering; that no entity is or possesses a substantial self; and that nirvāṇa is peace.

great unelaborate emptiness and, what's more, also affirm the vehicle of the tantras, [which teaches] the coalescence of bliss and emptiness. Because, then, in point of fact, their views and systems are similar, they are exceedingly close.

In thinking about other factions, [consider that] among non-Buddhists and barbarians, with whom we share not even tokens and dress, and who are [as numerous] as nighttime stars, we, who are just a few, like daytime stars, are approaching the completion of the teaching. While something of it remains, those who have entered into the domains of the teaching with common purpose ought to cultivate the perception that they are most closely related. Because mutual enmity will bring ruination, regard one another as does a mother her child, or as does a beggar a treasure, and so cultivate a perception of joy.[28]

Though sectarian antagonisms have remained undiminished among some Tibetans, the ideal of tolerance espoused here has become widespread, and in our times is embraced by H. H. the Fourteenth Dalai Lama.

BIBLIOGRAPHY AND SUGGESTED READINGS

Arguillère, S. (2007) *Vaste sphère de profusion, Klong-chen rab-'byams (Tibet, 1308–1364), sa vie, son œuvre, sa doctrine*. Orientalia Analecta Lovaniensa 167. Leiden: Peeters.

Cabezón, Jose Ignacio, and Geshe Lobsang Dargyay. (2007) *Freedom from Extremes: Gorampa's "Distinguishing the Views" and the Polemics of Emptiness*. Boston, MA: Wisdom.

Demiéville, P. (1952) *Le concile de Lhasa: une controverse sur le quiétisme entre bouddhistes de l'Inde et de la Chine au VIIIe siècle de l'ère chrétienne*. Bibliothèque de l'Institut des Hautes Études Chinoises, Volume VII. Paris: Imprimerie Nationale de France.

Dreyfus, Georges B. J. (2003) *The Sound of Two Hands Clapping: The Education of a Tibetan Buddhist Monk*. Berkeley/Los Angeles/London: University of California Press.

Dudjom Rinpoche, Jikdrel Yeshe Dorje. (1991) *The Nyingma School of Tibetan Buddhism: Its Fundamentals and History*, translated by Gyurme Dorje and Matthew Kapstein. Boston, MA: Wisdom Publications (2nd ed. 2002).

Gold, J. C. (2007) *The Dharma's Gatekeepers: Sakya Paṇḍita on Buddhist Scholarship in Tibet*. Albany, NY: State University of New York Press.

Goldfield, A., J. Levinson, et al. (trans.). (2006) *The Moon of Wisdom: Chapter Six of Chandrakīrti's Entering the Middle Way with Commentary from the Eighth Karmapa*. Ithaca, NY: Snow Lion.

Guenther, Herbert V. (1989) *From Reductionism to Creativity: Rdzogs-chen and the New Sciences of Mind*. Boston, MA: Shambhala.

Hopkins, J. (2004) *Maps of the Profound: Jam-yang-shay-ba's Great Exposition of Buddhist and Non-Buddhist Views on the Nature of Reality*. Ithaca, NY: Snow Lion.

Jackson, David. (1987) *The Entrance Gate for the Wise (Section III): Sa-skya Paṇḍita on Indian and Tibetan Tradition of Pramāṇa and Philosophical Debate*. 2 vols. Wiener Studien zur Tibetologie und Buddhismuskunde 17, 1–2. Vienna: Arbeitskreis für Tibetische und Buddhistische Studien Universität Wien.

28. Mi-pham, *Gzhan stong khas len seng ge'i nga ro*, Ser-lo dgon-pa (Nepal) xylographic ed.

KAPSTEIN, M. T. (2001) *Reason's Traces: Identity and Interpretation in Indian and Tibetan Buddhist Thought*. Boston, MA: Wisdom Publications.

KARMA PHUNTSHO. (2005) *Mipham's Dialectics and the Debates on Emptiness*. London: Routledge.

KLEIN, A. C., and GESHE TENZIN WANGYAL RINPOCHE. (2006) *Unbounded Wholeness: Dzogchen, Bon, and the Logic of the Nonconceptual*. New York: Oxford University Press.

KUIJP, LEONARD W. J. VAN DER. (1983) *Contributions to the Development of Tibetan Buddhist Epistemology*. Wiesbaden: Franz Steiner Verlag.

LOPEZ, D. S., JR. (2006) *The Madman's Middle Way: Reflections on Reality of the Tibetan Monk Gendun Chopel*. Chicago, IL: University of Chicago Press.

MAKRANSKY, JOHN J. (1997) *Buddhahood Embodied: Sources of Controversy in India and Tibet*. Albany, NY: State University of New York Press.

MATHES, KLAUS-DIETER. (2007) *A Direct Path to the Buddha Within: Gö Lotsāwa's Mahāmudrā Interpretation of the Ratnagotravibhāga*. Boston, MA: Wisdom.

NGAWANG SAMTEN and JAY GARFIELD. (2006) *Ocean of Reasoning: A Great Commentary on Nāgārjuna's Mūlamadhyamakakārikā*. New York: Oxford University Press.

PETTIT, JOHN. (1999) *Mipham's Beacon of Certainty*. Boston, MA: Wisdom Publications.

RUEGG, DAVID SEYFORT. (1989) *Buddha-nature, Mind and the Problem of Gradualism in a Comparative Perspective: On the Transmission and Reception of Buddhism in India and Tibet*. London: School of Oriental and African Studies.

STEARNS, CYRUS. (1999) *Buddha from Dolpo*. Albany, NY: State University of New York Press.

THUPTEN, JINPA. (2002) *Self, Reality and Reason in Tibetan Philosophy: Tsongkhapa's Quest for the Middle Way*. London: Routledge Curzon.

THURMAN, R. A. F. (1984) *Tsong Khapa's Speech of Gold in the Essence of True Eloquence*. Princeton, NJ: Princeton University Press.

TSONG-KHA-PA. (2001–2004) *The Great Treatise on the Stages of the Path to Enlightenment*, translated by Joshua Cutler et al. 3 vols. Ithaca, NY: Snow Lion.

WILLIAMS, PAUL. (1998) *The Reflexive Nature of Awareness: A Tibetan Madhyamaka Defence*. Surrey, England: Curzon.

CHAPTER 20

DZOGCHEN

ANNE CAROLYN KLEIN

DZOGCHEN (rDzogs chen) refers to an integrated set of texts, practices, philosophical perspectives, and theories of subjectivity unique to the most esoteric Buddhist and Bon traditions of Tibet. The philosophical core of Dzogchen is its emphasis on experiencing mind-nature (*sems nyid*) and understanding its relationship to ordinary mental states. To be fully and nonconceptually aware of one's nature is called open presence (*rig pa, vedanā*).

Dzogchen philosophy elaborates the issues and conundrums raised by this core tenet. Among Tibet's Buddhist traditions, it is only Nyingma (rNying-ma-pa), the most ancient school, that explicitly takes Dzogchen as its esoteric tradition.[1] Both Nyingma and Bon see Dzogchen as the highest in a ninefold system known as the Nine Vehicles. While the texts, lineage figures, and many details of Bon and Buddhist Dzogchen are different, they are also profoundly consonant. Their intertwined histories are a rich narrative of the extensive philosophical thinking and experiential exploration that has been part of Dzogchen communities in Tibet since at least the tenth century (Klein and Wangyal 2006, ch. 7).

Support of meditative experience is a concern of much Buddhist philosophy; it is particularly central to Dzogchen, for the role of intellect in this type of meditation is more limited than in other systems (Klein and Wangyal 2006, ch. I). Much of

1. Nyingma relies primarily on literature brought to Tibet during the ninth to eleventh centuries. This material includes a collection known as the Old Tantras, an important source for Dzogchen. There are three types of literature that expound on the ancient Nyingma tantras: scriptures (*lung sde*), instructions (*man ngag sde*), and reasoning (*rigs pa*). In addition, there developed numerous Dzogchen textual-cum-oral lineages in Tibet, such as the Heart Essence (*Nying Thig*) transmissions (see Klein 2009 and Thondup 1996). Both Nyingma and Bon categorize their Dzogchen material into sections on space (*klong sde*), mind (*sems sde*), and quintessential instruction (*man ngag sde*) but include different texts in these categories (Klein and Wangyal 2006, Appendix).

Dzogchen literature is in service of clarifying the stages, phenomenology, and practices of meditation.

We can best explore Dzogchen philosophy by contrasting it with other systems of Buddhist thought. We will do this in three ways: (1) by considering how Dzogchen differs from what Tibetans refer to as the "ordinary," or sūtra, vehicles, as well as from the "outer" tantric vehicles; (2) by relating central strands of Dzogchen perspective to the classic differentiation of the "Three Turnings of the Wheel," that is, the doctrines attributed to Buddha Shakyamuni; and (3) by showing how Dzogchen both differs from and incorporates Middle Way (Madhyamaka) philosophy's understanding of the ultimate, or emptiness. These three perspectives are intricately interrelated, so our account will move among them, rather than proceed through them in a strictly linear fashion.

Philosophically speaking, Dzogchen traditions reject the causal paradigm so prominent in what Tibetan doxographers refer to as "the lower eight vehicles" and the "Three Turnings of the Wheel." In these models, the practitioner's goal is to accumulate causes leading to realization. In Dzogchen traditions, the liberating wisdom that is the acme of Buddhist practice cannot and need not be caused; it is ever present. However, in ordinary beings it is unmanifest. This counterpoint at the heart of Dzogchen perspectives opens a number of difficult issues, many of them shared with Chan/Zen views. In Dzogchen—as in Chan/Zen—the claim of uncaused realization means that in a very fundamental sense there is no difference between Buddhas and non-Buddhas, nor between saṃsāra and nirvāṇa. As Longchen Rabjam (kLong chen Rab 'byams, 1308–1363) states in the first chapter of his *Naturally Liberated Mind:* "In the ultimate meaning there is no samsara and no wanderers in it. All are originally liberated" (Thondup 1996, 322). Likewise, the Bon Lishu Daring (Li shu sTa ring, eighth century) cites an ancient Bon Tantra, *Scripture of the Blissful Samantabhadra:* "Buddhas are not found by meditation, Nor lost by not meditating" (Klein and Wangyal 2006, 282).

Such claims leave Dzogchen with the philosophical challenge of explaining the place of practice in general and of study in particular. Dzogchen traditions do not agree with some other Buddhist schools that dualistic thought, even though considered "valid cognition" (*tshad ma, pramāṇa*), is capable of accessing the reality Dzogchen defines as ultimate. Thus, the intellect cannot participate in realization. But Dzogchen is not anti-intellectual. Writings by seminal figures such as the Lishu Daring and Dranpa Namkha (Dran-pa Nam-kha, eighth century) in Bon and Buddhist exemplars such as Rangzom (Rong zom Chos kyi bZang po, 1012–1088), Longchen Rabjam, Jigme Lingpa ('Jigs med gLing pa, 1729/30–1798), or Jigme Denbey Nyima ('Jigs med bDen pa'i Nyi ma, b.1765) as well as the modern-day Mipam Rinpoche ('Jam mgon 'ju Mi pham, 1846–1912), reveal them to be brilliant and creative thinkers, as well as poets and visionaries. Indeed, one of the hallmarks of Dzogchen, and much of Tibetan culture, is the way philosophical rigor is seamlessly conjoined with compelling artistic, mythological, or visionary accomplishment (Klein and Wangyal 2006 Introduction).

The Outer Three Vehicles

The first three vehicles correspond to what the Indian and Tibetan traditions more generally speak of as the hearer, solitary realizer, and bodhisattva vehicles. The philosophy and praxis of the hearers (*nyan thos, śrāvaka*)[2] center on understanding the Four Noble Truths and their sixteen aspects, including the selflessness of persons. Practitioners of the second vehicle, the solitary realizers (*rang sangs rgyas, pratyekabuddha*), emphasize the twelve links of dependent arising, further articulating the law of karma taught in connection with the second of the four noble truths, the truth of suffering's causes.

In both cases, what hearers and solitary realizers understand as the emptiness, or final reality, of persons is different from how they understand the emptiness of other phenomena—oceans, mountains, houses, and the like. The emptiness of persons that they realize is considered a coarser, and also more accessible, type of emptiness than that taught in the Middle Way. It is coarser because it negates, or contradicts, less of conventional, normative human conceptual and sensory experience.

The third vehicle is that of the bodhisattvas, whose purpose it is to realize emptiness as taught in Middle Way classics, especially Nāgārjuna's *Fundamental Wisdom of the Middle Way* and its commentaries.[3] The emptiness it teaches negates more than that of the previous two vehicles. For example, the Middle Way states that a person or thing designated to any configuration of parts is not identical with those parts. It is empty of being findable either in or as those parts. Thus, a steering wheel, engine, and so forth in a certain configuration are the basis of designation of a car, but they are not the car. Likewise, and more important, body and mind are the basis of designation of a person, but not the person itself. Upon investigation, no person is found, among its parts, nor can it be found separate from them.

Thus, the emptiness discussed in the Middle Way pertains equally to persons and phenomena other than persons. Emptiness is the ultimate truth, because it is nondeceptive. All other phenomena are conventional truths. Emptiness, however, is also empty of objective or independent existence; it too cannot be found when sought among its bases of designation. This unfindability so central to Middle Way thought is an important part of the Dzogchen view, especially with respect to the mind. For Dzogchen, however, mere unfindability is not, as in Madhaymaka, fully descriptive of the ultimate.

The Bodhisattva vehicle also emphasizes the six perfections as causes for enlightenment. These six (giving, ethics, patience, effort, concentration, and wisdom) are

2. Indo-Tibetan traditions say these are so called because they hear the teaching and then cause others to hear it. The "Solitary Realizers" of the second vehicle are so called because, having received all needed teachings in previous lives, practice in solitude, without a teacher in the current life. Although the nine vehicles discussed here are a Dzogchen doxographic perspective, the categories of Hearer and Solitary Realizer are recognized, and similarly identified, across the Buddhist traditions. In Jainism the term "Hearer" refers to a lay Jain follower.

3. For more on Madhyamaka (Middle Way) philosophy see John Dunne's chapter in this volume.

animated by the motivation to help all living beings attain enlightenment. Starting with the third vehicle, it is understood that even when utterly divested of mistaken views of self, one remains motivated by compassionate intention. Compassion and wisdom, like all phenomena, are empty of real or reified existence. Because they are empty, they can be cultivated and they can function. This seamless conjoining of the ultimate and the conventional occurs in a different guise in Dzogchen, which speaks in terms of an unconditioned reality's (*gzhi, ādhāra; chos nyis, dharmatā; chos dbyings, dharma dhātu*) capacity for dynamic expression (*rtsal*). For Dzogchen, the ultimate, while empty, is imbued with qualities that can emerge in positive and negative ways. As Jigme Lingpa famously stated, echoing Longchen Rabjam, "Because there is birth from the birthless, living beings are confused" (Klein 2009, 152). Fielding the philosophical issues associated with this perspective is central in the work of Longchen Rabjam, Jigme Lingpa, Mipam, and elsewhere.

Dzogchen is often explained in terms of three categories: view, meditation, and conduct. This last category, conduct, resonates with classic Bodhisattva teachings on ethics, for ethics is fundamentally the practice of not harming others, and is integral to the Bodhisattva's further goal of helping others. Therefore, as much as the Middle Way's emptiness or Dzogchen empty luminosity is emphasized as ultimate, ethics remains foundational. Padmasambhava (Pad ma 'byung gnas, eighth century), the source of Dzogchen in Tibet, famously stated that while his view was vast as the sky, when it came to conduct, his actions were as precise as finely ground barley flour. This means that, as a philosophical system and contemplative practice, Dzogchen has the challenge of centering itself in a normative state beyond good and evil while at the same time maintaining an ethic of good conduct.

Whereas in the third vehicle compassionate intention is associated with either a conventional or ultimate consciousness, Dzogchen posits an intrinsic, responsive dynamism as part of the mind's own nature. Both responsive and unconditioned, this dynamism is an aspect of reality and of mind-nature. The Tibetan term used to name the actual expression of such responsive dynamism is "*thugs rje*," the same word that in the context of the lower vehicles is appropriately translated as "compassion." *Thugs* means "heart-mind" and *rje* means "venerable, majestic, sovereign." In the Bodhisattva vehicle, compassion is something to be cultivated. And such cultivation is part of the training that, by long-established tradition, one engages in before taking up Dzogchen practice. In Dzogchen itself, however, "*thugs rje*" is not cultivated; it is an element intrinsic to mind-nature, not a conditioned consciousness. This is a crucial point distinguishing Dzogchen from other systems and supporting its view of itself as a discovery-oriented practice. For Dzogchen it is axiomatic that mind-nature, the way things are, is always at hand.

In Longchen Rabjam's and other discussions of the nine vehicles, the first three, or "outer," vehicles are partly analogous to what Buddhist traditions call the Three turnings of the wheel, three sequential groups of teachings attributed to the Buddha. Their description of the turnings accords with the other Indian and Tibetan Buddhist schools' understanding. However, whereas the Middle Way schools take the second wheel to be definitive, Mind-Only and Dzogchen, among others, take the third wheel to be definitive.

The first wheel emphasizes eradication of unwholesome physical, verbal, and mental acts as well as cultivation of wholesome ones. Eradication is achieved through counteragents, or antidotes, such as cultivating an understanding of impermanence to counter the mistaken impression that one's self or one's possessions are permanent. Antidotes are used to overcome two types of ignorance: ignorance regarding the cause and effect of actions (karma), and ignorance regarding the way things really are (empty or interdependent). From this perspective, the goodness and wisdom one cultivates is a cause, and enlightenment an effect. These causal or developmental systems face the philosophical challenge of explaining how any consciousness, which by definition is a conditioned phenomenon, can give rise to a wisdom that is by definition unified with the unconditioned emptiness. Dzogchen, as we have noted, faces a different philosophical challenge. If wisdom is unconditioned, how can it be attained? Why try to attain it? For if unconditioned wisdom is always present, then either enlightenment is of no use or all efforts to gain it are superfluous.

Mahāyāna sūtra systems understand Buddha-nature to be the mind's emptiness, that is, its lack of being self-enclosed, independent, or findable. Afflicted states of mind, being both conditioned and empty, can be dispelled through practice. Dzogchen, by contrast, emphasizes that the mind's empty nature is luminous with good qualities that are revealed as soon as mental stains are removed. In this it draws on Third Wheel discussions of Buddha-nature, such as those found in the *Tathagathagharba-sūtra.* Accordingly, Dzogchen understands that its practice does not change anything but reveals the nature that has always been. Jigme Lingpa writes: "In Dzogchen, having realized the changeless ultimate nature and by not moving from that state, the stains of both emotional and intellectual defilements are naturally purified without being abandoned" (Thondup 1996, 43).

Dzogchen traditions emphasize that when one is fully present to one's mind-nature, all defilements dissolve. There is no gradual process of dissipating them with an antidote, as in sutra, or even of transforming them into something else, a metaphor often used in tantra.

The sutras are those scriptures understood to have been spoken publicly by Śākyamuni Buddha; the tantras are scriptures understood to have been spoken to highly realized persons by a different Buddha-emanation, Vajradhāra. Buddhist traditions also distinguish between practices included within sutra or tantric perspectives. In the New Transmission of the Gelukpa Order (Dge-lugs-pa), the tantras are divided into the four classes of Action, Performance, Yoga, and Highest Yoga Tantra. In the Old Transmission, as presented in Nyingma's presentation of nine vehicles, these four are the fourth through ninth vehicles, with the seventh, eighth, and ninth vehicles being subdivisions of Highest Yoga Tantra. In terms of practice, sutra-based cultivation is causal or developmental, whereas Tantra is fruitional, a path of discovery, especially the discovery that oneself is the enlightened Buddha one seeks to emulate.

Most significantly for our discussion, whereas in the developmental style of sūtra practices, where reasoning and inference have an important role to play in dispelling ignorance, in the discovery style of Dzogchen, no amount of thinking can bring one to the nondual recognition of the mind's empty, luminous nature. In Middle Way philosophy, a cup's emptiness cannot be separated from the cup, although it is possible to think of one and not the other. In the language of that system, the cup is a conventional truth, its emptiness an ultimate truth. In Dzogchen, mind itself is the emptiness of which the Middle Way speaks, though mind is not a mere negative. This is partly because "the ultimate" is defined differently in these two systems. In Dzogchen, mind-nature is never an object; it is a nonconceptual mirror—like knowing one's nature as primordially pure in its essence (*ngo bo ga tag*), spontaneously luminous in its nature (*rang gzhin gsal ba*), and pervasively and compassionately responsive in its manifestation (*khyab byed thugs rje*).

In classic Middle Way thought, especially in Tsongkhapa's (Tsong-kha-pa, 1357–1419) interpretations of Nāgārjuna, the ultimate is emptiness, the object of a wisdom consciousness. This emptiness is described as spacelike, as simply the absence of a mistaken construction of what "person" is. It is a mere negative, with nothing findable or implied by it. In Dzogchen (and in some other systems as well) the ultimate reality, even when called empty, refers to what is spacious and dynamic. The Nyingma master scholar-practitioner Dodrupchen III (rDo-grub-chen, 1865–1926) points out that in Dzogchen the most subtle, authentic, and fundamental mind (*gnyug sems*) is the ultimate truth and the appearances of various phenomena, characterized by being adventitious and conditioned, are the conventional truths. The point is that here the ultimate truth refers to something fundamental and innate, and always existent (Gyatso 1984, 209), and also to something that is reflexively aware, or present to itself. This is not an object in the way that emptiness can be an object. Elaborating this is central to Dzogchen thought; realizing it is the goal of Dzogchen practice.

Thus, Madhyamaka and Dzogchen both understand the mind as empty, and Nyingma practitioners typically train in Middle Way study and practice in preparation for Dzogchen practice. Dzogchen itself, however, as indicated above, does not take emptiness, understood as a mere negative, to be the final view of mind's nature. For Dzogchen, direct experience reveals that the nature of mind is clear light[4]; this is the most subtle mind that sees emptiness. Considered uninterrupted and uninterruptible, it is not just a subjective state; it is mind's ultimate or final nature. Thus, the ultimate here is both knower and known. This mind-nature is simultaneously the goal of practice and its starting point. Practice reveals mind-nature, but does not bring it about. This is because the mind-nature one has now is itself enlightened mind. Mind-nature, reality, is not affected by circumstances, so it neither improves on enlightenment nor becomes flawed by the ignorance that prevents enlightenment. For

4. "Clear light" can refer also to a very subtle state of consciousness, such as occurs in deep states of meditation or at the time of death. This is known as a subjective clear light and the emptiness it knows is an objective clear light.

this reason Longchen Rabjam famously speaks of becoming "Buddha again." This is both an experiential conclusion of Dzogchen practitioners and a statement of the philosophical challenge it must continually address.

Third Turning of the Wheel: Extrinsic Emptiness and Luminous Buddha-Nature

Jigme Lingpa and Mipam, among others, take the Third Wheel to be the one that the Buddha meant literally. This contrasts with classic Middle Way identifications of the Second Wheel, the perfection of wisdom teachings on emptiness, as ultimate. Jigme Lingpa also states that Dzogchen—and specifically its view of the ultimate—includes all three Turnings of the Wheel.

Dzogchen's view of mind-nature as ultimate relates to an important debate across Buddhist traditions about whether emptiness refers to a lack of substantial or inherent existence or to something that is not specifically a quality of the object under consideration. The former is known as "self-emptiness" (*rang stong*), central to the teachings of Nāgārjuna as interpreted, for example, by Tsongkhapa and the latter is called other-emptiness (*gzhan stong*). Early proponents of other-emptiness include non-Dzogchen exponents such as Dolpopa (Dol-po-pa, 1292–1361), founder of what became known as the Jonang school, and another prominent Jonangpa, Tāranātha (1575–1634). The nonsectarian Nyingma lineage holder Jamgon Kongtrul Lodro Thaye ('Jam mgon Kong sprul bLo gros mTha' yas, 1813–1899) was a proponent of other-emptiness; Mipam was both critical and supportive of it. "Other-emptiness" emphasizes that the fundamental mind of clear light is empty of concepts and afflictions that are "other" than the luminosity itself. This innate mind of clear light is mentioned in Maitreya's *Sublime Continuum (Uttaratantra)* and *Discrimination of the Middle and Extremes Madhyāntavibhaṅga, dbU mtha' rnam 'byed)* (Gyatso 1984, 210).

To say that the fundamental innate mind is empty of adventitious afflictions does not mean that it is independent or ultimately real. This understanding of other-emptiness, which contradicts the Buddhist principle of dependent arising, was widely rejected in Tibet. Although the position of "emptiness of other" has for seven hundred years been pitted against the view of "emptiness of self," the fact that the former is devoid of inherent existence—the very definition of emptiness in the latter—means that the two views are not only compatible but also potentially complementary.

At the same time, although Dzogchen incorporates much of Nāgārjunian "self-emptiness" into its perspective, it does not, as we have seen, take this Middle Way emptiness as the final statement on reality or mind-nature. That status is reserved for the fundamental mind of clear light, which is sometimes in Dzogchen regarded as an example of "other-emptiness." In any case, Dzogchen is traditionally spoken of as "the clear light great completeness." The term "clear light" is in part a phenomenological reflection on the experiential state in which Dzogchen is centered and contrasts with the mere negative of classic Madhyamaka emptiness. Dzogchen further identifies this as the subjective clear light, in contrast to the objective clear light, which is emptiness.

Regarding this, Mipam points out that the primordially pure base, or mind-nature, is "empty" in lacking dualistic concepts and is also a luminous and dynamic "self-risen primordial wisdom." This is how he defines the "fundamental mind" and "natural mind of clear light." Because the mind of clear light is by definition empty of any kind of affliction, Mipam is pointing to the complementarity of these two views of emptiness. The Dalai Lama, in one of the most scholarly presentations of Dzogchen in print, writes that the emptiness that is a mere negative, a self-emptiness, is useful in establishing the view, and associating this with some type of affirmation is helpful in describing experience (Gyatso 2000, 166). Here again we see the importance of bringing together the phenomenological or experiential and pedagogical import of Dzogchen philosophy.

This fundamental mind that is empty of afflictions other than itself "is not some kind of subject that is the counterpart of an object—not a mere awareness that is a subject realizing emptiness from within a division into subject and object" (Mipam 2006, 56). From this perspective, again, we see that the Dzogchen path is not a matter of cultivating causes that bring about a state that hitherto did not exist. Dzogchen understands that awakening to open presence, a Dzogchen practitioner's ultimate attainment is a recognition of one's beginingless nature. This recognition is cultivated; the nature is not. Hence, again, path and fruit are identical.

Thus, instead of opposing nonvirtuous impulses as one might do in sūtra, and instead of harnessing coarse energies as one might do in tantra, in Dzogchen one takes primordial wisdom, the fundamental innate mind of clear light, as central to one's view and practice from the very start. Mipam states:

> Just this original basic clear light, the primordial way of being, is the final reality of all phenomena. All appearances of cyclic existence and nirvana shine forth from within it, and when they shine forth there is not a single phenomenon that is not continuously dwelling within it.... Since it is the source of all appearances of cyclic existence and nirvana, it is called an all- pervasive compassionate responsiveness. (Mipam/Sangpo, 2006, 52– 3)

This final reality, this fundamental mind, is devoid of afflictions, as other-emptiness theory asserts. It is also considered to be imbued with all the qualities that the Mahayana practitioner attains through cultivating the traditional six perfections as outlined by Candrakīrti and Śāntideva in India, Tsongkhapa, and others throughout Tibet. The tradition explains that *Dzog* (*rdzogs*) indicates there is no higher or more encompassing practice, and *chen*, meaning great, emphasizes the vast scope of this completeness. Together, these terms are meant to signify that Dzogchen holds all the meanings and accomplishments of sūtra as well as tantra and includes within it all the paths of practice and accomplishments present in those traditions (Sangpo, tr. Hopkins 1996, 13),

The Tantric Vehicles

We have already noted that Dzogchen is classified in Nyingma and Bon as the peak of the nine vehicles and we have considered how it distinguishes itself from the lower vehicles. Now we consider briefly its relation to the outer tantric vehicles.

The first three vehicles are sometimes referred to as the "sūtra" vehicles because their teachings are based on the scriptures attributed to Shakyamuni Buddha. The remaining vehicles are the tantric vehicles, based on the literature known as tantras. The fourth, fifth, and sixth vehicles are the outer tantras, known as Action (*krīya*), Performance (*cārya*), and Yoga Tantra. The remaining three are the inner tantras, known in Nyingma as Maha, Anu, and Ati, and can be considered subdivisions of Highest Yoga Tantra (bLa med kyi rgyud, Anuttarayogatantra).

Most who practice Dzogchen also study and practice tantra extensively. The principle objective of such tantra, as suggested briefly above, is not the application of an antidote to afflictions and the like, as in sūtra, but the transformation of afflictions through philosophical and contemplative understanding. This "transformation" is not understood as changing something into something else; it is not like making iron into gold. Rather, in keeping with the discovery orientation of Dzogchen, it is a transformation that occurs through recognizing the abiding purity (*gnas su dag pa*) in all things, and above all through seeing one's own mind in its true, unstained, and luminous state.

Tantric practice has two stages, creation and completion. The essence of the creation stage of tantra is awareness of emptiness and hence of the purity of all that appears to the senses. This in turn gives rise to bliss. Creation stage practice involves three types of meditative stability (*samādhi*): (1) stabilizing on reality (*de bzhin nyid*); (2) meditation on pervasive luminosity (*kun tu snang*), especially the cultivated sense of one's body and mind as that of an enlightened being resonant with compassion; and (3) focusing on a letter of light, understood to express the enlightened potentiality of that being (*rgyu'i ting nge 'dzin*).

The completion stage of tantra aims to unify one's energies, mind, and mental functioning (*rlung, sems, yid*) within the body's central channel. Thereby, it is believed, afflicted mental states can no longer be supported. In tantra this premise is based on an elaborately articulated phenomenology and epistemology of the body, which is also the basis for much medical practice. Thus, to dissolve afflictive energies—including those that sustain effortful and conceptual thought—is consonant with actualizing primordial wisdom. Here, an important Indo-Tibetan strand of body-based theorizing emerges in support of the fruitional, discovery orientation of Dzogchen.

There are both contemplative/philosophical and historical reasons why virtually all Dzogchen practitioners also engage in extensive tantric practice. The creation and completion stages of tantra were initially components of a single meditation manual, with the completion stage commencing immediately after the creation stage. Gradually, the two stages separated. Recent scholarship suggests that Dzogchen may have emerged in the eighth century as a third stage representing the culmination of the completion stage, and thus receiving the name Ati Yoga. Lochen Dharmaśrī (bLo chen, also known as Ngag dbang Chos dpal rGya mtsho, 1654–1717) writes: "*Atiyoga* is a means to liberate the meaning of primordial Buddhahood into its own state, and it is the nature of freedom from abandonments [of defilements] and taking up [of virtue] as well as hopes and fears" (Thondup 1996, 41). Again we see the premise of an already present state, complete and awaiting discovery.

Dongag Tenpe Nyima (mDo ngags sTen pa'i Nyi ma, 1907–1959) notes:

> According to the view of the *Ngagyur Nyingma* (Old Tantric Transmission), there are no differences between the sūtras and tantras in respect to (their views of) emptiness, the ultimate sphere. Because the absolute great emptiness of the great Middle Way, the absolute great equalness of the great Mahāyoga, the absolute Samantabhadrī, the mandala of "as it is" (*ji bzhin pa*) and the absolute great primordial purity (*ka dag*) of Ati Yoga (Dzogchen) are synonyms for the same truth. (Thondup, 1996, 9)

Moreover, we have seen that the primordial wisdom described in Dzogchen includes the views of the three lower vehicles. Primordial wisdom and open presence preclude the kind of self-identity that lower vehicles oppose through the use of their particular antidotes. Such errors have been overcome in the process of accessing one's own mind-nature. Thus, again, the sutra perspective is subsumed into the Dzogchen view.

When one is steadfastly present to the fundamental mind of clear light, one is free of the delusion of self-grasping that practitioners of the first three vehicles must also overcome—the hearers, solitary realizers, and bodhisattvas. Likewise, one's body, speech, and mind are experienced as pure, and hence "without the distortions of afflictive states." This accords with the realization of the outer tantras—the fifth, sixth, and seventh vehicles. And finally, this single moment of realization encompasses the realization of the inner tantras, the remaining vehicles, because the very subtle mind that is awakened is in deep meditative absorption.

Threefold Classifications of Open Presence in Dzogchen

As we have seen, Dzogchen is founded on the conviction that mind-nature is always unsullied and available. Dzogchen traditions must therefore explain how the notion of cultivation can be consonant with the idea that an unconditioned presence already exists. Both Bon and Buddhist Dzogchen traditions address this by subdividing open presence into three subcategories.

Dzogchen makes both a twofold and a threefold classification of open presence. In the first, it distinguishes the basic, or ground, open presence from the natural, or fruitional, open presence. From this basic open presence arises a mind that acts as the support of all predispositions that are like traces upon it. These traces perpetuate habits of mind and body, especially the ignorance that keeps one from seeing reality as it is. Both Dzogchen and Mind-Only use the term "support of all" (*kun gzhi, ālaya*) and also the related term "support of all consciousness." But the meanings are different in the two systems.

In Mind-Only, the consciousness called a support of all is understood to be a neutral continuum of consciousness that carries one's good and bad propensities from one life to another. Its classic description is in Asaṅga's *Ornament to the Sūtras* and its central significance for Mind-Only is in explaining the mechanism for rebirth. In Dzogchen, it is a particular type of dull consciousness. The natural (*rang bzhin*) open presence is experienced when, as a result of one's meditation practice, one gains direct experience of the subtle clear light that is the nature of mind.

These three types of open presence—basic, dynamic, and natural—are Buddhist Dzogchen's way of explaining how it can be a path in which the fruit is already present yet which, at the same time, requires practice to realize. A further point is that wisdom and delusion do not cancel each other out. Basic open presence is always complete and perfect. However, it takes practice to access either the dynamically displayed presence or the natural open presence.

Bon Dzogchen puts forward its own threefold enumeration of open presences. As with the Buddhist triad, this is a way of resolving the conundrum of the simultaneous existence of primordial wisdom and delusion. In Bon the three are known as pervasive, contemplative, and primordial open presence

The first, pervasive open presence (*kyab rig*) refers to the clarity that suffuses not only minds but also material objects as well and that, despite its name, is not itself an open presence. Contemplative open presence (*bsam rig*) arises through practice and in this sense is analogous to the natural presence identified by Nyingma. For Bon, contemplative open presence is aware of all the disparate displays inherent in its own nature, referred to as an unbounded wholeness. The third type, primordial open presence (*ye rig*) is a pristine state of awareness, always present in everyone, analogous to the basic presence discussed in Nyingma. This is complete and perfect whether one meditates or not. There is no approaching it or distancing from it. Another way to put this is to say that there is meditation and development with respect to the open awareness that dawns as dynamic display (*rtsal shar rig pa'i ye shes*) but not with respect to the actual primordial wisdom into which the open presence of dynamic display dissolves. Contemplative open awareness acts as a bridge from deluded unawareness to wisdom-awareness of the abiding condition, the direct recognition of the way things are. So while new understanding can arise through reading texts or through meditation, the primordial wisdom, also known as the primordial open awareness, does not itself newly arise. Recognition of it is cultivated; presence itself is simply present (Klein and Wangyal 2006, 106).

Bon and Buddhist Dzogchen traditions each have mainstream interpretations maintaining that open presence is not a mental state (Klein and Wangyal 2006, ch. I, II). In this view, the unchanging nature of open presence means that it is not a mental state because all minds are by definition impermanent and changing. "Mental state" (*sems, citta*) in many Buddhist texts is defined as "that which is clear and aware" (*gsal zhing rig pa*). In the context of Dzogchen's distinguishing such a mental state from open presence, "mental state" also explicitly refers to an awareness that is itself a caused phenomenon, and thus a conditioned and impermanent phenomenon as well. Such mental states are also subjective (*viṣayin, yul can*), and by definition apprehend objects (*viṣaya, yul*). Open presence, though sharing with mind the capacity for awareness, is for Dzogchen spontaneously complete (*lhun grub, anābhoga*). It is therefore neither conditioned, caused, nor impermanent. Moreover, being a reflexive open awareness (*rang rig, svasaṃedanā*), open presence has no object other than its own nature, unbounded wholeness (*thig le nyag gcig*). Thus, open presence is a state of awareness that has none of the usual mental characteristics. It is nondualistic; it does not change in response to an object. Its being unconditioned is an important corollary to the claim that it is discovered, not developed. As already suggested, this point is central for both philosophical understanding and contemplative cultivation.

Lopon Tenzin Namdak (sLob-dpon bsTan-'dzin rNam-dag, born 1926) in his *Treatise on the Mother Tantra* explains why open presence cannot be identified as any of the four types of direct perception well known in Buddhist descriptions of mind: sensory direct perception; mental direct perception; and the categories seemingly most compatible with Dzogchen discussions, yogic direct perception and reflexively open direct perception.

Dzogchen's open presence is neither sensory direct perception nor mental direct perception because neither of these well-known types of consciousness observe their own natural state. Another distinction between open presence and mental consciousness or sensory consciousness is that the latter depends on an immediately prior moment of consciousness. Visual consciousness, for example, comes about because of three conditions: an object that has form or color, a properly operating eye sense, and a previous moment of consciousness. The first two conditions alone cannot produce visual consciousness. Open presence, however, is not induced, or conditioned by, such an immediately prior condition.

For the same reason, the open presence of Dzogchen is not an instance of the yogic direct perception described in Indian and Tibetan philosophical literature. Yogic direct perception is famously defined as a union of calm abiding and special insight that acts as an antidote to ignorance. This description is in line with the causal approach of sūtra practice. By contrast, the open presence of Dzogchen is self-settled; there is no causal developmental process by which calm and insight are unified in order to precipitate it. Likewise, Dzogchen's open presence is not induced by a meditative stabilization that exists prior to it. As we already know, Dzogchen sees this open presence as a pristinely unconditioned state that includes all methods yet cannot be reached by any means other than itself. All other states are merely a dynamic display of open presence.

Finally, the open presence of Dzogchen is also different from the reflexive awareness (*rang rig*) described in the Mind-Only system. The latter necessarily has an ordinary consciousness as its explicit object (*dngos yul*). That is, a reflexive awareness associated with visual consciousness is aware of that visual consciousness, not its emptiness or ultimate nature. Unbounded wholeness is the ultimate that must be known in Dzogchen, just as emptiness is the ultimate that must be known in the Middle Way. However, unbounded wholeness must be known not as an object, but as the nature of one's own knowing itself. Thus, open presence can be described as a self-presence to its own unbounded wholeness.

In sum, consciousness is an impermanent phenomenon, whereas open presence and its nature, unbounded wholeness, are not. Consciousness necessarily arises from causes; self-arisen wisdom does not. As we have noted from the outset, it is a pivotal position within Dzogchen that primordial wisdom is neither an impermanent consciousness nor related with any cause, nor can it be a causeless impermanent thing. This is why, again, many Dzogchen traditions, Bon and Buddhist, maintain that primordial wisdom or open presence is not really consciousnesses at all. This is a unique and pivotal assertion of Dzogchen philosophy that dovetails well with its emphasis on the fundamental mind of clear light, an unbounded wholeness beyond subject and object.

BIBLIOGRAPHY AND SUGGESTED READINGS

Buswell, Robert. (1992). *Turning Back the Radiance: Chinul's Korean Way of Zen.* Honolulu, HI: University of Hawaii Press.

Candrakirti/Mipam. (2005) *Introduction to the Middle Way.* Boulder, CO: Shambala.

Gyatso, Tenzin, H. H. Dalai Lama. (2000) *Dzogchen: Heart Essence of the Great Perfection.* Ithaca, NY: Snow Lion.

———. (2007) *Mind in Comfort and Ease: The Vision of Enlightenment in the Great Perfection*, translated by Matthieu Ricard, Richard Barron, and Adam Pearcey; edited by Patrick Gaffney. Boston, MA: Wisdom Publications.

Dudjom Rinpoche, (trans. Kapstein and Dorje). (1991) *The Nyingma School of Tibetan Buddhism.* Boston, MA: Wisdom Publications.

Germano, David. (1992) *Poetic Thought in the Intelligent Universe: The Tantric Synthesis of Dzog Chen in Fourteenth-Century Tibet.* Ph. D. thesis, University of Wisconsin.

———. (1994) "Architecture and Absence in the Secret Tantric History of the Great Perfection *(rdzogs chen).*" *Journal of Indian and Buddhist Studies* 17.2, 209–334.

Karmay, Samten G. (1988) *The Great Perfection.* Leiden: Brill.

Khetsun Sangpo Rinpoche. (1996; revised from 1987) *Tantric Practice in Nyingma*, translated and edited by Jeffrey Hopkins, coedited by Anne C. Klein. Ithaca, NY: Snow Lion.

Klein, Anne Carolyn. (1987) *Knowledge and Liberation.* Ithaca, NY: Snow Lion.

———. (1991) *Knowing Naming and Negation.* Ithaca, NY: Snow Lion.

———. (2000). "Assorted Topics of the Great Completeness, Oral Commentary by Khetsun Sangpo Rinpoche." In *Tantra in Practice*, edited by David Gordon White. Princeton, NJ: Princeton University Press, 537–572

Klein, Anne Carolyn (Rigzin Drolma). (2009) *Heart Essence of the Vast Expanse: A Story of Transmission.* Ithaca, NY: Snow Lion.

Klein, Anne Carolyn, and Geshe Tenzin Rinpoche Wangyal. (2006) *Unbounded Wholeness: Dzogchen, Bon, and the Logic of the NonConceptual.* New York: Oxford University Press.

KVAERNE, PER. (1975) "The Great Perfection in the Tradition of the Bonpo." In *Early Ch'an in China and Tibet*, edited by Whalen Lai and Lewis Lancaster. Berkeley Buddhist Studies Series. Berkeley, CA: Asian Humanities Press, 367–392

MI-PAM GYA-TSO. (2006) *Fundamental Mind: The Nyingma View of the Great Completeness*, commentary by Khetsun Sangpo Rinpoche, translated and edited by Jeffrey Hopkins. Ithaca, NY: Snow Lion Publications.

NORBU, CHOGYAL NAMKHAI. (1989) *Dzogchen, The Self-Perfected State*, edited by Adriano Clemente, translated from Italian by John Shane. Ithaca, NY: Snow Lion.

———. (1989) *The Crystal and the Way of Light*. New York and London: Routledge and Kegan Paul.

PETIT, JOHN WHITNEY (trans.). (1999) *Mipham's Beacon of Certainty, Illuminating the View of Dzogchen*. Boston, MA: Wisdom.

SCHMIDTHAUSEN, LAMBERT. (1987) *Ālayavijñāna: On the Origin and Early Development of a Central Concept in Yogācāra Philosophy*. Tokyo. The International Institute for Buddhist Studies

SMITH, GENE. (1969) Introduction. In *Rang grol skor gsum and byang chu sems kin yed rgyal po'i don khrid rin chen grub: Soure for the Understanding of Rdzog chen Meditation*. Gantok: Ngagyur Nyingmay Sungrab Series, edited by Sonam T. Kazi.

SNELLGROVE, DAVID. (1967) *Nine Ways of Bon*. London: Oxford University Press.

THONDUP, TULKU. (1982) *The Dzogchen Preliminary Practice of the Innermost Essence*. Dharamsala: Library of Tibetan Works and Archives.

———. (1986) *Hidden Teachings of Tibet: An Explanation of the Terma Tradition of the Nyingma School of Buddhism*. London: Wisdom

———. (1996) *Practice of Dzogchen (Buddha Mind)*, introduced, translated, and annotated by Tulku Thondup; edited by Harold Talbott. Ithaca, NY: Snow Lion.

TULKU OGYEN RINPOCHE. (2006). *Confusion Dawns as Wisdom*, translated by Eric Hein Schmidt. Hong Kong: Rangjung Yeshe Publications.

VAN SCHAIK, SAM. (2004) *Approaching the Great Perfection*. Boston, MA: Wisdom Publications.

WANGYAL, TENZIN RINPOCHE. (1993) *The Wonders of the Natural Mind: Bonpo Dzogchen*. Barrytown, NY: Station Hill Press.

CHAPTER 21

BUDDHIST ETHICS

BARBRA R. CLAYTON

In what is remembered in Buddhist traditions as the first discourse of the Buddha, the Buddha outlined Four Noble Truths that framed the basic doctrine of the early Buddhist tradition and the Theravāda tradition today. The four truths specify that (1) existence is characterized by "unsatisfactoriness" or suffering, literally a lack of ease (*duḥkha*); (2) suffering has a cause, identified as aversion, craving, and ignorance; and (3) because suffering has a cause it can also come to an end, a state known as *nirvāṇa*. The fourth truth outlines the Noble Eightfold Path to the cessation of suffering. In one common formula, that path comprises "three trainings": insight (*prajñā*), moral conduct (*śīla*), and mental discipline (*samādhi*). While what precisely is meant by *śīla* in this context will be explored presently, this gives an indication that in some important sense ethics forms a central feature of the path to the ultimate spiritual goal for Buddhists. Furthermore, insofar as ethics is understood in the Socratic sense of "how one ought to live," all elements of the threefold training would be considered aspects of Buddhist ethics. For this reason, Buddhism has sometimes been considered an ethical system *par excellence*, and although there are other ways of understanding Buddhism, this is the lens through which Buddhism is viewed here. Buddhist practice and teachings vary widely, with three major branches or traditions (namely, Theravāda, Mahāyāna, and Vajrayāna), numerous schools of thought, and divergence in rituals and customs across Buddhist cultural areas. I have tried to identify the teachings that formed the basis of Buddhist moral traditions in India, where Buddhism originated, and which were more or less influential in the various traditions of Buddhism that spread across Asia and more recently to the West.

Foundations of Buddhist Moral Thought: Dharma and Karma

The root of Buddhist morality is not thought to be God or another supernatural being, nor even the Buddha himself, but Dharma, the "Law" or "Truth" of the nature of things, which the Buddha is said to have discovered and expounded. Dharma is the universal order of reality that embraces both natural and moral laws. The Buddha's teachings elucidate these laws, and they embody and are referred to as the Dharma. Dharma explains both the regular patterns apparent in the natural world, such as that of the seasons and planets, and the various states into which beings are born and reborn in the beginningless cycle of rebirth (*saṃsāra*). The pattern that explains the rebirth of beings is known as the law of karma, which reflects Dharma at the moral level. This law dictates that actions incur consequences that are consonant with the nature of the actions themselves. Generally speaking, according to karmic laws, good or moral deeds are a "shelter from anguish" (M.iii.171). They lead to happiness and pleasant conditions in this life, and better or "higher" states of rebirth, while bad or immoral actions lead to unpleasant results, suffering, and "lower" states of rebirth. For example, a life of hatred and violence is thought to cause rebirth in one of the many hells; selfishness and greed are said to lead to existence as a hungry ghost; ignorance and delusion produce rebirth as an animal. On the other hand, generosity, selflessness, and benevolence will yield a pleasant human life characterized by such things as wealth, good reputation, and freedom from fear and anxiety, and rebirth in a higher realm as a god (*deva*), or human. The latter is considered the most desirable rebirth, since the human realm is the realm from which it is easiest to attain liberation. To discern more clearly what "good" and "bad" actions mean in this context, we need to explore further the Buddhist approach to karma.

Karma, Intentions, and the Distinction between "Good" and "Bad" Actions

The term *karma* literally means "action," but like Dharma, it is a complex term with a range of meanings. It can refer, for example, to any or all of the following: an action itself, the agent of an action, the object of an action, or the results of an action. When referring to action, its meanings can include action in general, a habitual action, an occupation, or—echoing its original use in the context of Vedic ritual actions—ritualized action (s.v. "karma," PTS). While there are various traditions of karmic discourse in Buddhist texts that do not all cohere, one important development in Indian thought associated with the Buddha was the shift in emphasis from external actions to the motive behind actions as key to their nature and consequences. Indeed, in a well-known passage the Buddha declared that "it is intention (*cetanā*), O monks, that I call karma; having willed one acts through body, speech and mind" (A.iii.415). While the exact relationship between *cetanā* and the Western conception of "the will" are far from fully clear, this statement has been understood to mean that it is the mental impulses behind actions that are most decisive in shaping their nature, and in fact that actions are virtually equivalent to their motive.

This contributes to the standard view of Buddhist karma, which states that volitional actions lead to consequences that echo the nature of the volition, and that must inevitably be experienced by the agent. Because of the emphasis, it has sometimes been claimed—somewhat problematically—that "only intentional and ethically motivated actions have karmic effects"[1] and that "karmic actions are moral actions" (Keown 2005, 5). This emphasis on intention underlies a fundamental distinction in Buddhist thought between acts that are *kuśala* (P. *kusala*), "skillful" or "wholesome," and those that are *akuśala* (P. *akusala*), "unskillful" or "unwholesome." These terms are also understood and translated more generally as "good" and "bad."[2] More particularly, *kuśala* refers to actions or states that are "spiritually intelligent," that is, those that are grounded in wisdom, are salutary and lead to happiness, and are liberating in the sense of being conducive to *nirvāṇa* (e.g., A.i.263). *Nirvāṇa* is in fact equated with the complete elimination of all unwholesome qualities (S.iv.251). The psychological bases or "roots" (*mūla*) of wholesome actions are nongreed (*alobha*), nonhatred (Skt. *adveṣa;* P. *adosa*), and nondelusion (*amoha*), which can be understood positively as generosity or liberality, benevolence, and wisdom. Conversely, the causes of *un*wholesome actions are greed (*lobha*), hatred (Skt. *dveṣa;* P. *dosa*), and delusion (*moha*), which are also known as the three "poisons" or defilements (*kleśa*) at the root of suffering (M.i.47).

The criteria for deciding whether an action is *kuśala* or not corresponds with the range of meanings associated with it: the motivation in terms of greed, hatred, and delusion; the result (for the agent or others) in terms of happiness or suffering, and whether it contributes or hinders further wholesome states and progress along the path to liberation (Harvey 2000, 46–49). Thus, to call an action "good" or "bad" takes all of these into account, but it is its basis in greed, hatred, or delusion or not—what has been called its virtuous or unvirtuous motive—that is arguably the crucial distinguishing factor, and what fundamentally distinguishes good deeds from bad in Buddhism. Insofar as wholesome actions lead to further happiness, *kuśala* overlaps with another important concept, that of "merit."

1. Gananath Obeyesekere, *Imagining Karma: Transformation in Ameridindian, Buddhist, and Greek Rebirth* (Berkeley, CA: University of California Press, 2002), p. 130. For examples of where karma does not follow this normative model see Jessica Main, "The Karma of Others: Stories from the *Milindapañha* and the *Petavatthu-aṭṭhakathā*," in *Revisioning Karma: The eBook*, ed. Charles Prebish, Dale Wright, and Damien Keown (Journal of Buddhist Ethics Online Books, 2007).

2. For a discussion of the history and meaning of the term *kuśala* see Lance Cousins, "Good or skilful? *Kuśala* in Canon and Commentary," *Journal of Buddhist Ethics* 3(1996): 136–164.

Merit

The term "merit" (Skt. *puṇya;* P. *puñña*) refers to good or beneficial acts and their consequences, or to the quality of an action that is auspicious or brings fortune (Cousins 1996, 153). One useful translation of this term is "karmic fruitfulness" or "karmically fruitful" (Harvey 2000, 18), as it is suggestive of the common metaphor for karma as a "seed," whose consequences are its fruit (*phala*) or its "ripening" (*vipāka*). Generally speaking, it is thought that an act that is good or wholesome (*kuśala*) is also meritorious (*puṇya*), meaning that it is beneficial in itself and will lead to beneficial consequences. On the other hand, if an act has unwholesome motives, it is "evil" or fruitless (*pāpa*) and unmeritorious (*apuṇya;* P. *apuñña*), and will lead to unfortunate, harmful consequences.

It is thought to be necessary to accumulate merit in order to make progress on the spiritual path, and merit making is a crucial concept for understanding Buddhist norms of conduct. So, for example, the relationship between lay Buddhists and the monastic order or Sangha relies on a mutual exchange of merit: by offering food, clothing, and other forms of material support to monastics, laypeople earn merit, and monks in turn gain merit by offering guidance and, most important, the gift of the Dharma to laypeople. Of course, if either act is done with the aim of selfish gain, the karmic benefits are diminished. The idea that it is especially "fruitful" to give to monks and nuns is expressed in the idea that the Sangha is a "field of merit" (*puṇya-kṣetra*) (e.g., M.iii.255–257). The notion that the Sangha, as well as the Buddha and Dharma, is productive "merit-fields" permits the idea that merit can be acquired through ritual actions, such as chanting the names of *sūtras* and offerings to Buddhas and bodhisattvas. In this way, while what we might call a strict or orthodox reading of karma doctrine upholds an ethic of intention, it also makes way for an ethic of works, and the distinction between ethics and devotion is not always clear.

While the idea that merit can itself lead to *nirvāṇa* is not unknown in the Pali canon and other literatures,[3] one doctrinally significant canonical view is that meritorious deeds are necessary but not sufficient for attaining *nirvāṇa*, because *nirvāṇa* entails transcending the realm of karma and rebirth. That is, through eliminating the unwholesome roots of greed, hatred, and delusion, the Arhat—or "worthy one," who becomes awakened with the benefit of a Buddha's teaching—does not do anything karmically productive; all actions have ceased (S.iv.132–133). In this sense a liberated being is "beyond good and evil," that is, beyond *puñña* and *pāpa* (Sn 520, 636). This also implies that liberated beings act in ways that are spontaneously

3. See, for example, James Egge, *Religious Giving and the Invention of Karma in Theravāda Buddhism*, Curzon Studies in Asian Religions (Richmond, Surrey: Curzon Press, 2002), pp. 107–113. The idea that merit can itself lead to awakening is also found in the "lessons" (Sk. *avadāna;* P. *apadāna*). For a discussion of this literature see Richard Robinson, Willard Johnson, and Thanissaro Bhikkhu, *Buddhist Religions: A Historical Introduction*, 5th ed. (Belmont, CA: Wadsworth/Thomson, 2005), pp. 70–72.

wholesome: that is, they are virtuous (*kuśala*) by nature and do not need to deliberate about doing the "right thing" (Harvey 2000, 43–46).

Merit transference (*pariṇāmana*) is the idea that the benefits and blessings of good deeds can be shared with others. For example, a common Buddhist practice is to dedicate the merit of offerings to the welfare of deceased relatives in the afterlife. Though the idea of merit transfer is clearly related to the pan-Buddhist belief in fields of merit, the belief that Buddhas and bodhisattvas accumulate infinite stores of merit by which they can benefit devotees is particularly associated with Mahāyāna. This Mahāyāna belief lends an idea proximate to that of grace: the Chinese and Japanese terms suggest that Buddhas and bodhisattvas are "fields of blessings" (Ch. *Futian;* Jap. *fukuden*). Such thinking finds its fullest expression in the Pure Land traditions, which hold that by virtue of their great merit, the Buddhas create Pure Lands into which followers may be reborn and easily attain liberation. Indeed, in the True Pure Land tradition (Jōdo Shinshū) this is taken to the extent of denying the efficacy of the devotees' meritorious acts altogether.

The idea of transferring merit is "theologically" challenging in that it violates the karmic law that we are all inheritors of our own karma, and no one else's: that one will experience the results of one's own actions alone. Though it may be problematic in this way, the idea of merit transfer must be acknowledged in any thorough understanding of Buddhist moral thought and practice.[4]

Precepts and Virtues

In a verse from one of the most well-known and oft-translated texts of Buddhism, the *Dhammapada* (*Verses of the Dharma*), the teachings of the Buddha are succinctly summarized:

> The refraining from all that is harmful,
> the undertaking of what is skilful,
> the cleansing of one's mind
> that is the teaching of the Buddhas. (Dhp 183)

This summary can help us to comprehend the "three trainings" mentioned above, which condense the Noble Eightfold Path into moral practice (*śīla*), meditation or mental discipline (*samādhi*), and insight (*prajñā*). On one understanding, moral conduct (*śīla*) involves refraining from what is evil (*pāpa*) at the grossest, physical

4. For a discussion of merit transference and its apparent contravention of karma theory, see Obeyesekere, *Imagining Karma*, pp. 131–139.

level; mental discipline involves cultivating what is wholesome at the level of inner mental experience; and insight entails purifying one's mind at the most subtle level of consciousness. In this way we can see that *śīla* is not the only element of the Path that is relevant to Buddhist morality broadly understood, but it is certainly foundational, and it is to it that we now turn.

Śīla: The Moral Precepts

Though often translated loosely as "morality," "ethics," or "virtue," more helpfully *śīla* may be understood in terms of propriety,[5] specifically the good or proper conduct associated with awakening and awakened beings. In this it parallels the etymological meaning of the English term "ethics" (Gk. *ethikos*), in that it can refer to customary behavior. While *śīla* may also be used more broadly than this to refer to something like virtuous character or dispositions, in the context of the three trainings it refers to a set of moral injunctions or precepts. The five precepts (*pañca-śīla*) that all Buddhists, both lay and monastic, are expected to undertake, and which are therefore taken to be foundational moral norms, include the training precepts to refrain from:

1. Taking life
2. Taking what is not given
3. Harmful conduct in the pursuit of pleasure
4. False or misleading speech
5. Taking wine, spirits, and other causes of carelessness

The first precept against destroying life is associated with the pan-Indian value of "nonharming" (*ahiṃsā*), and is the most important precept in the sense that killing is the most blameworthy and karmically harmful deed. Because all sentient beings are "kin" in the cycle of samsara, and all share the wish to live and to avoid suffering and death, one should avoid harming all living beings, including animals and insects. The emphasis is on avoiding intentional harm, and so the accidental killing of insects, for example, is not considered a violation of the precept, even though the act of killing itself and the result (the death of the insect) would be considered karmically negative. Because the level of the virtue of the beings involved and the amount of effort involved in killing are factors in determining the degree of wrong, it is worse to kill a human than an animal, or a large versus small animal. The first precept and the ideal of nonharming underlie Buddhism's reputation for nonviolence, but it also has important implications for Buddhist views of the environment, abortion, and euthanasia.

5. Thank you to Jay Garfield for this suggestion.

The second precept against theft of others' property also includes the injunction to avoid fraud, cheating, borrowing without permission, and, in some interpretations, failing to repay loans and gambling. It entails numerous social responsibilities and has significant import for Buddhist perspectives on economics.[6]

The thrust of the third precept is to avoid harming others through one's sexual activity. For laypeople, this means eschewing adultery and other forms of illicit sex, such as rape and incest, and sex with inappropriate partners, such as prostitutes. Monks and nuns, on the other hand, are required to be celibate: in striving for awakening one is meant to curtail as much as possible all sensual attachments. Lying is considered an extremely harmful act, and the precept against it is closely associated with the injunction to avoid slanderous, abusive, and frivolous talk, which together are the four forms of wrong speech. Avoiding these upholds "right speech" on the Noble Eightfold Path.

The spirit of the fifth precept is that intoxication should be avoided because it undermines mindful conduct and obstructs seeing things "just as they are" (*yathābhūta*), the basis for wisdom. Intoxication is said to lead to various dangers, such as quarreling, illness, wasting money, and improper behavior, but the injunction to refrain from it is not necessarily interpreted as a complete ban on consuming alcohol, which has generally not been forbidden in Buddhist countries (Harvey 2000, 77–79). Because of their foundational place in Buddhist ethics, the five precepts are sometimes compared to the Jewish and Christian commandments, but they (and all the precepts) are perhaps better viewed as voluntary commitments to refrain from unwholesome (*akuśala*) and harmful actions (*pāpa*) (D.i.63). They are considered solemn commitments, however, and once taken on are thought to have negative repercussions if transgressed (see Harvey 2000, 69–82).

In addition to the five precepts, there are lists of eight precepts (*aṣṭāṅga-śīla*) undertaken by pious laypeople on holy days (*poṣadha;* P. *uposatha*), and ten precepts (*daśa-śīla*) taken up by novice monks and nuns. These include limits on the consumption of food and abstentions from personal adornment, entertainment, and certain luxuries. There are many other precepts—between 218 and 263 for monks and 279 and 380 for nuns—required of the Sangha, or the community of fully ordained monastics, reflecting their level of commitment to the attainment of *nirvāṇa*. This theoretically entails fully renouncing attachment to worldly life, including livelihood, home, and family, and so requires celibacy, minimal material possessions, and reliance on donations for food and clothing. In addition to elaborations on more explicitly "moral" rules against killing, lying, and sexual contact, the monastic code of conduct (Skt. *prātimokṣa;* P. *pātimokkha*)

6. For examples of the application of this precept, and Buddhist principles in general, to economics and political rule, see Russell F. Sizemore and Donald K. Swearer, *Ethics, Wealth and Salvation: A Study in Buddhist Social Ethics* (Columbia, SC: University of South Carolina Press, 1990), and Jeffrey Hopkins, *Nagarjuna's Precious Garland: Buddhist Advice for Living and Liberation* (Ithaca, NY: Snow Lion, 2007).

includes numerous rules of etiquette and general comportment, which might be thought to encourage monks and nuns to act like and have the bearing of an enlightened being.[7]

In general, the idea behind *śīla* is that unwholesome mental traits that lead to suffering are expressed in bodily actions such as stealing and killing, and verbal actions such as lying and malicious gossip. In taking on the precepts, one vows to refrain from acting in ways that express and nourish unwholesome dispositions. By making a conscious effort to refrain from such actions, one addresses the expression of such harmful dispositions at the grossest, physical or verbal level, and thereby "starves" the underlying unwholesome mental traits and helps to cultivate wholesome ones. The importance of cultivating positive, wholesome dispositions brings us to what we might call the Buddhist virtues.

Virtues

While the Buddhist discourses include various lists of virtues or wholesome qualities to be cultivated,[8] several stand out as distinctively important. We have already introduced liberality, benevolence, and wisdom, the "cardinal virtues" of Buddhism that oppose, respectively, greed, hatred, and delusion, the three root causes of suffering. The disciplinary precepts, though expressed as abstentions, are grounded in these positive qualities. For example, the first precept against destroying life and value of "nonharm" (*ahiṃsā*) entails not only a lack of hatred (*dveṣa*), but also an attitude of empathy and concern: a "trembling for the welfare of all beings" (D.i.4). In fact, such sentiments are the fundamental ground of buddhahood, for the Buddha is said to have come into being "for the welfare of the multitudes, for the happiness of the multitudes, out of sympathy for the world" (A.i.22).

Nonhatred (*adveṣa;* P. *adosa*) is associated with the two fundamental and related dispositions of friendliness and compassion. Friendliness or loving-kindness (Skt. *maitri;* P. *mettā*) is characterized by the wish for all beings to enjoy happiness. Compassion is the loving response to the anguish of fellow beings, and is characterized by the thought, "may all beings be liberated from suffering." Compassion (*karuṇā*) is particularly stressed as the preeminent virtue in the Mahāyāna tradi-

7. For studies of monastic discipline see John Holt, *Discipline: The Canonical Buddhism of the Vinayapiñaka* (Delhi: Motilal Banarsidass, 1981); Charles S. Prebish, *Buddhist Monastic Discipline* (Delhi: Motilal Banarsidass, 1996); and M. Wijayaratna, *Buddhist Monastic Life* (Cambridge: Cambridge University Press, 1990).

8. In the Theravāda tradition the ten perfections (*dasapāramitā*) is a well-known list of virtues. It includes generosity (*dāna*), moral practice (*sīla*), renunciation (*nekkhamma*), wisdom (*pañña*), energy (*viriya*), patience (*khanti*), honesty (*sacca*), determination (*adhiññhāna*), loving-kindness (*mettā*), and equanimity (*upekkhā*). For a list of Mahāyāna virtues, see "Mahāyāna developments" below.

tion, which emphasizes the development of "great compassion" or universal compassion for all sentient beings.[9]

Loving-kindness and compassion are said to counter unwholesome tendencies toward anger and the impulse to harm. Along with "sympathetic joy" (*muditā:* rejoicing in others' happiness) and "equanimity" (*upekṣā:* even-mindedness and impartiality), they are known as the "divine virtues" or "pure abodes" (*brahmavihāra*) because of their association with elevated meditative states and higher realms of rebirth (see Aronson 1980). Overall, we might summarize the cluster of virtues associated with the absence of hatred with a verse from the *Sutta-Nipāta*, one of the earliest texts of the tradition, which exhorts: "Just as a mother would protect her only child at the risk of her own life, even so, let him cultivate a boundless heart towards all beings" (Sn.v.149).

Nongreed (*alobha*) or liberality is the opposite of the impulse to cling to objects or ideas, and is the basis of generosity and giving (*dāna*). This is an extremely significant ideal in Buddhist traditions. As the Mahāyāna master Śāntideva defines it: "The perfection of generosity is said to result from the mental attitude of relinquishing all that one has to all people" (BCA v.10). Thus, generosity opposes greed in that it reflects the willingness to give up possessions and to renounce worldly attachments; hence, the word for generosity (Skt. *tyāga;* P. *cāga*) also means renunciation. The practice of generosity is the positive counterpoint to the precept against taking what is not given. In habitually giving, one is thought to nourish sensitivity to the needs of others, and to gain joy and peace of mind. Along with *śīla* and meditation, *dāna* was prescribed by the Buddha for laypeople as a foundational ethico-spiritual practice. It is the first of ten "bases for creating merit" (P. *puñña-kiriya-vatthus*) in the Buddha's discourses (e.g., D.iii.218) and the first in a standard list of "perfections" (*pāramitā*) or transcendent virtues in both Theravāda and Mahāyāna traditions.

The "generous patron" (*dānapati*) is therefore one of Buddhism's moral ideals, exemplified in the popular South Asian figure of King Vessantara, one of the previous incarnations of the Buddha who willingly gave up not only material possessions when asked but also his wife and child. Such heroic giving is characteristic of *bodhisattvas*, or beings who are dedicated to becoming fully enlightened Buddhas. While still a *bodhisattva* the Buddha also famously gave his life to feed a starving mother tigress,[10] and *bodhisattva* literature (e.g., *Jātaka* tales and Mahāyāna *sūtras*) abounds with such tales of supererogatory giving. But such exalted giving is thought to begin with small acts of generosity, such as the offerings of water often seen on Tibetan shrines.[11]

9. For a treatment of the role and different types of compassion in Mahāyāna see *Madhyamakāvatāra* in *Compassion in Tibetan Buddhism*, ed. and trans. Jeffrey Hopkins (London: Rider, 1980).

10. The story of the bodhisattva and the tigress occurs in Āryaśūra's (fourth century CE) *Jātakamalā*, available in translation in *Jātakamalā: The Marvelous Companion: Life Stories of the Buddha* (Berkeley, CA: Dharma Publishing, 1983).

11. For a discussion of gift giving in Buddhist cultures see Reiko Ohnuma, "Gift," in *Critical Terms for the Study of Buddhism*, ed. Donald Lopez, Jr. (Chicago and London: University of Chicago Press, 2005), pp. 103–123.

While loving-kindness, compassion, and generosity are foundational virtues in Buddhist traditions, in themselves they are insufficient for achieving the highest moral perfection and ultimate state of enlightenment. To attain liberation one must overcome ignorance (*avidyā;* P. *avijjā*), which is considered the greatest impurity and the primary cause of suffering and of continued rebirth (Dhp. v.241; A.iv.195). The perspicacity to see things "just as they are" (*yathābhūta*) is known as insight (*prajñā*). As one of the "three trainings" of the Noble Eightfold path, it comprises "right view" (understanding karma, rebirth, and the Four Noble Truths) and "right intention" (a resolve to turn away from malice and sensual attachments and toward calm loving-kindness), and relies on mental discipline cultivated through mindful awareness (*smṛti*) and concentration (*samādhi*). Insight is the primary distinguishing characteristic of the Buddha, whose enlightenment arose through awakening (*bodhi*) to the nature and origin of suffering and the way to its end. For the Arhat, insight into the "three marks" (*trilakṣana*) of reality—as impermanent (*anitya*), without self (*anātman*), and unsatisfactory—is what finally uproots the latent tendencies that impede enlightenment and thus purifies the mind. In the Mahāyāna tradition as well, insight into emptiness (*śūnyatā*), or the lack of inherent nature of all phenomena, including the self, cuts the impurities (*kleśa*) at their root by removing all basis for a sense of "me and mine" (e.g., ŚS 242.1–6). This allows for the bodhisattva's selfless concern for all sentient beings and "completes" or "perfects" (*pāramitā*) his or her other virtues. In this sense, the virtue of nondelusion (*amoha*), expressed positively as wisdom or insight (*prajñā*), is the most fundamental Buddhist virtue that transforms other "ordinary" (*laukika;* P. *lokiya*) virtues such as generosity and patience into transcendent (*lokottara;* P. *lokuttara*) ones that yield not just a better rebirth but full awakening.

Mahāyāna Developments

Mahāyāna Buddhism, a broad branch of Buddhism comprising numerous texts and schools, became the predominant Buddhist tradition in Tibet and East Asia. The goal in Mahāyāna is buddhahood rather than liberation from suffering (*nirvāṇa*) per se. A being who aims to become a fully enlightened Buddha (*samyaksambodhibuddha*) is a *bodhisattva* ("being for awakening"), and while already an ideal in Theravāda, the *bodhisattva* became a particular focus of Mahāyāna Buddhism, along with the doctrine of emptiness (*śūnyatā*).[12] The goal of buddhahood is taken to mean that one aims to become a being that liberates others. The ardent wish to devote oneself to the salvation of others is known as "the mind of awakening" (*bodhicitta*), and leads to the *bodhisattva*'s characteristic vow to remain in the endless rounds of rebirth working

12. See, in this volume, the chapters by Dunne, Powers, Klein, and Ziporyn.

for the welfare of all sentient beings. As Śāntideva expresses it: "For as long as there is a universe in space, I will remain, progressing in wisdom, doing the good of the world" (ŚS 363.13,14; s.a. BCA iii.6–21). This all-embracing compassion is the basis for the Mahāyāna's self-designation as the "great vehicle," and is reflected in the *bodhisattva* precepts taken by most East Asian monastics, based on the *Fan-wang ching* (*Sūtra of Brahma's Net*), which in some ways came to eclipse the Vinaya in importance in East Asian contexts. These precepts can be taken on by laypeople as well, and Mahāyāna schools outside of India in particular have tended to emphasize the accessibility of the bodhisattva path to all, lay and monastic.

Mahāyāna texts present varying accounts of the *bodhisattva's* path to buddhahood. The *Daśabhūmika-sūtra's* ten-stage process is one important example, with each stage corresponding to the perfection of a virtue: generosity (*dāna*), moral conduct (*śīla*), patience (*kṣanti*), energy (*vīrya*), meditation (*dhyāna*), insight (*prajñā*), skillful means (*upāya-kauśalya*), vows (*praṇidhāna*), power (*bala*), and knowledge (*jnāna*). There is an obvious continuity between these and non-Mahāyāna virtues, but there is also an increased focus on compassion and having the "skillful means" (*upāya-kauśalya*) to alleviate the suffering of sentient beings. There is also an expanded notion of *śīla* in Mahāyāna. In texts such as the *Mahāyāna-saṃgraha* and the *Bodhisattva-bhūmi, śīla* incorporates the "restraint" (*saṃvara*) of the lay precepts and monastic code, but adds to these the "collection of wholesome states" (*kuśala-dharma-saṃgraha*), achieved by practicing the perfections and "working for the welfare of beings" (*sattvārtha-krīya*) through ministering to their spiritual and practical needs. These practices yield infinitely vast stores of merit (*puṇya*) through which *bodhisattvas* and Buddhas are thought to be able to benefit sentient beings.[13]

To be a bodhisattva means that one's *raison d'être* is to save other beings from suffering, and this altruistic aim can at times "trump" obeisance to ordinary moral precepts (*śīla*). So, for example, Mahāyāna literature includes stories of *bodhisattvas* lying, stealing, and even killing out of the compassionate demand to help sentient beings (ŚS 140, 163f).[14] Such deeds are considered an aspect of the bodhisattva's skillful means, and are certainly one of the more striking features of Mahāyāna ethics. Succinctly put, the idea is that "even what is proscribed is permitted for a compassionate person who sees it will be of some benefit" (BCA v.84). These violations of standard moral precepts are only endorsed for bodhisattvas whose actions are grounded in an understanding of emptiness (*śūnyatā*), and whose compassionate motive is pure. In addition to instances where killing another being, stealing, lying,

13. This is in contrast to the Arhat, who (as indicated) in liberation is thought to transcend both evil (*pāpa*) and "good" vis-a-vis *puṇya*. See Barbra Clayton, *Moral Theory in śāntideva's śikṣāsamuccaya: Cultivating the Fruits of Virtue*, Critical Studies in Buddhism (Abington, UK: Routledge, 2006), pp.76–88. For descriptions of the bodhisattva path see Paul Williams, *Mahāyāna Buddhism: The Doctrinal Foundations*, London, Routledge, 1989), pp. 204–214; and *Asanga's Chapter on Ethics, with the Commentary of Tsong-Kha-Pa, The Basic Path to Awakening, The Complete Bodhisattva*, trans. Mark Tatz, (Lewiston/ Queenston: Edwin Mellon Press, 1986).

14. For a discussion of the skillful breaking of precepts in Mahāyāna see Harvey 2000, pp. 134–140, and Michael Pye, *Skilful Means: A Concept in Mahāyāna Buddhism* (London: Duckworth, 1978).

or engaging in sexuality are seen as necessary, the emphasis on selfless compassion also supports the ideal of heroic self-sacrifice, which might otherwise be prohibited as suicide and a violation of the first precept. The *Mahāprajñā-pāramitā-śāstra*, for example, advocates giving away one's head or marrow for others, and in the *Lotus Sūtra* (*Saddharmapuṇḍarīka-Sūtra*) the bodhisattva Bhaiṣajyarāja burns his body as a "living candle" in service and gratitude, which leads to his full enlightenment.[15] Skillful means has also been invoked to justify violence in defense of the Dharma, though the use of violence to defend Buddhism is not strictly a Mahāyāna phenomenon.[16] There is still the sense that such acts are ethically problematic in that they entail negative karmic repercussions, but the merit of the bodhisattva's altruistic willingness to endure such consequences—including aeons in hell—is thought to substantially or in some cases completely obviate any negative karma.

The Vajrayāna ("Diamond Vehicle") tradition as well, which became dominant in Tibet and influenced Buddhist schools in East Asia, is associated with antinomianism. The tantric texts that are the basis for the Vajrayāna upheld that since all phenomena lack inherent nature, unskillful qualities such as anger and lust could be transmuted into positive energies. These "impure" states could thus be used as tools for attaining liberation rapidly, even in this lifetime. This might entail the violation of conventional norms and moral precepts by eating meat, drinking wine, or engaging in sexual intercourse. Even if only enacted symbolically, these practices are generally thought to be the domain of only very advanced practitioners under guidance of a teacher, and (in the monastic context) on a foundation of adherence to monastic discipline and the *bodhisattva* vows. The predominant Gelug (dGe-lugs) school in Tibet emphasized such restrictions, and advocated the practice of "sexual yoga" as a meditative visualization only. However, some schools such as the rNying-ma have permitted the actual practice of sexual yoga, and unconventional behavior, both social and moral, is characteristic of exemplary tantric adepts (*mahasiddhas*). Thus, while it is perhaps true to say that transgressive behavior is most commonly enacted only symbolically and ritually, it is likely unwise to ignore the normative function of such behavior in the Tibetan tradition.[17]

15. Jan Yun-hua, "Buddhist Self-Immolation in Medieval China," in *History of Religions* 4 (1964–1965), pp. 256, 257. For a discussion of the phenomenon of self-immolation in the context of the Vietnam War, see Sallie B. King, "Those who burn themselves for peace: Quaker and Buddhist Self-Immolators during the Vietnam War," *Buddhist Christian Studies* 20(2000): 127–150.

16. For examples in the Sri Lankan context see Tessa J. Bartholomeusz, *In Defense of Dharma: Just War Ideology in Buddhist Sri Lanka* (New York: Routledge Curzon, 2002). On Buddhism and war in East Asia see Paul Demiéville, "Le Bouddhisme et la guerre: postscriptum à "L;Histoire des moines guerriers du Japon" in his *Choix d'études bouddhiques (1929–1970)* (Leiden: E. J. Brill, 1973), pp. 261–299, and Mikael S. Adolphson, *The Teeth and Claws of the Buddha: Monastic Warriors and Sōhei in Japanese History* (Honolulu, HI: University of Hawaii Press, 2007).

17. So argues Roger Jackson in "No/Responsibility: Saraha, 'Siddha Ethics' and the Transcendency Thesis," in *Universal Responsibility: A Felicitation Volume in Honour of His Holiness the Fourteenth Dalai Lama, Tenzin Gyatso, on His Sixtieth Birthday*, ed. Ramesh Chandra Tewari and Krishna Nath (Delhi: Foundation for Universal Responsibility, 1996), pp. 79–110. See also David Gray, "Compassionate Violence? On the Ethical Implications of Tantric Buddhist Ritual," *Journal of Buddhist Ethics* 14(2007): 239–271.

Contemporary Expressions: Engaged Buddhism

One of the marks of contemporary Buddhism is the effort by Buddhist scholars and thinkers to apply Buddhist principles to contemporary moral issues and social problems. This socially "engaged" turn draws on traditional Buddhist concepts such as no-self, emptiness, and interdependence; values such as compassion, loving-kindness (P. *mettā*), and nonharming (*ahiṃsā*); and the practice of meditation. Such ideas and values are seen to impel mindful work for the welfare of others through such efforts as building hospitals and hospices; doing peace, development, and justice work; serving prisoners by teaching meditation; and environmental activism. A growing body of literature by scholars, both Western and Asian, apply Buddhist perspectives to contemporary moral issues such as abortion, suicide and euthanasia, sexual ethics, human rights, and environmental issues.

Some of the more notable examples of engaged Buddhist thinkers and movements include Master Zhengyan (Cheng Yen), the Taiwanese Buddhist nun who founded the Tzu Chi Foundation. Her four-million-member organization focuses on charity, medical care, culture, and education, which she relates to the four "divine virtues" (*brahmavihāra*). Her work, which is part of a broader movement of "humanistic Buddhism" (*ren-sheng fojiao*), has, among other things, been instrumental in establishing free medical care in Taiwan. In Sri Lanka, the lay Buddhist leader A. T. Ariyaratna founded a grassroots movement for Buddhist-based development that has grown to be the largest nongovernmental organization in Asia (Sarvodaya Shramadana). His theory of development is based on his understanding of a Buddhist economics aimed at meeting basic needs (environmental, physical, social, cultural, and spiritual) rather than growth, and an analysis of the causes and cures for suffering at the village as well as individual level.

In pre-war Vietnam, the Zen leader Thich Nhat Hahn cofounded the School of Youth for Social Service to mobilize Buddhists to work for social welfare. He was a strong activist for peace during the Vietnam War and has continued this work through the Order of Interbeing since his exile. He writes and teaches tirelessly on "being peace" (Hanh 1987). Like Hanh, Tenzin Gyatso, the Fourteenth Tibetan Dalai Lama and exiled leader of the Tibetan people, has been profoundly influential to engaged Buddhism. The principled pacifism that has been his stance vis-à-vis the Chinese; his vision for world peace, which includes the creation of demilitarized "Zones of Peace" (Gyatso 2000, 222); and his emphasis on universal responsibility have developed Mahāyāna morality in a way that has been uniquely inspiring and applicable to a contemporary global audience, both Buddhist and non-Buddhist. There are numerous other "engaged" Buddhist leaders, including Daisaku Ikeda of Soka Gakai International, Cambodia's Maha Ghosananda, Aung San Suu Kyi of Burma, and Thailand's Sulak Sivaraksa, all known particularly for their advocacy of nonviolent means of reconciliation and innovative, Buddhist-based political and social reform.

In analyzing such movements, scholars have debated whether or not Buddhism can be understood to be inherently "socially engaged." Some emphasize that as a world-renouncing religion Buddhism is not fundamentally oriented to social change, and that contemporary Buddhist-based social change movements should be understood within the historical context of modern, Western and/or Christian-based influences.[18] Others dispute this perspective and point to a long history of Buddhist involvement with society and state in Asia.[19] Thich Nhat Hanh coined the term "engaged Buddhism" to reflect his view that all Buddhist practice has political and social import, insofar as the suffering that it aims to alleviate is experienced by humans and other beings who exist within social and political networks and institutions. In support, Sallie King (2005, 3) argues that if engaged Buddhism is assumed to be the result of Western influence, it problematically discounts the agency of engaged Buddhists themselves. Certainly it is apparent that if socially engaged Buddhism is *defined as* a Western-influenced movement, it begs the question as to the social relevance of Buddhism. It is clear in any case that many contemporary Buddhists, both in Asia and the West, employ uniquely Buddhist principles and practices in their approach to current moral and social issues.

Buddhist Moral Theory

The principle meta-ethical issue with which scholars have been preoccupied is how best to characterize Buddhist ethics using Western moral categories. Closely related to this issue is the place of ethics in Buddhist soteriology. Early on in such discussions, Winston King and Melford Spiro argued for a distinction between a "kammic ethic" of good works, practiced by laymen with the aim of gaining merit and a better rebirth, and a "nibbanic ethic" focused on meditation and insight, practiced by monks in the hope of *nirvāṇa*.[20] This view was aligned with an understanding of *nirvāṇa* as a nonmoral state of individual annihilation, and the idea that ethics (namely, *śīla* and moral virtues) are transcended in awakening. This analysis in turn supported a utilitarian reading of Buddhist ethics whereby *śīla* and other aspects of Buddhist morality are merely a means to the end of *nirvāṇa*, which, like the good in utilitarianism, is defined in terms of ending suffering.

Against this view, Damien Keown (1992) forcefully argued that Buddhist ethics could be better understood in terms of an Aristotelian virtue ethic. The utilitarian

18. Christopher S. Queen, "Introduction," in Queen and King, *Engaged Buddhism*, pp. 1–44.

19. For example, on the social involvement of monks in Sri Lanka see Walpola Rahula, *Heritage of the Bhikkhu: The Buddhist Tradition of Service* (New York: Grove Press, 1974).

20. See Winston L. King, *In the Hope of Nibbāna* (La Salle, IL: Open Court, 1964), and Melford E. Spiro, *Buddhism and Society: A Great Tradition and Its Burmese Vicissitudes* (New York: Harper and Row, 1970).

model is not appropriate to Buddhism, he claims, because the qualities reflected in Buddhist moral precepts and virtues embody wholesome (*kuśala*) qualities that are intrinsically related to the goal of awakening, rather than merely a means to that end. Because disciplined conduct (*śīla*) and virtues are goods in themselves, Keown asserts, Buddhist ethics must be understood to be teleological rather than consequentialist, and the basis for norms of character and conduct in Buddhism is that one should cultivate a certain type of character that instantiates the good of awakening.

Keown's rejection of the "transcendency thesis," or the idea that morality is only a means to the end of *nirvāṇa*, has been largely accepted, as has the framework of Buddhist ethics as a virtue ethic. However, some recent work on Indian Mahāyāna ethics has brought that analysis into question. In particular, the Mahāyāna idea that bodhisattvas may transgress moral precepts as a skillful means to help liberate sentient beings from suffering, and also the aim to maximize the benefit or merit of any given action, evinces a consequentialist form of reasoning that ill-suits a virtue ethic.[21] Neither does the bodhisattva's heroic aim of liberating *all* beings from suffering, even at the cost of his or her own well-being, sit well with an Aristotelian model of ethics, according to which actions or traits are endorsed if they contribute to the happiness or flourishing (*eudaimonia*) of the agent.[22] If so, Mahāyāna ethics might better understood as consequentialist rather than eudaimonist, and more aligned with utilitarianism than Aristotelianism, bringing the comparison of Buddhist ethics with Western moral theories full circle. This may in turn indicate that Peter Harvey (2000, 51) is right to suggest that no single Western moral theory adequately captures the complexities and diversity in Buddhist moral thought, though it should not preclude using Western ethics as a "skillful means" for understanding Buddhist texts and traditions.

Abbreviations

References in the form of "D.i.4" are to a collection (*nikāya*), volume (i), and page number (4) of the Pāli Text Society edition of the Theravāda Buddhist canon. The collections are abbreviated as follows:

D *Dīgha Nikāya*
M *Majjhima Nikāya*
A *Aṅguttara Nikāya*
S *Saṃyutta Nikāya*

21. Clayton, *Moral Theory*, pp. 102–106.

22. Charles Goodman, "Consequentialism, Agent-Neutrality, and Mahāyāna Ethics," in *Philosophy East and West* 58(1) (2008): 17–35.

BCA 1996. *Bodhicaryāvatāra/Śāntideva*. Trans. Kate Crosby and Andrew Skilton. Oxford: Oxford University Press

Dhp 2004. *The Dhammapada: Verses on the Way: A New Translation of the Teachings of the Buddha, with a Guide to Reading the Text*, by Glenn Wallis. New York: Modern Library.

PTS 1921–1925. *The Pali Text Society's Pali-English Dictionary*. Chipstead. Pali Text Society. (Available at http://dsal.uchicago.edu/dictionaries/pali/)

Sn 1994 [1985]. *The Sutta-Nipāta*. Trans. H. Saddhatissa. London: Routledge Curzon.

ŚS 1970. *Śikṣāsamuccaya: A Compendium of Buddhist Teaching, Compiled by Śāntideva*. Ed. Cecil Bendall. Bibliotheca Buddhica. I. Osnabrück: Biblio Verlag.

BIBLIOGRAPHY AND SUGGESTED READINGS

Aronson, Harvey. (1980) *Love and Sympathy in Theravada Buddhism*. Delhi: Motilal Banarsidass.

Cousins, L. (1996). "Good or Skilful? Kusala in Canon and Commentary," *Journal of Buddhist Ethics 3:* 136–164.

Gyatso, Tenzin. (2000) *Ancient Wisdom, Modern World: Ethics for the New Millennium*. London: Abacus.

Keown, Damien. (1992) *Nature of Buddhist Ethics*. London: Macmillan.

——— (ed.). (2000) *Contemporary Buddhist Ethics*. London: Curzon.

———. (2005) *Buddhist Ethics: A Very Short Introduction*. Oxford: Oxford University Press.

King, Sallie. (2005) *Being Benevolence: The Social Ethics of Engaged Buddhism*. Honolulu, HI: University of Hawaii Press.

Hanh, Thich Nhat. (1987) *Being Peace*. Berkeley, CA: Parallax Press.

Harvey, Peter. (2000) *Introduction to Buddhist Ethics*. Cambridge: Cambridge University Press.

Journal of Buddhist Ethics. Internet journal available at www.buddhistethics.org

Prebish, Charles S. (1992) *Buddhist Ethics: A Cross Cultural Approach*. Dubuque, IA: Kendall/Hunt.

Queen, Christopher S. (2000) *Engaged Buddhism in the West*. Boston, MA: Wisdom.

Queen, Christopher S., and Sallie B. King (eds.). (1996) *Engaged Buddhism: Buddhist Liberation Movements in Asia*. Albany, NY: State University of New York Press.

Saddhatissa, Hammalawa. (1970) *Buddhist Ethics: Essence of Buddhism*. London: George Allen Allen and Unwin (reprinted 1997, *Buddhist Ethics*. Boston, MA: Wisdom).

Sparham, Gareth (trans.). (2005) *Tantric Ethics: An Explanation of the Precepts for Buddhist Vajrayāna Practice: Tsongkhapa*. Boston: Wisdom.

PART IV

JAPANESE AND KOREAN PHILOSOPHY

EDITED BY KOJI TANAKA

JAPANESE AND KOREAN PHILOSOPHY

KOJI TANAKA

THE Japanese and Korean traditions of philosophy, when compared to other Asian traditions, present distinctive features. In China and India, the two main sources of philosophical inspiration in Asia, we can recognize distinctive subschools of thought. This is the case, for example, in the various Buddhist schools of thought that arose in China and India. Divisions between these schools are useful even when the boundaries are not well marked or have been questioned. In Japan and Korea, divisions are employed and maintained for "practical" purposes. For instance, some thinkers are identified as Confucians, some are Buddhists belonging to various sects of Buddhism, and so on. Philosophically, however, the notion of "schools of thought" is difficult to maintain in the Japanese and Korean context.[1] Whereas in China and India (as well as many other parts of the world), there is a tendency to maintain distinctions between schools of thought, philosophers in Japan and Korea tend to adopt and adapt the thoughts afforded by different traditions of philosophy. Instead of division, they are mostly interested in synthesis of thought. Creativity and ingenuity are considered to arise from the ways in which various thoughts can be synthesized in the formation of new ideas. As such, Japanese and Korean philosophers actively synthesize ideas found in the Chinese and Indian traditions (as well as others) into their own contexts.

1. This may be questioned in the case of the Kyoto school. However, philosophers in Japan, especially those at Kyoto University, don't identify it as a "school." Instead, they refer to it as Kyoto "style" philosophy.

Thomas Kasulis calls the philosophical orientation that can be seen to underlie the Japanese and Korean traditions one of *intimacy* as opposed to *integrity*.[2] Instead of pursuing the integrity of their philosophies, by distancing their views from that of others, Japanese and Korean philosophers often seek what is intimately relevant to them. In martial arts, for example, students are taught to absorb what the teacher has learned into their own experiences and practice, to acquire the teacher's knowledge "within their own skins" so to speak. The transmission of intimate knowledge is not unique to martial arts. Much of our knowledge, in fact, is of this kind. As babies learn how to behave, they replicate much of their parents' behavior in their own responses. In learning about the setting up of a computer, one is often shown what a friend has learned by trial and error. Hence, a concern with intimate knowledge is not unique to Japanese and Korean traditions of philosophy. What is unique, however, is that philosophers in Japan and Korea are primarily concerned with knowledge of this kind. This is not to say that they are only interested in theorizing about intimate knowledge. Rather, their philosophical activities are often carried out from this orientation and for the sake of acquiring such knowledge.

In making explicit such an orientation, one shouldn't insist that it is *essential* to Japanese and Korean philosophy. Such essentialization both overgeneralizes certain features and mischaracterizes the respective traditions. Nonetheless, it is useful to think of Japanese and Korean traditions as stemming from an orientation of intimacy since it allows us to make sense of the relevancy, significance, and value of the claims and arguments put forward by Japanese and Korean philosophers.

In this section, scholars of international standing not only describe the thoughts and ideas developed by Japanese and Korean philosophers, but also engage with the issues with which these thinkers grappled. In so doing, they exemplify one of the core philosophical values at the heart of these traditions, namely, that philosophy lies not in redescription but creative engagement with the ideas of "the old" when placed in a contemporary context. The authors of the chapters contained in this section focus on a mixture of important topics and prominent figures in Japanese and Korean philosophy viewed from a contemporary point of view.

The way in which the orientation of intimacy plays a role in Japanese and Korean thought can be best understood in the context of ethics. As a student of martial arts imitates the teacher, she or he *shares* the intimate wisdom of the teacher about martial arts. This sharing is made possible by the sense of compassion one has toward the other. Ethics that arises from the sense of compassion may not be rule driven or based on responsibility, but is based on the sense of *responsiveness* to everything around us. In the first article of this section, Robert Carter explores a sense of Japanese ethics that can be characterized in this way. It derives from elements of Confucian, Buddhist, and Shintō ethical traditions that, from a Japanese perspective, all share a common element: namely, charting a path toward becoming an ethical being and living an ethical life with a caring attitude toward the world

2. Thomas P. Kasulis, *Intimacy or Integrity: Philosophy and Cultural Difference* (Honolulu, HI: University of Hawaii Press, 2002).

and others. As Carter presents, the twentieth-century philosopher Watsuji Tetsurō[3] incorporates this element into his thought and presents Japanese ethics to be concerned with living in relationships with others, an ethics of social interaction. Japanese ethics, in his view, focuses on the practice of an ethical path and the cultivation of acting and being in the world of which we are a part.

This feature of Japanese ethics can, in fact, be found in artistic practices. As Mara Miller presents in the following chapter, Japanese aesthetics is concerned with a wider variety of experiences and objectives than its Western counterpart. Japanese aesthetics recognizes such experiences as *mononoaware* (awareness of the poignancy of things) and *shibui* (an acetic quality or astringency). These experiences often involve everyday objects and activities. *Haiku* is a good example of fine arts that have transformed everyday experiences into the expression of aesthetic values. Most important, Miller demonstrates how Japanese aesthetics is tied to the notions of cultivation and personal relationships that obtain between the practitioner and the audiences. Hence, arts are seen as expressions of one's identity as well as the cultivation of intersubjectivity (and/or cosubjectivity).

What is emphasized in both ethics and aesthetics is the practice, actualization, and realization of the ethical and artistic path. One's ethical and aesthetic agency is revealed in the way we *are* and *act* in the world. If this is the way that ethics and aesthetics are conceived in Japanese thought, there must be intimacy between the freedom one can express and the nature or world in which one is. In the chapter on natural freedom, Bret Davis shows that freedom for the Japanese isn't freedom *from* nature but is, in fact, an expression of nature. Nature is not thought of as an object of study but as a way of life. Naturalness is a way in which things, animals, plants, and people are. Freedom is to be found in the naturalness of our participation in nature. Given that one needs to practice being natural, it follows that freedom, in this sense, is an achievement. One achieves freedom by intimately engaging oneself with the everyday world. One becomes *responsive* to one's surrounding, whether in terms of a spontaneous compassionate act or in terms of a spontaneous artistic move, by means of actualizing freedom.

The Japanese focus on the realization of nature is given a soteriological character in Buddhism (and Shintō). Dōgen Kigen (1200–1253), often considered the most original and profound Zen thinker, centralizes practice or "enlightening engagement" with the world. Bret Davis engages with the intimacy, or rather inseparable nonduality, of practice and enlightenment as expressed by Dōgen in the following chapter. For Dōgen, enlightenment is a matter of verifying (in the sense of "making true"), realizing (in the sense of "actualizing"), and, thus, authenticating what one truly is in one's practice. In enlightening engagement with the world, however, one is not to assert one's subjectivity. Instead, one is to "drop off the body-mind" and openly and fully engage with the world. Enlightenment for Dōgen is, thus, an

3. In this introduction and the following chapters, Japanese names are given in the Japanese way, that is, surname/family name first followed by given name, unless the cited publication prints the name in another way.

ongoing journey of the authentication of the path of illuminating and appreciating the innumerable aspects of the world within the world. Such a journey is not one where the ego schematizes how things are but one where things are allowed to reveal themselves.

The orientation toward intimacy is manifested in many areas of enquiry in Japanese philosophy. What is the context or space in which this intimacy can be ascertained? for Nishida Kitarō (1870–1945), the originator of Kyoto "style" philosophy, it is "absolute nothingness." In his chapter on Nishida, John Maraldo delves deep into this absolute nothingness, a space in which everything is held together and from which all distinctions arise. The world of which we are a part, and in which we are embodied, has a structure composed of distinctions. What is the context in which this world can be found in its own integrity? *Absolute nothingness* is Nishida's answer. The integrity of the world "as one" must be negated, leaving absolutely nothing. Absolute nothingness must remain obscure and dark since the distinction between clarity and obscurity itself must swing back to nothing. In Nishida's view, it is, nevertheless, from this obscurity or darkness that light may shine to make clarity possible.

When the light shines through, however, the self is not posited as the center but, rather, is placed as only one among many jewels. In East Asian Buddhism, this idea is expressed as Indra's Net, in which each jewel is thought to reflect all other jewels. In her chapter on Korean Buddhism, Jin Park explores the Korean Buddhist development of this thought. For Ŭisang (625–702), considered as the founder of Hwaŏm (Ch. Huayan) Buddhism, all opposites (universal/particular, sameness/difference, integrity/fragmentation) coexist in each entity. The Sŏn (Zen) Buddhist, Pojo Chinul (1158–1210), focused on the nature of the mind and language and problematized the linguistic creation of the world in one's mind. For him, *hwadu* meditation promises to break out of the mind's activity of individuating being and event in terms of our language from the interpenetrated whole.

The development of Korean Buddhism is constituted by intimate and creative responses to Chinese and Indian Buddhism. For instance, the twentieth-century Buddhists T'oe'ong Sŏngch'ŏl (1912–1993) and Pŏpsŏng (1913–) rekindled the Chinese debate whether awakening is sudden or gradual by introducing a social and ethical dimension informed by Korean society. Pŏpsŏng, and earlier Wŏnhyo (617–686), a contemporary of Ŭisang, also emphasized the intimate relationship that obtains between individual and society as in Indra's Net.

As the reader might have noticed, many more articles in this section are devoted to engaging with the Japanese tradition than that of the Korean tradition. This is because contemporary studies have tended to focus more on the Japanese tradition and, as a result, have generated more philosophical interest among contemporary philosophers. This situation is regrettable, since it was partially because of the creative engagement of Korean philosophers with the Chinese and Indian material and its dissemination to Japan that Japanese philosophical thought was able to achieve its dominant position. Time may alter this situation. But, for now, more focus is given to Japanese philosophy.

Chapters of this section are written predominantly by philosophers who have exceptional grasp of the Japanese and Korean traditions. They are written in the format of an encyclopedia; yet each author was asked to not only present but also engage with the main issues and major figures of these traditions. It is hoped that readers can enter into Japanese and Korean philosophies and engage these traditions in their own philosophical work.

CHAPTER 22

JAPANESE ETHICS

ROBERT E. CARTER

Many philosophers working in the field of "Western" ethics find it difficult to come to grips with those approaches to ethics taken by the Japanese. To begin with, the Japanese perceive no hard and fast dividing line between religion and philosophy. While philosophy in Japan is grounded on evidence and rigorous thinking, much of the evidence comes from four major religious influences: Shintō, Confucianism, Buddhism, and Daoism. It would also not be wrong to include Zen Buddhism as a separate and distinctive source. In each of these religious traditions, a particular emphasis is placed on the transformation of the individual: a self-cultivation that requires following pathways to enlightenment marked out by these traditions, usually involving various meditative practices. Thus, not only are these pathways normative, but, more significantly, they are also transformative. Furthermore, for the Japanese, the "norm" in normative refers not to the average person but to those few, in any practice, who have reached excellence. As exemplars, these people act spontaneously out of a profound sense of compassion, which itself is based on the enlightened awareness of the fact that all things, human and nonhuman, are somehow connected. This comprehending of the "oneness of all things" grants sensitivity to the well-being of others that is not the result of mere ethical calculation or the following of rules. Rather, even though the results of calculated action may not seem to differ from those actions resulting from this deep sense of compassion, the source for each is radically different. However, "true" ethics is spontaneous caring and concern for others that has been achieved by lifelong practice yielding a transformation of both understanding and action. Thus, true ethical action results from *being* ethical through and through. For those of us who are en route, there are still rules, regulations, calculations, and precepts, but the goal and heart of ethics is the spontaneous and selfless expression of human-heartedness.

Past and Present

In giving an account of Japanese ethics, it is tempting to confuse the ideals of theory with the practices of a society. Peter Singer, in his recent book *How Are We to Live*, explores the textual traditions of scholarship on ethics, as well as examining present-day societies in his attempt to discover what is and what is not working, ethically speaking. To his great credit, he includes a chapter on "How the Japanese Live" in which he assesses whether or not Japanese society stands as a successful social experiment that the rest of the world ought to adopt. Singer concludes that, while there are numerous achievements in the way the Japanese live their lives, there are also ethical shortcomings to consider as well. Such a conclusion is both measured and unsurprising, insofar as one could sagely say the same of almost any society.

However, just as it is illegitimate to conclude that there is nothing in Western ethics to temper the rampant selfishness that so often manifests in the guise of individuality, so it would be wrong to conclude, as Singer does, approvingly quoting John David Morley, that "there is in Japanese ethics nothing corresponding to the key Christian injunction 'thou shall love thy neighbor as thyself'" (Singer 1995, 125). What is the basis of this conclusion? Surely it cannot be Morley's expertise, for his study is of the Japanese sex trade, in the form of a novel, with only the briefest analysis of Japanese ethics as casual observation.[1] A Japanese making a similar observation in New York, London, or Berlin might well conclude that such admonitions as to turn the other cheek or to love one's neighbor are, in any significant sense, ideals completely absent in Western ethics since they are almost nowhere practiced. Rather than a casual observation of behavior in the Ginza, or Soho in London, it is, I will argue, both imperative and instructive to seek out those underlying values that, taken together, serve as the background infusing ethics in contemporary Japan. That theory is not sufficiently put into practice is a fact common to both East and West. Nevertheless, the wellsprings of any society, to the extent that ethics is a concern at all, are to be found in the rich philosophical and religious traditions of that culture.

To begin, and in partial agreement with Singer, Hajime Nakamura (1911–1999), in *Ways of Thinking of Eastern Peoples*, has argued convincingly that the Japanese mind set has long given precedence to social relationships over that of individual concerns (Nakamura 1964, 409). The primary good is that which profits the social group, and the group is usually a "limited social nexus." While loyalty to the emperor, to one's community, or to one's family is strong enough to result in significant altruistic sacrifice, "only a few cases" of such sacrifice are made "for the sake of something universal, something that transcends a particular human nexus" (Nakamura 1964, 414). Nakamura concludes that Western people are more aware of the importance of transcending limited social human relationships in making moral judgments (Nakamura 1964, 415).

1. John David Morley, *Pictures from the Water Trade: Adventures of a Westerner in Japan* (New York: Perennial Library, 1985).

Nakamura's work in this area remains definitive with respect to Japanese culture, and yet it is less than obvious that Western peoples are as different as he intuits them to be. To take an example, Lawrence Kohlberg (1927–1987), whose study of the stages of moral development remains foundational, concluded that only at stage five of his six-level moral development scale does universalization in moral reasoning occur. Prior to that, it is preconventional and conventional moral reasoning that prevails, and the contexts of such reasoning range from one other person in one's group, to one's peer group, to one's country (right or wrong). Each of these is a limited social nexus. Only about 5 percent of U.S. citizens, Kohlberg concluded, are ever firmly at stage five of moral universalization.[2] Therefore, even though the U.S. Constitution is written in stage five language, it must be conceded that, at most, only a small portion of the population can understand it in a way that exceeds or transcends a limited social nexus. While the theory is stage five, the practice is stage one to four. The theory transcends any of the restrictions, while the practice is deeply entrenched in one of the limited nexuses. His longitudinal studies brought him to much the same conclusion for other Western countries. In short, most people operate from a limited social nexus. But now what both Singer and Kohlberg fail to appreciate is that universalization itself plays little or no role in ethics as conceived in Japan, or in classical China. Ethical decisions are concretely based, not abstractly rule or principle based, and are dependent on the character development of the ethical actor. More about this shortly.

Still, what is different in Nakamura's analysis is a de-emphasis of the importance of the individual in Japanese ethics and an increased emphasis on the importance of the group. About this I will say more later. However, it is important to understand here that the individual is not unimportant in Japan, but rather that the individual is always both an individual and a member of social groups. It is not an either/or logic that applies, but a both/and logic that must be conceded. To be a human person requires both individuality and social loyalty and cohesiveness.

On the basis of its Confucian background, it is certainly not accurate to conclude that a concern for the well-being of an ever-widening circle of people is rare or even absent in Japanese culture. This conclusion becomes even more convincing when the Buddhist and Shintō traditions are considered. Historically, Japanese ethics results from the confluence of three streams of thought and influence: indigenous Shintōism, Confucianism from China, and Buddhism from India, again by way of China. Chinese Daoism is a lesser, though important, influence as well, particularly in Zen Buddhism. Only Shintō is homegrown, while the other spiritual traditions underwent the Japanese alchemy of transformation, with aspects of the original importation altered to better fit Japan's cultural environment. Nevertheless, the bulk of the imported traditions remained basically what they were.

2. Kohlberg offered these percentages to me in a conversation. However, he was optimistic that the moral developmental level of U.S. citizens would improve. See Lawrence Kohlberg, *The Philosophy of Moral Development: Moral Stages and the Idea of Justice.* Vol. 1 of *Essays on Moral Development* (San Francisco, CA: Harper and Row Publishers, 1981), p. 237.

Confucianism, for example, is still viewed as the primary source of Japanese ethical values. To my mind, this understanding is too simplistic, for ethics in Japan is a complex mixture of the three traditions, and, in more recent times, Western influences must be added to the mix as well. Nevertheless, the importance of Confucian teachings is not to be minimized. Perhaps the first thing to note is that moral concern for an extended, if not universal, social nexus is paramount in Confucianism.[3] Confucius emphasized that *ren* (human-heartedness or benevolence) is the cornerstone of his philosophy. Centuries before the Christian era, Confucius taught that the meaning of *ren* is "do not impose on others what you yourself do not desire" (Hall and Ames 1987, 123 [12/2]). The *ren* person, or authoritative person, displays five attitudes: "respect, tolerance, living up to one's word, diligence, and generosity" (Hall and Ames 1987, 122 [17/6]). It is reasonable to conclude that the essence of Confucian ethical teaching is a selfless concern for others, without restriction, and a subsequent acting "on behalf of others" as one's duty as a conscientious moral being. Thus, the goal of one's self-development is to become spontaneously and effortlessly human-hearted. Hall and Ames point out that "Confucius does insist that the dissolution of the limiting ego-self is a necessary precondition for *ren* action..." (Hall and Ames 1987, 117). The *ren* person shows concern for "the widest possible range of interests" (Hall and Ames 1987, 117).

Given this brief review of the teachings of Confucius, and granted that Confucianism remains a major source of ethical thinking in Japan, it is impossible to conclude that there is nothing in Japanese ethics that corresponds to the Christian injunction to love one's neighbor as oneself.

The Buddhist emphasis in ethics is on a heartfelt, and eventually spontaneous, impulse toward compassionate identification with the joys and sorrows of others.[4] Codependent origination makes amply clear that everything arises and exists in relation to and interconnected with everything else. As radical empiricists, Buddhists in their epistemology have always rejected universals as "unreal" and were usually very careful to contextualize generalized claims. The Buddha clearly saw that universality is closely connected to rigidity, while simultaneously recognizing the pragmatic need for generalized statements. The compassion of the Buddha does not exclude any being in immediate experience, but not because of some universal principle. The Buddha simply *is* compassionate as evidenced by the constancy of his actions. Ethically speaking, what we have in place here is a "declaration of interdependence." We simply are connected to others, and to our environment, for we exist codependently from an experiential perspective. Psychologically, this translates into a strong feeling of kinship with other human beings, and with our environment as well. If I am not an independent, rigidly demarcated center of consciousness, but rather an aggregate of forces that persists only so long as the greater context of forces keep me afloat in a sea of nonsubstantial energy, then this so-called "I" really

3. See the chapters on Confucianism in this volume by Peimin Ni and Manyul Im.
4. See the chapter on Buddhist Ethics in this volume by Barbra Clayton.

has no boundary but extends out into the dynamic force field of nature. "I" am an energy center seemingly separate from but actually inextricably connected with and related to other things. In this sense, other things are a part of me, and I am a part of them. We are each other, and so it is only rational that I should treat others as I would be treated because they *are* me! Thus, rather than a limited social nexus at work, we have a fieldlike vision of the mutual interconnectedness of all "things" (each seemingly independent centers of awareness but in reality nonsubstantial) whereby each center is but a focus of awareness or consciousness in a seamless field of becoming. The Buddha went so far as to "advocate the treatment *of all beings* as ends in themselves" (Dhamasari 1989, 20). What is not given is a theory of ethics, but, instead, a path leading to one becoming ethical.

Likewise, Shintō does not provide an explicit catechism of rules for ethical living. Rather, it charts a pathway (*michi*) to follow in becoming naturally who one is that involves a cluster of attitudes defining what it means to be truly human. These attitudes include sincerity (*makoto*, whose meaning includes acting in accordance with the will of the universal divine energy), honesty or trustworthiness, purity, courtesy, group harmony, thankfulness, cheerfulness, and benevolence. The bite in all of this is that if one falls significantly short of these virtuous attitudes, or ways of walking with others in the world, one brings dishonor to oneself, to one's family, and to the group with which one is affiliated. Thus, it is honor that binds one to the ethical world. And while Singer concedes that it is impossible to say whether a culture is better in terms of its likelihood to put the interests of the group ahead of individual interests (Singer 1995, 123), he does conclude that the Japanese are able to eradicate the false dilemma between group and individual interests by believing that "the satisfaction of the individual is only to be found in commitment to the group" (Singer 1995, 122). While it is true that, for a Japanese, ethical satisfaction cannot be achieved if it does not include commitment to the group, it is simply incorrect to say that it is only to be found in such commitment, or that such commitment is ethically significant. The writings of Watsuji Tetsurō, which are still considered to be the definitive studies of Japanese ethics, make this abundantly clear. While Watsuji's account of Japanese ethics is primarily descriptive of Japanese ethics as it is lived and does not propose a theory of ethics, it lays the foundation for understanding the Japanese take on the nature of the individual in society.

Watsuji Tetsurō (1889–1960)

Nothing is more important to the Japanese than relationships. It is as though their ethics is a wholesale application of the Buddhist theory of codependent origination, with decidedly Confucian overtones. To the Japanese, an ethical person stands in the center of a complex intersection of relationships, such as father or mother, son or daughter, buyer or seller, teacher or learner, physician or patient, friend or enemy, nurturer or nurtured. Indeed, each of us is often both sides of these pairs at one and the same time; we can be fathers or mothers to our children, but also the children of our own mothers and fathers. Watsuji begins his analysis with the Confucian cardinal relationships of parent and child, lord and vassal, husband and wife, young and old, and friend and friend. Important as these relationships are in Japanese life, Watsuji himself went through a period of rejecting such seeming social conformity, while taking on a "Western" sense of the centrality of individualism. The more he came to live the life of individualism, however, the less satisfying he found it. In due course, he returned to his birth culture's emphasis on community, for he found that in an ethics of individualism, the individual loses touch with the vast network of interconnections that serves to make us individuals immersed in the world with others. Individualism is isolating, and the way around this was to get beyond the hard shell of the ego, becoming open to the countless possibilities of social interaction and interconnection. Thus, one becomes oneself within a community, which, further, is found in the "betweenness" (*aidagara*) between people, the space in which people interact with other people.

Ethics (*rinri*) is, for Watsuji, the study of the human being, and the word he uses for "human being" is *ningen*, which is composed of two characters. The first, *nin*, means "human being" or "person," and the second, *gen*, means "space" or "between." Watsuji adds the term *aidagara* to *gen* in order to draw out the fact that what is being referred to is the space or place in which people are located and socially interact. This space is always already etched with the criss-crossings of social interaction, past and present. Furthermore, *nin* indicates that human beings exist both as independent individuals and as socially imbedded members of a community. *Ningen*, then, makes plain that human beings are both individuals and social beings, within a space as the betweenness in which social interaction occurs. Betweenness includes all of the various human relationships in our life; it is the network that provides humanity with social meaning.

Thus, human beings have a "dual-nature," for we are individuals with individual personalities and unique histories, and yet we are inextricably connected to many others, for we exist in community from our first breath. It is not that individuality is lacking among the Japanese, but that the Japanese concept of a human being must never leave out the social dimension: we are both individuals and, at the same time, socially embedded in many different ways. It is Western individualism that is one-sided, for it assumes the priority of the individual, often to the exclusion of the social. For the Japanese, becoming an individual is an achievement, however, and not a fundamental starting point. Individuality emerges from within social relationships. Individuality arises last, rather than first. Society and culture provide the necessary resources (from emotional to physical needs; from language to customs) for realizing an individuality that is never created *ex nihilo* or *sui generis*.

In attempting to make clear what is distinctively Japanese about "human being" as *ningen*, Watsuji adopts a way of thinking originally provided by his colleague,

Nishida Kitarō: the identity of self-contradiction. In order to be an individual, it is necessary to reject the group, to stand against it; and yet, there must also be a group or groups against which an individual stands. Similarly, in order to be a member of a group, one must relinquish one's radical individuality; and yet, there must already be such individuality to set aside in becoming a member of a group. Each of us is both an individual as isolated, and necessarily interconnected with others in some community or other. We are *both*, in mutual interactive negation: as well as being determined by the group, we determine and shape this community as well. As such, we are living self-contradictions and, therefore, living identities of self-contradiction, or unities of seeming opposites in mutual interactive negation. The Japanese give more weight to participation in society than do those of us who have been brought up on a heavy dose of individualism. Yet it is important to notice that the Japanese do not emphasize the group at the expense of individuality—or at least they need not. It can be that one becomes swamped by the group, just as one can exaggerate one's individualism at the expense of others to the point of becoming egoistically antisocial. The ideal, however, is to be an individual in the world who is thoroughly comfortable in the various communities through which one is connected to others.

Watsuji also carried the idea of *nothingness*, ubiquitous in the Far East, into his analysis of ethics in Japan. Just as individuality and sociality are apparent self-contradictions preserved in the broader context of "a human person" that includes both in continual tension, so individuals and social groups are now understood to rest on a deeper ground that, itself, is neither individual nor social, but is that greater context out of which both the individual and the social arise, namely, nothingness, or that which is prior to all distinctions. Nothingness is the silence out of which sound arises, against which sound is contrasted, and in which sound becomes possible. In this nothingness, the ego-self disappears, and it is this annihilation of the self that "constitutes the basis of every selfless morality since ancient times" (Watsuji 1996, 134). To lose one's self in this way is to become authentically who one is, namely, a self-expression of the One as creative formless energy becomes formed. The result is the experience of a nondualistic connection between self and others that actually negates any trace of opposition; nondifferentiation replaces distinction making, and nondiscrimination replaces the ever-widening discrimination of ordinary consciousness. Dualistically comprehended, both the self and other are preserved, but nondualistically, each *is* the other, and together these constitute the basis for selfless, compassionate interaction with others.

What is clear from Watsuji's description is that the interests of the group ought not to deny the interests of the individual, not because the interests of the individual are taken to be the interests of the group, but because the interests of the group and the interests of the individual are both essential aspects of dual-natured human persons. Perhaps this accounts for some of the extraordinary pressures of Japanese life that Singer refers to (Singer 1995, 124); not only are they the result of having to walk the narrow lines of group approval that are so important in Japan, but also of trying to be a good citizen while maintaining one's own individual path in the short term.

It may be easier for a confirmed individualist to live simply because she or he can more or less ignore group responsibility. The "me" generation in North America has had just such a reputation.

Praxis

And how well do the Japanese live up to the standards of Confucian, Buddhist, and Shintō ethical traditions? Is the answer to such a question to be easily found? How well do Christians live up to the ideals of Christianity, Muslims to the ideals of Islam, or Jews to the teachings of Judaism? Few societies come even close to living up to their ethical ideals. It may be that the world is experiencing the great difficulties of the present precisely because the wise teachings of tradition are being ignored, or at least bent out of shape. Thus, it is unlikely that one will discover how we ought to live by examining how most people in a given society actually do live.

There is another possible approach: reconstruct or recover the ideals of a nation, culture, or religious tradition as *resources* for the ethical improvement of society. But what are the ethical wellsprings of a tradition, and how might they be employed to improve and enrich a people's understanding? In this chapter, I have already begun this enquiry by looking more closely at the Confucian, Buddhist, and Shintō perspectives on the individual's relationship to humanity at large and to the environment. But another distinctive aspect of the Japanese approach to ethics is to be found in the practice of the great arts. Some of this can be found in other East Asian societies, but the Japanese have honed such practices to a degree rarely found elsewhere. What is less understood is that these arts are ethically drenched: while they teach a specific set of skills, they also strive to bring about the transformation of the individual's character. Such self-cultivation moves one along the path of enlightenment, inescapably nourishing in the individual an awareness of one's interconnection with others, with nature, and with the cosmos. Such awareness supplies the lubrication that makes easier effective and appropriate interaction with others, ideally yielding a community of harmony, cooperation, good-heartedness, and nurturing. And the arts teach these indirectly, through the practice of something else entirely. Moreover, all of the arts, as meditative practices, gently but inexorably lead one to overcome the ego-self, replacing it with an expanding range of concern. Such a transformation of the person is central to ethics in Japan. Varela makes this point clearly when he writes that "an attitude of all-encompassing, decentered, responsive, compassionate concern" can only be "developed and embodied through *disciplines* that facilitate the letting-go of ego-centered habits and enable compassion to become spontaneous and self-sustaining" (Varela 1992, 73). So, true self-cultivation involves casting off the ego-dominated self, and this is achieved through the stilling of the ordinary mind by means of various meditative practices, with a resultant expansion of compassion and concern to a wider and wider field of application.

An inquiry into ethics as praxis in the Japanese arts might allow a glimpse of how practical ethics is taught in the present, while drawing on centuries of past tradition.[5] The arts (the Way of Tea, the Way of Flowers, the martial arts, haiku poetry, calligraphy, and so on) in Japan convey not only cultural specifics, but are meant to lead to self-transformation and provide ethical teachings about how one should relate to others. These "Ways" (*dō*) are unlike sports, or hobbies, or even vocational and commercial activities as we know them in the West. Each of the arts is a pathway, a road, a way of life. Not mere entertainment or distraction, they are all ways of self-development leading to the transformation of the participant. In short, each of these arts is, if seriously engaged in, itself a path to enlightenment and to ethical behavior.

The word "*shugyō*," when applied to the practice of a "Way," indicates a lifelong practice and is never a casual undertaking but a serious journey leading, it is hoped, to some form of spiritual awakening or realization. For this reason, true understanding is not just theory in Japan, but is meant to be everyday practice. Ethics is not a theoretical, intellectual "meta" search for the criterion of right or wrong but a way of "walking" (or being) in the world. Because this kind of approach to ethics is focused on the journey to enlightenment, it involves a recognition that we are inextricably intertwined not only with others but also with the entire cosmos. It is a manifestation of the aforementioned "declaration of interdependence" that serves as the basis of all ethical action. Thus, if I am one with my brothers and sisters, insofar as the enlightenment experience informs us that all that exists is a self-manifestation of the original creative energy called "nothingness," then to do harm to another human being is simply unthinkable. Varela says of nothingness that it is both threatening and paradoxical, for "it is no ground whatsoever; it cannot be grasped as ground, reference point, or nest for a sense of ego. It does not exist—nor does it not exist.... When the conceptual mind tries to grasp it, it finds nothing, and so it experiences it as emptiness. It can be known (and can only be known) directly" (Varela 1992, 68). Nothingness, emptiness, Buddha nature, no mind, and so forth, all refer to this same state of awareness. Out of this emptiness, compassion arises. This is an enlightened state that yields a "warmth toward the world" and a compassionate concern for others. Once the surface mind is quieted and the ego has "fallen off," there is then room for compassion to arise. One simply *is* other concerned now. One's horizon is far wider than ever before, and it manifests as specific action in specific situations. Enlightenment is not separate from practice, even though it is also an achievement (or a series of achievements) yielding a level of realization beyond the ordinary. In this way, ethics in Japan is not separate from the arts, or from the practice of religion, or from the everyday living of one's life. Self-cultivation

5. Those who wish to read more about Japanese ethics as theory might turn to my earlier work, *Encounter With Enlightenment* (Carter 2001).

means a transformation of personality, and it is from this that the strongest ethical insights arise: to see the "other," whether human or not, as a source of wonder and delight, of worth and as a potential friend, as inseparable from oneself, is a profound foundation for acting ethically. It is a way of being in the world that seeks to preserve and nurture, to embrace and assist whenever appropriate. To exemplify how the arts achieve this transformation, I will use examples from several of the Japanese arts.

The Japanese Arts

The Japanese arts are "ways of living" and providing discipline in specific techniques that are meant to be generalized as habits for living all of the aspects of one's life. These techniques, when regularly practiced, become internalized as spontaneous reactions to the varied occurrences of everyday life.

For example, learning to make tea is also a means to one's own self-cultivation as it is an act leading to increased spiritual awareness and a magnificent expression of courteous and compassionate behavior toward others. The former grandmaster of the Urasenke school of Tea, Dr. Soshitsu Sen XIV, stated that "Tea teaches us how to approach the people around us, and how to get along with them" (Carter 2007). The Way of Tea teaches that the world as ordinarily seen, as full of separate objects, is a fantasy created by the ego in its attempt to stabilize and solidify what is, in reality, ever-changing and impermanent. This insight—that the ordinary way of comprehending the world as made up of more or less independent, fixed, and permanent objects is a delusion—brings compassion to the fore, since the recognition that nothing exists separately means that it is interconnected with everything else in this flux of impermanence. The result is that everything and everyone is kindred in a sense far deeper even than blood ties. Furthermore, the Japanese Buddhist sense of the impermanence of all things is a central teaching of Tea as well: make tea as though this was your last opportunity to celebrate with others in this deliciously intimate way. Hōnen (1133–1212), in his *One Page Testament*, viewed the Way of Tea as an art "motivated and informed by a compassion for things and for one's fellows. In the love termed *suki*, artistic and religious aspirations are one.... [and] this love takes as its model the compassion of Buddha" (Hirota 1995, 110). The Buddha committed himself to the elimination of suffering for all beings by bringing them to enlightened awareness. To follow the Buddha's example is to abandon the self-centered perspective, which is also Singer's ethical goal.

Dr. Sen serves as a fine example of how the Japanese have moved away from the extremely limited social nexus perspective of feudal times and have joined Singer and others in adopting a more comprehensive perspective. As an ambassador of peace for the United Nations, and as president of the United Nations Association of

Japan, he remarks that he has "toured the world for more than a quarter of a century with the goal of 'Peace through sharing a bowl of tea.' The simple act of serving tea and receiving it with gratitude is the basis for a way of life called *Chadō*, the Way of Tea" (Sen 1979, front cover). "Tea is a way of communicating," he said to me in an interview in 2003. "Tea is *kokoro* to *kokoro*," or mind and heart to mind and heart, or soul to soul, or from thou to thou in Martin Buber's terms. This way of being with others "is contagious, for as the host attends meticulously to the feelings of his guests, then everyone else begins to attend to the feelings of the other guests." It is this quality, Dr. Sen urged, that gives Tea such an important role to play in the development of world peace. The sharing of tea is a communal act that, if successful, lifts each participant to a higher level of awareness, kindness, and appreciation where everyone is not only of equal rank but of no rank whatsoever.

Ethics is a part of the martial art of *aikidō; ai* means harmony; *ki* means energy; *dō* means way or path. Developed by Ueshiba Morehei (1883–1969) in the last century, *aikidō* has now spread all over the world. Ueshiba taught that *aikidō* is about the cultivation of body and mind and is based on the insight that each of us is already one with the universal (the ultimate source of all that exists). Influenced by both Shintō and Buddhist teachings, *aikidō* encourages human beings to become aware of this oneness with the cosmos. The term *michi* refers to the cosmic vitalizing force or energy, the spirit of the cosmos, and "is probably the most expressive term in the Japanese vocabulary of ethics and religion," for not only can it refer to a person of character or integrity, but it also links "the subject in some awe-inspiring way with the height and depth of the great All" (Herbert 1967, 45). A second key term is *makoto*, which means sincerity or integrity. It is the root of truthfulness, honesty, and trustworthiness, all of which are necessary for anything resembling dependable and worthwhile social interaction, and, as such, it is the foundation of all human relationships (Watsuji 1996, 48). One who *is makoto* is genuine, honest, and self-reflective such that one is vigilant in facing one's shortcomings and steadfast in working toward continuous character development. Such integrity inevitably leads to benevolence, faithfulness, and loyalty, since it is the fastidious attempt to keep oneself unsullied by selfish desire, hatred, ill will, or a shriveled sense of reality as purely material. One *aikidō* scholar and practitioner, Saotome, writes that "The laws of nature have come into being through the function of love, the absolute harmony found in the unfolding process of creation. It is imperative that those on the path of *Aikidō* practice with these things held deep within their hearts" (Saotome 1993, 67). Ueshiba further taught that "we all share the same divine origin. There is only one thing that is wrong or useless. That is the stubborn insistence that you are an individual, separate from others" (Gleason 1995, 6). Expanding on this very theme, Saotome writes that "The truth of I AM is that I am the other. I am a part of God. I am a part of the cosmos. I am a part of the earth. I am part of you. I Am is [the] true God [of] Consciousness, Universal Ego" (Saotome 1993, 152).

A major part of ethics is being able to recognize the value and worth of another. This is, in fact, the fundamental starting point of ethics, and education must be aimed at bringing this out, the ability to perceive the innate worth of another, an ability that arises from an attitude of human-heartedness, or fellow-feeling. We are kin in that we all come from the same cosmic womb. And, as surprising as this might be coming from a martial artist, Ueshiba taught that any worthy martial art teaches the art of loving. Even in swordsmanship, the spilling of blood and the aggressive behavior of the samurai gave way to the teachings of Zen Buddhism, which held that the sword is no-sword. That is to say, that swords should be carried, but not used. The metal sword was to be used for protection only. In *kendō* (the Way of Swordsmanship), the metal sword gave way to a practice sword of bamboo, split into several strands and yielding a broken sound when struck. The Zen love of paradox manifests in this way—the sword that killed can now be used to bring about nonaggression. One must be able to use the sword not as a sword. Through learning the use of the sword and following the path of self-cultivation and enlightenment, one can now live a life without ever having to draw a sword!

Perhaps the greatest modern-day teacher of *aikidō*, Tohei Koichi instructs that it is incumbent upon us not to fight (unless there is no other alternative, and even then it is "fighting" with the purpose of helping the other person, i.e., not allowing the other to hurt or be hurt), not to focus on winning or losing, and not to egoistically rank oneself as superior, but rather to "correct each other as whetstones, and mirror each other's actions" (Tohei 1966, 197). He stresses such character traits as openness, frankness, humility, perseverance, generosity, courtesy, harmony, fearlessness, wisdom, friendship, reconciliation, cooperation, empathy, respect, patience, having a calm mind, and being in control of one's anger. While this approach does not advocate a single rational criterion for recognizing what a right action is, it does emphasize, in the predictable Japanese way, what it will take to be an ethical and well-developed person in a demanding world. The focus is on character development, personal growth, and spiritual realization. It is little wonder, then, that those who practice *aikidō* do not speak of opponents, but only of "partners."

Likewise, in Japanese landscape gardening and design, the garden is much more than a garden; it is an expression of eternity, of the originary nothingness. The late Professor Nishitani Keiji (1900–1990), during a visit I had with him at his home in Kyoto, told me that most people who visit the great landscape gardens merely "look at the surface... at the beautiful rocks, the rippled patterns in the sand, the moss, and the earth-colored walls. But the garden is an expression of the landscape architect's own enlightenment!... Underneath our feet, where we stand in the garden, the garden is looking at us, for we are now a part of the actual manifestation of the garden architect's own personal self-transformation."

Masuno Shunmyo, a Sōtō Zen priest and one of Japan's foremost landscape architects, designed the Zen garden at the Canadian Museum of Civilization in Ottawa. He writes, "It is called *Wakei No Niwa*, which, roughly translated, means to understand and respect all cultures—their history, spirit, and people—which leads to cultural harmony" (Masuno 1999, 53). In designing a garden, Masuno first meditates and then establishes a "dialogue" with the space assigned to the garden, as well as with the rocks, plants, and trees. To accomplish this, one must empty the self in order to "hear" the garden elements speak. In discussions with him, he articulated his perspective on the ethics of gardening. Landscape gardening brings about a gentleness in the designer, the builders, and the caretakers. The garden teaches the suchness or intrinsic value of each thing, the connectedness, harmony, tranquility, and sacredness of the everyday. Developing a sense of respect for all things is no small step in becoming an ethical human being, both with respect to other humans and the environment at large. The garden teaches that we are always in relationship, and gardening requires us to respect the *kokoro* of each component of the garden. He added that the garden teaches by example: "the most important things cannot be expressed in words, and so the physical manifestations of the *dō* teach by example, rather than through abstract words—it is like pouring liquid from one cup to another." The garden raises you to a higher level of awareness and self-integration. The experience of the garden can convey to people a physical, emotional, and spiritual sense of how to live one's life in a very different way than before. One now lives as though walking or meditating in a garden. One is thereby engaged in practice, in self-cultivation, attempting to emulate the enlightenment experience of the designer. The result is far more than an intellectual lesson, for the resultant awareness involves the whole person in a gentle affirmation of one's connection with all of existence—a sense of genuine relationship with rocks and ferns, trees and insects, people and pets. And to viscerally experience one's kinship with all of these is a giant step toward becoming an ethical person, one who works in harmony with the things that exist in order to create beauty, to offer a glimpse of truth, and to express goodness. The landscape garden, in all of its forms, encourages each of us to cherish and nurture this world of which we are an integral part.

Conclusion

In my most recent book on the Japanese arts and ethics, I wrote the following: "If the Japanese approach to ethics is to develop the desired attitudes with which to face and greet life, then the practice of the various arts is central to the learning of these attitudes" (Carter 2007, 143). Rather than a single-minded focus on either the individual or membership in a group, Watsuji stressed both. And rather than an almost exclusive emphasis on theoretical reason that has no, or very little, impact on one's living, the Japanese way is to cultivate the heart through meditation and specific other-directed activities. In an abstract, intellectual approach to living, it is possible to think one knows what to do, ethically speaking, but so often either one does not act on that knowledge or takes no joy in doing so.

An ethical person will likely have a passion for acting well, for not causing undue pain to others, and for nurturing and protecting the environment at large. This passion arises out of the awareness that we are all interconnected, that we are one, that we are kinfolk, and the most powerful insight into this way of being is the experience of one's own empty self, which opens out to an interest in and concern for others. Varela contends that "authentic care resides at the very ground of Being," of nothingness (Varela 1992, 73). And while such passion may be no more universal among the Japanese than is observance of the Ten Commandments or the teachings of Jesus, Kant, or John Stuart Mill in Western cultures, it would be a colossal mistake to imagine that either Japan or the Western peoples are devoid of traditions that teach how one ought to live ethically in the fullest sense. Perhaps the surprise is that the Japanese have been able to create a modern-day culture in which guns play almost no part, where it is still remarkably safe to walk the streets and alleys at any time during the day or night. It is a culture that shows a high degree of respect for others in day-to-day encounters. The crucial mistake is to assume that a particular culture is missing essential resources in its depths rather than to recognize the advantages that might come from weaving insights from that culture into our own. Japanese culture and ethics are both deep and ancient. When explored in depth, rather than superficially, they offer new horizons of understanding that both nourish and offer insights into one's own culture and way of being in the world. Such a fusion of horizons, in the many ways that it might occur, may cause a rethinking of one's most cherished beliefs and ethical assumptions. And, if such a fusion occurred, it would further manifest that vital self-cultivation and personal growth leading toward self-transformation and enlightenment.

BIBLIOGRAPHY AND SUGGESTED READINGS

Carter, Robert E. (2001) *Encounter With Enlightenment: A Study of Japanese Ethics.* Albany, NY: State University of New York Press.

———. (2007) *The Japanese Arts and Self-Cultivation.* Albany, NY: State University of New York Press.

Dharmasiri, Gunapala. (1989) *Fundamentals of Buddhist Ethics.* Antioch, CA: Golden Leaves Publishing Co.

Gleason, William. (1995) *The Spiritual Foundations of Aikidō.* Rochester, VT: Destiny Books.

Hall, David L., and Roger T. Ames. (1987) *Thinking Through Confucius.* Albany, NY: State University of New York Press.

Herbert, Jean. (1967) *Shintō: At the Fountain-head of Japan.* London: George Allen and Unwin Ltd.

Hirota, Dennis. (1995) *Wind in the Pines: Classic Writings of the Way of Tea as a Buddhist Path.* Fremont, CA: Asian Humanities Press.

Masuno, Shunmyo. (1995) "Landscapes in the Spirit of Zen: A Collection of the Work of Shunmyo Masuno." *Process Architecture* Special Issue 7.

———. (1999) *Ten Landscapes*, edited by J. G. Truelove. Rockport, MA: Rockport Publishers Inc.

Nakamura, Hajime. (1964) *Ways of Thinking of Eastern Peoples: India-China-Tibet-Japan*, edited by Philip P. Wiener. Honolulu, HI: East-West Center Press.

Saotome, Mitsugi. (1993) *Aikidō and the Harmony of Nature.* Boston and London: Shambhala.

Sen, Soshitsu XV. (1979) *Tea Life, Tea Mind.* New York: Weatherhill (published for the Urasenke Foundation, Kyoto).

Singer, Peter. (1995) *How Are We to Live?: Ethics in an Age of Self-Interest.* Amherst, NY: Prometheus Books.

Tohei, Koichi. (1966) *Aikidō in Daily Life.* Tokyo: Rikugei Publishing House.

Varela, Francisco J. (1992) *Ethical Know-How: Action, Wisdom, and Cognition.* Stanford, CA: Stanford University Press.

Watsuji, Tetsurō. (1996) *Watsuji Tetsuro's Rinrigaku: Ethics in Japan*, translated by S. Yamamoto and R. E. Carter. Albany, NY: State University of New York Press.

CHAPTER 23

JAPANESE AESTHETICS AND PHILOSOPHY OF ART

MARA MILLER

JAPANESE aesthetics have exerted broad, deep, and important influences on arts, on politics and power structures, and on individual lives not only in Japan but, for the past hundred and fifty years, in Europe and America. As defined by modern Western philosophy, the definitive feature of aesthetics is the production and experience of distinctive forms of pleasure, specifically experiences of beauty, the sublime, and harmony, that are inherently valuable. Certainly the extraordinary global impact of Japanese aesthetics in the late nineteenth, twentieth, and twenty-first centuries results at least in part from their ability to produce such pleasure.

Unlike most Western aesthetics, however, which recognize (aesthetic) pleasure, independent of other values (truth and falsity, good and evil), as the primary value of aesthetic experience, the various Japanese aesthetics recognize a range of objectives and effects that is more complex. First, there is a wider range of types of aesthetic pleasure. Those best known and most influential in the West include *aware/mononoaware* (物の) 哀れ (an awareness of the poignance of things, connected to a Buddhist sense of transience and to passing beauty); *yūgen* 幽玄 (deep or mysterious and powerful beauty, especially in Noh theater); *wabi* 侘 (powerlessness, loneliness, shabbiness, wretchedness); *sabi* 寂, (the beauty accompanying loneliness, solitude, quiet); *shibui* 渋い (an ascetic quality or astringency, literally the sensation afforded by a pomegranate, which also imparts a rich but sober color to wood stains, etc.); *iki* 粋 (style or chic); *mingei* 民芸 (folk art, craft); and aesthetics of tea: *wa* 和 (harmony), *kei* 敬 (respect), *sei* 清 (purity), *jaku* 寂 (tranquility), etc., (Miner et al. 1985), together called categorical aesthetics.

Second, and more important, Japanese aesthetic experiences and activities are employed in the service of a wider range of objectives. These include (aesthetic) pleasure (however it be construed) and, in addition, the revelation of truth; self-cultivation that is not only artistic but also physical, social, emotional, psychological, and spiritual (even contributing to the attainment of salvation or enlightenment); the construction of personal, group, and national identity; and the formulation of relationships (intersubjectivity or cosubjectivity). Japanese arts and aesthetics amount to "cognitive prostheses" (to use a neologism from the fields of astronomy and information science) that extend the range of physical, cognitive, social, and emotional capabilities for both practitioners and audiences.

Pointing out these differences may wrongly suggest that many Japanese aesthetics and associated phenomena are inconceivable (or imperceptible) from a Western aesthetic point of view. It also raises the question of uniqueness, as problematic as that term may be.

This chapter begins with an overview of the issue of uniqueness. After that it examines several of the unique objectives of Japanese aesthetics in further detail.

Uniqueness of Japanese Aesthetics

Japan may be the only polity that has repeatedly tried to establish its national identity or self-definition on the basis of aesthetics. Indeed, one might claim that the persistent claim of uniqueness, by both Japanese and outside observers, is itself one of the unique features of Japanese culture and identity. In fact, a (primarily Japanese) preoccupation with questions of what defines the Japanese as a people and how they differ from other nations ("Japanese exceptionalism" or, in a stronger version, "uniqueness") has given rise to a field, *Nihonjinron* 日本人論 (the study of Japanese), as well as to counterarguments.[1]

Three major figures defined Japanese identity based on aesthetics. Motoori Norinaga 本居宣長 (1730–1801), a founder of *kokugaku* 国学 (national learning),[2] saw *mono noaware* as defining the Japanese. He argued that though *aware* is seen in poetry from the *Man'yōshū*万葉集 (late eighth or early ninth century, though some poems date to the fifth century), the idea as developed by Murasaki Shikibu 紫式部 (c. 973–after1014) in her novel *The Tale of Genji* 源氏物語 (ca. 1010), "enables . . . generalized sociality, transfiguring personal woes into a communal reverberation of sympathy" (Yoda 2004, 141). and Chinese literatures evinced nothing like Murasaki's concerns. *Aware* codiles Japanese life in ways still felt today. Kuki Shūzō 九鬼周造 (1888–1941) claimed a similar role for *iki*, the sense of style or elegance character-

1. Hardly a discipline, it is more a self- (or group) indulgence. See Lebra, 2004, and for a vehement critique of *Nihonjinron*, Dale 1986.

2. As opposed to Confucian or Buddhist studies, etc. His colleagues in the early *kokugaku* movement included Keichū 契沖 (1640–1701) and Kamo no Mabuchi 賀茂真淵 (1697–1769).

izing *bons vivants* in the Edo 江戸 period (1615–1868).[3] Yanagi Sōetsu 柳宗悦 (aka Y. Muneyoshi 義, 1889–1961) identified *mingei* 民芸 (folk arts) as the definitive aesthetic—although, ironically, his theory was partially based on the aesthetics of Korean ceramics (see Brandt 2007).

The issue of purported Japanese uniqueness is exaggerated. After all, Japanese aesthetic values cannot be unique to the Japanese, or the rest of the world would not have pursued them to the extent they have. Indeed, there are real problems with the concept of Japanese uniqueness. The claims of uniqueness are sometimes self-contradictory. Moreover, none of them applies to all Japanese or all segments of Japanese society. A vast number of Japanese know or demonstrate nothing of the pertinent aesthetics. Often the claim of uniqueness is countered by Japanese and Americans on the basis either of its reductive or essentializing effects that make such claims either mistaken or demeaning (and usually in a self-serving way). Peter N. Dale lists three problematic aspects of "uniqueness." First, it assumes that the Japanese constitute a culturally homogeneous racial entity, whose essence is unchanged from prehistorical times to the present day. (This is demonstrably erroneous on empirical and scientific grounds.) Second, it presupposes that the Japanese differ radically from all other known peoples. Third, it is consciously nationalistic, displaying a conceptual and procedural hostility to any mode of analysis that might be seen to derive from external, non-Japanese sources. In a general sense, then, the *nihonjinron* may be defined as works of cultural nationalism concerned with the ostensible "uniqueness" of Japan in any aspect, and that are hostile to both individual experience and the notion of internal socio-historical diversity (Dale 1986, ii).

Yet uniqueness itself need not entail essentialization of Japanese character or culture. In fact, a number of unique events features have significant aesthetic dimensions. The Jōmon 縄文, the earliest people in Japan, for example, are the only hunting-gathering people known to have developed pottery. Dance and music, used to entice the Sun Goddess out of her cave,[4] play unusual roles in creation myths and worship.[5] Japanese *shōgun* 諸軍 (medieval lords) may well be the only military rulers in world history who were also masters of aesthetics and connoisseurs, and whose closest advisors—including generals—were masters of aesthetics. (Sen no Rikyū 千利休 [1522–1591], the founder of modern tea ceremony aesthetics, was advisor to *shōguns* Oda Nobunaga 織田信長 [1534–1582] and Toyotomi Hideyoshi 豊臣秀吉 [1537–1598].) *Shōguns* even used aesthetic mastery and involvement in the arts as a strategy to preoccupy the warrior class and prevent fighting. The mainstreaming of women's voices in a civilization's canon is similarly without parallel,

3. Some have claimed that Kuki's theory was explicitly part of the rationalization of imperial expansion leading to World War II, but Kuki scholars are by no means in agreement on his intentions or complicity. See, for example, Nara 2004 and Pincus 1966. All names are in Japanese order.

4. This fundamental significance of dance—perpetuated in shrine festivals—was categorized by one Shinto priest, interviewed by Joseph Campbell, as the equivalent of Judeo-Christian theology (Joseph Campbell and Bill Moyers, *The Power of Myth* [New York: Doubleday, 1988], p. xix).

5. Tsuji 1994 speculates that dances for the gods may be the basis of decorative aesthetics (*kazari*).

and with ramifications yet to be explored (Miller 1993). Arts and aesthetics have contributed to the reconstruction of culture and values after the mass trauma of atomic attacks. These historical facts should not be used to essentialize Japanese character or culture. They do point to its exceptional reliance on aesthetics.

Contrasting Definitions of Aesthetics

Since the eighteenth century, when the term and the field of inquiry were introduced by Hume, Shaftesbury, Burke, and especially Kant, "aesthetics" in Europe and America has referred to the *study* of (1) certain kinds of intrinsically valuable experience (called aesthetic) of (perhaps numerous varieties of) pleasure, especially experience of the Beautiful and the Sublime; (2) the conditions arousing such experience (whether artistic or natural); and (3) certain kinds of related activity such as expression, self-expression, obfuscation or support of ideology, and so forth. A distancing or removal of experience from ordinary expectations of utility and from considerations of truth/falsity and good/bad is usually thought to be a necessary (but not sufficient) condition for aesthetic experience.[6]

One may think that the distancing or detachment from ordinary life that is characteristic of Buddhism characterizes Japanese aesthetics. Steve Odin, for example, emphasizes detachment in (Buddhist) aesthetics and presents Kyoto School philosophers such as Nishida Kitarō 西田 幾多郎 (1870–1945), Nishitani Keiji 西谷 啓治 (1900–1990), Hisamatsu Shin'ichi 久松真一 (1889–1980) as

> articulat[ing] a threefold dialectical Zen logic of emptiness that moves from "being" (*u*) to "relative nothingness" (*sōtaiteki mu*) to "absolute nothingness" (*zettai mu*), which in turn corresponds to a sliding scale of degrees of attachment and nonattachment. While the eternalistic standpoint of being is characterized by attachment to the separate ego and substantial objects, and the nihilistic standpoint of relative nothingness is characterized by attachment to nothingness itself, the middle way of absolute nothingness is characterized by a mental attitude of total nonattachment that affirms things in their concrete particularity without clinging to either being or nonbeing, existence or nonexistence, form or emptiness, presence or absence. (Odin 2001, 121)[7]

It is equally possible, however, to view the entire history of Japanese arts and aesthetics as just the opposite: a series of attempts to make every aspect of daily life an aesthetic experience, even possibly entailing attachment.[8] This may be a matter

6. There are, of course, exceptions. Marxist and neo-Marxist theories of art as superstructure providing justification for prevailing ideology comprise the major exceptions to this view.

7. See also Marra 2001, especially the chapter by Iwaki Ken'ichi 2001.

8. Some philosophical implications of such a view are explored by Crispin Sartwell 1995.

of attitude, like the detachment Odin describes, but it focuses more on actions and objects (or their arrangement or relations, or the space between them [*ma* 間).[9] As a result, in this view aesthetics are often tied to the notions of identity, self-cultivation, and personal relationships.

Before venturing into these exceptional aspects of Japanese aesthetics, we need to address the applicability of the term "aesthetics" in the context of Japan. As Michele Marra correctly points out, the term "aesthetics" was introduced only in the eighteenth century. Hence, he argues, applying it outside the modern West (and especially in Japan) is inappropriate (Marra 1999). Indeed, prior to the Japanese discovery of German philosophers in the Meiji 明治 period (1868–1911), nothing comparable to this strict usage of the philosophical term "aesthetic" was known in Japan.

Ever since Japanese writers began studying Western aesthetics in the Meiji, however, they have both studied its applicability to their own preexisting concepts and phenomena, and used it in their own ways.[10] Unless we accept these wider usages as "aesthetic," there is no ready way to refer to these various usages.

Marra's criticism, in any event, applies only to the strictest definition. For even in Western philosophy, the term "aesthetics" commonly has two additional meanings. It is also used by philosophers to denote *any* study within the philosophy of art (and the nonutilitarian use of nature), such as the ontology, epistemology, phenomenology of art, and so forth. This is the definition used by the American Society for Aesthetics and the British Society for Aesthetics and their journals. Also, the term is retrospectively applied to any philosophy of art or beauty, going back to Plato (427–347 BCE). Japan has a thirteen-hundred-year history of writing about art in these ways, and "aesthetics" is a useful way of referring to it so long as we do not mislead ourselves into thinking that what the earlier Japanese writers were doing is identical to or philosophically dependent on Western aesthetics.

Aesthetic Pleasure: Everyday Life

There have been several Japanese approaches that convert ordinary aspects of everyday life into an aesthetic work or act. Ornamentation of everyday objects through artistry, design, and embellishment is characteristic of Japanese material culture generally and even reveals the spiritual dimensions of everyday life and

9. As a principal operant within the arts, *ma* is clearly of ancient origins. However, it entered discussions of aesthetics relatively recently, in English primarily through the writings of architect Arata Isozaki 磯崎新 (1931–) (Isozaki 1978, 2006) and anthropologist/semiotician Emiko Ohnuki-Tierney (Ohnuki-Tierney 1994). See also Arima 1991; Kenmochi 1978; and Anon 1981.

10. The history of the introduction of the European philosophical concepts of "aesthetics" is presented and analyzed by Marra 1999, especially the Introduction and pp. 43 and 83; by nearly two dozen current Japanese philosophers in Marra 2001; and by Odin 2001.

objects (Tsuji 1994). A distinctively upper-class version is the Heian 平安 era (794–1185) notion of *miyabi* 雅, courtly elegance, described by Murasaki in *The Tale of Genji* and by Sei Shōnagon 清少納言 (c. 966–1017) in *The Pillow Book* (*Makura no Sōshi* 枕の草子, c. 990–1002). In a different context (the middle-class life of the pleasure quarters and the dandy about town), we can observe in the Edo period notion *iki* (varieties of chic or stylishness), in which every decision has aesthetic import, not only the choice of fabric for one's clothes, but also the angle of its drapery and physical posture.

Many people take Zen 禅 Buddhist aesthetics in a similar way: as a reworking of everyday objects, spaces, arrangements of objects, and activities to make them conform to aesthetic values and produce aesthetic experience. An ability to produce (certain kinds of) aesthetically satisfying works (calligraphy, painting, garden design) is sometimes seen as evidence of enlightenment. Artworks by Zen masters are valued largely for that reason.

In the case of Zen aesthetics, however, the value of aesthetic experience must be carefully examined. First, Dōgen Zenji 道元禅師 (aka Dōgen Kigen 希玄 1200–1253), the founder of the Sōtō 曹洞 school of Zen and the mastermind behind Zen aesthetics (Heine 1989, 1991; Yokoi Yūhō 1976), valued aesthetic experience, recommending it be incorporated into the daily life of monks (in his discussions of preparation of food, for instance). Yet his recommendation seems to have been for an *instrumental* reason—for the fact that if people enjoyed eating, they were less distracted from their ultimate purpose of seeking enlightenment. Second, it would seem that in Zen, the aesthetic contributes to the pursuit of enlightenment by eliminating unnecessary chaos and distraction, such as that provided either by lack of aesthetic awareness (clutter) or by other kinds of aesthetics: the gorgeous, the flamboyant, and so forth. It contributes a specific kind of tranquility to mental life that is valuable not only inherently but also instrumentally—for the ways it helps you attain larger goals, including (but not limited to) enlightenment. It is instrumental in that it contributes to reaching the spiritual goal that is distanced from the goals of ordinary life—finding food and shelter, accumulation of wealth, political advancement, and so forth.

Nonetheless, in the context of Buddhism, one must consider the possibility of more direct relations between aesthetic experience and enlightenment. Ananda K. Coomaraswamy drew attention to the recognition within even early Theravada Buddhism of aesthetic shock (Pali *samvega*) as an inherently valuable experience and a catalyst for enlightenment, and to the Theravada comparison of reactions to beauty with reactions to divinity (Coomaraswamy 1943). A sudden shift of *attitude* toward an ordinary object may provoke or be analogous to enlightenment.

Something strikingly similar seems to occur in Shinto—without, of course, a doctrinal connection to enlightenment: a sense of the power inherent in natural beauty that grabs one's attention and overwhelms one with its force. It is this awareness that is considered by some as the source not only of much early poetry but also of Murasaki's *aware*—and theorized by Motoori as the source of Japanese sociality and identity when shared with others through poetry (Yoda 2004, 129–130).

Not only decorated artifacts but also undecorated or natural objects may inspire specifically aesthetic experience. This tendency, which came to be called *aware* or *mononoaware,* the "ah-ness" of things, was well established by the time of the *Man'yōshū.* With *aware,* one recognizes aspects of the natural environment, such as blossoms falling, as worthy of contemplation and productive of enjoyment. *Waka* 和歌 (Japanese- as opposed to Chinese-style poems) focusing on such topics record the poet's initial perception or flash of insight and trigger another in readers. In *haiku* 俳句, too, we see that anything can inspire aesthetic experience, though in *haiku* it is expressed in ordinary, not poetic, language. For Matsuo Bashō 松尾 芭蕉 (1644–1694), the most cerebrated *haiku* poet, even the sound of water as a frog jumps in is worthy of aesthetic celebration.

Making, serving, and drinking tea, moreover, have been made into aesthetic experience, converted into fine art by complex means.[11] Aesthetic attitude is crucial: Sen tea ceremony uses peasant objects (iron teakettles, bamboo implements), local rather than exotic or out-of-season flowers, and architecture based on simple farmers' huts. They become valuable aesthetic objects through their recognition as such (as Yanagi showed with regard to Korean folk pottery, whose aesthetic value is ignored by the farmers who make and use it, and recognized only by the Japanese), by ritual, and by their new context. Taking them out of their original context does not mean eliminating use, however (unlike putting them into a museum). On the contrary, they are put to the purpose of transforming mundane activities (eating, drinking tea, sharing time with friends) into art of the highest order.

While all of these cases are distanced from everyday concerns in the sense of ordinary people's and society's obsessions, none is separated from either the pursuit of ordinary everyday activities (eating, washing up) or from the ultimate "interest" the individual has in his or her spiritual welfare. In the end, disinterestedness, so crucial to Western aesthetics, may not be of much use in understanding Japanese aesthetics, as the duality on which it is based is faulty.

Aesthetics, Art, and Truth

The first Japanese to theorize art was Kūkai 空海 (aka Kōbō Daishi 弘法大師, 774–835), for whom arts were forms of religious activity. Kūkai, a renowned Buddhist priest, calligrapher, and poet (in Chinese), studied esoteric Buddhism in China for two years, brought the Shingon 真言(True Word) school of esoteric

11. Tea Ceremony has had three phases of artistic development: its initial flowering into an opportunity to showcase beauty, stylishness, and gorgeousness; shaped by Sen no Rikyū, who studied Zen at Daitoku-ji 大徳寺, into an austere *wabi/sabi* aesthetic; and the global influence under Tenshin Okakura Kakuzō (天心) 岡倉覚三 (1862–1913) through *The Book of Tea* (1906), an immensely successful English explication of some Japanese aesthetics. (It was the last that influenced Frank Lloyd Wright.)

Buddhism back to Japan, and established the renowned Kōya-san 高野山 Temple. Kūkai identified four categories of religious activity: painting (especially *mandalas*) and sculpture; music and literature; "gestures and acts" (ritual, dance, and *mudrās,* religious hand positions of Indian origin used in meditation); and implements of civilization and religion. Awa Henro points out that "The importance that Kōbō Daishi... placed on architecture should not be underestimated, [he] went so far as to prescribe the ideal symmetry, shape and geometric forms suitable for use in an altar" (Awa 1983, 11).[12]

For Kūkai, arts were not only forms of religious rituals but also means to understanding truth, or wisdom, that language could barely approach. Kūkai reported that his Chinese master, Abbot Huiguo 恵果 (746–805):

> Informed me that the Esoteric scriptures are so abstruse that their meaning cannot be conveyed except through art.... In truth, the esoteric doctrines are so profound as to defy their enunciation in writing. With the help of painting, however, their obscurities may be understood. (Tsunoda, de Bary, and Keene 1958, 141)

Given the dramatic increases in intellectual understanding afforded in the modern and postmodern world by cartography, graphs, three-dimensional modeling, and so forth, we may now have a greater sympathy than we once had for the Buddhist claim that visual records can make complex realities clearer than can language. (If language seems to us today superior to visual arts in its ability to express ideas, it may be because we have in fact learned how to make ordinary language support conceptual innovation, and have developed philosophical thought—in natural, computer, logical and mathematical languages.)

It is important to note that, although the Buddhist view, like Plato's, is that the phenomenal world is an illusion, no view could be more diametrically opposed than Kūkai's to Plato's conception of art as imitation of an apparent "reality" that is itself only shadows of reality. That is, while the phenomenal world may be an illusion in both cases, there is in Buddhist metaphysics no ideal world behind it that is obscured. What we take to be reality may be an illusion, and language may inevitably distort our perceptions of reality, but visual arts may provide the clearest indication of reality (outside of its direct apprehension through enlightened meditation). Similarly, in sharp contrast to Plato's explicit dictum that "the poets lie too much," the Japanese view that art provides access to truth that is superior to that provided by language similarly privileges literary over literal (logical) language.

The driving force of Kūkai's impact derives from his own enlightenment, buttressed—and made evident for subsequent generations—by his masterful poetry and calligraphy. This initiates a tradition of grounding aesthetics in either

12. See Faure 1996 for the evolution of these issues in Kamakura Buddhism. Faure argues that architecture (especially *stupas*) established theoretical connections between different philosophies (p. 231). The same point could be made about *honji suijaku* mandara paintings 本地垂迹, which relate Buddhist and Shinto "deities" (Tyler 1992, ch. 5). Regarding the performative aspects of Buddhist objects, analogous to performative language, see Faure pp. 232, 253, 260, and *passim.*

enlightenment or total mastery of an art that continues through today. Japan's greatest theorists have often also been her great artists (at least until the introduction of Western philosophy in the late nineteenth century)—even when they also worked in the military, religion, or science.

The Construction of Personal and National Identity

In addition to the varieties of aesthetic pleasure (categorical aesthetics) that have been so appealing to the West, there turn out to have been also political and economic (and, I would argue, resulting emotional and psychological) motivations and forces to Japanese aesthetics as they have functioned within Japan, between Japan and the West, and between Japan and other parts of Asia. Ideological dimensions especially have received increasing academic recognition and investigation over the past three decades, including the roles played by aesthetics in rationalizing World War II, the invasions and occupation of Korea and China, and the historical roles played by poetry, poetic aesthetics, and Buddhist and Shinto architecture (and to a lesser extent painting and sculpture) in struggles for power and political legitimation (Ebersole 1989; Huey 1989; La Fleur 1983; Marra 1993).[13] Such complex investigations of Japanese aesthetics have helped eliminate mistaken assumptions of transcendence (and disinterest) that have been an important source of the justification and appeal of aesthetics in the West but are inappropriate when applied to Japan, where there is little philosophical or religious justification for using "transcendence." Such readings lead to an essentializing / "orientalizing" gaze that subjugates Japan to colonialist agendas—while ignoring Japan's own political agendas.

In the face of Westerners' exoticization of Japan, the Japanese found themselves needing to define, or redefine, themselves outside the essentializing, idealizing, demonizing, or demeaning Gaze (Davis 1996). Film director Kurosawa Akira 黒澤明 (1910–1998) achieved the apotheosis, taking the problem of the objectifying gaze of the other literally in *Rashōmon* 羅生門 (1950), restoring the victim to her position as Subject by allowing us to view her rape from her eyes[14]; his ascription of legitimacy to varying viewpoints of an event introduced "Rashomon" into English as a descriptor. But well before this, in the context of the large role played by the aesthetic in Japanese national identity, the Japanese had seized the initiative to make

13. See Faure 1996 for issues regarding visual arts and symbolism.

14. This type of shot was used again to great acclaim in Jonathan Kaplan's *The Accused* (1988) and in KumaiKei's 熊井啓 (1930–2007) *Sandakan No. 8* サンダカン八番 (1974), where, however, the victim's viewpoint has been edited out of prints by some American distributor(s), presumably because of a taboo in the United States about giving a victim's point of view.

themselves—and their points of view—known and *felt* to Americans and Europeans through the arts and aesthetics, by means of exhibitions, translations of texts, and performances. Industrial and fine-arts exhibitions allow viewers to see the objects Japanese see and adopt the Japanese subject position toward these objects. The impact can be surprisingly long-lasting: Japan's participation in the Centennial International Exhibition of 1876 held in Fairmount Park in Philadelphia, and the presence of a temple gate of historical significance ("Nimon" burnt 1955), were factors in deciding to award Shofuso Japanese House and Garden to that city after its initial exhibit at the Museum of Modern Art; as a result, it continues to make Japanese aesthetics publicly available today.

Translations of literature, of texts on aesthetics,[15] and of documentary and feature films both explain and demonstrate the aesthetics. Performing and martial arts also engage the audience as active participants, enabling them to *act in the ways* Japanese act. Film director Ozu Yasujirō 小津 安二郎 (1903–1963) was innovative in his insistence on the importance of shared point of view (Davis's "objectified spectatorship" [Davis 1996, 90–92]); he is famous not only for setting his cameras at the traditional sight level for people sitting in the traditional way on *tatami* mats, but also for screwing the cameras in place so they would not be moved.[16]

Even more interestingly, the Japanese have planted masses of cherry trees (in Washington, D.C., Philadelphia, and elsewhere) and built gardens (San Francisco, Philadelphia, and many "sister cities"). Film, performing arts, tree plantings, and gardens afford visitors opportunities to interact with Japanese environments and to see (and smell, hear, feel) things from cherished time-honored Japanese perspectives. Such activities are less a soliciting of the gaze of the other than the extension of invitations to the other to see the world from one's perspective; it is a mode of constructing an intersubjectivity, or cosubjectivity.

Analyses of Japanese arts and aesthetics have revealed the degree to which the Gaze is central to the construction of Japanese versions of selfhood and co- or intersubjectivities, including the studies of "objectified spectatorship" in "monument" Japanese film (Davis 1996), psychoanalysis of child-raising practices evinced in *ukiyo-e* 浮世絵 prints,[17] and poetry and prints (Miller 1998).

Collective identity, the shared sense of self, and the relations between arts, self-reflection, or interiority and identification with others have barely begun to be studied in the visual and performing arts, however. Due to the relative ease with which one can pin down differences between Indo-European and Japanese written

15. Among the most influential were Okakura 1906 (sufficiently influential that a mini-industry of criticism has grown around it); Anesaki 1932; Suzuki 1959; Kato 1971; and Kawabata 1968.

16. Both Kurosawa and Ozu have evoked a considerable literature; there are at least four books in English on Ozu. (see Bordwell 1988; Desser 1997; Richie 1977; Schrader 1988) and nine on Kurosawa.

17. Daniel Freeman, unpublished papers on mothers and infants sharing a gaze in ukiyo-e and on "Looking, Self-Regulation and Sensitivity to Feelings of Shame in Younger Japanese Children," International House in Tokyo, 1995; Doho University, 1995; the American Psychoanalytic Association of New York, 1995; Kyushu University, 1996; and Japan Psychoanalytical Association of Tokyo, 1996.

language (the avoidance of pronouns in Japanese, for instance) and to the intense self-awareness of early modern fiction writers in Japan, especially in the "I"-novel (Walker 1979, Suzuki 1996), these issues are better understood in of literary aesthetics, where they help explore "a political subject adequate to the task of resisting authoritarian rule" (Yoda 2004, 117), than in other arts (Karatani 1993; Lippit 2002; Miller, 2010/11; Nishiuchi 1997; see also Lebra 2004).

Aesthetics, Self-Cultivation, and Self-Realization

Drawing upon the early Buddhist—and Shinto—predilection for the aesthetic, and drawing further encouragement from exhortations in *The Lotus Sūtra* to build *stupas* and images of Buddhas, copy *sūtras,* and make music, early Japanese Buddhists took art making seriously. In addition to the many issues already mentioned, there is also the issue of the expansion of art and the aesthetic to forms of self-cultivation (shugyō 修業) fundamental to Confucian, Daoist, and Buddhist self-realization or self-actualization, and to the construction of persons and subjectivities, often resulting in an overlap of aesthetic and spiritual. (See, for example, Carter 2008; Miller 1993.) Artistic cultivation becomes both evidence of and a way (*michi* or *dō* 道, "road," "path") to self-actualization and ultimate realization: *gei dō* 芸道, the way of the arts. Because of this—and also as a function of the technology of ink painting and calligraphy, (shugyō 修業) which are highly susceptible to the artist's character and to spontaneous nuances of her mood and intentions—the person is revealed rather fully in the artwork. An artist's character is also evinced in the arts, including both innate temperament and the results of lifelong practices and discipline and overarching choices of what kind of person to be. In this way an artwork becomes, to the audience, an image of the artist.

By the time Kūkai traveled to China, artistic discoveries of enormous significance had already been achieved.[18] The greatest is the discovery of the expressive potential of calligraphic brushwork. This expressive potential has two sources. First, it is a function of the unique technology of East Asian calligraphy: an extremely pliant brush applying ink to paper or silk. The pliancy of the brush permits great variability in the width of lines and the beginnings and endings of strokes, permitting infinite variation—but also demanding complete control of the brush. The ink's incorrigibility demands total command, and this command requires both knowledge and physical training—physical training that is not limited to arm and hand but involves the entire muscular, breathing and circulatory systems as well.

18. They include the correlation of spatial with temporal progression to illustrate narrative; use of centrality, size, and elaboration to indicate spiritual or social importance of a figure; miniaturization of a landscape or plants to indicate the macrocosm on a microcosmic level; etc., as well as technical discoveries like lost-wax bronze casting.

The second source is the discovery by Wang Xizhi (Chinese: 王羲之, 303–361) that the act of writing could be like the flight of geese: not a pattern of disconnected lines and dots (like stone carving), but continuous lines, broken at the calligrapher's discretion (and the physical limits of the ink-holding capacity of the particular brush) rather than the pregiven ideal form of the character being written. From Wang Xizhi on, this expressive potential has been available for everyone who trains to the brush—that is, to every literate person. As a result, everyone who becomes literate receives the rudiments of an artistic education—which is also a somato-spiritual education (with emotional implications), and this basis for artistic expression has the potential for virtually infinite development, whenever the individual is ready to commit herself to it. The additional discovery of the expressive capacities of gradations of ink and, in Japan, of the expressive possibilities of the adornment of the paper, interweaves the physical features of the spatiotemporal world with the character, training, and mind-set of the calligrapher, allowing the interrelations of human being and physical world (the season, etc.) to be expressed as well.

This happy conflation of necessity and freedom, of physical and mental, of practical and aesthetic, of personal and situational, was seized upon by all the major Chinese religio-philosophical traditions (Buddhism, Confucianism, Daoism), and developed within both those and indigenous traditions in Korea and Japan as well, as one of a number of paths of self-cultivation. Artistry is thus not necessarily dependent on innate talent, or "genius," but on self-cultivation (Hahn 2007; Matsumoto 2007).

Calligraphy, then, provided a basic model for understanding other arts (and ways of self-cultivation). Arts came to be used to cultivate concentration, attention, and various kinds of noticing—all aspects contributing to selfhood and self-consciousness. Arts are accorded unusually important roles in the Confucian or Buddhist cultivation of personhood, in terms of ways of development in the arts, as a way of life, and as paths of spiritual development.

Relationship, Intersubjectivity, and/or Cosubjectivity in Japanese Aesthetics

Related to the issues of personal identity and self-cultivation is another important characteristic: the degree to which arts require active participation by the "audience" to fill in information, contribute actively to the process of completing the work. This active participation in the work by the audience presupposes even as it provides an aesthetic and artistic education on the part of the audience. This education is at once education in the arts and cultivation of the self, along spiritual, intellectual, emotional, and social terms that cannot always be differentiated. Within Confucian, Daoist, and Buddhist studies of self-cultivation, arts are now recognized in the West as highly significant (Carter 2008; Chang 1963).

The importance of the audience also suggests that the work of art is not achieved by the artist alone, but in company with the audience. There is a collusion or collaboration (not unremarked in Western aesthetics as well, of course), a topic requiring further study. This is not to suggest that Japanese arts are somehow imitative or collectively produced. On the contrary, aesthetics and arts provide arenas to develop extraordinary individuality and genius.

Nonetheless, "internal" awareness of oneself that in the West is a function of the development of the modern self or subject requires a special examination in the context of Japanese aesthetics. The modern Western notion of individual "self" may seem absent in Japanese arts, literature, and language (Miyoshi 1974), though this absence may be misleading (Miller 1997; Yoda 2004). As Thomas P. Kasulis has argued, the search for, creation of, and recognition of intimacy are fundamental dynamics and organizational structures in Japan (often at the expense of autonomy) (Kasulis 2002). In aesthetics, too, relationship is an important objective. Analysts have explored the numerous ways that Japanese arts and aesthetics constitute the structure of the self or subject and self-other relations, as various forms of subjectivity and shared subjectivity ("we-selves"): intersubjectivity and/or cosubjectivity. Pertinent to aesthetics is the well-marked tendency to view feeling (both emotional and aesthetic) as inhering in situations rather than individuals (Kasulis 1985; Miller 1998) Murasaki and Sei Shōnagon also developed feminist aesthetics (Miller 2011; Yoda 2004).

"Cosubjectivity" is a form of subjectivity (of inhabiting "subject positions") where two or more subjects share in a "we-self" (whether the latter is understood as permanent or temporary) (Miller 1998). Cosubjectivity is distinguished from the Phenomenological concept of "intersubjectivity" in which two autonomous subjects relate to each other and take each other into account. Intersubjectivity is at the core of many discussions of Japanese arts, such as tea and Noh performance (Nishiuchi 1997). In even the least "theoretical" (in modern terms) analyses of tea, the guest-host relationship, a special form of intersubjectivity, is central. It seems to be intersubjectivity that pertains, for instance, when one performs the tea ceremony before going into battle, where independent (yet coordinated) action will be called for. Yet before undertaking the battle, in which obviously one might be killed, there is a moment, orchestrated by the tea ceremony, in which to celebrate life—and the relationships one has with others who join in the tea. This is a moment in which the "otherness of the other" and, at the same time, the separation from oneself are of the utmost significance. This would seem to be a case of the arts functioning in ways that establish a We-Relation (in Alfred Schutz's phrase).

On the other hand, it is equally clear (*pace* Miyoshi) that the Japanese have at least a thousand-year history of several of the components of the modern Western notion of self (Miller 1997). We see in Murasaki, particularly in Kashiwagi's 柏木 "soliloquy" in *The Tale of Genji,* and in some *Man'yōshū* poets' reflections on time and on the unreliability of memory, for example, the habits of self-reflection and many components of the self, that we treasure in St. Augustine (who is commonly taken as the precursor of the modern self) and take as definitive of self-reflection.

Similarly, Buddhist debates between *jiriki* 自力 (self-power) and *tariki* 他力 (other-power) parallel Christian debates about Grace, and so forth.

The shared or collective sense of self described in the social science literatures on Japan is established by the collective—often with the (apparently) willing cooperation of the subjects themselves—by means of social institutions, customs, and rules. But individuals have choices: how far and in what ways to participate, and with whom. Arts take an active role in elaborating this realm of individual initiative—and use personal relationship to develop students' artistry (Hahn 2007).[19]

Conclusion: The Compass of Japanese Aesthetics

While few deny the pleasures provided by Japanese art and aesthetics, pleasure, important as it is, is only one of many ends or rewards derived from art and aesthetics in Japan. For twelve centuries, since the earliest philosophy of art, arts have been recognized as providing a privileged access to truth, superior in some cases to that of language. For several hundred years, Japanese writers have recognized aesthetics at the core of Japanese identity. For over a millennium, Japanese writers have attested that aesthetics provide what amount to "cognitive prostheses" for access to truth and for the development of special forms of self-cultivation, interiority, subjectivity, intersubjectivity, and cosubjectivity. Objectives and effects of Japanese aesthetics, then, differ from those commonly recognized in the West.

The value of Japanese aesthetics lies less in the knowledge they give us about the Japanese (whether they be "we" or "they"), intrinsically interesting as it is, than in the truths they expose about the human condition and about the views of it we construct, the means they provide for articulating—and strengthening—relationships (among living human beings, with our forebears and future generations, and with the natural world), the skills they impart (especially in various kinds of attention, concentration, noticing, and awareness), the conceptual tools and "cognitive prostheses" they provide for philosophical analysis of standard philosophical concerns (ethical, epistemological, metaphysical, the nature of self and community), and their ample provision of inexhaustible realms of delight.

19. Artists' sense of their individuality and the development of modern perceptions of their worth are only beginning to be studied. Melinda Takeuchi's study of "Ike(no) Taiga" 池 (野/の) 大雅 (1723–1776) is a pioneer in this regard, as is Lawrence Marceau's study of the early rise of *bunjin* 文人 ("literati") consciousness (Takeuchi 1994; Marceau 2004). See also Bullen 2010 and Miller 2007.

BIBLIOGRAPHY AND SUGGESTED READINGS

ANESAKI, MASAHARU. (1973 [1932]) *Art, Life, and Nature in Japan.* Rutland, VT: Charles E. Tuttle Co.

Anon. (1981) "'Ma': Space Full of Meaning in Japanese Culture." *The East* XVII, no. 9, 10, Sept.

ARIMA, MICHIKO. (1991) "Creative Interpretation of the Text and the Japanese Mentality." In *The Empire of Signs: Semiotic Essays on Japanese Culture*, edited by Yoshihiko Ikegami, Amsterdam-Philadelphia, John Benjamins Publishing: 33-55.

AWA HENRO. (1993) *A Bilingual Guidebook for Pilgrims in Tokushima.* Tokushima: AWA88.

BORDWELL, DAVID. (1988) *Ozu and the Poetics of Cinema.* London: British Film Institute.

BRANDT, KIM. (2007) *Kingdom of Beauty: Mingei and the Politics of Folk Art in Imperial Japan.* Durham, NC: Duke University Press.

BULLEN, RICHARD. (2010) "Refining the Past." *British Journal of Aesthetics* Vol. 50, Number 3, July, 243–254.

ÇARTER, ROBERT E. (2008) *The Japanese Arts and Self-Cultivation.* Albany, NY: State University of New York Press.

CHANG, CHUNG-YUAN. (1963) *Creativity and Taoism: A Study of Chinese Philosophy, Art, and Poetry.* New York: Harper Colophon Books.

COOMARASWAMY, ANANDA K. (1943, 1977) "Samvega: Aesthetic Shock." *Harvard Journal of Asiatic Studies* VII (republished in *Traditional Art and Symbolism,* edited by Roger Lipsey. Princeton, NJ: Bollingen Series, 1977).

DALE, PETER N. (1986) *The Myth of Japanese Uniqueness.* London: Croom Helm, and Oxford: Nissan Institute for Japanese Studies, University of Oxford.

DAVIS, DARRELL WILLIAM. (1996) *Picturing Japaneseness: Monumental Style, National Identity, Japanese Film.* New York: Columbia University Press.

DESSER, DAVID. (1997) *Ozu's Tokyo Story.* Cambridge: Cambridge University Press.

EBERSOLE, GARY L. (1989) *Ritual Poetry and the Politics of Death in Early Japan.* Princeton, NJ: Princeton University Press.

FAURE, BERNARD. (1996) *Visions of Power: Imagining Medieval Japanese Buddhism.* Princeton, NJ: Princeton University Press.

HAHN, TOMIE. (2007) *Sensational Knowledge: Embodying culture through Japanese Dance.* Middletown, CT: Wesleyan University Press.

HEINE, STEVEN. (1989) *A Blade of Grass: Japanese Poetry and Aesthetics in Dōgen Zen.* New York: Peter Lang Publishing.

———. (1991) *A Dream Within a Dream: Studies in Japanese Thought.* New York: Peter Lang.

HUEY, ROBERT N. KYŌGOKU *Tamekane: Poetry and Politics in Late Kamakura.* Stanford: Stanford University Press.

IWAKI KEN'ICHI. (2001 [1998]) "The Logic of Visual Perception: Ueda Juzō." In *A History of Modern Japanese Aesthetics*, edited by Michele Marra. Honolulu, HI: University of Hawaii Press, a translation of "*Shikaku no Ronri: Ueda Juzō.*" In *Nihon no Tetsugaku wo Manabu hito no Tame ni (Introduction to Japanese Philosophy)*, edited by Tsunetoshi Sōsaburō, Kyoto: Sekai Shisōsha, 1998, pp. 197–232.

ISOZAKI ARATA. (1978) "Ma: Space-Time in Japan" installation, Festival d'Automne, Paris.

———. (2006) *Japan-ness in Architecture,* translated by Sabu Kohso; edited by David B. Stewart. Cambridge, MA: The MIT Press.

KARATANI KOJIN. (1993) *Origins of Modern Japanese Literature,* translated and edited by Brett De Bary. Durham, NC: Duke University Press.

KASULIS, THOMAS P. (2002) *Intimacy or Integrity: Philosophy and Cultural Difference.* Honolulu, HI: University of Hawaii Press.

KATO, SHUICHI. (1971) *Form, Style, Tradition: Reflections on Japanese Art and Society.* Los Angeles and Berkeley, CA: University of California Press.

KAWABATA YASUNARI. (1968) *Japan the Beautiful and Myself,* translated by Edward S. Seidensticker. Tokyo: Kodansha International Ltd.

KEENE, DONALD. (1981) *Dawn to the West: Japanese Literature in the Modern Era,* Volume I. New York: Holt Rinehart and Winston.

KENMOCHI TAKEHIKO. (1978) *Ma no Nihon Bunka (Japanese Culture Characterized by Ma (Emptiness)).* Tokyo: Kodansha.

Kuki Shūzō. See Nara, and Pincus.

LA FLEUR, WILLIAM R. (1983) *The Karma of Words: Buddhism and the Literary Arts in Medieval Japan.* Berkeley, CA: University of California Press.

LEBRA, TAKIE SUGIYAMA. (2004) *The Japanese Self in Cultural Logic.* Honolulu, HI: University of Hawaii Press.

LIPPIT, SEIJI M. (2002) *Topographies of Japanese Modernism.* New York: Columbia University Press.

MARCEAU, LAWRENCE. (2004) *Takebe Ayatari: A Bunjin Bohemian in Early Modern Japan.* Ann Arbor, MI: University of Michigan.

MARRA, MICHELE. (1993) *Representations of Power: The Literary Politics of Medieval Japan.* Honolulu, HI: University of Hawaii Press.

———. (1999) *Modern Japanese Aesthetics: A Reader.* Honolulu, HI: University of Hawaii Press.

———. (2001) *A History of Modern Japanese Aesthetics.* Honolulu, HI: University of Hawaii Press.

MATSUMOTO, KOJI. (2007) *Japanese Spritiruality and Music Practice: Art as Self-cutivation.* New York: Springer International Handbooks of Education.

Miller, Mara. (1993) "Canons and the Challenge of Gender: Women in the Canon of Japan." *The Monist* (Special Issue on Canons), October.

———. (1997) "Views of Japanese Selfhood: Japanese and Western Perspectives." In *Culture and Self: Philosophical and Religious Perspectives, East and West,* edited by Douglas Allen. Boulder, CO: Westview Press.

———. (1998) "Art and the Construction of Self and Subject in Japan." In *Self as Person in Asian Theory and Practice,* edited by Wimal Dissanayake et al. Albany, NY: State University of New York Press.

———. (2007) "Identity, Identification, and Temperament in Emblematic Portraits of in Edo Japanese Literati Artists Taiga & Gyokuran: A Philosophical and Theoretical Analysis of the Ming-Qing Legacy." *MingQing Studies.*

———. (2010/2011). "Genji's Gardens: From Symbolism to Personal Expression and Emotion: Gardens and Garden Design in The Tale of Genji," in *States of Mind in Asia,* Santangelo, Paolo and Giusi Tamburello, eds, Naples: Universita degli Studi di Napoli "L'Orientale."

———. (2011) "Early Feminist Aesthetics in Japan: Murasaki Shikibu, Sei Shonagon, and A Thousand Years of the Female Voice," Ryan Musgrave, ed., *Feminist Aesthetics and Philosophy of Art: Critical Visions, Creative Engagements.* New York: Springer Press.

MINER, EARL, HIROKO ODAGIRI, and ROBERT E. MORRELL. (1985) *The Princeton Companion to Classical Japanese Literature.* Princeton, NJ: Princeton University Press.

MIYOSHI MASAO. (1974) *Accomplices of Silence: The Modern Japanese Novel.* Berkeley, CA: University of California Press.

NARA HIROSHI. (2004) *The Structure of Detachment: The Aesthetic Vision of Kuki Shūzō, with a translation of Iki no Kozo.* Honolulu, HI: University of Hawaii Press.

Nishiuchi Takeyoshi. (1997) *Theatre of the Rhetorical "I,"* University of California, Berkeley. Doctoral dissertation.

Odin, Steve. (2001) *Artistic Detachment in Japan and the West: Psychic Distance in Comparative Aesthetics.* Honolulu, HI: University of Hawaii Press.

Ohnuki-Tierney, Emiko. (1994) "The Power of Absence. Zero Signifyers and Their Transgressions." *L'Homme* 130, *avr.-juin*, XXXIV (2), pp. 59–76.

Okakura, Kakuzo. (1906) *The Book of Tea.* New York: Fox, Duffield and Company.

Pincus, Leslie. (c. 1966) *Authenticating Culture in Imperial Japan: Kuki Shūzō and the Rise of National Aesthetics.* Berkeley, CA: University of California Press.

Richie, Donald. (1977) *Ozu: His Life and Films.* Berkeley and Los Angeles, CA: University of California Press.

Sartwell, Crispin. (1995) *The Art of Living: Aesthetics of the Ordinary in World Spiritual Traditions.* Albany, NY: State University of New York Press.

Schrader, Paul. (1988) *Transcendental Style in Film: Ozu, Bresson, Dreyer.* New York: Da Capo Press.

Suzuki, Daisetz T. (1959) *Zen and Japanese Culture.* Princeton, NJ: Princeton University Press, Bollingen Series LXIV.

Suzuki, Tomi. *Narrating the Self: Fictions of Japanese Modernity.* Stanford, CA: Stanford University Press, 1996.

Takeuchi, Melinda. (1994) *Taiga's True Views: The Language of Landscape Painting in Eighteenth-Century Japan.* Stanford, CA: Stanford University Press.

Tsuji, Nobuo. (1994) "Ornament (Karazi): An Approach to Japanese Culture." In *Archives of Asian Art* 47, 35–45.

Tsunoda, Ryusaku, Wm. Theodore De Bary, and Donald Keene. (1958) *Sources of Japanese Tradition*, Volumes I and II. New York: Columbia University Press.

Tyler, Susan C. (1992) *The Cult of Kasuga Seen through Its Art.* Ann Arbor, MI: Center for Japanese Studies, The University of Michigan.

Walker, Janet A. (1979) *The Japanese Novel of the Meiji Period and the Ideal of Individualism.* Princeton, NJ: Princeton University Press.

Yoda Tomiko. (2004) *Gender and National Literature: Heian Texts in the Constructions of Japanese Modernity.* Durham, NC: Duke University Press.

Yokoi, Yūho, with the assistance of Daizen Victoria. (1976) *Zen Master Dōgen: An Introduction with Selected Writings.* New York: Weatherhill.

CHAPTER 24

NATURAL FREEDOM: HUMAN/NATURE NONDUALISM IN JAPANESE THOUGHT

BRET W. DAVIS

> Follow the creative transformations of nature; return to the creative transformations of nature!
>
> —Bashō

> If one has engaged in this practice for a long period of time, no matter in which direction one lets the mind go, it moves in a state of freedom.
>
> —Takuan Sōhō

"How should one live?"

"One should live freely and naturally."

An intuitively compelling response. And yet, can one have it both ways? Can one be both free and natural?

In fact, strong currents in the Western tradition tell us no. According to long-standing metaphysical dualisms, just as the mind or soul is distinct from the body, freedom is of an essentially different order than nature. While transcendently oriented religion tells us that we must ultimately free our souls from their embodiment in nature, modern science (albeit perhaps no longer quantum physics) tells us that nature is governed by deterministic laws that would seem to be the very antithesis of freedom as autonomy or self-determination.

Nevertheless, many of us today can neither swallow the metaphysical dogma that would separate our souls from the natural world nor bite the deterministic bullet and renounce our longing for—and inner sense of—freedom. The question, then, is: Can we find a path that leads beyond these apparent conflicts between freedom and nature? One thing seems clear: if there is such a path of reconciliation, it must entail along the way a radical rethinking of the very concepts of "nature" and "freedom."

What I mean to demonstrate in this essay is that Japanese thought has much to contribute to precisely such a rethinking of nature and freedom, a rethinking that sees them as nondually interrelated in their origins and as ultimately reconcilable through practice. By drawing on a number of traditional and modern thinkers, I shall explore here the philosophical sources in Japan for recognizing and realizing the possibility of a *natural freedom*.

The Intimacy of Freedom and Nature

The modern Japanese philosopher Kuki Shūzō wrote the following succinct and striking account of the fundamental differences between typically Western and typically Japanese conceptions of the relation between freedom and nature:

> In the Japanese ideal of morality, "nature" in the sense of what is "so of itself" [*onozukara na shizen*] has great significance.... If one does not reach the point of naturalness [*jinen*], then morality is not seen as completed. This is quite distinct from the West. Indeed, in Western conceptual configurations nature is often thought in opposition to freedom. By contrast, in Japanese practical experience there is a tendency for nature and freedom to be understood as fused together and identified. Freedom is something that naturally springs forth of itself. Freedom is not born as the result of a strained self-assertiveness. When the heart/mind of heaven and earth naturally comes forth of itself just as it is, that is freedom.[1]

According to traditional Japanese thought, then, freedom is not something gained by separating ourselves from nature, but rather is itself an expression of naturalness. It is not a freedom from nature, but rather a freedom in nature, a freedom of naturalness or a natural freedom.

This intimacy between freedom and nature is in fact reflected in the very language used to speak of "nature" and "freedom" in Japan. The *ji* of *jiyū* 自由 ("freedom" or, more literally, "arising-from-oneself") or of *jizai* 自在 ("freedom" or, more literally, "abiding-of-oneself") is written with the same character as the *shi* of *shizen* 自然 ("nature" or,

1. *Kuki Shūzō zenshū* (Tokyo: Iwanami, 1980), vol. 3, p. 276; also see ibid., vol. 2, p. 102. Unless otherwise noted, translations from Japanese sources are my own.

more literally, "what-is-just-so-of-itself"). The latter compound can also be read as *jinen* ("naturalness" or, more literally, "being-just-so-of-itself"). Moreover, the same character 自 (*shi* or *ji*)—a prefix meaning "self-" and originally a preposition meaning "from"—is also used, with only a slight variation in its phonetic modulation, to write both *onozukara* 自ずから and *mizukara* 自ら.[2] *Onozukara* is used as a noun or as an adjective signifying what is, or that something is, originally "so-of-itself," or as an adverb signifying that something occurs naturally "of-itself." *Mizukara*, on the other hand, can be used as a first-person pronoun or as a noun meaning "oneself," and it is often used as an adverb signifying that something is done "of-oneself," "by-oneself," or "from-oneself." The root meaning of "self" can also be found in these expressions in the *ono* 己, which refers generally to the self (*onore* 己 or *jiko* 自己), and in the *mi* 身, which refers more specifically to the "personal embodied self" (as in *mibun* 身分 or *jibunjishin* 自分自身).

As we shall see, what is striking in Japanese thought is precisely the *nonduality* between the personal initiative implied in the expression *mizukara* and the impersonal naturalness implied in the expression *onozukara*. In other words, the freedom (*jiyū* 自由) of the self (*jiko* 自己) is thought to accord with—rather than to stand in opposition to—the naturalness (*jinen* 自然) of nature (*shizen* 自然). Only by way of finding one's place of participation in what is naturally "so-of-itself" (*onozukara* 自ずから) can one recover the authentic ability to be freely "of-oneself" (*mizukara* 自ら). In taking part in nature, one is naturally free.

Freedom: Negative and Positive, Supernatural and Natural

As with the Western terms "freedom" and "liberty," Japanese words such as *jiyū* and *jizai* also imply, at least to begin with, a *freedom from* constraints. However, at the same time there is a keen awareness that a liberation merely from external restrictions can give way to an arbitrariness and even egoistic wantonness. Hence, Suzuki

2. *Mizukara* and *onozukara* are indigenous Japanese expressions that are sometimes written entirely in phonetic script (*hiragana*); more often, however, they are written in part with *kanji*, the ideograms adopted from China. I cannot discuss here the continuities/parallels and differences between Japanese and Chinese (specifically Daoist and Chan) conceptions of the intimacy of freedom and nature. I will also have to defer an examination of the many variations within Japanese thought, since my intent in this essay is to synthesize and reflect on a general sense of "natural freedom" that pervades much of this tradition. Nevertheless, it should be mentioned that, just as the Daoists, who pleaded for a return to naturalness, had their critics in the Legalists and some Confucians (Hanzi), who stressed an artificial reshaping of human nature, the prominent theme of recovering natural freedom was not always universally accepted in Japan. Maruyama Masao has argued, for example, that a rejection of the Neo-Confucian rooting of ethical and political principles in "nature" (*shizen*), and an attempt to see them as based rather on human "invention" (*sakui*), can be found in a number of thinkers (Ogyū Sorai in particular) in the Tokugawa period in Japan. Maruyama interprets this shift as a "modernization" that paved the way for Westernization. See Maruyama 1974, part 2.

Daisetsu draws a sharp distinction between "freedom" (*jiyū*) and "licentiousness" (*hōitsu*). Indeed, he claims that these are opposites, insofar as the latter involves a lack of self-control that leads to a slavery to the passions. (It is worth mentioning that Suzuki criticizes here the "Beat Generation"—many of whom ironically claimed to be inspired by Suzuki's own writings on Zen—for failing to make this crucial distinction between freedom and following one's whims.) The realization of true freedom, Suzuki claims, requires passing not only through a discipline of self-control, but ultimately through an existential "death" of the ego as the internal source of bondage.[3]

Unlike humans, inanimate things and nonhuman animals are not alienated from their own specific forms of natural freedom. "The pine tree is not the bamboo, and the bamboo is not the pine tree; each dwells in its own place, and this is the freedom of the pine tree and the bamboo." To call this "necessity" rather than "freedom," Suzuki remarks, is to take an outsider's perspective. For the pine tree to be a pine tree is the expression of its natural freedom, not the result of a denial of its desire to be something else. Natural necessity, experienced from within, is natural freedom. Nishitani Keiji also suggests a kind of compatibilism between natural freedom and natural necessity when he writes: "when someone tosses a crust of bread and a dog leaps up in the air to catch it, every 'thing' involved... [is] subject to certain physico-chemical laws.... [And yet,] the dog and the man *live* the laws of nature.... [Moreover,] their activities in some sense also imply an *appropriation* of the laws of nature."[4] In fact, as we shall see, in the Japanese tradition human freedom is thought to be compatible not only with the lawful regularity, but also with the radical indeterminacy and contingency of nature's unfathomable ways.

Yet humans, and apparently humans alone, are capable not only of naturalness but also of "falsity," that is, of a distorted and distorting view of their own place in the world and the range of possibilities open to this place. To be sure, we humans are not pine trees, and we have certain unique abilities and responsibilities for cooperatively shaping our environment. But it is a hubristic falsification for us to think of ourselves as supernatural masters of the natural world. We too have our own specific freedom within nature, not outside or opposed to it.

While Suzuki somewhat polemically claims that the (modern liberal) West has failed to think beyond a negative sense of freedom or liberty, in fact there have long been debates in Western political philosophy surrounding what Isaiah Berlin has referred to as "two concepts of liberty,"[5] namely, a "negative freedom" from constraints and a "positive freedom" to realize one's authentic potentials. Moreover, it is not the case that negative freedom has been thought only in the sense of political freedom from *external* constraints. According to Kant, for example, morality demands a freedom from *internal* compulsions (sensuous or natural "inclinations"), a negative freedom that in turn enables a positive freedom,

3. Suzuki Daisetsu, *Tōyō-teki-na mikata* (Tokyo: Iwanami, 1997), p. 68.

4. Nishitani 1982, 79–80.

5. See Isaiah Berlin, "Two Concepts of Liberty," in *Four Essays on Liberty* (London: Oxford University Press, 1969).

namely, the "autonomy" of giving the supersensuous or supernatural law of practical reason to oneself.[6]

Nevertheless, while Kant thinks of autonomy dualistically as requiring a supersensuous will free from natural inclinations, Suzuki thinks in nondualistic terms of an autonomous naturalness. Suzuki defines freedom as "the activity that naturally comes forth as it is—without any direction from another and without restriction—from the principle of nature." Far from seeing autonomy as an independence from nature, he stresses the linguistic as well as semantic intimacy between freedom, or "arising-from-oneself" (*jiyū* 自由)—autonomy in the sense of acting on one's own accord or "of-oneself" (*mizukara* 自ら)—and naturalness as a spontaneous activity that happens "of-itself" (*onozukara* 自ら).[7] On the one hand, then, Suzuki would agree with Kant that positive freedom requires a negative freedom, not just from external constraints, but also from internal compulsions. On the other hand, however, he would disagree with the idea that autonomy is gained by means of a supernatural freedom from and rational control of *all* natural inclinations. Autonomy is not gained by means of a complete independence from the supposed heteronomy of nature, but rather by means of harmonizing oneself with the truly natural Way that is the very origin of the self. Freedom is realized not by way of a dualistic disengagement from nature, but rather by way of a nondualistic engagement in nature.

In an early work, Nishitani suggests a dialectical path through a disengagement from egoistic self-will (what we might call our inauthentic, alienated, and alienating self-nature) toward a recovery of genuine naturalness (our authentic self-nature).[8] He acknowledges Kantian rational autonomy as a significant step on a way that ultimately, however, leads back to a realization of the nonduality of our authentic self with a radical naturalness. In his later attempts to think of this human/nature nonduality, where the self freely participates in nature, Nishitani turns increasingly to the tradition of Zen Buddhism. He quotes, for instance, the following passages from Musō Kokushi:

> Hills and rivers, the earth, plants and trees, tiles and stones, all of these are the self's own original part.... Out of the realm of the original part have arisen all things: from the wisdom of Buddhas and saints to the body-and-mind of every sentient being, and all lands and worlds.[9]

6. See Immanuel Kant, *Foundations of the Metaphysics of Morals*, 2nd ed., trans. Lewis White Beck (New York: Macmillan, 1990), p. 70 [452]. When Kant uses the term "nature" in the "widest sense" to mean "the existence of things under laws," he opposes the intelligible world of "supersensuous nature" to the empirical world of "sensuous nature." He claims that these worlds, or views of the world, are strictly distinct and yet somehow coexist in a manner incomprehensible to us. See Immanuel Kant, *Critique of Practical Reason*, trans. Lewis White Beck (New York: Macmillan, 1956), p. 44 [43], 102–103 [99–100].

7. Suzuki, *Tōyō-teki-na mikata*, p. 65. Note that Suzuki writes here *mizukara* and *onozukara* exactly the same, distinguishing them only by appended phonetic script (*furigana*).

8. See *Nishitani Keiji chosakushū* (Tokyo: Sōbunsha, 1986), vol. 1, pp. 85–90.

9. Nishitani 1982, 108.

When the self awakens to its own "original part," the core and source of its being, it realizes its participation in the dynamically interconnected whole of nature.

Nature as a Way of Naturalness

The question of freedom has taken us back to the question of nature. The contemporary Japanese psychoanalyst Kimura Bin draws a broad distinction between, on the one hand, a conception of nature that sets it in opposition to human culture and, on the other, a conception of nature that sees it as "pertaining to the innermost psychic reality" of human beings. The former conception, Kimura says, predominates in the Western tradition, whereas the latter is typified in the traditional Japanese understanding of nature.[10] Suzuki also claims that "Western 'nature' is dualistic and is set over against 'the human,'" while "Eastern '*shizen*' includes 'the human.'"[11] The Greeks did often set *technē* (art/craft) and *nomos* (convention) over against *physis* (nature); and a dualistic distinction between the natural body (*soma*) and the supernatural soul (*psychē*) gets repeated in one form or another from Plato through medieval Christian thought to Descartes. Of course, we can also find countercurrents to such dualisms throughout the Western tradition. But in Japan, a human/nature nondualism is the main current of thinking. As Yanabu Akira writes, the traditional Japanese notion of "nature" (*shizen*) signifies a world that either precedes the subject/object split or that entails the unification of subject and object.[12]

What, then, is this "nature" in which humans nondually participate? Today, *shizen* is used as a translation of the Western concept (or rather concepts) of "nature." In premodern (that is, pre-Westernized) Japan, however, "nature" as the totality of all natural things was referred to with such expressions as "mountains-rivers-grasses-trees" (*sansensōmoku*) and "the interwoven variety [literally the 'forest web'] of the myriad phenomena" (*shinrabanshō*). On the other hand, "Nature" as the order of the cosmos, or as a dynamic cosmological principle of transformation, was expressed with such terms as "heaven and earth" (*tenchi*), the Way (*dō* or *michi*), and "creative transformation" (*zōka*). Nature in the Japanese tradition is thus an inherently dynamic and creative whole unto itself. It is not the product of a transcendent Creator; indeed, even the Shintō gods are said to have emerged from mysterious yet natural processes.[13]

10. Kimura 1988, 4.

11. Suzuki, *Tōyō-tekihna mikata*, p. 220.

12. Yanabu Akira, "Shizen: Honyakugo no unda gokai," in *Honyakugo seiritsu jijō* (Tokyo: Iwanami, 1982), p. 133.

13. See Sagara Tōru, "'Onozukara' toshite no shizen," in *Sagara Tōru chosakushū* (Tokyo: Perikansha, 1995), vol. 6, pp. 148–149. Maruyama sees this as reflecting the fact that the Japanese historical consciousness is based, not on a teleological sense of creation, but on a sense of the natural dynamism of a continual becoming (*tsugi-tsugi ni nariyuku ikioi*). See Maruyama Masao, "Rekishi-ishiki no 'kosō,'" in *Chūsei to hangyaku* (Tokyo: Chikuma, 1992).

In many respects, this Japanese sense of "nature" does resemble a Greek sense of *kosmos:* that is, a self-contained world that includes the gods as well as all animate and inanimate beings, and in which humans are to find their proper place. But the Japanese did not attempt to develop a "cosmology" in the sense of a thoroughly logical account (*logos*) of a thoroughly rationally ordered world (*kosmos*). While nature is not thought of as simply chaotic, that is, while there are indeed principle patterns (*ri* or *kotowari*) that permeate the phenomenal flux, the rhyme and reason of nature's Way ultimately exceeds human calculation and intellectual reasoning. Nevertheless, while the principle of this fluid Way cannot be fixed in place by the objectifying intellect, it can be existentially realized by means of a holistically engaged praxis that includes, but is not limited to, discursive reasoning.

In the Japanese tradition nature is thus not so much an object of study as it is a way of life. The Japanese were concerned less with "nature" as the object of a theory of being, and more with "naturalness" as a principle of becoming and as a practical way of living. In fact, the Japanese word that is used today to translate the Western concept of "nature"—自然, read as *shizen*—was originally used as an adjective (natural) or as an adverb (naturally), rather than as a substantive (nature). Naturalness—自然, read as *jinen*—is an adverb describing the authentic way in which things, animals, and, ideally, people are. The human task is therefore not to learn to completely predict and externally control nature by fathoming its rational laws, but rather to bring oneself into accordance with the fluid principle of its Way.

A Way Beyond the Pitfalls of Naturalism and Supernaturalism

As we have seen, in traditional Japanese thought freedom is not found in a victorious or tragic struggle against nature, but rather in the naturalness of a participation in nature. But this free participation in nature is not in fact a given; the source of natural freedom must be retapped. And the path back to a radical wellspring of naturalness must avoid the pitfall of a superficial "naturalism." At the same time, as we shall see, Japanese thinkers attempted to avoid this pitfall without diverting the path away from a nondualistic this-worldly naturalness toward a dualistic otherworldly supernaturalism.

An affirmation of the soteriological efficacy of nature is a recurrent theme in Japanese Buddhism as well as in indigenous Shintō thought. The Buddha Way does not lead to a transcendence of nature, but entails rather a return to naturalness; and natural phenomena themselves help teach us this Way. Dōgen claims that "grass and trees" are the Buddha-nature.[14] "The sūtras," he says, "are the entire universe,

14. Dōgen 2002, 76–77.

mountains and rivers and the great earth, plants and trees," and we are counseled to listen to "the voices and figures of streams and the sounds and shapes of mountains" as they "bounteously deliver eighty-four-thousand *gāthās* [verses]."[15]

And yet, Dōgen was also keenly aware that the then-prevalent doctrine of the "original enlightenment" (*hongaku*) of all beings can easily mislead one to a superficial "naturalism" that permits a wanton indifference to practice.[16] In this regard he cites his teacher Rujin's warning: "If one says all sentient beings are from the first Buddhas, that would fall under the teaching of the non-Buddhist school of Naturalism."[17]

That a genuinely radical naturalness is not to be confused with the egoistic abandon of so-called naturalism is also clearly apparent in Shinran's ideal of "dharmic naturalness" (*jinenhōni*). For Shinran, such genuine naturalness is achieved precisely by disposing of all egoistic workings of "self-power" (*jiriki*) and opening oneself to the "other-power" (*tariki*) of Amida Buddha's grace. To Western ears, this may initially sound like a familiar sacrifice of naturalistic egoism for the sake of supernatural fideism, in other words, a giving up of self-will for the sake of obedience to God's Will. Yet, for Shinran, even the personified transcendence of Amida is ultimately to be understood as an "expedient means" for returning to a natural spontaneity and effortless compassion here and now.[18] And, we might ask, would not this dharmic naturalness then lie radically beyond the very dualism of self-power and other-power?

Nishida Kitarō writes that "in dharmic naturalness, we see God in a place where there is no God,"[19] and he explicitly suggests that dharmic naturalness must be understood neither in terms of the egoistic arbitrariness of an immanent naturalism nor in terms of a deferential obedience to a supernatural being.

> Something like what Shinran calls dharmic naturalness is not what is thought of as natural [*shizen*] in Western thought. It is not a matter of behaving arbitrarily and just following one's impulses. It is not a matter of so-called "naturalism" [*shizenshugi*]. Dharmic naturalness must involve exhaustively exerting the self in the face of things. It must include infinite effort, and must not merely be a matter of going with the flow. And yet, it should be recognized that one's efforts are themselves not one's own. There is something which of itself naturally allows things to happen [*onozukara shikarashimeru mono*].... [This] must not be [thought of as] something that moves the self either from the outside or from the inside, but rather [as] something that envelopes the self.[20]

15. Quoted from the "Jishō zammai" and "Keiseisanshoku" fascicles of the *Shōbōgenzō* in Kim 1987, 97, 256.

16. According to Takeuchi Seiichi, the "naturalism" (*shizenshugi*) of the "I novels" of early twentieth-century Japanese literature also fell into an analogous pitfall. See Takeuchi Seiichi, *"Onozukara" to "mizukara": Nihonshisō no kiso* (Tokyo: Shunjūsha, 2004), pp. 11–13, 20–21.

17. "Dōgen's Hōkyō-ki (1)," trans. Norman Waddell, *The Eastern Buddhist* New Series 10/2 (October 1977): 121.

18. Sagara shows how Shinran ultimately understands Amida and other-power as expedient means for realizing naturalness ("'Onozukara' keijijōgaku," in *Sagara Tōru chosakushū*, vol. 6, pp. 136–137).

19. Nishida 1987, 121, translation modified.

20. *Nishida Kitarō zenshū* (Tokyo: Iwanami, 1987–1989), vol. 12, p. 369.

True naturalness is not gained by simply passively submitting oneself to the Will of a transcendent being outside the self, any more than it can be gained by simply acting on the willfulness found immanent in the surface layers of the self. Rather, according to Nishida, the true individual discovers him- or herself to be "enveloped" by the "place of absolute nothingness"; and, realizing oneself as a "focal point" of the self-determination of this dynamic place, one truly becomes what one is, "a creative element in a creative world."[21]

Human/Nature Nonduality: Existence and Return

Nondualism is sometimes taken to be synonymous with distinctionless monism. However, while this may apply to the Advaita Vedanta school of Indian philosophy, in East Asian thought, and in Zen Buddhism in particular, nonduality (*funi*) tends to be thought rather in terms of "not one and not two" (*fuichi-funi*). As seen in the passage quoted above, Nishida was satisfied neither with a philosophy of sheer immanence nor with one of dualistic transcendence. Rather, he thought that the nondual relation between the self and the absolute must be understood in terms of "immanent transcendence" (*naizai-teki-chōetsu*).[22] Precisely because the finite self is "enveloped by" rather than externally opposed to the absolute, the absolute is found at the very heart of the finite self. Insofar as we understand nature to be the encompassing whole of reality,[23] in order to understand the relation of the finite self to nature, we must think in such terms of a nondual relation of immanent transcendence. The self is not simply submerged in nature, but neither is it something dualistically separate or separable from nature.

Kimura Bin helps us to understand this nondual relation between the self and nature by explaining it in terms of a literal sense of "existence." "The self, *mizukara*, is nothing but an 'existence' in the sense of a 'standing out' or 'emerging' of the intrinsic nature, *onozukara*, into the outer intersubjective reality of human life through the 'ex-it' of one's own body, *mi*."[24] The personal embodied self is thus an

21. See *Nishida Kitarō zenshū*, vol. 8, p. 339.

22. See Nishida 1987, 99, 110, 121.

23. Nishida himself does not in fact usually speak of the absolute or the ultimately enveloping and self-determining world as "nature." In his later thought, he tends to limit "nature" (*shizen*) per se to the realms of biology and physics, which he generally claims are enveloped by the historical world. However, in an important text from his later period, Nishida writes of the dialectically self-determining world in terms of "historical nature" (*rekishi-teki shizen*) (*Nishida Kitarō zenshū*, vol. 8, pp. 298ff.). In an early essay, Nishida had written that "nature and culture are not opposed to one another; nature is the root of culture. An artificial culture separated from a profound and vast nature cannot but degenerate" (*Nishida Kitarō zenshū*, vol. 13, p. 129).

24. Kimura 1988, 6.

ek-stasis, a standing outside oneself, insofar as it is an emergence from "the overall spontaneous activity of nature" that is the "very origin of the inner self."

Kimura suggests that mental health requires a dynamic balance between individuating existence and staying in touch with one's natural origins. While on the one hand the schizophrenic is unable to first achieve an individuating existence from nature, on the other hand the Zen practitioner seeks to radically return to the creative source of (human) nature. "If the goal of endeavor in Zen Buddhism is gaining access to the true Self before the differentiation of *mizukara* from *onozukara*, the basic disturbance of the schizophrenic psychosis can be seen in a difficulty to differentiate them."[25] While the schizophrenic fails to become an individual in the first place, the Zen practitioner attempts to transcend individual egoism and alienation by returning to the natural roots of humanity.

Freedom is thus not simply an innate given, but rather the achievement of a *regained* naturalness. The true self is a part of nature, but it is a part that dynamically stands out from and returns to nature. Natural freedom is not a static state of being, but rather a dynamic dialectic of existence and return.

The Unfathomability of Nature and Freedom

Insofar as we humans are one with nature, in other words, insofar as we come from nature and can return to nature, we can realize—awaken to and embody—the principle of its fluid Way. And yet, insofar as we stand out from nature as existing finite individuals, we can neither fathom its every rhyme and reason nor control every twist and turn of its flow.

As we have seen, the same characters 自然 can be read either as *jinen* or as *shizen*. While the former reading was used in the past, as it is still today, in the sense of "natural," without artificial intervention, the latter reading was traditionally used to refer to events that were unexpected, "one in ten thousand" (*man-ichi*). Analogously, the expression *onozukara* was used not only to refer to events that were "natural," that happen as a matter "of course," but also to events that occur "perchance" (*hyottosuruto* or *tamatama*).[26] Hence, the expressions *onozukara* and *shizen* evince, not a nature that is exhaustively ruled by laws of necessity that can be epistemologically fathomed and technologically manipulated, but rather a nature that can manifest itself also in radically contingent and surprising events.[27] Such events, that of death in particular, are

25. Ibid., 10.

26. See the entries for "*shizen*" and "*onozukara*" in *Kōjien* (Tokyo: Iwanami, 1991) and in *Iwanami kogojiten* (Tokyo: Iwanami, 1992).

27. It is not surprising that Kuki's philosophical investigation of "contingency" (*gūzen*) led him through European existentialism back to the Japanese conception of nature. See Tanaka Kyūbun, *Kuki Shūzō: gūzen to shizen* (Tokyo: Perikansha, 1992), ch. 5.

beyond our ken and control—and yet they too are natural.[28] Returning to a life of naturalness thus requires more than comprehending and attuning ourselves to the lawful regularities of nature; it also demands an openness to nature's unfathomable contingencies and a recognition of our own finitude and mortality in particular.

This conjunction of what is natural ("of course") with what is contingent and surprising is paradoxical only if we assume that the ways of nature can be reduced to the laws of human understanding and submitted to the calculations of egoistic desire. Yet, while this noncalculable contingency means that the natural world is beyond our control, the indeterminacy of nature is in fact also the source of our own freedom. An acknowledgment of the ultimate unfathomability of natural processes is at the same time an affirmation of the nondeterministic freedom of our participation in these processes. The spontaneity and creativity of nature and freedom is the complement of their contingency and unpredictability.

Freedom, after all, essentially cannot be explained—for to explain freedom would be to explain it away. What can be determined in advance is, strictly speaking, nothing new, but rather merely the mechanistic or teleological unfolding of what was already there. However situated and finite it may be, freedom is precisely what cannot be exhaustively determined by causes and conditions. Indeed, freedom (*jiyū* 自由) is as such an origin; it is a source from (自) which something new arises (由). It is not a predictable becoming based on determinate being, but rather a creative emergence out of an indeterminate "nothingness."[29]

The traditional Japanese Way of nature entails, then, a nondeterministic, uncontrollable, incalculable excess of originality and creativity. This natural Way both exceeds the control of our egos and is the very source of the freedom of our authentic selves. For, as Nishida puts it, we become true individuals when we realize ourselves as "creative elements in a creative world."

The Practice of Regaining Natural Freedom

As is implied in Bashō's call for us to "*return* to the creative transformations of nature," natural freedom is not simply a given; it must be achieved. This achievement, however, is a matter of radical regress rather than linear progress; that is to say, it entails stepping back to our forgotten roots, getting back in touch with the hidden source of spontaneous creativity and compassionate responsibility that lies underfoot.

28. See Sagara, "'Onozukara' keijijōgaku," pp. 124–125, and "'Onozukara' toshite no shizen," pp. 151–153.

29. See Nishitani 2005, 67–68.

The quest for natural freedom in the Japanese tradition thus always starts with a paradox of self-alienation: to begin with we are not who we are most originally.

Dōgen opens his *Fukanzazengi* with a version of this paradox: "From the beginning the Way circulates everywhere; why the need to verify it in practice? . . . And yet, if there is the slightest discrepancy, heaven and earth are vastly separated; if the least disorder arises, the heart and mind get lost in confusion."[30] Although the natural Way is everywhere, its ubiquity must be realized, that is, awakened to and actualized. Dōgen's solution to the acquired enlightenment (*shikaku*) versus original enlightenment (*hongaku*) dilemma is found in his notion of "the oneness of practice and enlightenment" (*shushō ittō*).[31] With this doctrine he manages to avoid the pitfall of a superficial naturalism that excuses humans from the task of *realizing* the originary ubiquity of the Buddha-nature. Practice is not a means by which we acquire a new essence; yet it is a way of expressly verifying our true being. As he tells us in *Bendōwa:* "Although the Dharma [cosmic law] amply inheres in every person, without practice, it does not presence; if it is not verified, it is not attained."[32] The natural freedom of our Buddha-nature is always already underfoot, and yet it must be appropriated by means of holistic practice (*shugyō*).

While there is no end to this practice of the realization of natural freedom (insofar as what one realizes is that practice is realization), one does pass from a more or less artificially forced discipline to what Takuan calls a state of "samadhic freedom" (*jiyū zammai*).[33] The practice (*keiko*) of serious discipline, Takuan writes, leads to a "state of freedom [*jiyū*]" in which one can let the mind go in any direction.[34] If one has learned to "throw the mind away in the entire body, not stopping it here or there," then, "when it does inhabit these various places, it will realize its function and act without error."[35] Freed from internal compulsion by means of strict external discipline, one finally lets go of the latter to realize a genuinely natural freedom in the midst of everyday activity.

As we have seen, the nonduality of this natural freedom does not imply a licentious naturalism, nor does it imply a distinctionless monism into which singular differences are dissolved and ethical responsibility abnegated. Although Takuan is sometimes accused of dissolving ethical distinctions, insofar as in his "lessons to the sword master" he says that the self, the opponent, and the sword are all to be viewed as "empty [of independent substantiality],"[36] in fact, the spontaneous freedom he teaches does contain significant ethical implications. It is necessary to cast off the dualistic discriminations of the ego, not in order to attain a blanket state of nondiscrimination, but rather in order to discriminate—that is, to make practical

30. My translation. For an alternative translation, see Dōgen 2002, 2–3.

31. The attempt to steer through the horns of acquired versus original enlightenment dualism did not remain unique to Dōgen. As Takeuchi points out, Ippen spoke of "the nonduality of acquired and original enlightenment [*shihon-funi*]" (*"Onozukara" to "mizukara,"* 19).

32. My translation. For an alternative translation, see Dōgen 2002, 8.

33. Takuan 1986, 82. Wilson translates *jiyū zammai* as "freedom in a meditative state."

34. Ibid., 36.

35. Ibid., 26, 31, translation modified.

36. Ibid., 37.

distinctions and ethical judgments—*freely and naturally*. This freedom from (artificial and egoistic) discrimination and freedom for (natural and nonegoistic) discrimination is what Takuan means when he says: "Without looking at right and wrong, he is able to see right and wrong well; without attempting to discriminate, he is able to discriminate well."[37] One finds the source of practical wisdom, not by intellectually disengaging oneself from the everyday world and transcending it to a supernatural realm, but rather by means of a holistic practice of intimately engaging oneself with the everyday world by nondually attuning oneself to the fluid principle—the natural Way—that pervades the singular events of the here and now.

To be sure, Zen masters and other Japanese teachers in the past and in the present have not always lived up to their ideal practices of returning to a free and responsible naturalness. At their worst, they have inhibited individual autonomy by conflating nonegoistic naturalness with conformity to the status quo of the community. On the path to recovering a nondual spontaneity, there are certainly perilous sidetracks that would confuse nonduality with homogeneity and pitfalls that would simply replace self-assertive activity with deferential passivity. But such aberrations and crude reversals should not divert our attention from genuine paths of recovering natural freedom. At their best, Japanese thinkers have conveyed ways of casting off both individual and collective egoism through practices of returning ever again to the wellsprings of a nondual naturalness that is a source of both compassionate responsibility and creative freedom.

BIBLIOGRAPHY AND SUGGESTED READINGS

Davis, Bret W. (2007) "Does a Dog See Into Its Buddha-nature? Re-posing the Question of Animality/Humanity in Zen Buddhism." In *Buddha Nature and Animality*, edited by David Jones. Fremont, CA: Jain Publishing.

Dōgen Kigen. (2002) *The Heart of Dōgen's Shōbōgenzō*, translated by Norman Waddell and Masao Abe. Albany, NY: SUNY Press.

Kim, Hee-Jin. (1987) *Dōgen Kigen: Mystical Realist* (revised ed.). Tucson, AZ: The University of Arizona Press.

Kimura Bin. (1988) "Self and Nature—An Interpretation of Schizophrenia." *Zen Buddhism Today* 6, 1–10.

LaFleur, William R. (1989) "Saigyō and the Buddhist Value of Nature." In *Nature in Asian Traditions of Thought: Essays in Environmental Philosophy*, edited by J. Baird Callicott and Roger T. Ames. Albany, NY: SUNY Press.

Maruyama, Masao. (1974) *Studies in the Intellectual History of Tokugawa Japan*, translated by Mikiso Hane. Tokyo: University of Tokyo Press.

Nishida Kitarō. (1987) *Last Writings: Nothingness and the Religious Worldview*, translated by David A. Dilworth. Honolulu, HI: University of Hawaii Press.

37. Ibid., 81, translation modified.

NISHITANI, KEIJI. (1982) *Religion and Nothingness*, translated by Jan Van Bragt. Berkeley, CA: University of California Press.

———. (2005) "On Nature," translated by Aihara Setsuko and Graham Parkes. In *Confluences: Studies from East to West in Honor of V. H. Viglielmo*, edited by William Ridgeway and Nobuko Ochner. Honolulu, HI: University of Hawaii Press.

SUZUKI, D. T. (1996) "The Role of Nature in Zen Buddhism." In *Zen Buddhism: Selected Writings of D. T. Suzuki*, edited by William Barrett. New York: Doubleday.

TAKUAN SŌHŌ. (1986) *The Unfettered Mind*, translated by William Scott Wilson. Tokyo: Kodansha.

UNNO, TAITETSU. (1998) *River of Fire, River of Water: An Introduction to the Pure Land Tradition of Shin Buddhism*. New York: Doubleday.

CHAPTER 25

THE PHILOSOPHY OF ZEN MASTER DŌGEN: EGOLESS PERSPECTIVISM

BRET W. DAVIS

> Carrying the self forward to verify-in-practice the myriad things is delusion; for the myriad things to come forth and verify-in-practice the self is enlightenment.
>
> ... [When] a person verifies-in-practice the Buddha Way, attaining one thing he or she becomes thoroughly familiar with that one thing; encountering one activity he or she [sincerely] practices that one activity. Since this is where the place [of the presencing of truth] is and the Way achieves its circulation, the reason that the limits of what is knowable are not known is that this knowing arises and proceeds together with the exhaustive fathoming of the Buddha Dharma.[1]

Dōgen Kigen (1200–1253), founder of the Sōtō school of Zen Buddhism, is undoubtedly one of the most original and profound thinkers in Japanese history. The focus of this chapter will be on Dōgen's *Genjōkōan*, which can be translated as "The Presencing of Truth."[2] This key text for understanding Dōgen's thought is the core fascicle of his major work, *Shōbōgenzō* (Treasury of the True Dharma Eye). It

1. Dōgen 1990a, 1:54 and 59; compare Dōgen 2002, 40 and 44. Most of my primary references will be to Dōgen 1990a, a reliable and readily available Japanese edition of the *Shōbōgenzō* in four volumes. Although all translations of quoted passages from Dōgen's texts will be my own, for the reader's convenience I will cross-reference available English translations in addition to citing the original Japanese texts.

2. For a full translation of this text, together with an essay that includes an explanation of the title as well as an earlier version of parts of the present chapter, see Bret W. Davis, "The Presencing of Truth: Dōgen's *Genjōkōan*," in *Buddhist Philosophy: Essential Readings*, ed. William Edelglass and Jay

is the "treasury of the true Dharma eye" that Śākyamuni Buddha (ca. 500 BCE) is said to have transmitted to his successor, Mahākāshyapa, by silently holding up a flower. This event is held to mark the beginning of the Zen tradition, which is characterized by Bodhidharma (ca. 500 CE) as "a special transmission outside the scriptures; not depending on words and letters; directly pointing to the human mind; seeing into one's nature and becoming a Buddha." Like Bodhidharma, who is said to have sat in meditation for nine years after bringing Zen (Ch. Chan) from India to China, Dōgen too placed great emphasis on the silent practice of "just sitting" (*shikantaza*).

Yet Dōgen's writings are not just expedient means to practice and enlightenment, fingers pointing at the moon; they are also literary and philosophical masterpieces in their own right. Indeed, Dōgen is considered by many to be the greatest "philosopher" in the tradition of Zen Buddhism.[3] Rather than merely insist on the limits of language and reason, he poetically and philosophically manifests their expressive potential. The "entangled vines" (*kattō*) of language are not treated simply as impediments to be cut through with the sword of silent meditation and ineffable insight. Instead, they are understood to have the potential to become "expressive attainments of the Way" (*dōtoku*) that manifest perspectival aspects of the dynamic Buddha-nature of reality.[4]

Dōgen accepts the delimited and delimiting nature of language and of thought in general. And yet, he does not think that the perspectival limits of all perception, feeling, and understanding are as such antithetical to enlightenment. Rather than an overcoming of perspectivism, enlightenment for Dōgen entails a radical reorientation and qualitative transformation of the process of perspectival delimitation. Nietzsche once wrote, "Egoism is the law of perspective applied to feelings."[5] Dōgen would say that "egoistic perspectivism" well describes a state of delusion. Enlightenment, on the other hand, is precisely a matter of shedding the egoistic will to posit oneself as the fixed center of the world. Nevertheless, according to Dōgen, enlightenment does not supplant perspectival knowing with an omniscient "view from nowhere." Rather, it involves an ongoing nondual engagement in a process of

L. Garfield (Oxford: Oxford University Press, 2009), pp. 251–259. Other translations of *Genjōkoan* include "Manifesting Suchness" (Waddell and Abe 2002), "Manifesting Absolute Reality" (Cook 1989), "The Realized Universe" (Nishijima and Cross 1994), "Actualizing the Fundamental Point" (Tanahashi 1985), and "Offenbarmachen des vollen Erscheinens" (Ōhashi and Elberfeld 2006).

3. Dōgen was first treated as a "philosopher" in Japan in the early twentieth century, most notably by Watsuji Tetsurō (1889–1960) and by Tanabe Hajime (1885–1962). Prior to that, the study of his texts had been confined to Sōtō sectarian exegesis, culminating in *Shōbōgenzō keiteki* (Tokyo: Daihōrinkaku, 1965, originally published posthumously in 1930), a detailed and influential commentary by Nishiari Bokusan (1821–1910). For an engaging example of a recent Zen master's commentary, which is frequently sharply critical of Nishiari's interpretations, see Yasutani 1996. Philosophical studies of Dōgen in the West include Abe 1992; Heine 1994; Kasulis 1981; Hee-Jin Kim 2004, 2007; and Kopf 2002.

4. See Dōgen 1999, 163–172, 179–184; Heine 1994, 243–249; and Cook 1989, 101–106.

5. Friedrich Nietzsche, *The Gay Science*, trans. Walter Kaufmann (New York: Vintage Books, 1974), p. 199 (§162); see also Friedrich Nietzsche, *The Will to Power*, trans. Walter Kaufmann and R. J. Hollingdale (New York: Vintage Books, 1967), p. 340 (§637).

letting the innumerable perspectival aspects of reality illuminate themselves. Enlightenment thus entails an egoless and nondual perspectivism.

Dōgen would agree with Heidegger that any manifestation of truth always involves both a revealing and a concealing.[6] As Dōgen puts it, "When one side is illuminated, the other side is darkened."[7] This epistemological principle is one of the central themes of his thought, and it can be found at work already in the famous opening section of the *Genjōkōan*. Since these programmatic yet laconic first four sentences of the text are often thought to contain the kernel of Dōgen's philosophy of Zen, let us begin by quoting and explicating them. As we shall see, these few lines can be read as a compact history of the unfolding of Buddhist thought from its foundational teachings through Mahāyāna philosophies to Dōgen's Zen.

Through Buddhism to Zen

> When the various things [*dharmas*] are [seen according to] the Buddha's teaching [Buddha Dharma], there are delusion and enlightenment; there is (transformative) practice; there is birth/life; there is death; there are ordinary sentient beings; and there are Buddhas.
>
> When the myriad things are each [seen as] without self [i.e., as without independent substantiality], there is neither delusion nor enlightenment; there are neither Buddhas nor ordinary sentient beings; and there is neither birth/life nor death.
>
> Since the Buddha Way originally leaps beyond both plentitude and poverty, there are arising and perishing; there are delusion and enlightenment; and there are ordinary sentient beings and Buddhas.
>
> And yet, although this is how we can say that it is, it is just that flowers fall amid our attachment and regret, and weeds flourish amid our rejecting and loathing.[8]

While the first sentence speaks from the temporal perspective of "*when* the various things are [seen according to] the Buddha's teaching...," the second sentence speaks from that of "*when* the myriad things are each [seen as] without self...." What is affirmed in the first sentence is strikingly negated in the second. What is Dōgen doing here in this overturning alteration of perspective? While the first sentence sets forth several fundamental distinctions that constitute the basic teachings of Buddhism—such as that between ordinary sentient beings and their delusion on the one hand and Buddhas and their enlightenment on the other—the second sentence, by focusing now on the central teaching of no-self (*anātman*), goes on to

6. See Martin Heidegger, "The Essence of Truth," in *Pathmarks*, ed. William McNeill (Cambridge: Cambridge University Press).

7. Dōgen 1990a, 1:54; compare Dōgen 2002, 41.

8. Dōgen 1990a, 1:53; compare Dōgen 2002, 40.

negate *the reification of* these oppositional designations. For readers familiar with Mahāyāna Buddhism's Perfection of Wisdom literature, such self-deconstructive negations in a Buddhist text do not come as too much of a surprise. *The Heart Sutra*, for example, radicalizes the early Buddhist doctrine of no-self into that of the emptiness (*śūnyatā*; i.e., the lack of independent substantiality) of all phenomenal elements of existence (*dharmas*) and linguistic conventions, even to the point of a systematic negation of (a reified misunderstanding of) traditional Buddhist teachings themselves, including the Four Noble Truths and the Eightfold Path. *The Heart Sutra* also speaks of no-birth, no-death, and no-attainment, rather than of nirvāna as the attainment of a release from samsāra as the cycle of birth and death.[9]

Furthermore, readers familiar with Mādhyamaka philosopher Nāgārjuna's notion of the "emptiness of emptiness" (i.e., the idea that emptiness itself is not an independently substantial entity, but rather is the nature of events of interdependent origination [*pratītya-samutpāda*]),[10] and with Tiantai (Jap. Tendai) philosopher Zhiyi's development of the Two Truths (i.e., the conventional truth of provisional designations and the ultimate truth of emptiness) into the Three Truths of "the provisional, the empty, and the middle,"[11] will be prepared for the third sentence of the *Genjōkōan*. No longer qualified by a "when . . .," the "middle" perspective expressed here resolves the tension between the first two perspectives so as to make possible the reaffirmation of distinctions, but now without reification. In fact, in its teaching of the ontological middle way of interdependent origination, Buddhism has always rejected nihilism and annihilationism along with substantialism and eternalism. The Buddhist account of the interdependent and dynamic nature of reality and the self is not subject to the "all or nothing" dilemma that plagues an ontology of independent and eternal substances. As Dōgen says here, "the Buddha Way originally leaps beyond both plentitude [i.e., substantial being] and poverty [i.e., nihilistic void]." Affirmatively thought, using the language of the Three Truths, the Buddhist *middle* way embraces the nondual polarity of the *provisional* "plentitude" of differentiated being and the "poverty" or substantial *emptiness* of ubiquitous interdependent origination.

It is possible to relate these first three sentences of the *Genjōkōan* not only to the Three Truths of Tiantai (Tendai) philosophy, but also to Chan Master Weixin's famous three stages on the way to enlightenment, according to which a mountain is first seen as a mountain (i.e., as a conceptual reification), then not as a mountain (i.e., as empty of independent substantiality and linguistic reification), and finally really as a mountain (i.e., in the suchness of its interdependent origination).[12] The path of the Buddha Way ultimately leads one back to the here and now.

9. See Hanh 1988, and Lopez 1988.

10. See Garfield 1995.

11. See Swanson 1995.

12. However, just as each of Tiantai's Three Truths is affirmed as a view of the truth, many traditional commentators (including Nishiari) stress that each of the first three sentences of the *Genjōkōan* ultimately has its own unassailable validity as a perspectival expression of the whole truth.

Be that as it may, and although we should bear in mind that Dōgen was first of all trained as a Tendai monk and was intimately familiar with doctrines such as the Three Truths, it is also important to recall that he was from an early age dissatisfied with the then-prevalent doctrine of "original enlightenment" (*hongaku*). What concerned the young Dōgen was that a premature and blanket affirmation of the self and the world of distinctions *as they are* tends to deny or at least downplay the importance of transformative practices of cultivation (*shugyō*). This dissatisfaction and concern finally induced him to come down from Tendai's Mt. Hiei on a path that led him to Zen.

The primary and ultimate standpoint of Dōgen's Zen is most directly expressed in the climactic—and, in a sense, intentionally anticlimactic—fourth sentence of the *Genjōkōan*. Here Dōgen calls for a return from the heights of reason (*ri*) to the basis of fact (*ji*), that is, to the nonidealized here and now of concrete experience, where "flowers fall amid our attachment and regret, and weeds flourish amid our rejecting and loathing." I would suggest that this crucial sentence, like so many in Dōgen's often polysemous texts, can be read in at least two ways. On the one hand, as the expression of the concrete experiences of enlightened existence, it signifies that nirvāna is not somewhere beyond the trials and tribulations of samsāra (the realm of desire and suffering). Rather, it is a matter of "awakening in the midst of the passions" (*bonnō soku bodai*). Like the Daoist sage's uninhibited weeping at his wife's funeral, Zen enlightenment is not an escapist dying to, but rather a wholehearted dying into a liberated and liberating engagement in the human life of emotional entanglements.

On the other hand, I think that this fourth sentence can also be read—on a less advanced but certainly no less significant level—as an acknowledgement that no amount of rational explanation of the nonduality of samsāra and nirvāna can bring about an actual realization of this truth. In *Fukanzazengi* Dōgen writes: "From the beginning the Way circulates everywhere; why the need to verify it in practice? . . . And yet, if there is the slightest discrepancy, heaven and earth are vastly separated; if the least disorder arises, the heart and mind get lost in confusion."[13] And he tells us in *Bendōwa*: "Although the truth [Dharma] amply inheres in every person, without practice, it does not presence; if it is not verified, it is not attained."[14] Religious practice is necessary, which, for Dōgen, involves not just the practice of meditative concentration, but also the practice of thoughtful discrimination. Hence, after the opening section of the *Genjōkōan* he proceeds to concretely describe—by means of what has been aptly called a "transformative phenomenology"[15]—the conversion from a deluded/deluding to an enlightened/enlightening comportment to the world.

13. Dōgen 1990b, 171; compare Dōgen 2002, 2–3.
14. Dōgen 1990a, 1:11; compare Dōgen 2002, 8; also see Dōgen 1985, 87.
15. See Elberfeld 2004, 382.

Verification: The Practice of Enlightenment

A deluding experience of the world, according to Dōgen, occurs when one "carries the self forward to verify-in-practice (*shushō*) the myriad things." On the other hand, "for the myriad things to come forth and verify-in-practice the self is enlightenment."[16] In order to appreciate this explanation of delusion and enlightenment, we need to first discuss Dōgen's peculiar notion of *shushō*. In this term, Dōgen conjoins two characters to convey the inseparable nonduality of "practice" and "enlightenment (verification)."[17] This key aspect of Dōgen's teaching is poignantly addressed in the concluding section of the *Genjōkōan*, where the action of the Zen master fanning himself (practice) is demonstrated to be one with the truth that the wind (Buddha-nature) circulates everywhere.

> As Chan Master Baoche of Mount Mayu was using his fan, a monk came and asked, "It is the wind's nature to be constantly abiding and there is no place in which it does not circulate. Why then, sir, do you still use a fan?"
>
> The master said, "You only know that it is the nature of the wind to be constantly abiding. You don't yet know the reason [more literally: the principle of the way] that there is no place it does not reach."
>
> The monk said, "What is the reason for there being no place in which it does not circulate?"
>
> At which time the master just used his fan.
>
> The monk bowed reverently.
>
> The verifying experience of the Buddha Dharma and the vital path of its true transmission are like this. To say that if it is constantly abiding one shouldn't use a fan, that even without using a fan one should be able to feel the wind, is to not know [the meaning of] either constantly abiding or the nature of the wind.[18]

Enlightenment, for Dōgen, is found not in inactive detachment, nor in a passive acceptance of the way things are, but rather in the midst of a holistic participation—an engaged playing of one's part—in the world.

The character for *shō*, which is Dōgen's favored term for enlightenment, normally means to verify, prove, attest to, confirm, or authenticate something. As a synonym for enlightenment, *shō* is a matter of *verifying* ("showing to be true" and literally "making true") and hence *realizing* (awakening to and thus actualizing) the fact that one's true self (*honbunnin*), one's "original part," is originally part and parcel of the dynamically ubiquitous Buddha-nature. In the *Busshō* fascicle of the *Shōbōgenzō*, Dōgen famously rereads the *Mahāparinirvāna Sūtra*'s claim that "all

16. Dōgen 1990a, 1:54; compare Dōgen 2002, 40.
17. See Dōgen 1990a, 1:28; Dōgen 2002, 19.
18. Dōgen 1990a, 1:60; compare Dōgen 2002, 44–45.

sentient beings have the Buddha-nature" to mean that "Buddha-nature is all that is" (*shitsu-u wa busshō nari*).[19] Enlightenment is a matter of *verifying-in-practice* this fundamental fact. It is a matter of *authentication*, of truly becoming what one in truth is: a unique expression of a universally shared Buddha-nature.

Learning to Forget the Self

The self is a participant in the dynamically interconnected matrix of the world. Delusion occurs when the self egoistically posits itself as the single fixed center—rather than existing as one among infinitely many mutually reflective and expressive focal points—of the whole.[20] In delusion the myriad things are seen, not according to the self-expressive aspects through which they show themselves, but rather only as they are forced into the perspectival horizon of the self-fixated and self-assertive ego. To borrow the language of Kant, the deluded and deluding ego willfully projects its own forms of intuition and categories of understanding onto the world. In contrast, through practicing the Buddha Way one comes to realize the empty (i.e., open and interdependent) nature of the true self.

Dōgen describes the steps of this process of practice and enlightenment in three of the most frequently cited lines of the *Genjōkōan*:

> To learn the Buddha Way is to learn the self.
> To learn the self is to forget the self.
> To forget the self is to be verified by the myriad things [of the world].[21]

The study of Buddhism, according to Dōgen's Zen, involves more than a cognitive grasp of the truth of the Buddhist teachings (Buddha Dharma; *buppō*). It involves a holistic practice of a way of life (Buddha Way; *butsudō*).[22] The central practice of the Buddha Way for Dōgen, and for the Zen tradition in general, is seated meditation (*zazen*),[23] rather than the study of scriptures, the performance of esoteric rituals, or calling on the grace of a transcendent savior. According to Zen, "what comes through the gate [i.e., from outside of oneself] is not the treasure of the house"; the truth

19. Dōgen 1990a, 1:73; compare Dōgen 2002, 61.

20. As with much of Zen thought, Dōgen's perspectivism is heavily influenced by Huayan (Jap. Kegon) philosophy, which in turn draws upon the *Avatamsaka Sūtra*'s image of the "jewel net of Indra" wherein each jewel reflects all the others. See Cook 1977 and Chang 1971.

21. Dōgen 1990a, 1:54; compare Dōgen 2002, 41.

22. Note the terminological shift from "Buddha Dharma" to "Buddha Way" in the first section of the *Genjōkōan*. In Japan, the terms traditionally used for "Buddhism" (now *bukkyō*) were *buppō* (Buddha Dharma or Law, which refers to the Buddhist teachings or the truth indicated by those teachings) and *butsudō* (Buddha Way, which refers to the practice of the way of the Buddha).

23. The very word "Zen" derives from the Sanskrit *dhyāna*, meaning meditation.

must be discovered within. Dōgen thus speaks of meditation as a practice of taking a radical "step back that turns the light around."[24]

The light of our unenlightened minds is generally directed outward, shining its objectifying gaze on things and on a projected image of the ego itself. Things and other persons become objects of attachment (or aversion), possessions (or enemies) of a reified conception of the self as ego-subject. But things and persons change and otherwise refuse to obey one's will, ever slipping from the grasp of the ego, which is itself constantly subject to mutation and otherwise fails to live up to the self-constructed image of itself. Hence, repeatedly disappointed and frustrated, the ego suffers the resistance of the world and, out of greed, hate, and delusion, inflicts suffering on others. Ironically, the Buddha Dharma itself, as with any teaching, can be turned into just another object of dogmatic and even fanatic attachment, diverting us from the root of the problem, namely, a false conception of ourselves and our relation to the world. Therefore, the Buddha Way first of all requires a penetrating examination of the self.

Yet when one turns the light around to reflect on the deepest recesses of the self, what one ultimately finds is—nothing. There is no substantial ego-subject underlying our thoughts, feelings, and desires. But neither is this nothingness—or emptiness—a nihilistic void. Rather, the ungraspable nothingness of the self is the very source of the open-minded, open-hearted, and creatively free activity of the true self. The true self is an open engagement with others. A thoroughgoing "learning the self" thus paradoxically leads to a "forgetting of the self" as an independent and substantial ego-subject.

Dōgen speaks of this "forgetting" most radically in terms of his own enlightenment experience of "dropping off the body-mind" (*shinjin-datsuraku*). Note that Dōgen does not speak dualistically of freeing the mind from the body. In fact, he explicitly rejects the mind/body dualism of the so-called Senika heresy, and speaks of the "oneness of body-mind" (*shinjin ichinyo*) along with the nonduality of the "one mind" with the entire cosmos.[25] Insofar as we have identified ourselves with a dualistic and reified conception of the mind, however, along with the body this too must be shed. Only through a radical experience of letting go of all reifications of and attachments to the mind as well as the body does one become open to the self-presentation of the myriad things.

Yet this openness must be realized, and this realization is neither static nor simply passive. When Dōgen says that "things come forth and verify-in-practice the self" (elsewhere he even claims that "original practice inheres in the original face of each and every thing"[26]), he is countering the willful self-assertion of unenlightened human subjectivity by calling attention to the "objective side" of the "total dynamism" or "undivided activity" (*zenki*) of a nondual experience of reality. Elsewhere he speaks of the *nonduality* of this experience as follows: "When you ride in a boat, body-and-mind, self-and-environs, subjectivity-and-objectivity are all together the

24. *Dōgen Zenji goroku*, 170; compare Dōgen 2002, 3.

25. See Dōgen 2002, 21–23, and Dōgen 1994, 41–46. On the notion of "body-mind" in Dōgen, see Yuasa 1987, 111–123; Nagatomo 1992, 105–129; and Shaner 1985, 129–155.

26. Dōgen 1990a, 1:18; compare Dōgen 2002, 14.

undivided activity of the boat. The entire earth as well as the entire sky are the undivided activity of the boat."[27] For our part, in order to authentically participate in this nondual event—and hence to verify or realize this or that aspect of reality—we must not only liberate ourselves from a self-assertive fixation on our body-mind by letting it drop off; we must also spontaneously pick up the body-mind again in an energetic yet egoless "total exertion" (*gūjin*) of "rousing the [whole] body-mind to perceive forms, rousing the [whole] body-mind to listen to sounds."[28]

Let us pause for a moment to review the pivotal paradoxes involved in Dōgen's path of Zen. (1) Turning to and from ourselves: By way of initially turning the light of the mind away from (a deluded view of) external reality and back toward ourselves, we discover an emptiness at the heart of the self that opens us up to an enlightened experience of the myriad things of the world. (2) Utter detachment and total involvement: This process of enlightenment entails a radical "dropping off the body-mind" that leads, not to a state of mindless disembodiment, but rather to a holistic integration of the body-mind and its unattached yet wholehearted employment in nondual events of enlightening perception and understanding.

Nondual Perspectivism

The intimately engaged yet egoless perception and understanding that Dōgen speaks of are, however, never shadowless illuminations of all aspects of a thing. The epistemology implied in Dōgen's understanding of enlightenment is plainly not that of simultaneous omniscience. Enlightenment does not entail the achievement of an instantaneous all-knowing view from nowhere, but rather the realization of being on an endless path of illuminating the innumerable aspects of reality, an ongoing journey of appreciating the "inexhaustible virtues" of things. Enlightenment is not a state of final escape to another world, but rather a never self-satisfied process of enlightening darkness and delusion within this world. Indeed, setting out on this never-ending Way of enlightenment entails awakening to the ineradicable play of knowledge and nescience. And thus, once again paradoxically, Dōgen tells us: "When the Dharma does not yet saturate the body-mind, one thinks that it is sufficient. If the Dharma fills the body-mind, one notices an insufficiency."[29] This is Dōgen's version of the Socratic wisdom of knowing one's ignorance.

27. Dōgen 1990a, 2:84; compare Dōgen 1999, 174.

28. Dōgen 1990a, 1:54; compare Dōgen 2002, 41. There are contrasting interpretations of this passage. Along with most scholars, I have interpreted this "rousing the [whole] body-mind to perceive and listen" in terms of enlightenment. Other scholars have read it in terms of delusion. For a noteworthy example of the latter interpretation, see "'Genjōkōan' to shizen," in *Ueda Shizuteru shū* [Ueda Shizuteru Collection] (Tokyo: Iwanami, 2002), 9:286ff.

29. Dōgen 1990a, 1:57; compare Dōgen 2002, 43.

Dōgen makes this epistemological point most clearly and forcefully in the section of *Genjōkōan* where he speaks of the inexhaustible aspects and virtues of the ocean.

> For example, if one rides in a boat out into the middle of the ocean where there are no mountains [in sight] and looks in the four directions, one will see only a circle without any other aspects in sight. Nevertheless, the great ocean is not circular, and it is not square; the remaining virtues of the ocean are inexhaustible. It is like a palace [for fish]. It is like a jeweled ornament [to gods]. It is just that, as far as my eyes can see, for a while it looks like a circle. It is also like this with the myriad things. Although things within and beyond this dusty world are replete with a variety of aspects, it is only through a cultivated power of vision that one can [intimately] perceive and apprehend them. In order to hear the household customs of the myriad things, you should know that, besides appearing as round or square, there are unlimited other virtues of the ocean and of the mountains, and there are worlds in all four directions. And you should know that it is not only like this over there, but also right here beneath your feet and even in a single drop [of water].[30]

When Dōgen speaks of a human being sitting on a boat in the middle of the ocean, looking out in all four directions and seeing only a vast empty circle, he is perhaps not only speaking literally but also metaphorically of a meditative experience of emptiness. We might refer in this regard to the "empty circle" or "circular shape" (*ensō*) that appears as the eighth of the *Ten Oxherding Pictures*,[31] which is often interpreted as a symbol for the absolute emptiness of the Dharmakāya (the Truth Body of the Buddha), or the Buddha-nature (*Busshō*) understood—as Dōgen and other Zen masters sometimes do—in terms of *mu-Busshō* ("no-Buddha-nature" or the "Buddha-nature-of-Nothingness").

In any case, what is crucial is that neither the *Ten Oxherding Pictures* nor Dōgen's Zen stops here at the empty circle. It may be necessary to pass through an experience of emptiness as a "great negation" of the ego and its reifying attachments, and as the realization of absolute equality and equanimity. But even emptiness must not become a "perspectiveless perspective" to which one becomes attached. In the all-embracing "one taste" of perfect equality, the differences between singular things are concealed. Here, too, "emptiness must empty itself" and allow for distinctions, such that true nonduality is a matter of "not one and not two" (*fuichi funi*). The universal truth of emptiness is not an overarching perspective that negates, but rather a pervading principle that enables the interplay between unique yet interconnected beings. In its "suchness," each thing, person, animal, or event is neither an independent substance nor an indistinct portion of an undifferentiated totality: rather, it is a unique perspectival opening within the dynamically interweaving web of the world.

30. Dōgen 1990a, 1:57–58; compare Dōgen 2002, 43.
31. See Yamada 2004.

Hence, even though one may perceive the ocean (or world) as a vast empty circle, Dōgen goes on to write: "Nevertheless, the great ocean is not circular, and it is not square; the remaining virtues [or qualities] of the ocean are inexhaustible. It is like a palace [for fish]. It is like a jeweled ornament [to gods]. It is just that, as far as my eyes can see, for a while it looks like a circle." Dōgen is drawing here on the traditional Buddhist notion that different sentient beings experience the world in different manners, depending on the conditioning of their karma. He is likely alluding specifically to the following commentary on the *Mahāyāna-saṃgraha*: "The sea itself basically has no disparities, yet owing to the karmic differences of devas, humans, craving spirits, and fish, devas see it as a treasure trove of jewels, humans see it as water, craving spirits see it as an ocean of pus, and fish see it as a palatial dwelling."[32] Dōgen writes elsewhere that one "should not be limited to human views" and naively think that what you view as water is "what dragons and fish see as water and use as water."[33]

The epistemology implied in Dōgen's view of enlightenment as an ongoing practice of enlightening, as an unending path of discovery, is thus what I would call an engaged yet egoless, a pluralistic yet nondual perspectivism. It is a perspectivism insofar as reality only shows itself one aspect and focal point at a time. On the one hand, in a deluded/deluding comportment to the world this aspect and focus get determined by the will of a self-fabricating ego that goes out and posits a horizon that delimits, filters, and schematizes how things can reveal themselves (namely, as objects set in front of a subject who represents and manipulates them). On the other hand, in an enlightened/enlightening comportment to the world, things are allowed to reveal themselves through nondual events in which the self has "forgotten itself" in its pure activity of egoless engagement. This engagement is neither simply passive nor simply active; for, originally, we are not detached ego-subjects who subsequently encounter (either passively or actively) independently subsisting objects. The original force at work in experience is neither "self-power" (*jiriki*) nor "other-power" (*tariki*). Rather, writes Dōgen, the "continuous practice" (*gyōji*) one participates in is "pure action that is forced neither by oneself nor by others."[34] At every moment of enlightened/enlightening experience there is—for the time being—but a single nondual middle-voiced event of "being-time" (*uji*)[35] as a self-revelation of a singular aspect of reality. Enlightenment is a matter of realizing that the world is in truth made up of such nondual self-revelatory events. And just as these interconnected yet unique events are infinite, so is the path of their verification-in-practice.

32. Quoted in Dōgen 2002, 43; see also Dōgen 1990a, 1:440.

33. Dōgen 1990a, 2:198.

34. Dōgen 1990a, 1:297; compare Dōgen 1999, 114.

35. In the *Uji* fascicle (Dōgen 1990a, 2:46ff.; Dōgen 2002, 48ff.), Dōgen famously reads the compound *uji*, not simply as "for the time being," but as a nondual event of "being-time." On this important aspect of his thought, see Heine 1985; Stambaugh 1990; and Elberfeld 2004.

BIBLIOGRAPHY AND SUGGESTED READINGS

ABE, MASAO. (1992) *A Study of Dōgen: His Philosophy and Religion*, edited by Steven Heine. Albany, NY: State University of New York Press.

CHANG, GARMA C. C. (1971) *The Buddhist Teaching of Totality: The Philosophy of Hwa Yen Buddhism*. University Park, PA: The Pennsylvania State University Press.

COOK, FRANCIS H. (1977) *Hua-yen Buddhism: The Jewel Net of Indra*. University Park, PA: The Pennsylvania State University Press.

———. (1989) *Sounds of Valley Streams: Enlightenment in Dōgen's Zen*. Albany, NY: State University of New York Press.

———. (2002) *How to Raise an Ox: Zen Practice as Taught in Zen Master Dogen's Shobogenzo*. Somerville, MA: Wisdom Publications.

DŌGEN. (1971) *A Primer of Sōtō Zen: A Translation of Dōgen's Shōbōgenzō Zuimonki*, translated by Reihō Masunaga. Honolulu, HI: University of Hawaii Press.

———. (1985) *Flowers of Emptiness: Selections from Dōgen's Shōbōgenzō*, translated by Hee-Jin Kim. Lewiston, ME: Edwin Mellen Press.

———. (1990a) *Shōbōgenzō*, edited by Mizuno Yaoko. 4 vols. Tokyo: Iwanami.

———. (1990b) *Dōgen Zenji goroku*, edited by Kagamishima Genryū. Tokyo: Kōdansha.

———. (1992) *Rational Zen: The Mind of Dōgen Zenji*. Translated by Thomas Cleary. Boston, MA: Shambhala.

———. (1994–1999) *Master Dōgen's Shobogenzo*, translated by Gudo Nishijima and Chodo Cross. 4 vols. Charleston, SC: BookSurge Publishing.

———. (1995) *Moon in a Dewdrop: Writings of Zen Master Dogen*, edited by Kazuaki Tanahashi. New York: North Point Press.

———. (1999) *Enlightenment Unfolds: The Essential Teachings of Zen Master Dōgen*. Boston, MA: Shambhala.

———. (2002) *The Heart of Dōgen's Shōbōgenzō*, translated by Norman Waddell and Masao Abe. Albany, NY: State University of New York Press.

———. (2004) *Beyond Thinking: A Guide to Meditation*, edited by Kazuaki Tanahashi. Boston, MA: Shambhala.

ELBERFELD, ROLF. (2004) *Phänomenologie der Zeit im Buddhismus*. Stuttgart: frommann holzboog.

GARFIELD, JAY. (1995) *Fundamental Wisdom of the Middle Way: Nāgārjuna's Mūlamadhyamakakārikā*. New York: Oxford University Press.

HANH, THICH NHAT. (1988). *The Heart of Understanding: Commentaries on the Prajñaparamita Heart Sutra*. Berkeley, CA: Parallax Press.

HEINE, STEVEN. (1985) *Existential and Ontological Dimensions of Time in Heidegger and Dōgen*. Albany, NY: State University of New York Press.

———. (1994) *Dōgen and the Kōan Tradition: A Tale of Two Shōbōgenzō*. Albany, NY: State University of New York Press.

KASULIS T. P. (1981) *Zen Action/Zen Person*. Honolulu, HI: University of Hawaii Press.

KIM, HEE-JIN. (2004) *Dōgen: Mystical Realist*. Boston, MA: Wisdom.

———. (2007) *Dōgen on Meditation and Thinking: A Reflection on His View of Zen*. Albany, NY: State University of New York Press.

KOPF, GEREON. (2002) *Beyond Personal Identity: Dōgen, Nishida and a Phenomenology of No-Self*. Richmond, Surrey: Routledge.

LaFleur, William R. (ed.). (1985) *Dōgen Studies*. Honolulu, HI: University of Hawaii Press.

Lopez, Donald S., Jr. (1988) *The Heart Sūtra Explained*. Albany, NY: State University of New York Press.

Nagatomo, Shigenori. (1992) *Attunement Through the Body*. Albany, NY: State University of New York Press.

Ōhashi, Ryōsuke, and Rolf Elberfeld. (2006) *Dōgen Shōbōgenzō: Ausgewählte Schriften*. Tokyo: Keio University Press.

Shaner, David Edward. (1985) *The Bodymind Experience in Japanese Buddhism: A Phenomenological Study of Kūkai and Dōgen*. Albany, NY: State University of New York Press.

Stambaugh, Joan. (1990) *Impermanence is Buddha-nature: Dōgen's Understanding of Temporality*. Honolulu, HI: University of Hawaii Press.

Steineck, Christian, et al. (eds.). (2002) *Dōgen als Philosoph*. Wiesbaden: Harrassowitz Verlag.

Swanson, Paul. (1995) *Foundations of T'ien-T'ai Philosophy: The Flowering of the Two Truths Theory in Chinese Buddhism*. Berkeley, CA: Asian Humanities Press.

Yamada, Mumon. (2004) *Lectures on the Ten Oxherding Pictures*, translated by Victor Sogen Hori. Honolulu, HI: University of Hawaii Press.

Yasutani, Hakuun. (1996) *Flowers Fall: A Commentary on Zen Master Dōgen's Genjōkōan*, translated by Paul Jaffe. Boston, MA: Shambhala.

Yuasa, Yasuo. (1987) *The Body: Toward an Eastern Mind-Body Theory*. Albany, NY: State University of New York Press.

CHAPTER 26

NISHIDA KITARŌ: SELF, WORLD, AND THE NOTHINGNESS UNDERLYING DISTINCTIONS

JOHN C. MARALDO

The Significance of Nishida Kitarō

Is there an ultimate context that encompasses not only the terms in which we conceptualize the world but also everything, every being, even the world itself? That question was a central concern of Nishida Kitarō (1870–1945) in the mature stage of his philosophy. Nishida, widely recognized as the most important Japanese philosopher of the twentieth century and the founder of the Kyoto School, authored some twenty volumes of essays influenced by Buddhist thought and deeply informed by the Anglo-European philosophy that was just beginning to be introduced to his country. Nishida began his work with the notion of "pure experience," the moment prior to any distinction between experiencing self and experienced object, as it founds the systematic development of our thinking about the world. After lengthy diversions into German and French dialectical thinking and Neo-Kantian philosophy to explain the nature of self-awareness, he returned to early Greek philosophy and Buddhist thinking and developed a novel alternative to the ways that philosophers have distinguished self and world and sought ultimate grounds for them.[1]

Nishida's alternative notion of "the place of absolute nothingness" that underlies all distinctions and contextualizes all grounds has profound significance for debates concerning the questions gathered under the labels of internalism and externalism, both cognitive and semantic. Once we see through his often forbidding language, his notion suggests a way to uncover the assumptions that both sides of the debate have in common. It points to the positive role that an obscure context plays in making distinctions. The "dazzling obscurity" that he called "the place of absolute nothingness" can be understood as the ultimate context of contexts, the common ground that makes distinctions possible—although it requires a modification in our usual conception of a *ground.* Just as Nishida's language is clarified by an analysis of distinction making, his own account of absolute nothingness, informed by Daoist and Zen Buddhist reflections, clarifies the relation between self and world.

Distinctions and the Opposition between Self and World

Making distinctions is at the heart of teaching and doing philosophy. Think of the importance of the distinctions—and often of the challenge to the distinctions—between what is and what ought to be, or between what something is and that it is, between synthetic and analytic, passive and active, empirical and transcendental, and so forth. More specifically, recall the distinctions that underlie disputes about the relation between self and world and between mind and world. Not only are the terms of the relation (*self* and *world* or *mind* and *world*) distinguished, but so too are the types of relationship in question: is mind self-contained and solely internal to the individual experiencing subject or are its contents dependent upon the environment and the world in general?

A primary interest shared by both sides in this dispute is to resist an overbearing imposition of our fallible minds and mental contents on the world, that is, to allow for resistance from the world as a corrective to our ideas. A second shared concern is to strictly preserve the features of experience that differentiate one individual from another. These concerns in turn imply two underlying distinctions, again shared by both sides of the dispute, namely, some distinction between mind and world, however disputed the bounds of the mind may be, and some distinction between individual minds. No matter how external or internal to the individual subject the content of her

1. *Pure experience* is developed in Nishida's first major work, *Zen no kenkyū* (Nishida 1911). I give a synopsis of the themes and development of Nishida's philosophy in Maraldo 2010. Davis 2010 places Nishida's work in the context of the Kyoto school.

mind and the meaning of her words may be, the mind is not thought to be wholly internal to the world; its fundamental distinction from world is maintained by both sides. These shared features conceal another, perhaps deeper, unsettled matter for both sides: the nature of the self in the background of this dispute. Is the self "self-contained" within the individual bodily subject, within one's skin so to speak, or does its extension reach beyond the body, at least the body as an object in the world? Is self rather a body-subject that reaches beyond the objective confines of the physical body? Is the "skin" of the self a perceptive organ that interacts with the environment and is not measurable by dimensions given by tape measures? Settling the dispute about the bounds of mind and its cognitions would require determining with much more precision the bounds of self and its transactions with the world. Yet again, whatever the position regarding the unsettled bounds of the self, the disputes presuppose its distinction from world. The talk of a "transaction" between perceptions, cognitions, or self on the one hand and world on the other implies this distinction. Even the most expansive notions of bodily self interacting with the world and with others, as we find in Merleau-Ponty, for example, assume a distinction between self and world. Heidegger's attempt to undermine commonplace assumptions by reformulating the terms and speaking of Being-in-the-World still differentiates between oneself and environment and between oneself and world as the ultimate context of meanings.

This chapter does not attempt to resolve these tangled issues or even describe them with more precision. Nor does it intend to question the fundamental distinction between self and world. Rather, it will present an alternative way, modeled after Nishida, to contextualize the distinctions and to understand the grounds of various levels of distinctions—both the grounds of distinctions like those mentioned above and the grounds of their various levels. It will present the ultimate "ground" as a nothingness with respect to all distinguished terms, and will thus call for a modification of the notion of ground. At the same time it will present a way to understand the meaning and function of *nothingness* in the philosophy of Nishida Kitarō and his East Asian sources.

Self and World in Nishida's Philosophy

Nishida developed a layered set of distinctions he took to be increasingly concrete, that is, inclusive of the terms abstracted out of their underlying context, and eventually he proposed "absolute nothingness" as the ultimate context.[2] Using his terms, we can begin with language and the logic of judgments and note the distinction

2. My variation here of Nishida's famous "logic of place" is geared toward an explication of a theory of distinctions and represents one among many interpretations. Nishida himself offered different versions during his career; one of the first is in essays in Nishida 1927. For other accounts see Maraldo 2010 and Wargo 2005, especially 121–178.

between the subjects and predicates of our judgments—without deciding whether or to what degree those predicates are internal or external to the judging individual. In judgments like "John is jealous of Mary" and "Eartheans mean H_2O to be water,"[3] we ascribe to a particular (grammatical) subject certain qualities or attributes, an emotion and a belief in these examples. The qualities or attributes "belong to" the grammatical subject. At the same time predicates name universals or at least general items not restricted to any particular subject. Judgments then are articulated states of affairs that form the context out of which grammatical subjects and predicates are distinguished. In other words, we can apprehend and then articulate a state of affairs that includes the subject and the predicate and that grounds the distinction between them—again without deciding the necessity or the degree of factors external to the individual who is judging.

Taken as the context that encompasses things and their characteristics or relations, the level of judgments leaves out the acts of mind or consciousness that formulate the judgments. Mind in the act of judging may be said to take the judgment, the articulated state of affairs (John is jealous of Mary, Eartheans think water is H_2O) as its proposed object for consideration—for confirmation or disconfirmation, for example. For Nishida, we must move to a more concrete context that includes both judgments and the mind as judging agent that is considering them. In Nishida's view, however, the acting mind is not simply one side of the distinction; rather, it includes both the act's object, the judgment, and the mind itself. This is because mind or consciousness in act is self-reflexive; however fallibly, it is aware of itself as well as of things in the world, and can thus distinguish between itself and things in the world.[4] Self-reflexive mind or consciousness forms the context out of which mind and things with their attributes are distinguished. The move to include judgments, with their grammatical subjects and predicates, within the context of self-aware mind might seem to imply some form of internalism and suggest that the content articulated in judgments is contained within an individual mind and thus independent of external factors in the world. Nishida's move as such, however, only acknowledges that judgments are the sorts of matters that are held, entertained, or proposed by minds. To use the previous example, Eartheans' belief that water is H_2O may or may not depend on factors outside Eartheans' minds, but the judgment about what Eartheans believe is proposed by someone and, for Nishida, belongs to the context of the self-aware mind considering the judgment. The appeal to a more inclusive context is not meant to settle the issue between internalism and externalism, but to show what both sides presuppose. We have seen how both assume a

3. The reference of water is to Hilary Putnam's famous "twin earth" thought experiment that generated much of the externalism-internalism debate: if *water* played exactly the same role in the thinking of two different societies but one usage referred to H_2O and the other to some other chemical compound, would the meaning of *water* be the same or not? See Hilary Putnam, "The meaning of 'meaning,'" in *Mind, Language and Reality: Philosophical Papers,* vol. 2 (Cambridge: Cambridge University Press, 1975).

4. For a more detailed analysis of Nishida's self-reflexive structure of consciousness and world, see Maraldo 2006.

distinction between mind and world and between one mind and another. If self-consciousness names a demarcation between self and others and self and world, then what is the context out of which these distinctions arise? We must proceed to the next level in Nishida's scheme to see their common ground.

The next level of concreteness is that of the world—not in the sense of some extramental reality, nor of a preexistent, nonhuman universe, nor of some projection or construction of mind, but rather world that creates knowing, embodied selves and is created by them. Nishida came to call this "the historical world" to emphasize the concrete and everyday space in which we live as embodied, enculturated selves immersed in the histories that we make and that make us.[5] The philosophical notions of minds as relatively isolated or self-contained units and of the world as a physical, nonhuman realm are abstracted from the historical world, as is any evidence supporting such notions. Here, too, we might ask whether the self-aware, judging mind is properly understood as a sole individual subject. To take the individual mind acting alone as the self-aware judging mind would be to abstract it from its context in a world of shared language, culture, and history—all factors that make judgments possible. Insofar as internalism and exernalism both recognize that meanings and beliefs are tied to language, culture, and history, they both can agree on this point. This is not to deny that there are individuals with their own mental features. But even to posit such individuating features requires a context of comparison that cannot be derived from any single such mind. Individual agents living in the historical world differentiate themselves from others and reciprocally are subject to differentiation; they create and are created by the historical world. The historical world thus is the context out of which actual, knowing selves are differentiated. This world displays a self-reflexive structure similar to that of self-aware minds, in that it refers to itself as including knowing, embodied selves.

If one were to understand the self-reflexive, historical world as a mind of a higher order, however, Nishida's scheme would amount to a form of panpsychism. This view either extends mind beyond individual subjects to some kind of universal mind or finds mind as a constitutive part of the universe. Mind in some sense is taken to be everywhere.[6] Panpsychism would collapse the distinction between mind and world that internalism and externalism hold in common. Nishida does not take that course, but instead maintains a distinction between individual selves as self-aware minds and the world that differentiates and contextualizes them. The world is "self-aware" in the sense that whatever is "in the world" is a reflection or mirroring of the world. In Nishida's parlance, the world "mirrors itself" in all that is

5. Nishida expanded this notion to the political realm when he spoke of a globally realized world, the world of worlds that are oriented to the entire world, which is possible in the present age as a place of unity-in-diversity. See, for example, Nishida 1943, 427.

6. Advocates of panpsychism are found on the side of materialism as well as idealism; for an example of the former see Galen Strawson et al., *Consciousness and its Place in Nature: Does Physicalism Entail Panpsychism?* (Exeter: Imprint Academic, 2006). For a survey of different positions see William Seager and Sean Allen-Hermanson, "Panpsychism," *The Stanford Encyclopedia of Philosophy* (Spring 2007 edition), ed. Edward N. Zalta. http://plato.stanford.edu/archives/spr2007/entries/panpsychism/

in it, but the individual, self-aware self is a "focal point" of the world. There is no outside to this world. In this respect Nishida's conception shares the assumption common to both internalism and externalism that, whatever the bounds of mind or sources of the mind's content, "world" represents the outermost boundary. Yet if world is the broadest existing context for differentiations, if there is no further existing context out of which terms can be distinguished, then what is the basis of the distinction between world and mind, or of the very conception of world?

Nishida's answer is: nothing that exists; indeed, *nothingness.* This obscure and difficult topic need not conjure up metaphysical specters that would be anathema to those who debate about self and world, however. We can clarify nothingness in terms of making distinctions, and making distinctions in terms of nothingness. Nishida's implicit account of distinctions casts light not only on his own philosophy but on the working of philosophical distinctions in general, and in particular their role in debates about the relation between self and world.

An Analysis of Distinctions

We can preface Nishida's particular account with Robert Sokolowski's illuminating analysis of distinctions in general. Sokolowski notes that making distinctions is not merely a matter of opposing one thing to another. We make distinctions when some obscurity stands in the way of clarifying an issue, and to understand them we must keep in mind the particular obscurity behind them. The obscurity "lets the distinction occur" even when it is meant to hold everywhere and always.[7] Making distinctions requires not merely that we separate or exclude terms, but that we first bring them together "so there is the activity of bringing together along with the annulment of their belonging together." The nondistinction does not come before the distinction; rather, the "ability to hold *two as one comes along with* the ability to hold *two together as distinguished*" from one another. Let us take these two "holds" one at a time. "Holding *two together as one* is holding them precisely as not distinguishable." Holding them together as *one* involves both "the possibility of their being distinguished and the denial [or perhaps the deferral] of that possibility." We might add that holding two together *as distinguished* reaffirms that possibility. Before the possibility of distinction, we have what Sokolowski calls mere assimilation, and we don't see the one *as* one. He calls distinction-making the "emergence of thinking and reasoning."[8]

With some appropriate shifts, to which we will return later, we can employ a similar analysis to understand Nishida's talk of nothingness. The stage of assimilation is what early Nishida called pure experience. This is not yet thinking and reasoning in

7. Robert Sokolowski, "Making Distinctions," in *Pictures, Quotations and Distinctions: Fourteen Essays in Phenomenology* (Notre Dame and London: University of Notre Dame Press, 1992), p. 56.

8. Sokolowski, pp. 62, 65.

that it is prior to the crucial epistemological distinction between subject experiencing and object experienced. Later, Nishida abandoned the talk of pure experience but retained the same priority of a unity in at least three notions: "knowing by becoming," where self and things in the world are seen as one; self-awareness as "a seeing without a seer"; and nothingness as a universal notion in which "there is no distinction between that which expresses and that which is expressed."[9] In his first works, Nishida was pressed to explain how distinctions and reflective thought could arise out of a state of unity; thus, we see him struggling with the themes of "intuition and reflection in self-awareness" (the title of one of his early books; Nishida 1917). He eventually gave up the logical and temporal priority of the assimilated state and moved to a kind of interdependence of unity and plurality, or identity and difference—the one comes along with the other. Nishida tried to express this sort of holding together in the enigmatic phrase "absolute contradictory self-identity," an identity that holds many together as one both as belonging together and as not belonging together, as bringing them together and negating the ability to keep them together.

This is part of what goes on in making distinctions: when we distinguish one thing from another, we first hold them together as being distinguishable but do not distinguish them. Then in distinguishing them we annul their belonging together. This annulment occurs in what Nishida calls the self-negation of nothingness, a negation of its nonduality. To elaborate, nothingness is not simply the initial oneness of the two, or the many, held together. And what holds them together cannot be any one thing; it cannot even be called what all things have in common, that is, "being" as the most universal concept. Nor can it be a second principle, different from being, like becoming, which would still need a third principle holding together these two, being and becoming, and differentiating them. Nothingness for Nishida is not so much a third principle (as in Hegel) as the obscurity that lets the (or any) distinction occur. Nishida calls this nothingness *absolute.* Literally, the Sino-Japanese term for absolute, *zettai,* means breaking through opposition, so absolute nothingness is not opposed to anything; it is the place where all things are held together as one, along with the negation of that oneness. As a universal, it is an attempt to name all things without opposing them. Individual things and persons emerge as the "self-determinations of nothingness" (to use Nishida's terms) just as items emerge into clarity and distinctness from the obscurity behind their distinction.

Nishida's talk of a self-determining context recognizes the impetus to clarify, which Sokolowski thinks precedes distinction and occurs within the obscurity that calls for it. But Nishida does not separately name this impetus or identify it as occurring within the obscurity. Rather, the obscurity (i.e., nothingness) is of itself infinitely determinable. In the term *absolute nothingness* Nishida combines the background obscurity and the cognitive impetus that give rise to distinctions. His talk of absolute nothingness brings to light the fundamental obscurity precisely as obscurity, not clarifying it away, but letting it work to generate clarity and

9. The quotation about the universal of nothingness is the formulation of Heisig 2001, 83.

distinctness.[10] Or, as he would probably rather say, absolute nothingness brings itself to light in the activity of self-awareness.

Two shifts are required to follow Nishida's moves. First, we must shift from a cognitive to an ontological account or, more precisely, a "me-ontological" account (from the Greek *το μεον*, nonbeing). This shift is from describing how thinking itself works (by making distinctions, etc.) to how reality or the "world" works. Nishida does call his mature philosophy a "logic of place" or of "topos" (*basho* in Japanese), but he articulates this "logic" as a kind of ontology (or me-ontology), not as a cognitive description of how mind or reason should operate. The introduction of me-ontology into debates in the philosophy of mind and language may seem a load that such debates are not meant to bear, but Nishida's logic is relevant insofar as it questions the assumptions of those debates regarding the means by which we distinguish self and world, for example. His logic of place undermines all anthropomorphic assumptions about the locus of awareness in the individual subject's mind. Making distinctions describes logically (if not causally) the emergence of the world out of nothingness as the place of nondistinction. The second shift we must make is from thinking of obscurity as something we must by all means eliminate to considering obscurity as something we can appreciate—even if it cannot be the last word. The positive role of obscurity and negativity are familiar to us through Daoism and its echoes in Zen sayings that speak of the darkness that harbors no discriminations, the darkness that lets light appear.

Let us delve a bit further into each of these shifts. The first involves the rather strange talk of absolute nothingness bringing itself to light and evincing self-awareness, rather than reflective human minds bringing things to light through the mental activity of making distinctions. Examples may help explain this shift further. Some distinctions imply a third term (Graham 1992, 211). Binary distinctions like *above/below* and *before/after* imply a hidden term that is a point of reference and indirectly leads to the one making the distinction. Some binary distinctions, like *up/down* and *left/right,* directly imply the maker of the distinction as the point of reference. Other binary distinctions such as between *I* and *you* or *I* and *it* do not allow for this hidden third term, "because the maker of the distinction is part of the distinction" (Hori 2000, 289). These types of distinctions hinge directly or indirectly on a self as the point of reference.[11] In the *right/left* kind of distinction, the point of reference is an embodied self that can be moved, so that what was right becomes left, for example—or even removed and not mentioned, so that we speak simply of right/left. But in the second type of distinction, between *I* and *it,* for example, the self-reference stays put.[12] Nishida wants to move this self-reference as it is located in the individual

10. In his seminal essay "Basho" [Place] in 1926, Nishida mentions the "dazzling obscurity" (in English) of Pseudo Dionysius Areopagita (Nishida 1927, 229).

11. The difference between the direct and indirect point of reference is my addition to Graham's and Hori's analyses.

12. Hori's point (2000, 289) is that the second type does not allow for an "identification of opposites" that can be understood intellectually; rather, "the nonduality of I/it, of subject/object... must be experienced."

to the logical space out of which it too emerges, along with its oppositions. The ultimate locus of these distinctions between self and other and between subject and object is his "absolute nothingness." This self-negating name points to the obscurity that gives rise to and by contrast makes evident all possible distinctions.

The steps through which Nishida tried to accomplish his shift were summarized earlier as the development of his logic of place, from the context of judgments through the context of self-awareness to that of the historical world and, ultimately, to absolute nothingness. This clarifies an element of making distinctions that is taken for granted by everyone who would clarify philosophizing by starting with the self as a cognizing agent.

For example, Sokolowski notes the difference between the thinking, reasoning person who begins to make distinctions and the unthinking person. He states that making distinctions is the emergence, the beginning, of thinking and reasoning, but he also implies that it is an achievement of reasoning. We can place the obscurity behind this emergence/achievement in the properly human self, which for Sokolowski (in another essay) means reason naturally ordered toward truth.[13] Such a self reaches for clarity and truth out of an inner impetus, the second element that Sokolowski must add to the obscurity in general to account for the activity of making distinctions. Although Sokolowski says this impetus is not to be differentiated from distinction in the way that identification is, so a deeper obscurity would not underlie both of them, nevertheless, we can ask what does hold the impetus and obscurity together. One might think that the impetus indicates a subjective or noetic side, whereas obscurity in general describes the noematic side or matter thought about. Both, then, are found "in" consciousness; that is, they are found as moments or nonindependent parts of consciousness.

If we recognize that obscurity is not merely a matter of the mind, not merely found in a consciousness striving for clarity and articulate speech, then we move in Nishida's direction. In his early attempts to formulate a logic of place, Nishida in fact did consider consciousness as the place or locus of the articulating subject/predicate distinction, and even called it "nothingness" (*mu* in Japanese) in the sense that it establishes the being or nonbeing of things.[14] Nishida noted, however, that one's very act of consciousness at any one time always eludes one's own objectifying consciousness. Eventually he tried to formulate something more basic, a deeper level as it were than the consciousness within which obscurities and distinctions are placed. Nishida's absolute nothingness deliberately conflates the self's urge to clarify and the rational agent—all into a greater, perhaps darker, background. And what is

13. Robert Sokolowski, *Introduction to Phenomenology* (Cambridge: Cambridge University Press, 2000), p. 206.

Husserl, whom Sokolowski is interpreting here, would call transcendental subjectivity (or the transcendental ego) the ultimate place of distinction-making; but this name would involve a similar problem, for it alone would not account for the obscurities it encounters.

14. See Michiko Yusa's account of the first formulations of "The Logic of the *Topos* (1924–1926)" in Yusa 2002, 202–204.

this background without foreground or opposite? There is simply no way to say—that is, no *what* to indicate. Nishida's talk of nothingness gainsays the notion that the thinking self is the ultimate reference point in making distinctions.

The Light Side of Obscurity

Nishida's shift to go beyond the thinking self requires a positive assessment of obscurity. We do not understand obscurity adequately when we treat it solely as an undesirable vagueness of expression. It is precisely the absence of articulation that Nishida appreciates in his talk of nothingness. We find precedents in classical Daoist texts and Zen dialogues. The writings ascribed to the Daoist Zhuangzi are full of examples, although there is no direct evidence that Nishida drew from them. Zhuangzi dares to speak of the Way, the Dao, that "has never known boundaries" and speech that "has no constancy." Boundaries come about when there is recognition of a "this" and a "that." Consider this passage, undoubtedly meant to humor the logicians and the normative philosophers of his day:

> Now I am going to make a statement here. I don't know whether it fits into the category of other people's statements or not. But whether it fits into their category or whether it doesn't, it obviously fits into some category [it is distinguishable]. So in that respect it is no different from their statements [it is behind such distinctions]. However, let me try making my statement.
>
> There is a beginning. There is a not yet beginning to be a beginning. There is a not yet beginning to be a not yet beginning to be a beginning. There is being. There is nonbeing. There is a not yet beginning to be nonbeing. There is a not yet beginning to be a not yet beginning to be nonbeing. Suddenly there is being and nonbeing. But between this being and nonbeing, I don't really know which is being and which is nonbeing. Now I have just said something. But I don't know whether what I have said has really said something or whether it hasn't said something. (Zhuangzi 1964, 38–39)

In this passage Zhuangzi playfully intimates the "dissolution of boundaries,"[15] as he calls it, that still preserves the possibility of distinctions. He also uses the metaphor of a hinge in its socket to express the "state in which 'this' and 'that' no longer find their opposites." "When the hinge is fitted into the socket, it can respond endlessly" (Zhuangzi 1964, 35). Although interpretations of such passages in Zhuangzi differ greatly,[16] we can think of these passages as a precedent to the positive appreciation

15. The dissolution of boundaries is also the theme of the famous butterfly passage: Zhuangzi dreams he is a butterfly, and then wakes up, but no longer knows that he isn't perhaps the butterfly dreaming he is Zhuangzi. "Between Zhuangzi and a butterfly there must be *some* distinction! This is called the Transformation of Things" (Zhuangzi 1964, 45).

16. Does the *Zhuangzi* teach a radical relativism or perspectivism that replaces the notion of "the Dao" with multiple *daos*, none of which is preferable? Does it advance an asymmetrical relativism that

of the obscurity that underlies distinctions. A good hinge turns freely and takes one appropriately in this direction rather than that; it articulates the sides.

Zhuangzi actually enjoins us to swing the door and use illumination or clarity:

> When the hinge is fitted into the socket, it can respond endlessly. Its right then is a single endlessness and its wrong too is a single endlessness. So I say, the best thing to use is clarity. (Zhuangzi 1964, 35)

Surely, it seems, we would want to distinguish clarity from obscurity. And out of what obscurity would that distinction arise? We are thrown back to the primordial obscurity, from which emerges the kind of clarity we ordinarily praise. Zhuangzi does an admirable job in clarifying obscurity without eliminating it.

Many Zen dialogues, which were influenced by Daoist texts and in turn inspired some of Nishida's thoughts, also show an appreciation of obscurity, often in the guise of darkness. The dark refers to a standpoint beyond or behind discriminations. *Black* and *dark* are words often used to describe the Buddhist notion of emptiness as the undifferentiated that comes to be manifest only in articulated forms.[17] Again we are reminded of making distinctions as a way of manifesting, presenting, or making present—but also of the positive role of the obscurity that underlies distinction-making. That appreciation of obscurity and the negative is what is gained from Nishida's talk of nothingness. And—to end with a distinction—what is gainsaid is the notion that clarity always takes precedence over obscurity in the practice of philosophy.

Distinctions that are crucial to discussions about the relation between self and world and mind and world refer at least implicitly to a common ground underlying the distinctions. In the philosophy of mind and of language, the intricate and often nuanced distinctions made in the debates between internalism and externalism likewise imply a common ground, usually left in the dark, that makes a debate intelligible to both sides. Nishida reflects on the role that such common ground plays in the specific distinctions at stake and in making distinctions in general, in an attempt to clarify the role that obscurity plays as a ground for making distinctions.

does not reduce Zhuangzi's own speaking to just another equally dismissible *dao?* Does it express a dialectical synthesis of opposites? Here I would not try to adjudicate the various interpretations, but rather point out what they have in common: the positive appreciation of the obscurity behind distinctions. This is not to equate Nishida's absolute nothingness with Zhuangzi's Dao. A. C. Graham notes that Zhuangzi's sequence of statements and of beginnings and nonbeginnings "are no doubt intended to lead to an infinite regress" (Graham 1981, 56). Nishida, on the other hand, ends (and begins) with absolute nothingness. Both Zhuangzi and Nishida, however, point to the inevitable remainder that gets left out of any distinction and analysis, as Graham mentions in the case of Zhuangzi (1964, 55).

17. According to the famous formula in the Heart Sūtra, "emptiness is nothing but form, form nothing but emptiness." The emphasis in the interpretation above is that form is necessary to manifest emptiness, just as emptiness is necessary for the existence of forms. The Indian Buddhist philosopher Nāgārjuna stressed the latter point (in chapter 24 of the *Mūlamadhyamakakārikāi*); Nishida's disciple, Nishitani Keiji, stressed the former point (Nishitani 1999, 180).

BIBLIOGRAPHY AND SUGGESTED READINGS

Davis, Bret W. "The Kyoto School." In *The Stanford Encyclopedia of Philosophy* (Summer 2010 Edition), Edward N. Zalta (ed.), URL=<http://plato.stanford.edu/archives/sum2010/entries/kyoto-school/>.

Graham, A. C. (1981) *Chuang-Tzu: The Inner Chapters.* London and Boston: Unwin Publishers.

———. (1992) *Unreason Within Reason: Essays on the Outskirts of Rationality.* LaSalle, IL: Open Court.

Heisig, James W. (2001) *Philosophers of Nothingness: An Essay on the Kyoto School.* Honolulu, HI: University of Hawaii Press.

Hori, Victor Sōgen. (2000) "Kōan and *Kenshō* in the Rinzai Zen Curriculum." In *The Kōan: Texts and Contexts in Zen Buddhism,* edited by Steven Heine and Dale S. Wright. Oxford and New York: Oxford University Press.

———. (2003) *Zen Sand: The Book of Capping Phrases For Kōan Practice.* Honolulu, HI: University of Hawaii Press.

Maraldo, John C. (2010) "Nishida Kitarô." In *The Stanford Encyclopedia of Philosophy* (Summer 2010 Edition), Edward N. Zalta, ed. url:<http://plato.stanford.edu/archives/sum2010/entries/nishida-kitaro/>.

———. (2006) "Self-Mirroring and Self-Awareness: Dedekind, Royce and Nishida." In *Frontiers of Japanese Philosophy,* edited by James W. Heisig. Nagoya: Nanzan Institute of Religion and Culture, 143–163.

Nishida Kitarō. (1911) *Zen no kenkyū,* translated as *An Inquiry into the Good* by Masao Abe and Christopher Ives. New Haven, CT: Yale University Press, 1992.

———. (1917) *Intuition and Reflection in Self-Consciousness,* translated by Valdo H. Viglielmo with Takeuchi Yoshinori and Joseph S. O'Leary. Albany, NY: State University of New York Press, 1987.

———. (1927) *Hataraku mono kara miru mono e [From That Which Acts to That Which Sees].* Volume 4 of *Nishida Kitarō Zenshū.* Tokyo: Iwanami, 1987. Partial translation by James W. Heisig, "The Logic of Place," in *Japanese Philosophy: A Sourcebook,* edited by James W. Heisig, Thomas P. Kasulis, & John C. Maraldo. Honolulu HI: The University of Hawaii Press, 2011, 647–657.

———. (1943) "Sekaishinchitsujo no genri" ["The Principles of the New World Order"]. In Volume 12 of *Nishida Kitarō Zenshū.* Tokyo: Iwanami, 1987. Translated by Yoko Arisaka in "The Nishida Enigma: 'The Principle of the New World Order,'" *Monumenta Npponica* 51/1 (1996), 81–106.

Nishitani Keiji. (1999) "Emptiness and Sameness." In *Modern Japanese Aesthetics: A Reader,* edited by Michele Marra. Honolulu, HI: University of Hawaii Press, 1999. This is Marra's translation of "Kū to soku," in Volume 13 of *Nishitani Keiji Chosakushū.* Tokyo: Sōbunsha, 1987, 111–118.

Wargo, Robert. (2005) *The Logic of Nothingness.* Honolulu, HI: The University of Hawaii Press.

Yusa, Michiko. (2002) *Zen & Philosophy: An Intellectual Biography of Nishida Kitarō.* Honolulu, HI: University of Hawaii Press.

Zhuangzi. (1964) *Chuang Tzu: Basic Writings,* translated by Burton Watson. New York: Columbia University Press.

CHAPTER 27

KOREAN BUDDHIST PHILOSOPHY

JIN Y. PARK

KOREAN Buddhism is a part of the East Asian Mahāyāna Buddhist tradition. During its fifteen-hundred-year history, which began in the fourth century and continues to today, Korean Buddhism has developed in a close relationship with Chinese Buddhism and at the same time generated its own unique views. Buddhism, together with Confucianism, constitutes one of the two veins of philosophical traditions in Korea. Five Buddhist thinkers are discussed in this essay: Ŭisang (625–702), Wŏnhyo (617–686), Pojo Chinul (1158–1210), T'oe'ong Sŏngch'ŏl (1912–1993), and Pŏpsŏng (1913–), with respect to the three themes of Hwaŏm (Ch. Huayan) Buddhism, Sŏn (Ch. Chan; Jap. Zen) Buddhism, and Buddhist ethics.

Ŭisang is credited as the founder of the Hwaŏm school. From 661 to 668, Ŭisang studied in Tang China with Zhiyan (602–668), the designated second patriarch of Chinese Huayan Buddhism. During this time, Ŭisang also became a colleague of Fazang (643–712), who later became the third patriarch of the tradition. Ŭisang's thought on Hwaŏm Buddhism is well articulated in a short piece titled *The Diagram of the Reality Realm of the One Vehicle of Hwaŏm Buddhism* (Hwaŏm ilsŭng pŏpkye to), which has had a significant impact on Korean Hwaŏm thought up to today.

Wŏnhyo, Ŭisang's contemporary, is one of the most influential Buddhist thinkers in Korean Buddhism. Wŏnhyo joined a monastery during his teens. Without specific teachers to guide him, he read widely and wrote commentaries on major Mahāyāna texts, making a significant contribution to the commentarial tradition in East Asian Buddhism. Wŏnhyo made two attempts to travel to China, neither of which was completed. A life-changing experience during his second unsuccessful journey to China is cited frequently as the moment of his awakening to the truth that the mind is the source of one's understanding of the external world.

Wŏnhyo left behind him a voluminous corpus, the themes of which include Hwaŏm Buddhist thought, Mind-Only (Cittamātra/Yogācāra) philosophy, the Lotus Teaching, and bodhisattva precepts, among others.

Pojo Chinul was a major figure in establishing the Sŏn Buddhist tradition in twelfth-century Korea and is considered one of the most important figures in Korean Sŏn Buddhism. Chinul joined a monastery at the age of eight (1165). Like Wŏnhyo, Chinul mainly trained himself without specific mentors until the age of twenty-five (1182), when he passed the governmental examination for monks. Instead of taking a governmental post, Chinul continued his own practice, traveling to different monasteries, and finally settled down at the Songgwang monastery in 1200, where he trained disciples, gave dharma talks, and wrote on Buddhism until his death. Chinul's Buddhism developed around the core Sŏn doctrine that the mind is the Buddha. In later days, Chinul adopted Kanhwa Sŏn and promoted it as the most effective way to attain awakening. The Kanhwa Sŏn tradition has remained the most prominent Sŏn tradition in Korea since Chinul's time, demonstrating his lasting impact on Korean Buddhism.

T'oe'ong Sŏngh'ŏl is one of the most important figures in the second half of the twentieth century in Korean Buddhism; he represents a Sŏn absolutist and subitist position. Pŏpsŏng might not be as well recognized as the other three thinkers introduced here; however, Pŏpsŏng's Buddhist thought represents engaged Buddhism in contemporary Korea, one of the important and emerging fields in Buddhist philosophy today. We will discuss Pŏpsŏng's engaged Buddhism together with Wŏnhyo's discussion of bodhisattva precepts. This will offer a response to the question of Buddhism's position in social philosophy and ethical theories, as has been raised in recent years among western Buddhist thinkers.

The Universal and the Particular in the Hwaŏm Thought of Ŭisang

Ŭisang discusses the ultimate vision of Hwaŏm Buddhism in his "Verse on the Dharma Nature" (Pŏpsŏng ke), which is included in the *Diagram of the Reality Realm of the One Vehicle of Hwaŏm Buddhism* (Hwaŏm ilsŭng pŏpkye to). The verse consists of 210 Chinese characters deployed in a diagram that demonstrates the interpenetration of all beings in the phenomenal world, the core theme of Hwaŏm Buddhism. In the Hwaŏm Buddhist tradition, the original nature of a being, frequently referred to as "the dharma nature," is characterized by its nonsubstantiality. The basic Buddhist doctrine postulates the identity of a being as conditional. A being in Buddhism is not an owner of independent and permanent substance but exists in the milieu of conditioned causality. Buddhism identifies its causal theory as dependent-arising. The traditional definition of the concept appears in early

Buddhist texts as follows: "Because this happens, that happens; because this ceases, that ceases." A being's identity is possible only as a differential notion in Buddhism, which challenges the identity principle in substantialist philosophy.

As one of the major East Asian Buddhist schools, Hwaŏm Buddhism emphasizes the reality of the conditioned causality at the entire level of the phenomenal world and discusses it especially through the relationship between the noumenal and the phenomenal. The ultimate teaching of the school is expressed frequently through the symbol of the jewel net of Indra. Imagine the universe as a net that stretches infinitely. Further envision that a glittering jewel sits in each knot of the net. The jewel itself is transparent and has no identity of its own. The identity of each jewel is constantly constructed through what it reflects. In the world of Hwaŏm Buddhism, each entity in the cosmos is like a jewel in the net. All beings exist within the net of dependent-arising. In this interrelated world, the identity of the subject is not defined by the independent and permanent essence of the subject but already includes its other. Ŭisang defines a being's identity in this nature as interfusion and nondual. The nature of what is reflected in each jewel cannot be analyzed systematically because of its quantitative immensity and its fluctuating quality. In the "Verse," Ŭisang describes the logic of Indra's net as follows: "Within the one is encompassed the all, and within the many is the one. / The one is the all and the many are the one."[1] The idea of mutual penetration reaches culmination in the signature Hwaŏm statement, as Ŭisang states: "In one particle of dust is contained the ten directions [the entire world]. / All other particles of dust are the same" (HPC 2.1a). In the logic of Hwaŏm Buddhism, any being, however infinitesimal it might be, is identified with the entirety of the world. Since all beings already exist within the net of conditioned causality, the one and the many are not separate. Ŭisang explains this relationship between the one and the many by using the example of the number "one" and the number "ten":

> In the teaching of the great dependent-arising, if there is no "one," the "many" cannot be established. [Practitioners] should be well aware of this nature. What is called the "one" is not the "one" by its self-nature. [By the same token], what is known as the "ten" is not the "ten" by its self-nature; the "ten" comes to be known as the "ten" by its relation to others [or by dependent-arising]. All of the beings produced out of dependent-arising do not have definite marks or a definite nature. Since there is no self-nature, beings do not exist independently, which suggests that birth actually means no-birth. No-birth means no need to abide, and no abiding means the middle path. (HPC 2.6b)

There exists no eternal, unchanging one-ness or ten-ness that grounds the nature of either the one or the ten. Both the "one" and the "ten" (and in that sense, any being

1. *Hwaŏm ilsŭng pŏpkye to* (Diagram of the Reality Realm of the One Vehicle of Hwaŏm Buddhism), *Han'guk Pulgyo chŏnsŏ* (Collected Works of Korean Buddhism, hereafter HPC), vol. 2, pp. 1–8, p. 2.1a. For a complete English translation of this work, see Odin 1982. Throughout this essay, English translations from Classical Chinese and Korean are mine.

in the world) earn their identities through the ever-changing causal transformation.[2] The logic of conditioned causality, however, does not negate the existence of individual beings on the phenomenal level: that is, the one and the ten are different. Despite the individuality that is recognized on the phenomenal level, Hwaŏm thought also consistently emphasizes the noumenal aspect of the phenomenally separated existence: hence, the one is the ten. Two issues deserve our attention here: first, the paradigm of one particle-qua-the world does not indicate that a specific one is the entire world all the time on every occasion. The one is the ten when we focus on the "one" at a given moment in a given situation, and the same can be said about any other entity in the world, which is represented in Ŭisang's "Verse" as "a particle of dust." When the notion of the one in "the one is the all" is interpreted as referring to exclusively a specific one—such as the emperor (the one) as opposed to the people (the all)—the Hwaŏm vision risks supporting a totalitarian vision. Second, the phenomenal (the one) and the noumenal (the all) are nondual, and so is the particular and the universal. The phenomenal and the noumenal are hermeneutically constructed concepts, not ontologically separated realities. These two issues should be the ground to respond to the criticism that Hwaŏm Buddhism is a form of a philosophy of idealism.

Ŭisang further elaborates the identity of the "one" and the "all" by using the concept of the six marks. The six marks consist of three pairs: universality/particularity (K. *ch'ongsang/pyŏlsang*), sameness/difference (K. *tongsang/yisang*), and integrity/fragmentation (K. *sŏngsang/koesang*). As in the case of the one and the ten, these seeming binary opposites coexist in the identity of an entity. The first in the pairs—universality, the sameness, and integrity—characterize the totality of the world as understood from the noumenal level. The second sets of each pair—particularity, difference, and fragmentation—characterize the individual entities at the phenomenal level like each jewel in Indra's net. The six marks making up the three pairs demonstrate the contradictory identity through which Hwaŏm Buddhism understands an entity. An individual entity is characterized by the marks of particularity, difference, and fragmentation, whereas the nature of its individual identity is constructed through its relationship with others, and its identity is inseparable from the marks of universality, sameness, and integrity.

In Chinese Huayan Buddhism, the mutual interpenetration of the noumenal and the phenomenal is explained through a theory known as the fourfold worldview. The fourfold worldview consists of (1) the world of the phenomenon (C. *shifajie;*

2. Fazang, the alleged Third Patriarch of Chinese Huayan Buddhism, explains the relationship of the one and the ten by employing the concepts of "the same body" (C. *tongti;* K. *tongch'e*) and "the different body" (C. *yiti;* K. *yich'e*). The one and the ten in the numerals one through ten are different entities (bodies) because the one is not the ten and the ten is not the one. However, they are the same body in the sense that the one cannot obtain its meaning without the rest of the number in the series of one through ten; the same is the case with the number ten. That the one is the same body and at the same time a different body with the number ten can be further explained through the Buddhist concept of identity known as the two levels of truth.

K. *sabŏpkye*), (2) the world of the noumenon (C. *lifajie;* K. *yibŏpkye*), (3) the world of the unobstructed interpenetration of the noumenon and the phenomenon (C. *lishi wuai fajie:* K. *yisa muae pŏpkye*), and (4) the world of the unobstructed interpenetration among phenomena (C. *shishi wuai fajie;* K. *sasa muae pŏpkye*). The first of the Huayan fourfold worldview represents the world that consists of individual existences; it is the world of the many, where diversity exists seemingly without a coherent system. The second stage of the fourfold worldview postulates a world that is understood from the perspective of the principle. However diverse existence in the phenomenal world might be, no being exists outside of conditioned causality, which is the structure of the world from the Buddhist perspective. Hence, the third layer of the fourfold worldview declares that there is no conflict between the world of diversity and the world of one principle. Considering the phenomenal diversity in light of the first three stages, Huayan envisions at its fourth level that all entities in the world are mutually influential and interconnected without conflicts.

Ŭisang explains the relationship between the noumenon (the universal) and the phenomenon (the particular) as follows: there is a mutual identity of the noumena (the universal) and the phenomena (the particular); there is a mutual identity of the noumenon and the noumenon, and there is a mutual identity of the phenomenon and the phenomenon (HPC 2.6a).[3] This is the world in which the universal and the particular, and the particular and the particular, are mutually interpenetrating due to their dependently arising nature. Ŭisang identifies the nature of things arising in the law of the dependent-arising as the "middle path." The Buddhist middle path does not indicate the meridian point of the two participating elements. Instead, it indicates that "all polarities are interfused" (HPC 2.5b). The one and the many, the noumenon and the phenomenon, the universal and the particular are interfused in the sense that neither has self-nature and that both exist in the midst of conditioned causal movements.

Language and Subjectivity in Chinul's Sŏn Buddhism

Zen Buddhism shares with Hwaŏm Buddhism the idea of the mutual interfusion of beings but develops its own paradigm that addresses the main concerns of the school. The basic premise of the Zen school claims that the sentient being is the Buddha. The premise is an oxymoron: if the sentient being is the Buddha, why are

3. The terms "nounema" and "phenomena" are translations of the Chinese character *li* (K. *yi*) and *shi* (K. *sa*), respectively. These terms are also translated here as the principle and the particular. Noumena and phenomena in this case are not related to Kantian philosophy or phenomenology in Continental philosophy, even though Huayan Buddhism can be understood as Buddhist phenomenology as I have discussed elsewhere. See Park 2008, especially ch. 8 and 9.

sentient beings still not enlightened? If the sentient being is the Buddha, what is the meaning of enlightenment? Zen Buddhism challenges the traditional logic of philosophy by answering these questions with the following statement: the sentient being is the Buddha, and yet the sentient being is the sentient being.

In approaching the paradoxical nature of the existential reality of a being, Pojo Chinul underlines the importance of understanding the nature of one's mind. In his *Encouragement to Practice: The Compact of the Samādhi and Prajñā Community* (*Kwŏnsu chŏnghye kyŏlsa mun* 1190), Chinul states, "When one is deluded about the mind and gives rise to endless defilements, such a person is a sentient being. When one is awakened to the mind and gives rise to endless marvelous functions, such a person is the Buddha. Delusion and awakening are two different states, but both are caused by the mind. If one tries to find the Buddha away from this mind, one will never find him" (HPC 4.698a). In this passage, one notices that the commonly held binary opposites, for example delusion and awakening, or the sentient being and the Buddha, are acknowledged but at the same time negated by attributing the ground of the existence of such dualism to the mind of a being. For Chinul, delusion arises not through a certain quality of an entity external or internal to the subject but through the subject's failure to see the nonsubstantial nature of one's ontological reality. Here one notes the fundamental difference of the focus between Hwaŏm and Sŏn Buddhism. Whereas Ŭisang's Hwaŏm Buddhism primarily concerns itself with the phenomenal world and understands each being within that structure, Chinul's Sŏn Buddhism gives priority to an individual's awakening to his own existential and ontological reality.

One way to interpret Chinul's Sŏn Buddhism is to understand it as an attempt to address the problem of subjectivity in the process of the individual's awareness of ontological reality, and the problem of subjectivity is closely linked to the subject's relation to language. As is well known, Sŏn Buddhism has been keen to the function of language in the subject's mode of thinking. However, Chinul points out that the emphasis on the limits of language and thought is not a Sŏn-specific feature but is found in most Buddhist schools. In explaining the meaning of Sŏn Buddhism, Chinul is especially aware of Fazang's fivefold taxonomy, in which Fazang placed Chan Buddhism (which he calls the Sudden school) at the fourth level, one step below the Huayan school. Fazang also characterized the teaching of the Sudden school as simply focusing on forgetting language and thoughts in an effort to create the undisturbed state of the mind. Responding to such characterizations of Chan Buddhism by Fazang, Chinul explains in his *Treatise on Resolving Doubts about Huatou Meditation* (Kanhwa kyŏrŭi ron) that all five stages of Buddhism in Fazang's fivefold doctrinal classification in their own way deal with the problem of language and of the thinking process. Chinul repeatedly emphasizes that the idea of cutting off language does not belong exclusively to the Sŏn school, nor is the nature of the achieved goal through Sŏn practice different from that described by other Buddhist schools, especially by Hwaŏm Buddhism. If we follow Chinul's logic here, we come to a rather interesting point. That is, the Sŏn school does not offer any doctrinal renovation of Buddhism; Chinul might even seem to say that the main concern of

Sŏn Buddhism is not Buddhist doctrine itself, since Buddhist doctrines are all already spelled out by existing Buddhist schools. At the same time, the Buddhist teaching Sŏn represents is not and cannot be different from the teachings expounded by other schools. Chinul's ready admission of the identity between Sŏn Buddhism and other Buddhist schools at the ultimate level leads one to ask the question: if there is no difference between the two, what is the identity of Sŏn Buddhism? For Chinul, Sŏn teachings, especially Sŏn *hwadu* meditation, facilitate a state through which the subject makes a radical change in his or her mode of thinking; the doctrinal schools offer a description of the Buddhist worldview and the Sŏn school teaches how to activate in the mind of the practitioner what has been stated in the doctrinal schools.

Chinul does not consider the linguistic rendering as found in Buddhist scriptures deficient as it is. However, Chinul points out that the linguistically rendered reality of the objective world is not always reflected in the existential reality of the subject. What, then, are the causes of the gap between the linguistically rendered reality and the reality of the subject? In this context, Chinul cites Chinese Chan Master Dahui Zonggao (1089–1163) to point out the structural problem in one's thinking process as a major cause that is responsible for such a gap: "The influence of established thought being so strong, the mind in search of enlightenment itself becomes a barrier and thus the correct knowledge of one's mind has rarely obtained a chance to manifest itself. However, this barrier does not come from outside nor is it something that should be regarded as an exception" (HPC 4.732c). The problems of the situation at this point become internalized and subjectivized.

At the beginning of the *Treatise*, Chinul juxtaposes Sŏn with Hwaŏm, equating them in terms of their vision of the ultimate reality and at the same time distinguishing them in terms of how to approach this reality. For Chinul, the investigation of one's mind is critical in this sense. The mind is allegedly the locus in which the gap between the existential reality of the subject and the hermeneutical reality represented in linguistic rendering of Buddhist teaching takes place. Hence, Chinul repeatedly emphasizes that "the mind is the Buddha," and Sŏn practice toward enlightenment, for Chinul, is to be awakened to the very nature of one's mind. In the later stage of his life, Chinul was firm in proposing that *hwadu* meditation can facilitate the environment in which the practitioner can attain this goal, and the capacity of *hwadu* in achieving this goal is closely related to the way in which language functions in *hwadu* meditation.

Chinul argues that language in Buddhist teachings other than Sŏn *hwadu* meditation functions simply as a tool to impart meaning. The *hwadu* meditation employs language not to communicate meaning but to facilitate an environment in which the subject makes a transition from being a mere receptor of the described meaning to an active participator in the reality described in language—that is, *hwadu* as it is does not present truth, nor does it offer a way to correct the problem that individuals might have. Chinul writes, "The moment one tends toward the slightest idea that the *hwadu* must be the presentation of the ultimate truth or that it enables one to treat one's defects, one is already under the power of the limitations set by linguistic expression" (HPC 4.733b). The *hwadu* is like a catalyst: as it is, it is not pertinent to what is happening to the subject; it simply facilitates a transformation in the subject without itself being involved or changed by the transformation. The transforming function of the *hwadu* is for Chinul what distinguishes Sŏn Buddhism from all other Buddhist schools.

In explaining the functioning of *hwadu* language, Chinul employs the distinction between the "live word" (K. *hwalgu*) and the "dead word" (K. *sagu*) and "the involvement with the word" (K. *ch'amgu*) and "involvement with meaning" (K. *ch'amŭi*), borrowing the concepts from Dahui. These distinctions are characterized by the language's relation to the subject rather than the specific nature of linguistic expressions themselves. Chinul criticizes passages like "In this endless world, between me and others, there is no gap even as infinitesimal as the thinness of a hair" (HPC 4.733a) as examples of dead words because "they create in the practitioner's mind barriers derived from understanding" (HPC 4.733a). As opposed to dead words, live words generate "no taste"; they create a dead-end situation to the practitioner in which the practitioner loses all of the resources to exercise his or her thinking process.

When Sŏn Buddhists criticize language and theorizing, it is because they are the very tools for the subject to carry out the process of domesticating the external world and tailoring it according to the mode of thinking most familiar to the subject. The *hwadu* meditation, especially the "live word" and the "direct involvement with word," are tools that put a break in the familiar world created by the subject. Dead words subjugate themselves to a sign-system and habituated mode of thinking. As opposed to dead words, live words become the mediator among the practitioner, language, and the world by disrupting the preexisting order and meaning structure of these three elements established in the subject's mind. The promise of *hwadu* meditation, for Chinul, is that this experience by the subject of the unfamiliar territory will lead the subject to the realization of her ontological reality, which from the Buddhist perspective is existence in the milieu of the conditionally arising process.

Nondualism and Mahāyāna Buddhist Ethics

Despite the differences in their emphasis, both Ŭisang's Hwaŏm Buddhism and Chinul's Sŏn Buddhism find their basis in the fundamental Buddhist vision of nondualism. In Ŭisang's Hwaŏm Buddhist thought, the particular and the universal, the phenomena and the noumena, are understood as being in a state of interpenetration; in Chinul's Sŏn Buddhism, the mind of the subject is the source of all delusions, and delusion in this context signifies understanding a phenomenon—be it an individual being, an event, or any abstract concept—as an independent occurrence instead of the result of a multilayered, causal process. If things are by nature void of independent essence and polar opposites are to be understood according to their mutual penetration, how does one construct an ethical system from such a nondual philosophy? In Ŭisang's Hwaŏm vision of the mutual interpenetration of entities, both good and bad, right and wrong, purity and impurity are understood as being empty. In this nondual world, as Ŭisang states, "saṃsāra and nirvāṇa are always harmonized together" (HPC 2.1a). The same applies to Chinul's Sŏn Buddhist world, as he says, "there being no purity or impurity, there is no right or wrong" (HPC 4.710c). Where do ethics stand in this antinomian world of Hwaŏm and Sŏn Buddhism? Given that Buddhism involves not only philosophical but also religious tradition, and that one of the fundamental functions of the latter is to provide practitioners with guidelines to follow in the process of Buddhist practice, the issue of Buddhism's position in ethical and moral systems makes us pause and wonder what kind of ethical paradigm it might offer.

The Mahāyāna Buddhist approach to ethics is well grounded in the fundamental Mahāyāna Buddhist position on the reality of existence. A being does not have an unchanging essence, nor do moral and ethical categories. The fact that a being exists only in the milieu of conditionally arising causal processes does not negate the individual's existence on the phenomenal level, and the same applies to moral and ethical categories. In other words, Mahāyāna Buddhism does not negate the necessity of moral values or ethical categories; however, it also underlines that precepts, moral rules, and ethical definitions exist and are acknowledged always in the context of their provisional nature. Wŏnhyo makes clear the double-edgedness of the Mahāyāna Buddhist position toward ethics in his discussion of bodhisattva precepts. The precepts by definition indicate rules that Buddhist practitioners are obliged to observe. When one observes a rule, what is the ground for this observation? Are moral rules and ethical categories given by the absolute power and thus to be respected in all circumstances, or are they abided by because of the beneficial consequences they promise to produce?

Wŏnhyo discusses bodhisattva precepts focusing on the provisional nature of the value category. Precepts are rules that Buddhist practitioners are required to abide by. However, even precepts cannot escape the dependently arising nature of the world, which means that no precepts, and in that sense, no moral or ethical categories, are to be accepted as having absolute independent values of their own. In *Essentials of Observation and Violation of Bodhisattva Precepts* (Posal kyebon chibŏm yogi), Wŏnhyo discusses the three categories of observing and transgressing the foundations of bodhisattva precepts. First, he discusses major and minor offenses; second, he shows the profound and shallow understandings of observing and transgressing precepts; and third, he presents the ultimate way of observing and transgressing precepts. In the first two sections, Wŏnhyo offers basic concepts of precepts and how the same precepts can be interpreted differently based on the subject's intention involved in a certain action. In these two sections, as in the case of most moral teachings, Wŏnhyo promotes the importance of respecting the existing rules. In the third section, titled "Ultimate Observation and Violation of Precepts," Wŏnhyo changes the direction of his discussion and revisits the very concepts of precepts and of observing and violating them. The result is to underline the fundamentally provisional nature of moral rules and ethical categories. Wŏnhyo writes:

> That precepts exist only based on multilevel conditional causes [and thus are empty] does not negate their existence in reality. Violating precepts is also like this; so is personal identity. In dealing with precepts, if one sees only their nonexistent aspect and says that they do not exist, *such a person might not violate precepts but will forever lose them*, because s/he denies their existence. Also, if someone relies on the idea that precepts do exist and thinks only on the existent side of precepts, even though s/he might be able to observe the precepts, *observation in this case is the same as violation*, because such a person negates the ultimate reality of precepts [which is emptiness]. (HPC 1.585a, emphasis mine)

When existence is understood through a differential notion instead of being anchored on substantial essence and the particular and the universal are intersubsuming, any attempt to create a closed value system faces a problem of appropriation. Appropriation requires an appropriator, and this logic cannot but question the validity of the created system. As Wŏnhyo states, the ambiguity of categorized values does not completely negate the necessity of a value system itself. Instead, the awareness of the multilayered contexts out of which a value system is constructed demands a constant readjustment of the existing system. Wŏnhyo's thought on bodhisattva precepts in its outlook proposes an ethical theory that challenges normative forms of ethics. It was, however, not until recent years that Korean Buddhist traditions began to seriously consider the position of Buddhism as an ethical theory. In contemporary Korean Buddhism, the issue of individual practice and awakening on the one hand and the social engagement and ethical dimension of Buddhism on the other has generated a polemic that makes the issue of Buddhist ethics more visible. Two Buddhist monk-thinkers took opposite positions: T'oe'ong Sŏngch'ŏl defined Buddhism as fundamentally based on the perfection of individual cultivation, whereas Pŏpsŏng claimed that individual cultivation cannot be achieved without being accompanied by social engagement. Sŏngch'ol's Buddhism kindled a debate known as the Sudden-Gradual debate, and Pŏpsŏng's Buddhism offers a philosophical paradigm for a form of engaged Buddhism known as Minjung Buddhism (Buddhism for the masses).

The idea of Buddhism for the masses first appeared in Korean Buddhism at the beginning of the twentieth century, when reform-minded Buddhist intellectuals proposed changing Buddhism to be more relevant to the life of the general public, especially those marginalized in society. As a movement, however, Minjung Buddhism began together with prodemocratic and antigovernmental movements in Korean society during the military dictatorship in the 1970s and 1980s. Critical of the subjectivist and solipsistic attitudes that appear in some forms of Buddhist practice, Minjung Buddhists emphasize the social dimension of Buddhist philosophy and contend that Buddhist liberation includes liberation from all forms of suppression. In doing so, Minjung Buddhists make appeals to the bodhisattva ideal and to compassion.

The Sudden-Gradual debate was ignited by Sŏngch'ŏl along with the publication of his book, *The Correct Path of the Sŏn School* (Sŏnmun chŏngno 1981), in which he criticizes the "sudden enlightenment with gradual cultivation" as a heretical teaching in the Sŏn school and defines "sudden enlightenment with sudden cultivation" as the authentic form of the Sŏn practice. The idea of sudden enlightenment is based on the fundamental Sŏn claim that sentient beings are already Buddha the way they are. On the surface, Minjung Buddhism and the Sudden-Gradual debate fall into two exclusively different categories of Buddhist thought: the former focuses on the social aspects of Buddhist philosophy, whereas the latter centers on the nature of individual cultivation. At a deep level, they cannot but reflect each other because, without a clear understanding of the nature of individual cultivation and awakening as explored in the Sudden-Gradual debate, Buddhist philosophy cannot maintain itself. However, if the subjective world of an individual cannot be linked to the public and objective domain of the social ethical realm, as Minjung Buddhism emphasizes, such a cultivation or awakening contradicts the basic Buddhist doctrines of dependent-arising and no-self. The Sudden-Gradual debate and Minjung Buddhism, then, represent the perennial core issues of Buddhism: that is, how to relate wisdom (realization of one's ontological reality) and compassion (sharing life with others).

Questions have been raised about whether attainment of wisdom (enlightenment) will naturally facilitate compassionate actions for others. Pŏpsŏng's discussion of sudden and gradual aptly applies to this issue. Instead of understanding sudden and gradual as a process from the former to the latter within the subject, Pŏpsŏng relates them to the subject's realization and the social and historical manifestation of that realization, that is, noumenal wisdom and its exercise through compassion in the phenomenal world. In doing so, he incorporates Hwaŏm Buddhist thought into his emphasis on the social and ethical dimensions of Buddhist enlightenment. Pŏpsŏng was not the first Korean Buddhist to resort to Hwaŏm Buddhism to underscore the relevance of Sŏn Buddhism to the social and ethical realities of the practitioner's life. From Chinul in the twelfth century to S'ŏngch'ŏl in the twentieth century, Korean Sŏn masters have frequently resorted to Hwaŏm Buddhist philosophy in an effort to clarify the relationship between the subject and the object in the Sŏn Buddhist worldview and between an individual's ontological awakening (wisdom) and its social dimension (compassion) in Sŏn practice.

Reminiscent of the Hwaŏm vision of the interpenetration of the phenomena and the noumena, Pŏpsŏng claims that the diversities characterizing the phenomenal world require endless engagement in bodhisattva activities in daily life, which Pŏpsŏng identifies as "history." History of Buddhism, as expressed through his term "historicization," is contrasted with a metaphysical or transcendental understanding of Buddhism. Sŏn Buddhist enlightenment, from Pŏpsŏng's perspective, cannot be related solely to individual spiritual awakening, nor can it be an asocial event, as has been argued previously. Pŏpsŏng contends that the *hwadu* of Sŏn Buddhism are not "dead words intuiting the inner spiritual mysticism. *Hwadu* meditation is epistemological activity that constantly negates the reification of ideas and self-absolutization of any entity; it is historical movement that actively accepts and refreshes the nature of dependent co-arising in one's existence."[4] Chinul prioritized *hwadu* meditation in Sŏn practice, emphasizing the capacity of *hwadu* to facilitate a fundamental change in one's mode of thinking. Pŏpsŏng took this possibility of Sŏn Buddhism further toward the social dimension and linked the change in an individual as a path toward a social change. Pŏpsŏng thus states, "Buddhist enlightenment is not a return to absolute reality; instead, it is a sudden liberation of all the essentialist views regarding one's consciousness and existence, self and the world."[5] This awakening or liberation of self-closure of an individual needs to take place constantly and continuously as life unfolds. This is a vision of the world in which human desire for a teleological completion needs to give way to the awakening to the openness of the world and of beings.

Wŏnhyo's bodhisattva precepts suggest an ethical theory that acknowledges rules but only to the degree that the moral rules and ethical categories are understood as provisional and do not have an essence of their own; Pŏpsŏng's engaged Buddhism explains the social dimension of Sŏn and Hwaŏm Buddhism, emphasizing the indissoluble nature of individual and society, or self and others in the Buddhist world. In both cases, the conventional rule-bounded moral theories are accepted only as a preliminary stage of social theory; in its place, the Mahāyāna Buddhism of Wŏnhyo and Pŏpsŏng proposes a context-bound ethical theory that requires a constant reawakening to one's existential and social reality as one lives in the milieu of the ever-changing causal processes of the Buddhist world.

BIBLIOGRAPHY AND SUGGESTED READING

BUSWELL, ROBERT E., JR. (trans.). (1983) *The Korean Approach to Zen: The Collected Works of Chinul.* Honolulu, HI: University of Hawai'i Press.

——— (trans.). (2007) *Cultivating Original Enlightenment: Wŏnhyo's Exposition of the Vajrasamadhi-Sūtra* (Kŭmgang Sammaegyŏng Non). Honolulu, HI: University of Hawaii Press.

JORGENSEN, JOHN. (2010) "Minjung Buddhism: A Buddhist Critique of the Status Quo-its History, Philosophy, and Critique." In *Makers of Modern Korean Buddhism*, edited by Jin Y. Park. Albany, NY: State University of New York Press, 275–313.

ODIN, STEVEN. (1982) *Process Metaphysics and Hua-yen Buddhism: A Critical Study of Cumulative Penetration vs. Interpenetration.* Albany, NY: State University of New York Press.

4. Pŏpsŏng, "Minjung Pulgyo undong ŭi silch'ŏnjŏk ipchang" (The Practical Standpoint of the Minjung Buddhist Movement), in *Chonggyo yŏn'gu* (Religious Studies) 6 (1990): 223–228, p. 223.

5. Pŏpsŏng, "Kkadarŭm ŭi ilsangsŏng kwa hyŏngmyŏngsŏng" (Commonality and Revolutionality of Enlightenment." *Ch'angjak kwa pip'yŏng* 82 (Winter 1993): 329–340.

Park, Jin Y. (2005) "Zen Language in Our Time: The Case of Pojo Chinul's Huatou Meditation." *Philosophy East and West* 55/1, 80–98.

———. (2008) *Buddhism and Postmodernity: Zen, Huayan, and the Possibility of Buddhist-Postmodern Ethics*. Lanham, MD: Lexington Books.

Yun, Woncheol. (2010) "Zen Master T'oe'ong Sŏngch'ŏl's Doctrine of Zen Enlightenment and Practice." In *Makers of Modern Korean Buddhism*, edited by Jin Y. Park. Albany, NY: State University of New York Press, 199–226.

PART V

ISLAMIC PHILOSOPHY

EDITED BY TAMARA ALBERTINI

REINTRODUCING ISLAMIC PHILOSOPHY: THE PERSISTING PROBLEM OF "SMALLER ORIENTALISMS"

TAMARA ALBERTINI

THIS is the place where readers expect to find a historic survey introducing them to authoritative figures and texts of the tradition to be studied. Whereas much historic information is included in the following narrative, the order of the ideas presented is determined not by chronology but by the discussion of a number of *orientalist* assumptions that continue to affect the status of Islamic thought, especially in the field of comparative philosophy. As Oliver Leaman put it, "[I]t is to be regretted... that the growing influence of the critique of Orientalism, which Said produced has yet to have much impact upon the study of Islamic philosophy, by contrast with its effect upon other disciplines in the area of Islamic studies" (Nasr and Leaman 1996, 1148). While Edward Said's groundbreaking *Orientalism* (1978) succeeded in bringing down the age of unchallenged orientalist theories invented to underscore the superiority of Western achievements over other world traditions, prejudices and biases remain in place. I call these the "smaller orientalisms" and do not necessarily find them less worrisome. Smaller orientalisms may not appear racist; they may even have the deceiving allure of objective statements. As a result, they are usually harder to detect and also more resistant to eradication.

In this introduction I discuss five common "orientalisms" regarding Islamic philosophy: that it is *medieval*, the expression of *Arab* thought, *Middle Eastern* in terms of its geographic expansion, mostly *Greek derived*, and/or merely of *religious* interest. They make Islamic philosophy appear to be not only limited in time and space but also with respect to its cultural appeal, its ability to formulate original ideas, and its general intellectual relevance. There is, therefore, an urgent need to redress these misconceptions and, in a way, to reintroduce Islamic philosophy as a living tradition of thought in its own right not to be solely measured by the standards and criteria of Western philosophy. While one may never avoid cultural and intellectual biases entirely—they are part of the hermeneutical encounter—one should be prepared to continuously review and, as needed, correct the assumptions with which one approaches another tradition.

Why Islamic Philosophy Is Not Medieval

A widespread perception is that Islamic philosophy "mattered" during the Middle Ages, when texts written by Muslim scholars became available in Latin translation and inspired generations of European philosophers and scientists. While Islamic intellectual achievements were instrumental in the shaping of Western thought and culture during the Middle Ages, and later periods, Islamic thought itself ought not be labeled "medieval." *First*, periodizations developed in and for one given tradition may not necessarily be transferrable to another tradition. While Europe had, indeed, a long "middle period" bridging ancient and modern times, Islamic civilization was peaking; it was not transitioning but rather blossoming. For lack of a better term, it is, therefore, best to speak of *classical* Islamic philosophy. *Second*, assigning Islamic philosophy to the Middle Ages in terms of chronology attaches to it connotations of being backward, unrefined, possibly even barbarous. While historians of the European Middle Ages are increasingly fighting this perception in defense of their field, and rightly so, there is even less grounds to apply any of these characterizations to Islamic civilization in the classical period. *Third*, referring to Islamic philosophy as medieval assumes that it is past and, therefore, dead. Because of this presumably "past character," all efforts made by later, including contemporary, Muslim scholars would be seen as futile attempts to reconnect to a glorious age never to return. *Fourth*, thinking of the Middle Ages as the sole period in which Islamic philosophy flourished reduces the pool of texts to be studied to works written roughly between the eighth and twelfth centuries, whereas Muslim thinkers have continued to make significant philosophical contributions to this day. *Fifth*, to scholars approaching Islamic thought from the field of medieval studies, it also suggests that only works once translated into Latin are to be included, thus leaving out works that medieval Western translators ignored or deliberately discarded because they considered them to be too closely connected to an Islamic religious worldview. Finally, since medieval "orientalists" by and large only read Arabic, texts written by Muslim philosophers in other languages were excluded. Even the nonspecialist may easily understand the limitations these highly selective criteria place upon what qualifies as an Islamic philosophical text.

The close association of Islamic philosophy with the Middle Ages explains to a great extent why this tradition of thought is still rather new to the field of comparative philosophy, and this, ironically, although it was the first non-Western tradition extensively studied by European philosophers. The study of Islamic philosophy, then, needs to be detached from medieval philosophy in Western scholarship. Whereas the story of the reception of Muslim ideas and achievements in the European Middle Ages has not been exhaustively explored and requires the continuous attention of experts of the Middle Ages, Islamic thought is not a subdomain of medieval philosophy.

Why Islamic Philosophy Is Not the Same as Arab Philosophy

While Arabic replaced Pahlavi (ancient Persian) and Greek under Islam's first dynasty (the Umayyads; seventh to eighth centuries) as the administrative and scholarly language of the Islamic empire, this does not mean that philosophy written in Arabic necessarily expresses a specific Arab worldview or a reflection on Arab language, literature, history, and culture. The latter was actually pursued within what used to be called the "Arab sciences," as opposed to the "Greek sciences" (Makdisi 1990, 202–227), and continues to represent a highly valued ideal of learning and self-cultivation (*adab*) in the contemporary Arab world.

Moreover, among Islam's numerous philosophers there were not only ethnic Arabs but also Persians, Syrians, Kabyls (Berbers), and Africans, and in more recent centuries also Turks (from Central Asia and the Ottoman empire), Bosniaks, and Indians. One has also to take into account that some Muslim philosophers did write even in the classical period, at least occasionally, in a language other than Arabic: depending on their ethnicity, typically in Persian, Turkish, or Urdu. The almost exclusive focus on Arabic as Islam's philosophical language thus explains why it was discovered only in the twentieth century that *The Aims of the Philosophers* (*Maqāṣid al-Falāsifa*), known in the Latin Middle Ages as *Intentiones Philosophorum* and attributed to al-Ghazzālī (also spelled al-Ghazālī), was actually the Arabic translation of a Persian text by Ibn Sīnā (Avicenna, d. 429/1037), entitled *Danesh Nameh Alā'ī* (*The Book of Sciences for 'Alā' al-Dawla*) (Goodman 1992, 37–38).

Why Islamic Philosophy Is Not "Middle Eastern"

To characterize Islamic philosophy as "Middle Eastern" is to deliberately ignore the vast territories from which Muslim thinkers have emerged and continue to emerge. In the first centuries of Islam, Muslim philosophers lived as far as Spain in the west and Central Asia and Northern India in the east. Ibn Rushd (Averroës, d. 595/1198), ethnically speaking an Andalusian Arab, would have been surprised to learn that he was a proponent of Middle Eastern thought. In his philosophical self-understanding he was a link in a long chain of thinkers that took its beginning with the Greeks, while his theology was clearly "western," in that it reflected both Mālikī legal training[1] and Almohad theological tenets as developed by Ibn Tūmart (d. ca 524/1130), the ideological founder of the Almohad dynasty in southern Spain. Al-Fārābī (d. 339/950), too, born in what is today Kazakhstan, speaking a Turkic or, more likely, a Persian idiom as his native tongue, and trained by Nestorian Christian scholars, would have had no use for a Middle Eastern affiliation. He may have lived in Baghdad, the heart of the Abbasid empire (eighth to twelfth centuries), for over forty years of his life and written exclusively in Arabic, and yet his mind was cosmopolitan. In an al-Fārābian world, knowledge is native to no land. It once traveled from the Chaldaeans to the Greeks and the Romans from whose territory it then wandered away to reach the Syrians, who eventually transmitted it to the Muslims. Knowledge was expected to continue its wanderings and engage the many more ethnic and religious communities living within the extraordinarily diverse Islamic empire. The same inner detachment from the Abbasid centers of culture and power is true of Ibn Sīnā. Born in the vicinity of Bukhara (today in Uzbekistan), Ibn Sīnā preserved a strong Persian identity throughout his life, making him seek the service of Persian princes only, which explains the writing of *Danesh Nameh* composed to introduce his revered Persian patron ʿAlāʾ al-Dawla to philosophy in his native language. The Persians—who hardly ever felt they belonged to the same world as Egyptians, Arabs, and Syrians—are yet to be recognized for their extraordinary cultural accomplishments since the inception of Islam. They were, indeed, for many centuries an essential conduit in the transmission of knowledge throughout the Islamic world, especially in Central Asia and Northern India. Thus, the scientific, philosophical, and artistic achievements of the Timurid empire in Central Asia (fourteenth to sixteenth centuries) and the Mughal reign (sixteenth to nineteenth centuries) are unthinkable without the strength of Persian intellectual contributions. Not surprisingly, Persian became the official language of Mughal India, and

1. Founded by Mālik ibn Anas (d. 179/795), the Mālikite *madhhab* (school of law) is one of four Sunnī schools still in existence. After the fall of Islamic Spain in the fifteenth century, it remained mainly represented in North Africa. The other legal schools are represented by the Ḥanafites, Ḥanbalites, and Shāfiʿites.

major scholarly works such as the monumental *Akbarnama* written in honor of emperor Akbar (d. 1605) by vizier Abū al-Faẓl (d. 1602) continued to draw from ancient Greek, Persian, and classical Islamic philosophical sources. The Indian-born, modern Muslim philosopher Muhammad Iqbal (d. 1938) wrote most of his works in Persian. (For the specifics of the Iranian school of thought after Ibn Sīnā see Hossein Ziai's chapter "Philosophy of Illumination.")

Why Islamic Philosophy Is Not Greek Derived

Much has been written about Europe's debt toward Muslim philosophical and scientific contributions ranging from the translation of Greek texts—some of which might have been otherwise lost to world philosophy—to elaborate commentaries adding not only insightful clarifications and explanations but also new interpretations (for the history of transmission see Shayegan 1996, and Daiber 2007). Clearly, no civilization begins from scratch but builds upon the achievements of preceding cultures. To fellow Andalusians who felt that Islam need not lean on the knowledge of previous cultures, Ibn Rushd replied in *Kitāb Faṣl al-Maqāl:* "But if someone other than ourselves has already examined that subject [Aristotelian demonstration], it is clear that we ought to seek help toward our goal from what has been said by such a predecessor on the subject, regardless of whether this other one shares our religion or not.... By 'those who do not share our religion' I refer to those ancients who studied these matters before Islam" (trans. by George F. Hourani, Lerner and Mahdi 1963, 166–167). So, Islamic philosophy *is* Greek derived? Understandably, the question has been discussed with great interest also among contemporary Muslim philosophers. The answer determines whether philosophy in Islam owes its inception to ancient Greeks (and/or other predecessors) or whether Muslim thinkers were able to create new means and methods of intellectual inquiry on their own. Differing views on this question have been expressed by two renowned Muslim scholars, Majid Fakhry and Seyyed Hossein Nasr. While the latter assumes that Peripateticism (Aristotelian philosophy) formed nothing but a short prelude to actual Islamic philosophy, the former maintains that Muslims wrote the last chapter in the history of Greek philosophy. Upon close scrutiny the two views turn out to be in less sharp opposition than they first appear, especially considering that Fakhry does point out that Muslims did develop their own schools of thought and their own questions independently from the Greeks. More recent research shows that rationalism predated the reception of Greek philosophy in Islam. It thus emerged out of the grammarian schools founded to support Qur'ānic studies (Daiber 2007, 19–39); dominated the teaching of Abū Ḥanīfa (d. 148/767), the founder of Islam's first school of law; and was clearly *the* mark of excellence among Mu'tazilites, Islam's first thinkers. (See Andrey Smirnov's chapter on Hellenistic philosophy.)

Thus, Islamic philosophy has some of its roots in the Greek tradition—and is then rightly called *falsafa* (Arabized term for Greek *philosophia*)—and some in its own intellectual resources. Islamic philosophy may exhibit Greek features but it is nevertheless a tradition of thought defined by its own paths of inquiry. The more interesting question is not, "Is Islamic philosophy Greek derived?" but rather, "How Greek is Islamic philosophy where it happens to be Greek derived?" Thus, when al-Fārābī wove together the political theories of Plato and Aristotle and invented in the process the ideal of the Prophet-Philosopher-King, did he realize that he had actually transformed the Platonic ideal? It is conceivable that he believed the notion of revelation (so central to Islamic doctrine) was integral to the ancient ideal, but it is more likely that he consciously adapted the Greek model to suit the intellectual *Weltanschauung* of his day. As with the ancient temple columns used for the colonnades within mosques, the materials may have been Greco-Roman, but the edifice was Islamic.

Why Islamic Philosophy Is Not Religious Literature

Depending on the author or work studied, an Islamic philosophical text may have been written in defense of religious values, merely include some religious themes and terms, or, to the contrary, not include any religious perspective. Islamic philosophy is as "religious" as Western thought was up to the nineteenth century, in the course of which religious views ceased to play a major role, positively or negatively, in the formulation of most philosophical positions. Intriguingly, the Islamic world witnessed the rise of atheists and other intellectual rebels mostly in the first centuries of its civilization, while the West developed openly atheistic positions rather late in its tradition. What is of greater importance, however, is that Islamic philosophy manifested a deep interest in reflection on religion, which is not the same as being religious. This type of reflection should not be understood as the expression of religious sentiments, certainly not in the ritualistic sense. Religion for most Muslim philosophers of the classical period was taken to be a matter of practical philosophy. Whereas the masses of believers depended on powerful images (Angel of Revelation, Throne of God, delights of paradise, fires of hell, etc.) to prompt in them good actions, philosophers felt they needed to understand the rationale behind religious injunctions in order to perfect themselves. An impressive example for such a rationale may be found in *Ḥayy Ibn Yaqẓān* (*Alive Son of the Awake*), a philosophical tale by Ibn Rushd's mentor, Ibn Ṭufayl (d. 501/1185, Abubacer). Ibn Ṭufayl has Ḥayy, his solitary protagonist and self-taught (Aristotelian) scientist, philosopher, and mystic, walk around a rock as in the Muslim pilgrimage to Mecca, not because he was commanded to do so but because he inferred that becoming like the stars would get him closer to God. In emulation of celestial bodies, Ḥayy thus moves along an invisible circumference or spins around his own axis, a technique still used by the Whirling Dervishes in Turkey. The thinly veiled message sent out by the novel is that for the philosopher the Ka'ba (i.e., the Meccan shrine that houses the Black Stone) is everywhere, because only the philosopher understands the true meaning of the circumambulation Muslims perform during the pilgrimage (i.e., moving ever faster until one's senses are shut and the soul is prepared to receive the divine). As a result, the philosopher's "religion" is mystical; it does not conflict with the rational but is borne of the rational. This is why philosophy in Islam may not be separated from Sufism (i.e. Islamic mysticism). (For Islam's rich, diverse, and widespread mystical tradition, see Erik S. Ohlander's chapter on Sufism.)

Similarly Kalām (i.e., rational theology) is not to be characterized simply as religious literature, in the same way as one wouldn't call Thomas Aquinas's (d. 1274) *Summa Theologica* a work written solely for the purpose of religious edification. While it is safe to assume that individual Muslim theologians were believers, their professional writings do not belong to the genre of pious literature. Mutakallimūn (followers of Kalām) were expected to apply pristine reasoning and follow the methodologies of their respective schools of thought. While there was some controversy as to the legitimacy of Aristotelian logic within theology (mostly because of its dependency on Greek language structures), philosophers like al-Ghazzālī (d. 505/1111) adapted Aristotelian logic for the use of theologians. Also, disputation rules such as dialectic (*jadal*) and disagreement (*khilāf*) were devised for teaching in the schools and also for public debates, which is why theologians were sometimes called people of dialectic (*jadaliyūn*). (For an overview of rational theology in Islam, both in the Sunnī and the Shī'a worlds to this day, see the chapter on Kalām by Eric Ormsby.)

Integral to theological studies in Islam is also jurisprudence; as in Judaism, Muslim theologians are at the same time lawyers. Law in Islam has two components, one normative (*sharī'a*), the other hermeneutic (*fiqh*). The latter ensures the continuous reviewing and adaptation of preexisting law to ever-changing historic conditions of life. While many controversies have shaken the Islamic legal system in its long history, common sense often prevails. Western scholarship has just begun to appreciate the intricacies of legal reasoning in Islam, some of which holds great potential for shaping the future of Muslim societies in the most innovative ways. Suffice it to reflect on the subtle differences between *istiḥsān* (lit., seeking the good), a Ḥanafī principle, and the Mālikī *istislāḥ* (lit., seeking what is wholesome), and how these principles could be applied alternately or in a complementary fashion to promote justice and equity. (See Robert Gleave's chapter "Muslim Jurisprudence," in which philosophical principles are extracted from the reasoning found in classical legal treatises.)

So, what is Islamic philosophy? Philosophy in Islamic sources has many names. It is clearly not only *falsafa* (i.e., Greek inspired). In a more encompassing sense it is *ḥikma* (wisdom), or *ḥikma ishrāqiyya* (illuminationist wisdom) as in the Iranian tradition. Depending on the sources examined, the pursuit of wisdom in Islam is called *'ilm* (knowledge), acquired and/or revealed, *ma'rifa* (mystical knowledge), *kalām*, or *fiqh*. As a result, Islamic philosophy is rational, at times even ultra-rational as in the early Mu'tazilite period; it may be Aristotelian or anti-Aristotelian, logical, mystical, theological, and/or jurisprudential in nature. One shouldn't necessarily think of Islamic philosophy as a "citadel" in which all knowledge that once entered it was "first Muslimized" (Nasr 1976, 9). A closed space is no abode for philosophical reflection. Remarkably, it is precisely the master-theologians of the past who understood that best by, for instance, choosing public debates as a means of inquiry. The adjective in *Islamic* philosophy does not apply to Islam the religion but to the intellectual culture of Islam to which, after all, non-Muslims contributed as well. While Islamic religion remains a defining moment of that culture, both in its Sunnī and various Shī'a expressions, it is by no means the sole criterion of what makes Islamic philosophy the rich and living tradition it is to this day.

BIBLIOGRAPHY

Albertini, Tamara. (1997) "Islamic Philosophy: An Overview." In *The Companion to World Philosophies*, edited by E. Deutsch and R. Bontekoe. Oxford: Blackwell Publishers, 99–133.

Butterworth, Charles E. (ed.). (1992) *The Political Aspects of Islamic Philosophy. Essays in Honor of Muhsin S. Mahdi*. Cambridge, MA: Harvard University Press.

Daiber, Hans. (1999) *Bibliography of Islamic Philosophy*. 2 vols. Leiden, Boston, Köln: Brill.

———. (2007) *Islamic Thought in the Dialogue of Cultures. Innovation and Mediation Between Antiquity and Middle Ages*. Sarajevo: Kult.

Fakhry, Majid. (2001) *Averroes: His Life, Works and Influence*. Oxford: Oneworld Publications.

———. (2004) *A History of Islamic Philosophy* (3rd ed.). New York: Columbia University Press.

Goodman, L. E. (1991) *Ibn Tufayl's Hayy Ibn Yaqzan. A Philosophical Tale* (3rd ed.). Los Angeles: gee tee bee.

———. (1992) *Avicenna*. London and New York: Routledge.

Lerner, Ralph, and Muhsin Mahdi. (1963) *Medieval Political Philosophy*. Ithaca, NY: Cornell University Press.

Makdisi, George. (1990) *The Rise of Humanism in Classical Islam and the Christian West: with Special Reference to Scholasticism*. Edinburgh: Edinburgh University Press.

Nasr, Seyyed Hossein. (1976) *Islamic Science. An Illustrated Study*. World of Islam Festival Publishing Company Ltd., Westerham Press Ltd., Westerham, Kent, U.K.

Nasr, Seyyed Hossein, and Oliver Leaman (eds.). (1996) *History of Islamic Philosophy*. London and New York: Routledge.

Ormsby, Eric. (2008) *Ghazali. The Revival of Islam*. Oxford: Oneworld Publications.

Sharif, M. M. (ed.). (1963) *A History of Muslim Philosophy*. 2 vols. Wiesbaden: O. Harrassowitz.

Shayegan, Yegane. (1996) "The Transmission of Greek Philosophy to the Islamic World." In *History of Islamic Philosophy*, edited by Seyyed Hossein Nasr and Oliver Leaman. London and New York: Routledge, 89–104.

Wahba, Mourad, and Mona Abousenna (eds.). (1996) *Averroës and the Enlightenment*. Amherst, NY: Prometheus Books.

Ziai, Hossein. (1990) *Knowledge and Illumination. A Study of Sohravardī's Ḥikmat al-Ishrāq*. Atlanta, GA: Scholars Press.

CHAPTER 28

THE HELLENIZING PHILOSOPHERS

ANDREY SMIRNOV

The Islamic thinkers who introduced Greek philosophy and Hellenistic approaches to doing philosophy are referred to as the "Hellenizing Philosophers." What did it mean "to Hellenize" in an Islamic cultural milieu? There is no single or uniform answer. The interplay of Islamic and Hellenistic ways of asking questions and constructing arguments to defend conclusions was varied. From some perspectives Greek and Islamic approaches to philosophy were complementary; in other respects there was a tension between two different ways of thinking.

The Hellenizing thinkers introduced Greek philosophy into a culture that already possessed a rich philosophical tradition. The great cities of that time (eighth to ninth centuries, Umayyad and early Abbasid period) were centers of intense polemics concerning the central questions of Islamic doctrine. The Muʿtazilites, the first really influential Islamic school of rational thought, at their "meetings" (*majālis*) made the most substantial contribution to this process.[1] From the beginning, in the early eighth century, they adopted the rational principle of seeking a sufficient, reasonable ground for any statement they made, and not relying on the authority of Revelation. This led them to pursue investigation as far as they could in response to the problems they raised. They introduced basic ontological categories (*wujūd-ʿadam-thubūt*, "existence-nonexistence-fixedness") and discussed the ontological status of things. They had debates concerning divine attributes that focused on the problem of oneness and unity of God and theory of action, and defended the doctrine of human autonomous action and free will. The Muʿtazilites also developed a sophisticated

1. See Ormsby's chapter, Islamic Theology.

physics—including atomistic theories of time, space, and matter—and a rigorous ethics. In addition to philosophical inquiry, the Muʿtazilites contributed to almost every significant field of Islamic science of that time, including jurisprudence and philology. Thus, while it was only through Arabic translations from the Greek that the Islamic world gained access to logical theory, there was much philosophical activity in the Islamic world prior to the translations of Greek philosophy.

Why did Muslim scholars embrace Greek philosophy? There are two primary reasons. First, Greek philosophy was regarded as perfect, accomplished wisdom. This distinguished it favorably from the Muʿtazilite theoretical quest. The Muʿtazilites rarely agreed among themselves. It was the questions, and not the answers, that they had in common, and even the core of their doctrine—the "five principles" (*al-uṣūl al-khamsa*)—were a subject of constant reinterpretation. Greek philosophy, viewed from an Islamic perspective, was completely different in that respect. It was an epitome of wisdom (*ḥikma*), which is "knowledge" (*ʿilm*) with the highest degree of "certitude" (*yaqīn*). Certain knowledge rules out debate, they believed, for it provides answers that are not subject to change. So, wisdom is not only perfect, but is also one; and it is one because it is perfect. When al-Fārābī (d. 339/950) wrote *Al-Jamʿ bayna Raʾyay al-Ḥakīmayn* (*The Harmonization of the Opinions of the Two Sages*), his main concern was to prove that Plato and Aristotle may have disagreed in their "wording" (*alfāẓ*) but they were in agreement in their "meaning" (*maʿānī*). The arguments of his adversaries that he seeks to refute, though, are so numerous that it makes clear that his contemporary Islamic intellectuals recognized the differences between Plato and Aristotle. Later, Shihāb al-Dīn al-Suhrawardī al-Maqtūl ("The Assassinated," d. 587/1191), the founder of the Ishrāqiyya school, declared that all the preceding philosophers and prophets, from Zoroaster and up to Ibn Sīnā (d. 428/1037), proclaimed one and only one wisdom. This testifies to the deep-rootedness of the Islamic version of the *philosophia perennis*—that all great sages share the same wisdom.[2]

The second reason Greek philosophy flourished in Muslim lands was the closing of the foremost schools of Greek learning under Roman emperors in the fifth and sixth centuries—for example, the Edessa School was closed by Zenon in 489 and the Athenian Academy by Justinian in 529. The teachers and students from these institutions were hosted by Persia where they resumed their activities. As a result, Greek learning was concentrated for the next several centuries in Iran and Central Asia. By the time of the Islamic conquests, Greek philosophy had been discussed and commented on by generations of non-Greek scholars. Numerous textbooks on Peripatetic philosophy and Aristotelian logic circulated in various languages, including Syriac, Persian, and Greek. Perhaps because of their own significant intellectual experience, scholars in the Muslim world were able to appreciate the accomplishments of the "ancients" (*qudamāʾ*) in philosophy, astronomy,

2. Ironically, al-Suhrawardī himself coins a new philosophical terminology and elaborates an original philosophy in his *Ḥikmat al-Ishrāq* (*Wisdom of Illumination*), rejecting *falāsifa* (Hellenizing philosophers) and yet proclaiming adherence to the eternal philosophical wisdom.

and medicine. As al-Kindī (d. 256/870) writes in a letter to caliph al-Mu'taṣim: wisdom is wisdom regardless of its origins; it is not tainted by the fact that non-Muslims were the first to develop it and Muslims should not be ashamed of adopting it. This sentiment manifests the value with which knowledge (*'ilm*) and its instrument, reason (*'aql*), are held in Islamic culture. Indeed, it is consistent with a well-known tradition according to which the Prophet urges believers to seek knowledge anywhere, even in the farthest lands of "China," thus transgressing cultural and religious borders. With the arrival of Greek knowledge—especially medicine, the sciences, and philosophy—in their own lands, the Islamic state sanctioned its appropriation and adaption to Islamic culture.

Transmission

The process of translation of Greek knowledge to Arabic was a long and painstaking one. Initially proceeding through the individual efforts of translators, the project was later sponsored by the caliph himself, when the famous *Bayt al-Ḥikma* (*House of Wisdom*) was established by al-Ma'mūn (d. 218/833). Translations into Arabic were made via Syriac or directly from Greek. At the beginning the focus was on Aristotle's logical texts. The first translations were made mainly by non-Arabs and/or non-Muslims, and were difficult to read; almost none of these survived. After several decades much more intelligible translations were produced, and Aristotelian logic started its triumphant march through Islamic philosophy and thought. The problem with the translations was not simply semantic; it also had to do with patterns of thought. Arabic language does possess means of expressing contradictions, but it uses them rarely. The negative particle *lā* may be used with any noun, but this way of constructing dichotomous sets of categories sounds unnatural in Arabic. This somewhat awkward and artificial style is still there in al-Kindī's writings, though it fades away in later authors' works.

Aristotle was the most important of Greek thinkers who found their way into Islamic philosophy. With one important exception, Muslim thinkers possessed a reliable Aristotelian corpus, including far more than the works on logic. That exception is the so-called Theology of Aristotle. Attributed to Aristotle, it is in fact a paraphrase of the last three books of Plotinus's *Enneads*. In addition to the works of Aristotle, Plato's dialogues (*Laws, Sophist, Timaeus*, and others) were circulating in Arabic. Galen was also widely read. Alexander of Aphrodisias' commentaries and Porphyry's *Isagoge* were studied as well. Neopythagorean and Stoic influences are also apparent in Islamic thought, though the textual sources are more difficult to locate.

This legacy of Greek thought was transmitted through professional translations and commentaries, aimed at a relatively narrow circle of scholars. At the same time, numerous encyclopedias and books of *adab* (moralizing instructions furnished in a refined literary style) helped disseminate Greek knowledge among the educated public. (The scope of learning and intellectual culture in Islamic lands during the classical period was much higher than in Europe.) Thus, Greek knowledge gradually became an important, and contested, part of the Islamic intellectual curriculum.

Metaphysics, Cosmology, and Physics

Aristotelianism, Neoplatonism, and Platonism, in addition to less prominent sources, made up an amalgam of what was thought to be a unified wisdom. Teachings of these different schools of thought were used in a way pieces of a puzzle are added one to another to build up a harmonious picture. Where Aristotelianism offered no confident answer, Neoplatonic doctrine was brought into play, disguised as a Peripatetic teaching in the *Theology of Aristotle*. Platonism was the least influential of the three. Most important, it was a resource for theories of the human soul and its faculties, ethical teachings, and al-Fārābī's utopia. However, in psychology and ethics Platonism was competing with the more dominant Aristotelianism. Plato's theory of forms was adopted as a sort of visionary mystical mythology rather than philosophy; idealism more generally has not flourished in Islamic thought.

As a rough scheme, the doctrine resulting out of the careful adjustment of heteronymous teachings was built along the following lines:

The First (the First Principle, the First Thing) is the One. It is perfect unity and absolute perfection. It is simple and nothing precedes it in the order of being. Its simplicity implies that its self (*dhāt*) is identical with its being. Its being is necessary (*wājib*), which means that it had never been nonexistent and can never become nonexistent. This amounts to saying that the First is eternal (*qadīm*).

The "First Thing" is a philosophical name for what religious doctrine calls "God." The "thing" (*shay'*) was understood since the days of the Mu'tazilites as a synonym of "fixed" or "established" (*thābit*), and this understanding prevailed regardless of a dispute over the question whether "fixedness" (*thubūt*) is identical with "being" (*wujūd*) or indicates a distinct ontological state. Since God is certainly "established," "the Thing" can denote Divinity. This identity entitled philosophers to claim the "real," "true" (*ḥaqīqī*) understanding of what religion knew only "metaphorically" (*majāzī*). Given the general Islamic quest for "certitude" (*yaqīn*), it implied that religion is inferior to philosophy; this implication was elaborated by Ibn Rushd (d. 595/1198) in his *Faṣl al-Maqāl* ("Decisive Statement").

In relation to all other things, the First Thing is the First Cause. Itself not caused by anything, the First Cause is the cause of everything, for all the intermediate causes are endowed with causal power derived from the First Cause. This marks an ontological distinction between the First Cause and the rest of the Universe: while the First is eternal and necessary, all the other things are contingent, shifting between nonexistence and existence. This is why our world is called the world of "origination and destruction" (*kawn wa fasād*).

As an absolute perfection, the First Thing is the source from which all other things emanate. The emanation of being (*fayḍ al-wujūd*) takes place not "because" of anything, since the First has no cause, and not "for the sake of" anything, since the absolutely perfect First is deprived of nothing and has no deficiency in itself. Thus, no will is involved in the emanation.

The emanation results in the hierarchy of being, from the perfect to the most contemptible. It is at the same time a hierarchy of unity and multiplicity; of general, particular, and individual; and of good and evil.

The emanation first produces cosmic intellects, from the first to the tenth. They correspond to the ten celestial concentric spheres. The lowest seven of those are occupied by the seven "heavenly bodies," with the Sun in the center and the Moon in the lowest sphere. Above those is the sphere of "fixed stars," after which another two spheres are added so that the whole number is ten. The intellect occupying the sphere of the Moon is the Active Intellect. It is a depositary of all the forms to be found in the sublunary world.

The sublunary world consists of four concentric spheres of the four elements: fire, air, water, and earth. The sphere of the earth is the planet we live on, situated in the center of the universe and by Divine wisdom and care deprived of strictly spherical figure. The mountains and plateaus are projected into the air from under the water high above their natural locus. This is what makes life on earth possible.

Each of the four elements possesses a pair of qualities, being either dry or humid, and either hot or cold. The reason for this variety is the effect of the celestial spheres' rotation and the heat this movement causes, for it gradually fades away as we move from the lunar sphere, under which the dry and hot fire is situated, toward the center where earth, the cold and dry element, is located.

Mixing of the four elements on the earth's surface accounts for the variety of earthly beings. There are three basic classes: minerals (*jamād*), plants (*nabāt*), and animals (*ḥayawān*), according to the three principal grades of the mixture's balanced subtlety (*iʿtidāl*). The more balanced and subtle the mixture is, the more it is ready to accept the soul and life donated from above and flowing through the universe. Minerals are deprived of soul. Plants possess vegetable soul with its faculty of growth. Animals, in addition to the vegetable soul, possess animal soul with its aggression and strive for pleasure. Those faculties are needed to repel enemies and reproduce. Human beings possess rational (*nāṭiq*) soul as well.

Beings in the sublunary world are corporeal. They are constituted by matter and form. The physical body by definition possesses three spatial dimensions. In theory, any body can be divided infinitely; in actuality, however, there always exists a limit to that division. Thus, no atoms exist, and Muʿtazilites' atomistic theories of matter were discarded as incompatible with Aristotelian continuity. Inferior spatial dimensions are limits of the superior, not their elements; thus, a line is a limit of a plane, constituted by the intersection of two nonparallel planes, but does not "consist of" dots and is not constructed by adding one dot to another. The Muʿtazilites argued for almost the opposite and thought that a juxtaposition (not addition) of two dots would produce a line, and so on; in Aristotelian perspective this argument was considered erroneous as well. Finally, the present is the limit between past and future, and time, being a measure of eternal celestial movement, is continuous and cannot be divided into basic atomic elements. Thus, the third of Muʿtazilites' atomistic theories is rejected.

Physical bodies "move," which means they can "act," which in turn runs contrary to the Muʿtazilites' view. Their sophisticated theories of movement "originating" (*mutawallid*) in physical bodies—which are only "metaphorical" (*majāzī*), and cannot be "real" (*ḥaqīqī*) actors, for they have no will, while "willing" (*irāda*), according to the Muʿtazilites, is essential for action—through a "real" agent (i.e., human being), are no longer needed to explain physical movement. It emerges naturally when an element is displaced and leaves its natural locus, and by that natural movement it returns to where it belongs; in all other cases the movement is coercive and requires application of a force.

Obvious examples testified to the validity of Aristotelian physics. The light of a candle always points upward, toward the natural locus of fire. Air encapsulated in a goatskin would not go under water unless forced to do so; it would naturally move upward and pops up from under the water when released because its natural locus is above water. The application of this theory was vivid and convincing, and the theory itself simple and elegant. Contrasted with Muʿtazilites' physics, which operated with notions not related directly to anything perceptible by the senses, Muslim scholars opted for the theory of less complexity and greater demonstrative force.

Everything in the sublunary world has four causes, namely, its matter, its form, the agent who produced it, and the goal for which the actor acted. Only when all four (*materialis, formalis, efficiens, finalis*) come together and any obstacle for their effectiveness is absent do they produce their fruit, bringing their effect into existence. In the world of generation and corruption, this process goes on endlessly without beginning. Thus, the world as a whole is eternal, though everything in it comes into existence and perishes.

Epistemology

According to the Islamic thinkers who appropriated Greek philosophy, the soul is the perfection of the body. The human soul has the faculty to detach forms from matter and operate with them; this faculty distinguishes it from all other beings endowed with soul. Two ways lead to the acquisition of forms. First, they are to be found in the world, in the beings around us. This is a way of exploration, of learning by experience. Second, they all are to be found in the Active Intellect, the intellect of the lunar sphere. If we access it, we acquire the forms immediately from their source and not by detaching them from matter. This is a way of gaining immediate knowledge. This general scheme is the basis for the interplay of two epistemological strategies, that of logical and of intuitive (not mystical) cognition, which we find in the Hellenizing philosophers' writings.

The former way, the way of exploration, is paved by logic, the instrument for operating with abstract forms. First, correct notions need to be constructed; second, they need to be organized correctly so that they produce "certain" (*yaqīnī*) knowledge. Correct notions are formed by definitions through *genus* and *differentia*, and later used in syllogisms. Aristotelian logic was catechized and popularized through innumerable treatises (this activity is associated mainly with al-Fārābī), and was valorized as an instrument.

Islamic authors, however, did not fail to point out its deficiencies. First, it requires tools to be applied in order to produce its fruit. Whenever the use of a tool is involved, there is always a threat of mistake: a notion might be formed erroneously, and a syllogism might be faulty. Thus, logic does not guarantee against errors. Second, the object of logical cognition is that which may be captured by correct notions, which means it should have a genus. This is not a problem for most things, yet it does not hold for the First Thing, which is the First Cause. However, we do not know anything truly unless we know the First Cause, which is the ultimate cause of everything; and knowing the First Cause, we know all the other things. So, what about the instrument of cognition that fails to grasp the First Cause? The argument for existence of a genus composed of only one individual, which some philosophers advanced, was too weak to close the gap.

As for the latter way, the way of intuition, it is devoid of both of these flaws. Being an immediate cognition, it uses no tool. When Ibn Sīnā started to develop his theory of intuition (*ḥads*), he pointed to human ego (*anā, anā'iyya*) and Divinity as two of its "objects," and later the Ishrāqiyya school declared everything to be cognizable intuitively through "illuminating conjugation" (*iḍāfa ishrāqiyya*). These advantages are balanced, though, by the difficulty of practicing intuitive cognition. While logic is accessible by anyone with enough intelligence and capacity to memorize its rules, there is no way to teach intuitive cognition. It is a gift rather than a fruit of goal-oriented action, though some propedeutic steps leading to it (like physical asceticism and moral piety) were considered helpful. The dialectic of the two ways of cognition was dwelt upon metaphorically by Ibn Sīnā in *Ḥayy Ibn Yaqẓān* (*The Living, Son of the Awake*) and later by al-Suhrawardī al-Maqtūl in *al-Ghurba al-Gharbiyya* (*The Western Outland*), and elaborated in detail by Ibn Ṭufayl (d. 501/1185) in his famous *Ḥayy Ibn Yaqẓān*.

Ethics and Aesthetics

According to the Hellenizing philosophers, the hierarchy of unity and multiplicity, paralleled by the hierarchy of general and particular, sets up the coordinates of human perfection, be it individual or collective. The way to individual perfection is twofold, as the way of cognition is. First, it is a path for acquiring virtues and expurgating vices. Aristotelian ethics explains how to do that: first, we have to realize that every virtue is a middle between the two extremes, which are vices; and second, we have to purify ourselves in accordance with that knowledge and practice virtues, not vices. Authors such as Yaḥyā Ibn ʿAdī (d. 974) and Miskawayh (d. 1030; *Tahdhīb al-akhlāq, Arrangement of Characters*, and *Risāla fī māhiyyat al-ʿadl, Treatise on the Quiddity of Justice*) gave rise to a whole tradition of treatises on virtues and vices, to be followed by giants like Naṣīr al-Dīn al-Ṭūsī (d. 672/1274). This way of knowledge and practice is focused on the world we live in, with its causes and effects; in this respect it is similar to the epistemological strategy of exploration.

Second, there is a path to individual perfection focused on the supreme cause, which is elevated above all the other causes and does not belong to this world. This supreme cause is sometimes identified with the Active Intellect of the lunar sphere, for it "administers" (*tadbīr*) the affairs of our world being the source of all forms. As philosophers shifted from an Aristotelian to a Neoplatonic perspective (which for them, though, was still understood to be Aristotelian), the supreme cause was identified with the First Cause. Only the soul, not the body, is capable of reuniting with the First Unity; therefore, our goal is to train it so that it can exercise its independence from the body, and even leave it before physical death, returning to it after some time. This is a way of mystical unity with the Divine, disguised as philosophy.

A way to collective human perfection is described in the famous *Ārā' Ahl al-Madīna al-Fāḍila* (*Views of the Virtuous City's Inhabitants*) by al-Fārābī. He constructs his "virtuous city" as a paraphrase of Plato's utopia. By their nature human beings need "community" (*ijtimāʿ*), since, if left to face the world alone, they perish because they are unable to attend to their needs. The city is the least possible level of human community, and it needs to be organized according to strict rules; it is an artificial construction, and never a natural phenomenon. The virtuous city is the one in which knowledge is matched by action, and both are perfect. Perfection of knowledge is provided for by adoption of philosophical wisdom; perfection of action is achieved through the proper hierarchical organization of society. The more general the science practiced in this or that profession, the higher its level, and the highest of all the sciences is the science of politics (*siyāsa*). Thus, there is only one type of virtuous city, while deviant, and therefore vicious, cities are many, depending on the degree to which knowledge and/or action are corrupted.

Greek aesthetics also influenced the Hellenizing philosophers, but to a lesser extent. In Islamic culture beauty and the beautiful relate not just to the perfection of form, but also to the perfection of correspondence between the "outward," the "external" (*ẓāhir*), and the "inward," the "internal" (*bāṭin*). This calls for particular means of artistic expression and accounts for the unique character of Islamic art throughout its various epochs and geographic diversity. Thus, while Muslim scholars did comment on Greek texts on aesthetics, especially Aristotle's *Poetics*, Greek thought did not have a major influence on Islamic poetics. Despite various Islamic attempts to adopt Aristotelian aesthetic theory, the metaphorical repertoire of

Arabic poetry had to be described and analyzed in terms developed by Islamic theorists.

Adoption by Islamic Intellectual Milieu

The vast teachings of Greek thought were adopted and appropriated by Islamic culture in several ways. It is helpful to consider the Hellenizing philosophers from at least three perspectives: first, the overall perspective of Islamic intellectual culture; second, a perspective of *falsafa* (Arabicized Greek *philosophia*), or more specifically philosophers working with Greek, especially Aristotelian, approaches; and third, a perspective of Islamic philosophy in general.

In the first perspective, the impact of Hellenistic wisdom was felt in nearly every branch of knowledge. *Adab* literature of all kinds, being an assemblage of wise and instructive pieces of knowledge, by its very nature was apt to incorporate the philosophical legacy of Greek antiquity. While the Muʿtazilites did not fall under the spell of Hellenistic philosophy, at its post-Muʿtazilite stages *Kalām* gradually mixed, to some extent, with Greek thought. In striving to build up Islamic doctrine, the Ash'arite *Kalām*, revising Muʿtazilite philosophy and restricting its rational character, drew on Greek wisdom, with which it also sometimes came into tension.[3]

These tensions are addressed at length by al-Ghazālī (d. 505/1111) in his *Tahāfut al-falāsifa* (*Inconsistencies of the Philosophers*). The most critical points of tension are (1) the God of the *falāsifa* is deprived of will and the knowledge of individuals (it has only general, unchangeable knowledge), which means it does not decide the fate of human beings; (2) the world is eternal, and not created, which contradicts scripture; and (3) Islamic doctrine insists on corporeal resurrection of the dead, while *falāsifa* acknowledged spiritual resurrection and denied the corporeal one.

Summarizing the classical period of Islamic culture, Ibn Khaldūn (d. 808/1406) says in his *Al-Muqaddima* (*Introduction*) that *falsafa* is widespread and taught everywhere in Islamic cities; however, one should be cautious and start learning it only after getting firmly established in Islamic doctrine and sciences. Otherwise, one's mind would be led to where there is no certainty. At the same time, he defended the view that logic is the best tool known to humankind.

In *fiqh*, Islamic law and jurisprudence, a number of great figures, among them the celebrated al-Ghazālī, advocated the adoption of Aristotelian syllogistics in order to replace the *qiyās*—"measurement" of a new legal case by a standard of the known, or precedent—practiced by *fuqahā'*; these attempts, however, were in vain. *Ikhwān al-Ṣafā'* (*Brethren of Purity*, tenth century) relied on Greek wisdom in their epistles, which aimed at enlightening society. And, of course, the sciences of

3. See Ormsby's chapter in this section.

medicine, astronomy, and mathematics were deeply influenced by and associated with Hellenistic philosophy.

The second perspective is shaped by *falsafa*; its representatives are called *falāsifa* (sing. *faylasūf*). This is a celebrated school of Hellenizing philosophers that flourished on Islamic soil. The pantheon of its most eminent adherents in the Eastern lands of Islam includes al-Kindī, "The Philosopher of the Arabs"; al-Fārābī, "The Second Teacher" (the first being Aristotle); and Ibn Sīnā, "The Head Master," while in the West it is represented by Ibn Bājja (d. 533/1139), Ibn Ṭufayl, and Ibn Rushd, the great "Commentator" of Aristotle.

Falāsifa did their best to preserve, comment on, and transmit the wisdom of the Greeks. In accomplishing this task they were remarkably successful, though this was not their only achievement. As they addressed the important metaphysical and ethical questions of their time, they followed their own, non-Greek, original lines of thought. This accounts for two aspects of *falsafa*, one consistent with the Greeks, and the other more or less independent.

This second side was brought into play already by al-Kindī, in *Fī al-Falsafa al-Ūlā* (*On First Philosophy*) and other treatises where he speaks about "horizontal" causality. This is accounted for by the four Aristotelian causes, which explain how beings of this world produce one another. Yet there is another, "vertical" causality, running from anything of this world up to the First Cause through intermediate causes. This line of causality is more important in quite a definite way, for any "acting" (*fā'iliyya*) cause would act only because it borrows its power of activity from the First Cause. To know the thing is to know its causes, al-Kindī says; and if we speak of "vertical" causality, we cannot know a thing unless we know the First Cause. It is the real and the true (*ḥaqīqī*) cause, while all the others are metaphorical (*majāzī*). This is the focal point of very different perspectives, that of Islamic doctrine with its central principle of *tawḥīd* (in one of its readings it means rendering all the causality to God); of Islamic ethical piety with its principle of "relying" (*tawakkul*) on God as the only real cause; and of Sufism with its striving to reach God as the only "basis" and "source" (*aṣl*) of being. When later Ibn Sīnā wrote in his *Al-Ishārāt wa al-tanbīhāt* (*Directives and Remarks*) that all the four causes boil down to the acting cause, he was following the same line of argument.

If the First Cause is the only Real Thing, what about all the other things? They are "possible" (*mumkin*), gaining their "necessity" (*wujūb*) from their cause, to which they get "attached" (*ta'alluq*), and this line of borrowing the necessity is identical with the line of vertical causality. When the thing is detached from its cause, or its cause is unable to act, it becomes "impossible" (*mumtani'*). Both necessity and impossibility are borrowed by the thing from "the other," that is, its cause (and ultimately from the First Cause), while the thing as such, taken in itself, is "possible." If necessity and impossibility are identified with being and nonbeing accordingly, possibility is the third ontological state, resembling what the Mu'tazilites meant by "fixed" (*thābit*) thing. This ontology was developed by al-Fārābī (*Fuṣūṣ al-Ḥikma*, "Bezels of wisdom"; *Al-Ta'līqāt*, "Comments") and Ibn Sīnā and later severely criticized as non-Aristotelian by Ibn Rushd.

Philosophical exploration in Islamic culture was not limited to *falsafa*. Muʿtazila, Ishrāqiyya, Ismāʿīliyya, and Ṣūfī schools of thought contributed to philosophy as well.[4] Only the Muʿtazila were not influenced by the Greeks, while the others responded to Greek knowledge or utilized its teachings. After the general perspective of Islamic culture and the school of *falsafa*, this is the third way in which Hellenizing philosophy was present in Islamic culture.

Al-Suhrawardī, the founder of the Ishrāqiyya school, is indebted to Ibn Sīnā inasmuch as the latter developed the theory of intuition (*ḥads*) and ontology of the thing "as such," regardless of its existence and nonexistence. However, al-Suhrawardī dismisses the teachings of *falāsifa* on the basis of his utmost nominalism (no general notion has any reality outside the mind) and sensualism (reality is basically simple and is perceptible only by senses). In the later elaboration of Ishrāqiyya by the "School of Isfahan" (Mīr Dāmād [d. 1041/1631], Ṣadr al-Dīn al-Shīrāzī [d. 1050/1640], and others), the lexicon of *falāsifa* was incorporated and their teachings mixed with early Ishrāqiyya doctrine.[5]

In Ismāʿīliyya philosophy, represented first and foremost by Ḥamīd al-Dīn al-Kirmānī (d. beginning of eleventh century) with his *Rāḥat al-ʿAql* (*Peace of Mind*), Aristotelian teachings are used to explain all that goes on in the sublunary world, while the ontological status of God, sociology, and very interesting historiosophy were elaborated on a non-Aristotelian and mostly non-Hellenistic basis. In Ṣūfī philosophy, which culminated in the writings of Ibn ʿArabī (d. 638/1240), the lexicon of *falāsifa*, as well as the lexicon of nearly all preceding philosophical and nonphilosophical schools of thought, is used; however, the well-known categories of antiquity are reinterpreted in the light of *waḥdat al-wujūd* (unity of being) philosophy, which shapes, for Ibn ʿArabī, the true perspective for interpreting *falsafa*.

Conclusion

As a result of the encounter with Greek thought, Islamic culture appropriated and adopted Greek philosophical knowledge. Oddly, this came at the expense of Islam's "homegrown" rationalist school of thought: Muʿtazilite philosophy. The *Mu'tazila* initiated and developed investigations in a number of the most important fields of philosophy, as well as philology and *fiqh*. These included philosophy of time and space, philosophy of language, and theories of action and ethics, to name only the most important ones. These theories were elaborated on a basis of rationality quite different from that of the Greeks.

Though *falsafa* was attacked by religious orthodoxy (*aqīda*), they both opposed followers of the *Mu'tazila* school—each for its own reasons. As a result, unable to

4. See the other chapters on Islamic philosophy in this volume.
5. See Ziai's chapter on Philosophy of Illumination.

face the double pressure of the overwhelming intellectual authority of the Greeks and dogmatic doctrinal religious authority, the Mu'tazilite influence waned and they were eventually forced out of the main intellectual centers of the Islamic world. The Ash'arite doctrinal dogmatic teaching replaced Mu'tazilite views as the dominant philosophical orientation. The Ash'arites preserved some central points of their earlier rivals, first and foremost their atomism; however, the search for the ultimate and unrestricted rational reasoning behind those theories was gone forever from *Kalām*. The opposite is true for *falsafa*. Rationalism was preserved, but the most creative and original findings of the Mu'tazilites were simply dropped and substituted by the adopted wisdom of the Greeks.

BIBLIOGRAPHY AND SUGGESTED READINGS

FAKHRY, MAJID. (2004) *A History of Islamic Philosophy* (3rd ed.). New York: Columbia University Press.

MOREWEDGE, PARVIZ (ed.). (1981) *Islamic Philosophy and Mysticism*. Delmar, NY: Caravan Books.

NASR, SEYYED HOSSEIN, and OLIVER LEAMAN (eds.). (1996) *History of Islamic Philosophy*. London and New York: Routledge.

RESCHER, N. (1964) *The Development of Arabic Logic*. Pittsburgh, PA: University of Pittsburgh Press.

SHARIF, M. M. (ed.). (1983) *A History of Muslim Philosophy*. Karachi: Royal Book Co. (first edition: Wiesbaden, Harrassowitz, 1963–1966).

WALZER, R. (1962) *Greek into Arabic. Essays on Islamic Philosophy*. Cambridge, MA: Harvard University Press.

WATT, M. W. (1962) ***Islamic Philosophy and Theology***. Edinburgh: Edinburgh University Press.

Primary Sources

AL-FĀRĀBĪ:

(1998) *On the Perfect State* (Mabadi' ara' ahl al-madinat al-fadilah), revised text with introduction, translation, and commentary by Richard Walzer. Great Books of the Islamic World, Chicago, IL: Distributed by KAZI Publications.

(2001) *Philosophy of Plato and Aristotle*, translated by Muhsin Mahdi. Revised edition. Ithaca, NY: Cornell University Press.

AL-GHAZĀLĪ:

(2002) *On the Boundaries of Theological Tolerance in Islam*, translated by Sherman A. Jackson. Oxford: Oxford University Press.

(1997) *The Incoherence of the Philosophers*. A parallel English-Arabic text translated, introduced, and annotated by Michael E. Marmura. Provo, UT: Brigham Young University Press.

AL-KINDĪ:

(1974) *Al-Kindi's Metaphysics*, translated by Alfred L. Ivry. Albany, NY: State University of New York Press.

IBN KHALDŪN:
(1967) *The Muqaddimah* (2nd ed.), translated from the Arabic by Franz Rosenthal. Princeton, NJ: Princeton University Press.
IBN RUSHD (Averroës):
(2001) *The Book of the Decisive Treatise Determining the Connection Between the Law and Wisdom, and The Epistle Dedicatory*, translation with introduction and notes by Charles E. Butterworth. Provo, UT: Brigham Young University Press.
(1982) *The Epistle on the Possibility of Conjunction with the Active Intellect*, with the commentary of Moses Narboni, a critical edition and annotated translation by Kalman P. Bland. New York: Jewish Theological Seminary of America.
(1954) *Averroes' Tahafut Al-Tahafut* (The Incoherence of the Incoherence). 2 vols. Translated by Simon van den Bergh. London: Luzac.
IBN SĪNĀ (Avicenna):
(1984) *Remarks and Admonitions*, translated by Shams Constantine Inati. Toronto, Ontario, Canada: Pontifical Institute of Mediaeval Studies.
(2004) *The Metaphysics of The Healing*, translated, introduced, and annotated by Michael E. Marmura. Provo, UT: Brigham Young University Press.
IBN ṬUFAYL:
(2003) *Ibn Tufayl's Hayy ibn Yaqzan*. A philosophical tale translated with introduction and notes by Lenn Evan Goodman. Los Angeles, CA: Gee Tee Bee.
MISKAWAYH:
(1968) *The Refinement of Character*. A translation from the Arabic of Ahmad ibn Muhammad Miskawayh's Tahdhib al-akhlaq by Constantine K. Zurayk. Beirut: American University of Beirut.
(1964) *An Unpublished Treatise of Miskawaih on Justice, or, Risala fi Mahiyat al-'Adl li Miskawaih*, edited with notes, annotations, English translation, and an introduction by M. S. Kahn. Leiden: E. J. Brill.
AL-MĀWARDĪ:
(1996) *Al-Ahkam as-Sultaniyyah*, translated by Asadullah Yate. London: Ta-Ha Publishers.
AL-ṬŪSĪ, NAṢĪR AL-DĪN:
(1964) *The Nasirean Ethics*, translated from the Persian by G. M. Wickens. London: Allen and Unwin.

CHAPTER 29

PHILOSOPHY OF ILLUMINATION

HOSSEIN ZIAI

Illumination (*Ishrāq*) is derived from the Arabic triliteral root: *sh-r-q;* its most basic meaning is "rising," or more precisely "rising of the sun" (Lane 1987, I:1539–1541). The term has been widely used in a range of Arabic and Persian texts in intellectual domains, including Persian poetry, with the semantic signification of nonnoëtic cognitive modes: "intuitive," "immediate," "a-temporal," "nonordinary," and "inspirational." A number of Persian thinkers have chosen *Ishrāq* as their "poetic name" (*takhalluṣ*), as exemplified in the poetic works of the seventeenth-century Persian philosopher Mīr Dāmād.

The Philosophy of Illumination (*al-Ḥikma*, or *al-Falsafa al-Ishrāqiyya*) was first introduced in the twelfth century as a holistic system distinct from both Ibn Sīnā's Peripateticism and the period's rising theological philosophy. The latter was presented in textbooks following Ghazzālī's guidelines to limit philosophy to the role of "handmaiden" of theology, and is best exemplified by Athīr al-Dīn Abharī's thirteenth-century Arabic text, *Ḥidāyat al-Ḥikma* (*Guide to Philosophy*), which together with numerous commentaries, glosses, and superglosses has been widely used in the Islamic philosophical curriculum, especially in the Iranian and Indian Madrasas, up to the present. The aim of the Philosophy of Illumination is to refine rational philosophy, not to refute it, and thus to provide an alternative approach to analytical and rational philosophy in response to al-Ghazzālī's attacks on rationalism in his *Incoherence of the Philosophers* (*Tahāfut al-Falāsifa*). The Philosophy of Illumination, while never attaining the mainstream acceptance bestowed on textbook philosophy defined by Abharī's work, was, however, elevated to the level of an independent school of philosophy, widely regarded as the most creative continuation of philosophical investigation after Ibn Sīnā (d. 428/1037).

The Philosophy of Illumination is constructed by the young Persian philosopher Shihāb al-Dīn Yaḥyā ibn Amīrak Sohravardī (also transliterated as Suhrawardī), born in 549/1155 in Northeastern Iran in the hamlet Sohravard, and executed in 587/1191 in Aleppo. In his short life he authored more than 50 works; the most famous is titled *Ḥikmat al-Ishrāq* (*The Philosophy of Illumination*),[1] which is aimed at refining philosophical problems.

The most important works of the new system are Sohravardī's four major Arabic texts: *The Intimations* (*al-Talwīḥāt*), *The Apposites* (*al-Muqāwamāt*), *The Paths and Havens* (*al-Mashāri' wa al-Muṭāraḥāt*), and *The Philosophy of Illumination* (*Ḥikmat al-Ishrāq*). These works constitute an integral corpus presenting the details of the new system, the Philosophy of Illumination.[2] Though of lesser philosophical significance, the Arabic treatises *The Imādin Tablets* (*al-Alwāḥ al-Imādiyya*) and *Temples of Light* (*Hayākil al-Nūr*) and the Persian *The Book of Radiance* (*Partow Nāmeh*) may also be added.

Sohravardī argues that the logical foundations of the Illumination system incorporate the principles and arguments of Islamic Peripatetic Philosophy (*al-Falsafa al-Mashshā'iyya*). Because these two systems appear similar, some scholars have suggested that the Philosophy of Illumination is mostly limited to Ibn Sīnā's Peripateticism, but retold in a symbolic language of light entities—existents (*mawjūdāt*)—in all realms of being. Most scholars, however, distinguish between the ontological, epistemological, and cosmological principles of the two systems. Sohravardī's innovative departure and refinement of sets of problems taken from the corpus of Islamic Peripatetic philosophy—mainly in Ibn Sīnā texts—are all presented in the major texts that comprise the Philosophy of Illumination. In sum, Sohravardī is accepted to this day as the founder of a new refined system of philosophy, a holistic construction named "Philosophy of Illumination."

Structure and Problems of the Philosophy of Illumination

Structure of Illuminationist Texts

Following Ibn Sīnā's magnum opus *The Healing* (*al-Shifā'*), theoretical Illuminationist texts are divided into three parts: Logic, the First Science; Physics, the Second Science; and a two-part Metaphysics (*generalis* and *specialis*), the Third

1. This text has been recently translated into English (Suhrawardī 2000).

2. See Ziai 1990b, 9–15, where I argue that based on Sohravardī's own explicit statements, these works together make up a corpus in which he carefully and systematically presents the genesis and development of the philosophy of illumination.

Science. The order in which subjects are covered in *al-Shifāʾ* are rearranged. Traditional questions treated in the canon of Aristotelian logic, known as the *Isagoge*, are reduced mainly to semantics of signification—things, terms, or names, and types and levels of signification, or meanings assigned to terms when used technically. Detailed attention is given to logical fallacies, which are grouped together with the presumed faults and shortcomings of Peripatetic philosophy. Another significant structural Illuminationist innovation is the addition of a Prolegomena (*Muqaddima*) to philosophical texts, where the author discusses "method" (*ṭarīq al-ʾilm*), "intention" (*qaṣd*), "terminology" and the notion of a constructed meta-language (*lisān al-ishrāq*, meaning "language of illumination), and a special view of the history of philosophy and ancient wisdom.

This special view of history presents an elaborate set of sources for the transmission of philosophical wisdom up to Sohravardī himself: the Greek (Pythagorean and "early" Greek, Hermetic, Platonic, and Aristotelian), the Indian (Brahmin sages), the ancient Iranian Khosravānī and Pahlavānī, and ninth-century Islamic pantheist mysticism (Abū Yazīd al-Bastāmī, Abū Ḥasan al-Kharraqānī, and Manṣūr Ḥallāj). In this lineage Sohravardī considers himself to be the one who has revived and harmonized the quintessence (*khamīreh*) of each tradition.[3] This type of Prolegomena on method is distinguished from the Peripatetic "Introduction" (*al-Madkhal*, i.e., Porphyry's *Isagoge*) to the *Organon*, and is considered the first step in the study of philosophy in all textbook compositions.

Epistemology and Methodology

Illuminationist philosophy challenges the Peripatetic position of the absolute, unchanging, and universal validity of "truths" discovered by applying Aristotle's method of science defined in *Posterior Analytics* (I.1 and 2) and *Metaphysics* (XII). The arguments focus on the epistemology of primary principles of science, whose problematic status is admitted by the great Stagirite himself. In response, Sohravardī's Philosophy of Illumination makes the attempt to construct a unified epistemological theory, named "Knowledge by Presence" (*al-ʿilm al-ḥuḍūrī*), where the entire range of knowing is defined in all domains, such as sense, intellect, dream, inspiration, and so forth. This includes "immediate knowledge," defined by Aristotle as the necessary indemonstrable first step of demonstrative science. The stipulated aim of the novel reconstruction is to advance the method of investigation by continually questioning universal validity of any "law" (*al-qawāʿid, al-ḥukūmāt, al-barāhīn*, etc.) deduced at a given time and place. The aim is to reconstruct a system through which a "new" scientific method, named "The Science of Lights" (*ʿIlm al-Anwār*), is defined to improve and expand philosophical inquiry applied to all realms, and specifically to rectify the dilemma of how the first step of science is obtained, by

3. See Ziai 1992.

focusing on what is the relation between knowing and being, and to analyze if primary knowledge is predicative or not. The new method takes the identity between the knower and the known as the first step in science, thus, *mudrik* (active agent for the verb *d-r-k* in Form IV, indicating knowing in the most general way, thus "knower," and *daryābandeh* in Persian).[4] The thesis of the "identity/sameness of the knower and known" replaces the Peripatetic thesis of "conjunction of the acquired intellect with the Active Intellect." Defining identity relations between knower and the known, or knowing and being, was considered a solution to the problem of determining the first step in science and the origin of its primary principles.

Philosophy of Illumination and Aristotelian Scientific Method

According to Aristotelian method, science is to be constructed on the most fundamental and best-known principles. Aristotle claims that such principles are *not* obtained by syllogistic demonstration (or, more precisely, by scientific syllogism). And, though he does state in more than one place that principles of science are known not by means of inference or demonstration, but by immediate knowledge, he never precisely distinguishes "immediate knowledge" (*nous*) from "opinion" (*doxa*).

Aristotle first names "primary knowledge" a kind of "immediate knowledge," or "intuition" (he uses the same term *nous* for both), and states that it is "a starting-point of knowledge," but then leaves unanswered the question of whether this type of preinferential knowledge is "opinion," *doxa*, valid by "common acceptance," or something known epistemically as "scientific knowledge." Sohravardī claims that his reconstructed system, which introduces a new and more consistent scientific method, the "Science of Lights" (*'Ilm al-Anwār*), resolves this ambiguity through its unified epistemological theory, Knowledge-by-Presence.[5] Sohravardī unequivocally posits primacy to atemporal, preinferential, and immediate knowledge, which is intuitive knowledge by the conscious self prior to differentiation between subject and object.

Illuminationist philosophy contests the Aristotelian position that the laws of science formulated as A-propositions (The Universal Affirmative, *al-mūjiba al-kulliya*) are both necessary and always true. Sohravardī argues that future contingency (*al-imkān al-mustaqbal*) is a scientific principle. Using this principle and others, he further argues that contrary to the Aristotelian position, laws of science cannot be universal,[6] since the validity of these principles are based on observations now and in the future.

4. *Mudrak* (known, *daryāfteh* in Persian) are "related" by *huwa huwa* or *'ayniyya*, indicating sameness.

5. See Ha'iri Yazdi 1992.

6. 3.2 The problem of universal propositions (*al-qaḍāyā al-kulliyya*) is introduced in formal logic. In the Illuminationist scheme, a conclusion reached by using a formally established syllogism has no epistemological value as a starting point in philosophical construction. The argument for this rests on the mode "necessary" (*al-wajh al-ḍarūrī*) and the modal "always" (*dā'iman*). For a universal affirmative

The impact of the Philosophy of Illumination has been most pronounced in epistemology, where it is widely known. Illuminationist logic, for example, is well known only to specialists. The epistemological priority status given to intuitive knowledge has dominated "speculative mysticism" (*al-'irfān al-naẓarī*) in Iran, and is still integral to mainstream intellectual Persian poetry. The way Persian poetic wisdom, for example, seeks to unravel the mysteries of nature is not through the principles of physics, but by means of the metaphysical world and the realm of myths, dreams, fantasy, and truths known intuitively, or in poetic language "illuminationist knowledge" (Per. *'ilm-e ishrāqī*) and "inspirational knowledge"—the poetic formulation of the "end" of Illuminationist theory of knowledge.

Logic

The Philosophy of Illumination examines the status of Aristotelian essentialist definition and its place in the foundations of scientific knowledge. The analysis of the place of essentialist definition and of its composition as the sum of the *summum genus* and the *differentiae* of the thing defined is elaborated in chapter 2 of the unpublished *Part One* (on logic) of Sohravardī's most extensive Arabic work, *al-Mashāri' wa al-Muṭāraḥāt* (*Paths and Havens*). Five types of definitions are classified. Sohravardī's fifth type of definition is a type of conceptualist definition, a "formula that makes something known by means of its concept."[7] The Illuminationist critique of Aristotelian essentialist definitions is closely paralleled in William of Ockham's *Summa Logicæ, Pars Prima*, as both Ockham and Sohravardī add the semantics of signification to their arguments.[8] In brief, the critique is based on the impossibility of combining the *summum genus* with all the *differentiæ* of the thing to be defined. Thus, knowledge of the thing's essence cannot be obtained by formulae named "definition." Knowledge of essence and knowledge of primary principles are obtained by an intuitive mode of cognition, which is "triggered" by the act of the self-conscious I-ness "in" (*fī*) a continuo us reality, where each individual constituent of the Whole (*al-Kull*) possesses a degree of self-consciousness, stated in terms of intensity of luminosity, including that of the most self-conscious Light of Lights in the entire continuum of existence.

proposition to have philosophical value as a foundation of scientific knowledge, it must be "necessary and always true." By introducing the mode "possibility" (*imkān*) and by giving it an extension in time as in "future possibility" (*al-imkān al-mustaqbal*), the universal affirmative proposition cannot be "necessarily true always." This is because of the impossibility of knowing, or deducing, all possible future instances.

7. See Ziai 1990b, ch. II and III.

8. See, for example, *Summa Logicæ, Pars Prima*, 12: "Second intentions," compared to *i'tibārāt 'aqliyya*, in the *Philosophy of Illumination, Part One*, III.3.1, §56ff; and especially, *Summa Logicæ, Pars Prima*, 26: "On Definition," which is remarkably similar to the *Philosophy of Illumination, Part One*, I.7, §13 through §16.

Ontology

The Illuminationist ontological position, called "primacy of quiddity," distinguishes philosophical schools of Islamic philosophy in Iran up to the present day. It is also a matter of considerable controversy. Those who believe in the primacy of being, or existence (*wujūd*), consider essence (*māhiyya*) to be a derived, mental concept (*amr i'tibārī*), while those who believe in the primacy of quiddity consider existence to be a derived, mental concept. The Illuminationist position is that existence must be considered an abstract, derived, mental concept. This is because if existence were real outside the mind (*mutaḥaqqaq fi khārij al-dhihn*), the real would consist of two things—the principle of the reality of existence *and* the being of existence, which requires a referent outside the mind (*miṣdāq fī khārij al-dhihn*), and since any referent outside the mind must also consist of two things, we would be landed in a vicious infinite regress, which is absurd.

Finally, the Philosophy of Illumination departs from Ibn Sīnā's Peripatetic philosophy in several ways. It has a different terminology. It prioritizes the intuitive over the purely deductive in its epistemology. The Philosophy of Illumination employs a language, reflective of its ontology, of light-entities to describe the continuum of all reality. And finally, it has a notion of "things" in each segment of the cosmos: Intellect, Soul, Matter, plus an added fourth realm called *'ālam al-khayāl, mundus imaginalis*, similar to the Platonic *paradigmata*. This Fourth Realm of "things" is best described as that of "things-as-ideas" prior to taking "shape," that is, prior to receiving "luminosity" (*istināra, nūriya)* from the One Source, the Light of Lights. However, the light received by each and every "monad" (*kull wāḥid wāḥid*) in the continuum has the same essence but differs from all other light-entities in respect to degrees of intensity. Luminosity propagates eternally and gives "shape" to the "idea-shape," making the entity "visible" and thus known. This Illuminationist ontology of continuum-essences—their differences being not in the thing's essence, but in terms of degrees of intensity of shared, "same" essence—that is, given to degrees of sameness in Platonic terms—is named "equivocal being" (*al-tashkīk bī al-wujūd*). All luminous entities, even the most "dim" (*al-nūr al-'adam*, equivalent to the Aristotelian Prime Matter) together constitute the "aggregate whole" (*al-kull al-'ijtimā'ī*, a novel Illuminationist term). They are coeternal with the source, the Light of Lights, that "propagates" eternally. The Light of Lights is one, but is neither beyond being nor nonbeing (Neoplatonists), nor does it have will; nor are the things generated by it the separate and numbered Intellects of Peripatetic cosmology (*al-'uqūl al-mufāraqa*). Each and every entity in the continuum whole is generated from the Light of Lights and possesses a degree of light-sameness. The Light of Lights is *one* with respect to all possible modes, known now or discovered in the future; it is *wāḥid min jamī' al-wujūḥ*, or *al-wāḥid al-muṭlaq* (Absolute One). Finally, Sohravardī is among the first philosophers to use a mathematical model to describe the process of becoming—multiplicity from One.

While this novel system was intended to refine the scientific method of the time, its widest impact, however, has not been in the domain of philosophy or science, but on Shī'ite political theory. Sohravardī's ideas regarding the scientist-philosophers of every era, who necessarily reexamine the principles of science, were employed by seventeenth-century Shī'ite thinkers. They used the Persian term "most learned of the era/time/period" (Per. *A'lam-e Zamān*) in the emerging Shī'ite doctrine as the epithet for the philosopher-sage who upholds the principles of science by continuously renewed observation.[9]

Sohravardī's most famous text, *The Philosophy of Illumination*, may be compared to William of Ockham's *Summa Logicæ*. Both Sohravardī and Ockham reject theological interpretations of Aristotelianism. Both clearly distinguish between the concepts "term" and "utterance." Both are critical of the Aristotelian essentialist definition as tautological and devoid of truth-value in scientific knowledge, and both distinguish between terms of primary intention and of secondary intention. There are also intriguing analogies between Sohravadī's project and Fichte's philosophy of science. Both were enraptured with the idea to construct a system that would yield unrestricted rational certitude. Both Sohravardī and Fichte seek to define an epistemology that would explain the process of obtaining "absolutely certain" first principles of science, and both posit a primary intuitive knowledge as the foundation of science.

Illuminationist Philosophy after Sohravardī

The Philosophy of Illumination was most popular in the thirteenth century, after the Mongol conquest when Ash'arite theology was no longer dominant. The lavishly endowed new School at Maragheh, directed by the Persian scientist-philosopher Naṣīr al-Dīn Ṭūsī, recruited many scholars from all parts of the vast empire ruled by the Mongol warlords. Many of these scholars were instrumental in the revival of intense scientific endeavor. This new spirit of inquiry, albeit short lived, was the reason for the recovery of Illuminationist texts from oblivion. Without the thirteenth- and fourteenth-century state-sanctioned centers of learning, the earlier

9. The term *'ilm*, in Islamic Philosophy in general is employed as equivalent to the Greek *episteme*, as used by Aristotle in his technical works, starting with *Posterior Analytics*, where science is defined as deduction from that which may be known through primary knowledge; this view is then further refined and expanded in the *Metaphysics* E.1, 1025bff, when Aristotle defines kinds of theoretical sciences; and in *Metaphysics* M.10, 1086b. 5ff, he examines the two notions of *science* and emphasizes that scientific knowledge is universal (the same as in *De Anima*, II.5, 417b). This basic view of science is consistently conveyed through the Arabic verb, *'-1-m;* and is fundamental to Avicennan Peripateticism, which was well-known to the seventeenth century authors—the same is paralleled in medieval Latin texts, as we often come across statements such as: *Scientia est universalium*, or stated differently: *Nulla est fluxorum scientia*. The term *'ilm*, and thus the concept *science* is given an additional meaning in the unified epistemological theory "Knowledge-by-Presence" by Sohravardī, and later confirmed and refined in the thirteenth century by Illuminationist authors such as Shahrazūrī and Ibn Kammūna.

scientific and philosophical achievements would have been lost. The main thirteenth-century Illuminationist scholars are Shams al-Dīn Muḥammad Shahrazūrī; Sa'd ibn Manṣūr Ibn Kammūna (d. 683/1284), whose commentary on *al-Talwīḥāt* became a textbook among Illuminationist philosophers in Iran; and Quṭb al-Dīn Shīrāzī.[10]

Shams al-Dīn Muḥammad Shahrazūrī's Illuminationist philosophical texts, such as *al-Shajara al-Ilāhiyya*, the first comprehensive and truly philosophical encyclopedia in Islamic thought, and his extensive text, *Sharḥ Ḥikmat al-Ishrāq* (*Commentary on the Philosophy of Illumination*), are demonstrative of thirteenth-century creative philosophical scholarship. Among the most important commentaries on Sohravardī's texts are the sixteenth-century works by Jalāl al-Dīn al-Davvānī and the seventeenth-century extensive Persian commentary by Muḥammad Sharīf Niẓ'ām al-Dīn Harawī.

Many authors are also known for having incorporated Illuminationist principles in their work, and for having written commentaries on Sohravardī's texts. The following is a selected list.

Naṣīr al-Dīn Ṭūsī (d. 672/1274) was a well-known Persian philosopher, astronomer, mathematician, and statesman whose commentary on Ibn Sīnā's *al-Ishārāt wa al-Tanbīhāt* has become one of the standard textbooks for the study of Ibn Sīnā's Peripatetic philosophy. Given the impact that Ṭūsī has had on all later Shī'ite authors, his Illuminationist position on the principles of knowledge should not be overlooked. Muḥammad ibn Zayn al-Dīn ibn Ibrāhīm Aḥsā'ī (d. after 878/1473), known as Ibn Jumhūr Ishrāqī Aḥsā'ī, is among Persian philosophers I have designated as "middle Ishrāqī" thinkers. Ghiyāth al-Dīn Manṣūr Dashtakī (d. 948/1542) also wrote a commentary on Sohravardī's *Hayākil al-Nūr*, titled *Ishrāq Hayākil al-Nūr li-Kashf Ẓulamāt Shawākil al-Ghurūr*. This is not a particularly important theoretical work but is indicative of Sohravardī's widespread impact. Muḥammad Bāqir ibn Shams al-Dīn Muḥammad (d. 1041/1631), well known as Mīr Dāmād, was perhaps the most significant philosopher of his age. He is among the few truly Illuminationist philosophers, a company that would include the immediate followers of Sohravardī, Shahrazūrī, and Ibn Kammūna, as well as in more recent times, Seyyed Kāẓ'em 'Aṣṣār. Ṣadr al-Dīn al-Shīrāzī, well known as Mollā Ṣadrā (d. 1050/1640, also transliterated as Mullā Ṣadrā), is regarded as the main originator of still another synthesis in Islamic philosophy, "The Science of Transcendental Metaphysics" (or "Metaphysical Philosophy" because of its singular emphasis on being, *al-Ḥikma al-Muta'āliya*). His theoretical work, as well as his philosophical interpretations of the traditional religious sciences, have had a significant impact on Shī'ite thought and the founding of clerical institutions in Iran from the seventeenth century to the present.

10. A Persian Illuminationist text has been recently discovered and published by M.-T. Danesh-Pajouh. The text is mainly a synthesis of Sohravardī's four major Arabic texts, but the controversial doctrines are left out. The author Ismā'īl ibn Moḥammad Rīzī composed a work, titled, *Ḥayāt al-Nufūs* in three parts, and dedicated it to the prince Yūsuf Shāh son of Alb Arsalān Urghūn son of Hezār Asp, Atābak of Loristān during the years 673–687/1274/1288.

In the thirteenth century the Philosophy of Illumination gave rise to two distinct interpretations. First, Shahrazūrī, whose commentaries on Sohravardī's texts, *Sharḥ Ḥikmat al-Ishrāq, Sharḥ al-Talwīḥāt*, and his independent *magnum opus*, the encyclopedic *al-Shajara al-Ilāhiyya*, emphasize the symbolic and distinctly non-Peripatetic components of Illuminationist philosophy. The inspirational, allegorical, and fantastic side of Illuminationist texts are extended and embellished. Second, Ibn Kammūna, who, in his *Sharḥ al-Talwīḥāt (Commentary on Sohravardī's* Intimations); in his major independent philosophical work, *al-Jadīd fī al-Ḥikma;* and in his shorter works, such as *Risāla fī al-Nafs* and *al-Ḥikma*, emphasizes the purely discursive and systematically philosophical side of Illuminationist philosophy.

BIBLIOGRAPHY AND SUGGESTED READINGS

Allers, R. (1952) "St. Augustine's Doctrine on Illumination." *Franciscan Studies* 12, 27–46.

Ha'iri Yazdi, M. (1992) *The Principles of Epistemology in Islamic Philosophy: Knowledge by Presence*. Albany, NY: State University of New York Press.

Lane, E. W. (1987) *Arabic English Lexicon*. London: Islamic Texts Society, I:1539–1541.

Merlan, Philip. (1963) *Monopsychism Mysticism Metaconsciousness*. The Hague: Martinus Nijhoff.

Merlan, Philip. (1968) *From Platonism to Neoplatonism* (3rd ed., rev.). The Hague: Martinus Nijhoff,

Suhrawardī. (2000) *The Philosophy of Illumination*. A new critical edition of the text *Ḥikmat al-Ishrāq* with English translation, notes, commentaries, and introduction by John Walbridge and Hossein Ziai. Provo, UT: Brigham Young University Press.

Walbridge, John. (1992) *The Science of Mystic Lights: Quṭb al-Dīn Shīrāzī and the Illuminationist Tradition in Islamic Philosophy*. Cambridge, MA: Harvard University Press.

Ziai, Hossein. (1990a) "Beyond Philosophy: Suhrawardī's Illuminationist Path to Wisdom." In *Myth and Philosophy*, edited by Frank E. Reynolds and David Tracy. Albany, NY: State University of New York Press, 215–243.

———. (1990b) *Knowledge and Illumination: A Study of Sohravardī's Ḥikmat al-Ishrāq*. Atlanta, GA: Scholars Press.

———. (1990c) "Vision, Illuminationist Methodology and Poetic Language." *Irān Nāmeh* VIII(1), 81–94.

———. (1992) "Source and Nature of Authority: A Study of Suhrawardī's Illuminationist Political Doctrine." In *The Political Aspects of Islamic Philosophy*, edited by Charles Butterworth. Cambridge, MA: Harvard University Press, 304–344.

———. (1998) *Suhrawardī's The Book of Radiance [Partow Nāmeh]*. A parallel English-Persian text, edited and translated with an introduction. Costa Mesa: Mazda Publishers.

———. (2005) "Suhrawardī on Knowledge and the Experience of Light." In *The Experience of Light: Divine Radiance and Religious Experience*, edited by Matthew T. Kapstein. Chicago and London: The University of Chicago Press, 25–44.

CHAPTER 30

SUFISM

ERIK S. OHLANDER

As situated within the Islamic tradition, Sufism (*taṣawwuf*) refers to the active process of discovering, developing, and actualizing certain spiritual verities within one's own person, normally in hopes of achieving an intimate, unmediated, or unitive encounter with God, who alone is the true ground of existence and the "really real" (*al-ḥaqq*). As situated within the purview of world philosophies, Sufism refers to the Islamic mystical tradition as a whole: an historical phenomenon composed of a diverse complex of attitudes, ideas, doctrines, practices, texts, and institutions that share certain features with the mystical traditions of Islam's cousin faiths, Judaism and Christianity. At the same time, however, while certainly validating the private concerns of individual world-renouncing ascetics and reclusive mystics, Sufism has typically been possessed of a public and social dimension that differentiates it from both the Judaic and Christian mystical traditions, in particular in terms of its diffuse historical persistence as a popular and enduring mode of religiosity prevalent across almost all Muslim societies past and present.

The term *taṣawwuf* appears neither in the Qur'an nor in the collected sayings and doings of the Prophet and his companions (the Hadith), and already in early Sufi tradition its etymology was a matter of debate. Proposed derivations included tracing it to the Arabic word *ṣafā*, which connotes the idea of "purity," whereas some linked it to the phrase "*ahl al-ṣuffa*" ("People of the Bench"), a particularly pious group of the prophet Muhammad's companions. The most probable interpretation connected it to the Arabic word for wool, *ṣūf*, in which case the verbal noun *taṣawwuf* refers to the practice of habitual "wool wearing." As a symbol of ascetic, penitential, and renunciative piety in the Late Antique Near East, the wearing of rough woolen garments was a common outward mark of the intentional religious *virtuoso*. This is particularly well attested in indigenous Near Eastern Christian anchoritic traditions in which the practice of renunciative spiritual athleticism was lauded as a particularly efficacious route to mystical realization.

Although such ideas and forms were naturally absorbed into early Muslim ascetic and mystical traditions, it is important to note that the development of a distinctive Sufi discourse drew much of its inspiration from an internalization of the Islamic revelation, something that in and of itself is possessed of marked mystical elements. Most notable in this regard is the paradoxical balance struck in the Qur'an between the absolute transcendence of the divine being and his immanence in creation:

> To God belong the East and the West; whithersoever you turn, there is the Face of God; God is All-embracing, All-knowing. (Qur'an 2:115)
>
> We indeed created man; and We know what his soul whispers to him, and We are nearer to him than the jugular vein. (Qur'an 50:16)
>
> In the earth are signs for those having sure faith; and in your selves; what, do you not see? (Qur'an 51:20–21)

This immanence is especially conspicuous in relation to humankind. As in the Hebrew Bible, the Qur'anic account of creation envisions God breathing something of his own spirit into Adam (Qur'an 38:72). As later Sufis were careful to point out, however, this was accomplished only in relation to a primordial covenant that God established with the first man's yet-to-be-engendered progeny, prior to the act of in-breathing itself: "And when thy Lord took from the Children of Adam, from their loins, their seed, and made them testify touching themselves, 'Am I not your Lord?' They said, 'Yes, we testify'" (Qur'an 7:172).

For the Sufis, the path to actualizing in the here and now the implications of this Qur'anic *in illo tempore* (the primordial "in-that-time") is preeminently grounded in the exempla of the prophet Muhammad (d. 632), the recipient of the revelation and its most perfect devotee. According to a hadith oft quoted in Muslim mystical literature, the Prophet himself hinted at this in saying: "the divine law (*sharī'a*) is my words (*aqwālī*), the mystical path (*ṭarīqa*) my actions (*a'mālī*), and the divine reality (*ḥaqīqa*) my interior states (*aḥwālī*)." Thus, experiences such as his first angelic visitation while meditating in a cave in the hills outside Mecca or his miraculous night journey to the Temple Mount in Jerusalem and subsequent ascension up through the seven heavens became the archetypal models of Muslim mystical experience, and his conspicuously ascetic attitudes and behaviors the prototypal means of realizing them.

Early History (Eighth to Tenth Centuries)

Although later Sufis would trace the teachings and techniques of *taṣawwuf* directly to the practice of the Prophet, the term itself did not gain currency until at least the first half of the ninth century. Historically speaking, its antecedents are properly located in the teachings of certain circles of Muslim ascetics who first appeared in Mesopotamia and Syria in the early eighth century. In no small part, this was a result of brute historical experience. As Islam began to make its transition from a provincial religious community to a transregional empire over the course of the later seventh through the early eighth century, certain individuals began to react to the increasing worldliness of a community whose spectacular military successes in the citied world of Persia and Byzantium had suddenly given it access to wealth and power unimaginable in the desert steppe of the Arabian Peninsula. These new Muslim religious *virtuosi*, such as the celebrated asan al-Baṣrī (d. 728), vigorously censured the increasingly worldly ambitions of prominent members of the emerging Muslim state and strongly condemned their vain pursuit of the things of this world at the expense of the world to come. asan al-Baṣrī attracted a sizable following of self-described renunciants (*zuhhād;* sing. *zāhid*) and pietists (*ʿubbād;* sing. *ʿābid*) who were impressed by his stern asceticism and fiery preaching. This group became united in their scrupulous observance of the divine law, their distrust of the world and its pleasures, and a dour and self-effacing outlook that often expressed itself in fantastic acts of contrition and self-mortification. This often took the form of supererogatory fasting, prolonged exposure to the elements, or ceaseless weeping. Although not a direct disciple of asan al-Baṣrī, the semilegendary figure Ibrāhīm ibn Adham (d. ca. 770) presents a particularly instructive example of this type of world-denying religiosity. Said to have been the scion of a powerful ruling family in the ancient Buddhist city of Balkh, like Siddhartha Gautama he is reported to have renounced his princely trappings and set off westward as a wandering ascetic, eating only what he could provide for himself or, more often than not, simply fasting or ingesting clay in adherence to his vow of complete trust in God (*tawakkul*), a key value in early Muslim asceticism (*zuhd*).

Near the end of the eighth century, a shift from this kind of world-denying religiosity to one rooted in an inner-worldly mysticism based on love of God began to appear within certain ascetic circles in Iraq. This proto-Sufi movement is synonymous with the fabled female ascetic of Basra, Rābiʿa al-ʿAdawiyya (d. 801). In this unmarried freedwoman we are presented with a paradigmatic ascetic whose surviving poetic utterances on seclusion, poverty, and absorption in God reflect the persistent memory of a decisive development in proto-Sufi tradition at the turn of the ninth century. In her legacy, we see the increasing use of elusive poetical language in which metaphors of erotic love and effacement in the beloved are used to describe mystical experience. After Rābiʿa, perhaps the most significant figure in this development is the enigmatic Dhū al-Nūn al-Miṣrī (d. 859). A Nubian born in Upper Egypt, Dhū al-Nūn was an insightful theoretician whose surviving logia infuse amorous descriptions of the relationship between God and the mystic with an abstract conceptualization of its ontological meanings. According to later Sufi tradition, he was the first to discuss, for example, the nature of the key Sufi concept of *maʿrifa*, a form of unmediated, immediate, and nondiscursive "knowing" through which the mystical lover directly apprehends his beloved.

In mid-ninth-century Baghdad these developments began to coalesce in the teachings of a number of figures calling themselves the *ṣūfiyya* ("Sufis"), a group that found itself in competition with equally vigorous ascetic and mystical movements flourishing in the northeastern Persian province of Khurasan. These latter movements—well represented in figures such as the famed Shaqīq al-Balkhī (d. 810), a disciple of Ibrāhīm ibn Adham—would quickly, however, lose ground to the former. Beginning with the influential moralizer, theologian, and psychologist al-Ḥārith al-Muḥāsibī (d. 857), who advocated a detailed program of introspection aimed at identifying those blameworthy dispositions of the soul (*nafs*) that estranged the spirit from God, it was the Sufis of Baghdad who would fashion the bulk of the epistemology, metaphysics, psychology, and associated technical language characteristic of the Islamic mystical tradition in the centuries to come.

Among this group, the most significant one to emerge was a young associate of al-Muḥāsibī named al-Junayd (d. 910). Arguably one of the greatest Sufi theoreticians of the first half-millennium of the movement, al-Junayd elaborated a model of mystical experience rooted in the notion of *fanā,'* a technical term denoting the annihilation or "passing away" of the individuated ego in the all-embracing unity of the "really real" (*al-ḥaqq*), nothing less than a return to the *in illo tempore* of the primordial covenant (*mīthāq*) spoken of in the Qur'an. However, according to al-Junayd, this dissolution does not mark the terminus of the mystic's journey but rather is followed, or completed, by an act of divine mercy in which the mystic is returned to his senses and ensconced in a state of "abiding in God" (*baqā'*), reindividuated but irrevocably changed.

Although using much of the same language, in contradistinction to the "sober" (*saḥw*) Sufism associated with the circle of al-Junayd, there were equally influential mystics of the time who embraced a markedly ecstatic, or "drunken" (*sukr*), approach to annihilation in God. Although there were others, such as the celebrated late-ninth-century Persian mystic Bāyazīd Bisṭāmī, the most controversial of these intoxicated Sufis was the abstruse and often extravagant Manṣūr al-Ḥallāj. Brutally executed in Baghdad on charges of heresy in 922, al-Ḥallāj's unabashed public displays of mystical ecstasy, such as his oft-cited apotheosizing "ecstatic elocution" (*shaṭḥ*) "I am the Truth!" (*anā 'l-ḥaqq*), scandalized the normally prudent and reserved followers of al-Junayd. Condemned by the authorities for preaching incarnationism and other seditious doctrines, it is little exaggeration to say that the affair of al-Ḥallāj marked something of a turning point in the history of Islamic mysticism. It marked a drawing of clearer boundaries between ecstatic, and often antinomian, mystics "martyred in love of God" and more temperate seekers who fastidiously attended to the demands of social and religious propriety.

Later Developments (Eleventh to Fourteenth Centuries)

A decisive systematization occurred within the Sufi movement beginning in the late tenth century, a development well evinced in the collective literary output of a series of unusually productive Sufi apologists such as Abū Naṣr al-Sarrāj (d. 988), Abū

Bakr al-Kalābādhī (d. 994), Abū ʿAbd al-Raḥmān al-Sulamī (d. 1020), ʿAbd al-Karīm al-Qushayrī (d. 1074), ʿAlī al-Hujwīrī (d. between 1072 and 1077), and ʿAbdullāh-i Anṣārī (d. 1089). Taking it as their task to secure a place for Sufism within the broader ambit of the Islamic religious sciences, these authors carefully sifted through the collective weight of the earlier centuries of Muslim ascetical and mystical discourse so as to paint a systematic picture of a contiguous tradition originating ultimately in the practice of the prophet Muhammad and his immediate companions. Almost without exception, this tradition was made to pass through the line of the *ṣūfiyya* of Baghdad, thus lending the "sober" Sufi tradition associated with al-Junayd and his circle a certain preeminence that it would continue to enjoy long thereafter.

This became an age of great Sufi biographical compendia and mystical handbooks, works that appropriated forms common to the Sunni jurisprudential, tradition-critical, theological, heresiographical, and exegetical sciences in order to construct a systematic discursive framework for the Sufi "science of the hearts" (*ʿilm al-qulūb*). Among the technical terminology defined in this new literature, the most significant is undoubtedly the two interrelated concepts of the "mystical station" (*maqām*) and the "mystical state" (*ḥāl*), notions as fundamental to the Islamic mystical tradition as the *sefirot* are to the Jewish Kabbalah. Here, the idea is that the mystical path (*ṭarīq*) is composed of various psycho-spiritual stopping points, or way-stations, through which the mystic must pass on his journey toward God. Realized through personal effort, the mystical stations are individual acquisitions serially arranged between "repentance" (*tawba*)—the starting point of any potential Sufi's journey—and the final goal, or "station," of annihilation (*fanāʾ*) and abiding (*baqāʾ*) in the divine unity. As described by the Sufi handbook-writers of the age, a wide range of discrete mystical stations fall in between these two points, including watchfulness (*waraʿ*), abstinence (*zuhd*), patience (*ṣabr*), fear (*khawf*), hope (*rajāʾ*), and contentedness (*riḍā*). In contradistinction to the mystical station, however, the mystical state is neither earned nor abiding; rather, it is an instantaneous and ephemeral grace freely bestowed upon the mystic as he or she proceeds through the mystical stations. In Sufi manuals such as al-Qushayrī's famous *Epistle*, these graces are often enumerated in dichotomous pairs such as "absence" and "presence" (*ghayba* and *ḥuḍūr*), "contraction" and "expansion" (*qabḍ* and *basṭ*), or "awe" and "intimacy" (*hayba* and *uns*). All appearances aside, it is important to note that these Sufi apologists were not particularly concerned with systematically enumerating the exact number or nature of the individual mystical stations and states, nor for that matter in agreeing upon whether or not a particular mystical experience, such as "love" (*maḥabba*) for example, was to be identified as a "station" or a "state." As with most discursive attempts to describe mystical experience, for the Sufi systematizers of the tenth and eleventh centuries, such terminology was considered summary and approximate at best.

The overall success of the Sufi systematizers in securing a place for Sufism within the ambit of mainstream Sunnism is well exemplified in the life and work of the celebrated late-eleventh-century theologian, jurist, and polemicist Abū Ḥāmid al-Ghazālī (d. 1111), most notably in his massive compendium of Islamic mystical piety *The Revivification of the Religious Sciences* (*Iḥyā' 'Ulūm al-Dīn*). Modeled in large part on the *Nourishment of the Hearts* (*Qūt al-Qulūb*), an encyclopedic manual of mystical piety composed by the Sufi author Abū Ṭālib al-Makkī (d. 996), *The Revivification* was the product of a deep personal struggle for certainty and truth that the author chronicles in his autobiographical *Deliverance from Error*. Systematically investigating the universalizing claims of dialectical theology (*kalām*); Hellenizing philosophy (*falsafa*); Ismā'īlī Shi'ism; and the sober, *sharī'a*-minded Sufism championed by the Sufi apologists, al-Ghazālī's existential crisis was resolved only when he came to realize that the Sufi way was the best of the four, furnishing the surest, most complete, and perfect enactment of the Islamic revelation in time and space. Accordingly, a major concern of his *Revivification* is to elucidate, often in great detail, the subtle spiritual meanings and mystical significances of the normative Islamic rituals and praiseworthy acts of piety, the result being an extensive synthesis of Islamic orthopraxy with the mystical idiom systematized by the Sufi manual writers of the previous century.

Building upon these developments, the period spanning the later twelfth through the first half of the thirteenth century witnessed a widespread flowering of Sufism. One of the more significant features of its development during this period was the appearance of a series of particularly outstanding Sufi masters who would come to lend their names to some of the most enduring of the early "Sufi orders": 'Abd al-Qādir al-Jīlānī (d. 1166) and 'Umar al-Suhrawardī (d. 1234) in Baghdad, Aḥmad al-Rifā'ī (d. 1182) in the marshland of southern Iraq, Najm al-Dīn Kubrā (d. 1220) in Transoxiana, Mu'īn al-Dīn Chishtī (d. 1236) in India, and Abū al-Ḥasan 'Alī al-Shādhilī (d. 1258) in North Africa. While the early Sufi orders, or *ṭarīqas* (literally "path" or "way"), associated with each of these eponyms—the Qādiriyya, Suhrawardiyya, Rifā'iyya, Kubrāwiyya, Chishtiyya, and Shādhiliyya, respectively—should not be imagined as having been as highly organized as the monastic orders of the medieval Christian West, they did share certain common features. Here, the practice of formal initiation ceremonies, a clear distinction between masters and novices, austere regimens of supererogatory devotion practiced in residential cloisters, and differences in respect to ascetic and contemplative practice, devotional literature, doctrinal position, codes of conduct, and costume and accoutrement between various confraternities stand out as primary.

However, as largely decentralized mystical teaching-lineages that ultimately derived their vitality from the charisma of individual Sufi masters rather than the particular "order" to which they might have belonged, the early Sufi brotherhoods are more aptly described as similar in scope and organizational logic to the Zen Buddhist schools of premodern Japan. Each Sufi initiatic lineage (e.g., the Qādiriyya as to the Rinzai school) looked back to an eponymous founder (e.g., al-Jīlānī as to Linji Yixuan) who was envisioned as having taught a particular "mystical path" or "method" (e.g., a unique "*ṭarīq*" as compared to a specific *dharma*) on the authority of an unbroken line of masters (e.g., a *silsila*, or "chain" of transmission as compared to the line of the Zen Patriarchs) stretching back, often through the key figure of al-Junayd (e.g., as compared to Bodhidharma), through an elect companion of

Muhammad (e.g., 'Alī as compared to Mahākāśyapa) to the person of the Prophet himself (e.g., as compared to the Buddha). Over the course of this period, intentional communities of mystical seekers attached to a particular Sufi master directing them in the "Sufi way" on the authority of such lineages became an increasingly ubiquitous feature of citied life across the Islamic world. Just as in premodern Japan, throughout the later medieval period outstanding mystical masters and their communities of erstwhile disciples were often viewed as desirable objects of patronage by Muslim political and economic elites looking to benefit from the spiritual authority and popular mystique concentrated in their cloisters.

In addition to the eponyms of the early Sufi orders, this period also played host to no small number of strikingly original and creative Sufi thinkers. Among the most influential, and controversial, is the Sufi theosophist Muḥyī 'l-Dīn Ibn 'Arabī (d. 1240). Known as *al-shaykh al-akbar* ("*doctor maximus*"), Ibn 'Arabī was born in 1165 in the city of Murcia in Muslim Spain and traveled extensively, eventually settling in Damascus where his tomb remains a place of pious visitation to this very day. A prolific author with a ranging mastery of the exegetical, philosophical, mystical, theological, and jurisprudential learning of his age, his works, in particular his voluminous *Meccan Revelations* (*al-Futūḥāt al-Makkiyya*) and the much shorter but just as weighty *Bezels of Wisdom* (*Fuṣūṣ al-Ḥikam*), elaborate an often dizzying system of Islamic monism whose orthodoxy has been long debated by admirers and detractors of equal energy in both Sufi and non-Sufi circles alike. Although it never occurs in his writings, the phrase *waḥdat al-wujūd* ("the unity of existence") has normally been used to describe the keynote of his system. Simply put, the idea is that God is the only true existent, with apparent extrinsic phenomena simply being the result of certain modulations of the divine attributes. Tied to this idea is his often discussed notion of the "perfect man" (*al-insān al-kāmil*), the polished mirror of the human microcosm that reflects the absolute unity of the godhead back unto itself—the self-revelation of God through man.

Whereas the complexity of Ibn 'Arabī's thought elicited a long string of commentaries that never seemed to exhaust its possibilities, this period also witnessed the blossoming of another important form of Sufi literature. Writing in Persian, the vernacular and literary language of the eastern half of the Islamic world, Sufi poets such as Sanā'ī (d. 1131) and Farīd al-Dīn 'Aṭṭār (d. c. 1221) excelled in communicating sophisticated mystical ideas in verse, in particular in the form of the *masnavī*, a poetic genre whose rhyming couplet scheme allows for lengthy and elaborate prose-like compositions. Arguably, the most celebrated of the Persian Sufi poets of the age was Jalāl al-Dīn Rūmī (d. 1273), an Afghani émigré to the southern Anatolian city of Konya (the Iconium of St. Paul) and eponym of the Mawlawiyya (Mevlevi) Sufi order (derived from his popular appellation "*mawlānā*," or "Our Master"). This order later became known to Europe as the "Whirling Dervishes." Rūmī is best known for his *Masnavī-yi ma'navī* (*Couplets of Inner Meaning*), a lengthy *masnavī* composed of some 26,000 verses that draws effortlessly from across the wide sweep of the classical Sufi tradition. One of the major draws of the work is found in its creative use of poignant metaphors, such as in its celebrated opening prologue, where the reed flute—a traditional Mevlevi accoutrement—is made to lament a painful separation from its own *in illo tempore* after having been torn from its marshy home only to be fashioned into a plaintive musical instrument.

Another element associated with this fecund period in the history of Sufism is the rise of deliberately unconventional, "drunken" forms of Sufi religiosity. This is perhaps no more vividly displayed than in the activities of various Qalandar movements that consciously rejected the measured, "sober" approach associated with the mainstream Sufi tradition. Holding the established Sufi masters in contempt for their slavish conformity to social custom and religious pedantry, various antinomian Sufi groups such as the Abdāls and Ḥaydaris roamed throughout the central and eastern regions of the later medieval Islamic world, drawing censure for their oftentimes shocking displays of intentionally deviant behavior. Known for their bizarre modes of dress and appearance, public nakedness, penchant for intoxicants, and often brazen flouting of basic religious duties, like the famed Sadhus of Hindu India these antinomian Sufis acted in accordance with a renunciative logic that finds a certain freedom in intentionally drawing blame to oneself (*malāma*) so as to be able to better focus one's efforts on the real task at hand.

Institutions and Practices

Although significant differences are to be found in expressions of mystical religiosity within and among the major Sufi teaching-lineages that began to emerge in the thirteenth century, there is a readily identifiable cluster of institutions and practices that have typically bound them together. For the most part, these characteristics have marked Sufism up to the present day. After the cloisters, hospices, and lodges that have traditionally furnished the actual physical space in which many of the activities associated with Sufi religiosity transpire, no institution has been more important than that of the master-disciple relationship. Inspired by the old Sufi dictum—said to have first been voiced by Bāyazīd Bisṭāmī—that "he who has no master takes Satan for his leader," general sentiment holds that successfully traversing the mystical path requires the guidance, if not the direct supervision, of one who has already traversed it himself. Normally claiming an initiatic lineage reaching back to the Prophet himself, it is the figure of the master (Ar. *shaykh;* Per. *pīr*) who stands at the center of a Sufi community, being responsible for auspicating new disciples (*murīd*, lit. "aspirant") into the Sufi path by way of a range of initiatory acts. This might include exacting a formal oath of allegiance (*bay'a*), the "inculcation of the mystical formula" (*talqīn al-dhikr*) distinctive to his teaching-lineage, or investiture with the Sufi habit (*khirqa*). However, the master was also responsible for overseeing the cloister's day-to-day affairs, presiding over communal ritual, directing individual aspirants in their mystico-ascetic and contemplative regimens, preaching and giving lectures, and offering spiritual counsel to audience seekers,

Sufi and non-Sufi alike. Ideally, the Sufi aspirant owes his master complete obedience, considering him to be both a "spiritual father" (*ab maʿnawī*) and a living "representative" (*nāʾib*) of the Prophet himself. The sincere aspirant should yield to his master, as is often said, "like a corpse in the hands of its washer."

At the wider social level, the spiritual charisma of particularly exemplary Sufi masters has often survived them after death, becoming ensconced in tomb-shrines where the holiness or "blessing" (*baraka*) they accrued during their lives can be accessed in the earthly residue of their physical remains. Throughout the later medieval period up through the present day, the tomb-shrines of such *awliyāʾ* (sing. *walī*), or "intimates" or "friends" of God, have traditionally served as places of popular petitionary devotion and pilgrimage among the Muslim masses, larger tomb-shrine complexes often staging annual festivals on the saint's birthday (*mawlid*) or, in South Asia, the day of his death, known as his *ʿurs*, or the "wedding" of his soul with God. From the earlier medieval period onward, Sufi tradition has also maintained the notion that each age is possessed of a *walī* who serves as the *quṭb*, the "pole" or "axis" of the cosmos. He presides over a hierarchy of lesser Sufi saints of various types and number (i.e., the forty, or seven, *abdāl*, or "substitutes" and the four *awtād*, or "pillars" being the most oft discussed), who together ensure the proper order and continued existence of the cosmos. Preeminent historical Sufi masters, such as the aforementioned eponym of the Qādiriyya order, ʿAbd al-Qādir al-Jīlānī, are often identified in hagiographic tradition as having been the *quṭb*, or *ghawth* ("succor"), of their age. Naturally, the shrine-tombs of such figures are places where common folk will go to seek intercession, often to the chagrin of non-Sufi Muslim religious scholars, who have often viewed such practices, especially in the present day, as misguided, if not potentially heretical.

Among the various mystico-ascetic and contemplative practices that mark active wayfaring on the Sufi path, it is the practice of *dhikr* (anamnesis) that takes pride of place. Possessing explicit Qur'anic associations—wherein believers are enjoined to "remember God often" (e.g., 62:10)—*dhikr* refers to the methodical and ritualized repetition of particular religious formulae, normally coupled with specific breathing patterns, visualizations, or bodily movements. A practice familiar to many mystical and contemplative disciplines (e.g., the Eastern Orthodox Hesychasm, certain Yogic and Bhakti practices in the Hindu tradition, or the mantra-centered practices of Vajrayāna Buddhism), the practice of *dhikr* can take many forms, being performed aloud or silently, alone or in congregation, in quantifiably set cycles or in endless repetition. Although marked differences exist between various Sufi teaching-lineages, each of which possesses its own set traditional collections of litanies and *dhikr* texts, the most common *dhikr* formula is drawn from the first half of the Muslim profession of faith, *lā ilāha illā ʾllāh*, "there is no god but God," which is often joined or combined with reciting any or all of the ninety names of God, such as *al-ḥayy al-qayyūm* ("the living, the self-subsisting"; a reference to Qur'an 2:255), or with a progressively shortened recitation of the Arabic third-person masculine singular pronoun *huwa* ("he"). In some Sufi confraternities, the communal performance of the *dhikr* is connected with the often much more effusive, and much more controversial practice of *samāʿ* (lit. "audition"). The *samāʿ* is best described as a type of "mystical concert," which might include the performance of music, the recitation of religious litanies or Sufi poetry, and—such as in the well-known case of the Mevlevis—the use of ritualized dance, all intended to induce mystical experience among those in attendance.

In addition to fastidious adherence to both the basic and supererogatory ritual obligations incumbent upon, or encouraged of, all Muslims (e.g., regular performance of prayer, fasting, Qur'anic recitation, etc.), other elements of mystico-ascetic praxis associated with the Sufi confraternities have traditionally included solitary retreat (*khalwa*)—in particular the forty-day retreat (Ar. *arbaʿīniyya;* Per. *chilla*)—the practice of reflective meditation (*fikr*), private audiences with the master in which spiritual experiences and dreams are described, and, in the premodern period, traveling as a mendicant from cloister to cloister.

Traditionally, it has been toward conceptualizing the subtle significances of the interiorization of the Qur'anic *in illo tempore*, the results of mystico-ascetic praxis rather than the praxis itself, that has commanded the most attention within the Sufi tradition itself. As such, it should be noted that such observable dimensions of Sufi ritual represent but the veneer of a much deeper life-orientational praxis subsumed under a complex set of inner principles and attitudes. This is perhaps no better displayed than in the famous "sacred precepts" (*kalimāt-i qudsiyya*) of the Naqshbandiyya teaching-lineage, a set of eight-plus-three prescriptions that orient the day-to-day activities of every Naqshbandī aspirant. Said to have been first formulated by the Persian-speaking Central Asian Sufi ʿAbd al-Khāliq Ghijduvānī (d. 1220), as later supplemented by the actual eponym of the order, Bahā' al-Dīn Naqshband (d. 1389), they run (1) awareness of breath (*hūsh dar dam*); (2) watching over one's steps (*naẓar bar qadam*); (3) self-introspection (*safar dar vaṭan*); (4) solitude in company (*khalvat dar anjuman*); (5) remembrance (*yād kard*); (6) self-restraint (*bāz gard*); (7) watchfulness (*nigāh dāsht*); (8) recollection (*yād dāsht;* or *dhikr*); and, related to the *dhikr* itself, (9–11) numerical pause (*wuqūf-i ʿadadī*), temporal pause (*wuqūf-i zamānī*), and the pause of the heart (*wuqūf-i qalbī*).

Contemporary Manifestations

Generally speaking, Sufism fared well in the later medieval and early-modern Islamic world, especially within the Ottoman and Mughal domains between the fifteenth and the eighteenth centuries. Although the Safavid dynasty itself began as a Sufi order, Sufis themselves did not fare as well in Persia, nor were they prevalent under their successors the Qajars. As with the wider societies in which Sufism was nurtured, the beginning of European colonial expansion and the introduction of Western modernity into the Muslim world signaled a major change in the fortunes of almost all Sufis. Of special note in this regard was the appearance of a number of

Sufi brotherhoods who directly challenged European colonial expansion in the Muslim world during the nineteenth century, in particular the Tijāniyya in West Africa, the Sanūsiyya in Libya, and the Naqshbandī-Khālidiyya in the northern Caucasus, it being members of these brotherhoods who formed the vanguard of Muslim anticolonial resistance against the French, Italians, and Russians, respectively. At the same time, in the later nineteenth through the early twentieth century the Sufi confraternities also found themselves needing to contend with the challenges brought by emergent Muslim reform and renewal movements. This has frequently taken the form of being censured as un-Islamic by fundamentalist and puritanical reformers, or being criticized as backward and superstitious by Muslim modernists.

In the late- and postcolonial period, the impact of this challenge on both secular and religious fronts is well evinced in the wholesale dismantling of the Sufi brotherhoods in Turkey in 1925 as part of Atatürk's program of secular modernization and, for a wholly opposite reason, the complete criminalization of Sufi associations, books, activities, and religious practices in the Kingdom of Saudi Arabia in accordance with the teachings of Wahhabism. Overall, contemporary Sufi groups have often chosen to remain relatively nondescript so as not to arouse negative attention, whether it be religiously motivated, such as in the case of the Islamic Republic of Iran, whose Shi'ite leadership have not always looked favorably upon the brotherhoods, or purely governmental, such as in the case of Egypt and Pakistan, where the quasi-nationalization of Sufi tomb-shrine complexes and their associated institutions provide the state not only with a source of revenue but also with a way to keep watch over large public gatherings. At the same time, Sufism has remained a vital force among Muslim communities in both North and Sub-Saharan Africa. On the other hand, across much of the Muslim world the past two decades have witnessed a certain repopularization of Sufi thought, especially among educated elites who have grown increasingly tired of the divisive nature of contemporary fundamentalist and puritanical discourse on the one hand, and the spiritual vacuousness of Western cultural norms on the other. This is perhaps no better evinced than in the vigorous and wide-scale publication and consumption of Sufi texts, especially translations and popular editions from the classical and medieval tradition, churned out in great numbers by publishers both major and minor in the Arab World, Turkey, Iran, Pakistan, and Indonesia.

The period from the later half of the twentieth century through the beginning of the twenty-first has also witnessed the spread of Sufism outside of the Muslim world through both migration and settlement, and, in recent years, the increasingly widespread diffusion and circulation of Sufi texts and media, as well as the creation of "virtual" Sufi communities and networks via the Internet. This phenomenon is especially prominent in Europe and North America, where Sufism can be described as serving a wide range of groups, being situated along an historically unprecedented continuum ranging from the preservation of traditional Sufi forms and practices among both immigrant and westernized Muslim communities, to its nearly complete acculturation as one of the "authentic world wisdom traditions" within the wider Euro-American New Age movement. Whereas apologists from the former tend to describe Sufism as the ecumenical, mystical quintessence of the Islamic tradition, apologists from the latter have tended to de-emphasize its Islamic origins, often presenting it as a universal mystical teaching that has little to do with Islam itself.

BIBLIOGRAPHY AND SUGGESTED READINGS

Primary Sources in Translation

Aflākī, Shams al-Dīn. (2002) *The Feats of the Knowers of God*, translated by John O'Kane. Leiden: Brill.

Arberry, A. J. (1955) *The Koran Interpreted.* 2 vols. London: George Allen & Unwin Ltd.

'Aṭṭār, Farīd al-Dīn. (1998) *The Speech of the Birds*, translated by Peter Avery. Cambridge: Islamic Texts Society.

Baqlī, Rūzbihān. (1997) *The Unveiling of Secrets: Diary of a Sufi Master*, translated by Carl W. Ernst. Chapel Hill, NC: Parvardigar Press.

al-Ghazālī, Abū Ḥāmid. (1999) *Deliverance from Error*, translated by R. J. McCarthy. Louisville, KY: Fons Vitae.

Hujwīrī. (1911) *The Kashf al-Maḥjúb: The Oldest Persian Treatise on Sufism*, translated by R. A. Nicholson. London: Luzac & Co.

Ibn 'Abbād. (1986) *Letters on the Ṣūfī Path*, translated by John Renard. New York: Paulist Press.

Ibn 'Arabī. (1980) *The Bezels of Wisdom*, translated by R. W. J. Austin. New York: Paulist Press.

Ibn al-Fāriḍ. (2001) *'Umar Ibn al-Fāriḍ: Sufi Verse, Saintly Life*, translated by Th. Emil Homerin. New York: Paulist Press.

Ibn al-Munawwar, Muḥammad. (1992) *The Secrets of God's Mystical Oneness*, translated by John O'Kane. Costa Mesa, CA: Mazda Publishers.

al-Iskandarī, Ibn 'Aṭā' Allāh. (2005) *The Book of Illumination*, translated by Scott Kugle. Louisville, KY: Fons Vitae.

al-Jīlānī, 'Abd al-Qādir. (1997) *Sufficient Provision for Seekers of the Path of Truth.* 5 vols. Translated by Muhtar Holland. Fort Lauderdale, FL: Al-Baz Publishing, Inc.

al-Kalābādhī. (1935) *The Doctrine of the Ṣūfīs*, translated by A. J. Arberry. Cambridge: Cambridge University Press.

Niffarī, Muḥammad b. 'Abd al-Jabbār. (1935) *The Mawāqif and Mukhātabāt of Muḥammad Ibn 'Abdi 'l-Jabbār al-Niffarī*, translated by A. J. Arberry. London: Luzac & Co.

Niẓām al-Dīn Awliyā. (1992) *Morals for the Heart*, translated by Bruce B. Lawrence. New York: Paulist Press.

Rāzī, Najm al-Dīn. (1982) *The Path of God's Bondsmen*, translated by Hamid Algar. New York: Delmar.

Renard, John (ed. and trans.). (2004) *Knowledge of God in Classical Sufism: Foundations of Islamic Mystical Theology*. New York: Paulist Press.

Rūmī. (1925–1940) *The Mathnawí of Jalálu'ddín Rúmí.* 8 vols. Translated by R. A. Nicholson. London: Luzac & Co.

AL-QUSHAYRĪ. (2007) *Al-Qushayri's Epistle on Sufism*, translated by Alexander Knysh. Reading, UK: Garnet Publishing Ltd.

SELLS, MICHAEL (ed. and trans.). (1996) *Early Islamic Mysticism: Sufi, Qur'an, Mi'raj, Poetic and Theological Writings*. New York: Paulist Press.

AL-SUHRAWARDĪ, ABŪ 'L-NAJĪB. (1975) *A Sufi Rule for Novices*, abridged translation by Menahem Milson. Cambridge, MA: Harvard University Press.

AL-SULAMĪ. (1999) *Early Sufi Women*, translated by Rkia E. Cornell. Louisville, KY: Fons Vitae.

Secondary Sources

ANDRE, TOR. (1987) *In the Garden of Myrtles: Studies in Early Islamic Mysticism*, translated by Birgitta Sharpe. Albany, NY: State University of New York Press.

ARBERRY, A. J. (1950) *Sufism: An Account of the Mystics of Islam*. London: George Allen & Unwin, Ltd.

BALDICK, JULIAN. (1989) *Mystical Islam: An Introduction to Sufism*. London: I. B. Tauris.

BÖWERING, GERHARD. (1980) *The Mystical Vision of Existence in Classical Islam: The Qur'ānic Hermeneutics of the Ṣūfī Sahl at-Tustarī*. Berlin: de Gruyter.

ERNST, CARL. (1997) *The Shambhala Guide to Sufism*. Boston, MA: Shambhala Publications.

HOFFMAN, VALERIE. (1995) *Sufism, Mystics, and Saints in Modern Egypt*. Columbia, SC: University of South Carolina Press.

DE JONG, FREDERICK, and BERNDT RADTKE (eds.). (1999) *Islamic Mysticism Contested: Thirteen Centuries of Controversies and Polemics*. Leiden: Brill.

KARAMUSTAFA, AHMET. (2007) *Sufism: The Formative Period*. Edinburgh: Edinburgh University Press.

KNYSH, ALEXANDER. (2000) *Islamic Mysticism: A Short History*. Leiden: Brill.

MALIK, JAMAL, and JOHN HINNELLS (eds.) (2006) *Sufism in the West*. London: Routledge.

MASSIGNON, LOUIS. (1982) *The Passion of The Passion of al-Hallāj: Mystic and Martyr of Islam*. 4 vols. Translated by Herbert Mason. Princeton, NJ: Princeton University Press.

NASR, SEYYED HOSSEIN (ed.). (1987–1991) *Islamic Spirituality*. 2 vols. New York: Crossroad.

RIZVI, ATHAR ABBAS. (1978–1983) *A History of Sufism in India*. 2 vols. New Delhi: Munshiram Manoharlal Publishers Pvt. Ltd.

SCHIMMEL, ANNEMARIE. (1975) *Mystical Dimensions of Islam*. Chapel Hill, NC: University of North Carolina Press.

SEDGWICK, MARK. (2000) *Sufism: The Essentials*. Cairo: American University in Cairo Press.

TRIMINGHAM, J. SPENCER. (1971) *The Sufi Orders in Islam*. London: Oxford University Press.

CHAPTER 31

ISLAMIC THEOLOGY

ERIC ORMSBY

The name for theology in both the Sunni and Shi'i traditions is *'ilm al-kalām*, literally, "the science of discourse." *Kalām* in Arabic means "speech" or "word." Muslim theologians were called *mutakallimūn*, "dialecticians," and *kalām* itself is best rendered as "dialectical theology." The designation may owe something to Christian antecedents but the term had strong indigenous resonance. The "word" is central to Islamic doctrine; the Qur'ān itself is considered God's "speech" (*kalām Allāh*). The notion of a "science of discourse" sometimes provoked derision among its critics. Strict upholders of orthodox tradition rejected the discipline as an impious "innovation," while philosophers, at the opposite extreme, dismissed it as flawed in its methods and aims. Nevertheless, the term "Kalam" is apt. Islamic theology thrived on *viva voce* debates and vehement disputations in which personal attacks and cutting sarcasm were as common as reasoned argumentation. Much was at stake: reputations and careers—and sometimes lives—hung in the balance, especially when disputations took place in a ruler's presence; occasionally the caliph himself judged the outcome of debate. Christians and Jews who debated Muslim opponents before a caliph found themselves delicately constrained; if they prevailed, they had to do so with becoming diffidence. The oral origins of Kalam continued to echo in the great compendia in which orthodox Islamic belief was later codified; intricate arguments are always structured in the patterns of spoken discourse: "If it be said" is routinely followed by "then I respond."

Kalam was polemical and apologetic, but it had another fundamental aim. It set out to give precise formulation to the articles of faith. Over the centuries, while Kalam grew steadily more systematic, it also became more capacious, eventually incorporating not only such foreign elements as Aristotelian logic but also broad metaphysical perspectives. This gradual process of refinement led to the creation of formal creeds, by which orthodox Islamic belief—both Sunni and Shi'i—defined itself. Distinctive "schools" of theology arose, each with its dogmatic agenda; inevitably, ever sharper conceptions of "heresy" also came into play. The theologians of such schools produced a vast array of formal treatises. Accompanied by commentaries and glosses, supercommentaries and superglosses, these formed the basis of doctrinal instruction in madrasas. By the early twelfth century, al-Ghazālī, a major figure in the Sunni tradition, could call Kalam "the most exalted of the religious sciences" because (unlike jurisprudence or exegesis) it was concerned with "universal truths." In fact, Kalam represents one of the most original and distinctive of the Islamic "sciences of religion," as comprehensive as it is intricate.

The basic tenet of Islamic belief is affirmed in the *shahāda*, the testimonial: "I testify that there is no God but God and Muḥammad is the emissary of God." To affirm this statement is to become a Muslim. The oneness of God and the primacy of Muḥammad's prophetic mission are the two indispensable components of the faith. The various orthodox creeds, from the ninth century onward, include many other articles about God's nature and attributes, the Prophet's mission and status, human freedom and responsibility, the life of the world-to-come, and the true meaning of belief and unbelief, among others. These formulations were hard-won. Behind the triumphant articles of faith, seemingly so immutable, lay centuries of fierce disagreement.

The Beginnings of Theology in Islam

The first stirrings of theological debate date from the early decades of the eighth century, when the Umayyad dynasty (661–750) began its irreversible collapse. In its origins, Islamic theology was shaped both by internal perplexities and by the pressure of events. Unlike philosophy (*falsafa*), which arose later under the influence of translations from Greek into Arabic, theology possessed its own dynamic. In part, this was impelled by difficulties in interpretation of the Qur'ān, for which no satisfactory solution could be found in the Traditions of the Prophet, the *ḥadīth*, in which Muḥammad's sayings and deeds had been recorded (and which served as a parallel source of revelation for Muslims). But the theological impulse was also driven by immediate practical concerns: the succession to the Prophet, the status of sinners, the nature of human action. These in turn had legal implications; and indeed, the development of Kalam occurred apace with the elaboration of Islamic jurisprudence (*fiqh*), with which it often overlapped.

Certain difficult problems arose from interpretation of the Qur'ān itself. In one of the earliest revelations (112:1), it is stated, "Say, He is God the One." That seems straightforward, and yet, it soon proved necessary to clarify that He is not "one" as in a numerical sequence, the first in a pantheon: He is unique. That further entailed stipulating that God has no "partner"—nor is He "begotten" or "begetting" (as Christians believe)—but in fact, is utterly incomparable to anything created. Nevertheless, in several Qur'ānic verses, God is given physical attributes. Verse 38:75 says that He "kneaded man with His own hands." God's "face" (55:26) is often invoked, as is His "hand" (3:73). These, and others, were the "verses of likening" (*āyāt al-tashbīh*); those who took them literally were said to uphold *tashbīh*, literally, "drawing comparisons" (in effect, "anthropomorphism"). In the early literature, there is much discussion about whether God has a body (and if so, what are its dimensions?) or, more basically, whether God can be described as a "thing" (*shay'*).

Such verses stood in apparent opposition to others that exalted God's transcendence, for example, "There is nothing like Him" (42:11) or "No one is comparable to Him" (112:4). Opponents of the "anthropomorphists" cited such verses to establish God's utter transcendence—an approach known as *tanzīh*. These two extremes clashed for centuries, with "likening" upheld by such sects as the Karrāmīya, long active in eastern Iran, and "transcendence" espoused by the Mu'tazilites, firmly ensconced in the centers of power, in Baghdad as well as in Basra and Kufa. For Shi'ites, too, the emphasis on God's transcendence was paramount, and so figurative interpretation prevailed; in the creed of the great Shi'ite traditionist and theologian Ibn Babūya (d. 991), it is stated explicitly: "'hand' means 'strength'" (Ibn Babūya 1982, 29).

Islamic theology is characterized not only by incompatible doctrinal extremes but also by recurrent efforts at reconciliation and dogmatic synthesis. Certain early thinkers tried to resolve the issue by declaring that while God had a body, it was a body "unlike other bodies," just as His voice was a voice "unlike other voices." A more influential solution lay in the formula *bi-lā kayfa*, by which one could affirm belief "without knowing how." The formula was apparently first employed by the great jurist Aḥmad ibn Ḥanbal (d. 855), but was integrated, with subtle modifications, in later Ash'arite theology, the dominant Sunni tradition.

The most momentous of the early questions concerned free will. The terms of the debate differed from parallel Christian discussions. In Islam, notions of free will collided with strong conceptions of divine omnipotence as well as justice. The possibility that humans might act in ways contrary to divine will—that they would choose "disobedience" over "obedience"—prompted questions about the efficacy of God's will. To admit free will implied that a mere creature possessed the power to oppose the divine will; to deny it implied that God, rather than the human agent, willed—and was responsible for—evil acts. This was but one of several fruitful dilemmas out of which the various schools of Islamic theology would develop.

Unlike the debate over anthropomorphism, the debate over free will was seldom theoretical; it was colored by events. After 661, when 'Alī ibn abī Ṭālib, the fourth "rightly guided" caliph (and the Prophet's son-in-law) was assassinated, the caliphate came under the control of Mu'āwiya, founder of the Umayyad dynasty, based in Damascus. Supporters of 'Alī, the *shī'at 'Alī* (or "party of 'Alī," from which the modern term Shi'ite derives) had militated at the time of the Prophet's death in 632 for 'Alī, the closest male relative of Muhammad, to succeed him. Instead, Abū Bakr, the Prophet's trusted companion (and the father of 'Ā'isha, his favorite wife) was chosen as the first "successor to the Emissary of God" (*khalīfat rasūl Allāh*)—the original designation of the office of "caliph." 'Alī would be passed over twice more, acceding to the caliphate only in 656. His supporters held that 'Alī had been unjustly deprived of his rightful succession, a grievance that continues to resound among Shi'ites (who curse the first three caliphs as "malefactors" to this day). The division was significant not only because of the enduring schism that it created but also because it fomented severe unrest among various factions who viewed the triumphant Umayyads as impious usurpers of a sacred office.

The issues raised were neither purely theological nor narrowly "political." If humans did not possess free will, then Umayyad "tyranny" had to be accepted as God's will; however, if humans did possess free will, they could move to oust unjust rulers. The debates had a dangerous edge; a proponent of free will might be considered—and often was—seditious. Several early advocates of free will ended up on the scaffold.

The proponents of free will came to be known as the Qadarīya, an ironic designation applied to them by their opponents; the Arabic word *qadar* actually means "predestination" (as in the classic traditional formula *qaḍā' wa-qadar*, "God's decree and foreordainment"). In Syria, the movement tended to be politically motivated; in Iraq, theological considerations predominated. The shadowy figure of Ma'bad al-Juhanī (d. 703) was, by most reports, "the first who talked about free will in Basra." Renowned as a legal authority, he participated in 701–702 in an insurrection against Umayyad rule, and was executed. A generation later, Ghaylān al-Dimashqī, the son of a Coptic convert to Islam, taught that while God ordained such matters as life span or sustenance, the power to rule could be won and held through human will and effort. He was crucified by order of the caliph in the 720s; his followers, the Ghaylānīya, perpetuated his teachings, but only fragments of his work survive.

Against the Qadarīya stood thinkers like Jahm ibn Safwān (d. 746), who held not only that human acts are compelled but that God is the only true agent. To speak of human agency is to speak figuratively: "God is the agent and men have acts ascribed to them only by way of metaphor" (Watt 1948, 99). God has implanted in humans a certain "power" (*quwwa*) that enables them to act, but this is a predetermined capacity, as fixed as height or skin color. Though widely repudiated, Jahm's influence endured. His espousal of a negative theology, his denial of divine attributes, and his insistence on the created nature of the Qur'ān were later incorporated within Mu'tazilite theology. His followers, the Jahmīya, would survive for two centuries after his death.

The mystical ascetic al-Ḥasan al-Baṣrī (642–728), an articulate exponent of free will, became a leading advocate of the Qadarīya. When the stirrings of the "free will" movement reached the caliph 'Abd al-Malik, he wrote to al-Ḥasan for clarification. His response constitutes the earliest surviving defense of free will in Islamic theology.

The "Letter" employs a two-pronged strategy. First, al-Ḥasan invokes Qur'ān 51:56–7 where God says, "I have created *jinn* and men only so that they will worship Me." He then turns to interpretation and argument—a classic example of what would become standard in Kalam: striking a balance between "tradition" and "rational argument" (a procedure epitomized by the rhyming formula *'aql wa-naql*, "reason and tradition"). The verse is astutely chosen. It establishes not only that God created human beings (and those fiery spirits known as *jinn*) solely to worship Him but also that God acts for a discernible purpose, not capriciously. If this is God's purpose, and He is just, He does not ordain worship only to obstruct it. Al-Ḥasan explains, "God ordered them to worship Him which is why He created them. God would not have created them for a purpose and then come between them and [the purpose] because He does not do harm to His servants." God's actions are thus both reasonable and just.

For al-Ḥasan, it is humans who choose to believe or not to believe; faith is not predetermined. This has the effect both of affirming human free will—and responsibility—and of clearing God of any imputation of wrongdoing. God is "He who determines and guides" (87:3), not He "who commands and leads astray." The "Letter" is as much a defense of God's justice as it is an argument for human agency.

Two disciples broke with al-Ḥasan over an issue that split the community: the status of sinners. That breach led to the creation of one of the most influential schools of Islamic theology, that of the Mu'tazilites, and indeed, to the establishment of Kalam as a formal "science."

The Khārijites, an extreme Shi'ite sect, regarded any Muslim guilty of a major sin (such as the murder of another Muslim) as guilty of "unbelief" (*kufr*). For others, such as the Murji'ites, a serious sinner remained a Muslim; Murji'ites practiced "suspension of judgment" (*irjā'*): judgment was God's prerogative. For al-Ḥasan, the sinner was a "hypocrite" (*munāfiq*), a Qur'ānic term of extreme opprobrium. Yet another position developed, the so-called intermediary position. In this view, the sinner persisted in a sort of moral limbo, neither Muslim nor unbeliever. The position had political as well as theological echoes, extending back to the "Battle of the Camel" in 656, at which 'Alī, in his struggle for the caliphate, had besieged and defeated troops loyal to 'Ā'isha, the Prophet's widow, who opposed his accession. For Muslims of the time, the problem was to know which of these sacrosanct figures—upstanding Muslims all—might be considered culpable in such a conflict; since it was not possible to know, it was preferable to uphold a neutral or "intermediate" position.

The Mu'tazilite School

This neutrality was expressed by the term *i'tizāl* ("withdrawal"), which designates the school of rationalist theology—the Mu'tazilite—of which Wāṣil ibn ʿAṭā' (699–748) and his colleague 'Amr ibn 'Ubayd (699–761?) are traditionally considered the founders. For a century, the Mu'tazilites wielded considerable influence: their boldly articulated theological positions were buttressed by state power. The school was united in name alone; its adherents interpreted its fundamental principles in widely differing, often opposing ways. Reportedly, "there were more than a thousand questions" on which the early Muʿtazilites disagreed; they were also at odds with other Muslims who resented both their rationalism and their intolerance. For certain critics they were "the Magians of the community," that is, dualists, because they ascribed evil to agencies other than God.

In Basra, where they were particularly active, Wāṣil ibn ʿAṭā' gained renown as a preacher while ʿAmr ibn ʿUbayd was revered for his asceticism; neither was really a theologian, or *mutakallim*, in its later sense, and yet, they articulated theological positions that dominated the Muʿtazilite agenda for centuries. ʿAmr, for example, argued in favor of human responsibility and its concomitant, the unimpeachable justice of God; typically, these took the form of fiercely debated questions: must God "keep His word" to humans? (ʿAmr held that He must); or can God impose impossible demands on His creatures? (no, because that would be contrary to His justice).

Both thinkers frequented circles in Basra where not only Muslims but also Zoroastrians and Buddhists, as well as outspoken sceptics, were present. Such exposure to divergent viewpoints strengthened their own doctrinal position even while subtly infiltrating it. Wāṣil engaged in polemics against dualism (*thanawīya* or *zandaqa* in Arabic); he also composed treatises defending divine unity (*tawḥīd*)—the central tenet of Muʿtazilism—explicating the Koran, and urging the necessity of repentance, not one of which survives. Sometimes foreign influences are discernible. The concept of the world as a "mixture" (*mizāj*), an old Zoroastrian idea, enters Muʿtazilite thought around this time; it appealed because it gave the human intellect, which Muʿtazilites exalted, the crucial function of discriminating between what is good and bad in human experience. The ninth-century Muʿtazilite polymath al-Jāḥiẓ would develop the concept extensively.

The Muʿtazilites espoused five cardinal principles of faith (*uṣūl*):

- Divine oneness (*tawḥīd*)
- Divine justice (*ʿadl*)
- The Promise and the Threat (*al-waʿd waʾl-waʿīd*)
- An intermediate position on grave sinners (*al-manzila bayn al-manzilatayn*)
- Commanding the Good and Forbidding the Bad (*al-amr biʾl-maʿrūf waʾl-nahy ʿan al-munkar*)

These principles took shape during the first century of Abbasid rule when Muʿtazilite theologians served as "court theologians." Though their doctrines were repugnant to much of the populace, as well as to traditional scholars, they were imposed by caliphal authority, especially during the reign of al-Maʾmūn (d. 833). It was not only specific doctrines, such as the "createdness of the Koran," that aroused opposition; the characteristic Muʿtazilite insistence on "the autonomy of the intellect" inspired revulsion. Matters ranging from the metaphysical (God's attributes) to the ethical (the nature of good and bad) thus came under the sway of reason rather than tradition. To their opponents this rationalistic emphasis seemed impertinent at best, and at worst, blasphemous.

Two outstanding theologians of the period were Abū al-Hudhayl al-ʿAllāf (d. 841?) and his nephew and one-time disciple Ibrāhīm ibn Sayyār al-Naẓẓām (d. 836). Both were formidable disputants, often against each other, and both brought philosophical as well as scientific factors into play in their theology. They were as curious about the physical structure of reality as about metaphysics. Al-Naẓẓām carried out experiments and wrote on such subjects as the migration of fish and the composition of scorpion venom. Abū al-Hudhayl espoused atomism as an integral aspect of his theology. The world, he taught, is made up of atoms and their accidents, both of which occur in "composition" (*ta'līf*).A body is nothing more than a created compound in which certain accidents, or nonessential qualities, are combined with a particular configuration of atoms, all brought into conjunction by God's will. Things have no essence, no intrinsic "nature." They are momentary compounds; their conjunction, like their dissolution, occurs by divine fiat, and the composition itself is an "accident." Change is a series of such compositions. Because these phenomena appear in time, becoming at one moment what they were not a moment before, some agency must have initiated the change from one composition to another; and this we call God. The argument represents the first proof of God's existence in Islamic theology.

Al-Naẓẓām disagreed; he rejected atomism. The elements of a body, he taught, interpenetrate one another. Change occurs when an element that was previously indiscernible becomes manifest on a body's surface. The only true accident is movement, which al-Naẓẓām explained by his notion of "the leap" (*ṭafra*). In humans movement results from free will; in nonhuman entities, it arises from a "creational compulsion," installed at creation. Knowledge, too, entails a kind of movement, and is therefore accidental, but it may produce an inner certainty, or "tranquillity of heart," a key concept in his thought.

Though both Abū al-Hudhayl and al-Naẓẓām were influential, especially in their strenuous polemics against dualism, their efforts to create a theology in which philosophical and scientific inquiry would play a part died with them; such concerns would pass to Muslim philosophers.

Much criticism of the Muʿtazilites centerd on their confident rationalism. Their doctrine of "the optimum" (*al-aṣlaḥ:* "the most beneficial") provides an example. If God is just, all His actions must be just. Not only can He not be held accountable for evil, but also He must always do what is best for His creatures. The doctrine was much contested, within the school and without. Most offensive to opponents was not merely its smug presumption but the corollary that God was somehow "obliged" to perform the optimum, both in this world and the next, for His servants. The word had juridical overtones. Reason tells us what justice means; justice is a value that God recognizes and observes: if we are obliged to be just, how much the more so God? Another corollary followed: good and evil are not determined by divine commandment; they are objective values, known to all; they exist independently of revelation.

The Mu'tazilite emphasis on divine oneness led them to practice *ta'ṭīl*, the rejection of any conception of divine attributes as discrete and separable qualities within God's essential nature, and so to condemn any form of "anthropomorphism" (Wensinck 1932, 207). This meant that for Mu'tazilites, God's hearing or knowing or willing occurred "essentially," flowing from His very nature rather than from any array of distinct and sharply delineated qualities; God did not know or will because of a "knowledge" or "will" lodged within His essence. To posit such attributes, which by their very nature would be coeternal with God, represented "polytheism" (*shirk*) in the Mu'tazilite view, threatening to turn God's essential oneness into a dubious composite. This position led unavoidably to the conviction that the Qur'ān, though "God's speech," was not eternal but "created." Most Muslims at the time—though it was not yet dogma—held that the Qur'ān had existed from all eternity in the form of a "preserved tablet" (*lawḥ maḥfūẓ*) and that it was, like God Himself, "uncreated." For the Mu'tazilites, such a belief infringed divine oneness; "speech" or "power" or "will" or any of the other attributes attested in the Qur'ān could not be considered separate, and coeternal, entities lodged in the godhead. When the caliph Ma'mūn promulgated the createdness of the Qur'ān as official doctrine, a kind of "inquisition" (*miḥna*) was instituted. Eminent scholars of law and tradition were hauled before the authorities and quizzed as to their beliefs; those who refused to accept the "createdness" of scripture were prosecuted. The great jurist Aḥmad ibn Ḥanbal, who held that the Qur'ān was uncreated, though "without knowing how," stood his ground; he was flogged and imprisoned. This persecution would have serious repercussions for the Mu'tazilites.

Abbasid support for the Mu'tazilites ended with the reign of al-Mutawakkil (r. 847–861) and the school began a long decline. Aḥmad ibn Ḥanbal was not only reinstated but became a Sunni popular hero, and his tradition-based doctrines prevailed. Mu'tazilism continued to be taught and expounded, most notably in the brilliant work of 'Abd al-Jabbār al-Asadābādī (d. 1025) and his circle. The last outstanding representative of the school was the lexicographer and exegete al-Zamakhsharī (d. 1144).

Classic Sunni Kalam

The Ash'arite school of Kalam, the dominant tradition of Sunni orthodoxy to this day, represents a persuasive synthesis of Mu'tazilite methods with Ḥanbalite doctrine. Abū al-Ḥasan al-Ash'arī (874–935) had been a Mu'tazilite, but around the year 912, he broke with his master Abū 'Alī al-Jubbā'ī (d. 915) over the doctrine of "the optimum." In his later works, al-Ash'arī employed structured syllogistic arguments to establish and defend the truths of traditional faith: he developed proofs for the existence of God; he argued for the reality of the attributes as discrete qualities "superadded to the divine essence"; he accepted the physical traits ascribed to God "without [asking] how"; he affirmed the direct vision of God in the afterlife; and he upheld predestination over free will. Against the Mu'tazilite insistence on free will, Ash'arite Kalam developed a notion of "acquisition" (*kasb*), which stated that humans acted by means of a capability "acquired" from God. His insistence on God's utter omnipotence led to the rejection of causality and the espousal of occasionalism: all that occurs is the direct result of God's "specifying will," atom by atom, and moment by moment.

Al-Ash'arī established Ash'arite Kalam as the classical mode of Sunni theological discourse. Abū Bakr al-Bāqillānī (d. 1013), celebrated for his defense of the "inimitability" (*i'jāz*) of the Qur'ān, Ibn Fūrak (d. 1015), Abū al-Ma'ālī al-Juwaynī (d. 1085), and others, further developed and codified the tradition. The immemorial questions persisted, despite increasing refinement and ever more exact formulation; their very intractability gave the Kalam its momentum. Thus, on the vexed question of divine attributes, it might be asked how such attributes as knowledge or will or power corresponded to their specific objects. If God's knowledge was indeed eternal and "uncreated," how explain, say, the fact that new circumstances, new "knowables," apparently came, more or less continually, into God's ken? Did His knowledge alter in conjunction with new facts? If so, how could it be called eternal, a preexisting fixture within His essence? But if it did not alter to accommodate new data, would this not compromise His omniscience? One "solution," propounded by the great thirteenth-century Ash'arite theologian Sayf al-Dīn al-Āmidī, was to argue that the divine attributes acted not directly on their objects, but rather stood in a "nexus" (*ta'alluq*) with them; it was not God's knowledge that changed with changing circumstances but the nexus between that knowledge and its objects. To some critics, such arguments seemed little more than tedious "hair-splitting." It could be argued, however, that it was precisely in such ever sharper refinement of terms and arguments that the true, and genuine, distinction—and the enduring influence—of Ash'arite Kalam ultimately lay.

Equally "orthodox" was the Sunni tradition of Kalam established by Abū Manṣūr al-Māturīdī (d. 944), a theologian born near Samarkand, whose doctrines, thanks to their adoption by the Ḥanafī legal school, became widespread in Central Asia. Though a dozen small points of dogma separated Māturīdism from Ash'arism, the major difference resided in the greater scope that al-Māturīdī allowed to human free will; in general, al-Māturīdī stood somewhat closer to Mu'tazilism on this vital issue. In his view, God creates in man the power to act, but man uses this power, not merely "figuratively" (as the Ash'arites held) but actually; human actions possess significance and man is responsible for them. Al-Māturīdī was critical of al-Ash'arī's rejection of free will because it led inevitably to a form of fatalistic determinism; in addressing Ash'arites, he stated bluntly, "Your doctrine amounts to depriving men of hope and fear; they will not fear on account of the evil in their acts, nor hope on account of the good in them."[1]

1. Al-Māturīdī's work survives imperfectly; a portion of his Qur'ān commentary has been published, as well as his *Kitāb al-Tawḥīd* ("The Book of Divine Oneness"), a major theological treatise, but neither has yet received the scholarly attention they merit.

Ash'arites and Māturīdites were not the only critics of Mu'tazilite rationalism. The one-time Mu'tazilite theologian Ibn al-Rāwandī (d. 859 or 864), ostracized as an "arch-heretic," sought to puncture their pretensions, espousing the position that given the frequent contradictions of theologians, their much-vaunted "proofs" were all "equivalent"—in other words, of dubious value. In Muslim Spain, a more formidable critic arose in the person of the jurist and litterateur Ibn Ḥazm (d. 1064), the major exponent of the Ẓāhirite school of law and theology that rejected all esoteric (*bāṭin*) scriptural interpretations in favor of purely exoteric (*ẓāhir*) readings; for him, God's clarity of expression was an aspect of His compassion. An irascible maverick, as well as a superb prose stylist, Ibn Ḥazm seemed to revel in provocation; for example, he was one of the very few medieval Muslim authors to argue forcefully that women could be prophets—a viewpoint that still sparks outrage among conventional theologians. Ibn Ḥazm also composed an encyclopaedic account of all sects and schools known to him, with scathing comments on both Ash'arite and Mu'tazilite doctrines; this major work represents a monumental contribution to heresiography, a fundamental genre of medieval Islamic theology.

The Transformation of Kalam

Abū Ḥāmid al-Ghazālī (1058–1111) was a legal scholar and theologian who turned to Sufism in 1095 after a spiritual crisis. In his autobiography he describes how the search for truth led him to explore Kalam (in which he wrote a classic treatise), Aristotelian philosophy, Sufi mysticism, and the teachings of the Ismā'īlīs, the Shi'ite sect known as "The Seveners" (because of their belief in a lineage of seven infallible imams). The philosophy of Ibn Sina (Avicenna) had a crucial influence on his thought; though he denounced twenty premises of the philosophers as heretical, his later works are permeated with Avicennian notions and made possible the gradual acceptance of both Aristotelian logic and Avicennian metaphysics within the Ash'arite tradition. Beyond such methodological and formal innovations, his celebrated work *The Revival of the Sciences of Religion* expounded an Islam in which traditional elements are boldly conjoined with mystical and philosophical considerations; it transformed theology and is still actively studied today. Though often described as a "synthesizer" of disparate disciplines, al-Ghazālī in fact revitalized Kalam from within, infusing traditional theological speculation with a fresh vision. His notion of a criterion "beyond the sphere of the intellect," which he identified with the faculty of "taste" (*dhawq*), emphasized the importance of direct, unmediated experience in the quest for truth; utter "certainty" (*yaqīn*), he argued, must be as indefinable but as unmistakable as the taste of something on the tongue. For al-Ghazālī, final truth, which is neither theological nor philosophical but experiential, is to be known, if at all, with the same certainty with which a person knows that one day he will die. (How this "certainty," which remains incommunicable, was to be verified, let alone articulated, remained an unanswered question, to which al-Ghazālī's characteristic response was invariably, "He who has tasted knows.") This new approach, laced with mystical Sufi elements, has been labelled "subjectivism," but it actually transcends so narrow a category. His guiding principle, expressed in the characteristic formulation "knowledge *and* action" (*'ilm wa-'amal*), was predicated on his conviction that knowledge and action were not merely interdependent but inseparable. This emphasis brought renewed vitality to Islamic theology; it broadened the discipline without lessening its rigor and it made possible the gradual introduction of new themes, new perspectives, fresh and sometimes surprising nuances. In the works of certain later thinkers, especially those of the "Illuminationist" (*Ishrāqī*) school, such as 'Ayn al-Quḍāt al-Hamadhānī (executed for heresy in 1131), or in the mystical theology of the celebrated Andalusian Sufi Muḥyi al-Dīn Ibn al-'Arabī (d. 1240) and his followers, al-Ghazālī's original insights—coupled with those of his younger brother Aḥmad al-Ghazālī (d. 1126), a far more radical thinker—would assume unexpected, and often monumental, dimensions.

In the voluminous works of Fakhr al-Dīn al-Rāzī (d. 1209), the tradition of Ash'arite Kalam was decisively extended. In addition to his major theological works, al-Rāzī composed a massive commentary (*tafsīr*) on the Qur'ān in which theological and philosophical considerations are seamlessly integrated; indeed, he expresses his views most creatively under the cover of exegesis. A combative metaphysician, he remains one of the greatest figures in the history of Kalam.

Later Ash'arite theologians include 'Aḍud al-Dīn al-Ījī (d. 1355), whose rigorous compendium of doctrine, the *Kitāb al-Mawāqif* ("The Book of Stations"), still dominates the curriculum at Al-Azhar University in Cairo, and whose principal commentators, Sa'd al-Dīn al-Taftāzānī (d. 1390) and al-Sayyid al-Sharīf al-Jurjānī (d. 1413), were significant theologians in their own right. The Ash'arite theological tradition became increasingly abstract and formulaic in later centuries; its last significant representative was Ibrāhīm al-Bājūrī (d. 1860).

It has long been commonplace to decry later Ash'arite Kalam as arid and rigid, if not downright ossified. (In their exhaustive *Introduction à la théologie musulmane* of 1948, Louis Gardet and M.-M. Anawati crisply dismiss it as "congealed.") That view is beginning to change. The great school compendia, their succinct, almost telegraphic texts ringed by commentary and supercommentary, gloss and supergloss, do present a forbidding aspect; they seem fortresses of dogma guarded by bristling battlements of antiquated debate. It is slowly becoming apparent, however, that the later Kalam possessed a lively dynamism, concealed in the numerous commentaries and "little treatises" (*rasā'il*), composed (sometimes literally) on the margins of the "official" dogmatic textbooks studied and memorized in the madrasas. In these ephemeral pamphlets and epistles, small, ostensibly minor subjects (the status of the Prophet's parents, the question of whether the despotic Pharaoh of the Qur'ān had died a believer or not) often developed into elaborate discussions of age-old topics—free will and predestination, the definition of belief and of unbelief—that had seemed long resolved but still smoldered stubbornly on. Much of this huge body of occasional writing consists of disputes, often quite vehement, between lesser-known theologians of Turkish or Central Asian origin (though most write in Arabic); moreover, these were disputes that continued from one generation to the next, with the issues and the solutions continually undergoing modification. At least one such debate, sparked by a remark by al-Ghazālī in the eleventh century, persisted until well into the nineteenth century; this eight-hundred-year debate, over the question of theodicy, involved numerous theologians of varying doctrinal persuasions and resulted not only in the vigorous airing of opposing views, echoing across the centuries, but also in the formulation of a novel version of a genuinely Islamic theodicy (Ormsby 1984). This is but one example of a hidden dynamic in the later "stagnant" period of Islamic theology, and which is only now coming under scrutiny.

Dissenting Traditions

Other, less "classic" theologians have also begun to receive fresh attention in recent years. The old specter of "anthropomorphism" re-emerged in the voluminous work of the prolific theologian Ibn Taymiyya (d. 1328), a brilliant jurist of the traditionalist Ḥanbalī school of law. He assailed virtually everyone, from Sufis to logicians—he was often considered to "have a screw loose" and spent time in jail—and espoused an extravagantly literalist interpretation of Islam. His vast body of thought underpins contemporary Wahhabi Islam in Saudi Arabia (where traditional Kalam is banned from schools), a fact that has tended to obscure the force and originality of his thought.

Though Mu'tazilism disappeared as a school, its doctrines and methods lived on—and continue to live on today—in Shi'ite Kalam, which affirmed the primacy of reason as well as human free will, together with an elaborate, often mystical doctrine of the Imamate. So central is the Imamate to Shi'ite thought that Shaykh al-Mufīd (d. 1022), a major early theologian, could declare that the very essence of Shi'ite belief is "loyal adherence to the Commander of the Faithful," that is, 'Alī ibn abī Ṭālib. For both Imāmī, or Ithnā ᶜAsharīya ("Twelver") Shi'ites, the majority of Shi'ites in Iran today, and the dissenting group known as the Ismā'īlīs (or "Seveners"), the figure of the imam is sacrosanct; often martyred, persecuted, and beleaguered, the imams in both Shi'ite traditions are considered divinely inspired, as well as sinless and infallible. They are the possessors of privileged knowledge, sometimes characterized in Shi'ite sources as "a luminous substance," which they impart to their followers. Another branch, the Zaydī Shi'ites—especially active in the Yemen—emphasized the importance of a "just imam" and rejected the doctrine of the "hidden imam," so fundamental to Twelver Shi'ism with its chiliastic expectations.

From its origins, Shi'ite theology was inextricably bound up with the study of both law and sacred traditions; indeed, much impetus was given to the development of Shi'ite theology in the tenth century by the protracted disputes over the proper way to study tradition between the so-called *Akhbārī* school, which favored a literal approach, and the *Uṣūlī* school, which favored more rationalistic methods. The latter tendency, represented by the commanding figure of Ibn Babūya (d. 991), a canonical authority in the Shi'ite tradition, would eventually prevail. Simultaneously, a rich tradition of philosophical theology arose among Ismā'īlī thinkers; in their work, mystical and esoteric concepts combined with Neo-Platonic doctrines to create an original and intricate synthesis. The Ismā'īlī "missionary" (*dā'ī*) and Fatimid agent Nāṣir-i Khosraw (d. ca. 1070) is particularly noteworthy in this respect: one of the greatest of Persian poets, he employed that language with striking sophistication in his theological treatises in an effort to reconcile Hellenistic thought with Ismā'īlī doctrine. Later thinkers, such as the versatile scientist, philosopher, and theologian Nāṣir al-Dīn al-Ṭūsī (d. 1274), originally an Ismā'īlī, would develop Shi'ite Kalam to a high level of formal distinction. His "Epitome of Belief" (*Tajrīd al-'Aqāid*), especially as embedded in the running commentary of his student Ibn al-Muṭahhar al-Ḥillī (d. 1325)—another Shi'ite theologian of canonical status—inspired more than two dozen commentaries and glosses well into the seventeenth century; it is one of the rare works of Shi'ite Kalam to be read and taught in Sunni madrasas.

The development of Shi'ite theology also gives the lie to depictions of later Islamic thought, and of theology in particular, as static and desiccated. Under the Safavid dynasty (1501–1732), when Iran officially adopted Twelver Shi'ite belief, theology as well as philosophy experienced a resurgence. Such original thinkers as Mīr Dāmād (d. 1631) and his one-time pupil Mullā Ṣadrā (Ṣadr al-Dīn Shīrāzī, d. 1640) created a philosophical theology of unusual scope and subtlety. They and their followers are difficult to categorize. They are at once philosophers, theologians, and mystics; this has occasionally given rise to the unfortunate designation of "theosophy" to their work, but that is seriously misleading. Mīr Dāmād's discussions of the nature of time in its various permutations, from "meta-time" to "mutable time" to "Non-Time," the realm of the timeless, impart a curiously modern cast to his metaphysics. The elaborate "philosophy of existence" of his pupil, and philosophical opponent, Mullā Ṣadrā, a commanding thinker by any criterion, stood the perennial essentialist tradition of Islamic thought, deriving from Ibn Sīnā, on its head. Being could no longer be seen as an adventitious "accident," superadded to essence, but constituted the authentic ground of reality. Both thinkers and their disciples in the "School of Isfahan" changed Islamic theology in Iran into a discipline at once soaring and exploratory and that continues, despite recent upheavals, to dominate the Shi'ite theological agenda.

Modern Developments

In the late nineteenth century, shaken by contact with Western powers, certain Muslim theologians began rethinking time-honored traditions. The Egyptian journalist and theologian Muḥammad 'Abduh (1849–1905), inspired by the charismatic Iranian reformer Jamāl al-Dīn al-Afghānī (1838–1897), sought to revive theology; though often banished, the two cofounded an influential journal from exile that had the aim of newly defining Islam's place in the modern world. When 'Abduh became a judge and then rector of Al-Azhar University, he used his position and his writings, especially his celebrated *Epistle on Unity* (*Risālat al-Tawḥīd*) of 1897, in the cause of reform—a reform designed largely to safeguard Islam against the influence of Western thought. Such rearguard efforts have attracted new spokesmen in recent years, most notably the Egyptian Islamist Sayyid Quṭb (executed 1966), a member of the extreme Muslim Brotherhood whose *In the Shadow of the Qur'an*, a vast (and inflammatory) Qur'ānic commentary, continues to inspire fundamentalist Muslims.

Contact with Western thought has been more fruitful for other modern Muslim theologians, even as they contest it; and European philosophy has been particularly influential. The Turkish theologian Mustafa Sabri (d. 1954), who served as Shaykh al-Islam, the highest (Sunni) spiritual authority under the Ottoman Empire, immersed himself in Western philosophy, especially the thought of Kant and Bergson, and incorporated certain of their insights into his own voluminous writings. The Iranian cleric Murtaḍā Muṭahharī (1920–1979), author of several important works in Persian, exhibited an unusual grasp of both the classic Islamic theological tradition and of Western philosophy from Plato to Schopenhauer and Hegel. His major treatise *Divine Justice* (1973) recasts venerable Mu'tazilite precepts in contemporary form. More generally, consideration of such current issues as medical ethics, social justice, women's rights, and heated debates over evolutionary theory, has now begun to jostle the abstract and studiously "timeless" realm of Islamic theology. Perhaps the most promising recent developments have been inspired by Western methods of Biblical hermeneutics, now increasingly—if cautiously—applied to the text of the Qur'ān. The Algerian-born scholar Mohammad Arkoun (b. 1928) has braved accusations of heresy to elaborate bold theoretical approaches not only to the study of the Qur'ān, but also to the unspoken preconceptions that govern traditional Islamic discourse. Finally, the Egyptian scholar Nasr Hamid Abu Zaid (b. 1943), through his controversial explorations of the historical context of the Qur'ān—studies for which he was exiled—has begun to provide illuminating perspectives as well as fresh impetus for the Islamic theology of the future.

BIBLIOGRAPHY AND SUGGESTED READING

Arkoun, Mohammad. (2002) *The Unthought in Contemporary Islamic Thought*. London: Saqi.

Al-Ash'arī. (1953) *The Theology of al-Ash'arī*, edited and translated by Richard J. McCarthy. Beirut: Imprimerie Catholique.

Ess, Josef, van. (2006) *The Flowering of Muslim Theology*. Cambridge, MA: Harvard University Press.

Frank, Richard M. (2005–2008) *Classical Islamic Theology*. 3 vols. Aldershot: Ashgate (Variorum).

Al-Ghazālī. (1980) *Freedom and Fulfillment: An Annotated Translation of al-Ghazālī's al-Munqidh min al-Ḍalāl and other relevant works*, translated by Richard J. McCarthy. Boston: Twayne.

Goldziher, Ignaz. (1966–1971) *Muslim Studies*. 2 vols. Edited by S. M. Stern. Chicago: Aldine Publishing Company.

———. (1981) *Introduction to Islamic Theology and Law*. Princeton, NJ: Princeton University Press.

Griffel, Frank. (2009) *Al-Ghazālī's Philosophical Theology*. Oxford: Oxford University Press.

Hamza, Feras, and Sajjad Rizvi, with Farhana Mayer. (eds.). (2008) *An Anthology of Qur'anic Commentaries. Volume I: On the Nature of the Divine*. Oxford: Oxford University Press.

Ibn Babūya. (1982) *A Shī'ite Creed*, translated by Asaf A.A. Fyzee. Tehran: WOFIS.

Al-Jāḥiẓ. (1969) *The Life and Works of Jāḥiẓ*, edited by Charles Pellat. Berkeley and Los Angeles, CA: University of California Press.

Al-Juwaynī. (2000) *A Guide to Conclusive Proof for the Principles of Belief*, translated by Paul E. Walker. Reading: Garnet.

Lawson, Todd (ed.). (2005) *Reason and Inspiration in Islam: Theology, Philosophy and Mysticism in Muslim Thought. Essays in Honour of Hermann Landolt*. London and New York: I.B. Tauris/The Institute of Ismaili Studies.

Madelung, Wilferd. (1997) *The Succession to Muhammad: a Study of the Early Caliphate*. Cambridge: Cambridge University Press.

McDermott, Martin J. (1978) *The Theology of al-Shaykh al-Mufid (d. 413/1022)*. Beirut: Dar El-Machreq.

Muṭahharī, Murtaḍā. (2004) *Divine Justice*. Qum: International Centre for Islamic Studies.

Nagel, Tilman. (2000) *The History of Islamic Theology from Muhammad to the Present*. Princeton, NJ: Markus Weiner.

Ormsby, Eric. (1984) *Theodicy in Islamic Thought: al-Ghazālī's "Best of All Possible Worlds."* Princeton, NJ: Princeton University Press.

———. (2008) *Ghazali: The Revival of Islam*. Oxford: Oneworld.

The Qur'an. (2004). Translated by M. A. S. Abdel Haleem. Oxford: Oxford University Press.

Taji-Farouki, Suha. (ed.). (2004) *Modern Muslim Intellectuals and the Qur'ān*. Oxford: Oxford University Press.

Tritton, A. S. (1947) *Muslim Theology*. London: Luzac.

Watt, W. Montgomery. (1948) *Free Will and Predestination in Early Islam*. London: Luzac.

Wensinck, A. J. (1932) *The Muslim Creed: Its Genesis and Historical Development*. Cambridge: Cambridge University Press.

Winter, Tim (ed.). (2008) *The Cambridge Companion to Classical Islamic Theology*. Cambridge: Cambridge University Press.

Wolfson, H. A. (1976) *The Philosophy of the Kalam*. Cambridge, MA: Harvard University Press.

CHAPTER 32

MUSLIM JURISPRUDENCE

ROBERT GLEAVE

MEDIEVAL Muslim legal literature is primarily characterized by casuistic modes of reasoning. That is, legal positions are principally developed through a question-and-answer process, whereby an author proposes a particular doctrine and objections to it are examined, one by one. These objections, often attributed to specific individuals, or (more generally) to one's opponents, are rebutted in turn. Often one's own position emerges as victorious not through a process of demonstrative reasoning resulting in a coherent position, but instead, one's views gain their authority from being the most defensible within the cut and thrust of academic debate. The dominance of this mode of reasoning restricted the development of a "theory" or an exposition technique that is "philosophical." That there is intellectual sophistication within legal literature is not in doubt. In general, though, Muslim legal theory is not presented as a "philosophical" system worked out from first principles or intellectual contemplation by an individual thinker, but rather as a series of questions (*masā'il*), the answers to which cascade, and exhibit a sort of intellectual chain reaction. The sum total of this process could be considered a legal philosophy, but this is not always explicit in the literature.[1]

Muslim jurists generally avoid developing comprehensive theories linking law and philosophy. One example of this is the manner in which metaphysical ideas are discussed in respect to a particular legal problem. The notion of purity and its transmission form a major chapter in works of Islamic jurisprudence (*fiqh*). However, Muslim jurists very rarely discuss the operations of "purity" (*ṭahāra*) in the abstract. An abstract, generalized theory of how purity status is breached, how purity and

1. The genre of literature known as the *masā''il* was a set of questions that had been posed to a jurist, followed by his answer. For an introduction to the importance of *masā''il*, see Susan A. Specktorsky, *Chapters on Marriage and Divorce Responses of Ibn Hanbal and Ibn Rāhwayh* (Austin, TX: University of Texas Press, 1993).

impurity are transmitted, and whether purity status has any physical (as opposed to metaphysical) character is rarely encountered. Such a "theory" does not emerge as a preoccupation of either medieval or modern Muslim jurists. Instead, any "theory" (or "philosophy") of purity has to be deduced from a series of *masā'il* (questions). Consider the following question and answer:

> The skin of a dog is not made pure by being tanned. This is what al-Shāfi'ī says. Abū Ḥanīfa says that it is purified thereby, and Dāwūd says this also. We say [it is not pure] and our proof is that the "whole group" has agreed this. Furthermore, there is the report [from the Prophet Muḥammad] that any [animal] whose meat is forbidden cannot be made pure through being slaughtered. There is also another report from the Prophet, in which he forbids all [animals] which have an incisor—and this is a general [ruling] for every instance.[2]

On the face of it, there is not much in this ritual issue to interest a philosopher. The author of this text, Muḥammad ibn al-Ḥasan al-Ṭūsī (d. 460/1067), was a Shi'ite theologian and jurist, and in this book, *al-Khilāf*, he lists the opinions of the different schools, ending with his own school's opinion (signaled by the section that begins, "We say…"). He provides a sketch of the reasons behind his school's opinion. *First*, all the Shi'ites (his code for this is "the whole group") have agreed that tanning does not purify dog skin. This is a proof known as *ijmā'* in Islamic jurisprudence (though al-Ṭūsī is using it in a specifically Shī'ī sense). That everyone believes something is not, philosophically speaking, a particularly convincing argument. *Second*, the dog is an animal whose meat is forbidden; the Prophet said that all parts (skin included) of impure animals were impure; therefore, dog skin is impure (a simple use of a syllogism). There was no mention of an exception for tanned dog skin. *Finally*, dogs have an incisor; the Prophet forbade anything that has an incisor; therefore, the dog is forbidden (another syllogism). In this last citation it is not clear what exactly is being forbidden here—it could be any number of activities. The report merely says that such animals were "forbidden" by the Prophet (forbidden to eat? forbidden to keep as pets? forbidden to hunt with?). There is a presumption that the Prophet is saying to eat the meat of an animal with an incisor is forbidden. Al-Ṭūsī argues that the prohibition is general (*'āmm*), applying to "every instance"; that is, there no indication that an exception is made for the tanned skin of a dog. This conclusion is shared by the great jurist al-Shafi'ī (more on whom is below) and his followers.

The dissenting opinion is that of Abū Ḥanīfa.[3] Like most of Abū Ḥanīfa's opinions, his opinion is recorded in later works by his followers rather than in any work

2. Muḥammad ibn al-Hasan al-Ṭūsī, *al-Khilāf* (Qum: Mu'assasat al-Nashr al-Islāmī, 1407AH), vol. 1, p. 66. All translations in this article are by the author.

3. Dāwūd al-Ẓāhirī (d. 270/883) is also said to have held the opinion that tanned dog skin is impure, though he was not as important a figure as Abū Ḥanīfa. On Dāwūd's school, see Ignaz Goldziher, *The Ẓāhirīs: Their Doctrine and their History* (Leiden: Brill, 2007). Al-Ṭūsī's convention here (as one finds in many works of *fiqh*) is to refer to the whole school by the name of the founder. So when he refers to Abū Ḥanīfa, he means his followers also (i.e., the Ḥanafis). The same is true when he mentions al-Shāfi'ī and al-Ẓāhirī.

he himself wrote. Al-Ṭūsī does not transmit it from him but knows it through the quotations of his followers. According to him, even though dogs are impure, their skin is not once it has been tanned. The argument is nested within a general exposition of the process of tanning and its ability to remove impurity. For the Ḥanafīs (the followers of Abū Ḥanīsfa), tanning a hide prevents it from decaying any further, effectively sealing it from the usual effects of the elements on animal skin. This sealing, for the Ḥanafīs, means that the hide can no longer transmit the impurity usually associated with the body parts of a cadaver (human or otherwise). Hence, all animal skins are made pure by the tanning process and available for ritual activity (such as being a ground surface for prayer). There are, however, two important exceptions: human skin and swine skin. For the Ḥanafīs, the reason for each exception is different. With respect to the human skin that has been tanned, this should not be produced, sold, bought, or used. The reason is not due to purity (human skin, once tanned, is pure just like any other skin), but out of respect for the human being who has died. While the dead bodies of animals can be used as a means, the dead body of a human cannot be (this principle raises interesting ethical questions regarding organ transplantation, which has been the subject of much debate in the modern period).[4] Swine skin is different from all other types of skin for a different reason. For the Ḥanafīs, pigs are the only animals that are essentially impure (*najas al-'ayn*). They are essentially impure for no physiological reason, but purely on a revelatory basis (God and the Prophet had indisputably said that pigs are impure). Dogs, they argue, cannot be essentially impure because essentially impure things cannot be bought and sold in a valid trade contract, and dogs can be bought and sold (pigs, on the other hand, cannot legitimately be bought and sold). Dogs, however, are impure (or, at least, are to be treated as if they are impure) not due to any essential impurity, but due to an accidental impurity that comes about because of their association with an impure object (such as carrion—a process called *tanjīs*).

In the Ḥanafī defense of their belief that a tanned dog skin is not impure, one sees the employment of philosophical categories. In particular, the essence/attribute distinction is utilized here in order to defend their particular categorization schema against that of opponents—the Shāfi'īs (the followers of Muḥammad ibn Idrīs al-Shāfi'ī), the Mālikīs (the followers of Mālik ibn Anas), and the Shī'a. The Shāfi'īs respond to this by asserting that dogs are essentially impure. Part of their argument is textual (they prioritize certain possible readings of texts over others, and accept some texts as authentic while rejecting others), but part of it refers to the manner in which essential impurity might be recognized and identified. For the Shāfi'īs, essential impurity refers to those things that cannot be considered pure in any circumstances. In all the revelatory evidence, and in all the laws regarding impurity developed by the jurists, dogs, when alive, are never considered pure. They transmit impurity on contact; when they lap from a bowl, the bowl must be washed (some

4. See Birgit Krawietz, "*Ḍarūra* in Modern Islamic Law: The Case of Organ Transplantation," in *Islamic Law: Theory and Practice*, ed. Robert Gleave and Eugenia Kermeli (London: I. B. Tauris, 1996), pp. 185–193.

reports refer to the need to wash the bowl seven times); if they drink from water, that water becomes impure and useless for ritual purposes. Now, with all this evidence, one must conclude that dogs, not withstanding their position as "animals," are in the same purity category as other "essentially impure" items, such as semen or feces. The Shāfiʿīs here are using an empirical test for the identification of an essential attribute. If, in all respects, an object's behavior within the purity system is identical to those items that are categorized as "essentially impure," then the object in question (in this case a dog) is an essentially impure thing. That is, this is a piece of inductive reasoning ("if it walks like a duck, looks like a duck and quacks like duck—it's a duck"). The Ḥanafīs, on the other hand, argue that essentially and accidentally impure objects may behave in an identical fashion within the purity system, but that the attribution of the purity/impurity attribute has a quite different mode of application in each case. It is just coincidence that accidental impurity appears identical to essential impurity in all known areas of the purity system: in fact, the essential status of each remains distinct (though not recognizable).

In the above discussion, the influence of categories and argument types developed within philosophical discourse (both within and outside of the Muslim tradition) is clear. However, the schema (even in its much debated form presented above) is never presented as developed from first principles. Instead, it is reactive, and the principal prompt for this reaction is revelatory material (the Qur'ān and the sayings and actions of the Prophet Muhammad, or in the case of the Shi'ites, the Prophet Muḥammad and the Shi'ite Imams). Revelation presents the individual jurist with a set of rules that require not justification but coherence (indeed, it could be argued that the fact that the rules are coherent is, in itself, the justification for their validity, since it proves divine construction of the whole scheme). That the rules form a consistent and comprehensive law authored by a single divine being is one of the rules of the game for Muslim jurists. They do not, in their works of jurisprudence, set about proving this proposition, but rather, they are concerned with constructing their own version of that coherent system, and in doing this they needed a set of rules whereby the texts could be interpreted and developed, and these rules were laid out in works of legal theory (*uṣūl al-fiqh*).

Islamic Legal Philosophy (*Uṣūl al-Fiqh*)

In a search for an Islamic legal philosophy, the most likely source is the genre of literature known as *uṣūl al-fiqh* ("the principles of jurisprudence"). Works of *uṣūl al-fiqh* have a reasonably predictable structure. Most begin with discussions of language and logic, giving way to discussions of the primary "sources" of the law, how the sources are to be established as authoritative (*ḥujjiyya*) and how they are to be interpreted, followed by a description of who it is who can interpret them (the so-called qualifications of independent reasoning, *sharā'iṭ al-ijtihād*). Whether or not the ideas contained within texts of *uṣūl al-fiqh* add up to a philosophy of law is not at all obvious. Taken as a whole, a work of *uṣūl al-fiqh* appears as a highly rarefied attempt to provide the law with a coherent theory that demonstrates its basic "rationality." I mean by this not that the writers of *uṣūl al-fiqh* (the *uṣūliyūn*, as they are often referred to, or *uṣūlīs*) attempt to demonstrate that legal rulings can be found through rational (philosophical?) contemplation without the need for (irrational) revelation (there was much debate on this matter, but it was not the primary concern of the *uṣūlīs*), But rather, that their primary concern is to demonstrate that the apparent disconnectedness of the various legal rulings provided by revelation actually mask an underlying consistency. Once one has discovered this underlying consistency, one can at least attempt to work out what the law might be in cases unmentioned in the revelatory texts. *Uṣūl al-fiqh* works may not have succeeded in doing this consistently and in an entirely convincing manner, but it was the *raison d'être* of the genre.[5]

The beginnings of Islamic jurisprudence are the subject of controversy and debate, both within and outside of the Muslim tradition. It seems clear, though, that the law of the newly instituted Muslim administration was not subject to extensive theoretical foundations, but evolved in an *ad hoc* manner. The requirement of the law of the Empire to conform to a detailed set of religious regulations came into force some time after the death of the Prophet Muhammad in 632. Pressure on military and administrative officials to enforce a law underpinned by the religious values of Islam grew primarily through the emergence of a scholarly class (*'ulamā'*) during the Umayyad period (650–750). The increasing influence of this class of society ran hand in hand with a desire to introduce a legal system that was Islamic, based not on the expediencies of government, but on the principles of law supposedly laid down by God in his revelation (*waḥy*—a term that was used by later jurists to refer both to the Qur'ān and to the example, or *Sunna*, of the Prophet Muhammad). The Qur'ān does include some legal rules relating to ritual law (prayer, fasting, pilgrimage), taxation (the *zakāt* tax, and alms more generally), inheritance, marriage, and divorce. However, the legal regime set out there is hardly comprehensive, and its effect on the administration of the law in early Islam is much disputed. Day-to-day legal decisions on individual cases, as much as can be deduced from the available sources, were made on the basis of the personal opinion of judges and jurists (*ra'y*), local expediency (including the continuation of the extant law in the conquered territories), and political ideology. Dissatisfaction with the fractured and incoherent nature of the law as practiced, and its general lack of reference to the law that was supposedly revealed to the Prophet, led to the emergence of a class of jurists (*fuqahā'*) who trained legal practitioners and at times advised rulers on the correct

5. More detailed introductions to the genre of *uṣūl al-fiqh* and its purpose can be found in Wael Hallaq, *A History of Islamic Legal Theories: An Introduction to Sunnī Uṣūl al-Fiqh* (Cambridge: Cambridge University Press, 1999), and Bernard G. Weiss, *The Spirit of Islamic Law* (Athens, GA: University of Georgia Press, 1998).

administration of the law. The *fuqahā'* eventually coalesced into schools (*madhāhib*), of which four emerged in the tenth century as preeminent among the Sunni scholars (Shī'ī scholars had their own schools of law). These "schools" back-projected their origins to the legal thought of particularly eminent jurists of the eighth and ninth centuries. These early jurists were given the role of school eponym and hence the Mālikī (named after Mālik ibn Anas, d. 179/795), Ḥanafī (after Abū Ḥanīfa, d. 150/767), Shāfi'ī (after Muḥammad ibn Idrīs al-Shāfi'ī, d. 204/820), and Ḥanbalī (after Aḥmad ibn Ḥanbal, d. 240/855) recognized each other as encompassing different (but generally mutually acceptable) interpretations of the law of God as revealed in the sources. In the debate that emerged between these schools, the theoretical underpinning of the law became a subject worthy of study, since if one wishes to prove an opponent wrong, one needs a valid reason for doing so, and the most persuasive reason was on the basis of the revelatory sources. Hence, theoretical reflection emerged around texts and their interpretation, the means of resolving conflicts within the texts, and the rules to be applied when the texts contained no clear law in a particular case. In short, Muslim reflection on the theoretical foundations of the law (as found in works of *uṣūl al-fiqh*) was inspired by the standard requirements of what we might, in a modern context, call hermeneutics.[6]

Al-Shāfi'ī's *al-Risala* ("Treatise") is regularly described in traditional accounts as the first work of *uṣūl al-fiqh*, though within it, there are only hints of the full-blown genre that became a staple element of legal training some 150 years later.[7] More extensive and comprehensive rules of the validation and interpretation of texts have survived from the late tenth century, and between al-Shāfi'ī and these later texts there appears to have been numerous works of *uṣūl al-fiqh* (or at least works that dealt with issues related to the later discipline of *uṣūl al-fiqh*), though mainly our knowledge of these works is restricted to references in later bibliographical works.[8] What defined the genre of *uṣūl al-fiqh* was a desire to demonstrate that the law was consistent and coherent, and to rebuff any criticism that claimed it was a random, unrelated collection of rules. Nearly all debates within works of *uṣūl al-fiqh* can be divided into one of three categories—provenance (how do we know that the texts we use as sources of the law are reliable?), interpretation (how are we to understand the texts?), and authority (who can interpret these texts?). The findings in all these areas were, naturally, debated.

The contested nature of the consistency of the law can be seen in the debates among *uṣūlīs* over the hermeneutic procedures known as *qiyās* and *istiḥsān*. *Qiyās* is

6. Differing theories on the emergence of Islamic law, both as a law that is practiced but also a theoretical body of rules, can be found in Norman Calder, *Studies in Early Muslim Jurisprudence* (Oxford: Oxford University Press, 1993); Harald Motzki, *The Origins of Islamic Jurisprudence: Meccan Fiqh before the Classical Schools* (Leiden: Brill, 2001); and Christopher Melchert, *The Formation of the Sunni Schools of Law, 9th–10th Centuries CE* (Leiden: Brill, 1997).

7. On the *Risāla* of al-Shāfi'ī see Joseph E. Lowry, *Early Islamic Legal Theory: The Risala of Muhammad Ibn Idris al-Shafi'i* (Leiden: Brill, 2007).

8. On this question generally, see D. Stewart, "Muhammad b.Da'ud al-Zahiri's Manual of Jurisprudence," in *Studies in Islamic Legal Theory*, ed. Bernard G. Weiss (Leiden: Brill, 2002), pp. 99–158.

normally understood as analogical reasoning (whereby the reason—'*illa*—for a rule in a known case is transferred to another, unknown case). In the classic example, God forbade the consumption of wine; he did so because it was intoxicating; all intoxicating liquors are therefore forbidden because they share the characteristic of wine that caused God to make it forbidden. There is a valid analogy (*qiyās*) between wine and other intoxicating liquids because the rulings share the same *'illa*. *Istiḥsān* is often seen as an alternative to *qiyās*. A rule is apparently indicated by analogical reasoning (i.e., it appears that the known case and the unknown case share the same *'illa*) but to follow analogical reasoning mechanistically appears to result in a violation of a more fundamental legal principle. The *qiyās* is, then, set aside since it conflicts with other, often general and overarching principles of law, and another rule is proposed because it is "preferred" (*istiḥsān*). Take, for example, the following example of the two procedures indicating different rulings. First of all, a solution is offered by *qiyās*:

> When a man from the [Muslim] army frees a slave girl who has been captured as war booty, then according to *qiyās*, this manumission is effective. This is because their [cf. the men in the army's] right [to do this] has been confirmed by the capture [of the slave girl]. Do you not see that the division of the war booty [by the Muslim leader after the conflict] is to determine what each one owns? The division [of booty] is to specify ownership, not to establish ownership. By this [specification] it becomes clear that ownership was already theirs previously. He has merely freed a slave who was jointly owned by himself and others. This, according to the principle of al-Shāfi'ī is the most evident position. Because he argues that the accomplishment [of capturing the booty] establishes them as having ownership [of the booty].[9]

Qiyās, then, is analogical reasoning: by capturing booty (slaves included) in war, the soldiers have ownership rights over it. Ownership of property gives rights of its disposal. Manumission is a type of disposal; therefore, the manumission is valid.[10] Sarakhsī, a Ḥanafī, however, rejects this argument:

> According to us, under *istiḥsān*, his act of manumission is not legally valid. This is because the effectiveness of an act of manumission requires ownership which is confirmed as being in place [for the specific object]. This is not present with respect to them [cf. the soldiers] before the division [of booty]. Do you not see that the *imām* [i.e., the leader of the Muslims] has the right to sell items of booty, and divide the price [among the soldiers]? [Do you not see] that he does not calculate [when doing this sale] the share of each [soldier] in the manner which takes place during the division of booty? This is a condition of valid manumission, and it is missing here. Hence the manumission is not valid.[11]

9. Shams al-Dīn al-Sarakhsī, *al-Mabsūṭ* (Beirut: Dār al-Ma'rifa, 1406/1986), vol. 10, p. 50.

10. Of course, the manumitter's share of the booty will be reduced by the value of the slave girl he has just freed. If, after the division of the booty, the manumitter's share is less than the value of the freed slave girl, he will owe the booty purse money. This does not, however, have any relevance for the legal validity of the manumission.

11. Sarakhsī, *Mabsūṭ*, vol. 10, p. 50.

What does *istiḥsān* mean here? It appears to mean that the analogy (*qiyās*) used by al-Shāfi'ī is invalid because one of its assumptions is incorrect. Both the Shāfi'īs and the Ḥanafīs accept that ownership of the booty is established by capture. Where they differ is over whether the right of disposal of property (in this case manumission) comes with that right of ownership before the booty has been distributed (i.e., before it is specified the amount due to each soldier). The Shāfi'īs, arguing from *qiyās*, say this right of disposal is created by capturing war booty, while the Ḥanafīs, arguing from *istiḥsān*, say it is not. *Istiḥsān* is the decision to reject a ruling derived from an analogy, because the validity of the analogy (and hence the ruling also) depends on an incorrect formulation of a basic principle of the law. In this case (Sarakhsī argues), the Shāfi'īs have not understood that shared ownership of property (here being booty) does not give the right of disposal of part of the property (i.e., manumission). For manumission to be valid, the ownership must be "confirmed" for a specified amount or proportion of the property. *Istiḥsān*, here at least, represents a rejection of an apparently persuasive analogy because it is based on an incorrect assumption about the stipulations of a particular legal act (namely, manumission).

While *istiḥsān* and *qiyās* in this example give different rulings, they share the common aim of bringing coherence to the law. A rule in one area of the law has an effect elsewhere. The law, since it is the product of a single law giver (namely, God), must be coherent. Both procedures (*qiyās* and *istiḥsān*) are designed to establish this consistency, even though they differ when applied to specific legal problems. The opponents of *istiḥsān* argued that it was merely arbitrary individual preference. The opponents of *qiyās* argued that it was slavish dedication to a principle of argumentation to the exclusion of the "bigger picture" of the law. The philosophical themes that underlie the legal issue of the slave girl are easy to identify. The difference between *potentia* and *actus* when applied to the right of ownership pervades Sarakhsī's analysis here—even if he does not use the terms explicitly. For the Shāfi'īs, the soldier's potentially specific ownership of the slave girl when the booty is distributed gives him an actual present right to manumit her prior to distribution. For the Ḥanafīs, potential specific ownership remains potential, with none of the rights of actual ownership. It is only the act of the Imam that makes the specific ownership actual. The division between actual and potential ownership around which this legal dispute resolves is, of course, Aristotelian, and their strict and fundamental distinction was developed in medieval scholastic philosophy ("*potentia et actus cum sint de primus differentiis entis*," as Thomas Aquinas expresses it).[12] As with the purity example above, the concerns here are broadly philosophical, but the method of their examination is through exempla (or *masā'il*). Once again, there is no detailed discussion in the books of legal theory of (for example) the *potentia/actus* division (or indeed the accident/essence distinction), though there is extensive employment of these categories in solving legal problems.

12. Thomas Aquinas, *Commentary on Aristotle's Physics* (London: Dumb Ox Books, 1999), III Phys., lectio 2, n. 285.

Ethics and the Law

The relationship between ethics and law is, perhaps, less problematic within the Muslim tradition than it was in Western thought. For Muslim jurists, the Sharī'a—God's law for his creation—was, for humans, an ethical code outlining the (morally) correct and incorrect ways of behaving. Every element of human existence is of concern to God, and hence every action has one of five assessments (*aḥkām*) made by God. These assessment categories were obligatory, recommended, neutral, discouraged, and forbidden. The performance of actions in each of these categories resulted in rewards or punishments. Performing obligatory actions, for example, gained one reward in the next life, and failure to perform them brought punishment. Legal theory was concerned with detailing the means whereby these assessments might be known. It was, then, an ethical as well as strictly legal system.[13]

One of the areas of *uṣūl al-fiqh* where there was a detailed philosophical discussion is the question of the ontological status of the moral qualities of actions. The question, which is also dealt with in works of *kalām* (theology), concerns whether or not the moral assessment of an action (such as lying) is wrong because God has declared it so, or because it has an external, objective moral quality of evil. In theological terms, the proponents of external moral qualities were the Mu'tazilīs (and the later Shiites), while their opponents were associated with the traditions of Abū al-Ḥasan al-Ash'arī (d. 324/935) and Abū Manṣūr al-Māturīdī (d. 333/944). The issue has obvious legal interest, hence its inclusion in works of *uṣūl al-fiqh*. In particular, performance of an act forbidden in the law leads to condemnation (*dhamm*) and punishment (*'aqāba*)—can the same be said of acts assessed as evil by reason? The Ash'arīs denied the relevance of the question. They argued that things were wrong because God had decreed them to be wrong—their position has been described as "divine subjectivism" (God's view on what is right or wrong is the only one that matters, and indeed the only one of which we can be sure).[14] The Mu'tazilīs and Shi'ites, on the other hand, were divided. Some argued that reason can recognize an action being evil, but it cannot recognize that it being evil necessarily leads to punishment. Others argued that reason could recognize both that an action was evil and that its performance led to punishment. Some went further than this and argued that the five legal categories (from obligatory to forbidden) can be linked to the assessment of reason in a direct manner, and hence revelatory sources (at least for some legal issues) can be entirely bypassed by the employment of reason. The question was, to an extent, ontological: did the moral quality of an act exist within that act to be recognized by reason (and if so, what were the legal implications of this)? Or, was the act devoid of moral qualities in itself, and the moral judgment of God had simply been "placed" on the act? The standard majority Sunni rejection of

13. On the ethical nature of Islamic legal theory, see A. Kevin Reinhart, "Islamic Law as Islamic Ethics," *Journal of Religious Ethics* 11(1983): 186–203.

14. See the studies of George Hourani, *Reason and Tradition in Islamic Ethics* (Cambridge: Cambridge University Press, 2007).

the former position (the idea that moral qualities were external, argued for by the Mu'tazilīs and Shi'ites) is succinctly expressed by al-Ghazālī:

> As for the first, claiming ['badness'] as being an essential characteristic [of an action], this is dogmatic assertion of the unintelligible. For, according to them [the Mu'tazilīs], killing is bad *per se*, provided that it is not preceded by a crime nor followed by compensation, such that it is permissible to inflict pain on animals and to slaughter them; and this is not regarded as bad on the part of God, for He will requite them in the afterlife. But killing *per se* has one essence that does not differ whether it is preceded by a crime or followed by pleasure. [It only differs] in terms of its relationship with the benefits and purposes [of the law]. Furthermore, [regarding] lying: how can it be bad *per se* even while it [may] be to protect a prophet's life through concealing his whereabouts from a transgressor aiming to kill him? In that case [lying] is good—rather, obligatory—and its abandonment would be sinful. Now, as for an essential characteristic, how can it be changed by relating it to circumstances?...

Al-Ghazālī's argument here is that for the Mu'tazilīs, killing or lying will always be essentially wrong because they believe in the essential "badness" of killing or lying. However, there are occasions when these actions are justified. Killing is justified when someone has committed a capital offense. Lying to the prophet's enemies concerning his whereabouts is good, as it protects a prophet's life. Killing and lying, therefore, cannot be essentially "bad" ("bad" *per se*), but are only bad in particular circumstances. Al-Ghazālī continues:

> They argue: We know with certainty that if truth and falsehood are set before a person, he will choose truth and be inclined to it— if he is rational. And this cannot be so except because of its [essential characteristic of] goodness. Even a great king, sovereign over many territories, when seeing someone weak and near death would be inclined to save him, even if the king does not believe in the principles of religion, nor if he expects requital or gratitude [from the weak man] or his objectives favoured, as well. In fact, he may be troubled by it. Indeed, rational people have argued for the goodness of patience, even when confronted by the sword to utter a declaration of unbelief or reveal a secret or break a promise, while this is contrary to the objective of the [one being] compelled. In general, regarding moral qualities as good, "giving generously" is something that no rational being would deny [as being essentially good] except through deliberate obstinacy.
>
> Our reply is that we do not deny the popularity of these propositions among the people and regard them as commonly praiseworthy. But their basis is either religion, following the *Sharī'a*, or personal objectives.[15]

For al-Ghazālī, then, although it may feel as if good acts have a quality of goodness inherent within them, this does not reflect their true nature. Because people agree that a particular action is good does not indicate, as the Mu'tazila claim, that that action is good because of an ontological category. Rather, for al-Ghazālī, the fact that

15. Abū Ḥāmid al-Ghazālī, *al-Mustaṣfā min 'Ilm al-Usūl* (Beirut: Dār al-Kutub al-Ýllmiyya, 1417/1996), vol. 1, p. 53.

the people agree over the goodness of an act is an indication of the success of religion in inculcating these values into the human mind. However, he argues, the reason why some things are good and some things bad is not linked to their physical makeup. Rather, he argues, a thing can only be good when it has been declared so by God. Before God, who has ultimate power over all qualities in creation, has declared a thing good or bad, it is impossible for it to be assessed by anyone. In a sense, the argument is over whether moral qualities are known through nature or nurture. The Mu'tazilīs argue that, by their nature, human beings are rational and able to recognize moral qualities external to themselves. For al-Ghazālī, human beings have to be taught what is right or wrong—that is the point of prophets and divine revelation. The reemergence of the essential/necessary versus contingent/accidental division on which this argument depends demonstrates, once again, the inescapable influence of philosophical terminology on the manner in which the law is discussed.

There were, of course, a number of theological issues linked to this area of discussion. If moral qualities are objective and external, God is compelled to follow them (otherwise God might be capable of performing evil acts). The Ash'arīs, of course, were deeply uncomfortable with the idea that God might be forced to do anything, let alone something as central to his being as his law, hence arguing that moral qualities were divinely imposed rather than externally existent, and saved God from being forced to do the good; instead, he defines what is good and then does it. Furthermore, if moral qualities exist independent of God's moral decree, then an act like punishing an individual for an action he or she could not help but commit would be unjust. Therefore, human beings must have free will in order that God can remain just.[16] These issues, however, were not the subject of much discussion in works of *uṣūl al-fiqh*. For a coherent theological vision, they were of course essential, but jurists (or at least scholars when writing works of jurisprudence) were not concerned with elaborating a coherent theological vision. Only those elements of theological discussions that had direct legal relevance were of interest. It was for this reason that the ability of reason to recognize moral qualities became a standard (usually introductory) chapter in works of *uṣūl al-fiqh*.

Conclusions

The influence of philosophical thought on Muslim jurisprudence was, in a sense, surreptitious. Outwardly the *uṣūlīs* condemned philosophical investigation (like most of their counterparts writing both *fiqh* and *kalām*).[17] However, within the details of their

16. For detailed examination of the interconnectedness of these issues, see Harry Wolfson, *The Philosophy of Kalam* (Cambridge, MA: Harvard University Press, 1976).

17. See Frank Griffel, *Apostasie und Toleranz im Islam. Die Entwicklung zu al-Gazalis Urteil gegen die Philosophie und die Reaktionen der Philosophen* (Leiden: Brill, 2000).

legal theory, one finds ample evidence of the influence of philosophical categories. These may have entered the discourse of *uṣūl al-fiqh* through theological discussions or directly from philosophical works (the exact trajectory is difficult to identify). However, dichotomies such as *potentia/actus*, essential/accidental, and necessary/contingent pervade the exploration of legal questions in works of *fiqh* (jurisprudence) and *uṣūl* (legal theory). Further evidence of this influence is that the technical terms used are, broadly speaking, those introduced into intellectual discourse in Arabic by thoroughbred Muslim philosophers or the translators of Greek works. While the study of philosophy (with its potential for slipping into heresy and antinomianism) was to be condemned by the *fuqahā'*, the achievements of Muslim philosophers and the translators gave the writers of *uṣūl al-fiqh* a vocabulary with which to analyze the details of the law. In this sense, though there were only ever hints of a full-blown philosophy of law as found in the Western academic tradition, there was considerable influence of philosophical thinking on the theoretical reflections of Muslim jurists.

BIBLIOGRAPHY AND SUGGESTED READING

Calder, Norman. (1993) *Studies in Early Muslim Jurisprudence*. Oxford: Oxford University Press.

Gleave, Robert. (2000) *Inevitable Doubt: Two Theories of Shī'ī Jurisprudence*. Leiden: Brill.

Goldziher, Ignaz. (2007) *The Ẓāhirīs: Their Doctrine and their History*. Leiden: Brill.

Hallaq, Wael B. (1999) *A History of Islamic Legal Theories: An Introduction to Sunnī Uṣūl al-fiqh*. Cambridge: Cambridge University Press.

———. (2009a) *An Introduction to Islamic Law*. Cambridge and New York: Cambridge University Press.

———. (2009b) *Shari'a: Theory, Practice, Transformations*. Cambridge and New York: Cambridge University Press.

Kamali, Mohammad Hashem. (1991) *Principles of Islamic Jurisprudences*. Cambridge: Islamic Texts Society.

Katz, M. (2002) *Body of Text: The Emergence of Sunni Law of Ritual Purity*. Albany, NY: SUNY.

Lowry, Joseph E. (2007) *Early Islamic Legal Theory: The Risala of Muhammad Ibn Idris al-Shafi'i*. Leiden: Brill.

Masud, Muhammad Khalid. (1989) *Islamic Legal Philosophy*. Delhi: International Islamic Publishers.

Melchert, Christopher. (1997) *The Formation of the Sunni Schools of Law, 9th-10th Centuries CE*. Leiden: Brill.

Motzki, Harald. (2001) *The Origins of Islamic Jurisprudence: Meccan Fiqh Before the Classical Schools*. Leiden: Brill.

Reinhart, A. Kevin. (1983) "Islamic Law as Islamic Ethics." *Journal of Religious Ethics* 11, 186–203.

Weiss, Bernard G. (1992) *The Search for God's Law: Islamic Jurisprudence in the Writings of Sayf al-Din al-Amidi*. Salt Lake City, UT: University of Utah Press.

———. (1998) *The Spirit of Islamic Law*. Athens: University of Georgia Press.

———. (ed.). (2002) *Studies in Islamic Legal Theory*. Leiden: Brill.

PART VI

PHILOSOPHY IN AFRICA AND THE AFRICAN DIASPORA

EDITED BY ALBERT MOSLEY AND STEPHEN C. FERGUSON II

PHILOSOPHY IN AFRICA AND THE AFRICAN DIASPORA

STEPHEN C. FERGUSON II

AFRICANA philosophy is broadly conceived to encompass African, Afro-Caribbean, and African American philosophy. Africana philosophy can be seen as a species of Africana intellectual thought. Africana philosophical traditions have historically tended to emerge from within the context of Africana intellectual culture rather than from the confines of the White academy. The claim here is not that the history of Africana philosophy is completely removed from European philosophy, only that it has a determinate identity and tradition.

Given its moorings outside the White academy, Africana philosophical discourse has a considerable and extensive history that requires linking the content of Africana philosophical inquiry to the broader dimension of its intellectual and social history. This requires highlighting, on the one hand, how philosophical inquiry addresses distinct problems and themes that are deeply rooted in the normative practices and traditions of academic philosophy. But it requires, on the other hand, understanding the particularities that emerge from concrete problems adjoined to Black intellectual and social history. So, while the history of Africana philosophy assumes its own specificity or particularity, it should not be seen as a bastard philosophy without any connection to the universal discourse of philosophy.

To advance Africana philosophy as a legitimate area of philosophy requires us to defend the category of particularity as it relates to the content and methodology of philosophy. To accent the particularity of Africana philosophy is not a dismissal of universalism tout court. The call for Africana philosophy is an attempt to link

Africa and the Africana diaspora to world philosophy. The truth of particularity resides in its dialectical relationship to universality. Though particularity and universality are distinct categories, they are, nevertheless, correlative categories. As correlative categories, they must of logical necessity be seen as a pair.[1] The relationship of particularity to universality is not an either/or proposition. Hence, the call for particularity is not merely an act of transferring the citadel of philosophy from Mt. Olympus to Mt. Kenya, but a recognition that world philosophy is not located in Europe.

Arguably, Africana philosophy developed in response to the false universalism of Western philosophy. Few Black philosophers are mentioned as part of the crucial episodes in Western philosophy. It is rare to find works by Black philosophers as foundational texts that make up the canon and the iconography of the Western philosophical tradition. As African American philosopher John Pittman writes, "'Philosophy' is usually introduced to college audiences by displaying the writings of some select group of 'dead White men,' all European or Anglo-American. This is traditional, and it is here that the weight of tradition is heaviest" (Pittman 1997, xi). In a similar tone, Charles Mills notes, "Philosophy has remained remarkably untouched by the debates over multiculturalism, canon reform, and ethnic diversity racking the academy; both demographically and conceptually, it is one of the 'whitest' of the humanities" (Mills 1997, 2)

In some philosophical circles, the idea of Africana philosophy is seen as a semantic monstrosity sort of like a square circle. Even today, questions continue to be raised about the legitimacy and necessity of Africana philosophy. And the continuing response of the philosophical guild to its presence confirms that its legitimacy is still not generally accepted. The universal character of philosophy, it is said, has no room for ethnic particularity. Though we speak of Greek philosophy, German philosophy, and even American philosophy, Africana philosophy is seen as a semantic monstrosity bordering on self-contradiction. Many Africana philosophers have argued that such criticisms rest on questionable presuppositions concerning the nature of philosophy, its method, and its analysis.

In response to the exclusion of Africana philosophers from the philosophical canon, many efforts have been made to engage the metaphilosophical question, "What is Africana philosophy?" Following Paulin Hountondji, some have argued that Africana philosophy encompasses a set of texts written by continental Africans and people of African descent and described as philosophical by their authors themselves (Hountondji 1983, 33). In contrast to Hountondji, the Afro-Caribbean philosopher Lewis Gordon defines Africana philosophy as a species of Africana intellectual thought that involves "theoretical questions raised by critical engagements with

1. As Aime Cesaire astutely notes, "My conception of the universal is of a universal rich with all that is particular, rich with all the particulars, the deepening and coexistence of all particulars." Aimé Césaire, *Lettre á Maurice Thorez* (Paris: Présence Africaine, 1956), 15 (*Letter to Maurice Thorez*, trans. Présence Africaine [Paris: Présence Africaine, 1957], 15).

ideas in Africana cultures and their hybrid, mixed, or creolized forms worldwide" (Gordon 2008, 1). Race, from Gordon's standpoint, functions as the organizing principle of a Black philosophy. Gordon argues that Africana philosophy as an area of philosophical research is limited to "the problems faced and raised by the African diaspora" (Gordon 2008, 13).

The Black philosopher William R. Jones, in contrast to Gordon, contends that Africana philosophy should be broadly conceived to include such factors as author, audience, ancestry, accent, and/or antagonist. To speak of Africana philosophy, from Jones's standpoint, means to "identify that the author is black, i.e., a member of a particular ethnic community, that his primary, but not exclusive, audience is the black community, that the point of departure for his philosophizing or the tradition from which he speaks or the world-view he seeks to articulate can be called in some sense the black experience" (Jones 1977–1978, 152–53). Jones further argues that the Africana philosopher may take on the role of an antagonist when criticizing academic racism in philosophy, especially as it relates to conceptual, curricular, and institutional issues.

Following Jones, we can draw an analytical distinction between *Africana philosophers* and *the philosophy of the Black experience*. The difference here is a qualitative one that is rooted, nonetheless, in a quantitative relationship. The former is more general in scope and is inclusive of all Black philosophers without regard for the exact nature of their philosophical works and practices. The latter, in turn, are those identifiable philosophical efforts toward elaborating on the precise characteristics and implications of the Africana experience.

Hence, it follows that "the philosophy of the Black experience" is one part of the more expansive category of "Africana philosophy"; "the philosophy of the Black experience" is a specific manifestation of the larger project "Africana philosophy." This is important to note because Africana philosophers historically and presently are not only concerned with philosophical issues and problems surrounding race, racism, Whiteness, blackness, and the like.

Black philosophers need not (and have not) exclusively engaged the Africana experience as an area of inquiry. Take, for example, the African American philosopher Berkley Eddins, whose primary area of scholarly interest was philosophy of history. Is Eddins's work not a part of the Africana philosophical tradition since it does not explicitly address the kinds of theoretical questions centered on Africana culture and experience that, according to Gordon, mark the realm of African philosophy? Gordon's conceptual framework would also exclude the work of Joyce Mitchell Cook—the first African American woman to be awarded a Ph.D. in philosophy (Yale 1965)—dealing with value theory. Or what about the African American philosopher Wayman McLaughlin, who published scholarly work on Ancient Greek philosophy? This list could be expanded to include the philosophical work of C. L. R. James on dialectics, Roy Morrison on philosophy of science, and many others. (Of course, such work on the part of African American philosophers, especially those who made the first forays into White academia, does not mean that the Black experience that marked each of them in their own lives did not function as a significant and formative condition of their thinking.)

As much as philosophical inquiry in Africa and the African diaspora has been concerned with the traditional subdisciplines in philosophy, arguably its primary focus has been what I have termed the philosophy of the Black experience. By drawing on a broad range of philosophical areas such as the history of philosophy, metaphilosophy, aesthetics, metaphysics, epistemology, philosophy of science, and social and political philosophy, contemporary Africana philosophers have attempted to address a range of philosophical issues related to the Black experience. For example, Africana philosophers have been greatly concerned with the origins of philosophy. As the traditional narrative goes, philosophical thought has its origins in Greece. However, the groundbreaking works of George G. M. James, Theophile Obenga, Cheikh Anta Diop, and Martin Bernal offer a different conception of the origin of philosophy, locating it instead in Africa. The most significant contribution to the ongoing debate about the African origins of philosophy is James's *Stolen Legacy*. The Guyanese-born philosopher presents a historico-philosophical interpretation of the African origins of philosophy. According to James, Greek philosophy was largely taken from classical African/Egyptian philosophy. Obenga—in the tradition of James—has done important work detailing the nature of classical African philosophy.

The following essays are provided to aid both students and teachers of philosophy as well as the general reader with interest in the field of Africana philosophy. These essays are by no means exhaustive. The aim of each essay is to provide a broad introduction to a significant area of Africana philosophy. Additionally, each chapter includes resources in the form of a bibliography and suggested readings for further inquiry. Four chapters are dedicated to examining developments in Africana, African, Afro-Caribbean, and African American philosophy. Tsenay Serequeberhan explores Africana philosophy as a broad philosophical movement. Barry Hallen discusses contemporary developments in African philosophy. Clevis Headley's contribution centers on Afro-Caribbean philosophy. John McClendon and Stephen Ferguson discuss African American philosophy. Finally, two chapters are dedicated to looking at the philosophy of the Black experience. In "Race in Contemporary Philosophy," Albert Mosley examines the philosophical significance of race. And, lastly, Rodney C. Roberts explores the philosophical implications of affirmative action.

BIBLIOGRAPHY AND SUGGESTED READINGS

Abraham, W. E. (1962) *The Mind of Africa*. Chicago, IL: University of Chicago Press.

Asante, Molefi, and Shaza Ismail. (2009) "Characteristics of Philosophical Thought in Ancient Africa." *Journal of Black Studies* 40(2), 296–309.

Coetzee, P. H., and A. P. J. Roux (eds.). (2003) *The African Philosophy Reader*. New York: Routledge.

Eze, Emmanuel C. (ed.). (1998) *African Philosophy: An Anthology*. Malden, MA: Blackwell Publishers.

Gordon, Lewis R. (2008) *An Introduction to Africana Philosophy*. Cambridge: Cambridge University Press.

Gyekye, Kwame. (1987) *An Essay on African Philosophical Thought: The Akan Conceptual Scheme*. New York: Cambridge University Press.

Hallen, Barry. (2000) *The Good, the Bad, and the Beautiful: Discourse about Values in Yoruba Culture*. Bloomington, IN: Indiana University Press.

——. (2002) *A Short History of African Philosophy*. Bloomington, IN: Indiana University Press.

Henry, Paget. (2000) *Caliban's Reason: Introducing Afro-Caribbean Philosophy*. New York: Routledge.

Hountondji, Paulin. (1983) *African Philosophy: Myth and Reality*. Bloomington, IN: Indiana University Press.

Imbo, Samuel O. (1998) *An Introduction to African Philosophy*. Lanham, MD: Rowman & Littlefield.

James, George G. M. (1954) *Stolen Legacy*. New York: Philosophical Library.

Jones, William R. (1977–1978) "The Legitimacy and Necessity of Black Philosophy." *The Philosophical Forum* 9(2–3), 149–160.

Lott, Tommy L., and John P. Pittman (eds.). (2005) *A Companion to African-American Philosophy*. Malden, MA; Blackwell Publishing.

Masolo, D. A. (1994) *African Philosophy in Search of Identity*. Bloomington, IN: Indiana University Press.

McClendon, John H. (1982) "The Afro-American Philosopher and the Philosophy of the Black Experience: A Bibliographical Essay on a Neglected Topic Both in Philosophy and Black Studies." *Sage Race Relations Abstracts* 7(4), 1–51.

——. (2005) *C. L. R. James's Notes on Dialectics: Left-Hegelianism or Marxism-Leninism?* Lanham, MD: Lexington Books.

Mills, Charles W. (1997) *The Racial Contract*. Ithaca, NY: Cornell University Press.

Mosley, Albert G. (ed.). (1995) *African Philosophy: Selected Readings*. Englewood Cliffs, NJ: Prentice Hall.

Nkrumah, Kwame. (1964) *Consciencism: Philosophy and Ideology for Decolonization*. New York: Monthly Review Press.

Obenga, Theophile. (2004) *African Philosophy: The Pharaonic Period, 2780–330 B.C.* Senegal: Per Ankh.

Oruka, H. Odera (ed.). (1990) *Sage Philosophy: Indigenous Thinkers and the Modern Debate on African Philosophy*. Leiden: E. J. Brill.

Outlaw, Lucius. (2007) "What is Africana Philosophy?" In *Philosophy in Multiple Voices*, edited by George Yancy. Lanham, MD: Rowman & Littlefield Publishers, Inc., 109–143.

Pittman, John P. (ed.). (1997) *African-American Perspectives and Philosophical Traditions*. New York: Routledge.

Serequeberhan, Tsenay (ed.). (1991) *African Philosophy: Essential Readings*. New York: Paragon House, 1991.

Valls, Andrew (ed.). (2005) *Race and Racism in Modern Philosophy*. Ithaca, NY: Cornell University Press.

Wiredu, Kwasi (ed.). (2004) *A Companion to African Philosophy*. Malden, MA: Wiley-Blackwell.

Yancy, George. (1998) *African-American Philosophers: Seventeen Conversations*. New York: Routledge.

Zack, Naomi (ed.). (2000) *Women of Color and Philosophy: A Critical Reader*. Malden, MA: Wiley-Blackwell.

CHAPTER 33

AFRICANA PHILOSOPHY: PROSPECTS AND POSSIBILITIES

TSENAY SEREQUEBERHAN

We are, at present, at a point in time when it is possible to think that the universe of Eurocentric dominance can be overcome by the multiverse of our shared humanity. From the fifteenth century to the middle of the twentieth century, victimized by the slave trade and colonial dismemberment, Africa was relegated to nonexistence. The Continent was immersed in darkness and its varied people, in the sight of Europe, were seen and presented as an arcane and exotic "prelogical" humanity (Lucien Lévy-Bruhl) in need of "development" in every sphere of human existence.[1] During this period, as Amilcar Cabral has noted, the existence of Africa was negated and blotted out of history.[2]

The horrors of World War II and the political revolt of the colonized created an auspicious setting in which the old assumptions of the Occidental mission to civilize the world were methodically put into question. The colonized, thus far demonized and vilified, rejected their subjugation and recommenced the struggles that had defined their existence prior to the harsh "pacification campaigns" that forced

1. Any discourse that utilizes the language of "development" is necessarily implicated in seeing Africa, and the non-European world as a whole, as retarded phases of humanity in need of "development" modeled on the Occident, which in this schema of things, is the proper manifestation of the humanity of the human as such. On this point see Robert Bernasconi, "Can Development Theory Break with its Past? Endogenous Development in Africa and the Old Imperialism." *African Philosophy* 11(1) (June 1998): 23–34.

2. Amilcar Cabral, "National Liberation and Culture," in *Return to the Source: Selected Speeches* (New York: Monthly Review Press, 1973), p. 41.

their submission. As Basil Davidson has noted, after "1945 the colonial powers could still resist" the process of decolonization but "they could not stop it."[3] The idea of a "singular" and "true" thread of human history, dominant thus far, had begun to gradually unravel.

Starting from 1957 and the independence of Ghana, Africa bit by bit established its political freedom. By 1960 most of Africa had attained the status of nominal independence. The early 1970s witnessed the end of Portuguese-NATO colonialism, and the early 1990s, with the demise of Apartheid South Africa, finally saw the fulfillment of Africa's struggle for political sovereignty. This victory, attained at great cost to the peoples of Africa, in and through which the Continent reinserted itself into history was a great achievement, yet much less than what had been hoped for. In the African Diaspora, it had an electrifying effect. As James Baldwin writing in 1961 tells us, the "emergence of Africa"[4] established the political-existential context in which "the American Negro can no longer, nor will he ever again, be controlled by white America's image of him."[5] In spite of shortcomings and paradoxes, the attainment of political independence fulfilled a felt need in the Black world and established a new *étape* from which more complex and protracted struggles could commence.

In view of all this, then: what is the philosophic situation of the present regarding the "ideas" and "conceptions" that, until recently, sanctioned supremacy and subjection? In what follows I will engage this issue by looking at recent developments in Continental philosophy and the fruitful confluence of these developments with what I take to be the prospects and possibilities of the contemporary practice of Africana philosophy.

Listening to Other Voices

Today, at the dawn of the twenty-first century, a great deal has changed and a much more encouraging situation prevails. Remarking on the contemporary scene that defines the climate of critical self-awareness, for example, Charles Taylor states:

> The days are long gone when Europeans and other Westerners could consider their experience and culture as the norm towards which the whole of humanity was headed, so that the other could be understood as an earlier stage on the same road that they had trodden.[6]

3. Basil Davidson, *Africa in Modern History* (New York: Penguin Books, 1985), p. 199.

4. James Baldwin, "East River, Downtown: Postscript to a Letter from Harlem," (originally published in 1961), in *Nobody knows My Name* (New York: Vintage Press, 1993), p. 77.

5. Ibid., p. 79.

6. Charles Taylor, "Understanding the Other: A Gadamerian View on Conceptual Schemes," in *Gadamer's Century*, ed. J. Malpas, U. Arnswald, and J. Kertscher (Cambridge, MA: The MIT Press, 2002), p. 279.

In the same vein, Hans-Georg Gadamer categorically affirms: "[W]e...need to accept our worldwide heritage not only in its otherness but also in recognizing the validity of the claims this larger heritage makes on us."[7] Indeed, as Gianni Vattimo has noted, "history [*la storia*], after the end of colonialism and the dissolution of Eurocentric prejudices, does not have anymore a unitary sense, it has been fractured into a number of stories [*di storie*] irreducible to a *single guiding thread*."[8] In and through these thinkers—against the historical grain of Western traditions—the lived actuality of a suppressed variegated humanity reasserts itself. A long-censored multiplicity is presently affirming itself, using for this purpose the spokesmen of Reason that had previously suppressed it.

These pronouncements indicate that, in principle, the days of Occidental arrogance and domination are *passé*. They indicate that the Eurocentric "single guiding thread" with which the Occident had firmly bound the world is *de facto* unraveling. And, as a task of the present, these pronouncements call for the hastening of this unraveling by the tangible articulation of *de jure* philosophic self-justifications of this multiplicity.

To be sure, until recently, such pronouncements were not acceptable in mainstream philosophy. It ought to be remembered that it was by clinging to this "single guiding thread" that Immanuel Kant, for example, could assert that the Occident "will probably give law, eventually to all the others."[9] And why should this be the case? Because, as Kant tells us, unlike animals, human beings need discipline (*Zucht*) in their tender years and cultural formation (*Bildung*) as they mature into adulthood; this is what completes the humanity of human beings. And, he adds, regarding non-Europeans:

> We see this also among savage nations, who, though they may discharge functions for some time like Europeans, yet can never become accustomed to European manners. With them, however, it is not the noble love of freedom which Rousseau and others imagine, but a kind of barbarism—the animal, so to speak, not having yet developed its human nature.[10]

To say the least, today such views, which unabashedly equate humanity with "European manners" and non-Europeans with "savage nations," are no longer acceptable. And yet, Gadamer, the self-same Gadamer who I quoted just now, urging us, in 2001, to be open to "our worldwide heritage," writing in 1978, refers to Kant as "the

7. Hans-Georg Gadamer, *Gadamer in Conversation*, ed. and trans. R. E. Palmer (New Haven, CT, and London: Yale University Press, 2001), p. 54.

8. Gianni Vattimo, *Credere di Credere* (Milan: Garzanti, 1996), emphasis added, p. 22 (*Belief*, trans. Luca D'Isanto and David Webb [Stanford, CA: Stanford University Press, 1999], pp. 31–32.

9. Immanuel Kant, "Idea for a Universal History from a Cosmopolitan point of View," originally published in 1784, edited and introduced by Lewis White Beck in *Kant on History* (Indianapolis, IN: Bobbs-Merrill Educational Publishing, 1963), p. 24.

10. Immanuel Kant, *Education* (Ann Arbor, MI: University of Michigan Press, 1964), p. 4. This text on pedagogy was originally published by Kant in 1803, one year before his death, and can be taken as Kant's final word on "savage nations."

greatest thinker of the idea of freedom who ever lived."[11] It is clear that we are here facing an inconsistency that is not, and yet needs to be, accounted for. For in our actions as well as in our words, as Socrates patiently explains to Crito, rigor and consistency are essential components of the practice of philosophic reflection.

Kant, furthermore, does not stand alone in holding and expressing the kind of views quoted above. By engaging in a methodic reading of the major figures of the Occidental tradition—Locke, Hume, Kant, Hegel, Marx, and the like—one can show how this Eurocentric "single guiding thread" has, thus far, constituted and defined *the Otherness of the Other* in terms of Europe's own self-flattering universalizing of itself. For in the view of the modern icons of the Tradition, Europe was humanity and humanity was Europe.[12]

That today major thinkers in European philosophy openly disavow this Eurocentric stance and endorse its critique means, among other things, that the Western tradition is coming to the realization that its picture of reality is but an image in a mosaic constituted by the multiple variance of human existence. It also means that the critical and/or de-structive[13] philosophizing of those of us who labor at and in the margins of this tradition has had a direct and/or indirect effect of deflating, or corroding, the cultural and theoretic hubris of the Occident. Within African philosophy (a component of Africana philosophy), this is what I have elsewhere referred to as "the critical-negative aspect" of this discourse.[14] To be sure, beyond the realm of European and African philosophizing, this promising theoretic situation of the present, avowed by the above-noted European philosophers, was created by the political and armed struggles of the formerly enslaved, segregated, and colonized. Indeed, the critically self-aware stance of Western thinkers and the de-structive reflections of Africana philosophers are both propitious theoretic effects brought about by the struggle against, and the final demise of, colonialism and unmitigated Western dominance. As Vattimo remarked:

> Many and more diverse things have come to pass: the "primitive" peoples, so called, [and] colonized by the Europeans in the name of the right of "superior" and more evolved civilization, have rebelled and made problematic *de facto* a unitary centralized history.[15]

This is what has made it possible for non-European voices, in the field of philosophy as in many other fields, to become audible. Again as Vattimo points out, "The 'other' cultures are finding their voice and asserting themselves as autonomous

11. Hans-Georg Gadamer, "Greek Philosophy and Modern Thought," in *The Beginning of Knowledge* (New York: Continuum, 2002), p. 123.

12. On this see Serequeberhan 2007.

13. I borrow this notion from Martin Heidegger. For an explanation of the way I utilize it please see endnote 4 of my article, "The Critique of Eurocentrism and the Practice of African Philosophy," in *Postcolonial African Philosophy*, ed. E. C. Eze (Cambridge, MA: Blackwell, 1997), p. 157.

14. Ibid., p. 142.

15. Gianni Vattimo, *La società trasparente* (Milano, Italy: Garzanti Editore, 1989), p. 11 (*The Transparent Society*, trans. David Webb [Baltimore, MD: The Johns Hopkins University Press, 1992], p. 4).

visions of reality, with which Europeans have to start a dialogue, which they can no longer simply 'civilize' or 'convert.'"[16] The words *civilize* and *convert*, which Vattimo places in quotation marks for emphasis, describe the violent operations through which the European colonizing venture nullified the Otherness of the differing peoples it conquered and whose histories it eradicated. Thus, within the discourse of European philosophy, a new awareness and recognition is coming to the fore regarding the historicity of the Occident and its negative violent effects on the rest of the globe. This recognition is not, and it should not be, a contrite atonement for past "sins." Rather, it should see and constitute itself as the opening of a possibility for the West to seriously engage itself, on an equal footing, with the other cultural-historical totalities that, in sum, constitute our world.

This is what Vattimo is pointing to when highlighting the possibility of "start[ing] a dialogue"[17] between former colonizers and colonized beyond Eurocentric constraints. For in consenting to this assessment, the above thinkers openly accede to the demise of the European empire of the mind and welcome the dialogue—or counterdiscourse—of a variegated humanity. The Occident in this context becomes, once more, an interlocutor among interlocutors in a multivocal dialogical situation. In this, what has to be noted is that what is coming to pass is the restoration on a more concrete level of the multiple voices that constituted our shared humanity before the coming of the modern age and European dominance. For it ought to be remembered that in the days of Marco Polo or the Crusades, our globe was constituted by multiple worlds in war and/or peace.

What is coming to pass today is a return of this multiplicity of existence, in full recognition that this is the more suitable condition for our shared and dependent humanity, dependent on both the individual and collective level. This is what Aimé Césaire means when he states: "My conception of the universal is of a universal rich with all that is particular, rich with all the particulars, the deepening and coexistence of all particulars."[18] Africana philosophy is thus a focal point and a situated source of dialogue, a component of this multivocal dialogical state of affairs. It is the eager philosophic voice of the formerly enslaved, segregated, and colonized that seeks, in liberation and freedom, shared venues for enhancing our mutually dependent humanity. This situation furthermore is, and has to be recognized as, the auspicious and unforeseen dialectical effect of the demise of Western global dominance.

16. Gianni Vattimo, *Nihilism and Emancipation* (New York: Colombia University Press, 2004), p. 52.

17. This openness to dialogue is a stance that has been advocated by the formerly colonized since the earliest days of political independence. As Patrice Lumumba emphatically noted in 1959: "We do not want to cut ourselves off from the West, for we are... altogether in favor of friendship between races, but the West must respond to our appeal. Westerners must understand that friendship is not possible when the relationship between us is one of subjugation and subordination." *Lumumba Speaks*, the speeches and writings of Patrice Lumumba (1958–1961), edited by Jean Van Lierde, translated from the French by Helen R. Lane, and introduced by Jean-Paul Sartre (Boston, MA: Little Brown and Co., 1963), pp. 72 and 73.

18. Aimé Césaire, *Lettre á Maurice Thorez* (Paris: Présence Africaine, 1956), p. 15 (*Letter to Maurice Thorez*, trans. Présence Africaine [Paris: Présence Africaine, 1957], p. 15).

Other Voices in Dialogue

What has to be recognized is that the colonial empires, in receding into history, have left behind a multitude of cultures and histories that are in the process of forming a new global community. In this situation Africana philosophy is a theoretic supplement: a philosophic component of the effort to "reintroduce," as Frantz Fanon has put it, "humanity into the world."[19] For in being *a* theoretic offshoot of our shared changing world, it is a self-conscious articulation of itself (from within a specific historicity) of the future possibilities that can be sighted and hoped for, from the vantage point made possible by this historicity, in the process of reclaiming itself.

In this reintroducing of humanity, multiple voices in dialogue[20] constitute the self-formative future of our shared world. In this regard Césaire, in his *Letter to Maurice Thorez* of 1956, in categorically affirming the right of non-European peoples to their own specific histories, has staked out the general parameters within which Africana philosophy, and other non-Occidental philosophies, can articulate and formulate their own theoretic engagements and concerns.

In the Atlantic Diaspora, thus far, these engagements have had to do with theoretic explorations of questions of race, racism, and the identity of black existence (the work of Lewis R. Gordon, Lucius Outlaw, and Leonard Harris, for example). Some of us have also engaged in a systematic de-structive reading of the Occidental tradition in view of how it constitutes and frames the *Otherness of the Other* in a flattering deference to itself. In this the aim is to supply a counterreading of the icons of the tradition and in so doing systematically dismantle the construct of concepts—the equilibrium of ideas—that sanction and justify, and thus humanize, the Western devastation of the globe.[21]

In this effort, the aim is to combat the metaphysical source of negative prejudice and cultivate or enhance what Gadamer refers to as productive or positive prejudice.[22] A central danger in all of this is the temptation to formulate an "overall" critical Africana philosophy. But what should be emphasized is a practice of solidarity in our reflective efforts aimed at our local and specific situations. For human existence is always concrete, specific, and particular and—in order not to be falsified by theory—it has to be dealt with in all of its specificity and particularity.[23]

19. Frantz Fanon, *Les damnés de la terre* (Paris: Éditions La Découverte, 2002), p. 103 (*The Wretched of the Earth*, transl.Constance Farrington [New York: Grove Press, 1968], p. 106).

20. On the question of dialogue, Evo Morales, the popular president of Bolivia, echoing Lumumba (see endnote 17) in the context of inter-American relations, recently stated: "We will never break off relations with the U.S. We're coming from a culture of dialogue, but dialogue without strong-arm pressures. We've met Señorita Condoleezza—a very nice woman—and they say they want to be partners with Bolivia. But I think we still need to understand each other's definition of democracy. "A Voice on the Left." *Time* 167(23) (June 5, 2006): 37.

21. For my efforts in this area see Serequeberhan 2007.

22. On this point see Hans-Georg Gadamer, *Truth and Method* (New York: Crossroad, 1982), pp. 246–247.

23. As is well known this is the central problem of Marxism, Marxism-Leninism, and any totalizing theoretic stance. For a critique of such a stance as it pertains to Africa see Serequeberhan 1994, 33–42.

On the other hand, the African philosophy component of Africana philosophy has been concerned with rigorously documenting the traditional philosophies of Africa (the work of Barry Hallen and Odera Oruka, for example) and simultaneously engaging the present socioeconomic crisis of the Continent. As is well known, on the occasion of Ghana's independence Kwame Nkrumah had asserted that "our independence is meaningless unless it is linked up with the total liberation of the African continent."[24] The question, then, is: what exactly does this mean? It is here that the calling of philosophy and of Africana philosophy comes into full play. For philosophy, above all else, is concerned with questions of meaning and existence. In other words, "our independence is meaningless" if it does not implicate us in the total transformation of the Continent. In making reference to "the total liberation of the African continent," Nkrumah has in mind not merely physical geography but, and more important, the lived spiritual or cultural horizon—the geography of existence—which postcolonial Africa must institute and freely establish for itself.[25]

Europe colonized Africa in the name of "civilization" and the general betterment of humanity. The project of de-colonization, the concerted reversal of this process, must necessarily involve a rethinking of the notions and ideas in terms of which Europe felt justified in conquering Africa. The contemporary practice of Africana philosophy has to thus be focused on, among other things, systematically engaging and undermining the symmetry of concepts that constituted, and still constitute residually, the theoretic buttress of supremacy and racism. It has to reclaim the humanity negated by colonial conquest out of the concrete needs and situations of the present.

In this regard it is useful to recall, for a moment, the origins of the contemporary discourse of African philosophy. In 1945, Father Placide Tempels, a Belgian missionary who had done extensive field work in the Belgian Congo, among the Luba (Baluba) people of the region, published a book *La Philosophie Bantoue.* The aim of the book, as Tempels informs us in Chapter 7 (with the revealing title "Bantu Philosophy and Our Mission to Civilize"), was to assist the European colonialist venture by supplying documentation and an explorative reading of the native's interior intellectual or spiritual life. It was aimed at the colonization, from within, of the consciousness of the colonized. It focused on the impossible task of fabricating a self-assured and contented colonized self-consciousness made to order in complete accord with the imperious specifications of European hegemonic ambitions.[26]

24. Kwame Nkrumah, *Revolutionary Path* (London: Panaf Books, 1980), p. 121.

25. For Nkrumah's efforts on this crucial concern see *Consciencism* (New York: Monthly Review Press, 1970), specifically ch. 3.

26. It goes without saying that a "contented colonized self-consciousness" is a contradiction in terms. The point I am making is the same as the one Frederick Douglass makes when he states that: "I have observed this in my experience of slavery,—that whenever my condition was improved, instead of its increasing my contentment, it only increased my desire to be free, and set me to thinking of plans to gain my freedom. I have found that, to make a contented slave, it is necessary to make a thoughtless one. It is necessary to darken his moral and mental vision, and, as far as possible, to annihilate the power of reason. He must be able to detect no inconsistencies in slavery; he must be made to feel that slavery is right; and he can be brought to that only when he ceases to be a man." *Narrative of the Life of Frederick Douglass an American Slave Written by Himself,* edited with an introduction by David W. Blight (Boston, MA: Bedford/St. Martin's, 2003), p. 106.

The native, according to Tempels, is in possession of a "philosophy" that he lives and yet is incapable of articulating. Thus, those engaged in the mission to civilize first need to articulate this silent interiority of those who are to be civilized. His basic concern was to penetrate the self-consciousness, or self-awareness, of the colonized and implant, from within, the "*mission civilizatrice*," and in so doing force the intellectual and cultural surrender of the native by colonizing the self-understanding that grounds, and is vital to, the native's own experience of life.

For Tempels, the failure of the colonialist project, attested to by the repeated rebellions and "reversions" of the *évolué*, was not a problem inherent in the incongruent nature of the colonialist project—that is, the effort aimed at fabricating domesticated human beings—but the result of a faulty theory of colonization. Tempels's project, if successful, would be a rectifying measure; by understanding the indigenous culture from within, it would implant the "*mission civilizatrice*" in the interiority of the native's own sense of himself and of his or her world. The colonialist project would thus stop being an external imposition and would become the manifestation of the native's own being-in-the-world. This was the simple, but sinister, agenda of *Bantu Philosophy*.

The unabashed colonialist intent of this book notwithstanding, it concretely subverted Lucien Lévy-Bruhl's established notion of a "prelogical mentality" that had justified the European colonial project. For Tempels, one had to recognize the humanity of the colonized in order to better colonize them. This stance created a fertile ambivalence, for the colonial project was predicated on the absence of humanity in the colonized, who thus needed to be colonized in order to be humanized.

The fruitful ambiguity of this stance, from the perspective of the colonized, is rather obvious. In the service of colonialism, and inadvertently, Tempels was forced to concede that the Bantu, or African (he uses these terms interchangeably), is not a mere "savage." A complex of interlocking and intricate notions and conceptions of the world, nature, the divine, human existence, the cosmos, and so forth, constitute the conscious and lived self-awareness of the colonized, centered on the idea of a core "vital force."

The contemporary discourse of African philosophy has to pursue further this documentary exploration, starting from a rigorously self-conscious awareness of contemporary needs. For as Frederick Douglass has noted, "We have to do with the past only as we can make it useful to the present and to the future. To all inspiring motives, to noble deeds which can be gained from the past, we are welcome,"[27] the obverse of this means that all those facets of the African tradition that have a retrograde aspect have to be critiqued and unhesitatingly rejected. Douglass is here suggesting what I would call an Africana hermeneutic or interpretative stance, which is both *critical* and *reverent* in its relation to the past. The flexibility of this *critical-*

27. Frederick Douglass, "What to the Slave Is the Fourth of July," in *Narrative of the Life of Frederick Douglass an American Slave Written by Himself*, Part Two, "Selected Reviews, Documents and Speeches," p. 154.

reverent stance is gauged in terms of the usefulness of the past in view of the concrete needs of the present and the hopeful possibilities of the future to come.[28]

On the other hand, African philosophy has to repay Tempels in kind by providing a reading and re-reading of the hegemonic European tradition in order to dismantle its untenable claims and presuppositions. In this effort it would basically be supplying a counterreading and, in so doing, clearing ground for itself and discarding the racist and Eurocentric conceptions that justified conquest and violence. In addition to the above, contemporary African philosophy has to also engage and systematically explore both the cultural inheritance of our precolonial past and the more recent intellectual advances produced by the African anticolonial struggle.

It has to be emphasized, as Douglass has noted, that it is in and through the needs of the present that what had value, in the past, sustains itself. The heritage of the past does not just endure by inertia. For it to be transmitted into the future it has to be sifted, explored, and appropriated in and out of the lived exigencies of the present. It is in this manner that the most fruitful aspects of our *effective-past* can be perpetuated into the future. In this regard we need to engage in exploring our past in order to self-consciously and critically document our African cultural-intellectual heritage. In this way, that which was of value in the past can be preserved and transformed in view of new developments and, in this light, new understandings of our future possibilities can be produced.

This, too, is the basic direction of thought that Amilcar Cabral's notion of a "return to the source" suggests: for the return is not to some cadaverous history but to the possibilities of a future that concretely originate in the lived needs of the present and are grounded in our *effective-past*. The "return" that Cabral calls for and which our present situation necessitates is not a return to the Africa victimized by colonialism but to the "Africa to come,"[29] an Africa that has left behind colonialism, its neocolonial residue, and the archaic dead past. What this "return" directs us to are those *effective* elements of our heritage that we have to learn to sift, utilize, and project into as our future.

A Different Region

Now, this husbanding of the past, this *hatäta*, is a paradigmatic philosophic task. As the seventeenth century Abyssinian philosopher Zär'a Ya'aqob has noted:

28. For my reading of this *critical-reverent* stance in Heidegger and Gadamer please see "Heidegger and Gadamer: Thinking as 'Meditative' and as 'Effective-Historical Consciousness.'" *Man and World* 20 (1987): 41–64.

29. This is part of the title of one of the last articles that Fanon wrote as an Algerian militant. "*Cette Afrique à venire*," in *Pour la révolution africaine* (Paris: François Maspero, 1964), p. 203; "This Africa to Come," in *Towards the African Revolution*, trans. Haakon Chevalier (New York: Grove Press, 1964), p. 177.

> Man aspires to know truth and the hidden things of nature, but this endeavor is difficult and can only be attained with great labor and patience.... Hence people hastily accept what they have heard from their fathers and shy from any (critical) examination.[30]

It is in and through this critical process of husbanding tradition (*hatäta*) that that which is deemed useful is preserved and that which is residual is discarded. For our past does not just endure, its vitality is sustained and cultivated by the concerns of the present; it is the present that solicits the vitality of the past out of its own needs and the exigencies that animate contemporary existence.

Thus, philosophy in present-day Africa and its Diaspora has its source in an anxious heeding, listening to, responding to, and creating the meaning of our freedom in the context of the contemporary world situation. This, furthermore, is what guarantees its relevance as a discourse. Here it should be noted that this listening to the call of the meaning of our being, our freedom, has always been the proper task of philosophic reflection. As Socrates reminds Crito, in the dialogue named after him, reflection should engage itself with its concerns in conscious awareness of, but without ever being deterred by, the limits imposed by its lived finitude. Its concerns are always the concerns of the day. It articulates the concerns of a concrete situation in view of contemporary exigencies. In this worthwhile effort *the past*, when properly engaged, explored, and critically appreciated, presents itself as a storehouse of reflective treasures.

Africana philosophy is thus both a negative critique of Eurocentrism and a positive *critical-reverent* appropriation of our precolonial heritage and the experiences gained in antislavery, anticolonial, and antisegregation struggles. It is in this manner that we can fruitfully engage our post–civil rights and postcolonial concerns. The aim in all of this is not to reject the West nor is it merely to embrace Africa; rather, the focus is on developing a concrete synthesis grounded in a *hatäta* of the resources of the past in view of the exigencies of the present that will enable us to utilize all of that which is useful for the betterment of our contemporary situation. In this the directing concern of our philosophic reflections will not be *authenticity* but the *pragmatic utility* of the cultural-intellectual resources to be found in our heritage—our variegated *effective-past.*

The task of Africana philosophy is thus an ongoing and perpetual conceptual purging of all that was imposed on us. It is also and concurrently a concrete reclaiming of our traditions in view of the hybridity of our contemporary Africana existence. It is in this context that questions to do with our "post–civil rights situation" and, internationally, to do with "development," "democracy," "terrorism," and so forth, have to be dealt with. For presently these are the *code-words* through which—beyond

30. Claude Sumner, *Classical Ethiopian Philosophy* (Addis Abeba: Commercial Printing Press, 1985), p. 235. As Sumner tells us, this *Ge'ez* word literally means "to question bit by bit, piece-meal; to search into or through, to investigate accurately; to examine; to inspect" (Ibid., p. 225). For a more extensive discussion of Zär'a Ya'aqob and "*hatäta*" see chapter 5 of my book, *Our Heritage* (Lanham, MD: Rowman and Littlefield, 2000).

segregation and colonial dominance—the old world, of domination and supremacy, hopes to perpetuate itself.

In engaging the issues named by these terms, our efforts would be directed at contesting the hegemony of the established order while *inventing* the ideas, notions, and practices through which we can better our Africana existence in the contemporary world. This, furthermore, is a critical task of the present. For as the old guises of supremacy and dominance are unmasked and recede into the dead past, new ones (democracy, the war on terror, etc.) are constantly being fabricated out of the residual imperious grounding *imaginaire*[31] of the dominant order. In other words, when Gadamer affirms that we need to "accept our worldwide heritage" and come to a full recognition of the "validity of the claims this larger heritage makes on us," it is necessary to emphasize that this "larger heritage" is *largely* the heritage of those who, until recently, were oppressed and dispossessed; and the "claims [of] this larger heritage" that still need to be taken seriously are, again, of those who until recently were colonized and segregated.

To be sure, the efforts of those like Gadamer, Taylor, and Vattimo are welcome gestures that need to be further expanded and consolidated. Those of us engaged in Africana philosophy have to fan these flames, for intellectual work is needed "to advance human freedom and knowledge."[32] These, then, are the prospects and possibilities of our efforts in Africana philosophy, the *raison d'être* of our reflections, grounded as they are, in the history and experience of the formerly enslaved and colonized.

BIBLIOGRAPHY AND SUGGESTED READINGS

Appiah, K. Anthony. (1992) *In My Father's House: Africa in the Philosophy of Culture.* Oxford: Oxford University Press.

Gordon, Lewis R. (2008) *An Introduction to Africana Philosophy.* Cambridge: Cambridge University Press.

Hallen, Barry. (2009) *A Short History of African Philosophy.* Bloomington, IN: Indiana University Press.

Masolo, D. A. (1994) *African Philosophy in Search of Identity.* Bloomington, IN: Indiana University Press.

Serequeberhan, Tsenay. (1994) *The Hermeneutics of African Philosophy: Horizon and Discourse.* New York: Routledge.

———. (2007) *Contested Memory: The Icons of the Occidental Tradition.* Trenton, NJ: Africa World Press.

Vattimo, Gianni. (1997) *Beyond Interpretation.* Stanford, CA: Stanford University Press.

31. On this point see Cornelius Castoriadis, *The Imaginary Institution of Society*, trans. Kathleen Blamey (Cambridge, MA: MIT Press, 1987).

32. Edward W. Said, *Representations of the Intellectual* (New York: Pantheon Books, 1994), p. 17.

CHAPTER 34

AFRICAN PHILOSOPHY

BARRY HALLEN

ANTECEDENTS

As time passes African philosophy becomes increasingly difficult to summarize. This is due as much to new discoveries about or orientations toward its past as it is to the ever-increasing publications of contemporary African philosophers concerned primarily with issues relevant to the present and future. With regard to the past, there is the enduring controversy surrounding the Afrocentric hypothesis (James 1954; Diop 1974), which maintains that the basis for Greek philosophy and, by historical extension, Western philosophy derives from Egyptian sources. What is clearly the case is that the peoples and cultures of the ancient Mediterranean did a good deal more of intermingling and exchanging of ideas than has sometimes been supposed (Bernal 1987, 1991, 2006).

Oral narratives from sub-Saharan Africa are being reevaluated and recast for their philosophical content (Imbo 2002). North African and Saharan thinkers who were previously excluded from the canon because of their ties to early Christianity (Tertullian, St. Augustine) or Islam (Ahmad Baba of Timbuktu) are now seen as substantively African in origin and orientation (Masolo 2004a; Diagne 2004). The Ethiopian thinker Zara Ya'acob (1599–1622), writing at roughly the same time as Descartes, invented a form of analytic thinking that would be compatible with its twentieth-century counterparts (Sumner 2004). The Ghanaian philosopher Anton Wilhelm Amo (c.1703–1758), who obtained higher degrees in philosophy and taught in German universities, wrote theses on Descartes and the rights of Africans in Europe (Abraham 2004).

Contemporary African philosophers are involved in vigorous debates about the character of philosophical thought in Africa's indigenous cultures (Bello 2004; Taiwo 2004). The consensus seems to be that Africans must make it a priority to be clear about the form and content of their various intellectual heritages. But, while giving the past its due, this need not in the least distract philosophers in the African context from prioritizing issues, problems, and topics directly and primarily relevant to that context, and from promoting intercultural philosophical dialogue (within Africa as well as with the West and the rest of the world).

Ethnophilosophy and the Postmodern

In the first half of the twentieth century a number of texts were published, primarily by European scholars, linking the word "philosophy" to the cultures of sub-Saharan Africa (Tempels 1949; Graiule 1965; Dieterlen 1951; Jahn 1961), which, in too many cases, exoticized Africa to a point where its peoples were presented as marginally rational in intellectual terms. This eventually provoked counterattacks in the form of systematic rebuttals and theoretical alternatives from a number of Africa's leading intellectuals as evidenced by, for example, Leopold Sedar Senghor and his theory of Negritude (Senghor 1971). Senghor insisted that the intellectual and cultural integrity of Africa must arise from an African rather than a Western paradigm. It was Western philosophy and psychology that had introduced a rigid distinction between reason and emotion and was seemingly obsessed with keeping the latter under control. But Africans did not share this paradigm, and African modes of understanding or epistemology were distinctive insofar as they did not arbitrarily attempt to isolate reasoning from feeling. Both were important to defining human being and therefore to human understanding.

More recently, Paulin Hountondji has argued that such texts (Senghor included) constitute clear examples of ethnography (he prefers the term "ethnophilosophy") insofar as they amount to little more than descriptions of communal African beliefs and practices, which do not correspond to philosophy as expressed by individual Western thinkers, and which in any case always end up ranking African thought as intellectually inferior to its possible counterparts in other cultures (1996).

In these texts, according to Hountondji, indigenous African cultures are said to be predominantly "traditional" in character, which entails at least the following attributes: (1) ethnophilosophy speaks only of tribal (Zulu, Akan, Yoruba) philosophies rather than of philosophy as the product of individual thinkers (Plato, Hegel, etc.); (2) ethnophilosophy's sources are in the past, in what are described as the "authentic" African cultures of precolonial times; (3) these sources are to be found primarily in oral literature: parables, proverbs, poetry, songs, myths, and so forth; (4) ethnophilosophy therefore tends to present African beliefs and practices as timeless, as things that do not change; and (5) the definitive meanings of these oral texts are often determined by non-African academics and scholars and then expressed in a non-African language in some form of discursive format. In any case, Hountondji goes on to argue, entirely too much importance, too much of an aura of cultural prestige, has come to be associated with philosophy as a benchmark of culture.

Africa would be better off prioritizing its educational resources for science and technology, fields that will inevitably give rise to second-order (theoretical) controversies that would be straightforwardly philosophical and directly relevant to the African cultural context.

Hountondji was immediately challenged by his colleague, H. Odera Oruka. Oruka felt that Hountondji was placing artificial, indeed un-African, limits on the definition of philosophical thinking if he so exclusively identified its form and content as having to conform to its counterpart in the West. Africa had always had its philosophical thinkers, whom Oruka referred to as "sages," in that rather than merely being the keepers of their cultures' traditions, they were also actively, uniquely, and eminently rationally critical of them. In numerous cases, which Oruka set out to carefully document, they displayed critical and analytic abilities that accorded them the status of genuinely philosophical thinkers (Oruka 1990).

The publication of V. Y. Mudimbe's *The Invention of Africa* in 1988 caused something of a sensation in African Studies generally, as well as in African philosophy. This text is grounded upon a meticulous critique of virtually every approach to philosophy in the African context. The more general point is that what distinguishes this body of writings is the fact that the methodologies applied, the paradigms invoked, and the resulting "texts" that were written about Africa have in virtually every instance been derived from non-African (Western, Christian, etc.) topical and methodological sources.

For example, with respect to Hountondji, his outright rejection of orature (oral literature and tradition) as a suitable source or basis for philosophy itself imposes a vision of philosophy that demands it be the product of individual thinkers, expressing themselves in writing, who would evidently constitute a kind of intellectual elite (Mudimbe 1998, 158–160). And since evidence of such efforts is absent from Africa's precolonial, indigenous cultures, so would be philosophy. But, if both the form and content of Africa's intellectual heritage may be different from that of the West, Mudimbe wonders whether the criteria for philosophical thinking that Hountondji stipulates might prove counterproductive.

What does Mudimbe say is the correct way to either understand or formulate philosophy in the African context? His text concludes with a paragraph that has become memorable in the canon:

> Gnosis[1] is by definition a kind of secret knowledge. The changes of motives, the succession of theses about foundation, and the differences of scale in interpretations that I have tried to bring to light about African gnosis witness to the vigour of a knowledge which is sometimes African by virtue of its authors and promoters, but which extends to a Western epistemological territory. The task

1. Mudimbe prefers the term "gnosis" (knowledge that has yet to be understood and digested beyond its cultural origins and therefore remains unknown) to "philosophy" at least in part because he is not convinced that conventional portraits of Africa's intellectual heritage have yet to do it justice.

> accomplished so far is certainly impressive. On the other hand, one wonders whether the discourses of African gnosis do not obscure a fundamental reality, their own *chose du texte*, the primordial African discourse in its variety and multiplicity. Is not this reality distorted in the expression of African modalities in non-African languages? Is it not inverted, modified by anthropological and philosophical categories used by specialists of dominant discourses? Does the question of how to relate in a more faithful way to *la chose du texte* necessarily imply another epistemological shift? Is it possible to consider this shift outside of the very epistemological field which makes my question both possible and thinkable? (Mudimbe 1988, 186)

In other words, numerous scholars have volunteered to write "on behalf of" Africa in their published work. But how many of them took the time to really "listen" to what Africa has to say? As a result, Africa remains silent, ready to speak, still waiting for those who are truly ready and willing to learn.

Phenomenology and Analytic Philosophy

On the other hand, Tsenay Serequeberhan attempts to adapt phenomenology and hermeneutics to the African context (1994, 2000, 2007), and argues that he has achieved compelling results by doing so. His response to the challenge that this involves applying a methodology derived from the West to the African context is that the results previously achieved by other Africana[2] colleagues using a hermeneutical approach, such as Frantz Fanon (1967a, 1967b), Amilcar Cabral (1970, 1979), and Aime Césaire (1972), have demonstrated that important and legitimate results can be achieved via such exercises (1994, 10–11). Phenomenological hermeneutics as enunciated by, for example, Gadamer (1999) acknowledges the primary importance of the fact that philosophy always occurs in a specific historical-cultural context, which must be explicitly taken into account. Indeed, one of Serequeberhan's priorities is to turn "Western" philosophy against itself by highlighting its cultural imperialism and the pejorative (indeed, racist) consequences it has inflicted upon the cultures of Africa.

African philosophers must rise above such philosophical corruption and establish their own, autochthonous philosophical priorities (1994, 114). The objectives of this kind of philosophical enterprise that Serequeberhan suggests are, first, that it would contribute to the full and final liberation of Africa from Western neocolonialism; second, that it will articulate the kinds of priorities that are truly germane to Africa's intellectual, political, and economic development; and, finally, that it can carry out a scrupulous reexamination and reevaluation of African traditions with a

2. "Africana" is a more inclusive term, in that it refers to intellectuals of African origin in the diaspora as well as in continental Africa.

view to reviewing them from a genuinely African point of view, and then determining which are worth preserving, even enhancing, and which should be, deliberately and finally, consigned to the past (1994, 100).

A wide variety of other important thinkers whose primary concern is philosophy in the African context are more difficult to classify. Perhaps the best approach would be to let them speak for themselves in this regard insofar as their fundamental philosophical orientations are concerned, although this too is not always easy to do.

Kwasi Wiredu is perhaps the most respected among this group. Mudimbe characterizes his approach as "very British" (1988, 161), which would seem to imply some form of analytic philosophy. Wiredu himself seems more comfortable with the terms "rationalism" and "humanism" (1980, 1992, 1996). The body of his work is, to say the least, substantive in both breadth and depth with regard to the variety of subjects and issues he addresses. His deliberate attempt to highlight the importance of reason in the African context has at least two priorities. One is to counter those accounts of the African cultural heritage that dismiss rationality (which, for Wiredu, cannot be anything but universal) as a key for understanding the cultures of Africa. On numerous occasions he engages in explorations of his native Akan culture, conceptually and otherwise, to illustrate and prove its reasoned orientations/rational content. Another is to encourage African philosophers to appreciate the heritage of the past by determining which elements of their indigenous and/or postcolonial cultures should be preserved and which revised or discarded. His commitment to humanism is evidenced by his concern to promote the recognition, cultivation, and endurance of those values evidenced by what he terms African communalism (1992, 193–206), insofar as it places considerably greater emphasis on an individual's moral responsibilities to and involvement with the community than is the case in the West.

Kwame Gyekye endorses a conceptual approach to African philosophy supplemented by fieldwork to clarify the use and meanings of oral literature. Since things like proverbs (which he characterizes as "philosophical nuggets") and parables are designed for practical application in everyday life, it is important for the academic philosopher to go to the appropriate members of an African community who are best qualified to expound upon them in a communal and practical context.

Gyekye too believes that philosophy is a universal undertaking, and therefore to be found in all cultures. What may differ between cultures, however, are the various philosophical positions taken with regard to a particular philosophical issue. For example, some cultures may enunciate a preference for determinism, while others come down on the side of free will. But whether the author of a particular oral text is known or unknown, it still almost certainly was originally the creation of an individual human being (thus further undermining Hountondji's arguments against ethnophilosophy). In other words, what one does find in every culture in the world are certain common philosophical concerns and questions (1995, xiv) to which different answers (destiny as opposed to free will) in different formats (proverbs as opposed to deductive arguments) have been proposed (2003).

It is the contemporary African philosopher's task and responsibility to take these various sources of philosophical expression and weave them together into more systematic and coherent wholes. Then again, philosophy must be a historical as well as a cultural enterprise, in that the issues and problems most relevant to philosophy in the African context today may not be the same as those that concerned Africans in the past (1995, xi-xii). It is on the basis of such an orientation that Gyekye then proceeds to do a philosophical review of his native Akan culture (1995), discussing such fundamental staples as causality, God, the person, ethics, logic, time, and the mind-body problem.

> For me, then, a philosophical discourse that critically interacts or communes with African culture and intellectual experiences...only needs to be the results of the reflective exertions of an African thinker, arrived at giving *analytical* attention to the intellectual foundations of African culture and experience. That is all. (1995, 211; my italics)

J. Olubi Sodipo and his colleague, Barry Hallen, chose to experiment with another form of analytic philosophy—ordinary language philosophy—in the context of the discourse and culture of the Yoruba people of southwestern Nigeria. The most prominent product of their collaboration (Hallen and Sodipo 1997) is devoted to identifying foundational epistemological terminology in Yoruba discourse—the terms supposedly equivalent to the English language "knowledge" and "belief." They then go on to demonstrate that the criteria governing the usage of these terms indicate that their meanings are fundamentally different from their supposed Western equivalents, that these differences negate the conventional definition of propositional knowledge as justified true belief, thereby enabling Yoruba epistemology to escape the ramifications of the Gettier counterexamples, and argue for the cultural relativity of propositional attitudes generally.

In a subsequent publication (Hallen 2000), this epistemological framework is extended so as to apply to ethics (how does one know whether a person is moral or immoral?) and aesthetics (how can one know whether or not a person or object is beautiful?). In a more recent volume (2006), Hallen discusses the possible positive consequences of an ordinary language approach for the study of philosophy in non-Western cultures generally.

Kwame Anthony Appiah is yet another philosopher of an analytic persuasion. At the present time he is probably best known for his advocacy of what he terms "cosmopolitanism" (2006). On what appears to be primarily an ethical basis, this involves all of humanity, in principle, recognizing our shared reasonableness just as much as our cultural differences, and engaging in various forms of cross-cultural dialogue that will promote mutual understanding and, possibly, compromise and eventual agreement on the controversial issues that have vexed humanity for millennia as well as today (torture, genocide, etc.). In doing so Appiah is invoking a form of universal rationalism (including moral principles) and advocating a form of humanism that would seem to be compatible with some of the points previously enunciated by Kwasi Wiredu.

However, with specific reference to philosophy in the African context, Appiah is much more flexible in that he has consistently advocated and encouraged African philosophers to experiment with a wide variety of methodological approaches as they attempt to come to terms with the African cultural heritage and introduce it to the world community (1992).

D. A. Masolo wrote the first truly comprehensive history of modern African philosophy (1994). In it he provides much more detailed accounts of the philosophers whose work is discussed in this chapter, as well as advancing his own original approach to the field generally. He expresses concern about an overly linguistic or conceptual approach to philosophy in the African context. He is wary of the possibility that academic philosophers who indulge exclusively and excessively in this kind of approach may end up espousing African "philosophies" that are not genuinely reflective or representative of the cultural heritages they presume to articulate.

Masolo also is wary of the artificial divide that has been created between those who espouse some form of universalism and those who espouse some form of relativism in African philosophy. Although he does not go so far as to suggest this is evidence of the fallacy of false extremes, he does insist that this kind of purely academic dispute may again detract from a genuine understanding and appreciation of the more specific issues and questions that should actually constitute an African philosophical canon (1994, 248). For this reason he prefers a more historical and contextual approach to philosophy in the African context. This is evidenced in his more recent writing about communalism as a distinctive theme of African social and moral philosophy (2004b), which he embraces as an indigenous alternative to the individualism linked to the Western Enlightenment, something that has been increasingly problematized by the moral concerns attendant upon urbanization, industrialization, the demise of the extended family, and the dubious values inherent in the ever-increasing importance assigned to self-interest.

Marxism and Feminism

Olufemi Taiwo has explored a variety of topics in his published work. In *Legal Naturalism: A Marxist Theory of Law* (1996), he challenges the orthodox Marxist view that "sees the law as the will of the ruling class in its efforts to make the subaltern classes cooperate with or accede to its dominance" (1996, 2). In other words, he argues that the conventional distinction between the economic substructure and its more explicitly moral, political, and legal superstructure is based on a failure to appreciate the underlying continuity between Marx's earlier and later writings (1996, 8).

If the body of Marx's writings is treated as a coherent whole, Taiwo argues, Marxism may be seen to embrace its own distinctive theory of natural law. Every variety of economic system, whether feudal, capitalist, socialist, or communist, has inherent in it a distinctive and defining set of natural laws that constitute part of its essence. These natural laws can then be identified and used to both evaluate and determine the limits of the positive legal system of the society or state concerned.

> "[L]awmakers" formulate... [the laws they do] because they have to operate within specific or specifiable limits imposed by the natural law of the given mode of production in which they are located. For example, if a social formation is feudal, no matter how determined the legislators are they cannot make or implement laws that will guarantee capitalist commodity production and exchange, or liberty, equality, etc. (1996, 67)

Nkiru Nzegwu is an artist, art historian, and scholar of Africana studies. She too has formulated a number of explicit critiques of both Western and African scholars who appear to have insufficient appreciation of African viewpoints in their subject areas. Most recently she has addressed herself to Western feminism and its consequences for women in Africa.

She views the feminist movement as a Western phenomenon that presumes to have a universal relevance without understanding or appreciating that the social status and role of women in non-Western societies may be fundamentally different from what is said to be the case in the West. Essentially, feminists see non-Western women as comparatively worse off than women in Western cultures.

Based on fieldwork in her native Igbo culture, Nzegwu argues, first, that it was a genderless society prior to European colonization insofar as social roles and status were concerned. The sexual differences between men and women (she calls it a "dual-sex system") were recognized, but were not used as a basis for making one sex inferior to the other (2006, 15). Nor was motherhood used to limit or segregate women. If anything, its status was appreciated as indispensably foundational to the welfare of the entire community, and therefore became a powerful force in its own right.

> By...centering the ideology of motherhood, we are able to see the understated sources of power and channels of influence of Igbo women... [T]he convergence of these channels on the mother...checked the development of patriarchal force by significantly curtailing the rights of fathers and husbands over daughters and wives. (2006, 19)

Conclusion

As was indicated at the outset, presenting a synopsis of a field as intellectually and geographically diverse as African philosophy is a delicate undertaking. The philosophers whose work has been discussed, therefore, provide only an introduction to the discipline; there are numerous other noteworthy scholars who have not been mentioned. Probably the best single and currently available source to turn to for additional information is *A Companion to African Philosophy* (2004), edited by Kwasi Wiredu. This substantial and important collection of specially commissioned contributions from forty philosophers in and of Africa on such diverse topics as aesthetics, epistemology, ethics, history of (African) philosophy, logic, metaphysics, methodology, and social and political philosophy is likely to remain an indispensable primary source of issues, topics, and problems most relevant to contemporary African philosophy for years to come.

Nevertheless, the above synopses provide clear evidence that today African philosophy is a dynamic and original field, animated by a number of continuing controversies that should be of cross-cultural interest to philosophers generally. What form must a text take if it is to be regarded as philosophical? How is the philosophical dimension to Africa's intellectual heritage to be distinguished from other elements of Africa's cultures? Must Africa conform to the paradigm(s) of the discipline as defined by the West? Or might it be the case that Africa will articulate its own, more flexible paradigm of the discipline that may relegate its Western version to a species rather than a genus? What will be the consequences if African philosophers do arrive at a consensus about preserving and enhancing their heritage of community-oriented moralities and societies? Why is it the case that much of what Western feminists have to say about the liberation of women is not relevant to the African context? What is clear, indeed indisputable, is that African philosophers are aware of all of these issues, and actively at work to enunciate them more clearly and work toward their successful resolution.

BIBLIOGRAPHY AND SUGGESTED READINGS

Abraham, W. (2004) "Anton Wilhelm Amo." In *A Companion to African Philosophy*, edited by Kwasi Wiredu. Malden, MA, and Oxford: Blackwell Publishing, 191–199.

Appiah, K. Anthony. (1992) *In My Father's House: Africa in the Philosophy of Culture*. Oxford: Oxford University Press.

———. (2006) *Cosmopolitanism: Ethics in a World of Strangers*. New York: W. W. Norton.

Bello, A. G. A. (2004) "Some Methodological Controversies in African Philosophy." In *A Companion to African Philosophy*, edited by Kwasi Wiredu. Malden, MA, and Oxford: Blackwell Publishing, 263–273.

Bernal, Martin. (1987) *The Fabrication of Ancient Greece*. Volume 1 of *Black Athena: The Afroasiatic Roots of Classical Civilization*. London: Free Association Books.

———. (1991) *The Archaeological and Documentary Evidence*. Volume 2 of *Black Athena: The Afroasiatic Roots of Classical Civilization*. New Brunswick, NJ: Rutgers University Press.

———. (2006) *The Linguistic Evidence*. Volume 3 of *Black Athena: The Afroasiatic Roots of Classical Civilization*. New Brunswick, NJ: Rutgers University Press.

Cabral, Amilcar. (1970) "National Liberation and Culture." In *The Program of East African Studies, Occasional Paper No. 57*. Syracuse, NY: Maxwell Graduate School of

Citizenship and Public Affairs, Syracuse University. (Republished in Cabral 1979, 138–154.)
———. (1979) *Unity and Struggle*. New York: Monthly Review Press.
Césaire, Aimé. (1972) *Discourse on Colonialism*, translated by Joan Pinkham. New York: Monthly Review Press.
Diagne, Souleymane. (2004) "Precolonial African Philosophy in Arabic." In *A Companion to African Philosophy*, edited by Kwasi Wiredu. Malden, MA, and Oxford: Blackwell Publishing, 66–77.
Dieterlen, Germain. (1951) *Essai sur la religion bambara*. Paris: Presses Universitaires de France.
Diop, C. A. (1974) *The African Origin of Civilization: Myth or Reality*, edited and translated by Mercer Cook. Westport, CT: Lawrence Hill and Company; and Paris: Presence Africaine.
Fanon, Frantz. (1967a) *Black Skin, White Masks*. New York: Grove Press.
———. (1967b) *The Wretched of the Earth*. Harmondsworth: Penguin.
Gadamer, Hans-Georg. (1999) *Truth and Method*. 2nd rev. ed. Translation revised by Joel Weinsheimer and Donald G. Marshall. New York: Continuum.
Gordon, Lewis. (2008) *An Introduction to Africana Philosophy*. Cambridge: Cambridge University Press.
Graiule, Marcel. (1965) *Conversations with Ogotemmeli*. Oxford: Oxford University Press.
Gyekye, Kwame. (1995) *An Essay on African Philosophical Thought: The Akan Conceptual Scheme* (rev. ed.). Cambridge: Cambridge University Press.
———. (2003) *Beyond Cultures: Perceiving a Common Humanity*. Accra, Ghana: Ghana Academy of Arts and Sciences.
Hallen, Barry. (2000) *The Good, the Bad, and the Beautiful: Discourse about Values in Yoruba Culture*. Bloomington, IN: Indiana University Press.
———. (2006) *African Philosophy: The Analytic Approach*. Trenton, NJ: Africa World Press.
———. (2009) *A Short History of African Philosophy* (rev. 2nd ed.). Bloomington and Indianapolis, IN: Indiana University Press.
Hallen, Barry, and J. Olubi Sodipo. (1997) *Knowledge, Belief, and Witchcraft: Analytic Experiments in African Philosophy* (rev. ed.). Stanford, CA: Stanford University Press.
Hountondji, Paulin. (1996) *African Philosophy: Myth and Reality* (rev. ed.). Bloomington and Indianapolis, IN: Indiana University Press.
Imbo, Samuel Oluoch. (2002) *Oral Traditions as Philosophy*. Lanham, MD, and Oxford: Rowman and Littlefield.
Jahn, Janheinz. (1961) *Muntu: An Outline of the New African Culture*. New York: Grove Press.
James, George G. M. (1954) *Stolen Legacy: Greek Philosophy Is Stolen Egyptian Philosophy*. New York: Philosophical Library.
Masolo, D. A. (1994) *African Philosophy in Search of Identity*. Bloomington, IN: Indiana University Press.
———. (2004a) "African Philosophers in the Greco-Roman Era." In *A Companion to African Philosophy*, edited by Kwasi Wiredu. Malden, MA, and Oxford: Blackwell Publishing, 50–65.
———. (2004b) "Western and African Communitarianism: A Comparison." In *A Companion to African Philosophy*, edited by Kwasi Wiredu. Malden, MA, and Oxford: Blackwell Publishing, 483–498.
Mudimbe, V. Y. (1988) *The Invention of Africa: Gnosis, Philosophy, and the Order of Knowledge*. Bloomington, IN: Indiana University Press.

Nzegwu, Nkiru. (2006) *Family Matters: Feminist Concepts in African Philosophy of Culture.* Albany, NY: State University of New York Press.

Oruka, H. Odera (ed.). (1990) *Sage Philosophy: Indigenous Thinkers and the Modern Debate on African Philosophy.* Leiden: E. J. Brill.

Senghor, Leopold Sedar. (1971) *The Foundations of "Africanite" or "Negritude" and "Arabite."* Paris: Presence Africaine.

Serequeberhan, Tsenay. (1994) *The Hermeneutics of African Philosophy.* London: Routledge.

———. (2000) *Our Heritage.* New York and Oxford: Rowman and Littlefield.

———. (2007) *Contested Memory: The Icons of the Occidental Tradition.* Trenton, NJ, and Asmara, Eritrea: Africa World Press.

Sumner, Claude. (2004) "The Light and the Shadow: Zera Yacob and Walda Heywat: Two Ethiopian Philosophers of the Seventeenth Century." In *A Companion to African Philosophy*, edited by Kwasi Wiredu. Malden, MA, and Oxford: Blackwell Publishing, 172–182.

Taiwo, Olufemi. (1996) *Legal Naturalism: A Marxist Theory of Law.* Ithaca, NY: Cornell University Press.

———. (2004) "*Ifa:* An Account of a Divination System and Some Concluding Epistemological Questions." In *A Companion to African Philosophy*, edited by Kwasi Wiredu. Malden, MA, and Oxford: Blackwell Publishing, 304–312.

Tempels, Placide. (1949) *La Philosophie bantoue.* Paris: Presence Africaine (translated in 1959 by A. Rubbens and Colin King, *Bantu Philosophy.* Paris: Presence Africaine).

Wiredu, Kwasi. (1980) *Philosophy and an African Culture.* Cambridge and New York: Cambridge University Press.

———. (1992) "Moral Foundations of African Culture." In *African-American Perspectives on Biomedical Ethics*, edited by H. E. Flack and E. D. Pellegrino. Washington, DC: Georgetown University Press (reprinted in 1992 in *Person and Community*, edited by Kwasi Wiredu and Kwame Gyekye. Washington, DC: The Council for Research in Values and Philosophy, 193–206).

———. (1996) *Cultural Universals and Particulars: An African Perspective.* Bloomington, IN: Indiana University Press.

Wiredu, Kwasi (ed.). (2004) *A Companion to African Philosophy.* Malden, MA, and Oxford: Blackwell Publishing.

CHAPTER 35

AFRO-CARIBBEAN PHILOSOPHY

CLEVIS HEADLEY

WRITING about Afro-Caribbean philosophy is a highly complicated affair due to the complexity of the idea of "Afro-Caribbeanness," on the one hand, and the concept of "philosophy," on the other hand. Analytic philosophy has gained hegemony in the English-speaking world, and while it does not consist of "a single, universally agreed-upon, precise definition," it was deeply motivated by developments in mathematical logic that sought to reduce philosophy to *a priori* logical analysis. On the other hand, Afro-Caribbean philosophy more closely resembles a naturalized philosophy precisely because Afro-Caribbean philosophy has borrowed much from less formalized disciplines. Indeed, Afro-Caribbean philosophy represents an interdisciplinary model of philosophical praxis precisely because Afro-Caribbean philosophy is the focal point of a constellation of overlapping marginalities and overlapping intertextualities. This site of intersection reveals the struggle by Afro-Caribbean philosophy to claim disciplinary identity, institutional visibility, discursive autonomy, and epistemological credibility. Nonetheless, there is the lingering assumption that the circumstances of Caribbean history preclude the possibility of philosophy taking roots in the Caribbean. Naipaul is of the view that "The history of the islands can never be satisfactorily told. Brutality is not the only difficulty. History is built around achievement and creation; and nothing was created in the West Indies" (Naipaul 1969, 29). One implication of Naipaul's position is that there is no Afro-Caribbean philosophy. However, since I disagree with Naipaul's negative conclusion, I will briefly discuss what makes one an Afro-Caribbean philosopher before launching into a more detailed discussion of Afro-Caribbean philosophy.

To be classified as an Afro-Caribbean philosopher does not require that one satisfy racial or ethnic essentialist criteria. Resisting the obvious urge to appeal exclusively to racial or ethnic criteria, my view is that being an Afro-Caribbean philosopher is a matter of being intimately grounded in the tradition of Afro-Caribbean philosophy and, more broadly, the Afro-Caribbean intellectual tradition. Being grounded in the tradition of Afro-Caribbean philosophy requires that one critically engage the canonical texts constituting this tradition, and engage with the problems and questions that constitute this tradition. Furthermore, another criterion of being an Afro-Caribbean philosopher requires that one be adequately integrated in the circuits of Afro-Caribbean philosophy, which means that one publishes scholarly work in relevant journals, attends conferences, and holds membership in scholarly organizations dedicated to the Afro-Caribbean intellectual tradition.

This essay will engage in a multidimensional exploration of Afro-Caribbean philosophy in an attempt to review some of the main elements constitutive of this tradition of thought. This brief study is by no means a thoroughly exhaustive overview of Afro-Caribbean philosophy. For, in addition to leaving out certain well-known areas of critical discussion, the focus will be mainly in the English-speaking Caribbean. Contestability, it seems, is inescapable.

Abandoning Misconceptions about Afro-Caribbean Philosophy

Let us begin by examining certain misconceptions about Afro-Caribbean philosophy that develop precisely because of a failure to appreciate the complexity of Afro-Caribbean philosophy.

It is easy to reduce the intellectual production of marginalized groups to biography or spontaneous ideology. But Afro-Caribbean philosophy is neither a "victim discourse" nor a "resistance discourse" that articulates the rage and desire for recognition of Afro-Caribbean subjects. Afro-Caribbean philosophy is not a tribalist manifesto concerned with cataloguing the worldview of the Afro-Caribbean community. Nor should Afro-Caribbean philosophy be construed as a "fashionable, Marxist-evolved revisionism" (Walcott 1998, 56). Finally, we must avoid representing it through the concepts and categories of the dominant philosophical traditions. Inevitably, efforts to reduce Afro-Caribbean philosophy, the Other, to the sameness of a universal discourse entangle Afro-Caribbean philosophy in a dialectic of recognition where it must contend with either invisibility or hypervisibility. Afro-Caribbean philosophy "should not be ghettoized into closed discursive boxes which marginalize [it], making [it] specific and unique only to what has loosely been called "the black experience" (Bogues 2003, 1).

Contextualizing Afro-Caribbean Philosophy

These warnings not to simplistically reduce Afro-Caribbean philosophy should not preclude appropriately situating Afro-Caribbean philosophy. Afro-Caribbean philosophy is indeed unique, but its uniqueness bears the scars of an exceptional history. We must recognize that Afro-Caribbean philosophy is a discursive singularity precisely because of its origins. Chamberlin writes:

> Blacks in the West Indies are not the only people with a history of oppression. But theirs is a special history, bringing with it a grim inheritance of someone else's images of difference and disdain, images that for five hundred years have conditioned their special and sometimes desperate need to determine for themselves who they are and where they belong. (Chamberlin 1993, 28)

In another context, George Lamming has also underscored the peculiar circumstances of Caribbean history. He writes:

> [T]he word colonial has a deeper meaning for the West Indian than it has for the African. The African, in spite of his modernity, has never been wholly severed from the cradle of a continuous culture and tradition. It is the brevity of the West Indian's history and the fragmentary nature of the different cultures which have fused to make something new; it is absolute dependence on the values implicit in that language of his colonizer which has given him a special relation to the word, colonialism. (Lamming 1992, 34–35)

Afro-Caribbean philosophy seeks to work through the dense complexity of this historical reality (Henry 2000). Hence, Afro-Caribbean philosophy cannot claim a pure origin but must be seen as philosophical activity taking place in the context of the Caribbean legacy of slavery and colonialism. This context is amplified by a distinctive inheritance that offers us an intercultural model of philosophy beyond the traditional binary of particularity and universality. Modernity serves as a transcendental opening for the emergence of Afro-Caribbean philosophy, marking the rise of both a specific universality (European) and a particularity (Afro-Caribbean) that dialectically sustains this universality, even as it calls it into question. Bogues writes:

> What is often elided is that the overarching framework for modernity's emergence was the rise of racial slavery, colonialism, and new forms of empires; that the conceptions of "rational self-interested subject" were embedded in a philosophical anthropology of bourgeois Enlightenment and Eurocentrism. (Bogues 2003, 2)

Critical engagements with the legacy of slavery and colonialism and their brutal intrusion into modernity constitute one of the core problems within Afro-Caribbean philosophy.

Contesting Modernity

Let us probe more deeply the connection between Afro-Caribbean philosophy and modernity (Bogues 2003). To the extent that the underside of modernity consists of the legacy of slavery and colonialism, a legacy premised upon notions of racial superiority, race emerges as an inescapable feature of modernity. Here, we should think of race in the socio-ontological sense, as a category of inclusion, as well as exclusion, complicit in the structuring of modern political arrangements. Closely aligned with the socio-ontological reality of race is the existential reality of blackness. Blackness, within the context of modernity, designates the lived reality of those who are bioculturally identified as descendants of Africans. Clearly, then, issues of race, blackness, slavery, colonialism, and modernity are canonical problems propelling the development of Afro-Caribbean philosophy. Indeed, partly because of this set of issues, Afro-Caribbean philosophy has been tasked with responsibilities aptly described by Walcott:

> What would deliver [the Caribbean subject] from servitude was the forging of a language that went beyond mimicry, a dialect which had the force of revelation as it invented names for things, one which finally settled on its own mode of inflection, and which began to create an oral culture of chants, jokes, folksongs, and fables; this, not merely the debt to history, was his proper claim to the New World. (Walcott 1998, 15)

The significance of Walcott's view for Afro-Caribbean philosophy is the idea of the creation of a new language for the renaming of things. This burden of utilizing the ontological resources of language, as will be discussed later, clearly suggests a distinctive trajectory that amplifies the uniqueness of Afro-Caribbean philosophy.

Afro-Caribbean Philosophy and the Nature of Philosophy

Engaging the idea of Afro-Caribbean philosophy requires critical involvement with a metaphilosophical inquiry regarding the nature, origin, scope, and objectives of philosophy. On the Afro-Caribbean view, philosophy is not about making hair-splitting distinctions and abstractions; nor is it the pursuit of abstract metaphysical questions or detached speculation that is alien to the materiality of human existence. There is no exaggeration in holding that Afro-Caribbean thinkers share Randall Collins's insights about the connection between the history of philosophy and philosophy itself. Collins states that the "history of philosophy is to a considerable extent the history of groups. [N]othing but groups of friends, discussion partners, close-knit circles that often have characteristics of social movements" (Collins 1998, 3). Outstanding groups of Afro-Caribbean thinkers certainly lend credence to this view. Aimé Césaire and Frantz Fanon were interlocutors from the French Caribbean; George Lamming, C. L. R. James, George Padmore, Kamau Braithwaite, Sylvia Wynter, Elsa Goveia, Wilson Harris, and Derek Walcott were interlocutors from the English-speaking Caribbean; and currently, Lewis Gordon, Paget Henry, and Charles Mills are representative of thinkers whose work has been strongly influenced by the discipline of philosophy. Even in those cases where these thinkers were not interlocutors, their intellectual development was profoundly shaped by the work of earlier generations of Caribbean thinkers.

From another perspective, Afro-Caribbean philosophy is also constituted by what Brian Stock has called textual communities: "microsocieties organized around the common understanding of a script" (Stock 1990, 23). Indeed, Afro-Caribbean philosophy's indebtedness to literature and history explains its interpretive struggles over literary and historical texts. Paget Henry has insightfully maintained that Afro-Caribbean philosophy "has largely been social and political in nature and concerned with problems of cultural freedom, political freedom, and racial equality. In the texts of this philosophy, history and poetics assume an ontological status as the domains in which Afro-Caribbean identities and social realities are constituted" (Henry 1993, 12). Viewing Afro-Caribbean philosophy from the perspective of textual communities explains the emergence of a Caribbean collective consciousness supported by the reading and interpretations of texts. Stock claims that "[i]n textual communities, concepts appear first as they are acted out by individuals or groups in everyday life. Only later, and within norms structured by texts, is there a collective consciousness" (Stock 1990, 13). Clearly, the forging of a collective consciousness has amplified the dominance of history for many Afro-Caribbean thinkers. For these thinkers, philosophy is not descriptively identical with its history but, rather, is to be understood through reference to its own historical development, so that philosophy then cannot be an ahistorical and acultural discursive practice. But it would be misleading to embrace an exclusive historicist characterization of Afro-Caribbean philosophy. Perhaps it would be more appropriate to characterize it as a form of radical empiricism, thereby understanding it as a courageous affirmation of experience in all of its untamed intensity and irreducible pluralism and flux. Furthermore, to frame Afro-Caribbean philosophy in generic terms as a radically empirical philosophy is to underscore its resistance to strategies of transcendence that escape material life.

In the context of the deconstruction of the metaphysics of presence and of foundationalism and realism, Afro-Caribbean philosophy, although not reducible to mere history, cannot be practiced independently of history. Such a philosophy earnestly situates philosophical ideas and habits within the flux and flow of our concrete lives. This puts Afro-Caribbean philosophy in solidarity with conceptions of philosophy that view truth, knowledge, and objectivity as the products of intersubjective agreement and not as matters strictly dependent upon faithfulness to an independent reality. This move away from seeking to reflect a reality totally independent of human language and concepts underscores the importance of understanding the self-legitimizing practices of distinctive human communities and the Afro-Caribbean form of life.

Models of Afro-Caribbean Philosophy

With the preceding background in place, it is appropriate to narrow the focus of this essay to an examination of some models of Afro-Caribbean philosophy. This exercise will reveal the ways in which Afro-Caribbean philosophy has been shaped by the circumstances of Caribbean reality. It would be incorrect to claim that mathematics, logic, or the natural sciences have served as the dominant structural model for Afro-Caribbean philosophy. Whereas some other traditions of philosophy have sought to erect philosophy on deductive models of argumentation, as well as the methods of the natural science, this has not been the case with Afro-Caribbean philosophy. Note, however, that this development does not indicate that Afro-Caribbean philosophy rejects argumentation and analysis. Indeed, although embracing argumentation and analysis, it has primarily utilized discursive styles of thought that were inspired by alternative models of human cognitive activity.

Afro-Caribbean Philosophy as Critical Ethnophilosophy

Patrick Goodin construes Afro-Caribbean philosophy as concerned with articulating the lived reality of the Afro-Caribbean subject (Goodin 2000). On Goodin's view, Afro-Caribbean philosophy will be a philosophy of existence in the sense of focusing on the style of existence common to Afro-Caribbean peoples. "Afro-Caribbean philosophy," writes Goodin,

> as a sub-division of Africana philosophy, must articulate itself out of its own sociopolitical/historical matrix. It must work its way to philosophy through a comprehensive understanding of its sociopolitical historical existence and not simply take over categories from the dominant group. It must self-consciously raise the question of what it means for an oppressed people to engage in the practice of philosophy. (Goodin 2000, 151)

Goodin makes a substantive case for an Afro-Caribbean philosophy by building upon Anthony Appiah's critical reflections on ethnophilosophy, for he shares Appiah's view that we should distinguish between philosophy, on the one hand, and what passes for philosophy but is really not philosophy, namely, ethnophilosophy, on the other. Whereas philosophy, in the proper sense of the term, is a normative undertaking, ethnophilosophy is descriptive and, accordingly, fails to qualify as proper philosophy. Appiah writes that "'ethnophilosophy,' [is] the attempt to explore and systematize the conceptual world of Africa's traditional cultures. This amounts, in effect, to adopting the approach of a folklorist or ethnographer: doing the natural history of traditional folk-thought about the central issues of human life" (Appiah 1992–1993, 17–18). Appiah claims that the ethnophilosophy that plausibly qualifies as true philosophy is critical ethnophilosophy. True philosophy, for Appiah, is an activity "in which reason and argument play a central role" (Appiah 1992, 86).

Goodin appropriates Appiah's strategy in order to offer his own insights about what constitutes a legitimate Afro-Caribbean philosophy. He maintains that critical ethnophilosophy should play a decisive role in Afro-Caribbean philosophy because of "the important issues raised by colonialism and postcolonial social and economic development and... the issues raised by race *vis-à-vis* justice" (Goodin 2000, 146).

Afro-Caribbean Philosophy as Philosophical Anthropology

Afro-Caribbean philosophy has also at times modeled itself as a form of philosophical anthropology. Because of the complex historical reality of the various religious, cultural, and social encounters among the various groups of people in the Caribbean (African, European, Indigenous, Asian), the Caribbean reality has provided the opportunity for critical reflections on the question of human existence. Indeed, Frantz Fanon (1967), Sylvia Wynter (2000), Lewis Gordon (1995b, 2000), and Paget Henry (1999–2000) have addressed the question of human existence precisely because of the existential *callaloo* of differences and similarities that were inconsistent with the ideal of rational self-interested individuals liberated from the burdens of religion, culture, and history. Furthermore, there is the immediacy of cultural diversity, the amazing hybridity of culture, religion, and music that flow from this tantalizing mixture and interaction of diverse peoples. This reinforces the project of critically reflecting upon the question of human existence.

Let us examine two treatments of Afro-Caribbean philosophy as philosophical anthropology.

Lewis Gordon's Existential Phenomenology

Lewis Gordon's work is of major significance within the context of Afro-Caribbean philosophy. He describes his own texts as "situated in what may be called black radical existential thought" (Gordon 2000, 22). Existential phenomenology, for Gordon, is the act of employing phenomenological analysis to investigate beings capable of raising questions about their own existence. He is drawn to existential phenomenology precisely because he wants to avoid the crude practice of using an abstraction "to avoid the human being in the flesh" (Gordon 2000, 43).

Gordon adds an additional layer of signification to his understanding of existential phenomenology by placing it within the broader context of postcolonialism, thereby situating phenomenology inside the scope of Afro-Caribbean philosophy. He describes his "existential phenomenological" approach to African-American and [Afro-Caribbean] philosophy, "[as] *postcolonial phenomenology*. It is a form of Afro-Caribbean phenomenology that comes out of the convergence of black existential thought and creolized forms of phenomenology" (Gordon 2006, 20).

Gordon grounds his existential phenomenological project in a critical investigation of black self-formation, focusing on historical strategies of racialization that have variously shaped this process. Implicit in this project is the acknowledgment of the asymmetrical material relations between blacks and whites. Consistent with his existential phenomenological project, he concentrates on the ontological (constitutive) dimensions of everyday black and white egos. This focus on the ontology of black and white ego formation is not a descriptive psychological task but a normative (critical) inquiry into the relations between these two ontologies. The relations between these ontologies have been dominated by a struggle for ontological space, namely, the space to claim creative human agency, to posit oneself, and to achieve this self-positing.

Gordon utilizes Sartre's notion of bad faith to anchor his take on the antagonistic relations between black and white egos. Bad faith, among other things, is the phenomenon of human beings evading their freedom, treating themselves as objects rather than as subjects. When operating in bad faith, human beings seek to evade or deny their lack of completion by presuming that they do not have to make choices. This tendency to deny incompletion leads to the pretense of completion, namely, the belief that one is indeed a well-integrated, fully present, self-contained, and autonomous self.

Gordon clarifies how race is manifested as significant within the context of self/other relations between whites and blacks. He maintains that race is inescapable precisely because "race has emerged, throughout its history, as the question fundamentally of 'the blacks' as it has for not other groups. It is not that other groups have not been 'racialized.' It is that their racialization . . . has been conditioned in terms of a chain of being from the European human beings to the subhuman on a symbolic scale from light to dark" (Gordon 2003, 37). In a racialized world, the battle for ontological space has taken the form of whites viewing themselves as complete and autonomous selves and as being in complete control of ontological space that is not available to blacks. Whites compensate for their own ontological failures and anxieties by instituting practices of racism that deny blacks authentic space. Whites become fully determinate subjects, whereas blacks remain deficient beings lacking ontological fulfillment. Indeed, Gordon maintains that white antiblack racism usually takes the form of a "projective non-seeing" of blacks. Black invisibility in an antiblack world leads to the disappearance of black humanity, and blacks come to be seen as lacking the agency that whites possess.

Gordon laments the fact that colonialism and racism have respectively functioned as "existential deviations" for blacks, negatively disrupting the project of black self-formation. Gordon's project of existential philosophy focuses on black self-formation and on the dynamics of bad faith that have contributed to the battle for ontological space.

Frantz Fanon: Afro-Caribbean Philosophy as Sociogenesis

Fanon explores the philosophical implications of the Afro-Caribbean reality through alternative phenomenological and psychoanalytic categories (Fanon 1967). He situates his thinking outside traditional ontological approaches to the study of human beings in favor of existential modes of interpretation and understanding. Furthermore, he provides us with a style of thinking called sociogenesis, which is more pertinent to the situation of the Afro-Caribbean subject. Sociogenesis is not an ontological approach to the study of human reality but, instead, focuses on the human responsibility for human institutions. Sociogenic features of things are essentially the meaning-constituting or meaning-signifying features of social existence.

Fanon's preference for the existential dimensions of human beings is ultimately directed at the methodologies of the European human sciences. He is critical of them precisely because they violate the singularity of the individual to the extent that they become infatuated with abstract methodological approaches to human beings. In this case, the European human sciences declare war on the Other. These approaches focus upon etiological features of generic individuals or individual species but not on the activities that provide insights about human beings as creators of meaning and values. Fanon, hence, favors a sociogenic approach to human beings, an approach rooted in the fact that human beings are interpretive, as well as valuing, beings. They are not things whose activities can be captured within nets of causal relations and causal explanations. According to Lewis Gordon:

> Fanon poses... the question of Man, the anthropological question, to remind all of us that one cannot legitimately study man without remembering that desires and values emanate from him and shake the contours of investigation. For Fanon, this amounts in one instance to the methodology of what he calls, a 'sociogenic' approach, an approach standing outside of phylogeny and ontogeny, an approach that involves the understanding that the problem and interpretation at hand must be addressed 'on the objective level as on the subjective level.' (Gordon 1995b, 9)

The European human sciences fail to register the collective singularity of blacks. Ontology becomes complicit with imperialism and, by extension, also conspires in the obliteration of ethics to the extent that ontology, in denigrating existence, exalts the human subject (white subject) but discards the black subject (the Other). Gordon quotes Fanon:

> In the *weltanschauung* of a colonized people there is an impurity, a flaw that outlaws any ontological explanation. Someone may object that this is the case with every individual, but such an objection merely conceals a basic problem. Ontology—once it is finally admired as leaving existence by the wayside—does not permit us to understand the being of the black man. For not only must the black man be black; he must be black in relation to the white man. (Fanon 1967, 109–110)

While agreeing with Fanon, Gordon confidently maintains that it is imperative for any attempt to construct a human science seeking to capture the lived experience of the black to appeal to the sociohistorical reality of black existence. Such efforts, according to him, should emerge from the core of sociogenesis, namely, realize that in considering black existence, historical, social, and cultural forces should not be ignored (Gordon 1997, 44).

Afro-Caribbean Philosophy as Anticolonial Intellectual Production

Afro-Caribbean philosophy is also a mode of anticolonialist intellectual production. Within this discourse, Afro-Caribbean thinkers utilize the language and the philosophy of their former colonial masters to undermine the system of racial and class oppression grounded in the idea of the superiority of Europe.

Anthony Bogues seeks to develop the idea of a black radical tradition of thought, expanding upon this idea of Afro-Caribbean philosophy as anticolonial intellectual production. Bogues's point of departure is his claim that "[t]here exists a deep political practice in [Afro-Caribbean] political thought that connects the lived social and political experiences of [Afro-Caribbean subjects] to the categories of political thought" (Bogues 2003, 21). Bogues does not model his conception of Afro-Caribbean philosophy on the traditional conception of philosophy as a sovereign discipline investigating transcendental questions. Indeed, on Bogues's view, it is not the aim of Afro-Caribbean philosophy to discover, analyze, and defend the fundamental principle of X such that X is understood as some universal phenomenon. Put differently, Afro-Caribbean philosophy does not limit itself to an exploration of the conditions of possibility of truth, knowledge, or experience. Afro-Caribbean philosophy's turning away from the traditional infrastructural concern of philosophy leads Bogues to construe Afro-Caribbean philosophy as a heretical and prophetic activity. Bogues writes that, for Afro-Caribbean philosophy, "'heresy' means becoming human, not white nor imitative of the colonial, but overturning white/European normativity" (Bogues 2003, 13). Afro-Caribbean philosophy, hence, is heretical not because it seeks to promote falsity but, rather, because it challenges the conceptual regime of the dominant tradition of philosophy. It appears heretical when judged by the categories and concepts of the very tradition that it challenges. Indeed, Afro-Caribbean philosophy must dialectically struggle with the Western philosophical tradition as it seeks to address the conditions of its own possibility as connected to the rise of Western modernity. It must critically engage this tradition.

For Bogues, Afro-Caribbean philosophy is "engaged in the creation of counter-hegemonic texts" (Bogues 2003, 13). As such, Afro-Caribbean philosophy will not need to seek recognition from the dominant Western tradition, even as it acknowledges its own emergence from a context determined by Western modernity. The ambivalent relation of Afro-Caribbean philosophy to Western modernity is aptly captured by Bogues: "[Afro-Caribbean philosophy as] radical intellectual production is not simply reducible to an application of western modernity... instead it is a critique of, and oftentimes a counterdiscourse about, the nature of western modernity" (Bogues 2003, 9).

Regarding what he calls the *redemptive prophetic voice* of Afro-Caribbean philosophy, Bogues maintains that it consists of those "who constructed a set of practices and rationalities that sustained Africans in the diaspora..." (Bogues 2003, 16). He attributes at least three elements to the prophetic stream of Afro-Caribbean philosophy: divination, healing, and prophecy. Within the prophetic tradition, knowledge is gained by nonrational means, namely, through revelation and dreams. Similarly, individuals within this tradition are often engaged in healing practices, and, finally, this tradition is also redemptive in the sense that "prophecy functions as a form of social criticism, a redemptive discourse that argues for the ending of colonial and racial oppression" (Bogues 2003, 19). Bogues attributes other significant features to the redemptive stream of Afro-Caribbean philosophy, citing its unique use of language. Indeed, Bogues underscores "its creative usage of language to describe social conditions and affirm their humanity. In these instances [language] becomes a weapon, a chant, and an invocation beating against the walls of oppression as well as an 'illocutionary force'" (Bogues 2003, 20). Finally, Bogues claims that the redemptive stream creates a "counter symbolic order." He maintains that the "[t]he creation of a symbolic order that then overturns the hegemonic racist or colonial order is not only a semiotic challenge but also, importantly, a battle for human validation" (Bogues 2003, 20).

Clearly, critical engagement with Western modernity is a core concern within Afro-Caribbean philosophy. This critical engagement is not a simplistic rejection of Western modernity but involves a double encounter with Western modernity: first, it engages it as an orthodoxy, and second, it offers a critique of it in order to develop different sets of political and social categories. Here, Afro-Caribbean philosophy seeks to promote alternative conceptions of things that might otherwise be rendered impossible by colonial reason. Afro-Caribbean philosophy resists the colonialization of reason as an exclusive prerogative of Europe.

Afro-Caribbean Philosophy as Ethics

Afro-Caribbean philosophy is also an ethics. By this, I do not mean that it follows traditional ethical theory in seeking to discover universal and formal principles of right conduct. Rather, Afro-Caribbean philosophy is modeled on a conception of ethics grounded in responsibility for the other. In this regard, faced with the hegemonic reign of the dominant Western philosophical tradition, Afro-Caribbean philosophy seeks to create a space for the Other, which is not immediately reducible to the concepts and norms of the Same. As a model of ethics, Afro-Caribbean philosophy is against "the subjugation and the marginalization of heterogeneity by self-centralizing, monolithic models" (Mackey 1993, 5).

Closely related with this emphasis on otherness and ethics is Afro-Caribbean philosophy's relation to music. Music enjoys the distinctive role of facilitating access to alternative realities, and this characteristic has motivated its influence as a model of social and epistemological dissent. Again, because of the infusion of music within Caribbean culture, musical influence has also affected philosophical activity in the region. The inherited African musical traditions—reggae, jazz, calypso, and salsa—have indelibly cross-fertilized Afro-Caribbean philosophy (Brathwaite 1967a, 1967b, 1968). The prevalence of music as a cognitive model has been noted by Mackey. He writes that music "serves many black writers as both a model and a highwater mark [*sic*] of black authority, a testament to black powers of self-styling as well as to the ability of such power to influence others" (Mackey 1993, 7).

Having reviewed various models of Afro-Caribbean philosophy, it is now appropriate to expand the focus of this study to consider some of the main currents in contemporary Afro-Caribbean philosophy.

Main Currents in Afro-Caribbean Philosophy

Let us briefly review the most recent attempts to impose a canonical structure on the diverse texts and thinkers within Afro-Caribbean philosophy. Paget Henry titles his text *Caliban's Reason: Introducing Afro-Caribbean Philosophy*. This act of naming is significant for, in referring to the character Caliban in the Shakespearean play *The Tempest*, a play about colonialism, Henry is announcing to us that Afro-Caribbean philosophy is metaphorically Caliban's response to Prospero, the character who teaches Caliban his language. Here, an Afro-Caribbean philosophy will not be captive to the language and logic of Sameness, identity, and totality but will speak in its own voice, the voice of the Other.

Not surprisingly, Henry situates Afro-Caribbean philosophy outside the closed discursive space of universalistic conceptions of philosophy. Philosophy, he claims, "is neither absolute nor a pure discourse. It is an internally differentiated and discursively embedded practice, the boundaries of which will continue to change as work in other fields requires the taking up of new philosophical positions" (Henry 2000, 3).

Similarly, Henry's construal of Afro-Caribbean philosophy does not fall prey to any insidious particularism that would "ghettoize" Afro-Caribbean philosophy. While advocating an intertexual strategy, Henry appropriately situates Afro-Caribbean philosophy within the project of decolonization. Accordingly, he writes that Afro-Caribbean philosophy is "a radically decolonized philosophical practice that [should] adequately meet the current postcolonial demands of the region" (Henry 1998, 25). The expectation is that such a philosophy will be concerned with the decolonialization of Afro-Caribbean consciousness, with decentering ways of thinking premised upon alien assumptions of life, and axioms of existence.

Consistent with the theme of doing philosophy from the underside of modernity, Henry articulates three important reforms that must be undertaken to facilitate the flourishing of Afro-Caribbean philosophy. He suggests that we change the patterns of creolization that are characteristic of Caribbean philosophy. To this end, he favors a process of creolization that is consistent with the aim of creating "a creole philosophy whose identity is closer to those of Caribbean literature, dance, theatre, calypso, reggae and other creole formations" (Henry 1998, 25). He demands that Afro-Caribbean philosophy be "capable of thematizing its own concerns, making distinct discursive contributions to knowledge production in the region.

The time has come for Caribbean philosophy to declare its independence from its historic intertextual subordination to ideological production" (Henry 1998, 26). Finally, Henry demands that there be a change in the intertexual address of Afro-Caribbean philosophy by making it a new critical writing. As a new critical writing, Afro-Caribbean philosophy will "help to link the founding categories of the subject in disciplines such as political economy and history to those of the arts, making dialogue and translation possible along these and other lines" (Henry 1998, 27).

Therefore, Henry, while delicately balancing the divide between intercultural and intracultural conceptions of philosophical activity, describes Afro-Caribbean philosophy as "an intertextually embedded discursive practice, and not an isolated or absolutely autonomous one. It is often implicitly referenced and engaged in the production of answers to everyday questions and problems that are being framed in nonphilosophical discourses" (Henry 2000, 2).

In charting his conception of Afro-Caribbean philosophy, Henry is not interested in sanctioning a hegemonic discourse premised on fuzzy notions of authenticity, and he clearly underscores the internal debates constitutive of the Afro-Caribbean philosophical landscape. In doing this, Henry identifies two schools of Afro-Caribbean philosophy: poeticism and historicism. He explicitly states that "Afro-Caribbean philosophy has concentrated its ontological efforts on the poetically or historically constructed nature of social reality" (Henry 1993, 12). Henry defines the poeticist tradition as a group of thinkers (Sylvia Wynters, Wilson Harris, Edouard Glissant) who claim that questions of identity, ego formation, and self must be resolved before there can be any constructive change in Afro-Caribbean society. Put differently, they claim that the conceptions of self and consciousness that infuse Afro-Caribbean literature are productive sources for existential and ontological change. Derek Walcott, who is perhaps one of the fiercest critics of historicism, but an enthusiastic supporter of poeticism, writes that:

> In the New World servitude to the muse of history has produced a literature of recrimination and despair, a literature of revenge written by the descendants of slaves or a literature of remorse written by the descendants of masters. Because this literature serves historical truth, it yellows into polemics or evaporates in pathos. The truly tough aesthetic of the New World neither explains nor forgives history. It refuses to recognize it as a creative or culpable force. This shame and awe of history possess [thinkers of the Caribbean] who think of language as enslavement and who, in a rage for identity, respect only incoherence or nostalgia. (Walcott 1998, 37)

Walcott clearly does not favor history as the basis of philosophy. Rather, he favors a philosophy rooted in the infinite resources of consciousness that are facilitated by the creative and the imaginative use of language.

On the other hand, the historicists (Frantz Fanon, C. L. R. James, Marcus Garvey, George Padmore) argue that external institutional change is the precondition to any meaningful transformation of consciousness of self within Afro-Caribbean societies. Here, the main idea is that social transformation directly connected to political economy must be seen as antecedent to the flourishing of a healthy Afro-Caribbean subjectivity. Poeticists favor projects that are attentive to the immateriality of consciousness, whereas historicists favor projects focused on overhauling the material structures of production, distribution, and consumption.

There are two other main currents of thought in Afro-Caribbean philosophy. One popular, but often misunderstood, school is negritude. The leading architect of negritude was Aimé Césaire (Césaire 2001). Many thinkers have chosen to interpret negritude as a vulgar nationalism premised upon the equally absurd notion of racial essentialism. According to these interpretations, negritude championed the idea of a unique African racial essence that explains the peculiar personality, aesthetic, and psychology of Africans and their descendants (Soyinka 1976). These complacent and simplistic readings of negritude, including Sartre's more positive reading (Sartre 1976) of negritude as an antiracist racism, fail to appreciate the more serious epistemological thrust of negritude. In this regard, Césaire utilizes negritude to critique Cartesian rationalist epistemology but does so in a language that deflates the sovereignty of reason. Hence, Césaire's more sophisticated conception of negritude does not uncritically suggest a celebration of blackness for purposes of racial pride. Instead, it works through this early positing to force a more critical rethinking of the Eurocentric monopoly on human cognition (Arnold 1981).

Another school of thought that has attracted the attention of Afro-Caribbean thinkers is existentialism. Indeed, we can find traces of existentialism in the early phase of Afro-Caribbean creative writing, when the consciousness of Afro-Caribbean subjects was ablaze with the idea of freedom and revolt against colonialism.

Lewis Gordon has made major contributions to black existentialist thought with his *Bad Faith and Antiblack Racism* (Gordon 1995a) and *Existentia Africana* (Gordon 2000), which have motivated Afro-Caribbean philosophy to escape its theoretical stasis. According to Henry,

> Gordon emerges as an important Caliban figure taking the claims of [the] old Caribbean voice in new philosophical directions and into new terrains. As such, it has brought new ideas and challenges to the field of Afro-Caribbean philosophy—a philosophy that has been dominated by its schools of...historicism and poeticism. [A]fro-Caribbean philosophy has tended to shy away from the existential and transcendental domains of experience that are so prominent in Gordon's thought. (Henry 2000, 146)

George Lamming appropriates the basic existentialist thesis of the radicality of human freedom. His well-known novel *In the Castle of My Skin* is considered a text that testifies to the "fusion of philosophy to experience" (Butler 1982, 39). Butler adds that "*In the Castle of My Skin* is the work where existentialist philosophy was first applied to personal experience" (Butler 1982, 38). Although other Afro-Caribbean writers flirted with existentialism, Butler maintains that "[f]ar from being frivolous or fashionable, Lamming's use of existentialism is experiential and functional.... The single intention running through all six [of] Lamming's novels is to depict man's rejection of freedom as he meekly accepts a definition given him by the Other, or to show him accepting that existential freedom and creating his own actions" (Butler 1982, 38).

Memory, Imagination, and Trauma

Because Afro-Caribbean philosophy utilizes available cognitive resources, memory and imagination have played major roles within Afro-Caribbean philosophy. Indeed, imagination is appreciated as a sphere of contestation, conflict, and struggle. Derek Walcott boldly proclaims that "the imagination is a territory as subject to invasion and seizure as any far province of Empire" (Walcott 1988). History, memory, and imagination are important within Afro-Caribbean philosophy precisely because of the need of Afro-Caribbean subjects to escape modes of thought and frames of consciousness that entrap them in notions premised upon the hopelessness and debilitating experience of the Afro-Caribbean reality (Webb 1992). The prospects of working through the violence and trauma of Caribbean history are considered impossible because the victims of this history are wounded beyond repair. However, cognitive paralysis and epistemological stasis are not the inevitable inheritance of Afro-Caribbean subjects precisely because there exists, within Afro-Caribbean philosophy, a keen appreciation of the art of "appropriating a *de facto* situation by endowing it with figurative meaning."[1] This emphasis upon transcending brutal material events through figurative transformation is insightfully addressed by Wilson Harris, who underscores the importance of imagination for the development of a philosophy of history that is adequate to the Caribbean reality. Harris insists upon the role of the arts in this project of fashioning a philosophy of history inspired by the arts of the imagination (Henry 2004). This, indeed, is one unique feature of Afro-Caribbean philosophy. Harris writes:

> I believe that the possibility exists for us to become involved in perspectives of renascence which can bring into play a figurative meaning beyond an apparently real world or prison of history. I believe a philosophy of history may well lie buried in the arts of the imagination. (Harris 1995, 18)

The primary motivation propelling Harris's belief in the emancipatory and redemptive capacity of the imagination is his belief in the possibility of a new "architecture of cultures" (Harris 1995, 20). Ultimately, then, Harris seeks "to free the Caribbean of a reductionist historiography that imprisons it in its deprivations" (Mackey 1993, 169).

Afro-Caribbean Philosophy and Postmodernism

Another issue that has played a crucial role in Afro-Caribbean philosophy is its involvement with postmodernism (Benítez-Rojo 1996; Glissant 1992; Henry 2000, ch. 5). Here, I will be using "postmodernism" loosely to include poststructuralism

1. Maurice, Merleau-Ponty, *The Phenomenology of Perception* (London: Routledge and Kegan Paul, Ltd.), p. 154.

and deconstruction. As to be expected, the postmodern turn is, to a large extent, preoccupied with the structuring role of language. Afro-Caribbean thinkers, such as Sylva Wynters, Wilson Harris, and Edouard Glissant, have variously engaged postmodernist modes of thought. Here, I will limit my discussion to Glissant.

Glissant has followed postmodernism in its resituating of the subject, rethinking of history, and phenomenological investigations of the concept of the Other. His involvement with postmodernist thought is not intended to sanction any nihilistic celebration of the death of the subject and the end of history or to exoticize the Other, but rather, to move beyond the conceptual stasis of the notions of the subject and history as they have been constituted by modernity.

Glissant's involvement with postmodernism is in the cause of creating alternative conceptions of subjectivity and history. Aware of the unique circumstances of the Caribbean situation, he questions the idea of a fully self-rational subject who serves as the transcendental ground of truth, knowledge, and meaning. Instead of embracing the idea of a fully self-rational subject whose consciousness qualifies as the authority of knowledge, Glissant favors the idea of a collective subject. The structuring elements of Afro-Caribbean consciousness are not the products of the psychological idiosyncrasies of isolated individuals or transcendental structures of consciousness but emerge from "landscape, community, and collective unconscious" (Dash 1992, xiii). Furthermore, in displacing the Cartesian *ego cogito* as a model for the Afro-Caribbean subject, Glissant locates the Afro-Caribbean subject in ongoing linguistic and cultural practices.

> Glissant's oeuvre in general and *Caribbean Discourse* in particular are predicated on a dislocation or deconstruction of the notion of individual agency in a post-Cartesian, post-Sartrean sense. There is a constant deflation of the solemnities of the self-certain subject in Glissant's critique of the longing for inviolable systems and pure origins, the sovereignty of self-consciousness, the solipsism of the structuring ego. In *Caribbean Discourse* Glissant is equally explicit on the limitations of the structuring, transcendental ego: 'man is not the privileged subject of his knowledge; he gradually becomes its objects.... He is no longer the mind probing the known-unknown.... The collective "We" becomes the site of the generative system, and the true subject. (Dash 1992, xii–xiii)

Not surprisingly, Glissant displaces the linear, hierarchical view of history that considers European culture as the highest evolutionary expression of culture. Again, Glissant is not denying history in the sense of ontologically renouncing the events of the past. Rather, he seeks to dethrone a conception of history that places Afro-Caribbean subjects at the periphery of history and that withholds from them the right to structure their own narratives of temporal existence (Taylor 1989). Indeed, Glissant refers to the presence of a nonhistory in the Caribbean as the "dislocation of the continuum, and the inability of the collective consciousness to absorb it all" (Glissant 1992, 62). Glissant rejects the Hegelian conception of history, a totalizing conception of history premised on the idea of the necessary development of freedom. History as the necessary development of freedom is, for Glissant, not an indisputable truth but the object of horrific desire. Glissant writes:

> "History ends where the histories of those peoples once reputed to be without history come together." History is a highly functional fantasy of the West, originating at precisely the time when it alone made the history of the world. If Hegel relegated African peoples to the ahistorical, Amerindian peoples to the prehistorical, in order to reserve History for European peoples exclusively, it appears that it is not because these African or American peoples "have entered History" that we can conclude today that such a hierarchical conception of the "march of History" is not longer relevant.... It is this hierarchical process that we deny in our own emergent historical consciousness, in its ruptures, its sudden emergence, its resistance to exploration. (Glissant 1992, 64)

Metaphor in Afro-Caribbean Philosophy

An important characteristic of Afro-Caribbean philosophy is its extensive use of rich metaphors. This extensive deployment of metaphor should be explained in terms of the importance of language in Afro-Caribbean thought and philosophy. Kamau Brathwaite has indicated that "it was in language that the slave was perhaps most successfully imprisoned by his master, and it was in his (mis-)use of it that he most effectively rebelled" (Brathwaite 1971, 237; Lamming 1992). Derek Walcott also underscores the importance of "renaming and finding new metaphors" (Walcott 1992, 25) in order to ground Afro-Caribbean existence. Whereas mainstream philosophy views metaphor as alien, Afro-Caribbean philosophy recognizes that Caribbean subjects have endeavored to grasp the rhythm of their existence through the agency of metaphor. Rejecting a representationalist view of language, Afro-Caribbean philosophy is concerned to produce new descriptions of things, as well as to institute self-legitimizing narratives. Here, we must understand metaphoricity as producing images to frame various characteristics of the life-world. Metaphoricity is not the opposite of conceptuality, but is intimately involved with illuminating the constitutive features of lived reality.

A plethora of root metaphors has infused Afro-Caribbean philosophical discourse: Anancy, Caliban, creolization, cross-culturality, fragments/fragmentation, hybridity, mestizaje, scar/wound, schizophrenia, submarine, and twilight. Chamberlin has called attention to Brathwaite's use of the metaphor of creolization to frame the historical, social, and cultural dynamic of racial interaction within Caribbean society (Brathwaite 1971, 1985). According to Chamberlin, when "Brathwaite uses the term creolization to describe the interaction between languages and between peoples, he is underlining its literary and political as well as its linguistic integrity" (Chamberlin 1993, 82). In another context, Ramazani describes the metaphor of scar as used by Walcott (Walcott 1990) as signifying "cultural convergence in the Americas without effacing its violent genesis" (Ramazani 2001, 61). The character Caliban has also played a dominant role in framing Afro-Caribbean intellectual activity, particularly the epistemological sovereignty of the Afro-Caribbean subject (Henry 2000; Bogues 1997). Bogues writes that the

> character [Caliban] in Shakespeare's 1623 play *The Tempest* has become representative of the thought of the "native" radical intellectual. C. L. R. James himself, in the epigraphs to *Beyond a Boundary*, invokes Caliban as the representative figure who, having learned the master's language, pioneers "into regions Caesar never knew." The Caribbean political novelist George Lamming, in *Pleasures of Exile*,... uses Caliban as representative of an anticolonial figure who contains "the seeds of revolt." (Bogues 2003, 15)

Lastly, Glissant describes Brathwaite's use of the metaphor of the submarine as indicative of the complex interplay of cultures in the Caribbean. In particular, he interprets this metaphor as signaling a rejection of uniformity and an embrace of difference. Glissant writes:

> We are the roots of a cross-cultural relationship. Submarines roots: that is floating free, not fixed in one position in some primordial spot, but extending in all directions in our world through its network of branches. We, thereby, live, we have the good fortune of living, this shared process of cultural mutation, this convergence that frees us from uniformity. (Glissant 1992, 67)

Conclusion

This essay has not examined every possible aspect of Afro-Caribbean philosophy. Developments in Afro-Caribbean religion and sociopolitical movements have not been covered. However, I hope it has succeeded in capturing some of the excitement and flavor of Afro-Caribbean philosophy.

BIBLIOGRAPHY AND SUGGESTED READINGS

Appiah, Anthony. (1992–1993). "African American Philosophy?" *The Philosophical Forum* XXIV, 1–3.

———. (1992). *In My Father's House: African In the Philosophy of Culture*. Oxford: Oxford University Press.

Arnold, James. (1981). *Modernism and Negritude: The Poetry and Poetics of Aimé Césaire*. Cambridge, MA: Harvard University Press.

Benítez-Rojo. (1996). *The Repeating Island: The Caribbean and the Postmodern Perspective*, translated by James Maraniss. Durham, NC: Duke University Press.

Bogues, Anthony. (1997) *Caliban's Freedom: The Early Political Thought of C. L. R. James*. London: Pluto Press.

———. (2003). *Black Heretics, Black Prophets: Radical Public Intellectuals*. New York: Routledge.

Brathwaite, Edward Kamau. (1967a) *Rites of Passage*. London: Oxford University Press.

———. (1967b) *The Arrivants: A New World Trilogy*. London: Oxford University Press.

———. (1968) *Masks*. London: Oxford University Press.

———. (1971). *The Development of Creole Society in Jamaica*. Oxford: Clarendon Press.

Butler, Janet. (1982). "The Existentialism of George Lamming: The Early Development of a Writer." *Caribbean Review* no. 4, Fall, 15, 38–39.

Césaire, Aimé. (2001). *Notebook of a Return to my Native Land*, translated by Clayton Eshleman. Middleton, CT: Wesleyan Press. Originally published Paris: Présence Africaine, 1968.

Chamberlin, J. Edward. (1993). *Come Back To Me My Language: Poetry and the West Indies*. Chicago, IL: University of Illinois Press.

Collins, Randall. (1998). *The Sociology of Philosophies: A Global Theory of Intellectual Change*. Cambridge, MA: Harvard University Press.

Dash, Michael. (1992). "Introduction." In *Caribbean Discourse*, translated by Michael Dash. Charlottesville, VA: University of Virginia Press.

Fanon, Frantz. (1967). *Black Skin White Masks*. New York: Grove Press.

Glissant, Edouard. (1992). *Caribbean Discours: Selected Essays*, translated by Michael Dash. Charlottesville, VA: University of Virginia Press.

Goodin, Patrick. (2000). "On the Very Idea of an Afro-Caribbean Philosophy." *Africana Philosophy*, 13(2).

Gordon, Lewis. (1995a). *Bad Faith and Antiblack Racism*. Atlantic Highlands, NJ: Humanities International Press.

———. (1995b). *Fanon and the Crisis of European Man: An Essay on Philosophy and the Human Sciences*. New York: Routledge.

———. (1997). *Her Majesty's Other Children: Sketches of Racism From a Neocolonial Age*. Lanham, MD: Rowman and Littlefield.

———. (2000). *Existentia Africana: Understanding Africana Existential Thought*. New York: Routledge.

———. (2003). "African American Existential Philosophy." In *A Companion to African-American Philosophy*, edited by Tommy Lott and John Pittman. Oxford: Blackwell Publishing, 33–47.

———. (2006). "African-American Philosophy, Race, and the Geography of Reason." In *Not Only the Master's Tools: African-American Studies in Theory and Practice*, edited by Lewis Gordon and Jane Anna Gordon. Boulder, CO: Paradigm Publishers.

Harris, Wilson. (1995). *History, Fable & Myth in the Caribbean and Guianas*. Wellesley, MA: Calaloux Publications. Originally published in 1970 by the National History and Arts Council, Ministry of Information and Culture, Georgetown, Guyana.

Henry, Paget. (1993). "CLR James, African and Afro-Caribbean Philosophy." *The CLR James Journal* Winter.

———. (1998). "Philosophy and the Caribbean Intellectual Tradition" *Small Axe* no. 4.

———. (1999–2000). "Wilson Harris and Caribbean Philosophical Anthropology." *C. L. R. James Journal: A Review of Caribbean Ideas* 7(1), 104–134.

———. (2000). *Caliban's Reason: Introducing Afro-Caribbean Philosophy*. New York: Routledge.

———. (2004). "Wilson Harris and Caribbean Philosophies of Art." *The CLR James Journal: A Review of Caribbean Ideas* 10(1), Winter.

Kirkland, Frank. (2003). "Modernisms in Black." In *A Companion to African-American Philosophy*, edited by Tommy Lott and John Pittman. Oxford: Blackwell, 67–86.

Lamming, George. (1953). *In the Castle of My Skin*. London: Michael Joseph.

———. (1992). *The Pleasure of Exile*. Ann Arbor, MI: The University of Michigan Press.

Mackey, Nathaniel. (1993). *Discrepant Engagement: Dissonance, Cross-Culturality, and Experimental Writing*. Tuscaloosa, AL: The University of Alabama Press.

NAIPAUL, V. S. (1969). *The Middle Passage.* Harmondsworth: Penguin.

RAMAZANI, JAHAN. (2001) *The Hybrid Muse: Postcolonial Poetry in English.* Chicago, IL: University of Chicago Press.

SARTRE, JEAN-PAUL. (1976) *Black Orpheus.* Paris: Presence Africaine.

SOYINKA, WOLE. (1976). *Myth, Literature and the African World.* Cambridge: Cambridge University Press.

STOCK, BRIAN. (1990). *Listening For the Text: On the Uses of the Past.* Philadelphia, PA: University of Pennsylvania Press.

TAYLOR, PATRICK. (1989). *The Narrative of Liberation: Perspectives on Afro-Caribbean Literature, Popular Culture and Politics.* Ithaca, NY: Cornell University Press.

WALCOTT, DEREK. (1988). "Caligula's Horse." Main lecture to the conference on "The Written Life: Biography/Autobiography in West Indian Literature." University of the West Indies, Kingston, Jamaica.

———. (1998). "The Muse of History." In *What The Twilight Says: Essays/ Derek Walcott.* New York: Farrar, Straus and Giroux, 36–64.

———. (1990). *Omeros.* New York: Farrar, Straus and Giroux.

———. (1992). "The Sigh of History." *The New York Times* December 8.

WEBB, BARBARA. (1992). *Myth and History in Caribbean Fiction.* Amherst, MA: University of Massachusetts Press.

WILSON-TAGOE, NANA. (1998). *Historical Thought and Literary Representation in West Indian Literature.* Gainesville, FL: University Press of Florida.

WYNTER, SYLVIA. (2000). "Africa, The West and the Analogy of Culture: The Cinematic Text after Man." In *Symbolic Narratives/African Cinema: Audience, Theory and the Moving Image,* edited by June Givanni. London: The British Film Institute, 25–78.

CHAPTER 36

AFRICAN AMERICAN PHILOSOPHY: A GENERAL OUTLINE

JOHN H. MCCLENDON III
STEPHEN C. FERGUSON II

THE history of African American philosophy and philosophers poses both empirical and conceptual problems. For example, who are the African American thinkers who have grappled with philosophical questions and problems? What type of training/education did they receive? What were the venues (institutional settings) available for their work? Were such outlets academic or nonacademic, or did both come into play? Did teaching or research matter more for the earlier generations of African American philosophers? What audience did they seek to address? And what means were at their disposal for reaching their audience? What subfields in philosophy did they explore and what schools of thought captured their allegiance? What philosophical movements—if any—were developed in light of the conditions faced by the masses of African Americans? What were the philosophical traditions that emerged from the history of African American philosophers? In this chapter we have addressed these questions by providing a general outline as a point of departure for both students and teachers of philosophy as well as the general reader with interest in the field.[1]

The virtual absence of African Americans from the history of philosophy, and the philosophical canon, in the United States is due to a history of neglect and

1. Although there are to date a number of studies on individual African American philosophers, there are no general histories on African American philosophers.

exclusion deeply rooted in academic racism.[2] Due to slavery and then segregation, and then racial quotas, African Americans had few opportunities to pursue philosophy as a profession. There were few opportunities for African Americans to enter the academy. Given this history of racism, in particular, the racism of academic philosophy over the last two centuries, it is necessary to call attention to the nonacademic sources of African American philosophy as well as its academic sources.

This exclusion of Black people, for the most part, from the academy does not in any way entail a lack of philosophical traditions among African Americans. In a quest for carrying out philosophical work, African Americans thinkers pursued academic as well as nonacademic avenues. Instead of emerging from the confines of the White academy, then, African American philosophical traditions have historically tended to emerge from within the context of African American intellectual culture. Furthermore, the content and direction of African American philosophical inquiry reflects the ongoing imperatives rooted in African American political and intellectual culture. Given its moorings outside the White academy, African American philosophical discourse has a considerable and extensive history. In fact, this history extends at least as far back as the eighteenth century.[3]

Despite these important nonacademic moorings, it would be incorrect to say that African American philosophy is essentially determined by the influence of these nonacademic (rather than academic) intellectuals. While nonacademic philosophers are often regarded as more intellectually influential than those actually trained as philosophers, and while such thinkers as Maria Stewart, Martin Delaney, Martin Luther King, and Malcolm X form a crucial part of the history of African American philosophy, African American academic philosophers have also played a critical role in the history of African American philosophy.

Through the Back Door: African American Philosophers and the Color Line

Contemporary discourse on African American philosophy views Cornel West, for example, as a canonical figure. His various positions at Ivy League institutions, his philosophical writings, and his extraordinary success as a public intellectual, for

2. Given this brief discussion of the beginnings of African American philosophy, it should come as little surprise that many African American philosophers are excluded from works that treat of the philosophical canon. A recent text on philosophy in the United States (Kuklick 2001) includes only one African American philosopher in passing, namely, W. E. B. Du Bois. On academic racism and philosophy see Valls 2005; Ward and Lott 2002; Harris 1995; Bernasconi and Cook 2003.

3. Percy Johnson offers an account of the origins of African American philosophical history starting with the writer Jupiter Hammon as among the first of African American thinkers to engage in philosophical discourse (Johnson 1970). Foremost on Hammon's philosophical agenda is the question of the ethical conduct of the slave vis-à-vis the slave-master (Pinn 2002).

some, position him as one of the most creative and insightful African American philosophers. Whatever merit there is to West's importance, we should not presuppose that African American philosophers only made "Giant Steps" in academic philosophy in recent times. We should not ignore the "lost voices" of African American philosophers who labored under the "Color Line," as W. E. B. Du Bois so aptly called Jim Crow. In this section, we give special attention to three African American philosophers who have been ignored—Patrick Healy, Thomas Nelson Baker, and Alexander Crummell. While these figures did not have the opportunity to publish many volumes of philosophical work, they are as significant and indispensable to the history of African American philosophy as more widely known contemporary Black philosophers.

Professional academic philosophy, like other disciplines in the White academy, is firmly rooted in institutionalized racism. This is not just the attitude or belief that some races are superior to others, but, more important, patterns of behavior and institutions that give material support to such attitudes and beliefs by the suppression of denigrated groups. Thus, academic racism is the practice associated with the complex of institutions such as colleges and universities, including the posture of the American Philosophical Association, that work together and assert institutional power by erecting standards that, under the guise of professionalization, were and are, in this sense, racist. This institutionalized academic racism is the context in which African American philosophers operate and the context in which their work must be interpreted.

Segregation determined that African Americans in the late nineteenth and on through most of the twentieth century were afforded little opportunity to pursue either undergraduate or graduate study in philosophy at White colleges. Therefore, prior to 1840, approximately no more than fifteen Black students attended White colleges.[4] And for the vast majority of African American philosophers who had in fact completed graduate work at White institutions, the "Color Line" of segregation also meant that they were either excluded from or had limited participation in the White academy, along with its ancillary professional organizations. (Beyond the discipline of philosophy, the general status of African American scholars was such that by 1936, there were only three Black Ph.D.s serving on the faculties of White colleges.[5])

Before Black institutions were viable alternatives for pursuing academic philosophy, several African Americans departed from the United States to engage in academic philosophy. For example, the antebellum philosopher Patrick Francis Healy became the first African American to earn a Ph.D. in philosophy. The son of a slaveholder and slave mistress, Healy's phenotype (he could pass for White) facilitated his rise in the White academy.[6] Healy earned his degree in 1865 from the

4. See Fleming 1974, 217–246.
5. See Winston 1971.
6. For more on Healy, see O'Toole 2002.

University of Louvain and became the only African American with a doctorate to teach philosophy at a White institution prior to the turn of the twentieth century. He taught philosophy at The College of the Holy Cross, St. Joseph's College (Philadelphia), and Georgetown University. He later became the president of Georgetown in 1874, making him the first African American to head a White institution of higher learning.

Crummell graduated from Cambridge University in 1853, where he studied with the Platonist William Whewell. Crummell's political philosophy was grounded in Platonic idealism. As such, he was opposed to materialist theories of race relations as reflected in Jeffersonian egalitarianism and Lockean contractarianism. In an implicit critique of Booker T. Washington, Crummell insisted, "Men are constantly dogmatizing theories of sense and matter as the salvable hope of the race. Some of our leaders and teachers boldly declare, now, that *property* is the source of power; and, then, that *money* is the thing which commands respect." But, Crummell lamented, these are "blind men!" (Crummell 1898, 4). Crummell's philosophical idealism formed the basis for his commitment to Christian civilization, his faith in the providential destiny of Black people, his authoritarian political philosophy, and his insistence on the importance of independent Black institutions.[7]

Crummell spent his entire philosophical teaching career outside of the United States, working in Liberia where he was professor of Mental and Moral Science. Crummell made a particular mark on the history of African American philosophers and their connection to Africa. After his return to the United States, Crummell founded the American Negro Academy, a Black intellectual society, in March 1897, for the purpose of racial uplift through the creation of African American high (bourgeois) culture and the adoption of Victorian moral standards.

The second African American to receive a Ph.D. in philosophy was Thomas Nelson Baker. Born on a slave plantation in Eastville, Virginia, his formal education included studying at Hampton Institute, the Mt. Hermon School (Gill, Massachusetts), as well as Boston University. Baker earned his doctorate from Yale in 1903, completing a dissertation on "The Ethical Significance of the Connection Between Mind and Body." In his dissertation Baker defends interactionism, arguing that the mind and body, though different, causally interact with one another. "We cannot remind ourselves too often that the mind and the brain are not identical, but that defective brain organization means, in one form or another, defective manifestation of mind," Baker argues. He continues, "The body does not produce the mind, nor does the mind produce the body, and in a sense they are independent of each other. They are independent as to their origin, but interdependent as to their development. The mental states affect greatly the bodily states and vice versa. The well being of the body is the condition for the well being of the mind. Degradation of the body is always accompanied by the degradation of the mind."[8]

7. See Moses 1989.
8. See Yancy 2001b, 62.

The "Color Line" restricted most African American philosophers prior to the 1970s to teaching at historically Black colleges and universities. The segregation of African American philosophers in often underfunded Black institutions limited their ability to pursue research and publication. Faced with enormous teaching loads, professional isolation, limited resources, and enormous administrative responsibilities, many African American philosophers were unable to publish their work.

Recently, the incipient Black feminism of Anna Julia Cooper has been credited as making a pioneering contribution to African American philosophy. Today, her feminism is often regarded as being grounded on a petit-bourgeois ideology of racial uplift, which measured racial progress from the standpoint of a late Victorian bourgeois sensibility distrustful of social democracy. Cooper did earn a doctorate in 1925 from the University of Paris-Sorbonne in French literature. Joyce Mitchell Cook, however, was the first African American woman to be granted a doctorate in philosophy, which she received in 1965 from Yale University. She was also the first woman appointed to teach at Yale and in the Howard University philosophy department (1959–1961 and 1970–1976, respectively). Between 1959 and 1961, she was the managing editor of *The Review of Metaphysics*. Both Cooper and Cook opened the door for future generations of Black women philosophers such as Anita Allen, Adrian M. S. Piper, Michele M. Moody-Adams, Blanche Radford-Curry, Joy James, Naomi Zack, Jacqueline Scott, Jennifer Lisa Vest, Anika Mann, and Kathyrn Gines, among others.

Excluded from the opportunity to participate in the White academy, African American philosophers were faced with a dual professional imperative: on the one hand, they undertook work that would gain the scholarly approval of their White counterparts. On the other hand, these segregated philosophers had a commitment to address the philosophical issues confronting the African American community. This dual imperative, which Du Bois had framed as double consciousness, remained a salient feature of the history of African American philosophers, up through the final decades of the twentieth century.

When addressing the problems raised by the African American experience, such as the nature and impact of racism, as well as philosophical problems and topics of interest to mainstream White philosophers, African American philosophers utilized resources available to them within the framework of Black institutions and often were forced to publish in Black publications. Such academic journals were generally focused on disciplines outside of philosophy. Nevertheless, Black philosophers actively continued to present their philosophical viewpoints in these journals. Wayman McLaughlin, for example, published "Symbolism and Mysticism in the Spirituals" in the African American journal *Phylon*. McLaughlin examines the double meaning of the spirituals, that is, the symbolic language used in and mystical meaning behind the spirituals. These songs, as McLaughlin notes, were "born out of the aches, pains, and joys of existence." However, in the tradition of philosophical personalism, McLaughlin emphasizes that the spirituals express an intuitive personal experience that African American slaves had with

God. When we unveil the mystical meaning of the spirituals, McLaughlin argues, we can see the spirituals as expressing the "direct communion of the soul with God" (McLaughlin 1963, 69).

Several African American religious journals provided outlets for Black philosophers. The *AME Church Review*, for instance, was a rich source of philosophical works by African American thinkers. Given the religious basis of the journal, idealism emerged as the dominant philosophical perspective. In his article on the "Philosophy of Progress" (1893), D. J. Jordan argues, "Philosophers tell us of the inertia of matter. According to the definition of inertia their teaching is correct; but no matter in all creation is inert; every particle and atom is acting upon every other."[9] Jordan eschews mechanical determinism and goes on to draw from his dialectical premise an ontological principle, which in turn constitutes a social philosophical perspective that conceptualizes how Black progress attains realization in the very process of history. Furthermore, we find in the pages of this religious journal an intriguing debate over the validity of Darwin's theory of evolution.[10]

While research opportunities for African American philosophers were restricted, a considerable number of these figures were pivotal mentors to social activists. An advocate of the philosophy of nonviolence with social democratic leanings, Samuel Williams was a key mentor to Martin Luther King Jr. King gained a philosophical foundation for his views on nonviolence from Williams's lectures and discussions. George D. Kelsey was another faculty member in the Philosophy and Religion Department of Morehouse College whose ideas contributed to King's development as an advocate of the philosophy of nonviolence; his role as a philosopher of nonviolence is a vital yet neglected chapter in the history of African American philosophy. Kelsey received his Ph.D. in philosophy from Yale in 1946 and would go on to write an important book representative of the Christian conception of nonviolence. Kelsey's *Racism and the Christian Understanding of Man* is a significant text for understanding African American contributions to the philosophy of nonviolence. William Stuart Nelson—who at Howard University developed the first academic course on the philosophy of nonviolence at an institution of higher education—advised King on the principles of nonviolence during the Montgomery bus boycott. Nelson was also founding editor of *The Journal of Religious Thought*, which remains a major source for intellectual discussion in the philosophy of religion. The import of Black journals such as *The Journal of Religious Thought* for understanding the history of African American philosophical inquiry cannot be overstated.

9. See Jordan 1893.

10. In addition to the *AME Church Review* and the *Journal of Religious Thought*, African-American journals such as the *Quarterly Review of Higher Education Among Negroes, Journal of Negro Education, Phylon, Freedomways, Journal of Negro History, Negro History Bulletin*, and *Western Journal of Black Studies* (among others) often served as the publishing outlets for African American work in philosophy (See Wiggins 1936; Golightly 1942; Locke 1950; Holmes 1965; Fontaine 1970; and Frye 1977).

What Is African American Philosophy?

To speak of African American philosophy could convey the impression that African American philosophers have a common philosophical perspective. In its most extreme presentation, African American philosophy is thought to be simply a system of collective thought, spontaneous, implicit, and unchanging, to which all Blacks adhere. In reaction to the false universalism of Western philosophy, proponents of Afrocentrism (the distant cousins of ethnophilosophy) such as Molefi Asante have argued along these lines.

A host of African American philosophers have tried to engage metaphilosophical questions such as, "What is African American philosophy?" and "What does it mean to be a philosopher of African descent in the American empire?"[11] Some years ago, William Banner took a stance against adjoining philosophy in any way to blackness. On the other hand, Roy D. Morrison envisioned Black philosophy as "an important instrument in the struggle for cultural and religious liberation" (Morrison 1976, 11).

Charles Mills suggests that all philosophical inquiry by African Americans has as its organizing principle subpersonhood. According to Mills, the notion of subpersonhood captures the defining features of the African American experience under White supremacy: "white racism so structured the world as to have negative ramifications for every sphere of black life—juridical standing, moral status, personal/racial identity, epistemic reliability, existential plight, political inclusion, social metaphysics, sexual relations, aesthetic worth" (Mills 1998, 6). Mills concludes, "African-American philosophy is thus inherently, definitionally *oppositional*, the philosophy produced by property that does not remain silent but insists on speaking and contesting its status" (Mills, 1998, 9).

Leonard Harris, taking up this theme, argues in *Philosophy Born of Struggle* (1983) that "a good deal of philosophy from the African-American heritage is a function of the history of the struggle to overcome adversity and to create" (Allen 1991, 273). Harris's view implies that African American philosophy is born of struggle against academic racism and the conceptual Whiteness of philosophy as a discipline. Hence, African American philosophy has a value commitment to serve the militant struggle of Black people. In a similar vein, Lucius Outlaw argues, "this issue of 'Black philosophy' is the expansion of the continuing history-making struggles of African and African-descended peoples in this country (and elsewhere) to achieve progressively liberated existence as conceived in various ways" (Outlaw 1996, 23).

Cornel West defends a similar view in "Philosophy and the Afro-American Experience" (1977–1978). In addressing the metaphilosophical question, "How does philosophy relate to the Afro-American experience?" West draws from Heidegger, Wittgenstein, and Dewey because they are all essentially "critical" of the Cartesian

11. West 1995, 356. See, for example, Jones 1977–1978; West 1977–1978; Outlaw 1992–93.

Weltanschauung, which posits philosophical problems as independent of culture, society, and history. West's utilization of Heideggerian, Wittgensteinian, and Deweyian resources results in an African American philosophy that is an "interpretation of Afro-American history, highlighting the cultural heritage and political struggles, which provides desirable norms that should regulate responses to particular challenges confronting Afro-Americans" (West 1977–1978, 122–123).

In contrast to these views, William R. Jones and John McClendon argue that African American philosophy should not be taken to mean a collective worldview or community with a shared metaphysics and *philosophical* vocabulary. After all, there are philosophers of African descent who are Marxists, existentialists, phenomenologists, and pragmatists who conceptually dwell within different and conflicting discourse communities. Jones's pioneering essay "The Legitimacy and Necessity of Black Philosophy: Some Preliminary Considerations" (1977–1978) argues that Black philosophy is another instance of the concrete particularity that in fact grounds philosophy in all of its universality.

Jones argues that the problem with the concept of "Black" in Black philosophy centers on the confusion of the meaning of "Black." Where "Black" is thought of as "exclusively a *racial* designation and, accordingly, race is the necessary organizing principle of a black philosophy...however...'black' connotes an ethnic or cultural—not a racial—group. The experience, history, and culture are the controlling categories for a black philosophy—not chromosomes" (Jones 1977–1978, 152). Jones suggests that the concept of "Black" in Black philosophy refers to such factors as author, audience, ancestry, accent, and antagonist. He explains "the intent appears to be one or more of the following: to identify that the author is black, i.e. a member of a particular ethnic community, that his primary, though not exclusive, audience is the black community, that the point of departure for his philosophizing or the tradition from which he speaks or the world-view he seeks to articulate can be called in some sense the black experience.... Special attention must be to "black" as a designation of the antagonist.... Accordingly, to call for a black philosophy, from this perspective, is to launch an implicit attack on racism in philosophy, especially in its conceptual, research, curricular, and institutional expressions" (Jones 1977–1978, 153). Hence, on this view, Black philosophy is simply philosophy that engages the Black experience and condition rather than a case of representing a unitary philosophical perspective, which is shared by all or even most Black people. In this connection, McClendon draws an important distinction between a *Black philosophical perspective* and the *philosophical comprehension of the Black experience*. As McClendon further explains:

> It is the case that Blackness provides my motivation (for doing philosophy) but not my (philosophical) orientation, that is, my specified philosophical perspective. For me, the issue is not about thinking in Black philosophical terms; rather it is to think philosophically about Blackness. So, therefore, even though I disagree with the Afrocentric notion that one must think in black or African modes of philosophizing, I do not accept William Banner's position that Blackness is outside of the concerns of philosophical thought and investigation.

> What it means to be Black is a philosophical question and my Blackness cannot be separated from what motivates and informs my philosophical research. (in Yancy 2005, 284)

So, while the history of African American philosophers is evidently tied to the material context of academic racism, it is important to see that not all African American philosophers resisted academic racism. In this respect, African American philosophy is intimately tied to African American intellectual history and culture. There are two salient, opposing (yet dialectically related) traditions within African American political and intellectual culture: one of accommodation and another of resistance to exploitation and oppression. The dialectic of accommodation and resistance contrasts with the more popular antithesis between assimilationist (integrationist) and separatist thought.[12]

Bernard Boxill deploys the assimilationist/separatist contrast. According to Boxill, "The history of African American political thought can be divided into two great traditions—the assimilationist and the separatist" (Boxill 1992–1993, 119). He adds that the differences holding between the two can extend beyond strategic concerns and may involve differences respecting ethics and philosophical anthropology. Cornel West follows Boxill along a similar path: the center of West's analysis is the W. E. B. Du Bois/Booker T. Washington debate. West views the Du Bois/Washington debate as essentially about the "framework for inclusionary African practices in the United States. The numerous black ideological battles between integrationism and nationalism, accomodationism and separatism are but versions and variations of the Washington/Du Bois debate" (West 1982, 40). Here West employs accommodationism as antithetical to separatism rather than the concept of resistance.

The assimilationist/separatist distinction, however, for some scholars is not entirely satisfactory as a lens through which to understand African American philosophy. This is because separatism is not inconsistent with an accommodationist (or conservative) posture.[13] The Nation of Islam's hostility toward "White devils" is an emotional substitute for political activism and essentially camouflages their avoidance of a political confrontation with racism. Elijah Muhammad's separatism has as its upshot the support of Black capitalism. In effect, Muhammad argues that racism is the manifestation of divine punishment and that racism actually functions as an opportunity for African Americans to begin the needed preparation for greater things in heaven.

Although it could be argued that Elijah Muhammad's "philosophy was born of struggle," its substance is emphatically accommodationist. Despite certain Black

12. McClendon 2004, 308–309. Although McGary makes a clear distinction between integration and assimilation, he acknowledges that oftentimes the two categories are conflated in discussions on separatism and integration. This is why we use the open parentheses around integration. Consult McGary 1983, 199–211.

13. West 1982, 40. For treatment of class affinities, Waldstreicher 1997, 317. The work of Wilson Moses clearly demonstrates that much of nineteenth-century Black Nationalist political philosophy, far from being progressive, was actually reactionary in character. See Moses 1988; McClendon 2003.

Nationalist presumptions about integrationism as intrinsically conservative, neither separatism nor integrationism stands on its own merits as progressive or conservative (Pinn 2002, 27–28). In contrast to the accommodationist tradition, Broadus Butler emphasizes the resistance tradition, arguing that the "preponderance of Black American philosophical inquiry...has been directed primarily toward change in the human condition and toward social and legal change in the pursuit of a clarification and perfection of the democratic ideal of justice. That pursuit always has combined ontological analysis with moral prescription" (Butler, in Harris 1983, 1).

African American Philosophical Perspectives and Trends

Given the plurality of philosophical perspectives, what are the dominant philosophical orientations, schools of thought, and trends among African American philosophers? In what follows we suggest the outlines of some of the variety of recent African American philosophical perspectives and trends.

Over the years, African American philosophers have undertaken the investigation of the philosophical ideas associated with particular Black thinkers. Perhaps the most widely studied African American philosopher is the first Black Rhodes scholar Alain Locke. He did considerable work in the area of value theory, particularly value relativism and cultural pluralism. Locke's widely published essay, "Values and Imperative" (1935), sought to ground truth and value on what he termed "feeling-attitudes and dispositional imperatives of action-choices."

William R. Jones's text, *Is God a White Racist?* is an example of African American philosophy of religion. Jones examines theodicy as the decisive category and methodological problematic for Black theology. Jones questions whether Black theology can be constructed on the foundation of a belief in an omnibenevolent God who has dominion over human history.

George G. M. James's *Stolen Legacy* set forth a radical departure from traditional scholarship in the history of philosophy. James outlines a controversial account of how Greek thought is largely borrowed from Egyptian philosophy. Consequently, the origins of philosophy, from James's perspective, rest in Egypt, not Greece. In the tradition of African Redemptionism, James argues that his book would enlighten the world "as to the real truth about the place of the African Continent in the history of civilization" and "race relations should tend to be normal and peaceful" (James 1954, 157).

Philosophers have also pursued research in the area of Black Studies. Charles Frye's pioneering work in the area of the African American Studies sought to anchor the philosophy of African American Studies in the tradition of hermetic idealism and mysticism (Frye 1977). This idealist tradition in the philosophy of African

American Studies continues with Jane and Lewis R. Gordon's recent efforts in *Not Only the Master's Tools: African American Studies in Theory and Practice* (2006).

African American philosophers are furthermore identified with a variety of schools of thought, such as pragmatism, personalism, humanism, ethnophilosophy, existentialism, phenomenology, analytic philosophy, and Marxism, to name only a few. The tradition of pragmatism in African American philosophy begins with Alain Locke. Arguably the most prominent African American pragmatist since Locke is Cornel West. Following Richard Rorty, West calls for a pragmatic reconstruction of philosophy. In a similar vein, Victor Anderson, Paul C. Taylor, Leonard Harris, and Eddie Glaude Jr. have advanced pragmatism to address philosophical problems associated with African American life and culture.

Some African American philosophers utilize the Anglo-analytical approach to the philosophy of the Black experience. The major proponents of this approach are Bernard Boxill, Tommy Lott, Howard McGary, Bill Lawson, Rodney Roberts, Adrian Piper, John Pittman, Laurence Thomas, Charles Mills, and Naomi Zack. Mills exemplifies this approach with his usage of contractarianism to understand the dynamics of White supremacy. In his magnum opus, *The Racial Contract*, Mills offers a conceptual reconsideration of contractarianism beyond the constraints of social contract theory to the submerged notion of the "the racial contract." He attempts to articulate a theory of justice that is attuned to the historical realities of White supremacy (Mills 1997).

Still other African American philosophers draw on the resources of the continental philosophical tradition, understanding the Black experience in terms of the theories and methods of phenomenology, existentialism, hermeneutics, structuralism, poststructuralism, French feminism, and the critical theory of the Frankfurt School. Some of the major proponents of this approach include Jesse McDade, Robert Gooding-Williams, Frank Kirkland, Richard McKinney, Lucius Outlaw Jr., Jaqueline R. Scott, Anika Mann, Robert Birt, George Yancy, Paget Henry, and Lewis Gordon. Lucius Outlaw, for instance, articulates a hermeneutics of the Black experience drawing on the work of Alfred Schutz (Outlaw 1996). McKinney was concerned with how philosophy, and specifically existentialism, could be linked to the civil rights movement, a project he pursued in his "Existential Ethics and the Protest Movement" in the *Journal of Religious Thought* (1965–1966). McDade's "Toward an Ontology of Negritude" is concerned with establishing a philosophical basis for a "black perspective." He holds to the notion that all Black people, regardless of demographic distinctiveness, share a "common Weltanschauung," or Black perspective (McDade 1977–1978; Gordon 1997; Yancy 2009).

Finally, there are African American Marxists in the academy who take a dialectical materialist philosophical perspective on the Black experience. These philosophers include Hubert Harrison, Eugene C. Holmes, C. L. R. James, Angela Davis, John H. McClendon, and Stephen C. Ferguson. Special mention should be made of Holmes, who made significant progress in developing a materialist conception of space and time. He also did work in the general area of the philosophy of the Black experience writing essays on African American sociopolitical philosophy, the aesthetics of Black art, and thinkers such as W. E. B. Du Bois, Langston Hughes, and Alain Locke. The Marxist philosopher and historian C. L. R. James embarked on an investigation of the role of dialectics in political struggle in his magnum opus, *Notes on Dialectics: Hegel-Marx-Lenin*. Angela Davis, one of the most widely known among past Communists of African American descent, has a distinguished career in activism and scholarship challenging racism, sexism, and supporting Black political prisoners (James 1998).

The various philosophers and philosophical trends discussed here are only a sample of the rich diversity of the overall field. The African American philosophical heritage is rich and vast, and constantly developing. For additional information, the reader should consult the Bibliography and Suggested Readings.

BIBLIOGRAPHY AND SUGGESTED READINGS

Allen, Norm R., Jr. (1991) "Leonard Harris on the Life and Work of Alain Locke." In *African-American Humanism: An Anthology*, edited by Norm R. Allen, Jr. Amherst, NY: Prometheus Books, 269–275.

Bernasconi, Robert, and Sybol Cook (eds.). (2003) *Race and Racism in Continental Philosophy*. Bloomington, IN: University of Indiana Press.

Boxill, Bernard R. (1984) *Blacks and Social Justice*. Totowa, NJ: Rowman and Allanheld.

———. (1992–1993) "Two Traditions in African American Political Philosophy." *The Philosophical Forum* 24(1–3), 119–135.

Crummell, Alexander. (1898) "Civilization, the Primal Need of the Race." In *American Negro Academy Occasional Papers, No. 3*. Washington, DC: The American Negro Academy.

Ferguson, Stephen C. (2003) "C. L. R. James, Marxism and Freedom." *American Philosophical Association Newsletter on Philosophy and the Black Experience* 2(2), 72–82.

Fleming, John E. (1974) *The Lengthening Shadow of Slavery*. Washington, DC: Howard University Press.

Fontaine, William T. (1970) "An Interpretation of Contemporary Negro Thought from the Standpoint of the Sociology of Knowledge." *Journal of Negro History* 25(1), 6–13.

Frye, Charles. (1977) "Black Studies: Definition and Administrative Model." *Western Journal of Black Studies* 1(2), 93–97.

———. (1978) *Towards a Philosophy of Black Studies*. San Francisco, CA: R & E Research Associates.

Golightly, Cornelius. (1942) "Negro Higher Education and Democratic Negro Morale." *Journal of Negro Education* 11(3), 322–328.

Gordon, Lewis R. (ed.). (1997) *Existence in Black: An Anthology of Black Existential Philosophy*. New York: Routledge.

——— (ed.). (2006) *Not Only the Master's Tools: African American Studies in Theory and Practice*. Boulder, CO: Paradigm Publishers.

Harris, Leonard (ed.). (1983) *Philosophy Born of Struggle*. Dubuque, IA: Kendall-Hunt.

———. (1995) "'Believe It or Not' or The Ku Klux Klan and American Philosophy Exposed." *American Philosophical Association Newsletter on Philosophy and the Black Experience* 68(5), 133–137.

HARRIS, LEONARD, and CHARLES MOLESWORTH. (2009) *Alain L. Locke: The Biography of a Philosopher*. Chicago, IL: University of Chicago Press.

HOLMES, EUGENE C. (1965) "W.E.B. Du Bois: Philosopher." *Freedomways* 5(1).

JACKSON, JOHN G. (1987) *Hubert Henry Harrison: The Black Socrates*. Austin, TX: American Atheist Press.

JAMES, GEORGE. G. M. (1954) *Stolen Legacy*. New York: Philosophical Library.

JAMES, JOY (ed.). (1998) *The Angela Davis Reader*. Oxford: Blackwell Publishers.

JOHNSON, PERCY E. (ed.). (1970) *Afro-American Philosophies: From Jupiter Hammon to Eugene C. Holmes*. Upper Montclair, NJ: Montclair State College.

JONES, WILLIAM R. (1974) *Is God a White Racist? A Preamble to Black Theology* Boston, MA: Beacon Press.

———. (1977–1978) "The Legitimacy and Necessity of Black Philosophy: Some Preliminary Considerations." *The Philosophical Forum* 9(2/3), 117–148.

JORDAN, D. J. (1893) "Philosophy of Progress." *The A.M.E. Church Review* (10)1.

KUKLICK, BRUCE. (2001) *A History of Philosophy in America, 1720–2000*. New York: Oxford University Press.

———. (2008) *Black Philosopher, White Academy: The Career of William Fontaine*. Philadelphia, PA: University of Pennsylvania Press.

LAWSON, BILL E., and FRANK M. KIRKLAND (eds.). (1999) *Frederick Douglass: A Critical Reader*. Malden, MA: Blackwell Publishers.

LOCKE, ALAIN. (1935) "Values and Imperatives." In *American Philosophy, Today and Tomorrow*, edited by Sidney Hook and Horace M. Kallen. New York: Lee Furman, 313–333.

———. (1950) "Self-Criticism: The Third Dimension in Culture." *Phylon* 11, 391–394.

LOTT, TOMMY L., and JOHN P. PITTMAN (eds.). (2005) *A Companion to African-American Philosophy*. Malden, MA: Blackwell Publishers.

MASON, ERNEST. "Alain Locke's Philosophy of Value." In *Alain Locke*, edited by R. J. Linnemann. Baton Rouge, LA: Louisiana State University, 1–16.

MCCLENDON, JOHN H. (1982) "The Afro-American Philosopher and the Philosophy of the Black Experience: A Bibliographical Essay on a Neglected Topic Both in Philosophy and Black Studies." *Sage Race Relations Abstracts* 7(4), 1–51.

———. (1983) "Eugene Clay Holmes: Black Marxist Philosopher." In *Philosophy Born of Struggle*, edited by Leonard Harris. Dubuque, IA: Kendall-Hunt, 36–50.

———. (1995) "The Afrocentric Project: The Quest for Particularity and the Negation of Objectivity." *Explorations in Ethnic Studies* (Special Issue Ethnicity: Global Perspectives) 18(1), 19–35.

———. (2003) "From Cultural Nationalism to Cultural Criticism: Philosophical Idealism, Paradigmatic Illusions and the Politics of Identity." In *Decolonizing the Academy: African Diaspora Studies*, edited by Carol Boyce Davies. Trenton, NJ: Africa World Press, 3–26.

———. (2004) "On the Nature of Whiteness and the Ontology of Race: Toward a Dialectical Materialist Analysis." In *What White Looks Like: African-American Philosophers on the Whiteness Question*, edited by George Yancy. New York: Routledge.

———. (2005) *C. L. R. James's Notes on Dialectics: Left-Hegelianism or Marxism-Leninism?* Lanham, MD: Lexington Books.

———. (2010) "On the Politics of Professional Philosophy: The Plight of the African American Philosopher. *Latin-American and African-American Philosophers on the Profession of Philosophy*, edited by George Yancy. Albany, NY: SUNY Press.

MCDADE, JESSE. (1977–1978) "Toward an Ontology of Negritude." *The Philosophical Forum* 9(2–3).

McGary, Howard. (1983) "Racial Integration and Racial Separatism: Conceptual Clarifications." In *Philosophy Born of Struggle*, edited by Leonard Harris. Dubuque, IA: Kendall/Hunt Publishing Company, 199–211.
McGary, Howard, and Bill E. Lawson. (1992) *Between Slavery and Freedom: Philosophy and American Slavery*. Bloomington, IN: Indiana University Press.
McKinney, Richard. (1965–1966) "Existential Ethics and the Protest Movement." *Journal of Religious Thought* 22(2).
McLaughlin, Wayman B. (1963) "Symbolism and Mysticism in the Spirituals." *Phylon* 24(1), 69–77.
Mills, Charles W. (1997) *The Racial Contract*. Ithaca, NY: Cornell University Press.
———. (1998) *Blackness Visible: Essays on Philosophy and Race*. Ithaca, NY: Cornell University Press.
Morrison, Roy D. (1976) "Black Philosophy: An Instrument for Cultural and Religious Liberation." *Journal of Religious Thought* 33(1), 11–25.
Moses, Wilson J. (1988) *The Golden Age of Black Nationalism, 1850–1925*. New York: Oxford University Press.
———. (1989) *Alexander Crummell: A Study of Civilization and Discontent*. New York: Oxford University Press.
O'Toole, James. (2002) *Passing for White: Race, Religion, and the Healy Family, 1820–1920*. Amherst, MA: University of Massachusetts Press.
Outlaw, Lucius. (1992–1993) "African, African American, Africana Philosophy." *The Philosophical Forum* 24(1–3), 63–93.
———. (1996) *On Race and Philosophy*. New York: Routledge.
———. (2007) "What is Africana Philosophy?" In *Philosophy in Multiple Voices*, edited by George Yancy. Lanham, MD: Rowman and Littlefield, 109–143.
Perry, Jeffrey B. (2001) *A Hubert Harrison Reader*. Middletown, CT: Wesleyan University Press.
Pinn, Anthony. (2002) *Moral Evil and Redemptive Suffering*. Tallahassee, FL: University Press of Florida.
Pittman, John P. (ed.). (1997) *African-American Perspectives and Philosophical Traditions*. New York: Routledge.
Valls, Andrew (ed.). (2005) *Race and Racism in Modern Philosophy*. Ithaca, NY: Cornell University Press.
Waldstreicher, David. (1997) *In the Midst of Perpetual Fetes: The Making of American Nationalism, 1776–1820*. Chapel Hill, NC: Omohundro Institute of Early American History and Culture.
Ward, J. K., and T. Lott (eds.). (2002) *Philosophers on Race: Critical Essays*. Malden, MA: Blackwell.
West, Cornel. (1977–1978) "Philosophy and the Afro-American Experience." *The Philosophical Forum* 9(2–3), 117–148.
———. (1982) *Prophesy Deliverance! An Afro-American Revolutionary Christianity*. Philadelphia, PA: The Westminister Press.
———. (1989) *The American Evasion of Philosophy: A Genealogy of Pragmatism*. Madison, WI: University of Wisconsin Press.
———. (1993) *Race Matters*. Boston, MA: Beacon Press.
———. (1995) "The Black Underclass and Black Philosophers." In *I Am Because We Are: Reading in Black Philosophy*, edited by Fred Lee Hord (Mzee Lasana Okpara) and Jonathan Scott Lee. Amherst, MA: University of Massachusetts Press.

WIGGINS, FORREST O. (1936) "Reflections on Education." *Quarterly Review of Higher Education Among Negroes* 13(1).

WINSTON, MICHAEL R. (1971) "Through the Back Door: Academic Racism and the Negro Scholar in Historical Perspective." *Daedalus* 100(3).

YANCY, GEORGE (ed.). (1998) *African-American Philosophers: 17 Conversations*. New York: Routledge.

———. (2001a) *Cornel West: A Critical Reader*. Malden, MA: Blackwell.

YANCY, GEORGE. (2001b) "History: On the Power of Black Aesthetic Ideals: Thomas Nelson Baker as Preacher and Philosopher." *AME Church Review* (October-December), 50–67.

YANCY, GEORGE (ed.). (2004) *What White Looks Like: African-American Philosophers on the Whiteness Question*. New York: Routledge.

———. (2005) *White on White, Black on Black*. Lanham, MD: Rowman and Littlefield.

———. (2009) *Black Bodies, White Gaze: The Continuing Significance of Race*. Lanham, MD: Rowman and Littlefield.

ZACK, NAOMI (ed.). (2000) *Women of Color and Philosophy: A Critical Reader*. Malden, MA: Wiley-Blackwell.

CHAPTER 37

RACE IN CONTEMPORARY PHILOSOPHY

ALBERT MOSLEY

TRADITIONAL racial realists assert that human beings are naturally divided into different races (realism), and that each race has distinctive physical and behavioral qualities shared by every member of the race (essentialism). Racists insist, not only that races are real and distinct, but that certain races are superior to and destined to rule over other races (heirachialism). Racists typically argue that the most prominent human achievements of a group are the result of inherited behavioral and morphological traits that can be only minimally influenced by environmental changes (determinism). Just as the webbed feet and love of water are inherited traits of the Labrador, so too, they claim, are fast twitch muscles and love of running inherited by Africans, and large brains and a love of science inherited by Europeans and East Asians (Sarich and Miele 2004). Many claim to be racialist rather than racist, arguing that group differences are real, but making no judgement of inferiority or superiority concerning differences.

Genetic determinism has come increasingly under attack, especially since Franz Boas showed in the early twentieth century how the cranial morphology of European ethnic groups changed dramatically before and after immigration. The atrocities of the Holocaust led many to deny that the Jews and Aryans were races, and many went further to deny that races exist altogether. The existence of races was construed as being of the same kind as the existence of witches: while witchcraft as a social practice exists (and should be eradicated), witches do not exist; and while racism as a social practice exists (and should be eradicated), races do not exist (Appiah 1999; Blum 2002).

It is from this perspective that many have called for a moratorium on the use of racial categories. They have argued that, while there may be geographical differences in the distribution of genetic variations, those differences do not correspond to the racial and ethnic categories we use to define our social identities (Rotimi 2004). Just as we have abandoned the use of phlogiston to explain combustion, race eliminativists argue that we need a paradigm shift that abandons altogether the use of racial categories to explain human differences (Royal and Dunston 2004). In this way, racists would be denied a necessary assumption of their position. Many who argue for eliminating racial categories go even further and characterize as racist anyone who advocates maintaining the use of racial categories.

Thus, Naomi Zack declares the general thesis of her book *Race and Mixed Race* to be "that black and white racial designations are themselves racist because the concept of race does not have an adequate scientific foundation" (Zack 1993, 3). Likewise, Anthony Appiah argues that racial classifications should be dropped because "the interests, in the political sense, that are served by talk of race are reactionary" (Appiah 1992, 10). Anthropologist Alan Goodman suggests that "those who continue to see race in biology but mean no harm by it are nothing more than 'kind racists.' By continuing to legitimize race, they inadvertently aid 'mean racists' who wish to do harm" (Goodman 1997, 25).

While the intent to eliminate racism by eliminating the use of racial categories is well intentioned, there remain reputable biologists, geneticists, and physical anthropologists who reject racism but also reject the claim that there is no biological rationale for the use of racial categories. Race conservationists argue that there are good biological and socio-historical reasons for distinguishing different human populations using traditional racial and ethnic categories, while simultaneously rejecting the traditional ideological rationales associated with those distinctions. To illustrate, most no longer believe that Africans, Asians, Europeans, and Native Americans are the progeny of Ham, Japheth, and Shem (the three sons of Noah). Nonetheless, it is true that Europeans are more than ten times more likely to have blood type A than Native Americans, East Asians are more than twice as likely to have blood type B compared with Europeans, and 98% of Native Americans have blood type O (Cavalli-Sforza 2000).

Suppose three individuals desperately in need of a blood transfusion self-identified as European, East Asian, and Native American, but we did not have the facilities to definitely determine the blood type of each individual. If we had one pint of A blood, one pint of B blood, and one pint of O blood, which individuals would be most likely to benefit from receiving which types of blood? This example may seem far-fetched, but physicians are often in situations where they do not have complete information and must make "educated guesses." We cannot expect them to always guess correctly, but we should expect them to make judgments that (over a large number of cases) are better than would be expected by chance.

Likewise, though many claim that differences between European ethnic groups are purely social, it is nonetheless true that the frequency of Rh-negative individuals among the Basques is almost three times higher than the frequency of such individuals among the Lapps (Cavalli-Sforza 2000). Why, then, should we deny that there is a biological rationale for distinguishing Basques and Lapps? For neo-pragmatists in contemporary philosophy of science, the key to whether or not racial categories are real is whether they are helpful. In medicine, if diagnoses and treatments are not improved by the use of racial categories, then they should be discarded. But if outcomes are improved beyond what would be expected by chance, the occurrence of misdiagnoses is no argument against their continued use.

Essentialist vs. Populational Definitions

The modern synthesis in biology replaced essentialist and typological conceptions of race with populational and phylogenic accounts. The essentialist belief that there is a "race gene," trait, or set of traits that is exclusive to each race, and that is the basis for all significant differences in physical and social differences between races, was rejected. Instead, a population perspective encourages us to think of races as ancestrally related, endogenous, inbreeding groups that differ by having a set of traits that occurs with higher frequency within one group compared with other such groups (Kitcher 2003; Outlaw 1996). Thus, while it is true that 97% of cases of sickle cell anemia in the United States occur among African Americans, it does not follow that sickle cell anemia in the United States only occurs among African Americans. A white patient afflicted with sickle cell anemia might well be misdiagnosed because the attending physician too strongly associates sickle cell with Africans rather than Europeans. But this is a flaw in racial essentialism, identifying one trait or disease exclusively with a particular race, rather than a flaw inherent in the use of racial categories.

Race and Biology

One of the most cited arguments against the existence of races is that there is more variation within so-called races than between races. Thus, two individuals chosen randomly from within a particular race are likely to be as different for a particular gene as two individuals randomly chosen from two different races. Eighty-five percent of all variation among humans occurs within each race, and only some 6 to 7 percent of human variation is accountable for on the basis of racial differences. This means that a randomly picked group of males and females from within a particular race could, if they became a founder population, reproduce 85 percent of all human genetic variation. This is taken to imply that most differences between human beings are independent of racial categories, and therefore render those categories superfluous. "Human racial classification is of no social value and is positively destructive of social and human relations. Since such racial classification is now seen to be of virtually no genetic or taxonomic significance either, no justification can be offered for its continuance" (Lewontin 1972, 397) This argument, proposed by R. C. Lewontin, has been used time and time again to justify the claim that racial categories are merely social constructs designed to justify exploitation, and otherwise have no basis in biology.

Lewontin's analysis does show that human beings are more alike than different. But conservationists reject the further inference that the differences that exist are insignificant. For, in fact, differences in the relative frequency of certain rare alleles (variants of a particular gene) tend to cluster into different subpopulations that correspond to the major continental races of Europe, Africa, East Asia, Australasia, and the Americas (Risch et al. 2002; Edwards 2003).

> Small differences in allele frequency... are still sufficient for generating clusters of individuals that correspond closely with groups defined by continental ancestry or self-identified race or ethnicity. The joint effect of small differences in allele frequencies at multiple neutral genetic markers provides the power to cluster individuals. (Mountain and Risch 2004, 551)

Studies in population genetics have shown that continentally separated groups exhibit the highest degrees of genetic clustering, and those clusters correspond to the five major racial groups: Africans, Europeans, Asians, Pacific Islanders-Australian Aborigines, and Native Americans. The major races consist of groups that, prior to the sixteenth century, were relatively isolated from one another. And within the major races there are ethnic groups that also were reproductively isolated from other groups because of geographic or cultural barriers. The genetic distance between these groups is often small, but real nonetheless. Genetic variation is geographically structured, as expected from partial isolation of human populations during much of their history. Because our traditional concepts of race are similarly correlated with geography, it is inaccurate to state that race is "biologically meaningless" (Jorde and Wooding 2004).

Using our current genetics and evolutionary biology, Robin Andreasen has proposed defining human races as clades, groups of modern homo-sapiens that are either African or founded by subpopulations from Africa that have evolved outside of Africa. Andreasen defines races as local populations that have branched off from a parent population and are reproductively isolated from the parent population and other local populations. When two populations have branched off from one another, mutations and drift increase their differences in certain gene frequencies, and the genetic distance between them can be used to estimate the amount of time they have been separated.

Using techniques of measuring genetic distance, a phylogenetic tree can be constructed showing a group splitting off from Africans some 200,000 years ago, another major split taking place some 100,000 years ago between South East Asians and North East Asians, and a split between North East Asians, Caucasians, and Native Americans some 40,000 years ago. These populations existed in relative isolation from one another until the fifteenth century and the age of European expansion.

Andreasen concludes that cladistic classification, in conjunction with current genetics, provides "a biologically objective definition of race. Races are...ancestor-descendant sequences of breeding populations, or groups of such sequences, that share a common origin" (Andreasen 1998, 214). But extensive interbreeding brought about by colonialism, imperialism, and globalization has blurred racial differences, so that though races once existed, Andreasen believes they exist no more.

Using measures of genetic distance to trace human evolutionary history, molecular biologists demonstrate how clades have split into clusters of contemporary human populations: Africans, non-European Caucasoids, Europeans, Amerindians, Arctic North East Asians, North East Asians, South East Asians, Pacific Islanders, and New Guineans and Australians. But Joshua Glasgow, in a recent article in the *Journal of Philosophy*, objects that this is nine races, while our common-sense notion of races "does not normally contain the nine races identified" (Glasgow 2003, 458–59).

Glasgow considers the notion that there are essentially three major races to be typical of common-sense notions: African, Asian, and Caucasian. While acknowledging that there is no common-sense agreement on how many races there are, he nonetheless considers it safe to say that "it is rare to hear a folk notion of race that involves more than four or five races." The central flaw of the cladistic approach, Glasgow concludes, is that the cladistic concept of race carves our ancestors into breeding populations, "but these populations are not what we call 'races.'" Likewise, while Naomi Zack acknowledges that cladism provides a way of giving race a biological basis, she denies that this grounds our current common-sense notions of race. Why? Because cladistics is based on changes in mitochondrial DNA, and this does not preserve the dependence of common-sense notions on observable phenic differences (Zack 2002).

But the claim that appearances play the major role in folk conceptions of race is debatable. Folk conceptions of racial identity have typically made ancestry and linage as, if not more, important than phenic similarities. The Jews were not considered a different race because they looked different from the Germans around them. Nor were the Irish considered a different race by Anglo-Saxon Englishmen because they had such dissimilar phenotypes. And Walter White, past president of the NAACP, was phenically indistinguishable from an American of European descent. Nonetheless, by the rule of hypo-descent, he was considered, by himself and others, as an African American.

In the science of human anthropology, paleontologists have favored definitions based on morphological similarities, while population geneticists have favored concepts defined around genealogical connections. Common sense, too, has vacillated between phenic and phylogenic considerations. A person's appearance is often taken as evidence of his or her ancestry, while knowing a person's ancestry is often taken as evidence for how that person is likely to act and look. But there is no doubt that ancestry plays an essential role in common-sense notions of race in Europe and the United States.

As Michael Root has argued, we should beware of assuming there is a concept of race that is true for all eras, places, and interests (Root 2005) Our ordinary conceptions combine elements from religion, science, business, and politics, and have never existed in isolation from other influences. Common-sense notions that classified whales to be more closely related to fish than to cows changed with the introduction of phylogenic considerations, and common-sense notions of race that classify African Americans and Australian Aborigines as more closely related than African Americans and European Americans must also change. What we mean by race should reflect current biology and current conceptions of justice.

Philip Kitcher proposes a definition of races as "reasonably reproductively isolated breeding populations" that is similar in many respects to Andreasen's. But in contrast to Andreasen, he argues that cultural barriers to interbreeding maintain a sufficient degree of genetic isolation between certain existing populations for those populations to be considered as races. For Kitcher, "the division of society into races on biological grounds maps onto a division into ethnic groups, ethnicities, marked out by alternative systems of cultural transmission" (Kitcher 2003, 233). Because economic inequalities, cultural differences, and racism make contact between Africans and other groups less likely, social mores act as isolating mechanisms that reinforce genetic distance. This provides an objective rationale for using the concept of race to identify biological divisions between contemporary African, European, and Asian Americans.

The racial ideologies that justified slavery and segregation have not simply disappeared, nor have their effects. Despite increasing rates of interracial marriage, African Americans remain an endogenous group in which 98% of African Americans marry other African Americans. Despite efforts to give racial categories objective definitions in terms of physical similarities, gene frequencies, and phylogenetic trees, our ordinary use of racial categories is overwhelmingly practical, varying by place, era, and social interest. Racial categories continue to shape our actions and the question is whether their use will be informed by current thinking or merely perpetuate historical biases and exclusions. Just as the assumption of Anglo-Saxon superiority justified the oppression of the Irish, so did the assumption that Europeans were superior to non-Europeans justify European colonization and imperialism. White supremacy induced poor Europeans to ally with rich Europeans in shifting the costs of modernity onto non-Europeans. The result is embedded in contemporary social practices determining how societies' opportunities and benefits are racially distributed (Harding 1993; Blaut 1993).

Social constructionists (Haslinger 2000, 2008; Mallon 2004, 2008) about race argue that the socio-historical forces that have shaped the distribution and inheritance of social wealth have exercised a far more important role than the biophysical factors that have shaped the distribution of alleles between different groups. Thus, many who are agnostic as to whether there is a legitimate biological basis for belief in the existence of races nonetheless insist on the social reality of races (Mills 1998; Taylor 2004; Blum 2002).

Social constructionists often use currency differences as a model of racial differences (Searle 1995). Clearly, differences in the physical constitution of money are not considered the cause of the differences in their exchange value. The difference in value between a $10 bill and a $100 bill does not derive from the differences in the physical constitution of the two bills. A counterfeit $100 bill could differ only slightly from an authentic $100, yet one is valuable and the other worthless. Even if two bills were physically identical, differences in the process by which they were produced could make one valuable and the other worthless. To illustrate, if X stole paper, ink, and press from the mint and produced bills indistinguishable from authentic bills, the illegally produced bills would still be worthless. It is social institutions and practices that make currencies valuable, not the physical constitution of the currencies. In a similar fashion, social constructionists argue that it is social institutions and practices that give racial significance to human groups, not the slight physical differences between them.

A typical ploy of racial determinists has been to use genetically based disparities such as the different rates of sickle cell anemia to construe social disparities as if they were genetically caused. Acknowledging the existence of differences in the frequency of certain rare alleles between races should not be used as an excuse to embrace genetic determinism and treat contingent social causes as if they were fixed and inevitable. For centuries, science has been used to legitimize unjust social arrangements and justify the most vicious forms of oppression on Africans and Native Americans. Portraying African and Native Americans as if they were genetically prone to higher rates of ill health, substance abuse, and criminal behavior continues a racist heritage in which science served the ideological function of justifying the "manifest destiny" of white supremacy (Lewontin 1993).

Racism has used biology to justify exploitative social arrangements by making it seem that social differences in the distribution of costs and benefits are primarily the effect of biological differences. Some contemporary philosophers continue to argue that the differential distribution of wealth between the races derives from genetically based differences in intelligence and moral worth (Levin 1997 Kershnar 2004; Pojman 1996). But the majority of contemporary philosophers, whether realists or constructionists, eliminativists or conservationists, reject the deterministic and hierarchical assumptions of racist thought.

BIBLIOGRAPHY AND SUGGESTED READINGS

ANDREASEN, ROBIN. (1998) "A New Perspective on the Race Debate." *British Journal for the Philosophy of Science* XLIX(2), June, 199–225.

———. (2000) "Race: Biological Reality or Social Construct." *Philosophy of Science* 67 (Proceedings), September, S653–S666.

APPIAH, K. ANTHONY. (1992) "Social Forces, 'Natural' Kinds." In *Exploitation and Exclusion: Race and Class in Contemporary US Society*, edited by Abebe Zegeye, Leonard Harris, and Julia Maxted. *African Discourse* series 3. Oxford: Hans Zell.

———. (1999) "Why There Are No Races." In *Racism*, edited by Leonard Harris. Amherst, NY: Humanity Books.

BLAUT, J. M. (1993) *The Colonizer's Model of the World*. New York: Guilford Press.

BLUM, LAWRENCE. (2002) *"I'm Not a Racist, But ...."* Ithaca, NY: Cornell University Press.

CAVALLI-SFORZA, LUIGI LUCA. (2000) *Genes, Peoples, and Language*. New York: North Point Press.

EDWARDS, A. W. F. (2003) "Human Genetic Diversity: Lewontin's Fallacy." *BioEssays* 25, 798–801.

GANNETT, LISA. (2001) "Racism and Human Genome Diversity Research: The Ethical Limits of Population Thinking." *Philosophy of Science* 68 (Proceedings), S479–S492.

———. (2004) "The Biological Reification of Race." *British Journal for the Philosophy of Science* 55, 323–345.

GLASGOW, JOSHUA. (2003) "On the New Biology of Race." *The Journal of Philosophy* 100, 456–474.

GOODMAN, ALAN. (1997) "Bred in the Bone?" *The Sciences* March.

HARDING, SANDRA. (1993) *The Racial Economy of Science*. Bloomington, IN: Indiana University Press

HASLINGER, SALLY. (2000) "Gender and Race: What Are They? What Do We Want Them to Be?" *Nous* 34(1), 31–55.

———. (2008) "A Social Constructionist Analysis of Race." In *Revisiting Race in a Genomic Age*, edited by Barbara Koenig, Sandra Lee, and Sarah Richardson. New Brunswick, NJ: Rutgers University Press.

JORDE, LYNN, and STEPHEN WOODING. (2004) "Genetic Variation, Classification and 'Race.'" *Nature Genetics Supplement* 36(11), November.

KERSHNAR, STEPHEN. (2004) *Justice for the Past*. New York: SUNY Press.

KITCHER, PHILIP. (1992) "Species." In *The Units of Evolution*, edited by Marc Ereshefsky. Boston, MA: MIT Press.

———. (2003) "Race, Ethnicity, Biology, Culture." *In Mendel's Mirror-Philosophical Reflections on Biology*. New York: Oxford University Press.

LEROI, ARMAND. (2005) "A Family Tree in Every Gene." *The New York Times*, March 14, A22–23.

LEWONTIN, R. C. (1972) "The Apportionment of Human Diversity." In *Evolutionary Biology*, edited by T. Dobzhansky, M. K. Hecht, and W. C. Steere. New York: Appleton-Century-Crofts, 381–398.

———. (1993) *Biology as Ideology*. New York: Harper.

LEVIN, MICHAEL. (1997) *Why Race Matters: Race Differences and What They Mean*. Santa Barbara, CA: Praeger Publishers.

MALLON, RON. (2004) "Passing, Traveling, and Reality: Social Construction and the Metaphysics of Race." *Nous* 38(4), 644–673.

———. (2008) "Naturalistic Approaches to Social Construction." *Stanford Encyclopedia of Philosophy*.

MILLS, CHARLES. (1998) "The Metaphysics of Race." In *Blackness Visible*. Ithaca, NY: Cornell University Press

MOUNTAIN, J. L., and NEIL RISCH. (2004) "Assessing Genetic Contributions to Phenotypic Differences among 'Racial' and 'Ethnic' Groups." *Nature Genetics* 36(11), November.

Pojman, Louis. (1996) "Are All Humans Equal?: A Critique of Contemporary Egalitarianism." In *EQUALITY: A READER*, edited by Robert Westmoreland and Louis Pojman. New York: Oxford University Press.

Outlaw, Lucius. (1996) *On Race and Philosophy*. New York: Routledge, ch. 6.

Risch, Neil, Esteban Burchard, Elad Ziv, and Hua Tang. (2002) "Categorization of Humans in Biomedical Research: Genes, Race, and Disease." http://genemebiology.com/2002/3/7/comment/2007.1

Root, Michael. (2005) "The Number of Black Widows in the National Academy of Sciences." *Philosophy of Science* 72(5), 1197–1207.

———. (2009) "Measurement Error in Racial and Ethnic Statistics"*Biology and Philosophy* 24 (11), June 375–385.

Rotimi, Charles. (2004) "Are Medical and Non-Medical Uses of Large-scale Genomic Markers Conflating Genetics and 'Race'?" *Nature Genetics Supplement* 36(11).

Royal, Charmaine, and Georgia Dunston. (2004) "Changing the Paradigm from 'Race' to Human Genome Variation." *Nature Genetics Supplement* 36(11).

Sarich, Vincent, and Frank Miele. (2004) *Race: The Reality of Human Differences*. New York: Basic Books.

Searle, John. (1995) *The Construction of Social Reality*. New York: The Free Press.

Taylor, Paul. (2004) *Race: A Philosophical Introduction*. Cambridge, UK: Blackwell Polity Press, ch. 3.

Zack, Naomi. (1993) *Race and Mixed Race*. Philadelphia, PA: Temple University Press.

———. (2002) *Philosophy of Science and Race*. New York: Routledge.

CHAPTER 38

AFFIRMATIVE ACTION

RODNEY C. ROBERTS

I.

"Affirmative action" is a term that has come to be associated with a variety of social policies that typically concern opportunities for employment or admission to institutions of higher learning. Such policies require that, in the process of hiring or admission, particular attention be paid to individuals who are members of groups thought to have been disadvantaged in the past. Although sometimes referred to as "preferential treatment" or "reverse discrimination," many philosophers have found these labels problematic, even fallacious. In the United States, affirmative action is usually directed toward women and members of ethnic minorities, especially African Americans. Affirmative action is not, however, a phenomenon unique to the United States. Although Malaysia recently abandoned an affirmative action policy for university admission that had been in place for over three decades, affirmative action policies remain in place around the world. Seats at colleges in Brazil are set aside for Black students, as well as for indigenous students and students with disabilities. Top students from rural and outlying areas in Israel have places made available for them at one of the country's most selective institutions, and disadvantaged students from immigrant families in France are recruited into one of that country's most prestigious public universities. In India, said to have the world's most extensive "quota system," seats are reserved at universities for lower-cast Indians. Finally, South Africa may have the quintessential example of a national commitment to affirmative action. The Bill of Rights in the Constitution of the Republic of South Africa allows for "legislative and other measures designed to protect or advance persons, or categories of persons, disadvantaged by unfair discrimination" in order to promote the achievement of equality (ch. 2, sect. 9). South Africa's constitution also has a diversity requirement in at least two important areas of government. First, the members of the nation's Commission for the Promotion and Protection of the Rights of Cultural, Religious and Linguistic Communities must not only be broadly representative of the main cultural, religious, and linguistic communities in South Africa (which has eleven official languages), but must also broadly reflect the gender composition of the country as well (ch. 9, sect. 186). Second, the process by which the country's judicial officers are appointed must include consideration of the need for a judiciary that broadly reflects South Africa's racial and gender composition (ch. 8, sect. 174).

While the Western philosophical literature includes discussion of affirmative action outside of Western contexts, and non-Western philosophers have addressed this controversial issue, both the idea of affirmative action itself and the bulk of philosophical discussion concerning it have come from the West. Moreover, while some discussion has focused on minority groups other than African Americans, or have focused exclusively on women, philosophical discussions of affirmative action typically focus on Blacks in the United States. Like the Fourteenth Amendment to the U.S. Constitution, affirmative action was initiated in large part out of a concern for the condition of Black Americans. President Lyndon Johnson recognized the historical injustices endured by Blacks in America when he employed the now classic hobbled runner metaphor in his 1965 commencement address at historically Black Howard University. He noted that one cannot take a person who has been hobbled by chains for many years, liberate that person, place that person at the starting line of a race, and then say, "you are free to compete with all the others" and be justified in the belief that one has been completely fair (Johnson 1966, 636). Johnson recognized that one of the fundamental reasons for the inequality faced by Black America is "the devastating heritage of long years of slavery; and a century of oppression, hatred, and injustice" (Johnson 1966, 638). The Black experience in America has been one of perpetual racial injustice from the arrival of the first Africans in the early seventeenth century to the present day. In his opinion in the landmark affirmative action case *Regents of the University of California v. Bakke* (concurring in the judgment in part and dissenting in part), Justice Thurgood Marshall observes that

> [I]t is unnecessary in 20th-century America to have individual Negroes demonstrate that they have been victims of racial discrimination; the racism of our society has been so pervasive that none, regardless of wealth or position, has managed to escape its impact. The experience of Negroes in America has been different in kind, not just in degree, from that of other ethnic groups. It is not merely the history of slavery alone but also that a whole people were marked as inferior by the law. And that mark has endured. The dream of America as the great melting pot has not been realized for the Negro; because of his skin color he never even made it into the pot (*Bakke*, 400–401).

A few months after his speech at Howard, President Johnson issued Executive Order 11246. The order states that government contractors "will not discriminate against any employee or applicant for employment because of race, color, religion, sex, or national origin." Moreover, it requires contractors to take "*affirmative action* to ensure that applicants are employed, and that employees are treated during employment, without regard to their race, color, religion, sex or national origin" (emphasis added).

A necessary part of doing Africana philosophy is having the problems facing the Black community at the forefront of one's thinking. Since Bernard Boxill and Albert Mosley exemplify the importance of this perspective through the issue of affirmative action, and since they are two of the most prominent philosophers of African descent in the affirmative action debate, the remainder of this discussion focuses largely on their ideas.

II.

Like many Black scholars of his generation, Bernard Boxill's scholarly interest was shaped by the tumultuous events of the 1960s, in his case in particular, the Watts (California) riots of 1965 and the rise of the Black Power Movement. Not surprisingly, therefore, Boxill has a tremendous concern for justice, especially the rectification of injustices perpetrated against Blacks in America (Boxill 1992, 2002). Although rectificatory or "backward-looking" grounds are still employed to justify affirmative action policies, only consequentialist or "forward-looking" justifications are recognized in U.S. law. Especially popular today are forward-looking arguments that appeal to diversity.

In *Gratz v. Bollinger* (2003), one of the most recent rulings by the U.S. Supreme Court on affirmative action in higher education, the Court held that the University of Michigan's use of race to admit underrepresented students to its College of Literature, Science, and the Arts was unconstitutional. However, in *Grutter v. Bollinger* (2003), the Court ruled that the use of race to achieve diversity in admissions at the University of Michigan's Law School was constitutional. The Court found that the latter policy included a "narrowly tailored" use of race in admissions decisions in order to further a "compelling interest in obtaining the educational benefits that flow from a diverse student body." By enrolling a "critical mass" of underrepresented minority students, the Law School's policy sought to ensure its ability to contribute to the objectives of the school and to the legal profession. More generally, the idea is that this sort of affirmative action produces better educational environments for all students. Discovery of the truth requires more than good reasoning skills. The premises of one's arguments, what one notices, are also an important factor. What one notices depends on one's background assumptions and attitudes. Since Black students and other students of color come to college with different background assumptions and attitudes than White students, and since the presence of a diversity of background assumptions and attitudes may dispose people to notice facts they might have otherwise overlooked, students are more likely to learn the truth in an atmosphere of diversity (Boxill and Boxill 2003, 123).

Another forward-looking approach that has appealed to many defenders of affirmative action is the argument from equal opportunity. On Boxill's view, this argument includes both an equal opportunity rationale and a principle of equal consideration of interests. Individuals who have the qualities and abilities to best perform the function of a position in society ought to be awarded that position. Equal opportunity forbids discrimination based on any characteristics that are irrelevant to the proper fulfillment of the position's function. The principle of equal consideration of interests holds that everyone should have the same chances to acquire qualifications or desirable positions in society. But because some societies, including the United States, have regularly violated the requirements of both equal opportunity and equal consideration of interests, Blacks and women are often absent from consideration for society's desirable positions. Therefore, affirmative action in favor of Blacks and women is, on this view, justified because it helps to ensure equality of opportunity.

A common objection to the equal opportunity argument is that it entails the violation of White male rights. According to this objection, since White males are most often the "best qualified" for desirable positions in society, giving "preference" to Blacks and women deprives White males of their right to obtain these positions. Boxill notes, however, that this objection rests on the assumption that the necessary qualifications are things like test scores, grades, and college degrees. But schools of higher learning exist to educate individuals so they can perform functions that impact upon society, not to reward high grades and test scores. Since affirmative action can help society give more equal consideration to the interests of all of its members, ethnicity or gender may be morally legitimate qualifications for admission. Hence, Boxill argues that the equal opportunity argument does not entail the violation of White male rights, and so the objection fails.

Boxill finds forward-looking arguments for affirmative action attractive, but he is not inclined to rely solely upon such arguments to justify affirmative action. This is because (*inter alia*) forward-looking justifications for affirmative action do not yield the consequences that flow from affirmative action as compensation for unjust harm. Missing from forward-looking justifications is the public conviction that society is acting justly toward Black Americans. This conviction could have greater positive consequences on societal welfare than diversity and equality combined. No forward-looking argument has yet been advanced showing that a reduction in economic inequalities reduces racial prejudice. A backward-looking approach, on the other hand, would not only address racial stratification but also address the continuing existence and justification of racism. On Boxill's view, the "fundamental" backward-looking argument begins with the fact that Black Americans have been and continue to be wrongfully harmed by the pervasive racism in American society (Boxill 1992). Given that wrongful harms ought to be compensated for, and that affirmative action is an appropriate form of compensation for Blacks, affirmative action policies that benefit Black Americans ought to be instituted. Boxill endorses the argument that since Black Americans have been denied full membership in society, and since employment will make them feel they have full membership, affirmative action is an appropriate form of compensation for the wrongful harms of American racism (Boxill 1978, 261).

Another version of the backward-looking compensatory argument holds that affirmative action is justified for present-day Blacks as compensation for their being wrongfully harmed by the unjust race-inspired treatment of their African and African American ancestors. Unlike the fundamental backward-looking argument, this argument is grounded in the injuries sustained to the ancestors of today's Black folk. One of the most popular objections to this argument claims that, since compensation aims at bringing the injured to the position they would have been in had the injury never occurred, and since present-day Blacks would not have come into existence had their ancestors not been enslaved, compensating present-day Blacks is impossible. However, Boxill observes that the objection fails to address the nature of the injury involved in this version of the backward-looking argument. The argument does not call for compensating present-day Blacks for the enslavement of their ancestors. Clearly, today's Black folk were not among those who were enslaved and therefore ought not to be compensated for being the objects of America's "peculiar institution." Rather, compensation is due to present-day Blacks for the injuries they themselves have sustained, some of which have resulted from the enslavement of their ancestors.

But why should we think that today's Black folk have been injured by the enslavement of their ancestors? Justice Marshall's observation that Black folk "have been discriminated against, not as individuals, but rather solely because of the color of their skins" suggests one rationale (*Bakke*, 400). Since there is clear evidence of direct harms to those individuals who were enslaved in North America, rectificatory compensation was due as a result of these harms. However, there are interdependencies and interrelationships among those who were enslaved and their descendents such that additional harms, consequent upon the direct harms to those who were enslaved, were transmitted to the descendents. These additional harms represent indirect harms to the descendants of American slaves. Moreover, there exists a negative stereotype of the members of the group that is culturally pervasive, a stereotype squarely grounded in the institution of slavery. Consequently, the descendants of American slavery have been harmed by slavery.

Boxill advances two reasons for thinking that today's Black folk have been injured by slavery. First, present-day Blacks begin with less wealth and education than Whites precisely because their ancestors were slaves. Since slaves typically had much less money, property, and position than free people, they have much less to bequeath to their descendants. Hence, contemporary Blacks typically begin with less wealth and education than those whose ancestors were not enslaved. This cripples the ability of present-day Blacks to achieve desirable places and positions in society, and constitutes a wrongful harm for which they ought to be compensated. Second, and perhaps more important, present-day Blacks are harmed by the enslavement of their ancestors because the legacy of slavery has intensified the racism against them. Indeed, there is a clear sense in which slavery is the genesis of racial injustice in America (Roberts 2006, 425). Black folk are hated and despised because of their slave heritage and the virulent antiblack racism originating with slavery has played a major role in constraining their social progress. So much lack of success can lead Black folk to conclude that the racism against them is both intense and effective in holding them down, thus making hopelessness a rational state of mind.

On this view, a pervasive and virulent antiblack racism has been a major cause of racial stratification. Since the reduction of racial stratification is a consequence of affirmative action, and since the reduction of racial stratification will result in increased success for Blacks in society, affirmative action will help to make the "American Dream" available to everyone, even if racism persists in some forms. Black hopelessness will cease to be rational. Affirmative action is justified, therefore, because it provides compensation in the form of restored hope for Black folk in America. For Boxill, affirmative action is justified by both forward-looking and backward-looking perspectives.

III.

Like Boxill, Albert Mosley emerged from his graduate education in the 1970s along with other influential African-descended philosophers like Anita Allen, Leonard Harris, Howard McGary, Lucius Outlaw, and Naomi Zack. However, unlike Boxill, Mosley denies that affirmative action is a morally legitimate part of rectifying the injustices perpetrated against Blacks in America (Mosley 2003). This is not to say that he opposes rectification, or that he opposes affirmative action, for he is in favor of both. What he opposes is the idea that affirmative action counts as rectificatory compensation. Mosley argues that affirmative action was not conceived as a form of reparation and it does not currently function as such. The rationale for establishing affirmative action policies is not to compensate the progeny of slaves for past wrongs. Rather, the point of affirmative action is to disrupt the practices of racism and sexism by putting qualified women and minorities into positions that most would have been denied in the past and probably would be denied in the present.

Some object that affirmative action is flawed because it benefits those Blacks who are best qualified, suggesting that most affirmative action beneficiaries are college-educated white-collar workers who have been harmed least by racism. Mosley maintains, however, that the primary impact of affirmative action has been in the blue-collar segment of the workforce. He points out that most of the major affirmative action cases that have come before the U.S. Supreme Court involving employment have not concerned white-collar positions. Rather, they have concerned jobs such as municipal workers, police officers and firefighters, admittance to labor unions, and training for skilled craft jobs (Mosley and Capaldi 1996, 39). Moreover, Blacks with higher levels of education were not disadvantaged least by slavery and racial discrimination, but were harmed progressively more so than other Blacks. This is shown by the fact that the proportion of White income received by Blacks varied inversely to their level of education and training. Low-skill jobs were more likely to pay Black workers nearly the same as White workers, but this was less likely in cases where the job required higher skill levels. Hence, relative to similarly situated Whites, Blacks on average saw their benefits decrease to the extent that their skills and education increased. There was thus a disincentive for Blacks to invest in obtaining higher levels of qualifications. By taking steps to ensure that the qualifications of Blacks are not discounted, affirmative action counters this historical phenomenon (Mosley 1992, 149). Mosley argues that equal opportunity "means more than simply moving Black people above the poverty line, for this would do nothing for those whose ability would likely have placed them far above the poverty line, were it not for the increasing hostility at higher levels of achievement" (Mosley and Capaldi 1996, 30). Finally, Mosley reminds us that helping Black folk with the highest levels of qualification ultimately helps those who are the least well off. Although one of the consequences of desegregation was the movement of Black physicians, lawyers, and other professionals out of the inner city, Black professionals continue to serve the Black community to a higher degree than those who are not Black (Mosley and Capaldi 1996, 35).

Like Boxill, Mosley takes issue with the notion of being the best "qualified" for a position. He thinks that being qualified for a position often presents "a classic case of Catch-22" for Black folk (Mosley 1998, 166). A necessary condition for developing requisite skills for being the best qualified for a position is having the opportunity to acquire those skills. However, if Blacks have been denied opportunities to acquire these skills, they cannot be among the best qualified for a position. When the relationship between the skills required for a position and actual performance on the job is suspect, this Catch-22 becomes even more pernicious. Moreover, since research shows that performance on timed paper-and-pencil tests like the Scholastic Aptitude Test (SAT) for college admission and the Law School Admission Test (LSAT) is not an accurate predictor of future performance, Mosley is suspicious of the assumption that those who perform best on such tests are indeed the best qualified. Also, with the advent of expensive test-preparation programs for many standardized tests, scores on the SAT, for example, have a higher correlation to household income than to future success in college. Insofar as IQ tests are concerned, a substantial number of educational psychologists in the United States continue to maintain that the variance between the average IQ score of Blacks and the average IQ score of Whites is due to inherited genetic factors, factors that are difficult if not impossible to change (Mosley 2005, 49). One prominent example of this position was advanced in the mid-1990s. However, as one author put it:

> *The Bell Curve* [1994] made the embarrassing mistake of confusing within-group variation and between-group variation. Many psychology and sociology textbooks have by now pointed out the mistake (and other mistakes) to introductory students, but the general public may have been left with the impression that Harvard professor Richard Herrnstein and his co-author Charles Murray were making a credible argument. (Crosby 2004, 54)

In response to the claim that White males have been harmed by affirmative action, Mosley shows how White males have instead been beneficiaries of affirmative action. By requiring that jobs and educational opportunities be publicly announced, affirmative action gives those White males who are not "insiders" a chance to take advantage of opportunities they otherwise would have been unaware of. Traditionally, union jobs and white-collar jobs like that of university professor were obtained through word of mouth. Without the proper personal recommendation, or attendance in the right circles, one had little chance of securing many desirable positions. In short, prior to affirmative action, many more jobs had membership in the "good 'ol boy club" as a necessary condition for consideration.

Finally, in response to the concern that racial discrimination in America may have ceased, and therefore that affirmative action is unwarranted, Mosley cites extant patterns of discrimination in both the public and private spheres. Discrimination persists in hiring, promotion, and lending practices both for personal property like loans for the purchase of automobiles and for mortgage loans on real property (Mosley and Capaldi 1996, 40–41). But even if it is acknowledged that racial discrimination still exists, some argue that addressing this sort of wrongdoing seems arbitrary and unjust when there are so many other kinds of wrongdoing that need to be addressed. Mosley argues that unlike the random victim of wrongdoing, one's race increases the likelihood of being the victim of injustice by means of fraud, denial of educational and vocational opportunities, assault, or even homicide. Racism increases the likelihood that members of a particular group will be the victims of wrongdoing.

Perhaps the most obvious context for underscoring this point is Black folk and America's legal system. Here the effects of discrimination can indeed be fatal. For example, while driving his late-model sports car through an all-White suburb of Pittsburgh, Pennsylvania, thirty-one-year-old Black businessman Jonny Gammage became a victim of what has come to be known as Driving While Black (D.W.B.). Unarmed and suspected of no crime, Gammage was asphyxiated to death by five police officers within seven minutes of being stopped. Charges were only filed against three of the officers, and two of those cases were dismissed. Following the acquittal of the remaining officer by an all-White jury, Gammage's mother remarked: "We gave the system a chance to work, and it didn't work. *I didn't believe the people who told us the system doesn't work for Blacks. I believed it would work. But I don't believe that anymore*" (Stolen Lives Project 1999, 16, emphasis added). Of course, one can become a victim of police brutality without D.W.B.; sometimes just sitting in a car suffices. This was the case with twenty-three-year-old Aswon Watson when he came out of a barber shop in Brooklyn, New York, and got into his car. One of the three plainclothes officers who approached him said, "You're dead, nigger!" and started shooting. Eighteen bullet wounds later, Watson was dead. A grand jury was convened, but the police were never indicted (Stolen Lives Project 1999, 25). Although many newspaper accounts fail to report the race or ethnicity of individuals killed by police, Blacks and Latinos are the main targets of police brutality in America (Stolen Lives Project 1999, iv). Even when Black folk survive contact with the police, "[f]rom initial charging decisions to plea bargaining to jury sentencing, African-Americans are treated more harshly when they are defendants, and their lives are accorded less value when they are victims" (Amnesty International USA 2007).

BIBLIOGRAPHY AND SUGGESTED READINGS

Amnesty International USA. (2007) "The Death Penalty iIs Racially Biased." http://www.amnestyusa.org/abolish/racialprejudices.html (accessed June 15, 2007).

Boxill, Bernard R. (1978) "The Morality of Preferential Hiring." *Philosophy and Public Affairs* 7(3), 246–268.

———. (1992) *Blacks and Social Justice* (rev. ed.). Lanham, MD: Rowman and Littlefield.

———. (2002) "The Morality of Reparation." In *Injustice and Rectification*, edited by Rodney C. Roberts. New York: Peter Lang, 124–130.

Boxill, Bernard R., and Jan Boxill. (2003) "Affirmative Action." In *A Companion to Applied Ethics*, edited by R. G. Frey and Christopher Heath Wellman. Malden, MA: Blackwell, 118–127.

Crosby, Faye J. (2004) *Affirmative Action Is Dead; Long Live Affirmative Action.* New Haven, CT: Yale University Press.

Johnson, Lyndon B. (1966) "Commencement Address at Howard University: 'To Fulfill These Rights,' June 4, 1965," Item 301 of *Public Papers of the Presidents of the United States,* Book II of II. Washington, DC: United States Government Printing Office.

Kershnar, Stephen. (1997) "Strong Affirmative Action Programs at State Educational Institutions Cannot Be Justified Via Compensatory Justice." *Public Affairs Quarterly* 11(4), 345–363.

Mosley, Albert. (1992) "Affirmative Action and the Urban Underclass." In *The Underclass Question*, edited by Bill E. Lawson. Philadelphia, PA: Temple University Press.

———. (1998) "Policies of Straw or Policies of Inclusion? A Review of Pojman's 'Case Against Affirmative Action.'" *International Journal of Applied Philosophy* 12(2), 161–168.

———. (2003) "Affirmative Action as a Form of Reparations." *University of Memphis Law Review* 33(2), 353–365.

———. (2005) "A Defense of Affirmative Action." In *Contemporary Debates in Applied Ethics*, edited by Andrew I. Cohen and Christopher Heath Wellman. Malden, MA: Blackwell, 43–58.

Mosley, Albert G., and Nicholas Capaldi. (1996) *Affirmative Action: Social Justice or Unfair Preference?* Lanham, MD: Rowman and Littlefield.

Roberts, Rodney C. (2006) "The Counterfactual Conception of Compensation." *Metaphilosophy* 37(3–4), 414–428.

Sher, George. (1999) "Diversity." *Philosophy and Public Affairs* 28(2), 85–104.

Stolen Lives Project. (1999) *Stolen Lives: Killed by Law Enforcement* (2nd ed.). New York: Stolen Lives Project. Cases Cited *Grutter v. Bollinger* 539 U.S. 244 (2003).

Gratz v. Bollinger 539 U.S. 306 (2003).

Regents of the University of California v. Bakke 438 U.S. 265 (1978).

PART VII

RECENT TRENDS IN GLOBAL PHILOSOPHY

EDITED BY CYNTHIA TOWNLEY

RECENT TRENDS IN GLOBAL PHILOSOPHY

CYNTHIA TOWNLEY

GLOBALIZATION has transformed philosophy and continues to transform philosophy. Non-Western philosophical communities are becoming more prominent in the global philosophical conversation, and the problems non-Western philosophers address, the solutions they propose, and the ideas they inject into world philosophy are coming to center stage. Constructive and critical exchanges between philosophical communities are increasing as new journals emerge. These interactions invite new thinking about philosophy itself—its history, scope, and boundaries; its relation to colonialism and its engagement with contemporary global concerns, such as environmental degradation and entrenched inequalities; and the ability of a discipline with mainly theoretical and abstract resources to engage with such concrete matters as transnational compensatory justice and fair inclusion and/or recognition without denial of difference.

The chapters in this section illustrate two aspects of globalization. First, increased interaction augments and alters existing or traditional philosophical conversations. Questions, problems, approaches, or presuppositions that might have appeared obvious or universal from a Eurocentric perspective often appear irrelevant, partial, or misguided when other vantage points are taken seriously. Feminism, environmentalism, and indigenous perspectives represent profound challenges to many aspects of European-inherited philosophy. Diverse experiences of gender, maternity, relationships, work, culture, and models of empowerment confront Western conceptions of and political priorities with respect to women, sexuality, family, and power. Diverse understandings of authenticity, representation, ownership, and rights to self-determination test and extend some (Western or liberal) assumptions about forms of and groundings for equalities and freedoms. Indigenous groups' understandings of and concerns about collective ownership and authorship, attitudes to ancestral remains, and rights over land, intellectual property, and creative works challenge an array of Western practices and philosophical assumptions. These new, or newly communicated, ways of thinking are important not just for their interest to philosophy, but also because a world facing climatic, population, and environmental challenges demands the resources of our best ideas.

Globalization also challenges us to rethink the nature of philosophy as a discipline and as a cultural activity. Previously unrecognized critical perspectives present challenges to Western philosophy as well as new opportunities for conversation and dialogue. The increased information traffic enabled by new technologies also might lead to appropriations, misrepresentations, or oversimplifications of ideas, so care and cultural competence are needed, in addition to goodwill from all sides. While many interactions with Western-style philosophy are marked by caution, recognizably philosophical ideas and approaches were never limited to the Western tradition and its academic focus. Thinkers informed by non-European traditions offer different ways of practicing philosophy, for example, in oral traditions. They challenge and encourage Western philosophers to reconsider some of the analytic categories and approaches to reasoning with which Western philosophers typically begin. Whether or not all parties welcome or accept the label "philosopher," and while the views and modes of expression are thoroughly diverse, the emergent conversations are arguably philosophical.

The works in this section discuss and partake in some of these conversations. The selection of topics is by no means exhaustive. The neglect of many worthwhile topics reflects the constraints of a single section within a larger volume in which difficult choices were necessary. While these chapters present some introduction to contemporary global philosophy, it is only an introduction. We hope that the issues raised in this section, as well as its lacunae, will prompt further thinking about the scope of philosophy in the contemporary world.

The five chapters in this section address topics in feminism, Native American philosophy, environmental philosophy, cosmopolitanism, and the theory of reparations. These topics are increasingly prominent in recent philosophical work as philosophers contend with global concerns and reflect on features of the profession, such as the domination of the profession by the West generally, and by privileged groups from Western communities in particular.

The chapter on global feminism takes a critical perspective, providing "an account of what feminism needs to be if it is to be truly global." It shows how feminism has shifted from a focus on erroneous assumptions that generalize from the conditions faced by some women to claims about all women, to recognize the need to respond to women's different experiences and diverse social positions in terms of race, class, ethnicity, and sexuality across countries and continents. This chapter demonstrates two important aspects of global philosophy: openness to the criticism and challenge of perspectives from beyond mainstream philosophy and the development and deployment of philosophical methods to develop and respond to such challenges.

The chapter on Native American philosophy also explores intersections between the philosophical mainstream and positions beyond it, in this case, the "outsider within" positions of Native American thinkers. While Eurocentric philosophers have sometimes denied that non-Western traditions can involve fully fledged philosophical practice, from their own side indigenous practitioners are sometimes explicitly reluctant to identify as philosophers, preferring to maintain their own distinct positions, and sometimes articulating robust critiques of Western philosophical practice and theory. This is an important way of engaging critically with philosophy; it resonates with some feminists' reluctance to identify as philosophers and it also motivates an interrogation of the nature of philosophy. Different Native American thinkers seek to maintain the integrity of their indigenous cultures and perspectives while mediating and negotiating with the intellectual traditions of the West in various ways.

Environmentalist philosophy has also treated Western philosophical assumptions with critical caution. Non-Western environmental philosophers, activists, and ecologists have presented views of the human relationship with the natural world that arguably avoid the anthropocentrism of much Western philosophy and form a basis for criticizing certain destructive, exploitative, and consumerist practices that are identified with the globally rich countries and corporations of the West. Significant ecofeminist work is initiated outside Western mainstream cultures and is informed by contemporary political activism as well as by alternative non-Western perspectives.

Globalization raises our awareness of the lives of distant others, and reinvigorates long-standing questions about cosmopolitanism and "our responsibilities to all in the global community." Yet in important ways, individual identity depends on national identity, cultural, religious, or racial belonging; and the integration of these affinities or partialities into a universal theory is both important and fraught with challenges. This chapter pays particular attention to John Rawls's *The Law of Peoples*, a focus of recent philosophical discussions of cosmopolitanism. Globalization has also seen "common points of struggle" bring together diverse groups over concerns related, for example, to farming, unionism, environmentalism, or indigeneity. This chapter shows how current global arrangements of resources and transnational regulations challenge and inspire new reflections about justice and what it requires, both in attending to identity and affinity groups, and to the negotiation of partial and universal moral claims and duties.

Philosophy's concern with the classic questions of the nature and scope of justice demands a response to current entrenched inequalities in a postcolonial world. Recent philosophical work on the moral implications for present people of the wrongs done in the past reveals the limitations of distributive justice arguments that depend on a neutral or ahistorical starting point. The reality of widespread ongoing state-sponsored violence also forces a rethinking of the nature and scope of ethical obligations between peoples. The chapter on reparations explores the definition, justifications, and moral value of reparations, and distinguishes reparation from forgiveness and reconciliation. Like the discussion of cosmopolitanism, this chapter engages with Rawls's *The Law of Peoples* and argues for including a principle of reparations in the suite of human rights principles that would be part of a Rawlsian "realistic utopia."

We hope that this section indicates a bit of the range of new discussions globalization has brought to philosophy and some of the range of contributions that reflective thinkers who come to philosophy from non-European traditions are making to our collective philosophical practice. We hope that it also shows the necessity of attending to the philosophical voice of the relatively marginalized or excluded majority of the world in discussions of cosmopolitanism, reparation, and justice. There is no reason to expect the positions articulated in these global discussions to converge, nor, if they do, to expect that they will converge on views advanced by European thinkers. This diversity of insights is to be celebrated.

CHAPTER 39

GLOBAL FEMINISM

CHRISTINE M. KOGGEL

UNLIKE well-known branches or kinds of feminism such as "liberal feminism," "socialist feminism," or "radical feminism," the concept "global feminism" is less about describing a common set of commitments or beliefs shared by "global" feminists than it is about providing a critical perspective on Western feminism as a theory and movement. The critique centers on the idea that as an intellectual and political movement, feminism has been dominated by the West and, specifically, by feminists in the United States. This critique has gained momentum in an increasingly globalized world and is reflected in contemporary feminisms variously described as "third-world feminism," "postcolonial feminism," "transnational feminism," and "global feminism." Given the enormous and rich development of different kinds of feminisms and movements over the past few decades, it is difficult and perhaps even futile to attempt to delineate global feminism from postcolonial or third-world or transnational feminism. The task of explaining "global feminism," therefore, may be best pursued by beginning with a discussion of each of the concepts that gives their juxtaposition the meaning it now has. The result is less a definition of global feminism than it is an account of what feminism needs to be if it is to be truly global in the sense of reflecting the interests and addressing the concerns of women from around the globe. In other words, the term "global feminism" is less indicative of a particular branch of feminism with clearly identifiable features than it is of an approach sensitive to the broad array of women's experiences shaped by local histories and conditions as well as by the contemporary context of globalization and the transnational initiatives that are made possible by it.

The second section that follows provides a general account of feminism as a way to capture what is common to all feminists and kinds of feminism as well as where differences emerge. This sketch of some of the history of feminism in the United States is used to explain, in section 3, the charge of false universalizing that emerged from within feminism. This critique had women of color and others in the United States and beyond reject and depart from many of the ideas and goals of mainstream second-wave feminists of the 1960s and 1970s. The fourth section outlines key features of a feminist theory and movement that moves beyond false universalizing or generalizing from the experiences of one group of women to all women. The fifth section describes features of the contemporary global context that are relevant to descriptions of kinds of oppression and to the feminist goal of alleviating women's oppression in its multilayered and multifaceted forms. The paper ends with a summary of insights central to a global feminism and with some examples of globalized networks of feminist movements and initiatives. Whether it is called "global," "postcolonial," "third world," or "transnational," these recent developments are meant to reflect a feminism attentive to a broad range of women's experiences of oppression in the contemporary global context and to transnational strategies and policies that emerge from this.

Defining Feminism: Commonalities and Differences

While there are many different kinds of feminisms, all feminisms can be said to have two common components. First, feminists believe that women have been and continue to be oppressed and to suffer various kinds of inequalities, injustices, and discrimination. This component is descriptive: inequalities, injustices, and kinds of discrimination are described in terms of the conditions and circumstances of women's lives. Second, feminists are committed to alleviating or eradicating that oppression and those inequalities, injustices, and discrimination. This component is normative or prescriptive: legislation, policies, or strategies are advocated in terms of what ought to happen or be implemented to remove conditions and circumstances of oppression, inequality, and injustice for women. All feminisms, then, can be said to have descriptive/intellectual/theory components and normative/prescriptive/political components. But capturing this much by way of commonality is misleading because it belies the disagreement.

As soon as feminists begin to outline aspects of one or the other component, substantial differences among feminists and kinds of feminisms appear. With respect to the descriptive component, feminists disagree about what counts as oppression and what sorts of injustice, inequality, and discrimination matter when describing women's experiences. Kinds of feminisms also differ in their descriptions of the sources of or explanations for oppression, inequality, injustice, or discrimination. Explanations have been given in terms of women's subordination in the family, women's role in reproduction, the sexual objectification of women, and so on. In other words, feminists and feminisms provide a wide range and variety of descriptions of women's experiences to back up their claims of inequality or injustice or oppression or discrimination. With respect to the normative and political component, feminists disagree about what kind of laws, policies, or strategies can or would be effective in eliminating or alleviating women's oppression, inequality, injustice, or discrimination. Often how inequalities or injustices are described connects with specific sorts of recommendations for policies that would work to alleviate those inequalities or injustices. Kinds of feminisms, therefore, reflect a wide range and variety of prescriptions for alleviating or eliminating women's oppression, inequality, injustice, or discrimination.

It may be useful to give substance to the complexity and variety underlying these components of feminism by working with one concept within one kind of feminism to show what can emerge by way of differences and disagreements: inequalities in the workplace as addressed by second-wave liberal feminists. While this risks oversimplifying the issues (and the kind of feminism), it can also help pinpoint a key issue that provoked challenges to and expansions of the descriptive and normative components of Western feminism. At issue is what has sometimes been referred to as essentialism. But because this concept has become mired in the biological/nature versus the sociological/culture debates over what it means, in essence, to be a woman, the issue may be less contentiously expressed as a charge that the experiences of some women have been taken to be representative of the experiences of all women. On this description, the charge is one of false universalizing or false generalization.

Before proceeding with explaining the pitfalls of and responses to false universalizing, a few warnings are in order. Sketching a small part of the history of second-wave feminism in the United States is tricky for a number of reasons. First, there is disagreement about how to distinguish the "waves" of feminism in the United States, let alone elsewhere. First-wave feminism is generally distinguished from second-wave feminism in terms of time periods, with first-wave feminism taking place in the 1920s and resulting in significant gains such as the right to vote and second-wave feminism beginning in the 1960s and building from the gains achieved by first-wave feminists much earlier. It is even more difficult, however, to delineate second- and third-wave feminism either in terms of time periods, central beliefs, or political goals and strategies. Though "waves" suggests that one kind of feminism was replaced by another, second- and third-wave feminism have each developed in complex and sophisticated ways that make it difficult to say that the second wave has ended or that the third wave is a significant rejection of second-wave feminism.[1] Second, many historical accounts of second-wave feminism have focused and continue to focus on what was being said and published by white middle-class women—thereby privileging what they produced by way of theory and

1. While not covered in this chapter, useful references on third-wave feminism are in edited collections by Findlen 1995; Walker 1995; Heywood and Drake 1997; and Baumgardner and Richards 2000.

achieved by way of political strategies. But this narrow focus also made it possible to bring to light the efforts of women of color, nonheterosexual women, and working-class women in the United States, who resisted domination before and after second-wave feminism of the 1960s—but did so outside mainstream theory and politics. By uncovering and challenging the descriptive and normative assumptions embedded in the mainstream feminist theory and movement, these feminists succeeded in motivating a generation of more sophisticated theory and politics that sought to avoid the charge and the resulting pitfalls of false generalization. Third, discussing the work of a few early second-wave feminists in the United States risks perpetuating a U.S.-centered perspective on feminism. The risk is counterbalanced when one considers that this feminist theory was prominent and mainstream in the United States and beyond and it was that against which challenges and critiques were launched by feminists whose theory and movement were marginalized or ignored. In other words, discussing one small part of second-wave feminism can highlight how the global feminism of today emerged from those early challenges to and departures from mainstream second-wave feminism in the United States. "Global feminism" can be said to extend the critique of the false universalizing of women's experiences, applied to and confronted in some feminist theory and movement in the United States, to accounts of women in a global context.

Universalizing Tendencies in U.S. Feminism and Feminist Critiques of It

The charge of false universalizing can be illustrated through a brief discussion of one kind of description and policy emerging from early second-wave feminism in the United States and reflected in the work of early liberal feminists such as Betty Friedan in *The Feminine Mystique* (1963) and Gloria Steinem in her role as founder, editor, and publisher of *Ms.* magazine. Here women's inequality was described in terms of their lack of access to the workplace and of women's dependence on men for their livelihood. From this description of women's inequality flowed prescriptions advocating the removal of the formal and informal barriers that prevented women from working outside the home. However, this description of women's inequality and of what ought to be done to remove it was easily contradicted by the experiences of women of color, nonheterosexual women, and poor and single women who were already in the workplace and needed to be in order to survive. In other words, in describing women's inequality in terms of unequal access to the workplace, many second-wave feminists of the time falsely generalized from the experiences of white middle- and upper-class women in the United States to the experiences of all women in the United States. The experiences of women of color, nonheterosexual women, poor women, and single women revealed a different set of inequalities: of not being able to care for their own children because they were holding jobs that had them care for the children of privileged women or of not having or wanting men on whom to depend or of experiencing racial or class-based discrimination in the jobs that they occupied.

The general point is that second-wave feminists who advocated policies for strengthening women's entry into and participation in the workplace ignored or failed to address the particular inequalities that many women experienced as women of color or as single women or as mothers who needed to work. The charge of false generalization was not limited to liberal feminist accounts of women's inequality in the workplace. Second-wave radical and Marxist feminists (Morgan 1970) were also accused of false generalization in explaining women's oppression in terms of their sexual subordination to men or the sexual division of labor or their role in reproduction. This challenge to the universalizing tendencies in the descriptive and normative components of mainstream second-wave feminism in the United States revealed that it was all too easy to assume the perspective of dominant white middle-class women and to generalize that all women share those same experiences of inequality, injustice, or discrimination.

The critique of mainstream feminism as paying little to no attention to differences among women on the basis of factors such as race, ethnicity, class, nationality, sexual orientation, religion, and so on is evident in the work of feminists of color such as bell hooks, who, in commenting on the feminist argument that women want rights equal to men, asks, "Which men do women want to be equal to?" (hooks 1984, 28). That the answer to this question is all too obvious reveals the assumed norm of white middle-class heterosexual males, who reside in rich and powerful countries and against whom others are judged and measured. This challenge from within second-wave feminism would turn out to play a central role in the development of feminist approaches and critiques within Western feminism generally and, more specifically, within U.S. feminist theory and movement. Work by lesbian feminists and feminists of color such as Audre Lorde (1984), bell hooks (1984), Patricia Hill Collins (1990), Gloria Anzaldúa (1987), and Cherríe Moraga (1981) were important for retaining the importance of describing women's experiences while challenging accounts by white feminists of what constituted those experiences and women's oppression more generally. The onus was now on feminists to show that their descriptions of inequalities or injustices were sensitive to differences in women's experiences and that the policies they were prepared to advocate could address the wide range of inequalities and kinds of discrimination experienced by a variety of women affected by factors other than gender.

As will be discussed later, global, postcolonial, transnational, and third-world feminists would expand this critique of false generalization. They would be the voices of women from developing countries who would self-identify as postcolonial and third-world feminists and be critical of histories and effects of colonialism in their home countries and beyond. They would embrace terms such as "postcolonial" and "third world" to develop accounts that put global relations of power at the forefront of the descriptive and normative components of this kind of feminist theory and movement (Narayan 1997; Alexander and Mohanty 1997; Mohanty et al. 1991). They would uncover biases in a feminism dominated by the West where the very account in terms of "waves" suggested that feminist theory and movements were contained within the United States and not evident across history, time, and cultures or present in locations outside the United States. In other words, just as second-wave feminists could be charged with assuming the perspective of privileged white women, Western feminism more generally could be charged with assuming the perspective of privileged white women in dominant countries and cultures. It is at this point that the concept of a global feminism begins to take shape and gain meaning.

Differences among Women within and across Borders

In the United States, the challenge to mainstream feminism's tendency to falsely universalize led to important developments such as the theory of intersectionality (Crenshaw 1991). Intersectionality holds that descriptions of women's inequalities and injustices need to be placed within a complex network of intersecting kinds of oppression. Women are not only women; gender intersects with one or more factors of race, class, ethnicity, disability, sexual orientation, age, and so on and in ways that call for attending to the specificity of those experiences and for advocating policies that are effective in removing the particular inequalities and injustices experienced by women at the intersection of multiple kinds of oppression. The fact that kinds of oppression intersect in ways that make it difficult to extract and privilege one factor is why it is too facile to claim that contemporary feminism is merely about describing and addressing *women's* oppression. If feminism's objective is to end women's oppression, then intersectionality explains that interlocking kinds of oppression call for a multipronged and integrated approach of describing oppression of all kinds and of dismantling domination in all its forms. As Elizabeth Spelman writes, "no woman is subject to any form of oppression simply because she is a woman; which forms of oppression she is subject to depend on what 'kind' of woman she is" (Spelman 1988, 52).

There have been other responses to the charge of false universalizing within Western feminism. Some third-wave feminists, for example, call for rejecting group meaning of and solidarity for "women" in favor of a focus on individual expression and freedom (Walker 1995; Heywood and Drake 1997). Postmodern and poststructuralist feminists focus on the role of discourse to argue that subjects are tossed to and fro by the contingencies of histories and the particularities of conditions and circumstances. There is, on this sort of account, no enduring subject to whom "women" can refer and who they should mobilize for change (Nicholson 1990; Scott 1990). These sorts of approaches have been challenged by other feminists (Okin 1994) who worry that feminism risks losing its political force: it is a slippery slope from acknowledging that women experience different forms of oppression to losing the ground from which to discuss groups at all or to mobilize as a group to effect change. It is important to note, however, that these descriptions of third-wave or postmodern feminism, like the description of early liberal feminism above, elide the range and variety of third-wave, postmodern, and poststructuralist contributions to feminist theory. That said, these kinds of feminism do pinpoint an important area of contention between Western and non-Western feminists, the latter charging that a focus on individual freedom and expression or on discourse reflects the perspective of privileged Western feminists who, in benefiting from gains achieved by women in the West, are positioned to ignore the importance of the normative and political.

Chandra Talpade Mohanty's seminal "Under Western Eyes: Feminist Scholarship and Colonial Discourses" is important not only for revealing the power and influence of Western feminism in the global context, but also for uncovering tendencies in Western feminist theory and methodology that result in women in third-world countries being depicted as a homogeneous group, all of whom are perceived to be suffering injustices and inequalities similar to but much worse than those suffered by women in Western countries. While she is careful not to accuse all Western feminists of falling prey to these tendencies, Mohanty targets those feminists who use categories of analysis such as "sexual division of labor" or "women as victims of male violence" in ways that falsely homogenize women's experiences of work or of violence across histories, cultures, and time—as though an analysis of the sexual division of labor, for example, can be abstracted from context and stand apart from the histories, cultures, and specificities of actual women's lives that give meaning to women's work in particular contexts. It may be, for example, that women in a particular context are responsible for agricultural or market work and that this matters for the description and analysis of the meaning of the division of labor in that context. Moreover, such universalizing tendencies tend to homogenize third-world women, no matter what the cultural differences and historical circumstances, as all experiencing oppression that is more severe or inequalities that are more entrenched than those experienced by first-world women, who are taken to be free of the worst effects of the sexual division of labor or of dependence on men. Without proper descriptions of the "historically specific material reality of groups of women," argues Mohanty, third-world women tend to be depicted as a monolith, all of whom are mere passive victims of male violence or of an entrenched sexual division of labor (Mohanty 1988). Not only does this deny agency to third-world women, who have always been and continue to be active in understanding and responding to oppression as it manifests itself in their specific contexts, but it also privileges Western feminist normative accounts of what can or ought to be done to "help" third-world women.

Mohanty's account and others by third-world feminists such as Uma Narayan in her critique of Western accounts of women and feminism in India are pluralist to the extent that they reject overarching or monocausal explanations, but still insist that descriptions and explanations of inequality, injustice, oppression, or discrimination can be and need to be given. Paying attention to how kinds of oppression interlock and are then reflected in and perpetuated by economic, political, legal, and cultural conditions shaped by particular histories and contexts does not mean giving up on explanations. Instead, it calls for fine tuning the descriptive components so that more accurate accounts of women's lives can be provided. With more accurate descriptions in hand, the idea is that more effective strategies can then be devised for removing oppression, inequality, injustice, and discrimination as it manifests itself in particular contexts and in the lives of women in those contexts. Using insights from Maria Mies's situated analysis of the "sexual division of labor" of women lace-makers in south India (Mies 1982), Mohanty writes: "if such concepts are assumed to be universally applicable, the resultant homogenization of class, race, religious and daily material practices of women in the third word can create a false sense of the commonality of oppressions, interests, and struggles between and amongst women globally" (Mohanty 1988, 76–77).

Women and Globalization: Feminism for a Global Context

If we think of intersectionality as having emerged from women marginalized in U.S. feminism and if we acknowledge that the resulting critical insights were crucial to feminist theory and feminist movement, then it is third-world, transnational, postcolonial, and global feminists who apply this analysis to the contemporary context of an increasingly globalized world. They describe women's experiences not only in terms of factors specific to particular locations and histories but also in terms of how these local factors are being shaped and reshaped in the contemporary global context. The global context is one that reflects an increasingly interdependent world, one in which features and factors of globalization shape the lives and experiences of all people. These features and factors, however, shape people's lives differently depending on who they are and where they live, whether they live in a rich or poor country, emerge from histories of colonization or imperialism, have beliefs about the inherent inequality of some fellow citizens, and so on.

In general terms, globalization represents increased flows—of things such as technology, trade, information, markets, capital, and people themselves. An overarching feature of globalization is that we live in a context of economic globalization, one in which open markets, multinational corporations, international financial institutions, powerful countries, and world trade organizations shape the issues and circumscribe their effects on people in a range of areas such as labor, migration, culture, education, health care, poverty, development, war, and the environment. More open markets, for example, have provided jobs where little opportunity existed before, jobs that have in turn increased household income and national wealth, improved access to education and health care, and challenged gender norms and practices in many parts of the world. But the corporate quest for profit has also resulted in the exploitation of workers in third-world countries and the destruction of families, ways of life, and communities when corporations move to countries with even lower wage labor or when rich countries or international financial institutions place paralyzing conditions on countries through aid or debt payment plans. While economic globalization may have positive effects, these sorts of negative effects have magnified relationships of power between rich and poor countries and rich and poor citizens within countries in ways that reduce the power they have, either individually or collectively, to change oppressive conditions (Koggel 2002, 2003, 2007).

These features of economic globalization undermine the idea that laws and policies can or should be restricted to what states do within their borders and for their own citizens. Rather, they create a need for transnational cooperation and regulation and for international policies and laws designed to address some of the detrimental effects of economic globalization in areas such as trade and the environment, for example. It is in this context of describing the complex effects of globalization that the detailed and contextualized accounts provided by feminists such as Mohanty and others variously referred to as third world, transnational, postcolonial, and global have become vitally important. They highlight the need to be aware of relations of power at both the global and local levels when providing accounts of women's oppression (Koggel 2002; Parpart et al. 2002; Kabeer 2004). They argue that many global processes and policies have had and continue to have a detrimental impact on women in domains such as the workplace, education, and health care, and for women's social, political, and economic status and participation (Salazar-Parreñas 2001). They point to the ways in which globalization intersects with gender, race, ethnicity, age, disability, and so on and in ways that exploit and perpetuate already existing forms of oppression, inequality, and injustice (Mohanty 1997; Fussell 2000; Benería et al. 2000; Koggel 2003). They show how globalization exploits formerly colonized countries at the same time as it reshapes the lives of people in and the futures of those countries (Ong 2006). This feminist work is reshaping both the conceptual terrain of these and other issues such as reproductive rights and the policies being framed and advocated by national and international organizations in countries around the world (Corea and Petchesky 1984; Molyneux 1988; Roa 2005). It is also reshaping feminist theory and the movement itself. Intersectionality is now applied to a postcolonial context fashioned by imperial and colonial pasts and impacted by the overarching influences of globalization.

These developments in feminism as theory and movement do not forego describing women as a group or mobilizing across differences to achieve change. Rather, they focus on providing detailed descriptions of women's lives in the contexts in which they are lived and as they are affected by interlocking practices, beliefs, social conditions, and political structures at the local level *and* by the overarching influences of globalization. These descriptions are starting points from which groups can mobilize on the basis of shared goals. The unity lies in coalition building around specific issues and causes and not in what it means to be a woman or a feminist. This does not mean that patterns or commonalities within and across social contexts cannot be discerned. It means acknowledging that such patterns need to be sensitive to historical and cultural variation and to the overarching impact of global factors and economic globalization itself.

Global Feminism and Globalized Networks

It can be said, then, that a feminism that aspires to be global needs to make use of a number of developments in and insights from contemporary feminisms from around the world. Global feminism should not be understood as assuming the perspective of, emerging through, or needing insights from feminists or feminisms in the West. It should seek to avoid Eurocentric versions of feminism that use categories of analysis that begin from the lives and experiences of women in first-world countries and end with generalizations about women in third-world countries as having lives and experiences similar to but worse than women in first-world countries (Mohanty 1997; Abu-Lughod 2001). Instead, a feminism that aspires to be global starts with the idea that women's movements and activism emerge from the material conditions and ideological circumstances that have shaped the inequalities and injustices experienced by women in their various contexts. It works with the idea that an account of third-world women's struggles against colonial and imperial forces is as relevant to an account of the history of feminist theory and movements as is the story of Western feminism that has been dominant thus far. As Ella Shohat puts it, "the activism of third-world women throughout the period of colonization and decolonization [is] a kind of subterranean, unrecognized form of feminism and, therefore, a legitimate part of feminist historiography" (Shohat 2001, 1270). When these are taken as elements of global feminism, possibilities for alliances, coalitions, and solidarity across cultures and histories can be explored and the shared goal of challenging local and global forces that create and perpetuate women's oppression can be pursued.

Women in transnational and globalized networks and alliances are crossing increasingly permeable borders through the Internet and in person to participate in international conferences, to engage in dialogue and discourse that speaks across differences, and to construct a women's movement that is understood as both local and global. Amrita Basu tracks these transnational initiatives in her historical account of the 1995 Beijing's women's conference and its aftermath of a growth of linkages, networks, and alliances among a diverse range of organizations, movements, and issue-based initiatives at the local and global levels (Basu 2000).

Sometimes strategies call for using international law or the discourse of human rights, sometimes they call for challenging the laws or extending the meaning of human rights, and sometimes they call for action and policy specific to the local level. Through these processes local movements not only learn about the experiences and successes of other local movements, but also gain strength from mobilizing and strategizing at the global level. Examples of such mobilizing and strategizing include the Association for Women's Rights in Development (AWID), an "international network striving to support proactive and strategic gender equality research, activism, and policy dialogue" (http://www.awid.org); Development Alternatives with Women for a New Era (DAWN), "a network of women scholars and activists from the economic South who engage in feminist research and analysis of the global environment and are committed to working for economic justice, gender justice and democracy" (http://www.dawnnet.org); the International Association for Feminist Economics that collects "scholars, policy professionals, students, advocates, and activists interested in empowering and improving the well-being of women—and other under-represented groups—around the world" (http://www.iaffe.org/); Feminist Approaches to Bioethics, an international organization of feminist bioethicists "dedicated to the interests of women as patients, citizens, parents, practitioners and carers" (http://www.fabnet.org/); and the United Nations' WomenWatch, "a central gateway to information and resources on the promotion of gender equality and the empowerment of women throughout the United Nations system, including the United Nations Secretariat, regional commissions, funds, programmes, specialized agencies and academic and research institutions" (http://www.un.org/womenwatch/about/).

The account of global feminism provided here started with the claim that it is becoming more and more difficult to delineate kinds of feminism. This is as true for current versions of and revisions to liberal and radical feminism as it is for new forms of feminism variously labeled as postcolonial, postmodern, poststructuralist, third world, global, or transnational. In the case of each new or revised version of feminism, however, there remains a responsibility to accurately describe women's oppression as it exists in the contemporary context of globalization and to devise strategies and policies that are truly effective for ending that oppression. Feminists have had to learn lessons from false universalizing. A feminism that aspires to be global must stand ready to uncover biases in accounts from perspectives of privilege, power, and authority, accounts that fail to recognize the effects of these biases on women in a postcolonial and globalized world. It must also stand ready to revise descriptive and normative accounts that may succeed in explaining or alleviating women's oppression in one context only to ignore or worsen it another. As Felicity Nussbaum puts it, "the current despair and pessimism about feminism and its theory might be reimagined as a redirection away from white feminism to a global feminism. Women of color and lesbian women of all 'races' are already engaged in radical redefinition rather than in nostalgia for what once was, and they have recharged feminism's batteries. White feminism is in crisis, not feminism itself" (Nussbaum, 1993, 269).

BIBLIOGRAPHY AND SUGGESTED READINGS

ABU-LUGHOD, LILA. (2001) "Orientalism and Middle East Feminist Studies." *Feminist Studies* 21(1), 101–113.

Alexander, M. Jacqui, and Chandra Mohanty (eds.). (1997) *Feminist Genealogies, Colonial Legacies, Democratic Futures.* New York: Routledge.

ANZALDÚA, GLORIA. (1987) *Borderlands. La Frontera; The New Mestiza.* San Francisco, CA: Aunt Lute Books.

Association for Women's Rights in Development. (2006) *Achieving Women's Economic and Social Rights: Strategies and Lessons from Experience.* Toronto: Association for Women's Rights in Development.

Baumgardner, Jennifer, and Amy Richards (eds.). (2000) *Manifesta: Young Women, Feminism, and the Future.* New York: Farrar, Straus and Giroux.

BASU, AMRITA. (2000) "Globalization of the Local/Localization of the Global: Mapping Transnational Women's Movements." *Meridians* 1(1), 68–109.

BENERÍA, LOURDES, MARIA FLORO, CAREN GROWN, and MARTHA MACDONALD. (2000) "Introduction: Globalization and Gender." *Feminist Economics* 6(3), vii–xviii.

COLLINS, PATRICIA HILL. (1990) *Black Feminist Thought: Knowledge, Consciousness, and the Politics of Empowerment.* Boston, MA: Unwin Hyman.

CORREA, SÔNIA, and ROSALIND POLLACK PETCHESKY. (1984) "Reproductive and Sexual Rights: A Feminist Perspective." In *Population Policies Reconsidered,* edited by Gita Sena, Adrienne German, and Lincoln C. Chen. Cambridge, MA: Harvard University Center for Population and Development Studies.

CRENSHAW, KIMBERLÉ. (1991) "Mapping the Margins: Intersectionality, Identity Politics, and Violence Against Women of Color." *Stanford Law Review* 43(6), 1241–1299.

Findlen, Barbara (ed.). (1995) *Listen Up: Voices from the Next Feminist Generation.* Seattle, WA: Seal Press.

FRIEDAN, BETTY. (1963) *The Feminine Mystique.* New York: Norton.

FUSSELL, ELISABETH. (2000) "Making Labor Flexible: The Recomposition of Tijuana's Maquiladora Female Labor Force." *Feminist Economics* 6(2000), 59–79.

Heywood, Leslie, and Jennifer Drake (eds.). (1997) *Third Wave Agenda: Being Feminist, Doing Feminism.* Minneapolis, MN: University of Minnesota Press.

HOOKS, BELL. (1984) *Feminist Theory: From Margin to Center.* Boston, MA: South End Press.

———. (1988) *Talking Back: Thinking Feminist, Thinking Black.* Toronto: Between the Lines.

KABEER, NAILA. (2004) "Globalization, Labor Standards, and Women's Rights: Dilemmas of Collective (In)action in an Interdependent World." *Feminist Economics* 10(1), 3–35.

KOGGEL, CHRISTINE. (2002) "Equality Analysis in a Global Context: A Relational Approach." *Canadian Journal of Philosophy. Supplementary Volume: Feminist Moral Philosophy* 28, 247–272.

———. (2003) "Globalization and Women's Paid Work: Expanding Freedom." *Feminist Economics. Special Issue: Amartya Sen's Work and Ideas* 9(2 and 3), 163–183.

———. (2007) "Empowerment and the Role of Advocacy in a Globalized World." *Ethics and Social Welfare* 1(1), 8–21.

LORDE, AUDRE. (1984) *Sister Outsider: Essays and Speeches.* Freedom, CA: The Crossing Press.

MIES, MARIA. (1982) "The Dynamics of the Sexual Division of Labor and Integration of Rural Women into the World Market." In *Women and Development: The Sexual*

Division of Labor in Rural Societies, edited by Lourdes Benería. New York: Praeger, 1–28.

Mohanty, Chandra. (1988) "Under Western Eyes: Feminist Scholarship and Colonial Discourses." *Feminist Review* 30(Autumn), 61–88.

———. (1997) "Women Workers and Capitalist Scripts: Ideologies of Domination, Common Interests, and the Politics of Solidarity." In *Feminist Genealogies, Colonial Legacies, Democratic Futures,* edited by M. J. Alexander and C. Mohanty. New York: Routledge, 3–29.

Mohanty, Chandra, Ann Russo, and Lourdes Torres (eds.). (1991) *Third World Women and the Politics of Feminism.* Bloomington, IN: Indiana University Press.

Molyneux, Maxine. (1988) "The Politics of Abortion in Nicargua: Revolutionary Pragmatism—Or Feminism in the Realm of Necessity?" *The Feminist Review* 29(May 1988), 114–132.

Moraga, Cherrie, and Gloria Anzaldúa (eds.). (1981) *This Bridge Called My Back: Writings by Radical Women of Color.* New York: Kitchen Table, Women of Color Press.

Morgan, Robin (ed.). (1970) *Sisterhood is Powerful; An Anthology of Writings from the Women's Liberation Movement.* New York: Random House.

Narayan, Uma. (1997) *Dislocating Cultures: Identities, Traditions, and Third World Feminism.* New York: Routledge.

Narayan, Uma, and Sandra Harding (eds.). (2000) *Decentering the Center: Philosophy for a Multicultural, Postcolonial, and Feminist World.* Bloomington, IN: Indiana University Press.

Nicholson, Linda J. (ed.). (1990). *Feminism/Postmodernism.* New York: Routledge.

Nussbaum, Felicity. (1993) "White Anglo-American Feminism in Non-US/Non-us Space." *Tulsa Studies in Women's Literature* 12(2), 263–270.

Okin, Susan Moller. (1989) *Justice, Gender, and the Family.* New York: Basic Books.

———. (1994) "General Inequality and Cultural Differences." *Political Theory* 22(1), 5–24.

Ong, Aihwa. (2006) "Sisterly Solidarity: Feminist Virtue under 'Moderate Islam.'" In *Neoliberalism as Exception: Mutations in Citizenship and Sovereignty.* Durham, NC: Duke University Press.

Parpart, Jane, et al. (eds.). (2002) *Rethinking Empowerment: Gender and Development in a Global/Local World.* London: Routledge.

Roa, Monica. (2005) *Challenging Abortion Law in Columbia: An Interview with Monica Roa* http://www.womenslinkworldwide.org/pdf_programs/prog_rr_col_articles_25.pdf (accessed October 11, 2009).

Salazar-Parreñas, Rhacel. (2001) *Servants of Globalization: Women, Migration and Domestic Work.* Palo Alto, CA: Stanford University Press.

Scott, Joan W. (1990) "Deconstructing Equality-Versus-Difference: Or, the Uses of Poststructuralist Theory for Feminism." In *Conflicts in Feminism,* edited by Marianne Hirsch and Evelyn Fox Keller. New York: Routledge.

Shohat, Ella. (2001) "Area Studies, Transnationalism, and the Feminist Production of Knowledge." *Signs: Journal of Women in Culture and Society* 26(4), 1269–1272.

Spelman, Elizabeth. (1988) *The Inessential Woman.* Boston, MA: Beacon Press.

Walker, Rebecca (ed.). (1995) *To Be Real: Telling the Truth and Changing the Face of Feminism.* New York: Anchor Books.

CHAPTER 40

NATIVE AMERICAN PHILOSOPHY

ADAM AROLA

It is a popular contention, articulated by thinkers as disparate as Aristotle and Enrique Dussel, that only organized, urban societies permit the practice of philosophy. A class of people who we would call philosophers—those who consider why the world is the way it is—can only emerge within a social setting that permits sufficient leisure for some people to move away from the basic human labors of acquiring food and shelter. In asking whether or not there is such a thing as American Indian philosophy, many people are thus inclined to look for a class of people within traditional native cultures who exhibit this kind of sustained and organized questioning. Nearly every indigenous culture throughout the world has something resembling a class of what Westerners would want to call religious leaders. The *tlamatinime* within Nahuatl culture or the *midewiwin* within Ojibwe Anishinaabe culture are just two examples. In both cases these segments of the population were (and are in the case of the Ojibwe) responsible for ceremonial practice, for interpreting dreams, and for helping people through the trials and tribulations of their lives via articulating the place of any individual lives within the structural whole that is the cosmos. Even Miguel León-Portilla, a scholar sympathetic to the brilliance and peculiarity of Nahuatl culture, refuses to ever fully characterize the *tlamatinime* as philosophers. Instead, scholars are often criticized for daring to categorize such thinkers as philosophers, and quite often this critique is leveled precisely because the segment of the population that is responsible for this practice either have recourse to forms of language (poetry, song, prayer) that are considered nonphilosophical or explicitly articulate and interpret the world through the cosmological framework of their culture, which often includes references to deities and other spiritual entities. Accordingly, such people could be said to articulate the ramifications of what it means to have the philosophy that they do without ever really questioning the validity and soundness of their "worldview." Thus, Western scholars often grant that pre-Columbian (and even post-Columbian) indigenous populations had religious traditions, beliefs, and practices that may have even resembled theology; many scholars, however, resist calling such intellectual practices philosophy.

One of the most pernicious tendencies in engaging indigenous populations is the tendency to seek the primitive, the primal, the unadulterated, the pre-Columbian. To ask whether or not American Indian populations *did* philosophy is to forego asking the question of whether or not American Indian populations *do* philosophy, today. Such a tendency is often accompanied by a desire to lambast and critique contemporary indigenous populations for betraying their authentic Indian roots and steering toward syncretism. This tendency to seek out the authentically native is a voyeuristic and damaging fantasy perpetrated by much of the West from those who would call Indians primitive barbarians to those acolytes of Carlos Castañeda who would hope to find an authentic medicine man to help them find their spirit animal while smoking peyote. In both cases, the voices of indigenous populations are silenced. The outsider who approaches assumes the authority to tell Indian populations what it would mean for them to be authentically indigenous.

While I do not assert that one has nothing to learn from looking back at records of pre-Columbian ceremonial practices, or from attempting to derive the ontological implications of traditional Indian stories, or from reading a brilliant text such as Neihardt's *Black Elk Speaks*, I take a different tack in introducing Native American philosophy here. I will introduce the central thinkers of contemporary American Indian philosophy by discussing concerns including, but not limited to, the nature of experience, meaning, truth, the status of the individual and community, and finally issues concerning sovereignty.

The impossibility of carving up the intellectual traditions of contemporary Native scholars in North America into neat and tidy disciplines must be kept in mind. The first hallmark of American Indian philosophy is the commitment to the belief that all things are related—and this belief is not simply an ontological claim, but rather an intellectual and ethical maxim.

Experience and Truth

The work of V. F. Cordova provides an account of how truth is conceptualized within Native American philosophy. Cordova died in 2003, but a collection of her essays and poems was published in 2007 under the title, *How It Is: The Native American Philosophy of V.F. Cordova*. In this text, Cordova never develops any kind of overt doctrine of "how it is"; rather, she exhibits a univocal comportment of questioning. She does not seek to rest in the stasis of an answer that could respond to the question of "how is it?"—a desire Cordova frequently aligns with Euro-American philosophical and scientific tendencies. She explains, "The Euro-American conducts his attempts to understand his world on the assumption that there are definitive explanations to be discovered.... there will be one universal—all encompassing—and absolute—beyond question—Truth" (Cordova 2007, 69). Such a conception of truth can only be borne out of a conception of the world as static, unchanging.

Nevertheless, Cordova exhibits constancy in her philosophical comportment. Confronted with any concept, Cordova argues that philosophy happens when one asks, "In what sort of world would this concept make sense?" (Cordova 2007, 56). The answer points toward a matrix, which she defines as a "view, or description [that] consists of three very basic items: a description of the world, a description of what it is to be human in that world, and a description of the role of humans in that world.... [T]he matrix forms a foundation upon which all else is explained" (Cordova 2007, 61).

According to Cordova, most of the time we live unaware of the matrix that enables us to engage the world as we do. For Cordova, a matrix is most often exposed when two conflicting conceptual frameworks come into contact with one another; she exhibits this fact most clearly in her own autobiographical writings, explaining how she always found herself in the midst of multiple matrices. This encounter with the limits of our knowledge, the ungrounded foundations of our explanatory frameworks, is where we confront the fact of the matrix. Cordova argues that this happens more often for indigenous folks in colonial circumstances than for the colonizers, as indigenous populations are constantly confronted with not only another matrix, but a matrix that dominates how all conversation and discourse must take place—a theme to which we return in discussing sovereignty.

As there is hegemony of Euro-American belief systems in North America, it is rare that people who encounter the world via the matrix of the West need account for their beliefs. This fact, more than anything, motivates Cordova's writing. Taking stock of the rise of multiculturalism, she writes, "While the Native American, as an *artifact*, is undergoing a resurgence of popularity, the Native American as he actually exists is ignored" (Cordova 2007, 163). Cordova's exposure of the matrix that underpins Euro-American knowledge systems, in effect, exposes the particularity, peculiarity, and relativity of Western claims of universality. In turn, this creates space for contemporary indigenous voices to speak for themselves.

Contrary to many Western philosophical tendencies, which take their root in Platonistic understandings of truth as pure presence, pure stability, and immutability, Cordova argues that stability in the native world is about knowing how to ensure that consistency can be found amidst complexity. This task will always be circumstantial, environmental, and ongoing. "Each perspective, in its own environment, or circumstances, will be 'true' or 'valid'—in *that* environment, in *those* circumstances....He does not assume the 'incorrectness' of the other's perspective when it does not coincide with his own" (Cordova 2007, 71). For Cordova, the nature of indigenous matrices is rooted in the ontology that undergirds them: the combined emphasis on monism and the diversity and specificity of creations implies that not only are practices particular to places, but also all practices are instantiations of and simultaneously responses to the univocity of being named variously "'nilch'i' by the Navajo, 'najoji' by the Blackfoot, 'usen' by the Apache, 'manitou' by the Ojibway" (Cordova 2007, 104). Cordova thus argues that there is no universal Truth, while maintaining that certain referential frameworks are appropriate to situated manifestations of "the unidentifiable *is*" (Cordova 2007, 107). The Western model fails from the beginning by assuming that infinite complexity can be subsumed under one template.

This claim—that there are truths that could be categorized as universal within a particular matrix but that are not universal *tout court* insofar as what is manifests itself in particular places and sites—may strike a reader as odd and even paradoxical. Yet it is a claim that resonates with even more emphatic claims made by other indigenous philosophers. Both Brian Yazzie Burkhart and Vine Deloria Jr. argue that one of the fundamental characteristics of indigenous conceptions of experience is that there is no distinction between the ordinary and the extraordinary. What this claim amounts to is that an indigenous comportment is essentially phenomenological. An indigenous comportment toward what is must perpetually attend to the fact that the manner in which what is shows itself will be multifarious and unpredictable. Any attempt to fully conceptualize how things will appear to us prior to our experience of them will place undue limits upon the presencing of things. J. Irving Hallowell recounts a conversation with an old Ojibwe man regarding the capacity of stones and other apparently inanimate objects to speak to humans. Noting that stones "are grammatically animate," he recounts that he "once asked an old man: Are *all* stones we see about us here alive? He reflected a long while and then replied, 'No! But *some* are" (Tedlock and Tedlock 1992, 147). Deloria, Burkhart and others (including Lee Hester) would not necessarily interpret this assertion to mean that this old man had actually spoken to a stone before, but rather that he would not close off the possibility that he could learn something from interacting with a stone. If we approach the stone as an inanimate object in advance, assuming that it is nothing but a mute object that sits in front of us, at our disposal to use as we will, we will never encounter a stone as anything more than such a mute object. And if we were hypothetically to have an encounter with any kind of object that we encountered as anomalous with regard to the expectations imposed upon experience by our matrix, Burkhart and Deloria argue that we will cast such an experience aside and ignore it. An indigenous manner of conceptualizing experience would perpetually attend to the way in which things show themselves to us, attempting to broach the world as something that can never exhibit anomalies, precisely because anything and everything is possible.

The previous paragraph's account does not, however, resolve the apparent paradox of Cordova's assertion. In order to understand how and why she is justified in asserting the relative universality of truth claims within indigenous matrices, it helps to appreciate the affinity between a pragmatist's account of truth and that which is often advocated for by many Native American thinkers. While running the risk of engaging in an act of essentializing, Deloria's pan-Indian tendencies lead him to be quite emphatic that for "the indigenous mind," truth is tantamount to function. Something is believed to be true if it is verified by experience to have sufficient explanatory power to enable a person to accomplish tasks. Scott Pratt has extensively traced this account of truth and its affinity to pragmatism in his *Native Pragmatism*. He argues that many of the major trends of American philosophy are borne of interactions between Europeans and American Indians. The otherwise idealist tendencies of late-nineteenth-century American philosophy were mitigated by border encounters between whites from the Northeast and the Haudenosaunee confederation. This argument points to the shared tendency in the pragmatic tradition and the indigenous philosophical traditions of North America to have a conception of truth that is both universally applicable but also eminently revisable; for any account of truth *qua* function can be communicated as the *best* thing to believe, the *best* way to accomplish a task, that we know so far. But openness to the possibility that experience may show us superior ways to accomplish a task indicates that this conception of truth is always understood to be flexible and at the mercy of what is shown in experience. Gregory Cajete further vindicates this claim in his *Native Science*, arguing that indigenous knowledge practices at both the ontological level and the practical level—that is, planting crops, building irrigation systems—are always based on a process of trial and error. Indigenous populations learn from what has succeeded and modify the way in which they conceive of the world to accord with results, always aware that there is more to be learned from experience, all the while maintaining a full awareness that anything understood as true or appropriate to believe in any given moment is always transient and revisable through further experience and further dialogue with the world. It is this openness toward the perpetual transformation of one's views that delineates indigenous thinking from many—but certainly not all—philosophical tendencies one may encounter throughout the world.

The Community and the Individual

Yet this account raises the question of what kinds of experiences and interactions are things from which we can learn. To fully understand what could count as an experience from which one could learn, we must first discuss how exactly it is that indigenous thinkers conceptualize identity. Without an account of how the identity of a knower, or a thing to be known, is conceived, there is no way to arrive at an understanding of what would count as an epistemic experience.

While it is fair to say that the array of indigenous philosophers present within North America would not completely agree about how to conceive of identity, I will offer an account that I believe captures the most basic sense and convictions held by indigenous thinkers. First and foremost, we must understand that identity is not understood as something that is given to anything in isolation. Scott Lyons claims in his article "Rhetorical Sovereignty" that Indian cultural understandings of what it means to be a political human being are very different from this model of ipseity and self-determination. The individual self does not have primacy as in the Kantian tradition, wherein the state is a collective of already mini-sovereigns, individuals, who get together and form the nation-state. Lyons rejects this view for a concept of a nation-people. A people here is defined as "a group of human beings united together by history, language, culture, or some combination therein—a community joined in union for common purpose: the survival and flourishing of the people itself" (Lyons 2000, 454). Thus, the status of the individual takes a backseat.

Within indigenous communities one often hears the adage, "we are all related." For Deloria, Lyons, Sandy Grande, Cajete, and many others, truth and identity are terms best understood through how we conceive of our relatives—I refer to it as relational identity: the identity of any particular entity in the world can never be discovered by distilling the essence out of a particular object such that one could arrive at an eternal *eidos* that shines out of this particular encapsulation; rather, identity emerges through the constant act of relating. Deloria describes this as follows: "everything in the natural world has relationships with every other thing and the total set of relationships make up the world as we experience it" (Deloria 1999, 34). That is to say, the essence of any particular thing *is what it is only insofar as it relates to what it is not*. If this is the case, and the identity—insofar as this is understood as something that one seeks in epistemic inquiry—of a particular bird is sought, the only way in which to come to know "what" this bird is is to understand the web of relations in which it participates in a particular place at a particular time. In other words, to know the bird means to know the "personality" of the bird insofar as it plays a part in a structure that is larger than the body of the bird itself. This, then, necessitates that one has an understanding of the causal nexus that the bird participates in to make the web of relations to which it belongs behave the way it does. Knowing the particular bird, then, would mean knowing what the bird eats, where it builds its nest, and what its different songs can tell us about this particular place. But these things are only knowable insofar as we have an understanding of the whole in which the bird participates. Here, then, the universal—or the genus, for example—is eschewed in lieu of knowledge of the network that this bird sustains and that, in turn, sustains the bird.

There is a further complication in this account of identity. Given the emphasis upon not only relation but also the act of *relating*, the nature of any particular thing is perpetually in process and thus perpetually changing. Accordingly, the bird—take a thrush, for example—is never knowable in exactly the same way twice. Therefore, one must be perpetually open and responsive to the manner in which the thrush shows itself at a particular moment in a particular place in order to be confident that one can learn something from, or about, the thrush. We can now see why the account of experience given in the work of Burkhart and Deloria places such a radical emphasis upon the lack of distinction between the ordinary and the extraordinary in indigenous conceptions of experience. That which is to be an object can never be encountered as what it is insofar as one attempts to appropriate a static object. Only insofar as the matter of experience is encountered in the singular manner of its happening can we have an experience that can teach us something about ourselves and about the world around us. And both of these claims are tantamount to claims of self-knowledge, for knowing oneself within Native American thought necessitates knowing how one is constituted by and simultaneously perpetually constituting the world that one inhabits.

With this understanding of identity in mind, we can thus get a handle on the apparent peculiarities of many Native American conceptions of the individual human and their place within a human community. First and foremost, the individual is not simply conceived of as an epiphenomenon of a community. This view that would privilege the tribe over its members may have currency in some circumstances, yet in many cases it is far too simple of a characterization of indigenous conceptions of community. Asserting that indigenous conceptions of identity are community centered whereas Euro-American conceptions of identity are individual centered is an account that too simply accepts the basic coordinates of univocal emergence from a preexisting, static entity, whether that entity happens to be an individual or a community. Within Native conceptions of the individual and the community, these two moments are always reciprocally determining. There is no individual prior to a community, nor is there any community prior to the individual. We cannot conceptualize either half of this supposed opposition without the other.

Thinking of ourselves in our sociality, or in our belonging to nature, it would be clear to say that for this indigenous conception of personhood or identity, an individual cannot be said to exist without the "people"—and we see how broadly this must be construed insofar as it includes all of our relationships. Insofar as personhood is extended not only to nonhuman animals, but even to the things of the world that are often considered inanimate, the question of who is to flourish is no longer about individuals within a structure that serves them, but rather the people as a whole. And that people as a whole is thus to be understood as the whole web of existence in which any singular being inheres. And here, we get a sense of how the ontological commitments of Native American philosophy overlap with the political commitments; in fact, I would argue, one cannot make sense of one without the other.

Sovereignty

This leads us to the final major theme of Native American philosophy: sovereignty. Lyons points out that a native model of sovereignty "is probably best understood as the right of a people to exist and enter into agreements with other peoples for the sole purpose of promoting, not suppressing, local cultures and traditions, even while united by a common political project—in this case, the noble goal of peace between peoples" (Lyons 2000, 456). One need only think about the Haudenosaunee confederation to get a sense of what Lyons is getting at: tribes united for the sake of all of their flourishing, which would seem to require an awareness of their dependence on one another. The Great Law of Peace as established in the 117 Codicils "were," as Charles Mann puts it, "concerned as much with establishing limits on the great council's powers as on granting them" (Mann 2006, 372). Interestingly enough, the council that represented the Five Nations—constituted by male sachems chosen by female clan heads within specific tribes—could not declare war, but only negotiate peace treaties. War declaration was left to the particular nation-people. And within the great council, all decisions had to be unanimous, a step away—it would seem—from representative democracy wherein individuals battle, wage war, within a parliamentary system so as to win a majority (Mann 2006, 372). Respect and reciprocity, not autonomous abuse of power—this is the key moment of political life in indigenous conceptions of community.

Nevertheless, in thinkers such as Lyons, Dale Turner, Taiaiake Alfred, and others, we find a complaint about traditional multicultural education in American universities as it bears upon issues of tribal sovereignty. Lyons writes, "Mainstream multiculturalism may focus on the *people* but typically not the *nation* and thus isn't necessarily the practice or honoring of Indian sovereignty" (Lyons 2000, 457). The battle for Indian sovereignty is the battle for political recognition—and this battle is covered over in lieu of a quasi-cultural voyeurism by the majority of multiculturalists in America. In Dale Turner's *This Is Not a Peace Pipe: Towards a Critical Indigenous Philosophy*, he articulates precisely this problem. Attempts by tribal governments to interact politically with the Canadian and American governments are nearly always foiled in advance insofar as North American governments conceive of sovereignty and identity in accordance with a liberal political model that is premised upon a variety of quite specific ontological and epistemological commitments. North American governments traditionally misrecognize the variant nature of indigenous conceptions of identity and sovereignty either because they are overdetermined by their own conception of the good life[1] or because Native populations are themselves overdetermined by the interpretative framework imposed upon them by the image of Indians in the North American

1. Turner would argue that the Canadian 1969 White Paper is an example of precisely this tendency. The White Paper was a policy document issued by then head of Aboriginal affairs Jean Chrétien as an attempt to overturn the policies of the Indian Act—a legislative act that had greatly curtailed the civil rights of Aboriginal peoples in Canada, subjecting them to land claims and giving them a peculiar status as separate and unequal to other citizens of Canada. In large part, the goal of the White Paper—from Chrétien's perspective—was to eliminate the status of "Aboriginal" as an identity recognized by the Canadian government. Instead, the objective was to assimilate Aboriginal populations into the broader Canadian population, thus making them Canadian citizens first, who just happened to be Aboriginal. As Turner elucidates, many Aboriginal groups responded to the White Paper by insisting that the attempt to assimilate them into a modern, liberal society without attending to the particular understanding of what it means to be a person, to be a citizen, to be sovereign, was tantamount to continued colonization by other means.

imagination as Deloria would put it. If there is no good-faith effort made to encounter indigenous populations on their own terms, particularly with regards to how they conceive of themselves politically, any attempt at negotiation—whether those negotiations be regarding simple facts of daily life such as hunting rights or about larger issues concerning rights to self-determination—between North American and tribal governments will fail. Within such a circumstance, dialogue is simply not possible. For this reason, Turner advocates for what he calls "word warriors":

> An Aboriginal mediator—a word warrior—is an indigenous person who engages the imposed legal and political discourses of the state guided by the belief that the knowledge and skills to be gained by engaging in such discourses are necessary for the survival of all indigenous peoples. (Turner 2007, 92)

As he explains, a word warrior must thereby be a person who in a certain sense belongs to both an indigenous community while also being able to speak the language of Euro-American philosophy, law, and politics. The task of such a person, as the above quote indicates, is to mediate between these two worlds—and in fact, insofar as such a person "belongs" anywhere, we may have to say that they belong to this *between*. Here Turner is respectfully critiquing indigenous thinkers such as Taiaiake Alfred, who explicitly advocate for a kind of separatism wherein indigenous intellectuals carve out and create their own communities, distinct from—and hopefully uninfluenced by—the academic and legal discourse of the Euro-American world. Contrary to Alfred, Turner writes:

> I am suggesting that instead of carving out their own communities and asserting their intellectual sovereignty within them, Aboriginal intellectuals must develop a community of practitioners *within* the existing dominant legal and political intellectual communities, while remaining an essential part of a thriving indigenous intellectual community. (Turner 2007, 90)

The objective is thus that word warriors will be able to simultaneously sustain and defend the integrity of indigenous life and culture by employing, working on, and working with the intellectual traditions of the West while still being rooted in indigenous culture.

Whether or not Turner's objective is actually realizable is uncertain. Many thinkers such as Gordon Christie and Taiaiake Alfred would likely disagree with Turner's thesis. For many indigenous thinkers, the desperation over the failure of past attempts to interact with North American governments in a manner that was productive for indigenous populations has proven to be too great an obstacle to overcome with any theoretical apparatus. Yet Turner's response would certainly be that indigenous populations must press forward, and doing so as mediators, negotiators, and interpreters is the only authentically indigenous manner of doing so. One of the primary ramifications of the claims that I have made thus far is that the conception of experience described above demands that indigenous peoples are perpetually in the process of negotiating with the world around them to be who and what they are. If this is the case, then Turner's thesis about word warriors would seem to be the most appropriate manner of engaging governments insofar as one wishes to be true to his or her indigeneity.

The activity and comportment of those who word warriors encounter in the courthouse, the parliament, or the classroom has just as much of an impact on the nature of the encounter. And to the extent that I am advocating, just as Turner is for a "critical indigenous philosophy," let us hear him out. This is what Turner has in mind when advocating for a critical indigenous philosophy. Explaining the approach that word warriors are to take in the academy, he writes:

> ...[this] approach makes an investigation of the meaning and praxis of colonialism a central activity of an indigenous intellectual community. The dialogue between indigenous intellectuals and their non-indigenous counterparts created by unpacking colonialism from the history of ideas generates the philosophical battleground for word warriors. This kind of intellectual dialogue can lead us to what I call a "critical indigenous philosophy." (Turner 2007, 101)

To the extent that our encounters with the history of philosophy, for example, can amount to the unpacking of colonialism, we can only be successful to the extent that people have ears to hear what we are saying. Insofar as people continue to carry themselves monologically, our encounter with the history of ideas will be *precisely* a battleground—a conflict between two opposing sides, one that insists that dialogue can actually happen and thus would hopefully not try to see this dialogue as a *battle*, and another that insists that all conversation is, in fact, a battle. For most people who comport themselves in accord with the narcissism of monologue, the monologue of the sovereign that is above the law, actually engaging in open, incomplete dialogue—actually negotiating—is unthinkable and impossible. Yet Turner's vision is for me worth striving for and is consonant with the account of Native American thought that I have presented.

Conclusion

We have concluded this account with Turner's writing on sovereignty. Yet this account could have begun and ended with any of the concepts discussed. For indigenous conceptions of sovereignty are wedded to conceptions of the nature of being, which are in turn wedded to conceptions of what it would mean to live well and what it would mean to know; all of these allegedly separable disciplines are what they are only insofar as they are perpetually in the process of relating to one another. The conception of the identity of any particular thing that we discussed earlier must also—and does—apply to the different objects of study broached within indigenous thought. All of the seemingly disparate disciplines are themselves dependent on one another to be what they are. One cannot have a full understanding of any aspect of indigenous thought without attending to all others. And it is in this simple fact that we find, perhaps, the most fundamental quality of Native American philosophy.

BIBLIOGRAPHY AND SUGGESTED READINGS

ALFRED, TAIAIAKE. (1999) *Peace, Power, Righteousness: An Indigenous Manifesto*. Don Mills: Oxford University Press.

American Indians in Philosophy Newsletter from the American Philosophical Association, edited by Adam Arola. www.apaonline.org/publications/newsletters/americanindians.aspx

AROLA, ADAM. (2007) "'A Larger Scheme of Life': Deloria on Essence and Science (in Dialogue with Continental Philosophy)." *American Indians in Philosophy Newsletter from the American Philosophical Association* 7, 1.

———. (2008) "Dialogue and Identity: Worries About Word Warriors." *American Indians in Philosophy Newsletter from the American Philosophical Association* 8, 2.

———. (2009a) "How It Is: The Native Philosophy of V.F. Cordova." *Canadian Journal of Native Studies*. In press.

———. (2009b) "Taking on the Tradition: Sovereignty and Self-Identity." In *Philosophy and Aboriginal Rights: A Critical Dialogue*, edited by Lorraine Mayer and Sandra Tomsons. Cambridge: Oxford University Press.

CAJETE, GREGORY. (1994) *Look To the Mountain: An Ecology of Indigenous Education*. Durango, CO: Kivaki Press.

———. (2000) *Native Science: Natural Laws of Interdependence*. Santa Fe, NM: Clear Light Publishers.

CORDOVA, V. F. (2007) *How It Is: The Native American Philosophy of V.F. Cordova*, edited by Kathleen Dean Moore, Kurt Peters, Ted Jojola, and Amber Lacy. Tucson, AZ: University of Arizona Press.

DELORIA, VINE, JR. (1999) *Spirit & Reason: The Vine Deloria, Jr. Reader*. Golden, CO: Fulcrum Publishing.

———. (2003) *God Is Red: A Native View of Religion*. Golden, CO: Fulcrum Publishing.

DELORIA, VINE, JR., and CLIFFORD LYTLE. (1983) *American Indians, American Justice*. Austin, TX: University of Texas Press.

———. (1984) *The Nations Within: The Past and Future of American Indian Sovereignty*. Austin, TX: University of Texas Press.

DELORIA, VINE, JR., and DANIEL WILDCAT. (2001) *Power and Place: Indian Education in America*. Golden, CO: Fulcrum Publishing.

GRANDE, SANDY. (2004) *Red Pedagogy: Native American Social and Political Thought*. New York: Rowman and Littlefield.

LEON-PORTILLA, MIGUEL. (1992) *Aztec Thought and Culture: A Study of the Ancient Nahuatl Mind*. Norman, OK: University of Oklahoma Press.

LYONS, SCOTT RICHARD. (2000) "Rhetorical Sovereignty: What Do American Indians Want from Writing?" *CCC* 51, 3.

MANN, CHARLES. (2006) *1491: New Revelations of the Americas Before Columbus*. New York: Vintage.

Pratt, Scott. (2002) *Native Pragmatism: Rethinking the Roots of American Philosophy*. Bloomington, IN: Indiana University Press.

Tedlock, Barbara, and Dennis Tedlock. (1992) *Teachings from the American Earth: Indian Religion and Philosophy*. New York: Liveright Press.

Turner, Dale. (2007) *This Is Not a Peace Pipe: Towards a Critical Indigenous Philosophy*. Toronto: University of Toronto Press.

Waters, Anne. (2004) *American Indian Thought*. Oxford: Blackwell Publishing.

Whitt, Laurie. (1995) "Indigenous People and the Cultural Politics of Knowledge." In *Issues in Native American Cultural Identity*, edited by Michele K. Green. New York: Peter Lang.

CHAPTER 41

INDIGENOUS ENVIRONMENTAL PHILOSOPHY

WORKINEH KELBESSA

FACING massive resource depletion, species extinction, and pollution overload—most significantly leading to climate change, with its far-reaching consequences—environmental challenges and their impacts on humans and other animals have become thematized in virtually every discipline. Although some Western thinkers emphasized the relationship between humans and the natural environment in ancient, medieval, and modern periods, it was not until the twentieth century, largely prompted by environmental crises, that environmental philosophy became a field in its own right. Today, the rubric of "environmental philosophy" includes most prominently environmental ethics, but also environmental aesthetics, ecojustice, and certain kinds of explorations of epistemology; metaphysics and ontology; language; architecture, place, and dwelling; philosophy of science and technology; political theory and political action; global justice; economics; education; theology and religion; animal ethics and animal studies; agriculture; tourism and travel; and so forth. Indeed, virtually every aspect of human culture is now being studied in its relation to the more-than-human world, and philosophers are reflecting on these relations.

At the same time as Western philosophers have been developing the field of environmental philosophy, scholars have been documenting the worldviews of some peoples in America, Asia, Africa, and the Pacific, especially indigenous cultures, and they have stressed that indigenous environmental knowledge has had a paramount role in addressing environmental challenges. Non-Western traditions are, for this reason, often held up as models for how to live in harmony with the more-than-human world. Indeed, in a famous and influential article, Lynn White Jr. claimed it was the devaluation of nature and pervasive anthropocentrism characteristic of Western philosophical and religious traditions that constituted the root cause of environmental crises. In contrast, he suggested, Asian traditions, which conceive of human beings as wholly interdependent with the natural world, presented a more ecologically sustainable way of thinking and, therefore, way of life. In recent years scholars have produced more nuanced studies of both Western and non-Western views and practices. Moreover, some critics argue that indigenous traditions had no awareness of the kinds of ecological crises we face today; it would be a mistake to project contemporary environmental sensibilities, now part of the global discourse of modernity, back upon ancient ideas and practices. Still, non-Western traditions remain a fertile source for many thinkers attempting to reconceive the culture-nature relationship and envision a theoretical foundation for sustainable living. This is especially true of many scholars from Asian, African, Latin American, Pacific, and indigenous traditions, who have found conceptual resources in their own traditions to formulate an approach to contemporary environmental and social challenges. My purpose in this chapter is to present a very brief introduction to the environmental thought and worldviews of some traditions in Asia, the Americas, Africa, and the Pacific.

Many environmental ethicists have pointed out that Eastern thinking is holistic in the sense that the human and the natural worlds are inextricably entwined within an organic whole. Culture and nature are inseparable. Jainism, Buddhism, Hinduism, Taoism, and Confucianism, it is often claimed, emphasize that humans are interdependently linked with the natural environment.

Buddhism, in particular, is often characterized as environmentally friendly. Buddhist metaphysics and ontology, for example, are based on the doctrine of interdependence, which is interpreted as an articulation of the interdependence some thinkers regard as the dominant characteristic of ecological relationships. The Huayan image of the Jewel Net of Indra, in which every node reflects every other, is widely employed in environmental writing. The doctrine of a pure, original Buddha-nature, which is said to be present in all sentient beings, and in some Buddhist traditions also in nonsentient nature, is employed to argue that Buddhists recognize the intrinsic value and moral considerability of nonhuman natural beings, an important element of much contemporary environmental thought. Buddhism shares with other Indic traditions a view of transmigration through human and nonhuman animal forms, and because even deities and enlightened beings appear in narratives as nonhuman animals, Indic traditions are sometimes said to present us with accounts of sentient life that are not, to use Peter Singer's term, "speciesist."

Indic psychology and moral thought,[1] with its analysis of how desire leads to suffering, provide a robust critique of consumerism, which plays a significant role in pollution overload and resource depletion. The precepts against killing and the

1. See, for example, the chapters in this volume by Clayton and Long.

widely practiced cultivation of compassion are understood not just as oriented toward other humans, but also toward other sentient beings. Indeed, the Indic ideal of nonviolence is employed as a model that presents the aspiration to relieve the suffering that human practices inflict on nonhuman life. Indic traditions, then, are claimed to have an ecological insight into the interdependence and value of all life.

Today, these traditions are often employed both in formulating environmental worldviews and in justifying environmental activism and sustainable practices. In Thailand, for example, old growth trees have been ordained as monks to preserve them from logging corporations.

Living in harmony with nature is also a prominent aspect of Chinese traditions. Indeed, the most fundamental practice of Daoism is learning to live in harmony with nature, with the way (*dao*) of things. Ancient philosophers conceive Dao as the way of transformation and the fountainhead of all forms of life in the world. Confucian and Neo-Confucian thinkers took metaphysical holism as their central theme. They considered the cosmos to be a dynamic, organic whole, an interdependent, ecological system. It was the duty of human beings to conform to this system, for nature is both inherently valuable and morally good. Thus, for Confucians, nature is the basis of human cultural values and practices. Indeed, human self-realization is achieved in relation to nature.

The earth-based spirituality of Native American peoples has inspired some environmental ethicists who favor responsible attitudes toward the environment. Native American religions generally have worldviews that support nature-friendly grand narratives. Native Americans have developed genuine respect for the welfare of other life-forms. For many Native Americans, all of Earth is sacred. They regard Earth as a living being, inspirited, and sacred in all her parts; they do not strive to conquer nature but to live in harmony with it, recognizing their own interdependence with the natural world.

Australian Aboriginal peoples believe that human beings are united with the land and with the other forms of life on the land; the natural environment is regarded as a sentient being, which can communicate with them. Individuals are identified with specific tracks of land. They employ graphic and cognitive systems to symbolically represent the bonds between the people and the landscape. Mythic symbols (the Dreaming) and physical symbols (the land) are connected through Warlpiri graphic arts. Countries that are homes for different beings and the landforms that sustain their lives are created by Dreamings. People are required to take care of their country and their human and nonhuman kin.

Likewise, the Maori people in New Zealand conceive the environment as a community of kin rather than as resources to be exploited. They believe that everything is linked, more or less directly, to everything else. In the Maori view, all creatures have a life force, or *mauri*, that joins them into an interdependent whole and enables them to flourish. Thus, all creatures are seen as both our cousins and our ancestors, and must be treated with respect. In Maori culture, *whakapapa*, or genealogy, is important because the people use it to express their identity by reference to their mountain and river, and to their ancestral dwelling place within the tribal landscape. It enables us to know ourselves and other things.

African worldviews involve environmentally friendly beliefs and laws that have encouraged or enforced limits to the exploitation of biological resources. The relation between responsible use of the planet's resources and ethics remains apparent in many cultural and social systems of traditional Africa. Indeed, a number of cultural groups have an environmental ethic that is functioning for them. Today, there are still indigenous environmental thinkers sharing their wisdom orally.

Among others, ancient Egyptians recognized the unity of humans and nonhuman, and developed a holistic view of the universe. For ancient Egyptians, *nun*, the primeval chaotic water, is the source of the universe. In the beginning, the sun-god as *Ra-Atum* appeared from *nun* by his power of self-development to start the existence of all beings. Accordingly, the self-development of matter resulted in spirit. *Ra* then became the source of life and rationality. Thus, in ancient Egyptian ontology, there is no radical distinction between spirit and matter.

Maat, the ancient Egyptian ethical and spiritual principle, integrates the sacred with a mundane or secular situation. It governs all aspects of creation and change. *Maat* is the totality of all things and the orderliness of the totality of existence, and represents things in harmony and in place. Moreover, ancient Egyptians personified the cosmic order as the goddess *Maat*. Without *Maat* there would be no order, no truth, and no justice. Disorder, chaos, disease, and moral decay prevail in the absence of *Maat*.

The Egyptian worldview is not anthropocentric. Spell 125, *The Declaration of Innocence* in the *Book of the Dead*, states the responsibility of a human being for both fellow human beings and nonhuman beings. "I have not deprived the orphan of his property...I have not caused pain, I have not made hungry, I have not made to weep, I have not killed, I have not commanded to kill" (Faulkner 2005, 134). Also, humans should not undermine the place of nonhumans. "I have not deprived herds of their pastures, I have not trapped the birds from the preserves of the gods, I have not diverted water at its season, I have not built a dam on flowing water" (Faulkner 2005, 134). Moreover, as Maulana Karenga notes, "[i]n Maatian theology and ethic, humans are the guardians of the earth as dutiful sons and daughters" (Karenga 2008, 177). The well-being of humans relies on the well-being of nature.

African worldviews emphasize the communal relationships among human beings. In Africa, the person is linked with the community and the extended family. Interdependence and connectedness are prominent features of traditional African society. The interconnectedness of beings is manifested through cultural concepts such as *ubuntu. Ubuntu*, a concept found in the languages of East, Central, and Southern Africa, recognizes the connections of all people and the importance of relationships and of building communities. It captures the essence of what it means to be human. It means a person is a person through other persons, and I am what I am because of what we all are. We affirm our humanity when we acknowledge that of others. Traditional African worldviews also recognize the interconnection between the natural and supernatural, physical and metaphysical, visible and invisible dimensions of the world. Currently living human and nonhuman beings, ancestors, the yet unborn, and the natural world are interconnected.

Ubuntu also captures the relationship between humanity and the natural environment. Many African peoples envision a kinship relationship between themselves and the natural world. They have developed an organic conception of nature that promotes an ecological interdependency among human, plant, and animal life. For example, the Oromo, the largest ethnic group in Ethiopia, believe that *Waaqa* (God), *Lafa* (Earth), and all other creations are interconnected. *Saffuu* or *ceeraa fokko*, an ethical principle, governs the relationship between the creator and the created, generations, families, human beings and nonhuman beings, and so on. *Saffuu* governs the use of natural resources.

For some Africans, spirits dwell in nature. The Oromo, for instance, recognize some trees as sacred trees based on what are essentially *spiritual* values. Certain trees are believed to have a special association with *Waaqa. Qoloo* or *Abdaarii* trees, trees around the *Qaalluu*, Oromo religious institution, wells, springs, and other places of worship are held to be sacred and are believed to be inhabited by some powerful spirit. Cutting sacred trees is believed to result in annoying the spirits and may cause death. Moreover, animals have a considerable place in African worldview. Some lineages have believed in the kinship of human beings and animals. They have developed the system of totemism, and refrained from harming, killing, and eating their totem.[2]

Some ethnic groups in Africa have developed discriminatory hunting practices to avoid depletion of breeding stocks. The Oromo largely kill male wild animals. Wild species may be hunted when there is sufficient reason to do so, but not extinguished. They have, thus, developed judicious use and conservation of the natural resources of their area. Like some environmental ethicists, they hold the belief that animals have the right to continued existence, and it is unnatural to destroy the whole species as such. Oromo environmental ethics also teaches that humans have special moral responsibility for domestic animals. Domestic animals should not be severely maltreated. They should be allowed to graze healthily and continue to exist. Those who violate the rights of animals are subject to punishment.

Besides their reverence for the natural environment, like other indigenous people in the world, many African peoples have all along been actively manipulating it. The people exploit natural resources in a respectful and just way. They do not abuse nature's generosity by consuming more than what is needed. Thus, in traditional Africa, human beings have developed an attitude of *live and let live* toward nonhuman beings.

Modern environmental ethicists can make use of the wealth of biological and ecological insights and sustainable resource management systems developed by various cultural groups around the world in order to effectively deal with environmental problems. An important lesson that can be learned from indigenous people is the

2. The totem of a clan is some animal with which that particular lineage had established a special relationship in the distant past.

capacity for an intrasubjective relationship with the nonhuman environment. In the West, it is believed that humans are the only conscious subjects. Dialogue always takes place from one human being to another. When there is a larger world that is vocal, communicative, subjective, intelligent, and interactive that may be speaking to us, people are not listening and hearing. So, the capacity for listening to and hearing the communicative discourse of the nonhuman world can be an extremely valuable lesson from indigenous traditions.

On the other hand, peasant farmers, pastoralists, and other indigenous people can learn from ecologists, conservation biologists, and so on. The most important point is that learning has to be contextualized and to promote partnership that does not seek to replace useful indigenous practices. Instead, learning must enhance local indigenous practices, making them more efficient or better adapted to the environments from which they arose.

One might dismiss, perhaps, indigenous environmental ethics as irrelevant to global environmental problems. It can be argued that indigenous ideas have not intensively addressed modern problems, and that they have been difficult to make modern. While it may be true that some indigenous traditions lack a global consciousness and an awareness of some contemporary environmental problems, it is also true that indigenous traditions are proving to be rich resources not just for environmental philosophers and ecotheologians, but also for many natural scientists and social scientists in search of local knowledge of the natural world or wanting to understand the varied possible relations between human societies and the more-than-human world.

BIBLIOGRAPHY AND SUGGESTED READINGS

Badiner, Allan H. (ed.). (1990) *Dharma Gaia: A Harvest of Essays in Buddhism and Ecology*. Berkeley, CA: Parallax Press.

Burnett, G. W., and Kamuyu wa Kang'ethe. (1994) "Wilderness and the Bantu Mind." *Environmental Ethics* 16(2), 145–160.

Callicott, J. Baird. (1994) *Earth's Insights. A Survey of Ecological Ethics from the Mediterranean Basin to the Australian Outback*. Berkeley, Los Angeles, and London: University of California Press.

Chapple, Christopher K. (2002) *Jainism and Ecology: Nonviolence in the Web of Life*. Cambridge, MA: Harvard University Press.

———. (2003) "Jainism and Buddhism." In *A Companion to Environmental Philosophy*, edited by Dale Jamieson. Oxford: Blackwell Publishing, 52–66.

Chapple, Christopher K., and Mary Evelyn Tucker. (2000) *Hinduism and Ecology: The Intersection of Earth, Sky, and Water*. Cambridge, MA: Harvard University Press.

Cheng, Chung-ying. (1986) "On the Environmental Ethics of the Tao and the Ch'I." *Environmental Ethics* 8(4), 351–370.

Curtin, Deane. (2005) *Environmental Ethics for a Postcolonial World*. Lanham, MD: Rowman and Littlefield Publishers.

DE SILVA, LILY. (1998) "The Buddhist Attitude Toward Nature." In *Environmental Ethics: Divergence and Convergence* (2nd ed.), edited by Richard G. Botzler and Susan J. Armstrong. Boston, MA: McGraw-Hill, Inc., 284–290.

FAULKNER, RAYMOND O. (trans.). (2005) [1972], *Ancient Egyptian Book of the Dead.* Austin: University of Texas Press.

FAULSTICH, PAUL. (2005) "Mapping the Mythological Landscape: An Aboriginal Way of Being-in-the-World." In *Environmental Philosophy: Critical Concepts in the Environment*, Volume V: *Issues and Applications*, edited by J. Baird Callicott and Clare Palmer. Routledge: London and New York, 293–313.

FOLTZ, RICHARD C. (2003) *Worldviews, Religion, and the Environment: A Global Anthology.* Belmont, CA: Thomson Wadsworth.

GIRARDOT, N. J., JAMES MILLER, and XIAOGAN LIU. (2001) *Daoism and Ecology: Ways within a Cosmic Landscape.* Cambridge, MA: Harvard University Press.

GOODMAN, RUSSELL. (1980) "Taoism and Ecology." *Environmental Ethics* 2(1), 73–80.

GRIM, JOHN A. (2001) *Indigenous Traditions and Ecology: The Interbeing of Cosmology and Community.* Cambridge, MA: Harvard University Press.

GRUVER, D. M. DUSTY. (1994) "The Earth as Family: A Traditional Hawaiian View with Current Applications." In *Philosophy, Humanity and Ecology. Philosophy of Nature and Environmental Ethics*, Volume 1, edited by Henry Odera Oruka. Nairobi: ACTS Press, 301–305.

HARRIS, IAN. (1995) "Getting to Grips with Buddhist Environmentalism: A Provisional Typology." *Journal of Buddhist Ethics* 2, 173–190.

INATOY, ENRIQUE. (1995) "Protection of Forests and Other Natural Resources: A View from Central America." In *Social Aspects of Sustainable Dryland Management*, edited by Daniel Stiles. Chichester and New York: John Wiley and Sons, 189–192.

IP, PO-KEUNG. (1998) "Taoism and the Foundations of Environmental Ethics." In *Environmental Ethics: Divergence and Convergence* (2nd ed.), edited by Richard G. Botzler and Susan J. Armstrong. Boston, MA: McGraw-Hill, 290–295.

JAMES, SIMON P. (2009) "Asian Philosophy." In *Encyclopedia of Environmental Ethics and Philosophy*, Volume I, edited by J. Baird Callicott and Robert Frodeman. Detroit, MI: Macmillan Reference, Gale, 70–73.

KARENGA, MAULANA. (2008) "The Moral Anthropology of Marcus Garvey: In the Fullness of Ourselves." *Journal of Black Studies* 39(2), 166–193.

KASSAM, ANEESA, and GEMETCHU MEGERSSA. (1994) "Aloof Alollaa: The Inside and the Outside: Boran Oromo Environmental Law and Methods of Conservation." In *A River of Blessings: Essays in Honour of Paul Baxter*, edited by David Brokensha. Syracuse, NY: Maxwell School of Citizenship and Public Affairs, 85–98.

KAZA, STEPHANIE, and KENNETH KRAFT (eds.). (2000) *Dharma Rain: Sources of Buddhist Environmentalism.* Boston, MA: Shambhala Publications.

KELBESSA, WORKINEH. (2005) "The Rehabilitation of Indigenous Environmental Ethics in Africa." *Diogenes* 207, 17–34.

———. (2009) "Africa, Sub-Saharan." In *Encyclopedia of Environmental Ethics and Philosophy*, Volume I, edited by J. Baird Callicott and Robert Frodeman. Detroit, MI: Macmillan Reference, Gale, 10–18.

———. (2010) *Indigenous and Modern Environmental Ethics: A Study of the Indigenous Oromo Environmental Ethic and Modern Issues of Environment and Development: Ethiopian Philosophical Studies. I.* Washington, DC: The Council for Research in Values and Philosophy.

Kimmerle, Heinz. (2006) "The World of Spirits and the Respect for Nature: Towards a New Appreciation of Animism." *The Journal for Transdisciplinary Research in Southern Africa* 2(2), 249–263.

Langton, Marcia. (1998) *Burning Questions: Emerging Environmental Issues for Indigenous Peoples in Northern Australia*. Darwin: Centre for Indigenous Natural and Cultural Resource Management.

Momaday, N. Scott. (1994) "Native American Attitudes to the Environment." In *The Environmental Ethics and Policy Book. Philosophy, Ecology, Economics*, edited by Donald VanDeVeer and Christine Pierce. Belmont, CA: Wadsworth Publishing Company, 102–105.

Omari, C. K. (1990) "Traditional African Land Ethics." In *Ethics of Environment and Development: Global Challenge, International Response*, edited by J. Ronald Engel and Joan Gibb Engel. Tucson, AZ: University of Arizona Press, 167–175.

Rose, Deborah Bird. (2009) "Australian Aborigines." In *Encyclopedia of Environmental Ethics and Philosophy*, Volume I, edited by J. Baird Callicott and Robert Frodeman. Detroit, MI: Macmillan Reference, Gale, 80–83.

Swearer, Donald K. (2006) "An Assessment of Buddhist Eco-Philosophy." *Harvard Theological Review* 99.2, 123–137.

Tangwa, Godfrey B. (2004) "Some African Reflections on Biomedical and Environmental Ethics." In *A Companion to African Philosophy*, edited by Kwasi Wiredu. Oxford: Blackwell Publishing Ltd., 387–395.

Tucker, Mary Evelyn. (2009) "Confucianism." In *Encyclopedia of Environmental Ethics and Philosophy*, Volume I, edited by J. Baird Callicott and Robert Frodeman. Detroit, MI: Macmillan Reference, Gale, 163–166.

Tucker, Mary Evelyn, and John Berthrong. (1998) *Confucianism and Ecology: The Interrelation of Heaven, Earth, and Humans*. Cambridge, MA: Harvard University Press.

Tucker, Mary Evelyn, and Duncan Ryūken Williams (eds.). (1997) *Buddhism and Ecology: The Interconnection of Dharma and Deeds*. Cambridge, MA: Harvard University Press.

White, Lynn, Jr. (1967) "The Historical Roots of our Ecological Crisis." *Science* 155, 1203–1207.

Whitt, Laurie Anne, et al. (2003) "Indigenous Perspectives." In *A Companion to Environmental Philosophy*, edited by Dale Jamieson. Oxford: Blackwell Publishing, 3–20.

CHAPTER 42

COSMOPOLITANISM

GILLIAN BROCK

On one common account of what cosmopolitanism is, the key idea is that every person has global stature as the ultimate unit of moral concern and is therefore entitled to equal respect and consideration no matter what her citizenship status or other affiliations happen to be. If this is interpreted to mean (as it sometimes is) that national, ethnic, or local attachments are therefore irrelevant to questions of distribution, fairness, and equality, this would seem to set cosmopolitanism on a collision course with the views of most people in the world. For many people, individual identity crucially depends on national or ethnic identity, a sense of cultural, religious, or racial belonging, and is characterized by strong attachments to local communities, neighborhoods, friends, and, of course, families. Are these affinities and partialities necessarily in tension with cosmopolitan views of our universal entitlements? And if they are, does this not mean so much the worse for cosmopolitanism? In order to see why there is not necessarily the conflict imagined, in this chapter I discuss several types of cosmopolitanisms and their commitments and implications. I also give the reader a sense of other current debates in the field of cosmopolitanism.

This article is structured as follows. In the next section I discuss the origins of the idea of cosmopolitanism and some contemporary theses typically associated with cosmopolitanism—that it includes both a thesis about identity and one about responsibility. In the following section I distinguish cosmopolitanism from some concepts closely associated with it and discuss the connections among the ideas of cosmopolitanism, globalization, and global justice. The next sections distinguish varieties of cosmopolitanism and cosmopolitan justice. One cannot fully understand the arguments of prominent cosmopolitans, especially concerning cosmopolitan justice, without understanding the debate between Rawls and his critics about *The Law of Peoples*, so we discuss that next. Finally, we are in a position to assess whether cosmopolitanism is compatible with other commitments that fill human lives with meaning, and that is discussed in the last section.

The Cosmopolitan as a Citizen of the World

Early proponents of cosmopolitanism included the Cynic, Diogenes, and Stoics such as Cicero (Nussbaum 1996).[1] These cosmopolitans rejected the idea that one should be primarily defined by one's city of origin, as was typical of Greek males of the time. Rather, they insisted that they were "citizens of the world." The Stoics' idea of being a citizen of the world neatly captures the two main aspects of cosmopolitanism, especially as it is frequently understood today. These are a thesis about identity and one about responsibility. As a thesis about identity, being a cosmopolitan indicates that one is a person who is marked or influenced by various cultures. Depending on attitudes to the various influences or markings, the word "cosmopolitanism" could have both negative and positive connotations. It has had positive connotations when, for instance, it has been thought to mean that a person is worldly and well traveled rather than narrow-minded or provincial. It has had more negative connotations, for instance, in the case of Jews and Bolsheviks, who, at one time, were considered to be dirty or foreigners, a threat to the community's purity (Sypnowich 2005, 56). Cosmopolitanism as a thesis about identity also denies that membership in a particular cultural community is *necessary* for an individual to flourish in the world. Contra Will Kymlicka's prominent claims on the matter, cosmopolitans deny that such membership is necessary for an individual's having a social identity or her living a fulfilling life (Waldron 1992). Belonging to a particular culture is not an essential ingredient in personal identity formation or maintenance: one can pick and choose from the full smorgasbord on offer, or reject all in favor of other options, as Waldron maintains.

Cosmopolitanism as a thesis about responsibility generates much discussion, as we will come to see.[2] Roughly, the idea is that as a cosmopolitan, one should appreciate that one is a member of a global community of human beings. As such, one has responsibilities to other members of the global community. As Martha Nussbaum elaborates, one owes allegiance "to the worldwide community of human beings," and this affiliation should constitute a primary allegiance (Nussbaum 1996, 4). As a thesis about responsibility, cosmopolitanism guides

1. For an excellent history of cosmopolitanism, see Pauline Kleingeld 2006.

2. For an overview of some of this debate see Brock and Brighouse 2005 and Brock and Moellendorf 2005.

the individual outward from local obligations, and prohibits those obligations from crowding out responsibilities to distant others. Cosmopolitanism highlights the responsibilities we have to those whom we do not know and with whom we are not intimate, but whose lives should be of concern to us. The borders of states, and other boundaries considered to restrict the *scope* of justice, are irrelevant roadblocks in appreciating our responsibilities to all in the global community.

Globalization and Global Justice

Talk about cosmopolitanism is often closely aligned with discourse about globalization and global justice. These are, in general, different topics entirely, but often have strong points of intersection, as we see.

What is the subject matter of global justice? What is the field of global justice concerned with or what should it be about? If we examine actual global justice movements in the world, as represented by (say) the World Social Forum,[3] the first thing we might notice is that there are a number of quite different groups that can be identified as concerned with issues of global justice. To pick out just a few, these include trade unionists, farmers, indigenous peoples, environmentalists, and so forth. They often have common grievances and points of resistance, such as opposition to the way globalization is unfolding in the world today, the dominance of multinational corporations or economic interests throughout the globe with a feared withering away of local cultures, devastation for local economies, intensified destruction of the environment, deepening exploitation, the apparent unconcern with the most vulnerable and marginalized, and so forth. Though members of the so-called Global Justice Movement have common points of struggle, they often resist congealing into an overarching political program, despite occasional victories (such as those achieved at, or represented by, the World Social Forum). A central claim made by some of these marginalized groups is that they want to be left alone. Perhaps despairing of ever getting any meaningful chance to be given a real voice and input in decisions that crucially affect them, perhaps also skeptical given bad histories of interference, domination, or oppression, given their current and expected future marginalization, they (apparently) frequently ask now simply to be left alone to live their lives as they see fit. Others, perhaps more hopeful about what their activism can accomplish, demand changes to our global governance arrangements (such as the rules governing the World Trade Organization). Chief among

3. More information about this organization can be found at their official home page: http://www.forumsocialmundial.org.br/.

these would be changes that take more seriously fairness for the world's worst off and most vulnerable, by distributing the costs and benefits of globalization more evenly.

Academic theorizing about global justice has, in some important ways, been more narrowly focused, though it does incorporate the concerns of such activists. Theorizing about global justice has been dominated by issues of global distributive justice over the last two decades or so, though this is not to say that other issues have been entirely neglected. Various theorists advocate different models of global justice that might consist of several components, such as advocating that every person be well positioned to enjoy the prospects for a decent life; a more equal distribution of resources globally or that every person have enough to meet her basic needs; more global equality of opportunity; universal promotion of human rights; promotion of the autonomy of peoples who stand in relations of equality with one another; or criteria governing intervention, especially military intervention, in the affairs of states. There is also much debate about how best to realize the desired elements, what principles should govern our interactions at the global level, and how to improve the management of our global affairs, including how best to govern globalization. Contemporary theorizing on global justice has been enormously influenced by John Rawls's work, especially his *The Law of Peoples*, and the position known as "Cosmopolitanism," which is discussed in more detail below.

For the antiglobalization movement, cosmopolitanism is sometimes feared because it is construed as another way to justify the relentless spread of capitalism throughout the globe and the liberal discourse associated with cosmopolitan values is nothing more than global capitalism's useful handmaiden. This view involves a misconception about the diversity of positions that are rightly construed as cosmopolitan. One could see oneself as a member of a global community of human persons for all sorts of reasons, such as religious commitments—Christianity is often thought of in this connection—and there is also a strong Marxist justification for holding this position as well. There is no need to suspect at the outset that talk of cosmopolitanism necessarily entails commitment to neo-liberal, capitalist views about economic justice. The question of what cosmopolitan justice entails is very much a current topic of debate, with people defending a full spectrum of views. Indeed, the critical mass of scholars actively working on the topic today endorse forms of egalitarianism that would be quite antithetical to the neo-liberal agenda, as I discuss.

There are economic forms of cosmopolitanism, some proponents of which advocate free trade (these include Adam Smith and Milton Friedman). However, there are also as many communist and socialist versions of economic cosmopolitanism as well (as advocated by, say, Marx, Engels, and Lenin), which encourages proletarians of the world to unite and to recognize their common interests in promoting a global economic order more aligned with workers' interests rather than those of capital. What is cosmopolitan about both of these familiar economic views is simply the idea that the preferred economic model transcends the boundaries of a nation-state. Current debates about what cosmopolitan justice consists in typically bypass the debate about modes of production.

Varieties of Cosmopolitanism

Several distinctions are in use in the literature and it may be useful to review these next.

Moral and Institutional Cosmopolitanism

The crux of the idea of moral cosmopolitanism is that every person has global stature as the ultimate unit of moral concern and is therefore entitled to equal consideration no matter what her citizenship or nationality status. Thomas Pogge gives a widely cited synopsis of what are thought to be the key ideas:

> Three elements are shared by all cosmopolitan positions. First, individualism: the ultimate units of concern are human beings, or persons—rather than, say, family lines, tribes, ethnic, cultural, or religious communities, nations, or states. The latter may be units of concern only indirectly, in virtue of their individual members or citizens. Second, universality: the status of ultimate unit of concern attaches to every living human being equally—not merely to some sub-set, such as men, aristocrats, Aryans, whites, or Muslims. Third, generality: this special status has global force. Persons are ultimate units of concern for everyone—not only for their compatriots, fellow religionists, or such like. (Pogge 1992, 48–49)

Cosmopolitanism's force is best appreciated by considering what it rules out. For instance, it rules out positions that attach no moral value to some people, or weights the moral value some people have differentially according to their race, ethnicity, or nationality. Furthermore, assigning ultimate rather than derivative value to collective entities such as nations or states is prohibited. If such groups matter, they matter because of their importance to individual human persons rather than because they have some independent, ultimate (say, ontological) value.

A common misconception is that cosmopolitanism requires a world state or government. A distinction is sometimes drawn in the literature between moral and institutional cosmopolitanism (also referred to in the literature variously as "legal" or "political" cosmopolitanism). Institutional cosmopolitans maintain that fairly deep institutional changes are needed to the global system in order to realize the cosmopolitan vision adequately (Cabrera 2004; Held 1995). Moral cosmopolitans need not endorse that view; in fact, many are against radical institutional transformations (Nussbaum 2006). Cosmopolitan justice requires that our global obligations (such as protecting everyone's basic human rights or ensuring everyone's capabilities are met to the required threshold) are effectively discharged. However, a number of suitable arrangements might do this effectively. There are various possibilities for global governance that would not amount to a world state. These include mixtures of delegating responsibilities for particular domains to various institutions, with multiple agencies able to hold each other accountable, and other ways of reconfiguring the structure of governance bodies at the global level (such as the United Nations) so they are brought into line better with cosmopolitan goals (Held 1995; Weinstock 2006; Grant and Keohane 2005).

Extreme versus Moderate Cosmopolitanism

This terminology was initially introduced by Samuel Scheffler (2001 115–119). Using this terminology, Scheffler actually distinguishes at least two forms of cosmopolitanisms, giving rise to two distinctions. One concerns the *justificatory basis* of cosmopolitanism and the other concerns the content of what cosmopolitan justice consists in. An extreme cosmopolitan with respect to *justification* considers the underlying source of value to be cosmopolitan and it is with respect to cosmopolitan principles, goals, or values that all other principles of morality must be justified. A moderate cosmopolitan can take a more pluralistic line on the source of value, admitting that some noncosmopolitan principles, goals, or values may have ultimate value as well. In particular, moderate cosmopolitans need not reduce our special obligations to principles of cosmopolitan value, which might be construed as devaluing and distorting the meaning of the special attachments that people have (Scheffler 2001, 115; Tan 2004, 2005).

We can best appreciate the force of the second kind of cosmopolitanism, cosmopolitanism about the *content of justice*, by considering the question: are there any norms of justice that apply within an individual society and not to the global population at large? The extreme cosmopolitan denies that there are *at the level of fundamental principle*, whereas the moderate cosmopolitan believes that this is possible. On this latter view, principles of social justice are constrained but not replaced by principles of global justice (Scheffler 2001, 116; Miller 2007).

Weak versus Strong Cosmopolitanism

The way in which this distinction is typically drawn (e.g., Miller 2000, 174) is that weak cosmopolitanism underwrites, as requirements of justice, only the conditions that are universally necessary for human beings to lead minimally decent lives, whereas strong cosmopolitans are committed to a more demanding form of global distributive equality that will aim to eliminate inequalities between persons beyond some account of what is sufficient to live a minimally decent life. So, what is weak or strong on this account is the extent of one's commitments to redistribution.

While this distinction does have some value in distinguishing positions in the literature, it also glosses over other issues that seem just as important. If, for instance, one endorses a relational view of equality, such that what matters about equality is people's standing in relations of equality to one another, that is to say, in relations characterized by equal respect and lacking domination or oppression—having equal standing, for short—is this a weak or a strong form of cosmopolitanism? Presumably to answer that question we will need to look at the distributive implications of such a view. Let us say they demand redistribution up to the lower threshold but not beyond. It looks like we have a weak form of cosmopolitanism. But, its proponents might object, this classification as "weak" is pejorative and misleading if indeed it is the proper account of that with which cosmopolitanism should rightly be concerned. Furthermore, this distinction seems to exclude almost no one with defensible views on global justice. Even Rawls ends up as a weak cosmopolitan on this account (a label he himself explicitly rejected). This distinction needs to be replaced with more nuanced ones to play some continuing, useful role in the literature.

Cosmopolitan Justice

Cosmopolitan justice can be argued for from a number of theoretical perspectives. After all, there are different conceptions of how to treat people equally especially with respect to issues of distributive justice, and this is often reflected in these different accounts. Cosmopolitan justice could be argued for along various lines, including utilitarian (prominently Singer 1972), rights-based accounts (Shue 1980; Jones 1999; Pogge 2002), Kantian lines (O'Neill 2000), Aristotelian (Nussbaum 2000, 2006), and contractarian (Beitz 1979; Pogge 1994; Moellendorf 2002). In recent years, one popular way of arguing for cosmopolitan justice has taken contractarian forms, following a very prominent debate between John Rawls and his critics. Because of its enormous dominance in current debates on cosmopolitan justice, I discuss this next.

Rawls's *Law of Peoples* and Some of His Prominent Cosmopolitan Critics

In *A Theory of Justice*, John Rawls sets out to derive the principles of justice that should govern liberal societies and, by employing all the apparatus attached to the original position (the hypothetical choosing situation used to select principles of justice in which we are deprived of knowledge of who we are in society), he famously endorsed two principles; namely, one protecting equal basic liberties and a second permitting social and economic inequalities when (and only when) they are both to the greatest benefit of the least advantaged (the Difference Principle) and attached to positions that are open to all under conditions of fair equality of opportunity (the Fair Equality of Opportunity Principle). In *A Theory of Justice*, Rawls's focus is on the principles that should govern closed communities—paradigmatically, nation-states. Cosmopolitans such as Charles Beitz (1979) and then Thomas Pogge (1989) argued that these two principles should apply globally. After all, if the point of the veil of ignorance is to exclude us from knowledge of factors that are morally arbitrary, surely where one happens to have been born (or citizenship) qualifies as one of those quintessentially arbitrary factors from the moral point of view?

It was something of a disappointment, then, when Rawls later weighed in on the issue explicitly against such a suggestion. He argued that, though the two principles should apply within liberal societies, they should not apply across them. Rather, in the international arena, Rawls thinks different principles would be chosen (in a second original position occupied by representatives of different, well-ordered peoples) and these would include principles acknowledging peoples' independence, their equality, that they have a right to self-defense, and that they have duties of nonintervention, to observe treaties, to honor a limited set of rights, to conduct themselves appropriately in war, and to assist other peoples living in unfavorable conditions. In the space provided, I cannot do justice to all the complexities of Rawls's sophisticated account, but for good exposition of the views and critical discussion of these see Martin and Reidy (2006), Moellendorf (2002), and Tan (2004). Here I focus on just a few commonly identified points of tension between Rawls and his cosmopolitan critics.

In *The Law of Peoples*, Rawls engages directly with central claims made by some cosmopolitans, namely, those who argue that the Difference Principle should apply globally. He takes up Beitz's claim that, since a global system of cooperation already exists between states, a Global Difference Principle should apply across states as well. Rawls argues against this, for a couple of reasons, but notably, because he believes that wealth owes its origin and maintenance to the political culture of the society rather than (say) to its stock of resources. Furthermore, any global principle of distributive justice we endorse must have a target and a cut-off point. Rawls believes we do have a duty "to assist burdened societies to become full members of the Society of Peoples and to be able to determine the path of their own future for themselves" (1999, 118). Unlike his understanding of cosmopolitan commitments to a Global Difference Principle, Rawls believes his principles have a target, which is to ensure the essentials of political autonomy and self-determination.

Rawls's *Law of Peoples* has generated much criticism. One of the most frequently raised objections is that the background picture Rawls invokes incorporates outmoded views of relations between states, peoples, and individuals of the world. Rawls presupposes that states are (sufficiently) independent of one another, so that each society can be held largely responsible for the well-being of its citizens, at least in the case of well-ordered peoples (that is, those reasonable, liberal, and decent peoples not suffering unfavorable conditions). Furthermore, according to Rawls, differences in levels of wealth and prosperity are largely attributable to differences in political culture and the virtuous nature of its citizens. Critics point out, however, that Rawls ignores both the extent to which unfavorable conditions may result from factors external to the society and that there are all sorts of morally relevant connections between states, notably that they are situated in a global economic order that perpetuates the interests of wealthy developed states with little regard for the interests of poor, developing ones. Those of us who live in the affluent, developed world cannot thus defensibly insulate ourselves from the misery of the worst off in the world, because we are complicit in keeping them in a state of poverty.

Thomas Pogge has done much to show the nature and extent of these incriminating connections (1994, 2001, 2002, *inter alia*). According to Pogge, two international institutions are particularly worrisome: the international borrowing privilege and the international resource privilege. Any group that exercises effective power in a state is recognized internationally as the legitimate government of that territory, and the international community is not much concerned with how the group came to power or what it does with that power. Oppressive governments may borrow freely on behalf of the country (the international borrowing privilege) or dispose of its natural resources (the international resource privilege), and these actions are legally recognized internationally. These two privileges have enormous implications for the prosperity of poor countries (for instance) because these privileges provide incentives for coup attempts, they often influence what sorts of people are motivated to seek power, they facilitate oppressive governments being able to stay in power, and, should more democratic governments get to be in power, they are saddled with the debts incurred by their oppressive predecessors, thus significantly draining the country of resources needed to firm up fledgling democracies. All of this is disastrous for many poor countries. Because foreigners benefit so greatly from the international resource privilege, they have an incentive to refrain from challenging the situation (or worse, to support or finance oppressive governments). For these sorts of reasons, the current world order largely reflects the interests of wealthy and powerful states. Local governments have little incentive to attend to the needs of the poor, since their being able to continue in power depends more on the local elite, foreign governments, and corporations. Those of us in affluent developed countries have a responsibility to stop imposing this unjust global order and to mitigate the harms we have already inflicted on the world's most vulnerable people. As an initial proposal for us to begin to make some progress in the right direction, Pogge suggests that we impose a global resources tax of roughly 1 percent to fund improvements to the lives of the worst off in developing societies (Pogge 1994).

So, critics point out that Rawls ignores the extent to which societies suffering unfavorable conditions frequently results from factors external to that society, and that national policies are often shaped, or even decided by, international factors. They also argue that the boundedness and separateness of political communities is difficult to sustain in our world today, due to phenomena such as globalization and integration (Hurrell 2001). Rawls assumes we can talk coherently of bounded political communities that can constitute self-sufficient schemes of political cooperation. However, critics argue this is an untenable assumption. Some authors concentrate on showing that we actually have a system of global cooperation between societies and how this would give rise to obligations to the worst off (Hinsch 2001). Others believe that it is insulting to characterize the relations between states of the world as cooperative, since in reality the relationship is rather one of domination and coercion (Forst 2001).

Several critics, then, argue that the basic global structure is a scheme of coercive institutions that importantly affects individuals' life prospects. It should be transformed so that it becomes a fair scheme of cooperation among all citizens of the world. For many of these critics, this is best modeled by considering a global original position in which decision makers have no knowledge of any morally arbitrary features, including country of citizenship. Using this kind of strategy, popular claims are that we should endorse a Global Difference Principle (permitting economic inequalities just in case they work to improve the situation of the worst off in the world) or Global Equality of Opportunity, though other options, such as arguing for a needs-based minimum floor account of global distributive justice, are also attractive (Brock 2005).

Several other kinds of criticisms are also voiced, including that the notion of a people is not sufficiently clear or important to do the work Rawls thinks it can do (Pogge 1994; Kuper 2000). Furthermore, since Rawls often takes the boundaries of states to mark off distinct peoples, his view runs into difficulties. If we take a people to be constituted by commonalities such as shared language, culture, history, or ethnicity, then the official state borders and peoples do not coincide well. National territories are not typically composed of a single people, nor is it clear that individuals belong to one and only one people (Pogge 1994).

Another common observation is that Rawls's arguments for his abridged list of human rights is defective. For one thing, critics charge that Rawls's failure to include democratic rights is quite mistaken. Amartya Sen, for instance, provides extensive evidence to support the claim that nondemocratic regimes have severely adverse consequences for the well-being and human rights of those over whom they rule (1999, 147–148, 154–155). Sen also argues that respect for human rights and ideas of democracy are not simply Western values, but rather that substantial elements of these ideas can be found in all major cultures, religions, and traditions.

Rawls argues for a respectful relationship between states (as representatives of peoples). Indeed, he argues that liberal democratic regimes have an obligation to deal with illiberal decent hierarchical regimes as equals, and not to endeavor to impose their values on them. Some might think that Rawls's views appropriately acknowledge the importance of our cultural or national affiliations. Andrew Kuper (2000) argues that Rawls may take cultural pluralism seriously but he does this at the expense of taking seriously the reasonable pluralism of *individual persons*. Well-ordered hierarchical societies may well contain individuals who hold liberal ideas. Rawls's account incorporates the wrong kind of toleration for such societies at the expense of liberal values. Rawls's view is not sufficiently sensitive to the individuals within states. Indeed, it would seem that Rawls, in defending nonliberal states as he has, would be forced to defend the rights of states to impose inegalitarian policies on its citizens, even if a majority of the citizens were vigorously against such policies (Blake 2005, 23).

Rawls aims at a realistic utopia, but critics charge that the result is neither sufficiently realistic nor utopian (e.g., Kuper 2000). It is not sufficiently realistic because, critics claim, he has not taken account of all the relevant realities, for instance, of interdependence or domination in the global arena. To the extent that he has not captured all the salient realities, his Law of Peoples is not as "workable" and likely to sustain ongoing cooperative political arrangements and relations between peoples. Furthermore, the view is not very utopian in that the political (moral) ideals used are too tame to constitute much of an advance over the status quo. In his bow to realism, Rawls has tried to ensure that the Law of Peoples results in stability, yet the Law of Peoples he endorses is potentially very unstable because, arguably, stability is only really achieved when just arrangements are in place, and Rawls has offered us nothing more than a *modus vivendi* with oppressor states.

Reconciling Cosmopolitanism with Other Commitments

Can cosmopolitans take account of the special attachments and commitments that fill ordinary human beings' lives with value and meaning?

A common misconception about cosmopolitanism concerns how a cosmopolitan must view her relations to those in local or particular communities, namely, that she must eschew such attachments in favor of some notion of impartial justice that the individual must apply directly to all, no matter where they are situated on the globe. But this is by no means entailed by several of the sophisticated accounts of cosmopolitanism on offer today (see, for instance, Brock and Brighouse 2005). Indeed, most contemporary cosmopolitans recognize that for many people, some of their most meaningful attachments in life derive from their allegiances to particular communities, be they national, ethnic, religious, or cultural. Their accounts often seek to define the legitimate scope for such partiality, by situating these in a context that clarifies our obligations to one another. Cosmopolitan justice provides the basic framework or structure and thereby the constraints within which legitimate patriotism may operate (see, for instance, Tan 2004, 2005). Cosmopolitan principles should govern the global institutions, such that these treat people as equals in terms of their entitlements (regardless of nationality and power, say). However, once the background global institutional structure is just, persons may defensibly favor the interests of their compatriots (or conationals, or other more particular groups), as long as such partiality does not conflict with their other obligations, for instance, to support global institutions. So cosmopolitan principles should govern the global institutions, but need not directly regulate what choices people may make within the rules of the institutions. One of the strengths of Tan's view is that even though cosmopolitan justice provides the justification for the limits of partiality toward group members, the value of those attachments is not reduced to cosmopolitan considerations, which is arguably a flaw with other attempts (e.g., Nussbaum 1996).

A simple way to show how there is a gap between the cosmopolitan's position and what anticosmopolitans fear is this. Cosmopolitanism is essentially committed to these two central ideas: first, the equal moral worth of all individuals, no matter where they happen to be situated on the planet and what borders separate them from one another. Second, there are some obligations that are binding on all of us, no matter where we are situated. But acknowledging these two ideas still leaves plenty of room to endorse additional obligations, which derive from more particular commitments, and the preference some may have to spend discretionary resources and time on particular communities or attachments important to one's life plans and projects. In order to know just what constitutes our discretionary resources, and what our basic obligations to one another are, we need the input of cosmopolitan justice. So long as we act in ways consistent with those commitments, there are no residual ethical concerns. Whether or not there is still room for conflict depends on how much is packed into cosmopolitan justice. Very strong forms of egalitarian duties might leave little room; weaker ones might leave more. And yet we can appreciate that conceptually, at least, there is no tension here as feared.[4]

BIBLIOGRAPHY AND SUGGESTED READINGS

Beitz, Charles. (1979) *Political Theory and International Relations*. Princeton, NJ: Princeton University Press.

Blake, Michael. (2005) "International Justice." In *Stanford Encyclopedia of Philosophy*. http://plato.stanford.edu/entries/international-justice/

Brock, Gillian. (2002) "Liberal Nationalism versus Cosmopolitanism: Locating the Disputes." *Public Affairs Quarterly* 16, 307–327.

———. (2005) "Egalitarianism, Ideals, and Cosmopolitan Justice." *Philosophical Forum* 36, 1–30.

———. (2009) *Global Justice: A Cosmopolitan Account*. Oxford: Oxford University Press.

Brock, Gillian, and Harry Brighouse. (2005) *The Political Philosophy of Cosmopolitanism*. Cambridge: Cambridge University Press.

4. Recall that this sort of solution to the issue of how our global responsibilities can be reconciled with our local ones applies primarily to the issue of global *distributive* justice. Other principles may certainly be overlaid on these to deal with rectifying past injustices. For more discussion on how to reconcile particular and cosmopolitan commitments see, for instance, Brock 2002.

Brock, Gillian, and Darrel Moellendorf. (2005) *Current Debates in Global Justice.* Dordrecht, The Netherlands: Springer.

Cabrera, Luis. (2004) *Political Theory of Global Justice: A Cosmopolitan Case for the World State.* London: Routledge.

Caney, Simon. (2005) *Justice Beyond Borders: A Global Political Theory.* Oxford: Oxford University Press.

Forst, Rainer (2001) "Towards A Critical Theory of Transnational Justice." *Metaphilosophy* 32, 160–79.

Grant, Ruth, and Robert Keohane. (2005) "Accountability and Abuses of Power in World Politics." *American Political Science Review* 99(1), 29–43.

Held, David. (1995) *Democracy and the Global Order: From the Modern State to Cosmopolitan Governance.* Stanford, CA: Stanford University Press.

Hinsch, Wilfried. (2001) "Global Distributive Justice." *Metaphilosophy* 32, 58–78.

Hurrell, Andrew. (2001) "Global Inequality and International Institutions." *Metaphilosophy* 32, 34–57.

Jones, Charles. (1999) *Global Justice.* Oxford: Oxford University Press.

Kleingeld, Pauline. (2006) "Cosmopolitanism." In *Stanford Encyclopedia of Philosophy.* http://plato.stanford.edu/entries/international-justice/

Kymlicka, Will. (1995) *Multicultural Citizenship: A Liberal Theory of Minority Rights.* Oxford: Oxford University Press.

Kuper, Andrew. (2000) "Rawlsian Global Justice: Beyond the *Law of Peoples* to a Cosmopolitan Law of Persons." *Political Theory* 28, 640–674.

Martin, Rex, and David Reidy. (2006) *Rawls's Law of Peoples: A Realistic Utopia?* Malden, MA: Blackwell.

Miller, David. (2000) *Citizenship and National Identity.* Cambridge: Polity Press.

———. (2007) *National Responsibility and Global Justice.* Oxford: Oxford University Press.

Moellendorf, Darrel. (2002) *Cosmopolitan Justice.* Boulder, CO: Westview Press.

Nielsen, Kai. (1988) "World Government, Security, and Global Justice." In *Problems of International Justice*, edited by Stephen Luper-Foy. Boulder, CO: Westview Press.

Nussbaum, Martha. (1996) "Patriotism and Cosmopolitanism." In *For Love of Country: Debating the Limits of Patriotism*, edited by Joshua Cohen. Boston, MA: Beacon Press.

———. (2000) *Women and Human Development.* Cambridge: Cambridge University Press.

———. (2006) *Frontiers of Justice: Disability, Nationality, Species Membership.* Cambridge, MA: Belknap Press.

O Neill, Onora. (2000) *Bounds of Justice.* Cambridge: Cambridge University Press.

Pogge, Thomas. (1989) *Realizing Rawls.* Ithaca, NY: Cornell University Press.

———. (1992) "Cosmopolitanism and Sovereignty." *Ethics* 103, 48–75.

———. (1994) "An Egalitarian Law of Peoples." *Philosophy and Public Affairs* 23(3), 195–224.

———. (2001) "Priorities of Global Justice." *Metaphilosophy* 32, 6–24.

———. (2002) *World Poverty and Human Rights.* Cambridge: Polity Press.

Rawls, John. (1971) *A Theory of Justice.* Belknap, MA: Harvard University Press.

———. (1999) *The Law of Peoples.* Cambridge, MA: Harvard University Press.

Scheffler, Samuel. (1999) "Conceptions of Cosmopolitanism." *Utilitas* 11, 255–276.

———. (2001) *Boundaries and Allegiances.* New York: Oxford University Press.

Sen, Amartya. (1999) *Development as Freedom.* Oxford: Oxford University Press.

Shue, Henry. (1980) *Basic Rights: Subsistence, Affluence, and U.S. Foreign Policy.* Princeton, NJ: Princeton University Press.

Singer, Peter. (1972) "Famine Affluence, and Morality." *Philosophy and Public Affairs* 1(3), 229–243.
Sypnowich, Christine. (2005) "Cosmopolitans, Cosmopolitanisms, and Human Flourishing." In *The Political Philosophy of Cosmopolitanism*, edited by Gillian Brock and Harry Brighouse. Cambridge: Cambridge University Press, 55–74.
Tan, Kok-Chor. (2004) *Justice Without Borders: Cosmopolitanism, Nationalism, and Patriotism*. Cambridge: Cambridge University Press.
———. (2005) "The Demands of Justice and National Allegiance." In *The Political Philosophy of Cosmopolitanism*, edited by Gillian Brock and Harry Brighouse. Cambridge: Cambridge University Press, 164–179.
Waldron, Jeremy. (1992) "Minority Rights and the Cosmopolitan Alternative." *University of Michigan Journal of Law Reform* 25(3), 751–793.
Weinstock, Daniel. (2006) "The Real World of (Global) Democracy." *Journal of Social Philosophy* 37(1), 6–20.

CHAPTER 43

REPARATIONS

J. ANGELO CORLETT

It is the increasing concern of many that certain historical injustices of serious proportions against groups be remedied by way of compensatory justice. Yet there are numerous philosophical and ethical questions that arise when considering such matters. This is particularly the case concerning compensatory justice to groups that have suffered from serious harmful wrongdoings such as genocide, enslavement, unjust wars, or other forms of undue violence, theft, and fraud. Reparations have been the main legal remedy for such injustices. Yet the problems of reparations stand in acute need of resolution for the sake of rectificatory justice.[1] What are reparations, why are they important, and what are the primary considerations that would make them justified on moral grounds, especially concerning historic injustices? This essay explores the nature, value, and possible justification of reparations for historic injustices. It does so in terms of rights.

The Problems of Definition, Valuation, and Justification

The issues of reparations include those of definition, valuation, and justification. The definition of "reparations" concerns the nature of reparations, which differs from the value or justification of reparations. While the nature of reparations involves the giving to a group its due, questions of valuation and justification are

1. Significant portions of this paper are drawn from Corlett 2003, 149f.

more complex. The reason for this is that reparations can have an economic, legal, political, and otherwise social or moral value, and the same might be said of their justification.

The economic value of a reparation might be that a group that has been wrongfully and seriously harmed is restored to its previous economic status so as to suffer no undue financial burden. The political value of a reparation might be that the wrongfully harmed group retains its political power within a larger society, which in turn can have an effect on how the law functions in that society. The social value of a reparation might be that it respects the compensatory rights of a group so that it suffers no undue social disadvantage. And the moral value of a reparation might be that it supports a system of rights that protects individual and collective autonomy, and allows groups and their respective members to be able to predict when they ought to suffer conflict with legal, social, or political authorities. In other words, reparations provide a means to effect peace between parties, one of which has been unduly harmed by the other. In so doing, reparations can serve to support morally just political and legal institutions.

The justification for reparations might take an institutional or noninstitutional form. That is, reparations might be justified by law or morality, or both. When justified according to law, a reparation satisfies a set of requirements deemed appropriate by law. However, when reparations are morally justified, they are justified according to a set of moral principles, principles of a morally enlightened conscience. It is the balance of human reason that grounds such principles, rather than legal rules. This discussion of reparations, like most philosophical ones, will focus mainly on the matter of the moral justification for reparations.

Whether institutional or not, reparations can be justified in at least two senses.[2] First, there is the justification of the very institution of reparations. Then there is the justification of particular instantiations of it. An adequate theory of reparations must account for both such justifications, as it does little good to justify a particular awarding of reparations if the very institution of reparations is itself morally odious. Likewise, if the institution of reparations is justified, yet the reparation cannot in practice be awarded justly, then the reparation is inefficacious and thus problematic. Most of what follows is an attempt to address the problem of the general justification of reparations as an institution, as the investigation of particular instances of reparations is far beyond the scope of this article.

Reparations are forms of rectification that are typically made between groups, and are species of compensatory justice between a harmful wrongdoer to its victim(s) regarding severe instances of injustice. Although there seems to be no conceptual barrier to thinking that reparations can be owed by or to individuals, they are typically paid by and to groups, whether countries, nations, organizations, corporations, companies, ethnic groups, and so forth. Paradigmatic instances of

2. This distinction is borrowed from a similar distinction about punishment found in Quinton 1954; Rawls 1955; and echoed in Benn 1958.

historical cases of reparations include Germany's post–World War II reparations to Israel for Nazi Germany's genocide against European Jews and the payment of reparations to some Japanese families by the United States for the internment of those Japanese American families subsequent to the Japanese attack on Pearl Harbor on December 7, 1944.

The Nature of Reparations

Reparations involve restitution, which is the act of restoring something to its rightful owner, the act of making good or giving equivalent for a loss, damage, or injury. One who is unjustly enriched at the expense of another owes reparations to the injured party. As Joel Feinberg states, "Reparations 'sets things straight' or 'gives satisfaction'.... for redress or injury" (Feinberg 1970, 74–75). By this understanding of the nature of reparations, they might amount to monetary payments normally paid in one lump sum or over time by way of general tax revenues by the wrongful party (Levinson 1973, 250), or return or repair of property, unjustly taken, acquired, or damaged, to its rightful owner.

The Value of Reparations

The value of reparations is that they serve to protect the rights of those who would suffer at the hands of harmful wrongdoers. In so doing, reparations have a complex expressive function that is similar to the expressive functions of punishment articulated by Feinberg (Feinberg 1970, ch. 5). Like punishment, reparations disavow the harmful wrongdoings committed and state that the harmful wrongdoers had no right to perform such wrongs. Moreover, they, like punishment, say publicly that such harmful wrongdoings do not represent society's highest aims and aspirations. In democratic societies, reparations speak in the name of the people against such harmful wrongdoings, upholding the genuine standards of law in the face of past failures of the legal system to carry out true justice. Furthermore, like punishment, reparations seek to separate a reasonably just society from its corrupt history, absolving it of its historic evils. Reparations "can express sympathy, benevolence, and concern, but, in addition, it is always the acknowledgement of a past wrong, a 'repayment of a debt,' and hence, like an apology, the redressing of the moral balance of the restoring of the *status quo ante culpum*" (Feinberg 1970, 76). More generally, the expressive function of reparations is to make public a society's or organization's own liability concerning the harmful wrongdoings it has wrought on a group. It is to offer an unqualified and unambiguous apology to the wronged parties (or their successors) without the presumption of forgiveness or mercy. It is to acknowledge in a public way the moral wrongness of the act, along with its gravity. Reparations also act as a reminder of the rights violation so as not to repeat it. Reparations send a message to all that justice and fairness are top priorities. The value of reparations in a reasonably just society, then, is to protect and honor rights of innocents.

But the protection of the rights of innocents implies further, deeper values of reparations. In protecting the rights of innocents, reparations promote self-respect, respect for others, and self-worth. Feinberg notes these as features of rights more generally (Feinberg 1973, 1980). As a compensatory right, reparations (when respected by a viable legal system) send the message that innocents can depend on certain valid claims or interests withstanding the test of violation, providing a certain level of personal and social security for those in a reasonably just society, or one that is attempting to be just. The result of a society's not respecting the right to reparations, or in its doing so sporadically or capriciously, is that justified resentment and distrust accrues between innocent victims of oppression and those who benefited from the oppression.

The Justification of Reparations

Most of the discussion of reparations centers on whether they are morally justified or even morally required in a particular case. By this is meant whether or not the balance of human reason, informed by a morally enlightened conscience, supports reparations in a particular case. As noted by Bernard Boxill, there are at least two general kinds of arguments: backward looking and forward looking (Boxill 1972, 113–122).[3] In either case, reparations, in order to be morally just, must conform to principles of proportionality in compensation.

In the case of forward-looking arguments for reparations, a utilitarian tack is usually taken, placing emphasis on social and economic programs that would benefit those individuals who themselves belong to groups that have been victimized by severe injustice. Thus, forward-looking arguments for reparations take a distinctly conciliatory and integrationist approach vis-à-vis the oppressors and their respective victim groups. This can be construed as presumptuous by the victims themselves, as compensatory justice normally does not require either that the victims of injustice establish or continue to have social relationships with those who harm them, or that victims have to somehow earn (in the case of affirmative action programs of employment) their court-ordered "compensation." Furthermore, those seeking to ground reparations in forward-looking utilitarian arguments face an

3. For a discussion of backward-looking and forward-looking arguments on the related question of affirmative action, see Roberts's chapter in this volume.

even deeper problem. It is that such an emphasis is placed on the overall happiness of society that reparations are not taken as a compensatory *right* that outweighs social utility considerations. This implies that considerations of social utility can override valid moral claims to or interests in reparations, no matter how severe the injustice experienced by the victimized group. Yet a "right" that can be overridden by social utility considerations is no right at all, and a more backward-looking justification for reparations is sought. Thus, forward-looking arguments for reparations seem to not be arguments about reparations at all insofar as reparations are compensatory *rights*, but rather some form of distributive justice wherein the least advantaged are assisted for a variety of reasons, including the relief of poverty and general equality. Indeed, the problem of reparations often distinguishes forward-looking utilitarians from backward-looking rights-based theorists.

Backward-looking reasons theorists in favor of reparations construe a reparation as a compensatory right that cannot be outweighed by considerations of social utility because they are based on valid moral claims or interests. A basic reparations argument runs as follows:

(1) Instances of clear and substantial rights violations that result in harmful wrongdoings against groups ought to be compensated by way of reparations;
(2) X has clearly committed substantial rights violations that resulted in harmful wrongdoings against Y;
(3) Therefore, X ought to pay reparations to Y,

where "ought" implies that if the compensation is not paid, then there remains a duty unfulfilled and one is morally wrong for not fulfilling it. Thus, the backward-looking reasons approach to reparations favored by Boxill, J. Angelo Corlett, and Howard McGary construes reparations as a fundamental compensatory right similar to other compensatory rights within a morally and reasonably just legal system. As such, reparations are part of the rights that support a group's self-respect and respect for others.

In particular cases of reparations, most of the discussion revolves around (2) of the above reparations argument. For even if it can be determined who X and Y are and that they are currently existing groups with reasonably identifiable members, and even if it is possible to identify a particular and serious harmful wrongdoing against Y that X is responsible for, it might still be asked *how* X violated Y's right(s). This central point in reparations theory is answered by an appeal to moral principles. For example, the principle of morally just acquisitions and transfers can be marshaled to ground the rights of indigenous groups to reparations for the theft of land by colonizers: "Whatever is acquired or transferred by morally just means is itself morally just; whatever is acquired or transferred by morally unjust means is itself morally unjust"[4] (Corlett 2003, 155). This moral principle is based on Immanuel

4. This principle is a modification of one found in Nozick 1974, 150.

Kant's point that those who acquire stolen property have a responsibility to "investigate" the historical chain of acquisitions and transfers of property, and if, unbeknownst to her, the property she deemed she purchased legitimately was the actual possession of another, then "nothing is left to the alleged new owner but to have enjoyed the use of it up to this moment as its possessor in good faith" (Kant 1996, 82). Such a principle reveals who X and Y are by way of thorough historical investigation, and in turn tells us who owes reparations to whom, and why. Similar moral principles can be devised in terms of unjust usurpation of a person's wages or labor value as the result of, say, morally unjust enslavement, and for cases of human rights violations associated with enslavement and colonial appropriation of land. And yet similar moral principles can be brought to bear in cases where unjust wars justify reparations to victims. In that case, the basic principles of just war theories can be brought to bear to ground the injustice and in turn to justify the reparation.

Reparations as a Human Right?

John Rawls (Rawls 1999) and others[5] who have analyzed human rights seem not to have included compensatory rights as part of a legitimate package of human rights. In *The Law of Peoples*, Rawls sets forth and defends "principles and norms of international law and practice" (Rawls 1999, 3) and "hopes to say how a world Society of liberal and decent Peoples might be possible" (Rawls 1999, 6). His view is of one of a realistic utopia to the extent that "it extends what are ordinarily thought of as the limits of practical political philosophy" (Rawls 1999, 6) and "because it joins reasonableness and justice with conditions enabling citizens to realize their fundamental interests"[6] (Rawls 1999, 7). In working toward his realistic utopia, Rawls employs a modified version of the original position thought experiment employed in his earlier works (Rawls 1971, 1993). However, his conception of the veil of ignorance is "properly adjusted" for the problems of international justice: the free and equal parties in the original position do not know the size of the territory or population or relative strength of the people whose basic interests they represent (Rawls 1999, 32). Although such parties know that reasonably favorable conditions possibly exist for the foundation of a constitutional democracy, they do not know the extent of their natural resources, the level of their economic development, and so forth (Rawls 1999, 33). Moreover, Rawls states:

> Thus, the people's representatives are (1) reasonably and fairly situated as free and equal, and peoples are (2) modeled as rational. Also their representatives are

5. See Nickel 1987, 2005. For a discussion of how the right to reparations can satisfy each of Nickel's conditions for a human right, see Corlett, 2010.

6. See Rawls 1999, 11–23, for his elaboration of the nature of a realistic utopia.

> (3) deliberating about the correct subject, in this case the content of the Law of Peoples.... Moreover, (4) their deliberations proceed in terms of the right reasons (as restricted by a veil of ignorance). Finally, the selection of principles for the Law of Peoples is based (5) on a people's fundamental interests, given in this case by a liberal conception of justice (already selected in the first original position). (Rawls 1999, 33)

From this procedure, Rawls argues, the following "principles of justice among free and democratic peoples" will be selected:

> 1. Peoples are free and independent, and their freedom and independence are to be respected by other peoples.
> 2. Peoples are to observe treaties and undertakings.
> 3. Peoples are equal and are parties to the agreements that bind them.
> 4. Peoples are to observe a duty of nonintervention.
> 5. Peoples have the right of self-defense but no right to instigate war for reasons other than self-defense.
> 6. Peoples are to honor human rights.
> 7. Peoples are to observe certain specified restrictions in the conduct of war.
> 8. Peoples have a duty to assist other peoples living under unfavorable conditions that prevent their having a just or decent political or social regime. (Rawls 1999, 37)

Various questions might be raised here, including one concerning the possible lexical ordering of such principles because such an ordering is essential to the proper application of such principles under conditions of uncertainty and rights conflicts (Wilkins 2007, 161–175). But regardless of whether or not, and, if so, how, the principles ought to be lexically ordered, this set of principles is importantly incomplete, especially in light of Rawls's repeated claim that "decent" peoples have rights to property, territory, and life. And consonant with Rawls's admission that "other principles need to be added" (Rawls 1999, 37), some have proffered an international principle of justice that complements Rawls's own list, one that includes a human right of severely and wrongfully harmed groups to reparation (Corlett 2009).

However, it might be argued that Rawls's eight principles of international justice seem to lack any mention or guarantee of compensatory justice between peoples. Yet without such a principle, there can hardly be a realistic global utopia, as Rawls desires, in that part of what helps to ensure social stability at the global level would be absent: remediation through compensation when certain rights are violated. Insofar as Rawls's international principles of justice are to protect basic rights that would best ensure global stability, and insofar as rights remediations are basic rights along with substantive rights,[7] then Rawls's principles seem to lack what is essential to international justice in a realistic utopia, the objection goes. The concern is that liberal and decent peoples simply must compensate those whom they

7. Hence the old legal adage: "Absence of remedy is absence of right."

wrongfully harm. It is their duty correlated with the right of those they wrongfully harm to be compensated. And it simply will not do, the objection continues, to argue in Rawls's defense that matters of compensatory justice are not the proper domain of Rawls's theory of international justice, as Rawls's principles reflect a concern for conditions of war and poverty and so imply remedial rights. Thus, it is argued that it is an omission on Rawls's part—as well as on the parts of various other philosophers who write on global justice[8]—that there is not even a mention of a basic principle of compensatory justice. This would imply that reasonably just societies have no duties to compensate other societies they have harmed by way of, say, reparations for past and severe injustices. Because such injustices are so prevalent, even in societies that Rawls believes are reasonably just, the issue of compensatory justice is especially important. This line of reasoning asks: why would a party in the international original position select principles 1–8 above without some principle(s) of remedial rights that help(s) to guarantee them—either by their deterrent effect or by their ability to grant the authority to an international court of justice to award reparations or other appropriate compensation to wrongfully harmed peoples by those who have wrongfully harmed them? It is only reasonable and rational for those peoples in the original position to select not only Rawls's principles, but also principles of compensatory justice that properly and fairly undergird them. But precisely what might some such principle be in the context of international justice?

Consider the "principle of international compensatory justice," which is intended to supplement Rawls's eight principles of international justice, though in such a way that it does not indicate a lexical ordering:

> To the extent that peoples wrongfully harm other peoples, they have the primary duty to compensate those they wrongfully harm in proportion to the harm caused them, all things considered.

According to this principle of international justice, peoples who wrongfully harm other peoples have a duty of compensation to them pursuant to the corollary rights version of the compensatory principle of international compensatory justice:

> Peoples have a right to be compensated in proportion to the harms wrongfully suffered, all things considered, at the hands of their primary offender(s).

One point here is that no third-party peoples have a duty to compensate what another people has a primary duty to compensate. Additionally, what Rawls himself refers to as "outlaw" states or societies are not to escape their compensatory duties toward those they have wrongfully harmed. And it is inconceivable that free and equal parties in the Rawlsian international original position would ignore compensatory justice considerations. For if they were to do so, then the Law of Peoples would lack a basic component to any legitimate and workable legal order.

8. See, for example, Buchanan 2005; Pogge 2002; and Singer 2002.

And recall that it is Rawls himself who seeks to articulate and defend principles of international justice that can be implemented with reasonable workability in a *realistic* utopia. Even in a realistic utopia rights are violated now and then, and require rectification if it is to remain a reasonably just social scenario. Nothing about Rawls's international original position excludes the possibility of the international principle of compensatory justice. Indeed, it implies it.

Moreover, this principle of international compensatory justice fits well into Rawls's list of eight principles. It supports his first principle in that it provides a basic rule in cases wherein a peoples' rights to independence and freedom are disrespected by other peoples. Peoples wrongfully harming other peoples are to compensate those they harm to the extent of their harming them, all things considered. Furthermore, the principle of international compensatory justice implies that Rawls's fourth and fifth rules can be broken by decent peoples in certain cases where the ninth rule is violated in a flagrant manner by an outlaw state. Indeed, third-party peoples might consider it their duty to confront the guilty peoples who refuse to adequately compensate the wronged party. In cases wherein an outlaw state refuses to compensate peoples it has wrongfully and severely harmed, Rawls's fifth principle must be supplemented by a corollary one stating that, in defense of others, war and certain other forms of political violence may be justified. I have in mind here cases where generations of race-based slavery (a case Rawls himself discusses) go uncompensated, or where indigenous peoples are victimized by genocide for the sake of societal expansion—again, without adequate compensation. In such instances, it is clear that Rawls's fifth principle can be broken in light of his claim (a claim that he never recanted) that at times militancy is justified (Rawls 1971, 368). Indeed, it would appear that the principle of international compensatory justice upholds Rawls's sixth principle insofar as it is plausible to think that the first principle relies on such general rights being protected by compensatory rights. The principle of international compensatory justice further implies that, in the waging of war or other means of political violence, certain restrictions are to be obeyed in terms of going to war or engaging in political violence for the sake of enforcing laws of compensation and protecting compensatory rights. Finally, as mentioned earlier, the principle of international compensatory justice is congruent with Rawls's eighth principle in that the former allows for the assistance of third-party peoples to involve themselves in the administration of compensatory justice in cases where offender peoples refuse to compensate those peoples whom they have wrongfully harmed, or where such compensation is forthcoming but grossly inadequate to return the compensated peoples to a decent level of living subsequent to the harms caused by the wrongful action of the offender peoples.

Thus, a plausible principle of international compensatory justice is both necessary for the Rawlsian analysis of international justice and congruent with many of the Rawlsian principles as stated. The human right and duty of compensatory justice should be added to Rawls's eight principles in order to better locate peoples in Rawls's realistic utopia. For if consistently respected, such a principle would serve to maintain stability between peoples with good intentions regarding a reasonably just global order.

Of course, Rawls's not including reparations on the list of human rights is not the same as his disallowing it in principle. Further, nothing that is argued about human rights by Rawls or others who analyze them philosophically rules out reparations as a human right.[9] Yet if the fullness of justice is to accrue in the world, and in light of the several and continuing human rights violations throughout the world, it behooves human rights theorists to include compensatory rights among the list of human rights. And it seems natural to think that reparations would rank high on the list of such human compensatory rights. Indeed, it is counterintuitive to deny the importance of the human right to reparations, as some cosmopolitan liberals do. But how might human rights of groups be protected if not by human rights such as reparations? Reparations provide the International Criminal Court and any war crimes tribunal a means by which to institutionalize the world's attitude toward those governments or agencies that would violate the rights of groups. And it provides each group with an important measure of assurance that global legal institutions and policies respect them. Of course, as with all rights, they must be properly and consistently respected in order to be effective. But this is a matter of practice, rather than of principle. So there is no principled manner by which to deny the importance of the human right of groups to reparations from their harmful wrongdoers—that is, if there are human rights in the first place.

Objections to Reparations

However, there are numerous objections to the very idea of reparations (Corlett 2003, ch. 8–9) or whether or not they are a human right, and these will vary depending on the case in question. In regard to cases of historic injustice, the concern about a possible moral statute of limitations arises. But this concern has been met with the following rebuttals. First, those who argue in favor of a moral statute of limitations on historical injustice have the burden of argument in demonstrating that such a statute exists, or should exist.[10] Yet no successful arguments have been provided along these lines[11] (Roberts 2003, 115–138; 2007, 177–192).

Another general concern with reparations is the extent to which it is difficult to identify perpetrators and victims of injustice. This objection can take one of two forms. First, it might be asked how ethnic groups, for instance, might be identified. After all, if it is impossible to adequately identify the members of groups that have

9. See Corlett, 2010.
10. For a negative argument against such a claim, see Corlett 2003, 152, 214.
11. For positive arguments against the proposal, see Roberts 2003, 2007.

been wrongfully harmed, then it would appear that the case for reparations to such groups is unjustified because it would be implemented in a morally arbitrary manner. Second, it might be asked how the complexities of history might render the awarding of reparations capricious in that the facts about which group did what to whom might well be convoluted to the extent that the facts of the case are insufficiently clear to make a particular case for reparations. But the ethnic group identity matter is reasonably resolvable, as there are analyses of ethnicity based on existing models of identifying members of groups precisely for compensatory justice purposes (Corlett 2003, ch. 2–3). Moreover, no case of reparations is complete to the extent that it is overly complex, that is, where the case is weak. Only strong and convincing evidence should be taken as sufficient for reparations awards. Plausible cases for reparations are not arguing that all reparations claims are valid. Rather, the point is that some such cases might be to the extent that they are adequately supported by clear evidence.

Whether justified by way of forward- or backward-looking reasons, reparations are typically tied to the collective liability responsibility of the harmful wrongdoer, on the one hand, and the victim group, on the other (Corlett 2003, 157–160, 197–213; McGary 1999, ch. 5). As Feinberg argues, collective liability can obtain absent fault, or even guilt. Thus, a society can owe damages to a group even though those who committed the harmful wrongdoings against it are no longer alive to pay restitution. But retrospective collective liability responsibility,[12] like its individualist counterpart, admits of degrees, as not every member of a group is as coresponsible as another for harmful wrongdoings caused by the group. Principles of proportional responsibility and compensation must be brought to bear in attempting to clarify more precisely collective responsibility for harmful wrongdoing. One effective manner by which to do this is to require that prior to forcing a collective to itself pay damages to a victim group, all reasonable efforts must be made to force those individuals within the group most responsible for the harmful wrongdoing to compensate the wronged group. Only after all such assets are expended and more is owed to the wronged group ought the collective owing reparations be forced to pay them.

Moreover, if it is morally justified to inherit wealth, it is also justified to inherit debt. Of course, even if inheritance is not morally justified, say, due to the fact that good or bad moral luck vitiates claims to *deserved* inheritance, it would still not rule out reparations as a duty of wrongdoing groups to those whom they have wronged. Thus, rectificatory justice is supported by but is not contingent on the moral status of inheritance.

It is a grand confusion indeed to conflate reparations with affirmative action programs, as most forward-looking theorists seem to do.[13] Affirmative action pro-

12. For a philosophical analysis of the concept of collective moral responsibility, see Corlett 2006, ch. 7.

13. For a discussion of the philosophical questions related to affirmative action, see Roberts in this volume.

grams tend to justify "reparations" in terms of preferential treatment programs for "disadvantaged" groups in society, providing members of such target groups with education, job training, and employment opportunities. Yet this construal of reparations mistakes reparations as a means of compensatory justice with social welfare programs. In no way is compensatory justice a matter of what one earns in employment, or in education or job training. Courts typically do and should award compensation based on the merits of a case, without regard to how the decision is to affect society as a whole. Stolen goods are not to be rectified by way of a court-ordered system of victims' working for the values of those goods stolen from them. Indeed, it is the thief who is to rectify her victim! Thus, the confusion of reparations with affirmative action is a category mistake.

The category mistake of confusing reparations with affirmative action has in the United States led to unfortunate results in affirmative action whereby several groups targeted as "disadvantaged" include both ethnic and gender groups, each of which has experienced wrongdoing at greatly varying kinds and degrees. Furthermore, this difficulty is complicated by the fact that some such groups have served as oppressors of others, yet they are all treated as legitimate targets of affirmative action, and for the betterment of society as a whole. The most obvious case is that white women have benefited more by affirmative action than even the most oppressed groups combined, as evidenced by their respective social, political, and economic standings in the United States.

One further moral problem with this approach to reparations is that the principle(s) of proportional compensation is totally ignored under such a provision, and often the most advantaged groups within the "disadvantaged" benefit most from affirmative action. So it is not just that those who benefit most from affirmative action programs are, historically and otherwise, oppressive of other groups within the group of disadvantaged ones; it is also that they benefit more than the least well-off and most deeply oppressed by the most advantaged of the disadvantaged groups! Thus, the forward-looking confusion of reparations with affirmative action programs has deleterious effects that, ironically, no self-respecting utilitarian could accept. Thus, reparations must be grounded in a backward-looking moral justification, though one that does not necessarily reject forward-looking considerations after the backward-looking ones play their primary justificatory roles. This is likely, though not guaranteed, to run afoul of some cherished principles of political egalitarians, at least regarding those whose egalitarianism is sufficiently crude that it would disallow for the awarding of compensatory justice that would eventuate in economically unequal groups. Yet to take such a line would disregard group rights to compensatory justice and the values thereof. One problem here is that no sophisticated egalitarianism has been brought to bear in the philosophical discussions of reparations.

To the extent that reparations are morally justified in a given case of injustice, to what ought they amount? The answer to this question depends on the facts of a given case. In the case of American Indian genocide and gross land theft, reparations must include damages for both the land theft and the genocidal acts against them by the U.S. government. This might include awarding of damages part of which would include the return of certain especially sacred lands and full mineral rights to Indian peoples. In the case of blacks in the United States whose ancestors were enslaved in the U.S., land is not so much the issue as financial awards. In either case, it is important that presumptions of reconciliation be left totally in the hands of the members of the victimized groups. For only this policy would begin to accord to each group the autonomy and sovereignty each deserves but has never experienced given their oppression by the U.S. federal, state, and local governments.

Reparations can also be owed for war crimes, including the declaring and commencing of an unjust war (Walzer 2000). While some of the genocidal acts against American Indians would qualify as war crimes, more straightforward cases include (but are surely not limited to) the U.S. use of weapons of mass destruction on civilian populations in Hiroshima and Nagasaki in 1945, where over 100,000 Japanese civilians were killed and many hundreds of thousands maimed; the hundreds of thousands of Vietnamese civilians who were killed at the hands of U.S. military during its morally unjust involvement in the Vietnam conflict; the U.S. military invasion and occupation of Iraq in 2003 and for years thereafter in which hundreds of thousands of Iraqi civilians were killed by U.S. troops; and the Israeli usurpation and occupation of parts of Palestinian territory and its subsequent military oppression by state terrorism against Palestinian terrorists (who responded to Israeli attacks in self-defense) and innocent Palestinian civilians. Other cases that qualify for reparations but are more difficult to classify as war crimes reparations include but are not limited to the oppression of South African blacks by the white South African government during the official South African apartheid regime.

So other than instances such as the indigenous ones wherein both land and money are awarded to victimized groups by perpetrating ones, money seems to be the manner by which reparations are awarded. But this does not rule out the sincerity of reparations being accompanied by official apologies issued by the leadership of the governments or organizations most responsible for the atrocities that justified the reparations in the first place, as argued by McGary (McGary 1999, ch. 12). While this is desirable, one must bear in mind that integrative reconciliation ought never to be presumed to be the legitimate aim of forgiveness, even though it requires forgiveness. But forgiveness requires genuine apology, which in turn requires rectification of past wrongs by the harmful wrongdoer (Corlett 2006, ch. 6). Thus, without rectification there can be no apology, no forgiveness, and no reconciliation. Reparations, then, serve as a necessary condition for reconciliation that is required for justice and peace, though it is a popular view today (not among reparations theorists, however) to deny this claim. However, it is a presumptuous mistake to think, on the one hand, that reparations are sufficient for reconciliation or forgiveness, or on the other hand, that reparations are contingent on either for their moral justification. Just as compensatory justice in general is not contingent on reconciliation or forgiveness, neither are reparations.

BIBLIOGRAPHY AND SUGGESTED READINGS

Benn, E. Stanley (1958) "An Approach to the Problems of Punishment." *Philosophy* 33, 325–341.

Boxill, Bernard. (1972) "The Morality of Reparation." *Social Theory and Practice* 2, 113–122.

Buchanan, Allen. (2005) *Justice, Legitimacy, and Self-Determination*. Oxford: Oxford University Press.

Corlett, J. Angelo. (2003) *Race, Racism, and Reparations*. Ithaca, NY: Cornell University Press.

———. (2006) *Responsibility and Punishment* (3rd ed.). Dordrecht: Springer.

———. (2009) *Race, Rights, and Justice*. Dordrecht: Springer.

———. (2010) *Heirs of Oppression*. Lanham, MD: Rowman & Littlefield.

Feinberg, Joel. (1970) *Doing and Deserving*. Princeton, NJ: Princeton University Press.

———. (1973) *Social Philosophy*. Englewood Cliffs, NJ: Prentice-Hall.

———. (1980) *Rights, Justice, and the Bounds of Liberty*. Princeton, NJ: Princeton University Press.

———. (1992) *Freedom and Fulfillment*. Princeton, NJ: Princeton University Press.

Kant, Immanuel. (1996) "The Metaphysical Elements of Justice. " In *The Metaphysics of Morals*, translated by Mary Gregor. Cambridge: Cambridge University Press.

Levinson, Sanford. (1973) "Responsibility for Crimes of War." *Philosophy and Public Affairs* 2, 250.

McGary, Howard. (1999) *Race and Social Justice*. London: Blackwell Publishing.

Nickel, James W. (1987) *Making Sense of Human Rights*. Berkeley, CA: University of California Press.

———. (2005) "Poverty and Rights." *The Philosophical Quarterly* 55, 385–402.

Nozick, Robert. (1974) *Anarchy, State and Utopia*. New York: Basic Books.

Pogge, Thomas. (2002) *World Poverty and Human Rights*. London: Polity Press.

Quinton, Anthony M. (1954) "Punishment." *Analysis* 14, 133–142.

Rawls, John. (1955) "Two Concepts of Rules." *The Philosophical Review* 64, 3–13.

———. (1971) *A Theory of Justice*. Cambridge, MA: Harvard University Press.

———. (1993) *Political Liberalism*. New York: Columbia University Press.

———. (1999) *The Law of Peoples*. Cambridge, MA: Harvard University Press.

Roberts, Rodney C. (2003) "The Morality of a Moral Statute of Limitations on Injustice." *The Journal of Ethics* 7, 115–138.

———. (2007) "More on the Morality of a Moral Statute of Limitations on Injustice." *The Journal of Ethics* 11, 177–192.

Singer, Peter. (2002) *One World*. New Haven, CT: Yale University Press.

Walzer, Michael. (2000) *Just and Unjust Wars* (3rd ed.). New York: Basic Books.

Wilkins, Burleigh T. (2007) "Principles for the Law of Peoples." *The Journal of Ethics* 11, 161–175.

Index